iDentities

PAUL SELIGSON,
PAT CHAPPELL AND DAMIAN WILLIAMS

Teacher's Book 2

Richmond

Contents

Language Map	3
Introduction	6
Features Presentation	15
Unit 1	20
Unit 2	40
Review 1	60
Unit 3	64
Unit 4	84
Review 2	104
Unit 5	108
Unit 6	128
Review 3	148
Unit 7	152
Unit 8	172
Review 4	192
Unit 9	196
Unit 10	216
Review 5	236
Unit 11	240
Unit 12	260
Review 6	280
Grammar expansion	284
Grammar expansion answer key	308
Audio scripts	311
Song activities	341
Phrasal verb list	356

Language Map

	Speaking / Topic	Grammar	Vocabulary / Strategies	Writing
1.1	What are your earliest memories of school?		Expressions for reminiscing; Phrasal verbs with *off*	
1.2	What innovative businesses do you know?	Subject-verb agreement: portions and indefinite pronouns; units of measurement, collective nouns, asides, and verbs as subjects		
1.3	How many ways can you use a brick?		Figurative expressions for ideas (*pop into your head*, *hit you*, etc.)	
1.4	What do the 2000s make you think of?	Using perfect tenses: simple past vs. present perfect; present perfect vs. present perfect continuous; past perfect vs. past perfect continuous	Uses of *set* (*put, design, establish, schedule*)	
1.5	Have you ever had a dream come true?		Informal responses (*That's for sure; I'll say*, etc.)	An autobiographical narrative: functions of the word *as*, both neutral and slightly more formal
2.1	What would you change about your lifestyle?		Expressions for decision making; Expressions for expressing goals	
2.2	What's the biggest house you've ever been to?	Avoiding repetition: affirmative and negative statements (*but I really should have; but my friends aren't*, etc.)	Plural-only nouns	
2.3	Do you like to spend time alone? (Authentic reading: article on dining and traveling alone)		Understanding metaphor; Common verb / adjective + noun collocations (*convey an idea, ubiquitous presence*, etc.)	
2.4	Are you more of a morning or an evening person?	Using *so* and *such*: *so, so much, so little, so many, so few, such* and *such a(n)*		
2.5	Can an apartment be too small?		Expressions from video for discussing city problems	A compare-and-contrast email: considering two things together, adding supporting points, and offering contrast
Review 1 *p.26*				
3.1	What language would you least like to learn?		Expressions to discuss learning (*out of your depth, pick something up*, etc.)	
3.2	Are you into tweeting?	Information focus: subject and object clauses (*What I did was to ... ; Why ... is unclear I'm not really sure.*)	Making your attitude clear (*to put it mildly, to say the least*, etc.)	
3.3	Can someone learn to be a good speaker? (Authentic reading: article on public speaking)		Expressions with *word* (*by word of mouth, get a word in edgewise*, etc.)	
3.4	What's the ideal age to learn a language?	Using participle clauses to express result, time, and reason (*When driving to work, I used to ... ; Supported by his parents, Ben is in no hurry ...*); Perfect participles (*Having played the trombone ...*)		
3.5	What can't you learn through practice?		Expressions related to giving advice (*Practice makes perfect; You need to hit a middle ground*, etc.)	An expository essay: participle clauses for linking ideas; making suggestions with modal verbs
4.1	How often do you remember your dreams?		Productive suffixes (*-conscious, -friendly, -related*, etc.)	
4.2	Do you believe everything you're told?	Emphatic inversion: inverted subject and verb (*Rarely do we find such realistic sound effects, Not since ... has there been so much excitement.*)		
4.3	When did you last hear something illogical? (Authentic reading: article on why people believe in conspiracy theories)		Nouns and adjectives from phrasal verbs (*break-in, throwaway*, etc.)	
4.4	How would you describe your personality?	Formal relative clauses with *which* and *whom* (*most of whom, about which*, etc.)		
4.5	Would you ever hire a former criminal?		Expressions for honesty (*be up front, on the table*, etc.)	A letter to the editor: fixed expressions to support arguments in formal writing
Review 2 *p.48*				

Language Map

		Speaking / Topic	Grammar	Vocabulary / Strategies	Writing
5	5.1	Why do good plans sometimes fail?		Expressions for failed plans (*on the verge of, call something off*, etc.); Talking about disappointments	
	5.2	Do you ever make resolutions?	Formal conjunctions and prepositions for reason and purpose (*in view of; with the aim of; so as to*, etc.)		
	5.3	How well do you deal with failure? (Authentic reading: article on making peace with failure)		Expressions for evaluating success (*keep in perspective, take stock*, etc.)	
	5.4	Have you ever had a wrong first impression?	Levels of formality in nouns, object pronouns, and possessive adjectives + *ing* form (*I appreciated him / his considering our project*, etc.)		
	5.5	How bad are drivers where you live?		Expressions for making proposals (*airtight, rationale*, etc.)	A proposal: adverbs and adverbial expressions to link ideas and signal the next point; Formulaic expressions for formal proposals and emails
6	6.1	Do you still read paper books?		Phrasal verbs with *out*	
	6.2	Do you ever watch dubbed movies?	Adverb clauses of condition (*in case, even if, as long as*, etc.)	Using the expression *out of*	
	6.3	Who are your favorite authors? (Authentic literature: short story by Roald Dahl *The Way Up to Heaven*)		Evocative language: vivid verbs	
	6.4	What do you think of graffiti art?	Emphasis with auxiliaries (*I really did like it*, etc.)		
	6.5	Are musicals popular where you live?		Expressions for making recommendations	A book review: techniques and expressions to capture the reader's attention and maintain suspense
	Review 3 *p.70*				
7	7.1	What are our most important years?		Expressions for describing milestones (*come of age, make it through*, etc.)	
	7.2	Would you like to live to be 100?	Future perfect vs. future continuous	Expressions for clarifying opinions (*What I mean is that …*, *What I was trying to say is that …*, etc.)	
	7.3	Do babies ever surprise you? (Authentic reading: article on surprising things babies can do)		Adjective-noun collocations in writing and speech	
	7.4	Do you seem younger or older than you are?	Cleft sentences: subject and object (e.g. *It's my grandmother who can walk three miles.*)		
	7.5	What would your ideal job be?		Expressions for making formal requests	An application letter: more formal alternatives to cleft sentences (*Working in a hotel is rewarding*, etc.)
8	8.1	What makes a restaurant special?		Expressions with *take* for discussing events; Describing negative experiences	
	8.2	Are you a demanding customer?	Subjunctive: verbs and expressions (*I insist that …, it's important that …* etc.)		
	8.3	What are the worst aspects of air travel? (Authentic reading: article about amazing customer service)		Expressions of help (*took it upon himself to, went to great lengths to*, etc.)	
	8.4	Have you ever borrowed money?	Information focus: adverb clauses to emphasize conditions or contrasts (*As useful as the manual may be, it didn't help; However reasonable the price may seem, its too high*, etc.)	Money terms (*borrow, loan, profit, inherit, tax*, etc.)	
	8.5	What was the last complaint you made?			A formal complaint letter (formulas: *to no avail, to resolve the matter*, etc.; passive expressions: *It was my understanding that …, I was led to believe that …*, etc.)
	Review 4 *p.92*				

Language Map

	Speaking / Topic	Grammar	Vocabulary / Strategies	Writing
9.1	Would you like to be a teacher?		"Out-verbs" (outsmart, outnumber, etc.); Drawing tentative conclusions	
9.2	What is alternative medicine?	Passive expressions with active and passive infinitives (The treatment is thought to work well, Patients are known to have been helped, etc.)	Three-word phrasal verbs (come down with, give up on, etc.)	
9.3	What unconventional families do you know? (Authentic reading: article about single parenting)		Common collocations and compounds (fictitious belief, fairytale ending, etc.)	
9.4	How often do you work out?	Overview of verb patterns: with base forms, infinitives, and -ing forms	Fitness words (treadmill, stretching, etc.); Verbs ending in -en (whiten, lengthen, etc.)	
9.5	What are the pros and cons of dieting?		Reacting to new information (I should reserve judgment, Did I hear you correctly?, etc.)	A report on pros and cons: using consistent style in lists
10.1	Why do friends drift apart?		Expressions with say and tell (it goes without saying, truth be told, etc.); Friendship idioms (the life of the party, a breath of fresh air, etc.)	
10.2	Who's the oldest person you know?	Degrees of comparison with the ... the, more / ... er, and as ... as (the more friends you have, the happier you'll feel, friends are nowhere near as important as family, etc.)		
10.3	How easy is it to make friends where you live? (Authentic reading: the nature of American friendship)		Words with both prefixes and suffixes (double affixation) (dis-, il-, im-, in-, ir-, un- + root + -able, -al, -ful, -ible, -ive -ity)	
10.4	Have you ever met someone new by chance?	Inverted conditional sentences for present, past, or future time (Had she not gone to the party, we wouldn't be married today, etc.)	Expressions with odds (What are the odds that ...?, etc.)	
10.5	How persuasive are you?			A persuasive opinion essay: logically building an argument (review of topic sentences; words appealing to common sense, conjunctions, and time markers)
Review 5 *p.114*				
11.1	What was the last risk you took?		Risk-taking expressions (play it safe, err on the side of caution, etc.); Expressing hesitation and encouragement (There's just too much at stake, What do you have to lose?, etc.)	
11.2	Do you enjoy riding a bike?	Special uses of modals (expectation, suggestion, refusal, annoyance)	Expressing danger and fear (He froze in his tracks, He screeched to a halt, etc.)	
11.3	Are you in favor of online dating? (Authentic reading: article on online dating safety)		Strategies for whether to look up words (guessing words in context, deciding whether they're for active use, etc.)	
11.4	What does the sea make you think of?	Definite and indefinite articles: general and specific use (countable and non-count nouns, first mention, adjective + number, shared knowledge, adjective for a group)		
11.5	Have you ever had an allergic reaction?		Talking about symptoms (itching, swelling, etc.)	A statistical report: subject-verb agreement (fractions, percentages, half, one, a number, the number, etc.)
12.1	What brands are the wave of the future?		Verbs describing trends (skyrocket, plummet, etc.); Expressing cause and reason (stem from, is closely related to, etc.)	
12.2	What songs have changed the world?	Passive forms with gerunds and infinitives (I remember being told about it; New facts seem to be discovered all the time, etc.)	Transitive and intransitive phrasal verbs	
12.3	What futuristic programs have you seen? (Authentic reading: predicting the future 100 years ago)		Looking up words	
12.4	How unpredictable has your life been?	The passive with get and be; the causative with get and have (get passive to express informality, emphasis, negative intent, and unintended consequences)	Expressions with worth (worth the effort, worth my time, etc.)	
12.5	What will make a better society?		Whatsoever to emphasize negative ideas	An opinion essay: using verb phrases and noun phrases to avoid repetition
Review 6 *p.136*				

Grammar expansion *p.138*   **Selected audio scripts** *p.162*   **Phrasal verb list** *p.164*

Introduction

iDentities 2 is the second in a ground-breaking, two-level course for adults, younger and older, at Upper-Intermediate (B2) and Advanced (C1). With an eye-catching design, highly original, largely authentic texts, motivating topics and constant opportunities for personalization in both levels, just like iDentities 1 and the English iD series, iDentities 2 will continue to help your students progress faster and be able to express their identity both fluently and ever more accurately in English.

iDentities works either as a free-standing course, or as a natural follow-on from English iD 0-3.

Unique features of iDentities

iDentities offers many familiar features from English iD and adds new ones specifically designed for students at a higher level. These include:

- Two extra units for a total of twelve, with skills development and writing fully integrated into the unit.
- Contemporary, highly original topics that cater to adult learners, both younger and older with truly interesting twists, new angles, and a good deal of humor too.
- Higher level listening skills, such as notetaking and making inferences. Listening always leading to speaking on the same topic.
- More challenging **Make it personal** activities that include students' own ideas on a wide range of topics, enabling them to express their identity ever more fully in English.
- Pronunciation fully integrated with speaking.
- An increased emphasis on inductive grammar and more focus on the subtleties of language. Students will be able to express themselves with more precision in many different contexts, both formal and informal.
- An original and expanded **Grammar expansion** section with new aspects of structures taught and accompanying activities, as well as unique activities on the grammar of song lines.
- A rich vocabulary syllabus with an expanded level-appropriate focus on phrasal verbs, collocations, idioms, discourse markers, word formation and dictionary definitions.
- New **How to say it** sections that present conversation strategies, formulaic language, and higher level, natural ways of performing functions.
- Increased focus on register contrasts, where relevant.

- More systematic attention to writing with a full page per unit.
- A brand new **Keep talking** section that not only leads into writing, but is preceded by listening, for a rich integrated skills lesson.
- A two-page review unit after every two units for a total of six.
- A 4-page **Phrasal verb list** with a comprehensive list of separable and inseparable phrasal verbs and their meanings.
- At least one search online task per unit to encourage personalization.
- Helene, the cyber teacher who provides clear definitions and examples of new vocabulary, including phrasal verbs and idioms.

At the same time, the key features of English iD are retained:

- Question titles as an instant ready-made warmer for every lesson, now serving as schema builders for higher level topics.
- Song lines in every lesson offering authentic, memorable relevance to help English come alive and show sts how much they already know.
- **Common mistakes** continued at a higher level.
- A **Make it personal** speaking activity to end every phase.
- Visual pronunciation, highlighting stress on syllables, as well as pronunciation activities throughout the book.
- The **World of English** concept, now with specific names for boxes to capture the language points covered.
- Plus the light, humorous style, student-friendly, and teacher-friendly approach, now with a fully interleaved Teacher's Book for easy classroom management.

Like English iD, iDentities will enable your students to be able to express their own identity in English more fluently and with greater accuracy.

If English iD was all about learning to be yourself in English, iDentities is about pushing, developing, and polishing your English-speaking self, in order to feel ever more "at home" in English.

Introduction

What do upper-intermediate and advanced-level adults expect from an English course?

You might want to note down your own answers before you read on.

Our research suggests that, above all, learners at any level expect:

- to become fluent listeners and speakers as quickly as possible;
- confidence building, quick results, and a strong sense of progress;
- contemporary, interesting largely authentic content, i.e., real-life, adult relevance with lots of personalization;
- overt teaching of grammar and vocabulary, a systematic approach to pronunciation, plenty of skills practice, with ever lengthening texts to reflect the higher level and potential exam needs, and useful study tips;
- an appropriate, adult teaching style combined with strong self-study elements, including autonomous learning tools to speed up their learning: we provide keys to most of the material, audio for all longer texts, and all the listening and video activities are available on the platform for self-study;
- value—both for the time they invest and the money they spend.

As sts' level gets higher, it's harder to notice progress, so motivation to continue studying is best fostered by successful achievement of more challenging tasks and learning more complex expressions leading to tangible progress. In iDentities sts can expect:

- increased focus on accuracy, as well as fluency to give them the necessary self-confidence to express more complex arguments;
- to be able to express themselves with greater control, depth and precision, using a wider range of words, expressions and grammatical structures, leading to fluency and spontaneity in English;
- recycling of familiar structures with new and more subtle distinctions (e.g., perfect tenses, modal verbs, future forms, phrasal verbs, expressions, etc.)

Methodology

Like English ID, iDentities is in every sense a communicative course, teaching learners to speak in as short a time as possible and focusing on both fluency and accuracy. You will note, for example, the large number of speech bubbles (to model and cue speaking activities) and the **Common mistakes** (anticipating likely L1 transfer errors that should be avoided) presented in most lessons.

Learners need to be given opportunities to express their own ideas and opinions. English ID and iDentities progressively adapt as the series evolves to reflect the best learning practices at each of the learner's advancing levels. At advanced levels, there is an increased focus on levels of formality, as a student's need to master various registers gradually increases.

The same goes for the lexis—where the initial simple task of matching vocabulary to pictures in the early levels of English ID becomes more abstract and contextualized in iDentities—and grammar, where spoon-feeding is reduced and inductive learning increased, as learners' confidence and foreign language learning experience grow.

iDentities provides the tools to allow you, the teacher, to incorporate your own pedagogical identity into the course, as well as to emphasize what you think will be more relevant for your learners.

Flexi-lessons

iDentities follows on from English ID to offer a unique flexi-lesson structure because one lesson is never enough to practice and consolidate all of its content. iDentities, therefore, gives students more opportunities than most books to revisit, consolidate or extend what they first learned in the previous lessons.

Constant and consistent recycling of language is essential for memorization, making learning much more likely. iDentities regularly builds bridges between lessons rather than packaging lessons in "artificially neat" units just to fit a notional design. Besides, every lesson / institution / teacher is different, with its own identity. A lesson structure where there is little or no connection between lessons is unlikely to foster efficient or optimum learning—hence our flexi-lessons. As students are now at a higher level, you will also notice that topics are pursued in more depth, with sub-themes of broader topics developed through the unit.

Key concepts

English promotes the three friendlies: it is language-friendly, learner-friendly, and teacher-friendly.

1. Language-friendly

iDentities, like English ID is not just another international series. It is a language-friendly series, which embraces

Introduction

students' existing language knowledge—a fundamental pillar of all foreign language learning for example, through exploiting cognates, familiar structures, famous songlines, and local cultural background—to help them better understand how English works.

2. Learner-friendly

iDentities respects the learner's need to be spoken to as an adult, so students explore a full range of topics requiring critical thinking. iDentities also helps students to negotiate and build their own new identity in English.

In addition, iDentities:

- supports students, helping them avoid obvious errors in form, word order, and pronunciation;
- motivates students, as they discover they can recognize a lot of English, which they already have "inside themselves";
- offers a vast range of activities, resources and recycling in order to ensure students have enough practice to finally learn to speak English.

3. Teacher-friendly

iDentities respects each teacher's need to teach as he or she wants to. Some wish to teach off the page with minimal preparation, others dip in and out, while others largely follow the Teacher's Book. All these options have been built into iDentities from the start.

The flexi-lesson structure helps teachers to individualize, personalize and vary classes, as well as focus on what is important for them.

The Teacher's Book has a teaching-friendly visual code, providing a straightforward "quick route" or a substantially longer one. Everything that is essential is clearly separated from all the optional extras.

Key features

1. A 60-question syllabus

Every lesson begins with a question as the title, which serves as a natural warm-up activity to introduce and later review each lesson topic. At higher levels, these questions serve the very important role of schema building, as topics logically become more complex, varied, and include more authentic language and information.

Therefore, these questions offer:

- an introduction to the lesson topic, an essential component for a good lesson, as, in some cases, topics may be new to students;
- a ready-made short lead-in to create interest, paving the way for the integration of skills, grammar, and content;
- an opportunity for sts to get to know and feel comfortable with each other before the lesson begins, facilitating pair and group work;
- an instant revision or speaking activity, whenever you need one: sts in pairs can look back at the map of the book and ask and answer random questions;
- a wonderful expression of syllabus;
- a useful placement test. Asking some of the 60 question when sts are being level-tested is a good way to help place them appropriately.

2. A balanced approach to grammar

Our rich grammar syllabus offers an eclectic approach to meet the needs of all students. It offers an innovative combination of:

- inductive grammar, with students discovering patterns and completing rules for themselves in and around the lesson-page grammar boxes;
- deductive grammar, through interesting facts about language and regular reminders of key rules, in addition to important usage notes;
- a discrete degree of proactive, contrastive grammar analysis, by showing what not to say via **Common mistakes**;
- a wide variety of extra grammar practice in review units, the Workbook, on the Richmond Learning Platform, as well as suggestions for extra contextualized writing in the Teacher's Book;
- a new **Grammar expansion** feature at this level, containing 24 pages of explanation and exercises (two per unit) focusing on more advanced language points. This section can be done in class, or assigned as homework. The corresponding core lesson is indicated in each case.

3. It has to be personal

Not only the 60 lesson question titles, but each phase of every lesson (and most Workbook lessons) ends with **Make it personal** activities: real, extended personalization—the key stage in any language practice activity. Students expand all topics and main language items into their own lives, opinions, contexts, and experiences. This is how students continue to construct and consolidate their English identity. Successfully "making it personal" is what makes students believe that they can be themselves in English.

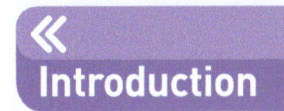

4. Avoid common mistakes to speak better, more quickly

Many lessons include **Common mistakes**, a flexible resource to foster accuracy. We highlight what to avoid before, during and / or after any lesson. **Common mistakes** helps maximize self- and peer-correction too. Students are enabled to help and teach themselves, by anticipating and therefore more quickly avoiding, reviewing, and remembering typical learner errors. At the high-intermediate and advanced levels, these sections help reinforce language as it is taught, thereby avoiding L1 transfer and fossilization.

If short of time, as teachers so often are, **Common mistakes** can help you cut through a longer, more inductive presentation and get to the practice activity more quickly. They are flexible, too: you can refer to them at any time in the lesson, usually the earlier the better.

5. Integrated skills

The fifth lesson in each unit is an integrated skills page, which gives students the opportunity to immerse themselves in a highly-engaging, contemporary topic and practice all four skills in real-world activities.

6. Useful language boxes

In iDentities these boxes have specific names like *Common uses of get*, *Types of noun modifiers*, or *More about can and could*, which immediately focus student and teacher attention on the point covered, enabling classes to use their time more efficiently.

7. Classic song lines to "hook" language

iDentities continues on from English iD with its use of music in exercises, cultural references, images, and, most obviously, the authentic song lines in each lesson. In addition, music as a theme features prominently in several lessons.

Why music? Songs are often the most popular source of authentic listening practice in and out of class. Most students have picked up a lot of English words through songs, ads, TV theme tunes, movie soundtracks, etc. But often they don't realize they know them or the exact meaning of what they're singing.

The song lines empower both teachers and students by offering useful language references and pronunciation models; and an authentic source of student-friendly input to elicit, present, practice, personalize, extend, and "hook" almost anything.

Unique to English iD and iDentities, the song lines have a direct link to each lesson, whether to illustrate grammar, lexis, or the lesson topic, and are designed to provide an authentic hook to help students remember the lesson

Introduction

and the language studied. Looking for the link provides an additional fun, puzzle-like element to every lesson. Students should also enjoy the **Language in song** bonus activities in the **Grammar expansion** section.

iDentities Teacher's Book offers a highly original useful **Song activities** bank of cultural, background and procedural notes for every song line, including the artist's name, suggestions on exactly where and how to exploit it, and optional activities. You can find this useful resource on pages 341-355.

> **Tip**
>
> Of course, we don't suggest you use these songs in full, just the extract we've chosen. Besides, many aren't actually appropriate when you look at the complete lyrics, but the lines we've chosen are globally famous and should be easy to identify, find on the internet, and be sung by at least some students. Obviously, with your own classes you can exploit the song lines in a variety of ways.

Some ways to use song lines in iDentities:

- Play / show (part of) the song as students come into class
- Sing / hum the song line and / or look for links to the song at an appropriate time during the class to help students remember the lesson later
- Read and guess the artist's gender, message, etc.
- Analyze the song for pronunciation: rhyme, repeated sounds, alliteration
- Expand. *What comes before / after this line? What's the whole song about?*
- Change the tense or some words to make it more or less formal and see how it sounds. *Why did the artist choose this tense?*
- Provoke discussion around a theme / issue
- *What do you associate the song with?*, e.g., a moment, vacation, dance, movie
- Search online for other songs that connect to the lesson in some way
- Use sections of the song as a class warm-up, review, listening for pleasure, an end of the lesson sing-along, etc.
- Board or dictate the line but add, subtract or change some words for sts to correct it (similar to **Common Mistakes**)

Course structure and components

English coursebooks have often been too long, too repetitive or inflexible, meaning teachers have either to

Introduction

rush to get through them—denying students the practice they need to achieve an adequate degree of fluency—or start omitting sections, often leaving students feeling frustrated. iDentities was designed to be flexible, so you can tailor it to fit your schedule. It provides 80-100 class hours of teaching.

iDentities has …

- twelve core units, each comprised of five approximately one-hour lessons. That's 60 lessons containing listening, grammar, vocabulary, speaking, reading, and writing
- authentic video
- 24 pages of Grammar expansion + corresponding exercises
- selected audio scripts that encourage students to focus on specific listening points
- a comprehensive list of separable and inseparable phrasal verbs and their meanings
- Workbook: one page of review and extra practice material per lesson
- Richmond Learning Platform for iDentities, which can be accessed using the code on the inside front cover of the Student's Book
- Digital Book for Teachers: IWB version of the Student's Book

Vocabulary

iDentities focuses on high-frequency words and expressions in context, and provides a variety of word-building tools, including a 4-page **Phrasal verb list** on page 164 of the Student's Book. This summarizes the most common phrasal verbs used in English and is a great resource for cover-and-test-yourself memorization, as well as a "mini dictionary" for reading and listening. If time permits, encourage students to write what are often the more formal Latinate equivalents alongside them in pencil and learn both.

By limiting new vocabulary sets to only seven items per section, iDentities ensures that students are never overloaded and will transfer to their productive use the new words and expressions presented.

Skills

Speaking

iDentities teaches spoken English and prioritizes oral fluency.

In order to learn both quickly and well, students should be given every opportunity to try to express their ideas and opinions in comprehensible English at every stage of every lesson. After all, practice and personalization are the best way to improve and self-correct, and whatever method you use, accuracy will always be the last element of competence learners will acquire. In iDentities every lesson, be it a listening, vocabulary, grammar, reading or writing focus, is full of controlled oral practice and personalized speaking opportunities, clearly marked and modeled by multiple speech bubbles on every page.

iDentities offers fluency, accuracy and pronunciation practice at every opportunity. **Keep talking** sections consolidate and put into practice the language learned and lead directly into **Writing** on the facing page, where students can choose from among topics they've already discussed. This significant unique feature not only encourages the integration of skills, but develops the very important skill of distinguishing levels of formality and registers. The presentation of more formal language and register contrasts is expanded further in iDentities 2.

Finally, at the upper-intermediate and advanced levels, the importance of language strategies and speech acts increases, as anyone who has to function in a foreign language begins to realize. "Fluent" English consists of far more than grammatical sentences. For that reason, iDentities offers a new **How to say it** section, which highlights expressions and responses especially useful for managing conversations successfully.

Listening

iDentities has more listening than most other high-intermediate and advanced courses: frequently 13 to 16 activities per unit that include scripts of increasing length, more challenging activities focusing on inference, as well as gist and detail listening, and numerous "Listen to check" activities that provide additional language information for students.

Listening homework should be set as often as possible as what students most need is to spend the maximum time in the company of English in order to become truly confident when expressing themselves in English. These days this is relatively easy—they can listen while doing other things, at home, traveling, at the gym, etc.

In addition to the material included in the course itself, teachers may find some of the following suggestions helpful, either in or out of class:

- have students create their own listening practice at this level—listening to music or podcasts, watching TV or movies, using bi-lingual websites to figure out what words mean, sending each other recordings in English via, e.g., Whatsapp;

- dictogloss short sections of any listening activity—listen and remember (or write down) all you can, then compare in pairs;
- pause at any time in any listening to check comprehension: *What do you think was said?* after any short section is a key question in trying to teach rather than keep testing listening.

If time permits ...

- sensitize students to how words blur and have a variety of sound shapes in connected speech and elicit/explain how pronunciation changes;
- expose students to "the difficult," e.g., phoneme variations in connected speech; dictate multiple examples of phrases containing the same weak forms;
- model processes used by L1 listeners: decoding sounds into words / clauses and building larger scale meaning;
- transcribe elision as they hear it: old people = *ole people*, a blind man = *a bly man*, etc;
- study and interpret, e.g. pairs: *He said he called* vs. *He said he'd call*.

The following are some ideas for listening homework that you could set your students:

- Listening to recordings of the class itself (flipped)—instructions, stories, pair work, roleplay, etc.
- Web-based listening: songs, podcasts, searching online for the huge number of online lessons available now, YouTube, radio, audio books, TV (with subtitles in L1 & L2)
- Homework partners—call / record messages, check answers with partner, dub favorite movie scene, etc.

Reading

In iDentities, reading texts become longer and in iDentities 2 consist almost exclusively of authentic material. To prepare students to read such material, both levels include a wider range of reading skills. Activities focus on such areas as pronoun reference; new lexical sets where students can see words and expressions in context; predicting; capturing the essence of a section and the author's intention; and perhaps most importantly, interacting with the content of the text. **Make it personal** activities in **Reading** lessons allow students to react to and evaluate the author's ideas by presenting their own.

Just because texts are necessarily longer should not mean classes have to be dull, with long, silent "heads down" periods. We strongly suggest you break them up, giving short tasks:

- Keep tasks to 2 or 3 minutes tasks, then have sts share what they remember, and predict what comes next before reading on. You can do this several times in some of the longer texts, making classes much livelier and allowing you to see and hear how fast individuals read, how much they have taken in, and what help they need.
- Sts in pairs each read a different paragraph to create an information gap, then tell each other what they read.
- Give sts (via the digital board, cut up slips, or let them choose) random samples of the texts—a couple of lines from different paragraphs, or the first and last line of each paragraph, etc., to share what they understood and speculate about what else they will read, before doing so to check.
- With any text you can get sts to cover it with a sheet of paper, read one line at a time, guess what comes next in pairs, then unveil the next line to see if they were right. They then do the same with the next line, and so on.
- Make each st in a group responsible for finding the answer to one of the questions, then share with the group.
- Help sts experience different reading skills: skimming, scanning, etc., even within the same text, by setting different tasks, and perhaps giving them reading role cards for different paragraphs or columns of text: *A) Read and translate the text word by word.; B) Read the text in order to memorize as much of the information as you can.; C) Read the text for the general idea.; D) Read the text aloud quietly to yourself at a comfortable speed.*

These ideas and many more you will find expanded in the Teacher's notes.

Writing

The fifth and final lesson in each unit is different from the others. The first page leads to a substantial **Keep talking** activity; the second is dedicated to process writing.

Our writing syllabus is primarily covered by these twelve activities, with twelve different genres and additional attention to writing in the Review units and Workbook. Here students are given a clear written model, a variety of tasks to analyze it, specific writing tips and a structured model to draft, check, then share with a classmate, before finally submitting it to you or posting on the class learning platform / wiki. The intention is to protect you, the busy teacher, from having to dedicate time to excessive marking of avoidable mistakes, as well as to help students be more in control of their own writing. Indeed, we strongly suggest you show sts that you are not their editor but their teacher, and insist they see helping with and improving writing as a class responsibility.

Introduction

For this reason, we suggest you try partial marking, underlining (key) errors for sts to self-correct, using a marking code (there are many online), etc., so that sts become more aware of the options and, above all, work at least as hard as you do at correction.

The left-hand page of each lesson introduces the topic through listening, via genres such as radio shows, lectures, or dialogues. Additional development of listening skills then moves into open-ended speaking, the **Keep talking** section that synthesizes the unit through discussion, personalized role-playing, surveys, or problem-solving situations. This section frequently presents **How to say it** expressions to facilitate the activity.

A unique feature of iDentities is to include only authentic genres in the twelve units.

Pronunciation

To the extent that you choose to work on pronunciation, any of the following ideas may be helpful:

- Emphasize the relevance of the pronunciation tasks to improve listening comprehension and increasingly natural sounding English.
- Make sure sts understand that their pronunciation does not need to be "perfect" or "near native," but it does need to be clear and facilitate communication. To that end, focus on features that most impinge on international communication with your particular learners.
- Explore what sts already know, e.g., from song lines, TV, their travels, etc., and have them record and listen to themselves imitating texts they like or wish to deliver better.
- Model new words in context rather than in isolation, e.g., in a phrase: *the environment* not just *environment*, so they get used to stressing and reducing. In this way, the focus on intonation, phrase or sentence stress, word boundaries, etc. increases.
- Respond naturally to incorrect models or effects of "wrong" intonation and encourage repetition to say it better, e.g., say *Excuse me?* in response to incorrect pronunciation or flat intonation.
- Highlight linking (a line between words: *an_orange*), pauses (/ = short pause, // = longer pause) and sentence stress shift (eliciting different meanings according to which words are stressed).
- Work on transcripts, e.g., shadow read text and sub-vocalize to self; notice and underline most stressed words / pauses / links. Turn any audioscript into a proper listening / pronunciation teaching vehicle.
- Spot the music, e.g., help them hear changes of pitch
- Track, shadow, rehearse, imitate, repeat, and record themselves

Systematic visual pronunciation activities give real help in many lessons. Pink syllables have been retained in iDentities to show you how to stress new, poly-syllabic words when they first appear in reading texts.

Therefore, iDentities offers real help with all aspects of pronunciation.

Review lessons

There is ample opportunity for review and recycling throughout the book via the six review lessons. These include many additional activities focusing on speaking, grammar, listening, reading, writing, self-test (error-correction), and point of view (debate). Some skills alternate across the review units, but all are thoroughly covered. Don't forget, you can always look back at the song lines and re-use the lesson question titles, too!

Learner autonomy

iDentities offers a clear layout, lessons that progress transparently, and many language explanations. While these features greatly facilitate classroom teaching, they also allow for easy review and autonomous learning. Depending on the classroom hours available, many activities in the course (e.g., selected vocabulary, grammar, reading, and writing tasks) could be assigned for homework. The student-friendly grammar boxes, with additional explanation in **Grammar expansion**, also allow for easy review. The actual review units can be assigned for homework also.

Another way to encourage learner autonomy is with the brand new **search online tasks** included in iDentities. These days, we all depend more and more on online search tasks, seeking information or translations, purchasing items, etc. The classroom should be no different, so students are invited individually or in groups to look online for their own texts and authentic information to bring greater personalization, individualization and localization, to many activities. These can be done before, during or after class, depending on your needs and the availability of technology (and time!). Students are also encouraged to search for additional information they may need to develop their arguments for **Keep talking** activities or writing tasks.

Introduction

If it seems feasible, you may wish to consider "flipping" more of your classes, too. Before any major presentation or review activity, have students search online for material to support the next lesson. This is especially useful for weaker students, who might be struggling to keep up, but also works for stronger students, who might even be able to lead the next class themselves.

A key element in the thinking behind both iDentities and English ID has been to produce textbooks which are not too long. iDentities 2 is made up of twelve ten-page units, which leaves teachers more time to do whatever is most needed, including searching online and, of course, customizing lessons with local names, places, and references.

Richmond Learning Platform for iDentities

This extremely useful and user-friendly blended learning tool has been developed in parallel with the series and combines the best of formal and informal learning to extend, review and test core lesson content. The full range of resources is available to teachers and students who adopt either of the iDentities levels. The Richmond Learning Platform will be regularly updated with new features and content, and we believe both students and teachers will enjoy and benefit from its content. The Richmond Learning Platform for iDentities includes:

- interactive activities to cover all language points in iDentities Student's Books
- Skills Boost: extra reading and listening practice available in interactive format
- Tests: Unit Tests and Review Tests
- Resources for teachers
- Downloadable audio
- Access to authentic video material

To access the platform, go to richmondlp.com and use the access code on the inside front cover of the Student's Book.

Workbook

In the Workbook, a single page corresponds to each Student's Book lesson, designed to consolidate and reinforce all the main language. Exercises can be used in class, e.g., for fast finishers, or extra practice of specific areas.

The Workbook includes:

- a variety of exercises, texts, and puzzles to scaffold, continue practicing and extend the main grammar and vocabulary of each lesson;
- Skills Practice: several listening activities per unit to continue practicing the most important skill outside class, plus plenty of short, enjoyable reading texts
- Song lines: students are asked to look back at the five song lines in the unit and find the link to the lesson—a fun way of reviewing each unit

Interleaved Teacher's Book

iDentities offers a rich, complete, teacher-friendly, lesson plan for every left and right hand page of each lesson. It provides a complete step-by-step lesson plan from beginning to end, offering:

- lesson overviews and aims
- an optional books-closed warm-up for every lesson
- an alternative books-open warm-up based around the question title
- step-by-step notes and suggestions for each on-page activity, including background information and language notes where appropriate
- help with identifying the focus of each activity and any new language being presented; additional help (where relevant) on presenting increasingly complicated grammar
- teaching tips to vary and hone your teaching skills
- suggestions for multi-level classes (ideas for both stronger and weaker students)
- extra writing options for every lesson
- a complete answer key and audioscript
- a bank of original ideas for exploiting each songline in a different way, as well as background information and step-by-step, teaching notes for the song lines

Digital Book for Teachers / IWB

The Digital Book for Teachers is a separate medium containing all the pages of the Student's Book. Teachers can use this resource to promote variety in their classes, at all stages of any lesson, so that students can see the images on the IWB instead of looking at the book. It's particularly useful for operating the audio, zooming images and adding zest and color to your classes!

On the next pages you will find detailed information about all the features of iDentities.

iDentities

STUDENT'S BOOK 2

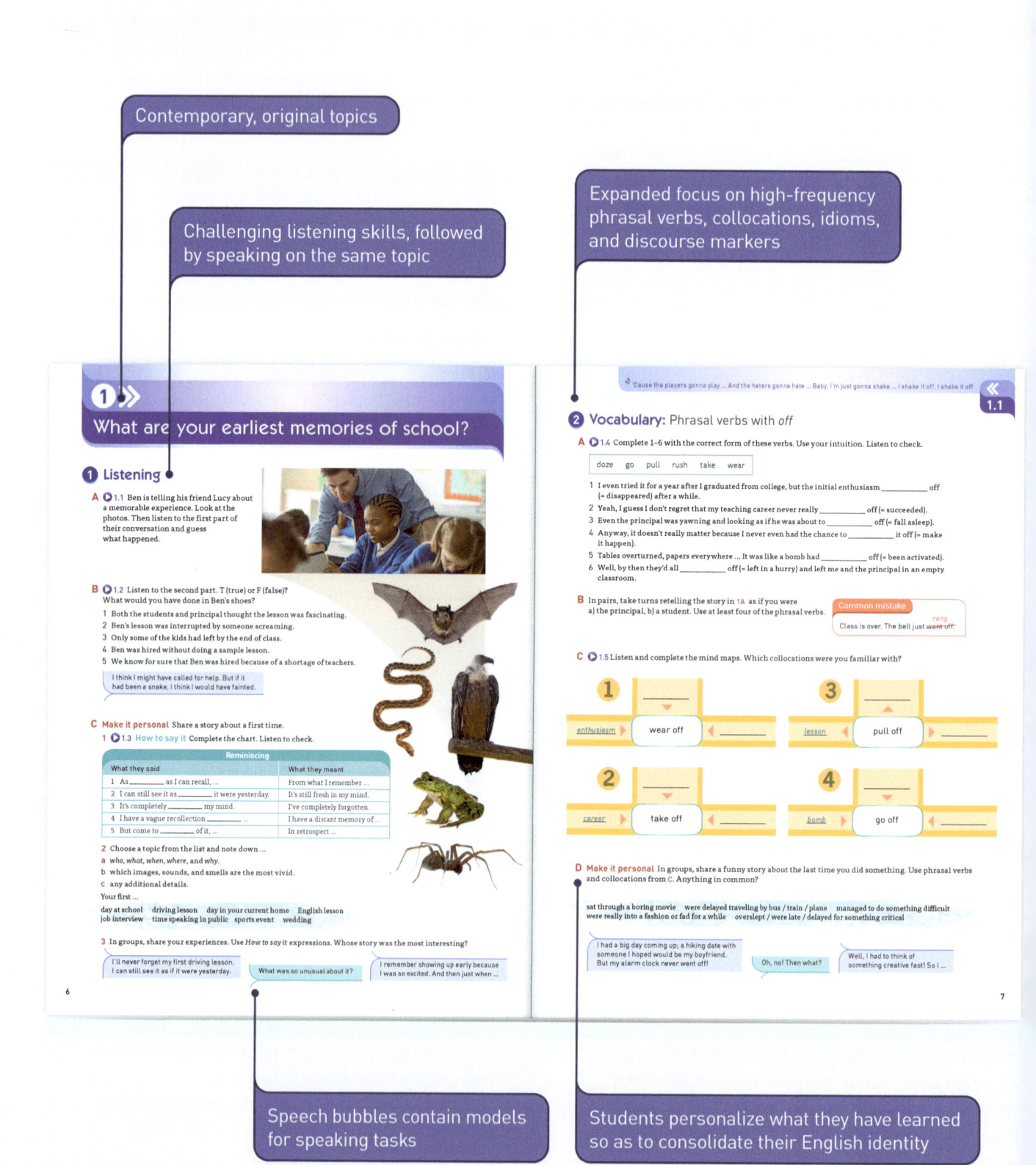

Contemporary, original topics

Challenging listening skills, followed by speaking on the same topic

Expanded focus on high-frequency phrasal verbs, collocations, idioms, and discourse markers

Speech bubbles contain models for speaking tasks

Students personalize what they have learned so as to consolidate their English identity

---

1 » What are your earliest memories of school?

1 Listening

A ▶1.1 Ben is telling his friend Lucy about a memorable experience. Look at the photos. Then listen to the first part of their conversation and guess what happened.

B ▶1.2 Listen to the second part. T (true) or F (false)? What would you have done in Ben's shoes?
1 Both the students and principal thought the lesson was fascinating.
2 Ben's lesson was interrupted by someone screaming.
3 Only some of the kids had left by the end of class.
4 Ben was hired without doing a sample lesson.
5 We know for sure that Ben was hired because of a shortage of teachers.

> I think I might have called for help. But if it had been a snake, I think I would have fainted.

C Make it personal Share a story about a first time.

1 ▶1.3 *How to say it* Complete the chart. Listen to check.

Reminiscing	
What they said	What they meant
1 As _____ as I can recall, …	From what I remember …
2 I can still see it as _____ it were yesterday.	It's still fresh in my mind.
3 It's completely _____ my mind.	I've completely forgotten.
4 I have a vague recollection _____ …	I have a distant memory of …
5 But come to _____ of it, …	In retrospect …

2 Choose a topic from the list and note down …
a who, what, when, where, and why.
b which images, sounds, and smells are the most vivid.
c any additional details.
Your first …
day at school   driving lesson   day in your current home   English lesson
job interview   time speaking in public   sports event   wedding

3 In groups, share your experiences. Use *How to say it* expressions. Whose story was the most interesting?

> I'll never forget my first driving lesson. I can still see it as if it were yesterday.

> What was so unusual about it?

> I remember showing up early because I was so excited. And then just when …

♪ *Cause the players gonna play … And the haters gonna hate … Baby, I'm just gonna shake … I shake it off, I shake it off* « 1.1

2 Vocabulary: Phrasal verbs with *off*

A ▶1.4 Complete 1–6 with the correct form of these verbs. Use your intuition. Listen to check.

doze   go   pull   rush   take   wear

1 I even tried it for a year after I graduated from college, but the initial enthusiasm _____ off (= disappeared) after a while.
2 Yeah, I guess I don't regret that my teaching career never really _____ off (= succeeded).
3 Even the principal was yawning and looking as if he was about to _____ off (= fall asleep).
4 Anyway, it doesn't really matter because I never even had the chance to _____ it off (= make it happen).
5 Tables overturned, papers everywhere … It was like a bomb had _____ off (= been activated).
6 Well, by then they'd all _____ off (= left in a hurry) and left me and the principal in an empty classroom.

B In pairs, take turns retelling the story in 1A as if you were a) the principal, b) a student. Use at least four of the phrasal verbs.

> **Common mistake**
> Class is over. The bell just ~~went off~~. *rang*

C ▶1.5 Listen and complete the mind maps. Which collocations were you familiar with?

1 *enthusiasm* → wear off
2 *career* → take off
3 *lesson* → pull off
4 *bomb* → go off

D Make it personal In groups, share a funny story about the last time you did something. Use phrasal verbs and collocations from **C**. Anything in common?

sat through a boring movie   were delayed traveling by bus / train / plane   managed to do something difficult
were really into a fashion or fad for a while   overslept / were late / delayed for something critical

> I had a big day coming up; a hiking date with someone I hoped would be my boyfriend. But my alarm clock never went off!

> Oh, no! Then what?

> Well, I had to think of something creative fast! So I …

Introduction

Lesson titles are questions forming a ready-made warm-up activity and schema-builder to lead students naturally—and personally—into the topic.

Emphasis on inductive grammar and focus on the subtleties of language

1.2 What innovative businesses do you know?

3 Language in use

A 🔊 1.6 Listen to the start of a podcast. What's it about?
- ☐ People who want to innovate and turn their ideas into a small business.
- ☐ Big companies that try to meet people's changing needs.

B 🔊 1.7 In pairs, look at the photos and the slogans. What exactly do you think each start-up does? Listen to the rest to check. How close were you?

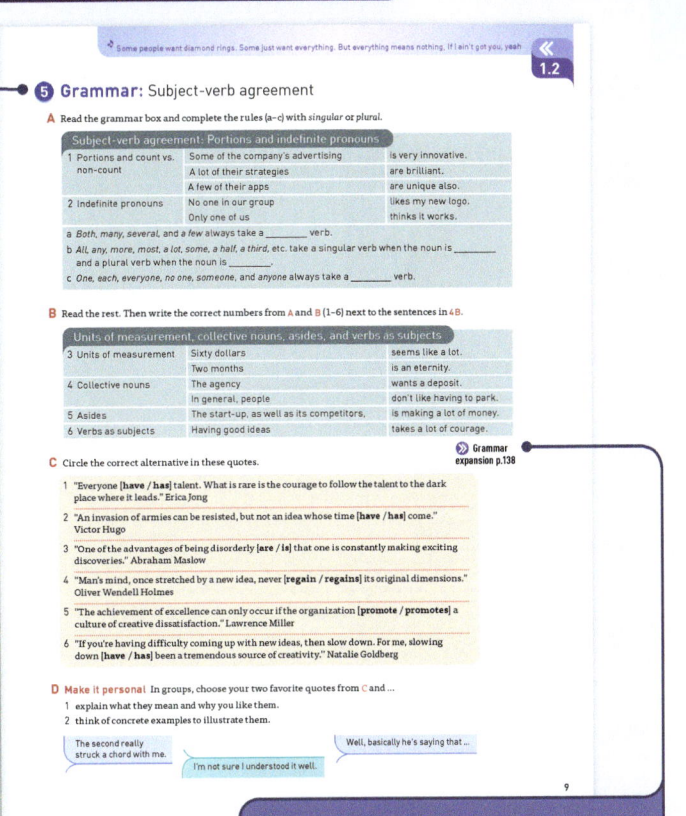

C In pairs, which start-up would be more successful where you live? What kinds of problems might each one face?

> *Lists and Twists* would be a hard sell. Maybe it's just me, but I'd hate to wear something that's been worn before.

4 Pronunciation: Final consonant clusters

A 🔊 1.8 Read and listen to sentences 1 and 2. Cross out the letters you hardly hear at all, or don't hear, in the **highlighted** words. Then circle the correct word in the rule.

1. IT manager Elena Fernández left her job and created *Lists* and *Twists*, a company that has shipped more than 100,000 dollars in **products** since 2015.
2. The app **asks** where you're going and invites you as you make your way to your destination – just like your **parents** used to do on the week**ends**.

A consonant cluster is a group of consonants with no vowels between them. In final clusters ending in /sts/, /kts/, /sks/, /nts/ and /ndz/, the [**first** / **second** / **third**] consonant is very weak or not pronounced.

B 🔊 1.9 Listen and complete 1–4 with words that end in consonant clusters. Then listen again and repeat.
1. One of our _____ seven articles of clothing. ☐
2. Our team _____ new clothes based on your _____ and purchase history. ☐
3. If 60 dollars _____ like a lot of money, that's nothing compared to what most designer clothing usually _____ . ☐
4. The feedback we've been getting from our _____ , as well as the number of positive press reviews, _____ our commitment to excellence. ☐

C Make it personal Complete 1–6 to create your own innovations. Which is the class favorite?
I'd like to see a start-up / an NGO / an app / a robot that …
inspects [1]_____ free of charge.   scans our hard disks for [2]_____ .
looks for the best discounts in [3]_____ ,   lists [4]_____ in our area.
reinvents the way we [5]_____ .   defends the rights of [6]_____ .

> I'd like to see a robot that inspects my car free of charge. I'm tired of getting ripped off by mechanics!

5 Grammar: Subject-verb agreement

A Read the grammar box and complete the rules (a–c) with *singular* or *plural*.

Subject-verb agreement: Portions and indefinite pronouns		
1 Portions and count vs. non-count	Some of the company's advertising	is very innovative.
	A lot of their strategies	are brilliant.
	A few of their apps	are unique also.
2 Indefinite pronouns	No one in our group	likes my new logo.
	Only one of us	thinks it works.

a *Both*, *many*, *several*, and *a few* always take a _____ verb.
b *All*, *any*, *more*, *most*, *a lot*, *some*, *a half*, *a third*, etc. take a singular verb when the noun is _____ and a plural verb when the noun is _____ .
c *One*, *each*, *everyone*, *no one*, *someone*, and *anyone* always take a _____ verb.

B Read the rest. Then write the correct numbers from A and B (1–6) next to the sentences in 4B.

Units of measurement, collective nouns, asides, and verbs as subjects		
3 Units of measurement	Sixty dollars	seems like a lot.
	Two months	is an eternity.
4 Collective nouns	The agency	wants a deposit.
	In general, people	don't like having to park.
5 Asides	The start-up, as well as its competitors,	is making a lot of money.
6 Verbs as subjects	Having good ideas	takes a lot of courage.

C Circle the correct alternative in these quotes.
1. "Everyone [**have** / **has**] talent. What is rare is the courage to follow the talent to the dark place where it leads." Erica Jong
2. "An invasion of armies can be resisted, but not an idea whose time [**have** / **has**] come." Victor Hugo
3. "One of the advantages of being disorderly [**are** / **is**] that one is constantly making exciting discoveries." Abraham Maslow
4. "Man's mind, once stretched by a new idea, never [**regain** / **regains**] its original dimensions." Oliver Wendell Holmes
5. "The achievement of excellence can only occur if the organization [**promote** / **promotes**] a culture of creative dissatisfaction." Lawrence Miller
6. "If you're having difficulty coming up with new ideas, then slow down. For me, slowing down [**have** / **has**] been a tremendous source of creativity." Natalie Goldberg

D Make it personal In groups, choose your two favorite quotes from C and …
1. explain what they mean and why you like them.
2. think of concrete examples to illustrate them.

> The second really struck a chord with me.
> I'm not sure I understood it well.
> Well, basically he's saying that …

➡ Grammar expansion p.138

Refers students to new aspects of the structure and extra activities

A wide range of reading skills encourage students to interact with the texts

1.3 How many ways can you use a brick?

6 Reading

A Read the first paragraph. In pairs, what creative ideas or solutions have occurred to you in the shower? List as many as you can in two minutes.

> I've figured out the solution to some crossword clues.

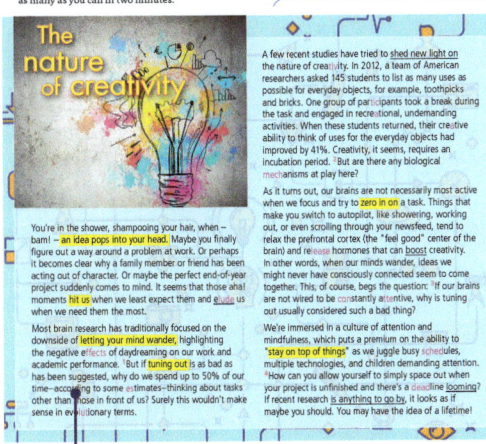

The nature of creativity

A few recent studies have tried to shed new light on the nature of creativity. In 2012, a team of American researchers asked 145 students to list as many uses as possible for everyday objects, for example, toothpicks and bricks. One group of participants took a break during the task and engaged in recreational, undemanding activities. When these students returned, their creative ability to think of uses for the everyday objects had improved by 41%. Creativity, it seems, requires an incubation period. [2]But are there any biological mechanisms at play here?

You're in the shower, shampooing your hair, when – bam! – an idea pops into your head. Maybe you finally figure out a way around a problem at work. Or perhaps it becomes clear why a family member or friend has been acting out of character. Or maybe the perfect end-of-year project suddenly comes to mind. It seems that those aha! moments hit us when we least expect them and elude us when we need them the most.

As it turns out, our brains are not necessarily most active when we focus and try to zero in on a task. Things that make you switch to autopilot, like showering, working out, or even scrolling through your newsfeed, tend to relax the prefrontal cortex (the "feel good" center of the brain) and release hormones that can boost creativity. In other words, when our minds wander, ideas we might never have consciously connected seem to come together. This, of course, begs the question: "If our brains are not wired to be constantly attentive, why is tuning out usually considered such a bad thing?"

Most brain research has traditionally focused on the downside of letting your mind wander, highlighting the negative effects of daydreaming on our work and academic performance. [3]But if tuning out is as bad as has been suggested, why do we spend up to 50% of our time—according to some estimates—thinking about tasks other than those in front of us? Surely this wouldn't make sense in evolutionary terms.

We're immersed in a culture of attention and mindfulness, which puts a premium on the ability to stay on top of things as we juggle busy schedules, multiple technologies, and children demanding attention. [4]How can you allow yourself to simply space out when your project is unfinished and there's a deadline looming? If recent research is anything to go by, maybe you should. You may have the idea of a lifetime!

B 🔊 1.10 Read and listen. In pairs, match the questions (1–4) in the article to the most likely answers (a–e). There's one extra.
a. ☐ We are expected to be focused.
b. ☐ Creative ideas need time to develop.
c. ☐ Students who daydream get better grades.
d. ☐ It's the best way to have a creative idea.
e. ☐ When you're distracted, the pleasure centers of your brain react positively.

C Find 1–5 in the article and circle the most likely meaning in the context.
1. *elude* (paragraph 1): We [**escape from** / **fail to achieve**] them.
2. *shed new light on* (paragraph 3): They [**explain** / **define**] it in a new way.
3. *boost* (paragraph 4): They [**amplify or increase it** / **push it up from below**].
4. *looming* (paragraph 5): It [**appears as a large form** / **is about to happen**].
5. *is anything to go by* (paragraph 5): It [**can be followed** / **should be obeyed**].

Interesting and useful language points

D Make it personal In groups, debate which statements are good advice. Find evidence in the article for or against. Has anyone ever said them to you?
1. "Stop daydreaming! You won't get your homework done in time again."
2. "Take a short break. Come back to it when you're fresh, and something will occur to you."
3. "You have to learn to concentrate or you won't get ahead!"
4. "Stop worrying so much about the deadline. Let's go out and have some fun. You might have a brilliant idea!"

> My parents used to say number 1 all the time.
> But look, in paragraph 3, it says …

7 Vocabulary: Figurative expressions for ideas

A Look at the **highlighted** expressions in the article in 6A. Then match them to pictures 1–6.

B In pairs, explain what the expressions mean. Use an online dictionary, if necessary. Then add them to the chart. Which images in A best help you remember them?

Having an idea	Getting distracted	Staying focused

> One meaning of *pop* is to "explode" or "burst open", so if an idea pops into your head, it "explodes" or "appears suddenly".
> Yes, like a burst of energy. So if I say, "An idea popped into my head," it means it was very sudden and wasn't there before.

C Share true sentences about yourself using at least three of the expressions in B.

> Yesterday when I was walking home from school, a great idea hit me …

D Make it personal In pairs, share your creative process.
1. Think of a time when you couldn't think of an idea.
2. Where / When / How did the solution finally come to you?
3. Have you applied your strategy to any new situations since then? Did it work?
4. Have you ever used any of the suggestions in the article?

> I took a very demanding art course, and it was hard to stay on top of all the projects. One day, an idea just wouldn't come to me.
> So what did you do?

Word stress highlighted in pink in reading texts

15

Introduction

Students activate the language in real-world situations

Song lines help English come alive!

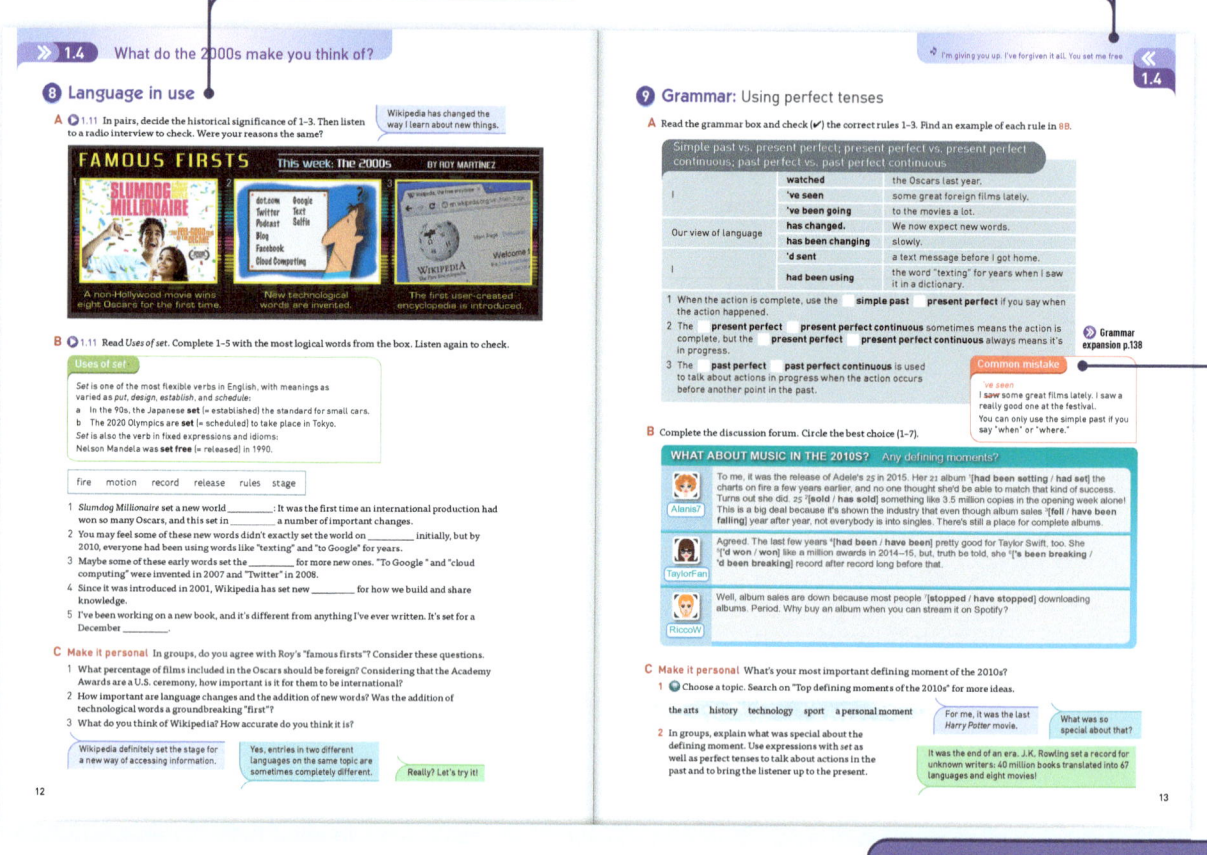

1.4 What do the 2000s make you think of?

8 Language in use

A ▶ 1.11 In pairs, decide the historical significance of 1-3. Then listen to a radio interview to check. Were your reasons the same?

Wikipedia has changed the way I learn about new things.

FAMOUS FIRSTS — This week: The 2000s — BY ROY MARTINEZ

- SLUMDOG MILLIONAIRE — A non-Hollywood movie wins eight Oscars for the first time.
- dot.com, Google, Twitter, Text, Podcast, Selfie, Blog, Facebook, Cloud Computing — New technological words are invented.
- WIKIPEDIA — The first user-created encyclopedia is introduced.

B ▶ 1.11 Read *Uses of set*. Complete 1-5 with the most logical words from the box. Listen again to check.

Uses of set
Set is one of the most flexible verbs in English, with meanings as varied as *put, design, establish,* and *schedule*:
a. In the 90s, the Japanese **set** (= established) the standard for small cars.
b. The 2020 Olympics are **set** (= scheduled) to take place in Tokyo.
Set is also the verb in fixed expressions and idioms:
Nelson Mandela was **set free** (= released) in 1990.

| fire | motion | record | release | rules | stage |

1. *Slumdog Millionaire* set a new world _____: It was the first time an international production had won so many Oscars, and this set in _____ a number of important changes.
2. You may feel some of these new words didn't exactly set the world on _____ initially, but by 2010, everyone had been using words like "texting" and "to Google" for years.
3. Maybe some of these early words set the _____ for more new ones. "To Google " and "cloud computing" were invented in 2007 and "Twitter" in 2008.
4. Since it was introduced in 2001, Wikipedia has set new _____ for how we build and share knowledge.
5. I've been working on a new book, and it's different from anything I've ever written. It's set for a December _____.

C Make it personal In groups, do you agree with Roy's "famous firsts"? Consider these questions.
1. What percentage of films included in the Oscars should be foreign? Considering that the Academy Awards are a U.S. ceremony, how important is it for them to be international?
2. How important are language changes and the addition of new words? Was the addition of technological words a groundbreaking "first"?
3. What do you think of Wikipedia? How accurate do you think it is?

Wikipedia definitely set the stage for a new way of accessing information.
Yes, entries in two different languages on the same topic are sometimes completely different.
Really? Let's try it!

9 Grammar: Using perfect tenses

I'm giving you up. I've forgiven it all. You set me free

A Read the grammar box and check (✓) the correct rules 1-3. Find an example of each rule in 8B.

Simple past vs. present perfect; present perfect vs. present perfect continuous; past perfect vs. past perfect continuous

	watched	the Oscars last year.
I	've seen	some great foreign films lately.
	've been going	to the movies a lot.
Our view of language	has changed.	We now expect new words.
	has been changing	slowly.
I	'd sent	a text message before I got home.
	had been using	the word "texting" for years when I saw it in a dictionary.

1. When the action is complete, use the ☐ simple past ☐ present perfect if you say when the action happened.
2. The ☐ present perfect ☐ present perfect continuous sometimes means the action is complete, but the ☐ present perfect ☐ present perfect continuous always means it's in progress.
3. The ☐ past perfect ☐ past perfect continuous is used to talk about actions in progress when the action occurs before another point in the past.

Common mistake
've seen
I saw some great films lately. I saw a really good one at the festival.
You can only use the simple past if you say "when" or "where."

→ Grammar expansion p.138

B Complete the discussion forum. Circle the best choice (1-7).

WHAT ABOUT MUSIC IN THE 2010S? Any defining moments?

Alanis?: To me, it was the release of Adele's 25 in 2015. Her 21 album ¹[had been setting / had set] the charts on fire a few years earlier, and no one thought she'd be able to match that kind of success. Turns out she did. 25 ²[sold / has sold] something like 3.5 million copies in the opening week alone! This is a big deal because it's shown the industry that even though album sales ³[fell / have been falling] year after year, not everybody is into singles. There's still a place for complete albums.

TaylorFan: Agreed. The last few years ⁴[had been / have been] pretty good for Taylor Swift, too. She ⁵[‘d won / won] like a million awards in 2014–15, but, truth be told, she ⁶[‘s been breaking / ‘d been breaking] record after record long before that.

RiccoW: Well, album sales are down because most people ⁷[stopped / have stopped] downloading albums. Period. Why buy an album when you can stream it on Spotify?

C Make it personal What's your most important defining moment of the 2010s?
1. ★ Choose a topic. Search on "Top defining moments of the 2010s" for more ideas.
   the arts   history   technology   sport   a personal moment
2. In groups, explain what was special about the defining moment. Use expressions with *set* as well as perfect tenses to talk about actions in the past and to bring the listener up to the present.

For me, it was the last Harry Potter movie.
What was so special about that?
It was the end of an era. J.K. Rowling set a record for unknown writers: 40 million books translated into 67 languages and eight movies!

Anticipate and prevent errors

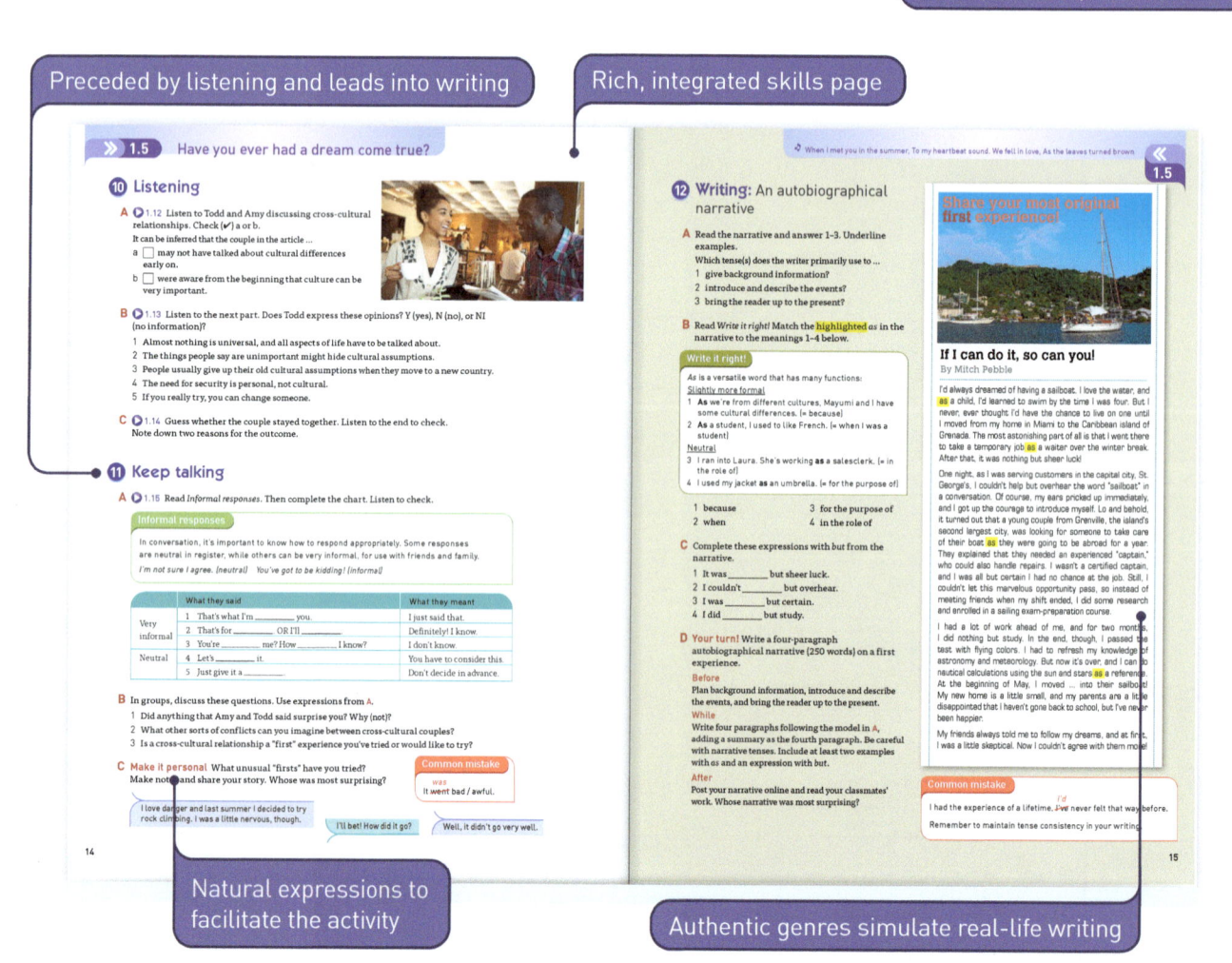

Preceded by listening and leads into writing

Rich, integrated skills page

1.5 Have you ever had a dream come true?

When I met you in the summer, To my heartbeat sound. We fell in love, As the leaves turned brown.

10 Listening

A ▶ 1.12 Listen to Todd and Amy discussing cross-cultural relationships. Check (✓) a or b.
It can be inferred that the couple in the article …
a ☐ may not have talked about cultural differences early on.
b ☐ were aware from the beginning that culture can be very important.

B ▶ 1.13 Listen to the next part. Does Todd express these opinions? Y (yes), N (no), or NI (no information)?
1. Almost nothing is universal, and all aspects of life have to be talked about.
2. The things people say are unimportant might hide cultural assumptions.
3. People usually give up their old cultural assumptions when they move to a new country.
4. The need for security is personal, not cultural.
5. If you really try, you can change someone.

C ▶ 1.14 Guess whether the couple stayed together. Listen to the end to check. Note down two reasons for the outcome.

11 Keep talking

A ▶ 1.15 Read *Informal responses*. Then complete the chart. Listen to check.

Informal responses
In conversation, it's important to know how to respond appropriately. Some responses are neutral in register, while others can be very informal, for use with friends and family.
I'm not sure I agree. (neutral)   *You've got to be kidding!* (informal)

	What they said	What they meant
Very informal	1. That's what I'm _____ you.	I just said that.
	2. That's for _____ OR I'll _____.	Definitely! I know.
	3. You're _____ me? How _____ I know?	I don't know.
Neutral	4. Let's _____ it.	You have to consider this.
	5. Just give it a _____.	Don't decide in advance.

B In groups, discuss these questions. Use expressions from A.
1. Did anything that Amy and Todd said surprise you? Why (not)?
2. What other sorts of conflicts can you imagine between cross-cultural couples?
3. Is a cross-cultural relationship a "first" experience you've tried or would like to try?

C Make it personal What unusual "firsts" have you tried? Make notes and share your story. Whose was most surprising?

Common mistake
was
It went bad / awful.

I love danger and last summer I decided to try rock climbing. I was a little nervous, though.
I'll bet! How did it go?
Well, it didn't go very well.

12 Writing: An autobiographical narrative

A Read the narrative and answer 1-3. Underline examples.
Which tense(s) does the writer primarily use to …
1. give background information?
2. introduce and describe the events?
3. bring the reader up to the present?

B Read *Write it right!* Match the highlighted *as* in the narrative to the meanings 1-4 below.

Write it right!
As is a versatile word that has many functions:
Slightly more formal
1. **As** we're from different cultures, Mayumi and I have some cultural differences. (= because)
2. **As** a student, I used to like French. (= when I was a student)
Neutral
3. I ran into Laura. She's working **as** a salesclerk. (= in the role of)
4. I used my jacket **as** an umbrella. (= for the purpose of)

____ because   ____ for the purpose of
____ when   ____ in the role of

C Complete these expressions with *but* from the narrative.
1. It was _____ but sheer luck.
2. I couldn't _____ but overhear.
3. I was _____ but certain.
4. I did _____ but study.

D Your turn! Write a four-paragraph autobiographical narrative (250 words) on a first experience.
Before
Plan background information, introduce and describe the events, and bring the reader up to the present.
While
Write four paragraphs following the model in A, adding a summary as the fourth paragraph. Be careful with narrative tenses. Include at least two examples with *as* and an expression with *but*.
After
Post your narrative online and read your classmates' work. Whose narrative was most surprising?

Share your most original first experience!

If I can do it, so can you!
By Mitch Pebble

I'd always dreamed of having a sailboat. I love the water, and **as** a child, I'd learned to swim by the time I was four. But I never, ever thought I'd have the chance to live on one until I moved from my home in Miami to the Caribbean island of Grenada. The most astonishing part of all is that I went there to take a temporary job **as** a waiter over the winter break. After that, it was nothing but sheer luck!

One night, **as** I was serving customers in the capital city, St. George's, I couldn't help but overhear the word "sailboat" in a conversation. Of course, my ears pricked up immediately, and I got up the courage to introduce myself. Lo and behold, it turned out that a young couple from Grenville, the island's second largest city, was looking for someone to take care of their boat **as** they were going to be abroad for a year. They explained that they needed an experienced "captain," who could also handle repairs. I wasn't a certified captain, and I was all but certain I had no chance at the job. Still, I couldn't let this marvelous opportunity pass, so instead of meeting friends when my shift ended, I did some research and enrolled in a sailing exam-preparation course.

I had a lot of work ahead of me, and for two months, I did nothing but study. In the end, though, I passed the test with flying colors. I had to refresh my knowledge of astronomy and meteorology. But now it's over, and I can do nautical calculations using the sun and stars **as** a reference. At the beginning of May, I moved … into their sailboat! My new home is a little small, and my parents are a little disappointed that I haven't gone back to school, but I've never been happier.

My friends always told me to follow my dreams, and at first, I was a little skeptical. Now I couldn't agree with them more!

Common mistake
I'd
I had the experience of a lifetime. I've never felt that way before.
Remember to maintain tense consistency in your writing.

Natural expressions to facilitate the activity

Authentic genres simulate real-life writing

Introduction

Reviews systematically recycle language and review skills, grammar, vocabulary, and common mistakes

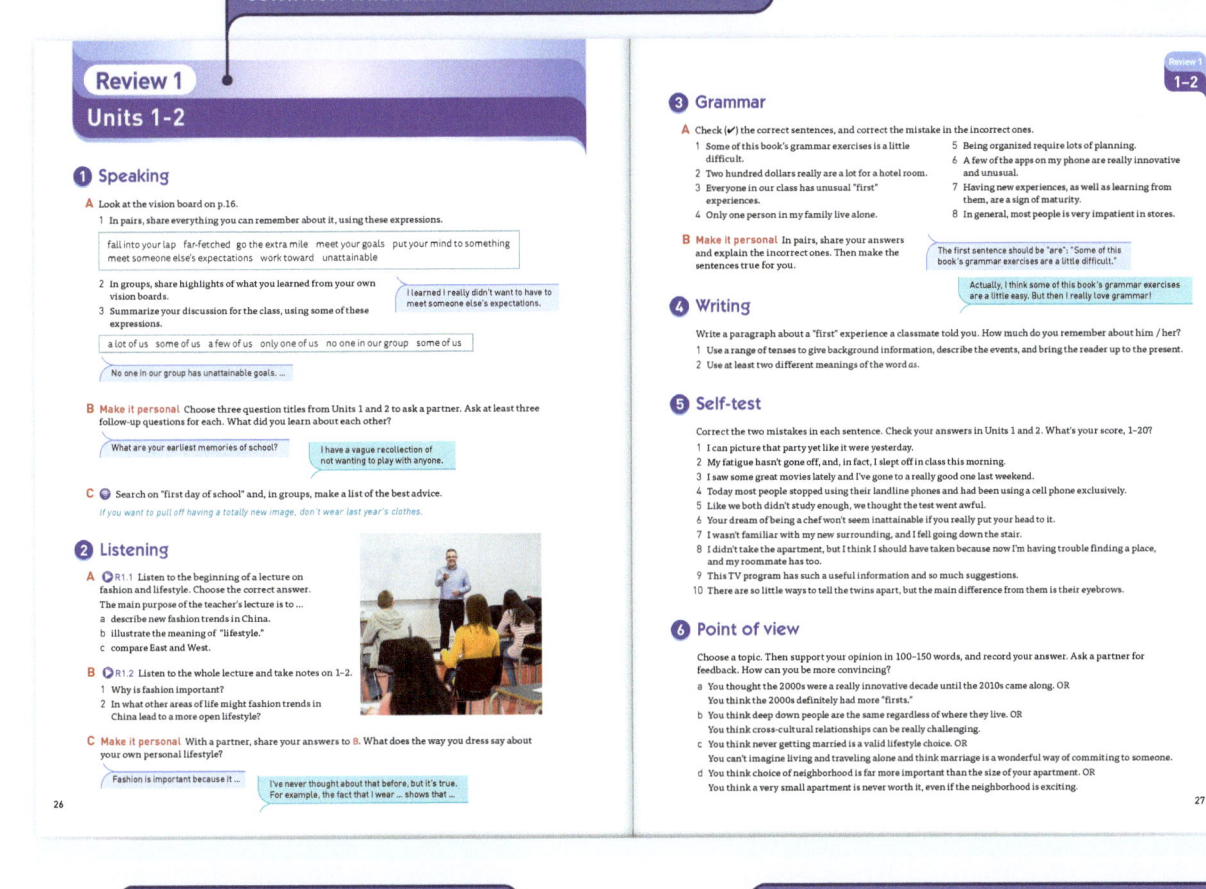

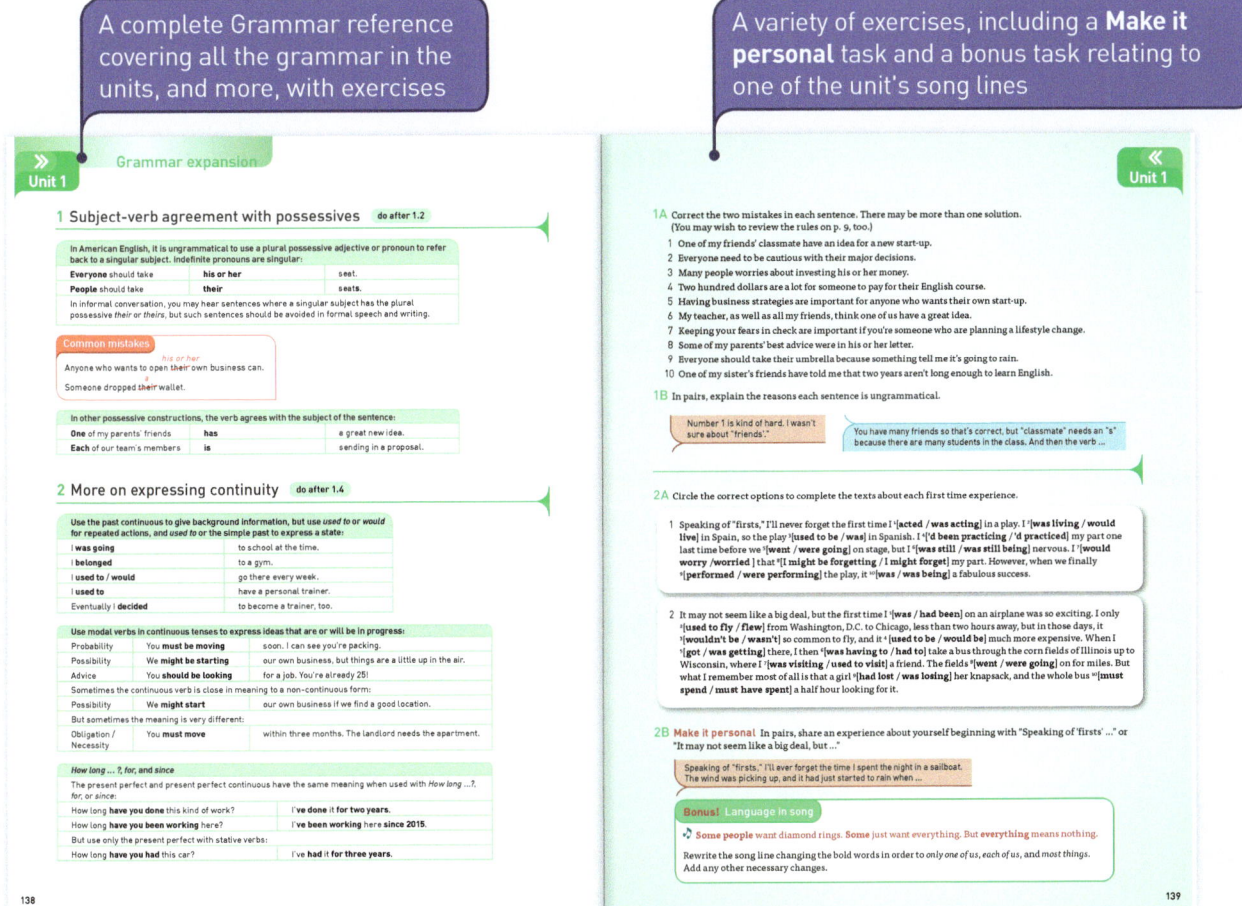

Review 1
Units 1-2

1 Speaking

A Look at the vision board on p.16.
1 In pairs, share everything you can remember about it, using these expressions.

fall into your lap far-fetched go the extra mile meet your goals put your mind to something
meet someone else's expectations work toward unattainable

2 In groups, share highlights of what you learned from your own vision boards.
I learned I really didn't have to meet someone else's expectations.
3 Summarize your discussion for the class, using some of these expressions.

a lot of us some of us a few of us only one of us no one in our group some of us

No one in our group has unattainable goals. ...

B Make it personal Choose three question titles from Units 1 and 2 to ask a partner. Ask at least three follow-up questions for each. What did you learn about each other?

What are your earliest memories of school?
I have a vague recollection of not wanting to play with anyone.

C Search on "first day of school" and, in groups, make a list of the best advice.
If you want to pull off having a totally new image, don't wear last year's clothes.

2 Listening

A R1.1 Listen to the beginning of a lecture on fashion and lifestyle. Choose the correct answer.
The main purpose of the teacher's lecture is to ...
a describe new fashion trends in China.
b illustrate the meaning of "lifestyle."
c compare East and West.

B R1.2 Listen to the whole lecture and take notes on 1-2.
1 Why is fashion important?
2 In what other areas of life might fashion trends in China lead to a more open lifestyle?

C Make it personal With a partner, share your answers to B. What does the way you dress say about your own personal lifestyle?

Fashion is important because it ...
I've never thought about that before, but it's true. For example, the fact that I wear ... shows that ...

---

3 Grammar

A Check (✓) the correct sentences, and correct the mistake in the incorrect ones.
1 Some of this book's grammar exercises is a little difficult.
2 Two hundred dollars really are a lot for a hotel room.
3 Everyone in our class has unusual "first" experiences.
4 Only one person in my family live alone.
5 Being organized require lots of planning.
6 A few of the apps on my phone are really innovative and unusual.
7 Having new experiences, as well as learning from them, are a sign of maturity.
8 In general, most people is very impatient in stores.

B Make it personal In pairs, share your answers and explain the incorrect ones. Then make the sentences true for you.

The first sentence should be "are": "Some of this book's grammar exercises are a little difficult."
Actually, I think some of this book's grammar exercises are a little easy. But then I really love grammar!

4 Writing

Write a paragraph about a "first" experience a classmate told you. How much do you remember about him / her?
1 Use a range of tenses to give background information, describe the events, and bring the reader up to the present.
2 Use at least two different meanings of the word as.

5 Self-test

Correct the two mistakes in each sentence. Check your answers in Units 1 and 2. What's your score, 1–20?
1 I can picture that party yet like it were yesterday.
2 My fatigue hasn't gone off, and, in fact, I slept off in class this morning.
3 I saw some great movies lately and I've gone to a really good one last weekend.
4 Today most people stopped using their landline phones and had been using a cell phone exclusively.
5 Like we both didn't study enough, we thought the test went awful.
6 Your dream of being a chef won't seem inattainable if you really put your head to it.
7 I wasn't familiar with my new surrounding, and I fell going down the stair.
8 I didn't take the apartment, but I think I should have taken because now I'm having trouble finding a place, and my roommate has too.
9 This TV program has such a useful information and so much suggestions.
10 There are so little ways to tell the twins apart, but the main difference from them is their eyebrows.

6 Point of view

Choose a topic. Then support your opinion in 100-150 words, and record your answer. Ask a partner for feedback. How can you be more convincing?
a You thought the 2000s were a really innovative decade until the 2010s came along. OR
You think the 2000s definitely had more "firsts."
b You think deep down people are the same regardless of where they live. OR
You think cross-cultural relationships can be really challenging.
c You think never getting married is a valid lifestyle choice. OR
You can't imagine living and traveling alone and think marriage is a wonderful way of commiting to someone.
d You think choice of neighborhood is far more important than the size of your apartment. OR
You think a very small apartment is never worth it, even if the neighborhood is exciting.

A complete Grammar reference covering all the grammar in the units, and more, with exercises

Grammar expansion
Unit 1

1 Subject-verb agreement with possessives *do after 1.2*

In American English, it is ungrammatical to use a plural possessive adjective or pronoun to refer back to a singular subject. Indefinite pronouns are singular:

Everyone should take	his or her	seat.
People should take	their	seats.

In informal conversation, you may hear sentences where a singular subject has the plural possessive *their* or *theirs*, but such sentences should be avoided in formal speech and writing.

Common mistakes
Anyone who wants to open ~~their~~ *his or her* own business can.
Someone dropped ~~their~~ wallet.

In other possessive constructions, the verb agrees with the subject of the sentence:

One of my parents' friends	has	a great new idea.
Each of our team's members	is	sending in a proposal.

2 More on expressing continuity *do after 1.4*

Use the past continuous to give background information, but use *used to* or *would* for repeated actions, and *used to* for the simple past to express a state:

I was going	to school at the time.
I belonged	to a gym.
I used to / would	go there every week.
I used to	have a personal trainer.
Eventually I decided	to become a trainer, too.

Use modal verbs in continuous tenses to express ideas that are or will be in progress:

Probability	You must be moving	soon. I can see you're packing.
Possibility	We might be starting	our own business, but things are a little up in the air.
Advice	You should be looking	for a job. You're already 25!

Sometimes the continuous verb is close in meaning to a non-continuous form:

| Possibility | We might start | our own business if we find a good location. |

But sometimes the meaning is very different:

| Obligation / Necessity | You must move | within three months. The landlord needs the apartment. |

How long ...?, for, and since
The present perfect and present perfect continuous have the same meaning when used with *How long ...?, for,* or *since*:

How long **have you done** this kind of work?	I've **done** it **for** two years.
How long **have you been working** here?	I've **been working** here **since** 2015.

But use only the present perfect with stative verbs:

| How long **have you had** this car? | I've **had** it **for** three years. |

A variety of exercises, including a Make it personal task and a bonus task relating to one of the unit's song lines

Unit 1

1A Correct the two mistakes in each sentence. There may be more than one solution. (You may wish to review the rules on p. 9, too.)
1 One of my friends' classmate have an idea for a new start-up.
2 Everyone need to be cautious with their major decisions.
3 Many people worries about investing his or her money.
4 Two hundred dollars are a lot for someone to pay for their English course.
5 Having business strategies are important for anyone who wants their own start-up.
6 My teacher, as well as all my friends, think one of us have a great idea.
7 Keeping your fears in check are important if you're someone who are planning a lifestyle change.
8 Some of my parents' best advice were in his or her letter.
9 Everyone should take their umbrella because something tell me it's going to rain.
10 One of my sister's friends have told me that two years aren't long enough to learn English.

1B In pairs, explain the reasons each sentence is ungrammatical.

Number 1 is kind of hard. I wasn't sure about "friends."
You have many friends so that's correct, but "classmate" needs an "s" because there are many students in the class. And then the verb ...

2A Circle the correct options to complete the texts about each first time experience.

1 Speaking of "firsts," I'll never forget the first time I ¹[acted / was acting] in a play. I ²[was living / would live] in Spain, so the play ³[used to be / was] in Spanish. I ⁴['d been practicing / 'd practiced] my part one last time before we ⁵[went / were going] on stage, but I ⁶[was still / was still being] nervous. I ⁷[would worry / worried] that ⁸[I might be forgetting / I might forget] my part. However, when we finally ⁹[performed / were performing] the play, it ¹⁰[was / was being] a fabulous success.

2 It may not seem like a big deal, but the first time I ¹[was / had been] on an airplane was so exciting. I only ²[used to fly / flew] from Washington, D.C. to Chicago, less than two hours away, but in those days, it ³[wouldn't be / wasn't] so common to fly, and it ⁴[used to be / would be] much more expensive. When I ⁵[got / was getting] there, I then ⁶[was having / had to] take a bus through the corn fields of Illinois up to Wisconsin, where I ⁷[was visiting / used to visit] a friend. The fields ⁸[went / were going] on for miles. But what I remember most of all is that a girl ⁹[had lost / was losing] her knapsack, and the whole bus ¹⁰[must spend / must have spent] a half hour looking for it.

2B Make it personal In pairs, share an experience about yourself beginning with "Speaking of 'firsts' ..." or "It may not seem like a big deal, but ..."

Speaking of "firsts," I'll ever forget the time I spent the night in a sailboat. The wind was picking up, and it had just started to rain when ...

Bonus! Language in song
♪ **Some** people want diamond rings. **Some** just want everything. But **everything** means nothing.

Rewrite the song line changing the bold words in order to *only one of us, each of us,* and *most things*. Add any other necessary changes.

Introduction

Workbook to practice and consolidate lessons, including regular listening exercises and **Make it personal** tasks.

---

1 » 1.1 What are your earliest memories of school?

A 1 Listen to Chris telling his friend Janet about his first day at college. Number pictures a–e in the correct order.

B 1 Listen again. True (T) or false (F)?
1 Chris went to bed very late the night before his first class.
2 He arrived late for class because he stopped for coffee on the way.
3 The lecturer saw him fall asleep.
4 Chris doesn't think he was as embarrassed as the lecturer.
5 He apologized and asked to talk to her at the end of class.

C Circle the correct options.

I used to work in an office. I enjoyed it at first, having my own desk and talking to customers on the phone, but after a few years, the novelty ¹*wore off / rushed off*. It wasn't the most interesting job to be honest, and my career never really ²*pulled off / took off*, so I decided to leave and go back to college. But on my last day, I thought I'd have some fun, and managed to ³*go off / pull off* a trick on one of my coworkers. He was quite lazy, and every day after lunch he used to shut himself in his office and ⁴*doze off / wear off* for a while. He thought nobody knew what he was doing, but we all did, and thought it was quite funny. So on my last day, he went into his office as usual, and I stood outside his office and called him. I knew he would just listen to the message on the answering machine on his desk and only pick up if he wanted to. I heard his phone ⁵*ring / rush off* and then go to the answering machine. I said, "David, this is the area manager, and I'm five minutes away from the office. I'm coming in to do an inspection." Well at that, he jumped up, opened the door and ⁶*wore off / rushed off* towards the exit, shouting, "If anyone comes, say I'm sick!" We all had a good laugh about that.

D **Make it personal** Complete the sentences so they're true for you.
1 My enthusiasm for _____ wore off when _____.
2 I have a vague recollection of _____.
3 I can still see _____ as if it were yesterday.

» 1.2 What innovative businesses do you know?

A Complete the conversations with the correct form of these verbs. There are two extra.

| allow | be | have | say | seem | taste | try |

1 A: Have you heard Jack's latest business idea?
   B: No, and I don't want to. Having good ideas _____ one thing, but he never acts on them.
2 A: Have you been to the new vegetarian diner on 16th Avenue?
   B: Yes! Some of their burgers _____ amazing!
3 A: How's the new business going, Sarah?
   B: Terrible. I hired a new assistant and everyone _____ complained about him.
4 A: Is this price correct?
   B: Yes sir, why do you ask?
   A: It's just that two hundred dollars _____ like a lot to me.
5 A: What are the results of the latest research, Diane?
   B: Well, more and more of our customers _____ they'd like us to improve our support service.

B 2 Circle the correct forms. Listen to check.

Why do most new businesses FAIL?

Statistics ¹*vary / varies*, but it is generally believed that almost all new start-ups ²*fail / fails*. Some people say the figure is as high as 90 percent, which ³*seem / seems* high, but it is a reality. Everyone ⁴*have / has* at least one great idea, but building a successful company ⁵*take / takes* a lot of work and courage. Knowing a few basic facts first ⁶*help / helps*. For example, is the market already crowded? Several hours using search engines ⁷*is / are* a good place to start. Many start-ups also ⁸*has / have* hidden costs that often no one ⁹*discover / discovers* until it's too late. In general, people ¹⁰*make / makes* mistakes with start-ups. Make sure it's not you!

C Complete the sentences with an appropriate form of the verbs in parentheses.
1 The company, as well as its customers, _____ at all happy with its level of service. (be)
2 Everyone in the meeting _____ the new product will be a success. (think)
3 One of the managers _____ the new logo. He said it was too old-fashioned looking. (like)
4 Two years _____ a long time to develop a new product. It usually takes about 12 months. (be)
5 About a third of new businesses _____ successful this year. That's a great result. (be)

D **Make it personal** Complete the sentences so they're true for you.
1 Everyone in my class _____.
2 Both my parents _____.
3 These days, a lot of people _____.

How many ways can you use a brick? 1.3 «

A Read the first paragraph. Is the article going to contain good advice?

The art of procrastination

Do you have what it takes to be a good procrastinator? Or do you worry that you don't spend enough time worrying about not working on that important project? Well, now you don't have to worry, with this helpful guide. Read on to find out how you, too, can join the millions of other successful procrastinators out there, and avoid staying on top of things.

1 _____

Before you start work, make sure everything is in place. You need the right amount of space, the correct temperature, and enough light. You shouldn't be too hungry or too full, and you need to be able to tune out any unnecessary distractions. Don't even think about starting work until these conditions are met. Otherwise, you won't be able to produce the best work you can do. And only the very best is good enough.

2 _____

You have to answer every email as soon as it comes in. No one likes being ignored, and people hate it when you don't reply for a long time. Besides that, you might miss out on some fantastic deals and offers from that company you once bought a specific type of coffee from online. How could you, after they went to all the trouble of sending it to you? Only you can do.

3 _____

Changing your environment might just let your mind wander. It might even stimulate your brain, and you don't want to lose that winning idea to just that you like that. You need to zero in on exactly what you're doing!

4 _____

There's no way you can do any meaningful work if you don't keep abreast of current affairs. This means, obviously, trawling as many news sites as you can, as well as cross-checking facts between sites. You don't want to be ignorant!

5 _____

And I mean everything. When you're about a third of the way into a task (shame on you for getting so far), stop and ask yourself, "Is this really any good? Can I do better?" If an idea pops into your head about how to do something differently, follow up on it. The best way forward at this point is usually just to tear it up and start from scratch.

Finally, the most important thing: if it's too difficult, just leave it. Never do today what you can put off until tomorrow.

B Read the rest. Put the headings back into the article 1–5. Then circle the best advice.

| Keep up with the world. | Don't be rude. | It has to be perfect. |
| Question everything. | Always work in the same place. | |

C Complete the sentences with one missing word.
                                                                                    wander
1 If you have trouble thinking of ideas, it can be good to just let your mind ^ for a while.
2 It's really hard to work with all that noise going on, I keep tuning _____.
3 That's when it hit: I could give my presentation as a story.
4 Some people listen to music while they work, but I need silence to really zero _____ on what I'm doing.
5 Sally's best ideas usually pop her head when she's on the bus to work.
6 You need to prioritize these tasks if you're going to stay on _____ of things.

» 1.4 What do the 2000s make you think of?

A 3 Complete the interview with the correct form of the verbs in parentheses. Listen to check.

PRESENTER: Hello and welcome to *Movie Watch*. Joining me today is movie director Jermaine Gómez. Jermaine, in your opinion, what ¹_____ (be) the most important movies of the decade so far?
JERMAINE: Well for me, one of the best films I ²_____ (see) in the last few years is *Her*, which came out in 2014. Until then, nobody ³_____ (make) a movie that was such an honest portrayal of impossible romance. I mean, yes, directors ⁴_____ (try) to do something similar with movies for years, but it had exactly the right combination of script, music, and acting that made it such a success.
PRESENTER: I agree, it's a great movie. Are there any others?
JERMAINE: Have you seen *Boyhood*? Critics ⁵_____ (describe) it in glowing terms, and they're not wrong. The makers of this movie did something no one ⁶_____ (ever do) before. They filmed it over 12 years, with the same actor as he aged from 6 to 18.
PRESENTER: I ⁷_____ (not watch) it yet, actually, but I'm definitely going to!
JERMAINE: Perhaps the best movie of the decade, though, is *Inception*, in my opinion. With this movie, they ⁸_____ (create) an insanely complicated story, which is thrilling to watch from start to finish, and great fun to try to figure out!

B Circle the correct options.

What ¹*has / had* been the most important technological innovation of the twenty-first century so far?

Many people would argue that it was the iPod. Until it came out, people ²*have / had* bought music on CDs, and some had huge collections that took up vast amounts of space in their home. Others might say the invention of social networking ³*has had / had had* the most influence on our lives, but it ⁴*hasn't helped / didn't help* our privacy, as we now share pretty much everything online with the rest of the world. For me though, one of the biggest milestones was when IBM's computer "Watson" competed on the U.S. quiz show *Jeopardy*, and won against the two all-time champions. It was important because it showed just how far we ⁵*have come / have been coming* in developing artificial intelligence. Until this point, many companies ⁶*had / have been* trying to develop computers capable of independent thought, and since then, this field ⁷*has / had* been developing rapidly. So much so that you can even talk to your cell phone and have it search the Internet for you.

C Match 1–5 to a–e to make sentences.
1 Usain Bolt set
2 3D printing is yet to set
3 The latest album by Robotix is set
4 The government has recently set
5 Video-sharing websites have set

a ☐ for a March release.
b ☐ the stage for a new generation of entertainers.
c ☐ a new world record for the fastest 100 meters in 2008.
d ☐ the world on fire, but is expected to become more popular in the next few years.
e ☐ new rules for opening a small business.

Introduction

Richmond Learning Platform for Identities, includes:

- **Interactive activities** to cover all language points in Identities Student's Books
- **Skills Boost:** extra reading and listening practice available in both interactive and PDF format
- **Tests:** Unit Tests and Review Tests delivered in separate A and B versions
- **Resources** for teachers
- Downloadable **audio**
- Access to **video**

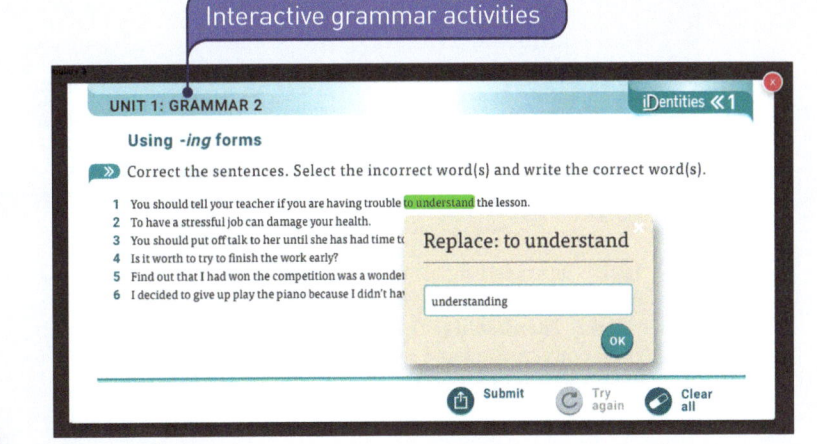

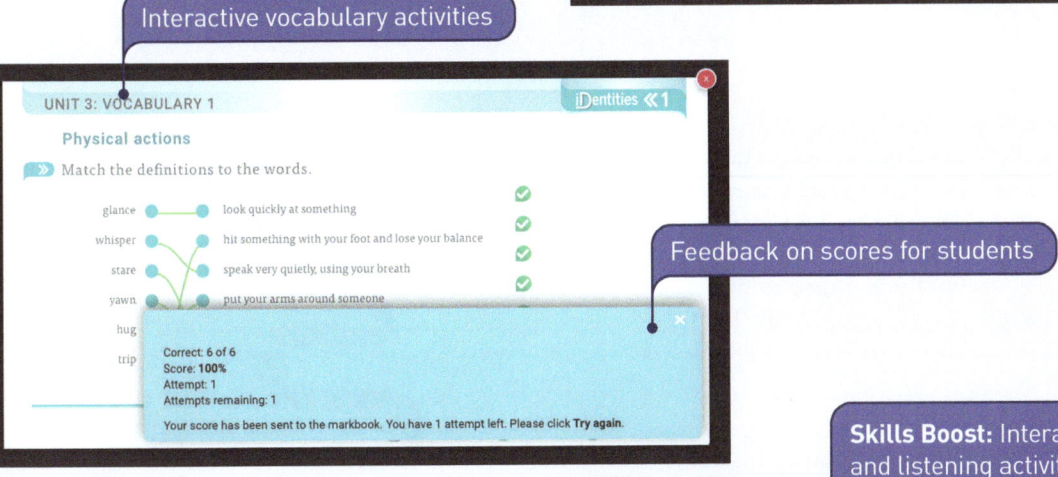

Interactive grammar activities

Interactive vocabulary activities

Feedback on scores for students

Skills Boost: Interactive reading and listening activities

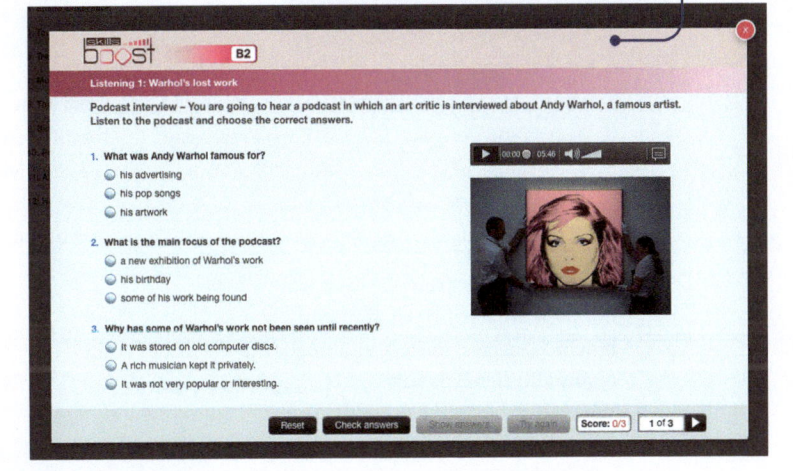

Scores visible for teachers in Markbook

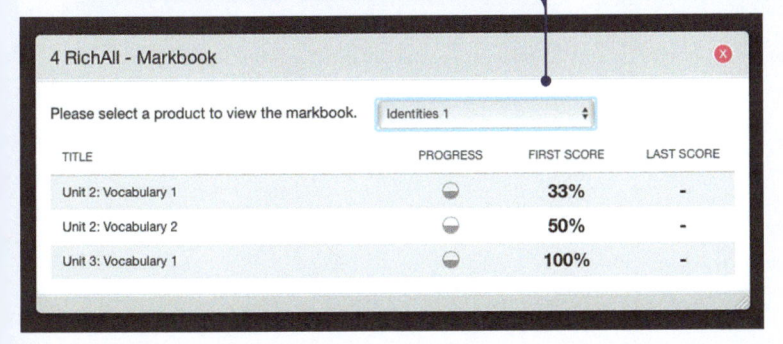

1 » What are your earliest memories of school?

1 Listening

A ▶ 1.1 Ben is telling his friend Lucy about a memorable experience. Look at the photos. Then listen to the first part of their conversation and guess what happened.

B ▶ 1.2 Listen to the second part. T (true) or F (false)? What would you have done in Ben's shoes?
1 Both the students and principal thought the lesson was fascinating.
2 Ben's lesson was interrupted by someone screaming.
3 Only some of the kids had left by the end of class.
4 Ben was hired without doing a sample lesson.
5 We know for sure that Ben was hired because of a shortage of teachers.

> I think I might have called for help. But if it had been a snake, I think I would have fainted.

C Make it personal Share a story about a first time.

1 ▶ 1.3 **How to say it** Complete the chart. Listen to check.

Reminiscing	
What they said	What they meant
1 As _____ as I can recall, ...	From what I remember ...
2 I can still see it as _____ it were yesterday.	It's still fresh in my mind.
3 It's completely _____ my mind.	I've completely forgotten.
4 I have a vague recollection _____ ...	I have a distant memory of ...
5 But come to _____ of it, ...	In retrospect ...

2 Choose a topic from the list and note down ...
a *who, what, when, where,* and *why.*
b which images, sounds, and smells are the most vivid.
c any additional details. 
Your first ...

day at school   driving lesson   day in your current home   English lesson
job interview   time speaking in public   sports event   wedding

3 In groups, share your experiences. Use *How to say it* expressions. Whose story was the most interesting?

> I'll never forget my first driving lesson. I can still see it as if it were yesterday.

> What was so unusual about it?

> I remember showing up early because I was so excited. And then just when ...

6

What are your earliest memories of school? 1.1

Lesson Aims: Sts reminisce and share memories of "first experiences," and learn phrasal verbs with *off*.

Skills	Language	Vocabulary
Listening to someone talking about a memorable experience Sharing experiences and memories Telling funny stories	Talking about the past, e.g. *From what I remember..., It's still fresh in my mind, I have a distant memory of...*	Expressions for reminiscing Phrasal verbs with *off* Collocations with *wear off, pull off, take off,* and *go off*

Warm-up

As this is the first lesson, you might want to begin with a general opener. Ask sts to think of five questions to ask another st in the class, e.g. *How do you get to school? Do you go to a gym?* Sts ask each other the questions. Ask one or two sts to report back to the class.

Books open. Ask the lesson title question: *What are your earliest memories of school? Did you enjoy it? Do you remember your first day? Do you remember any of your teachers? Did you like them? Who was your favorite?*

1 Listening

A ▶ 1.1 Focus on the photos. Elicit or pre-teach the words for the animals (*bat, snake, vulture, frog, spider*). Ask sts to listen and find out what Ben's job is (a psychologist) and what "first experience" he is talking about (his first job interview).

Have them guess what happened. Don't confirm or deny their guesses at this stage.

Weaker classes: Before sts listen for the first time, board the following questions:
1 Has Ben always wanted to be a psychologist?
2 How long was he a teacher for?
3 What did they ask him to do in addition to the interview?
4 How did he feel about it?
5 Do you think it went well or badly?

≫ See Teacher's Book p.311 for Audio script 1.1.

B ▶ 1.2 Play the second part of the audio for sts to check their guesses. Have sts read through sentences 1–5, then play the audio again for them to answer True or False. Peercheck, then classcheck. Highlight the meaning of *afford (not) to do something* in the audio (to be able to do something without risk of undesirable consequences). Elicit the alternative meaning of *afford to do something* (to have enough money to do something) which sts will be more familiar with.

Have sts discuss in pairs what they would have done in Ben's shoes. Highlight the pronunciation of *might have* (mighta) in the speech bubble. Class feedback, and invite volunteers to share their ideas. Ask: *Have you had or heard of any similar experiences?*

Answers
1 False. The principal was yawning.   2 True.
3 False. The classroom was empty.   4 True.
5 False. Ben says: "I guess [the principal] couldn't afford not to take me on ..."

≫ See Teacher's Book p.311 for Audio script 1.2.

Tip

After a listening or reading activity, give sts a chance to peercheck in pairs before eliciting answers in a classcheck. This will increase sts' confidence and help them get any answers they may have missed.

C Make it personal

1 ▶ 1.3 **How to say it** Focus on the chart. Sts complete it, then listen and check. Classcheck. Model pronunciation of the phrases, and have sts practice saying them in pairs.

Answers
1 far 2 if 3 slipped 4 of 5 think

2 Focus on the topics. Ask individual sts: *Do you remember your first day at school / your first driving lesson / ...? How did you feel?*

Have sts choose a topic from the list and make notes for a, b, and c. Brainstorm a few examples for a. Ask: *At your first job interview ... who interviewed you? / Where was the interview?* Monitor and give help.

Tip

Before asking sts to share personal information, give a personal model of your own first. This will allow you to demonstrate the type of story you want to hear and also help to build the classroom dynamic between you and your sts.

3 Put sts in groups to share their experiences.

Weaker classes: Have sts share their experiences in pairs, beginning with *I'll never forget ...* or *I remember ...* as in the examples. Encourage the use of follow-up questions to find out more information about each other's experiences.

While sts are working, monitor and make a note of common errors or good uses of English to discuss in class check.

1.1

> Song lyric: See Teacher's Book p.341 for notes about the song and an accompanying activity to do with the class.

2 Vocabulary: Phrasal verbs with *off*

A ▶1.4 Remind sts that phrasal verbs are a special group of verbs which consist of two or three words: verb + adverb, verb + preposition, or verb + adverb + preposition. Sts read the sentences and complete with the correct form of the verbs. Play the audio for sts to check their answers.

> **Answers**
> 1 wore off   2 took off   3 doze off   4 pull it off
> 5 gone off   6 rushed off

Stronger classes: Have sts write their own sentences with each of the phrasal verbs. They can blank out the verbs and have their partner try to complete them.

Elicit other phrasal verbs with *off* that sts have come across, e.g. *get off, take off, leave off, drop off, keep off, pass off, show off, set off, turn off.*

B Put sts in pairs to retell the story. If necessary, replay audio 1.2 to remind them of the story while sts make notes. Focus on the **Common mistake**. Tell sts that we don't use *go off* with bells. We usually use the verb *ring*.

Tip

For fun, now set your phone alarm to ring at the end of the lesson, to elicit what happened to review this phrase as they leave.

While sts are retelling their stories, encourage their partners to respond appropriately or ask questions for elaboration. Elicit and board phrases, e.g. *Really? That's incredible. How? And then what? What a nightmare! How terrible! Oh, boy! What did you do then? You what? No way! You've got to be kidding! What do you mean? Oh, no!* (They should remember most of these from the audio.)

Choose one or two sts to retell their stories to the whole class.

C ▶1.5 Focus on the mind maps. Explain or elicit what the direction of the arrows means (whether the verb comes before or after the noun, i.e. whether it is transitive or intransitive). Demonstrate with the examples on the mind map: *The enthusiasm wore off. I pulled off the lesson.* Play the audio for sts to complete.

Weaker classes: Before sts do the completion task, board the definitions for the phrasal verbs (activate / explode; gradually disappear / stop; accomplish / make it happen; succeed / get started) and have sts match them with the correct phrasal verbs.

Paircheck. Classcheck. Ask: *Which collocations did you know before the lesson?*

> **Answers**
> 1 b novelty   c effect
> 2 b plane   c business
> 3 b trick   c crime
> 4 b alarm clock   c fire alarm

> See Teacher's Book p.311 for Audio script 1.5.

Optional activity

Play collocations "tennis." Put sts in pairs and ask them to sit, facing their partner. Each st takes turns "serving" by saying a phrasal verb. The other st then "returns" with a collocation and another phrasal verb and they repeat, e.g.

A: Get out.

B: Get out of bed in the morning. Get off

A: Get off the bus at the last stop.

When one partner can't think of a collocation, the other st wins a point and they start again. Let sts play for five minutes. The st with the most points in each pair wins.

D **Make it personal** As a warm-up, and to prompt sts' memories, ask: *When was the last time you … watched a boring movie / overslept / managed to do something difficult?* Use the examples to set this up. Sts can then ask and answer the questions in pairs to maximize speaking practice and help them brainstorm one story to expand on at the next group stage.

Have sts think of an anecdote about a "last time" and note down what happened. Tell them to use the phrasal verbs and collocations from A and C, e.g. *The movie was so boring I dozed off. The plane was delayed and didn't take off for two hours. It was such a difficult job but I pulled it off.*

Sts take turns sharing their stories in groups. Encourage other sts to listen carefully, and to respond where appropriate with the phrases given in the TB notes for B. Class feedback. Have one or two sts share their stories with the whole class. Ask: *Did anything similar happen to you or your friends / family?*

Optional activity

Ask sts to write a paragraph about their story, including the language from the unit. When they have finished, collect the stories and pin them up around the room. Ask the class to walk around, read the stories, and choose their favorite one.

> Workbook p.3.

🎵 'Cause the players gonna play … And the haters gonna hate … Baby, I'm just gonna shake … I shake it off, I shake it off « 1.1

2 Vocabulary: Phrasal verbs with *off*

A ▶ 1.4 Complete 1–6 with the correct form of these verbs. Use your intuition. Listen to check.

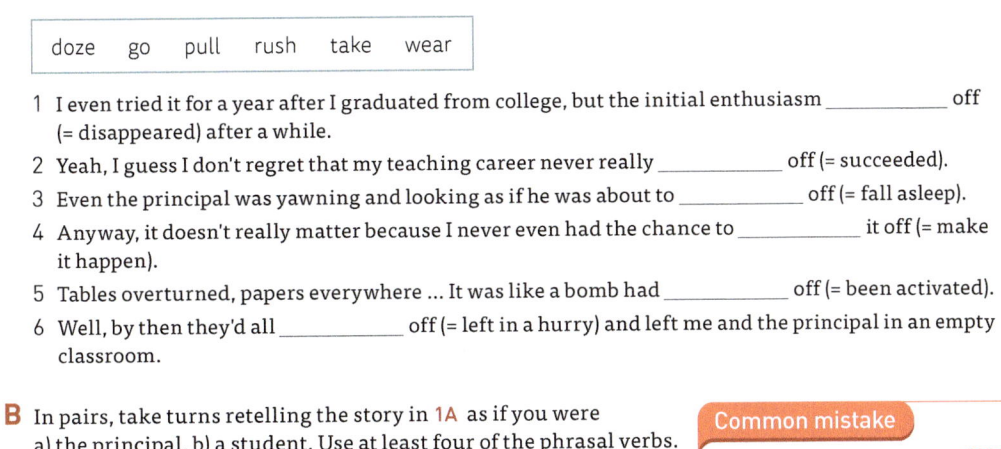

| doze | go | pull | rush | take | wear |

1 I even tried it for a year after I graduated from college, but the initial enthusiasm _____ off (= disappeared) after a while.
2 Yeah, I guess I don't regret that my teaching career never really _____ off (= succeeded).
3 Even the principal was yawning and looking as if he was about to _____ off (= fall asleep).
4 Anyway, it doesn't really matter because I never even had the chance to _____ it off (= make it happen).
5 Tables overturned, papers everywhere … It was like a bomb had _____ off (= been activated).
6 Well, by then they'd all _____ off (= left in a hurry) and left me and the principal in an empty classroom.

B In pairs, take turns retelling the story in **1A** as if you were a) the principal, b) a student. Use at least four of the phrasal verbs.

> **Common mistake**
> *rang*
> Class is over. The bell just ~~went off.~~

C ▶ 1.5 Listen and complete the mind maps. Which collocations were you familiar with?

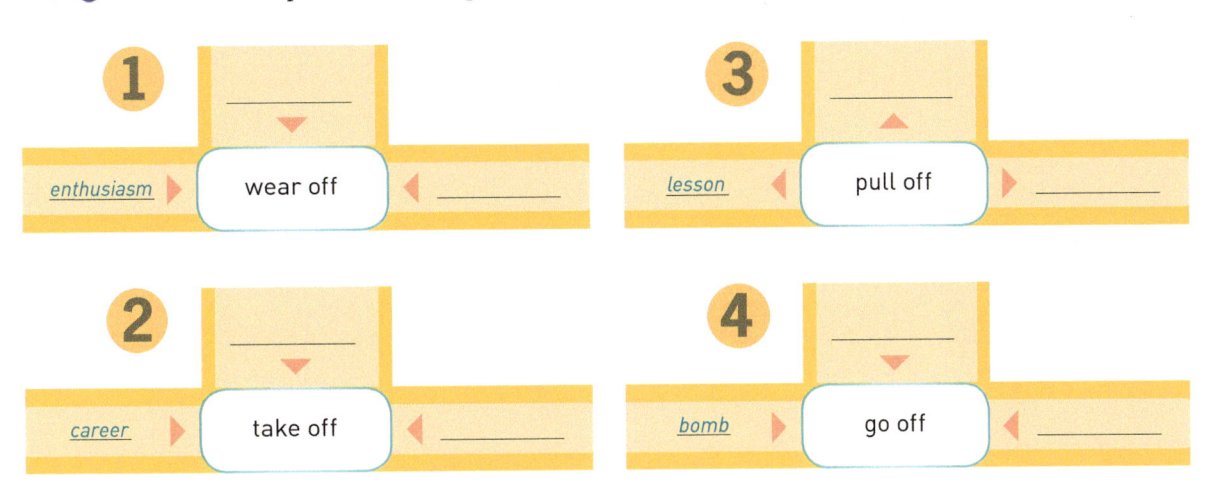

1 _____
enthusiasm ▶ **wear off** ◀ _____

3 _____
lesson ◀ **pull off** ▶ _____

2 _____
career ▶ **take off** ◀ _____

4 _____
bomb ▶ **go off** ◀ _____

D **Make it personal** In groups, share a funny story about the last time you did something. Use phrasal verbs and collocations from **C**. Anything in common?

> sat through a boring movie · were delayed traveling by bus / train / plane · managed to do something difficult
> were really into a fashion or fad for a while · overslept / were late / delayed for something critical

> I had a big day coming up; a hiking date with someone I hoped would be my boyfriend. But my alarm clock never went off!

> Oh, no! Then what?

> Well, I had to think of something creative fast! So I …

23

» 1.2 What innovative businesses do you know?

3 Language in use

A ▶ 1.6 Listen to the start of a podcast. What's it about?
☐ People who want to innovate and turn their ideas into a small business.
☐ Big companies that try to meet people's changing needs.

B ▶ 1.7 In pairs, look at the photos and the slogans. What exactly do you think each start-up does? Listen to the rest to check. How close were you?

How come no one thought of that before?   This week: Innovative start-ups

LISTS AND TWISTS 'Never wear it twice.'

Personal Attendant 'We make parking fun.'

C In pairs, which start-up would be more successful where you live? What kinds of problems might each one face?

> *Lists and Twists* would be a hard sell. Maybe it's just me, but I'd hate to wear something that's been worn before.

4 Pronunciation: Final consonant clusters

A ▶ 1.8 Read and listen to sentences 1 and 2. Cross out the letters you hardly hear at all, or don't hear, in the highlighted words. Then circle the correct word in the rule.

> 1 IT manager Elena Fernández left her job and created *Lists* and *Twists*, a company that has shipped more than 100,000 dollars in products since 2015.
> 2 The app asks where you're going and tracks you as you make your way to your destination – just like your parents used to do on the weekends.
>
> A consonant cluster is a group of consonants with no vowels between them. In final clusters ending in /sts/, /kts/, /sks/, /nts/ and /ndz/, the [**first / second / third**] consonant is very weak or not pronounced.

B ▶ 1.9 Listen and complete 1–4 with words that end in consonant clusters. Then listen again and repeat.
1 One of our _____ _____ seven articles of clothing. ☐
2 Our team _____ new clothes based on your _____ and purchase history. ☐
3 If 60 dollars _____ like a lot of money, that's nothing compared to what most designer clothing usually _____. ☐
4 The feedback we've been getting from our _____, as well as the number of positive press reviews, _____ our commitment to excellence. ☐

C Make it personal Complete 1–6 to create your own innovations. Which is the class favorite?

I'd like to see a start-up / an NGO / an app / a robot that …

inspects [1] _____ free of charge.   scans our hard disks for [2] _____ .
looks for the best discounts in [3] _____ .   lists [4] _____ in our area.
reinvents the way we [5] _____ .   defends the rights of [6] _____ .

> I'd like to see a robot that inspects my car free of charge. I'm tired of getting ripped off by mechanics!

What innovative businesses do you know? 1.2

Lesson aims: Sts talk about innovative ideas and review subject-verb agreements.

Skills	Language	Vocabulary	Grammar
Listening to a podcast about start-up companies	Explaining, e.g. *Well, basically he's saying …*	Units of measurement Collective nouns, e.g. *company* Determiners e.g. *all, most, some*	Subject-verb agreement: portions and indefinite pronouns; units of measurement, collective nouns, asides, and verbs as subjects Singular / plural verbs with countable / uncountable nouns, indefinite pronouns, determiners, e.g. *No one in our group likes my blog. A few of their apps are unique.*

Warm-up

Board the word *innovative*. In pairs, ask sts to define it and list as many related adjectives as possible, e.g. *original, inventive, ingenious*. Discuss the lesson title question with them, and brainstorm businesses they think are innovative, and why. Encourage use of the adjectives in their answers.

3 Language in use

A ▶ 1.6 Play the audio and ask sts to listen for gist and say what the podcast is about.

> **Answers**
> People who want to innovate and turn their ideas into a small business.

≫ See Teacher's Book p.311 for Audio script 1.6.

B ▶ 1.7 Focus on the photos and the slogans. Discuss the meaning of *start-up* (a new company or venture, which is entrepreneurial and, typically, fast-growing).

In pairs, sts discuss what they think the start-ups do. Play the audio for sts to check their ideas. Classcheck. Ask sts: *What service does each company offer? How much does it cost? Would you be interested in either of these services? Why / why not? Do you think they are good value for money?*

> **Answers**
> Lists and Twists is a clothing subscription service. It costs 60 dollars a month. You rent clothes (a bag of seven items at a time) which you can keep and wear as long as you like. When you have finished with them you return them, and receive a new bag.
> City Valet Driver is a parking service. You pay 8 dollars a day. A parking attendant meets you at your destination and parks your car for you, then returns it when you need to leave.

≫ See Teacher's Book p.311 for Audio script 1.7.

C Sts discuss which company they think would be more successful and why. If necessary, prompt them by asking: *What type of people would the service appeal to? What type of people live in your area? Does a similar service exist? Is parking a problem in your area?* Class feedback.

Optional activity

Put sts in pairs. Ask half the pairs to think of and note down disadvantages of each start-up in their area, and the other half to think of advantages. Monitor and help where necessary. Then combine pairs into groups of four, to share their ideas and debate whether each is a good idea or not. At the end, nominate a st from each group to share their ideas with the class.

4 Pronunciation: Final consonant clusters

A ▶ 1.8 Sts listen and read sentences 1 and 2. Sts cross out the letters, then circle the correct word in the rule. Have them practice pronunciation of the words by modeling and drilling each word separately.

> **Answers**
> Li~~s~~ts and Twi~~s~~ts   products   a~~s~~ks   paren~~t~~s   weeken~~d~~s
> Second

B ▶ 1.9 Have sts try and complete the sentences from memory before they listen. Play the audio for them to check. Play the audio again, and have sts repeat.

> **Answers**
> 1 stylists, selects   2 suggests, comments
> 3 sounds, costs   4 clients, reflects

Tip

After sts repeat after a model, ask them to use their mobile devices to record themselves saying the sentences, then listen back to them. This can be a useful exercise for sts in identifying their own strengths and weaknesses in pronunciation.

C Make it personal Sts complete 1–6 with their own ideas. Put sts in groups to compare. Ask each group to select the three innovations they would most like to see. Have each group report back to the class, and then vote on the three best innovations.

25

1.2

5 Grammar: Subject–verb agreement

A Focus on the heading. Elicit examples of *portions* (a piece of pie, a slice of pizza) and indefinite pronouns. Read through the examples in the grammar box with the class.

Weaker classes: Have sts underline the verbs and say whether they are singular or plural.

Sts complete rules a–c. Peercheck. Classcheck. Elicit other examples for each determiner, e.g.

a Both companies are innovative.
   Many companies sell second-hand clothes.
   Several businessmen left the company.
   A few women worked there.
b All our family lives in England.
   Most of the families live in New York.
   A lot of the government workers supported his new ideas.
   Many governments think that economic progress is the main goal.
c Everyone is happy at this company.
   Each product is more innovative than the last.

> **Answers**
> a plural   b singular, plural   c singular

» Song lyric: See Teacher's Book p.341 for notes about the song and an accompanying activity to do with the class.

B Read through the examples in the second grammar box. If you have sts of Romance languages, highlight the fact that units of measurements in English are singular, e.g. *$60 **is** a lot. Two months **is** a long time.* Focus on 4 and elicit other examples of collective nouns, e.g. *Our family, The government*. Highlight that *people* in English always takes a plural verb.

Refer sts back to the sentences in 4B on page 8, and have them figure out which of the rules 1–6 in the grammar box apply to each sentence. Peercheck. Classcheck. Board the following sentences from audio 1.7, and ask sts which rules apply to these:

1 … that's nothing compared to what most of the designer clothing available usually costs. (Rule 1)
2 Meeting your needs is our number 1 priority! (Rule 6)

As follow up, ask sts which of the rules for singular / plural verbs are different in their language.

> **Answers**
> 1 rule 2   2 rule 4   3 rule 3   4 rule 5

» Refer sts to the **Grammar expansion** on p.138.

Stronger classes: Sts work alone and write a further example sentence for each of the rules 1–6. Monitor and check sts are using the language correctly. When they have finished, put sts in pairs. Sts take turns reading out their sentence to their partner for them to guess which rule it is.

C Sts read the quotes and circle the correct alternatives. Classcheck. Ask sts which of the rules in A/B they applied to each sentence. (1 – rule 2; 2 – rule 1; 3 – rule 2; 4 – rule 5; 5 – rule 4; 6 – rule 6)

Discuss any unknown vocabulary in the quotes. Ask sts if they have come across any of the quotes before, and when.

> **Answers**
> 1 has   2 has   3 is   4 regains   5 promotes   6 has

Tip
With quote exercises like these, it's usually a good idea to ask if sts know any other similar quotes, and, for fast finishers, to allow them to search for further examples of their own.

D Make it personal Put sts in groups and explain that they are going to discuss the quotes in C and tell each other what their two favorite quotes are.

Weaker classes: Discuss the meaning of each quote first as a class before sts discuss in groups.

Focus on the models in the speech bubbles, and elicit meaning of *strike a chord* (to affect you or to have an emotional impact on you). Ask sts to decide as a group on their two favorite quotes by taking a vote on each quote. Class feedback, and invite groups to tell the rest of the class their choices and why.

» Workbook p.4.

♪ Some people want diamond rings. Some just want everything. But everything means nothing, If I ain't got you, yeah

1.2

5 Grammar: Subject-verb agreement

A Read the grammar box and complete the rules (a–c) with *singular* or *plural*.

Subject-verb agreement: Portions and indefinite pronouns		
1 Portions and count vs. non-count	Some of the company's advertising	is very innovative.
	A lot of their strategies	are brilliant.
	A few of their apps	are unique also.
2 Indefinite pronouns	No one in our group	likes my new logo.
	Only one of us	thinks it works.

a *Both, many, several,* and *a few* always take a _____ verb.
b *All, any, more, most, a lot, some, a half, a third,* etc. take a singular verb when the noun is _____ and a plural verb when the noun is _____.
c *One, each, everyone, no one, someone,* and *anyone* always take a _____ verb.

B Read the rest. Then write the correct numbers from A and B (1–6) next to the sentences in 4B.

Units of measurement, collective nouns, asides, and verbs as subjects		
3 Units of measurement	Sixty dollars	seems like a lot.
	Two months	is an eternity.
4 Collective nouns	The agency	wants a deposit.
	In general, people	don't like having to park.
5 Asides	The start-up, as well as its competitors,	is making a lot of money.
6 Verbs as subjects	Having good ideas	takes a lot of courage.

» Grammar expansion p.138

C Circle the correct alternative in these quotes.

1 "Everyone [**have** / **has**] talent. What is rare is the courage to follow the talent to the dark place where it leads." Erica Jong

2 "An invasion of armies can be resisted, but not an idea whose time [**have** / **has**] come." Victor Hugo

3 "One of the advantages of being disorderly [**are** / **is**] that one is constantly making exciting discoveries." Abraham Maslow

4 "Man's mind, once stretched by a new idea, never [**regain** / **regains**] its original dimensions." Oliver Wendell Holmes

5 "The achievement of excellence can only occur if the organization [**promote** / **promotes**] a culture of creative dissatisfaction." Lawrence Miller

6 "If you're having difficulty coming up with new ideas, then slow down. For me, slowing down [**have** / **has**] been a tremendous source of creativity." Natalie Goldberg

D **Make it personal** In groups, choose your two favorite quotes from C and …
1 explain what they mean and why you like them.
2 think of concrete examples to illustrate them.

> The second really struck a chord with me.

> I'm not sure I understood it well.

> Well, basically he's saying that …

9

1.3 How many ways can you use a brick?

6 Reading

A Read the first paragraph. In pairs, what creative ideas or solutions have occurred to you in the shower? List as many as you can in two minutes.

> I've figured out the solution to some crossword clues.

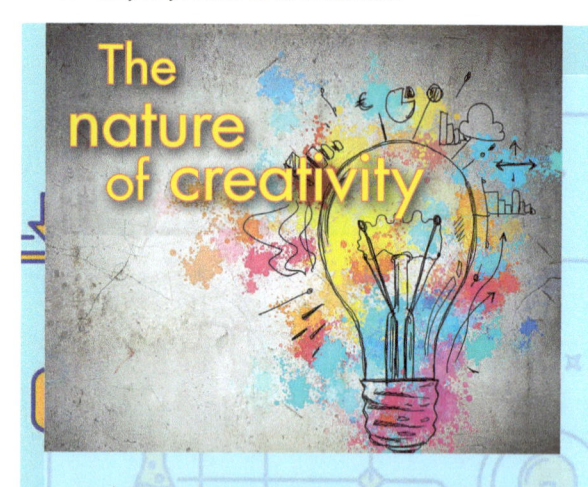

The nature of creativity

You're in the shower, shampooing your hair, when – bam! – an idea pops into your head. Maybe you finally figure out a way around a problem at work. Or perhaps it becomes clear why a family member or friend has been acting out of character. Or maybe the perfect end-of-year project suddenly comes to mind. It seems that those aha! moments hit us when we least expect them and elude us when we need them the most.

Most brain research has traditionally focused on the downside of letting your mind wander, highlighting the negative effects of daydreaming on our work and academic performance. [1]But if tuning out is as bad as has been suggested, why do we spend up to 50% of our time—according to some estimates—thinking about tasks other than those in front of us? Surely this wouldn't make sense in evolutionary terms.

A few recent studies have tried to shed new light on the nature of creativity. In 2012, a team of American researchers asked 145 students to list as many uses as possible for everyday objects, for example, toothpicks and bricks. One group of participants took a break during the task and engaged in recreational, undemanding activities. When these students returned, their creative ability to think of uses for the everyday objects had improved by 41%. Creativity, it seems, requires an incubation period. [2]But are there any biological mechanisms at play here?

As it turns out, our brains are not necessarily most active when we focus and try to zero in on a task. Things that make you switch to autopilot, like showering, working out, or even scrolling through your newsfeed, tend to relax the prefrontal cortex (the "feel good" center of the brain) and release hormones that can boost creativity. In other words, when our minds wander, ideas we might never have consciously connected seem to come together. This, of course, begs the question: [3]If our brains are not wired to be constantly attentive, why is tuning out usually considered such a bad thing?

We're immersed in a culture of attention and mindfulness, which puts a premium on the ability to "stay on top of things" as we juggle busy schedules, multiple technologies, and children demanding attention. [4]How can you allow yourself to simply space out when your project is unfinished and there's a deadline looming? If recent research is anything to go by, it looks as if maybe you should. You may have the idea of a lifetime!

B ▶ 1.10 Read and listen. In pairs, match the questions (1–4) in the article to the most likely answers (a–e). There's one extra.

a ☐ We are expected to be focused.
b ☐ Creative ideas need time to develop.
c ☐ Students who daydream get better grades.
d ☐ It's the best way to have a creative idea.
e ☐ When you're distracted, the pleasure centers of your brain react positively.

C Find 1–5 in the article and circle the most likely meaning in the context.

1 elude (paragraph 1): We [**escape from** / **fail to achieve**] them.
2 shed new light on (paragraph 3): They [**explain** / **define**] it in a new way.
3 boost (paragraph 4): They [**amplify or increase it** / **push it up from below**].
4 looming (paragraph 5): It [**appears as a large form** / **is about to happen**].
5 is anything to go by (paragraph 5): It [**can be followed** / **should be obeyed**].

How many ways can you use a brick? 1.3

Lesson Aims: Sts learn figurative expressions and read about the nature of creativity.

Skills
Reading a text about how to encourage creativity
Discussing the creative process

Vocabulary
Figurative expressions for ideas: *pop into your head, hit, let your mind wander, tune out, zero in, stay on top of things*

Warm-up

Board the lesson title question: *How many ways can you use a brick?* Put sts in small groups and ask them to note down as many ideas as they can. Class feedback. Have sts share their ideas. Ask: *Which group thought of the most ideas? Which is the most original idea?* Discuss with the class how they went about thinking up ideas. Ask: *Do you think you are creative? What situations help you to think creatively? Do you know any other examples of creative use of simple resources?*

6 Reading

A Focus on the picture and the title of the text. Try to elicit the phrase *light-bulb moment* (moment of inspiration) and have sts figure out the connection between the title and the picture.

Ask: *Who invented the light bulb? Thomas Edison (U.S., 1847–1931) Do you know the famous quote by him?* ("Genius is one percent inspiration and ninety-nine percent perspiration". Or "I have not failed. I've just found 10,000 ways that won't work."

Have sts read the first paragraph of the text. In pairs, sts discuss any creative ideas they have had in the shower, and list as many as they can. Classcheck, and ask who has the most creative ideas. Ask: *Were most of your ideas related to problem solving or were they new ideas?*

B ▶ 1.10 Have sts listen to the audio while they follow the text in their books. Suggest they underline questions 1–4 in the text to make the task easier. In pairs, sts discuss the most likely answers from a–e. Make sure they realize that they need to deduce the answers using their general understanding of the text, i.e. they won't find the answers directly in the text.

Weaker classes: Play the audio and pause after each of the questions 1–4 to give time for sts to match.

Tip

You might want to let sts read the text at their own pace first before they listen and read. In this case, have them read the text, do the task, and then listen and read the text a final time to listen for pronunciation of new or difficult words.

Answers

Sts' own answers, but the most likely answers are:
1 d / b 2 e 3 a 4 b / d

Weaker classes: To ensure sts have a good understanding of the text, ask the following comprehension questions or board them:

1 What two aspects of our lives does daydreaming have a bad effect on, according to a lot of traditional brain research? (work and academic performance)
2 According to research, how much time do we spend on the immediate task we are doing? (less than 50%)
3 In research carried out in 2012, what type of activities were shown to improve our creative ability? (recreational undemanding activities)
4 What do activities like showering, working out, scrolling through your newsfeed have in common? (they make you switch to autopilot)

Classcheck. Ask: *Did you find the article interesting?* Elicit, and if appropriate, drill the pronunciation of new words (stressed in pink) or play the audio again and have sts listen carefully to the pronunciation. Pause the audio after the new words and have sts repeat.

Tip

As a listening task, whenever there are pink-stressed words in texts, ask sts to echo the words as they hear them during the listening, and/or, then in pairs, to remember the pronunciation of these words after they have heard the texts.

C Sts find the words in the text and circle the correct meanings. Peercheck. Classcheck. To check sts have understood the meanings, ask them to come up with new examples of their own including each of the words.

Answers

1 escape from
2 explain
3 amplify or increase it
4 is about to happen
5 can be followed

1.3

D Make it personal Divide the class into groups of three or four. Review phrases for agreeing / disagreeing. Board them for sts to refer to during their debate.

Stating an opinion: *In my opinion … If you ask me … The way I see it …*

Asking for someone's opinion: *How do you feel about that? Do you agree? What do you think?*

Agreeing: *I agree with you 100%. I couldn't agree more. That's so true. Absolutely! That's exactly how I feel.*

Disagreeing: *I'm afraid I disagree. That's not always true / the case. I totally disagree.*

Weaker classes: Allow sts time to prepare their arguments before the debate starts, and write down their views on the statements.

Focus on the model in the speech bubbles. Give sts time to debate the statements in their groups. Monitor and check they are supporting their opinions with evidence from the article.

7 Vocabulary: Figurative expressions for ideas

A Focus on the pictures. Ask: *What can you see?* Try to elicit: *brain with feet, woman not paying attention to a man who is talking to her, woman standing on a pile of books, arrow hitting the bullseye, a man being punched in the face, man with a ball dropping into a hole in his head.*

Sts do the matching activity. Peercheck. Classcheck. Ask: *Do you have direct equivalents for these expressions in your language?*

> **Answers**
> 1 letting your mind wander
> 2 tuning out
> 3 stay on top of things
> 4 zero in on
> 5 hit us
> 6 an idea pops into your head

» Song lyric: See Teacher's Book p.341 for notes about the song and an accompanying activity to do with the class.

B Put sts in pairs. Tell them to choose three expressions each, and look up the meanings in a dictionary. Sts explain to each other the meanings of their expressions. Tell them to use the models in the speech bubbles to help them. Encourage sts to ask their partner for clarification if they don't understand the explanation.

Sts add the expressions to the chart. Classcheck. Discuss with the class which of the pictures best helps them remember the expressions.

Tip

If you're using a digital board, use an online dictionary to flash up further examples to help them see the phrases in other contexts.

C Give sts a few minutes to think of some ideas.

Weaker classes: Sts write down their sentences.

In pairs, have sts tell each other their sentences. Classcheck. Have some sts tell the class their sentences.

Optional activity

Stronger classes: Instead of having sts write three true sentences, ask them to write two true sentences and one false one. Monitor and help where necessary. When they have finished, put sts in pairs to read out their sentences to each other. Their partner asks follow up questions, then tries to guess which sentence is false.

Tip

Some sts find it difficult to generate ideas from scratch like this. If so, give them some prompts to help, e.g. different places they've been, homework and other work they've done, websites they've visited.

D Make it personal Ask: *Do you have to be creative in … your job / your studies? What types of creative tasks do you have to do?*

Tip

With all exercises like these, it's a good idea to get the class to ask you the questions first. Your answers will help them know more about both you and your difficult task of teaching them (!), and just as importantly, exemplify and give them more time to begin to shape their own answers.

In pairs, sts discuss questions 1–4. Ask sts to swap partners and share their ideas with their new partner. Class feedback. Have some sts report back to the class any new ideas they learned from their classmates.

Tip

While sts are doing a freer speaking activity such as in D, monitor and listen carefully to what sts are saying. Note down any common or important errors with grammar, lexis, and pronunciation, and also any particularly good use of language you hear. In feedback, board any good examples of language and drill them with the class. Write up errors and ask the class to correct them together. Keep a record of these for yourself and go over them again at the beginning of the next lesson.

» Workbook p.5.

♪ Take you with me if I can. Been dreaming of this since a child. I'm on top of the world

1.3

D Make it personal In groups, debate which statements are good advice. Find evidence in the article for or against. Has anyone ever said them to you?
1 "Stop daydreaming! You won't get your homework done in time again."
2 "Take a short break. Come back to it when you're fresh, and something will occur to you."
3 "You have to learn to concentrate or you won't get ahead!"
4 "Stop worrying so much about the deadline. Let's go out and have some fun. You might have a brilliant idea!"

> My parents used to say number 1 all the time.

> But look, in paragraph 3, it says …

7 Vocabulary: Figurative expressions for ideas

A Look at the highlighted expressions in the article in **6A**. Then match them to pictures 1–6.

B In pairs, explain what the expressions mean. Use an online dictionary, if necessary. Then add them to the chart. Which images in **A** best help you remember them?

Having an idea	Getting distracted	Staying focused

> One meaning of *pop* is to "explode" or "burst open", so if an idea pops into your head, it "explodes" or "appears suddenly".

> Yes, like a burst of energy. So if I say, "An idea popped into my head," it means it was very sudden and wasn't there before.

C Share true sentences about yourself using at least three of the expressions in **B**.

> Yesterday when I was walking home from school, a great idea hit me …

D Make it personal In pairs, share your creative process.
1 Think of a time when you couldn't think of an idea.
2 Where / When / How did the solution finally come to you?
3 Have you applied your strategy to any new situations since then? Did it work?
4 Have you ever used any of the suggestions in the article?

> I took a very demanding art course, and it was hard to stay on top of all the projects. One day, an idea just wouldn't come to me.

> So what did you do?

11

1.4 What do the 2000s make you think of?

8 Language in use

A ▶1.11 In pairs, decide the historical significance of 1–3. Then listen to a radio interview to check. Were your reasons the same?

> Wikipedia has changed the way I learn about new things.

FAMOUS FIRSTS This week: The 2000s BY ROY MARTÍNEZ

1. A non-Hollywood movie wins eight Oscars for the first time.
2. New technological words are invented.
3. The first user-created encyclopedia is introduced.

B ▶1.11 Read *Uses of set*. Complete 1–5 with the most logical words from the box. Listen again to check.

> **Uses of *set***
>
> *Set* is one of the most flexible verbs in English, with meanings as varied as *put*, *design*, *establish*, and *schedule*:
> a   In the 90s, the Japanese **set** (= established) the standard for small cars.
> b   The 2020 Olympics are **set** (= scheduled) to take place in Tokyo.
> *Set* is also the verb in fixed expressions and idioms:
> Nelson Mandela was **set free** (= released) in 1990.

| fire | motion | record | release | rules | stage |

1. *Slumdog Millionaire* set a new world _____: It was the first time an international production had won so many Oscars, and this set in _____ a number of important changes.
2. You may feel some of these new words didn't exactly set the world on _____ initially, but by 2010, everyone had been using words like "texting" and "to Google" for years.
3. Maybe some of these early words set the _____ for more new ones. "To Google" and "cloud computing" were invented in 2007 and "Twitter" in 2008.
4. Since it was introduced in 2001, Wikipedia has set new _____ for how we build and share knowledge.
5. I've been working on a new book, and it's different from anything I've ever written. It's set for a December _____.

C Make it personal In groups, do you agree with Roy's "famous firsts"? Consider these questions.
1. What percentage of films included in the Oscars should be foreign? Considering that the Academy Awards are a U.S. ceremony, how important is it for them to be international?
2. How important are language changes and the addition of new words? Was the addition of technological words a groundbreaking "first"?
3. What do you think of Wikipedia? How accurate do you think it is?

> Wikipedia definitely set the stage for a new way of accessing information.

> Yes, entries in two different languages on the same topic are sometimes completely different.

> Really? Let's try it!

12

What do the 2000s make you think of? 1.4

Lesson Aims: Sts listen to an interview about defining historical moments of the 2000s, and review perfect tenses.

Skills	Language	Vocabulary	Grammar
Listening to a radio interview with an author about key moments of the 2000s Discussing personal defining moments	Talking about events in the past using present perfect tenses, e.g. *Most people have stopped downloading albums. Since it was introduced in 2001, Wikipedia has set new rules for how we build and share knowledge.*	Expressions with *set*, e.g. *set on fire, set in motion, set a record*	Simple past vs. present perfect; present perfect vs. present perfect continuous; past perfect vs. past perfect continuous

Warm-up

Focus on the lesson title question: *What do the 2000s make you think of?* In pairs, ask sts to note down events or developments which they think had a major impact on the landscape of society in their country and / or globally. Elicit a few examples to begin with, e.g. the Game of Thrones books and TV series, the iPod, the launch of Facebook, the U.S. electing their first black president. Put sts in groups to pool their ideas, and ask them to rank their top five in order. Class feedback.

8 Language in use

A ▶ 1.11 Focus on the pictures, and elicit what sts know about them. Ask sts to read the text under the pictures. In pairs, sts discuss the historical significance of each one. If necessary, prompt sts by asking: *What nationality were most of the actors in Slumdog Millionaire? Do you think it was easy for Indian actors to gain international recognition before this movie? How many new words can you think of related to social media (to google, to text, to snap chat)? Who are the authors of Wikipedia? How accurate is the information in it?*

Tell sts they are going to hear Roy discussing his defining moments of the 2000s. Have sts listen and compare the speaker's views with their own.

Weaker classes: Play the audio in three parts, pausing to paircheck, then classcheck after he explains each of his choices.

» See Teacher's Book p.312 for Audio script 1.11.

Background information

Slumdog Millionaire tells the story of a boy from a poor background in India who wins a fortune on the gameshow *Who Wants to be a Millionaire?* but is accused of cheating by the police. He then recounts the history of his life and how it enabled him to answer the questions.

The Dot.com bubble refers to the collapse of many internet start-ups from 1999–2001, after wildly exaggerated expectations of their success.

Wikipedia was launched in 2001 as a way of creating a reference work which users could edit. The English version is the largest, with over five million articles. In its early days it had issues with the accuracy of the articles published, but recent studies have shown it to be much more accurate overall.

Optional activity

Board the following statements. Have sts listen again and circle the correct answers.

Roy ...

1 [hopes / **is sure**] *Slumdog Millionaire* will make the Academy more inclusive
2 [**enjoyed** / was not impressed by] the movie.
3 says texting was a new [activity / **word**] in 2004.
4 [doubts / **expects**] that new words will continue to be added in the future.
5 believes today's social networks [tried to copy / **were made possible by**] Wikipedia.
6 suspects people criticize Wikipedia because it's [too democratic / **not always dependable**].

B ▶ 1.11 Go through the **Uses of set** with the class.

Have sts complete sentences 1–5 with the correct word in the box. Peercheck, then classcheck by playing the audio. When they have finished, ask them to write E (established), S (scheduled), or FE (fixed expression) by each sentence depending on what the meaning of *set* is. Classcheck.

> **Answers**
> 1 record (E); motion (FE) 2 fire (FE) 3 stage (FE)
> 4 rules (E) 5 release (S)

» Song lyric: See Teacher's Book p.342 for notes about the song and an accompanying activity to do with the class.

C Make it personal Put sts in groups to discuss Roy's "famous firsts." Before they begin their discussions, read through the questions with the class and focus on the models in the speech bubbles. Ask sts to think about how historically significant they think each event was; and what they would have included in their famous firsts for the 2000s: same or different?

Class check, and have sts share their views with the rest of the class.

33

1.4

9 Grammar: Using perfect tenses

Tip

It's a good idea to use the headings as an initial brainstorm before going into the grammar boxes. First cover the box and ask: *How many perfect tenses do you know? What kind of actions are they used for? What they have in common?* In pairs, sts brainstorm answers. Monitor and help as necessary, but don't confirm too much yet.

A Go through the grammar box and check understanding of the example sentences.

Have sts read through the rules and choose the correct options. If necessary, review negative forms by asking sts to write their own personalized examples for each category in the table, one affirmative and one negative, e.g. *I watched a Spanish movie last night. / I didn't watch the Oscars last year. I've seen some fantastic Japanese movies. / I haven't been to the movies in ages.*

Weaker classes: It might be useful for sts to compare the following sentences to show the difference between the present perfect and the past perfect: *I've been going to the movies a lot these last few months. I had been going to the movies a lot before they closed the theater.*

Note: Point out that in American English we often avoid the past perfect in informal speech, e.g. *I sent a text message before I got home, I was using the word for years before I saw it*, are common examples.

Answers

1 simple past
2 present perfect; present perfect continuous
3 past perfect continuous

Refer sts to the **Common mistake**. If necessary, explain that *lately* does not tell us specifically "when" this person saw some great movies but refers to a vague period of time, which is why we don't use the simple past. Board the following sentence for sts to compare: *I saw a great movie last week / on Friday.*

Tip

To find out more about their learning experiences, try to personalize the **Common mistake**. Ask: *Did you used to make this type of mistake? How long has it taken you to learn the present perfect? When did you finally feel it had become "a friend"?*

» Refer sts to the **Grammar expansion** on p.138.

Optional activity

Ask sts to go online and watch a video clip from a video-sharing website. Ask them to note down any uses of the present perfect they hear, then share them with the class.

B Have sts read the discussion forum quickly to get the gist. Ask: *Which artists are mentioned?* Sts read again and choose the correct options for 1–7. Peercheck. Classcheck.

In pairs, ask sts to discuss what they think are the defining moments for them in music in the 2010s. Class feedback. Elicit some of their favorite artists and songs, and remind them to suggest them as alternatives to the song lines in the book if they think of any that match the lesson topics, language, or grammar.

Answers

1 had set   2 sold   3 have been falling   4 have been
5 won   6 'd been breaking   7 have stopped

C Make it personal Explain what sts have to do. Brainstorm ideas with the class if they don't have access to the Internet, and make a class list of defining moments.

To prompt them, ask: *What events that have occurred in the 2010s do you think will be in future text books? What effect do you think social media has had on the Arts? What aspect of technology from the 2010s do you think you could not live without?*

Have them choose a topic, and make notes about the most defining moments relating to their topics. Put sts in groups to share their ideas. Refer them to the models in the speech bubbles. Class feedback. Ask: *Which topics were most popular?*

Tip

For these online search tasks, once you get to know the book, it's a good idea to ask them to do the searching as homework **the lesson before**.

In class, having sts work in pairs, sharing one phone to access the information can be more productive and means you need fewer phones, too! Try to stick to a sensible time limit, so classes don't drift.

Where time is short, set this as the homework task for the next lesson, and stick to what's on the page.

» Workbook p.6.

🎵 I'm giving you up. I've forgiven it all. You set me free

1.4

9 Grammar: Using perfect tenses

A Read the grammar box and check (✔) the correct rules 1–3. Find an example of each rule in 8B.

Simple past vs. present perfect; present perfect vs. present perfect continuous; past perfect vs. past perfect continuous

I	watched	the Oscars last year.
	've seen	some great foreign films lately.
	've been going	to the movies a lot.
Our view of language	has changed.	We now expect new words.
	has been changing	slowly.
I	'd sent	a text message before I got home.
	had been using	the word "texting" for years when I saw it in a dictionary.

1 When the action is complete, use the ☐ **simple past** ☐ **present perfect** if you say when the action happened.
2 The ☐ **present perfect** ☐ **present perfect continuous** sometimes means the action is complete, but the ☐ **present perfect** ☐ **present perfect continuous** always means it's in progress.
3 The ☐ **past perfect** ☐ **past perfect continuous** is used to talk about actions in progress when the action occurs before another point in the past.

>> Grammar expansion p.138

Common mistake

've seen
I ~~saw~~ some great films lately. I saw a really good one at the festival.

You can only use the simple past if you say "when" or "where."

B Complete the discussion forum. Circle the best choice (1–7).

WHAT ABOUT MUSIC IN THE 2010S?   Any defining moments?

Alanis7: To me, it was the release of Adele's 25 in 2015. Her 21 album ¹[**had been setting** / **had set**] the charts on fire a few years earlier, and no one thought she'd be able to match that kind of success. Turns out she did. 25 ²[**sold** / **has sold**] something like 3.5 million copies in the opening week alone! This is a big deal because it's shown the industry that even though album sales ³[**fell** / **have been falling**] year after year, not everybody is into singles. There's still a place for complete albums.

TaylorFan: Agreed. The last few years ⁴[**had been** / **have been**] pretty good for Taylor Swift, too. She ⁵[**'d won** / **won**] like a million awards in 2014–15, but, truth be told, she ⁶[**'s been breaking** / **'d been breaking**] record after record long before that.

RiccoW: Well, album sales are down because most people ⁷[**stopped** / **have stopped**] downloading albums. Period. Why buy an album when you can stream it on Spotify?

C Make it personal What's your most important defining moment of the 2010s?

1 🌐 Choose a topic. Search on "Top defining moments of the 2010s" for more ideas.

the arts   history   technology   sport   a personal moment

For me, it was the last *Harry Potter* movie.

What was so special about that?

It was the end of an era. J.K. Rowling set a record for unknown writers: 40 million books translated into 67 languages and eight movies!

2 In groups, explain what was special about the defining moment. Use expressions with *set* as well as perfect tenses to talk about actions in the past and to bring the listener up to the present.

13

1.5 Have you ever had a dream come true?

10 Listening

A ▶ 1.12 Listen to Todd and Amy discussing cross-cultural relationships. Check (✔) a or b.

It can be inferred that the couple in the article …

a ☐ may not have talked about cultural differences early on.
b ☐ were aware from the beginning that culture can be very important.

B ▶ 1.13 Listen to the next part. Does Todd express these opinions? Y (yes), N (no), or NI (no information)?

1 Almost nothing is universal, and all aspects of life have to be talked about.
2 The things people say are unimportant might hide cultural assumptions.
3 People usually give up their old cultural assumptions when they move to a new country.
4 The need for security is personal, not cultural.
5 If you really try, you can change someone.

C ▶ 1.14 Guess whether the couple stayed together. Listen to the end to check. Note down two reasons for the outcome.

11 Keep talking

A ▶ 1.15 Read *Informal responses*. Then complete the chart. Listen to check.

> **Informal responses**
>
> In conversation, it's important to know how to respond appropriately. Some responses are neutral in register, while others can be very informal, for use with friends and family.
>
> *I'm not sure I agree.* (neutral)   *You've got to be kidding!* (informal)

	What they said	What they meant
Very informal	1 That's what I'm _____ you.	I just said that.
	2 That's for _____. OR I'll _____.	Definitely! I know.
	3 You're _____ me? How _____ I know?	I don't know.
Neutral	4 Let's _____ it.	You have to consider this.
	5 Just give it a _____.	Don't decide in advance.

B In groups, discuss these questions. Use expressions from A.

1 Did anything that Amy and Todd said surprise you? Why (not)?
2 What other sorts of conflicts can you imagine between cross-cultural couples?
3 Is a cross-cultural relationship a "first" experience you've tried or would like to try?

C Make it personal What unusual "firsts" have you tried? Make notes and share your story. Whose was most surprising?

> **Common mistake**
>
>   *was*
> It ~~went~~ bad / awful.

> I love danger and last summer I decided to try rock climbing. I was a little nervous, though.

> I'll bet! How did it go?

> Well, it didn't go very well.

Have you ever had a dream come true? 1.5

Lesson Aims: Sts listen to a discussion about cross-cultural relationships, and write a narrative about a first-time experience.

Skills	Language	Vocabulary
Listening to a discussion about cross-cultural relationships Writing an autobiographical narrative using narrative tenses, and the conjunction *as* Responding appropriately during conversation	Informal / formal responses, e.g. *How would I know? I'll bet. Let's face it.*	Expressions with *but*, e.g. *It was all but …, I couldn't help but …, I was all but …, I did anything but …*

10 Listening

Warm-up

Focus on the lesson title question and discuss with the class. Try to think of an example yourself to set up the discussion. Begin by saying: *When I was young I always dreamed of … then when I was in my twenties I had the chance to …* Invite volunteers to tell the class about their dreams and whether they have come true yet.

A ▶ 1.12 Focus on the photo. Elicit their guesses as to what the listening may be about. Then explain that sts are going to hear the couple in the photo discuss an article about an American man who moved to Japan and married a Japanese woman. Ask: *What type of problems do you think this couple might have come up against?*

Play the audio. Sts check the correct option a or b.

Answer

a

» See Teacher's Book p.312 for Audio script 1.12.

B ▶ 1.13 Have sts read opinions 1–5 and discuss the meaning together. Ask if they agree / disagree with the statements. Play the next part of the audio. Sts write Y, N, or NI next to each opinion.

Weaker classes: Pause the audio after each answer or after each relevant bit of the audio.

Classcheck. Have sts review their own performance of the task. Ask: *Did you find the audio difficult? Did you find it too fast? Was the vocabulary too difficult? Would you like to hear it again?* If they found it very difficult, have them follow the audio script on p.313 of the TB as they listen again.

Answers

1 Y   2 Y   3 NI   4 N   5 N

» See Teacher's Book p.312 for Audio script 1.13.

Tip

When going through the answers, ask sts to justify their Y and N answers by telling you what the speakers said.

C ▶ 1.14 Sts discuss in pairs whether they think the couple stayed together. Play the audio for them to check their guesses.

Answers

The couple did stay together. Possible reasons: they could express themselves well, as they spoke each other's languages, they both tried to merge a little (he joined her family business and she stopped taking things for granted / assumed things were just common sense).

» See Teacher's Book p.313 for Audio script 1.14.

Optional activity

Put sts in groups, and ask them to make a list of "top tips" for foreigners starting a relationship with someone from their country.

11 Keep talking

A ▶ 1.15 Read **Informal responses** with the class. Model stress and pronunciation of the example phrases. Have sts repeat them. Sts complete the chart, then play the audio for them to check.

Re-play the audio, pausing after each phrase so sts can repeat. Have them practice saying the phrases in pairs.

Answers

1 telling   2 sure, bet   3 asking, would   4 face   5 try

B In groups, sts discuss the questions. Encourage them to use the expressions from A. During class feedback, if anyone in the class has experienced a cross-cultural relationship, invite them to share their experiences with the class (if they are happy to!).

C Make it personal Give an example of something you have tried for the first time to get sts started. Focus also on the example in the speech bubbles. Give sts time to think of a "first experience" and make notes. Make some suggestions, e.g. first time they did a sport or hobby, first day at a new job, a first date.

Sts share their stories in pairs. Encourage them to respond to each other using the phrases in A.

Focus on the **Common mistake**. Point out that we need to use an adverb after *go*, e.g. *It went badly* or an adjective after *was*, e.g. *It was bad*.

1.5

> Song lyric: See Teacher's Book p.342 for notes about the song and an accompanying activity to do with the class.

12 Writing: An autobiographical narrative

A Focus on the title. Ask the class: *What was the last biography you read? Have you ever read an autobiography? Which was the best biography you ever read and why?*

Focus on the photo and title of the text. Ask: *What can you see in the photo?* (sailboats, seaside, hotel, blue sky). *Where do you think it is? What experience do you think is described in the text? Have you ever been sailing?*

Ask sts to read the text quickly for gist and see if they guessed correctly. Give them a time limit to encourage them to read quickly. Sts read the text again and underline examples of 1–3.

Weaker classes: Elicit an example of each before sts begin.

Classcheck. Don't forget to ask their opinion of the text, the author and his experience, and if they enjoyed reading it.

Answers

1 past perfect, simple past
Examples: I'd always dreamed of having a sailboat.
… as a child, I'd learned to swim by the time I was four.
But I never, ever thought I'd have the chance to live on one.

2 simple past, past continuous
I went there to take a temporary job as a waiter over the winter break.
One night, as I was serving customers in the capital city, St. George's, I couldn't help but overhear the word "sailboat" in a conversation.
Of course, my ears pricked up immediately, and I got up the courage to introduce myself.
… it turned out that a young couple from Grenville, the island's second largest city, was looking for someone to take care of their boat as they were going to be abroad for a year. They explained that they needed an experienced "captain," who could also handle repairs.
I wasn't a certified captain, and I was all but certain I had no chance at the job.
I did some research and enrolled in a sailing exam-preparation course.
I had a lot of work ahead of me
… for two months, I did nothing but study.
I passed the test with flying colors.
I had to refresh my knowledge of astronomy and meteorology.
At the beginning of May, I moved … into their sailboat!

3 present perfect, simple present
But now it's over, and I can do nautical calculations using the sun and stars as a reference.
My new home is a little small …
… my parents are a little disappointed that I haven't gone back to school, but I've never been happier.

Tip

If you want to ensure sts read quickly for gist, rather than setting a time limit, have them do it as a race. Ask sts to close their books and tell them that the first person to find the answers is the winner. When they are ready, say *Go!* and let them read quickly to find the answers.

B Go through **Write it right!** Ask sts what word they would use for *as* in sentences 1–4 in their language. Sts find the examples of *as* highlighted in the text and match them with meanings 1–4. Peercheck. Classcheck.

Answers

1 because: as they were going to be abroad for a year.
2 when: as a child, I'd learned to swim by the time I was four.
3 for the purpose of: using the sun and stars as a reference.
4 in the role of: I went there to take a temporary job as a waiter over the winter break.

C Tell sts to find sentences 1–4 in the text and fill in the missing words. Classcheck. Elicit other sentences with the *but* phrases to check sts' understanding, e.g. *It was nothing but hard work. I couldn't help but laugh at her. It was all but over. I did nothing but sleep.*

Answers

1 nothing   2 help   3 all   4 nothing

D Your turn!

Go through the **Common mistake**. Ask: *Why do we use the past perfect in this case, and not the present perfect?* Refer sts back to the Grammar on page 13 to remind them of the rules.

Tell sts they are going to write their own narratives on a "first experience." Tell them they can write about the experience they shared in 11C or choose a different one.

While sts plan, monitor and give help where necessary. They can write up their narratives for homework if you need more time.

When they have finished, ask sts to swap them with a partner, and correct any mistakes they find, paying particular attention to use of tenses. Finally, sts post their work online and read their classmates' stories. Class feedback. Ask: *Whose did you find most surprising / interesting? Did you have any similar experiences? Which student's autobiography would you most like to read?*

> Workbook p.7.

🎵 When I met you in the summer, To my heartbeat sound. We fell in love, As the leaves turned brown

1.5

12 Writing: An autobiographical narrative

A Read the narrative and answer 1–3. Underline examples.

Which tense(s) does the writer primarily use to …
1 give background information?
2 introduce and describe the events?
3 bring the reader up to the present?

B Read *Write it right!* Match the highlighted *as* in the narrative to the meanings 1–4 below.

Write it right!

As is a versatile word that has many functions:
<u>Slightly more formal</u>
1 **As** we're from different cultures, Mayumi and I have some cultural differences. (= because)
2 **As** a student, I used to like French. (= when I was a student)
<u>Neutral</u>
3 I ran into Laura. She's working **as** a salesclerk. (= in the role of)
4 I used my jacket **as** an umbrella. (= for the purpose of)

1 because
2 when
3 for the purpose of
4 in the role of

C Complete these expressions with *but* from the narrative.

1 It was _____ but sheer luck.
2 I couldn't _____ but overhear.
3 I was _____ but certain.
4 I did _____ but study.

D **Your turn!** Write a four-paragraph autobiographical narrative (250 words) on a first experience.

Before
Plan background information, introduce and describe the events, and bring the reader up to the present.

While
Write four paragraphs following the model in A, adding a summary as the fourth paragraph. Be careful with narrative tenses. Include at least two examples with *as* and an expression with *but*.

After
Post your narrative online and read your classmates' work. Whose narrative was most surprising?

Share your most original first experience!

If I can do it, so can you!
By Mitch Pebble

I'd always dreamed of having a sailboat. I love the water, and **as** a child, I'd learned to swim by the time I was four. But I never, ever thought I'd have the chance to live on one until I moved from my home in Miami to the Caribbean island of Grenada. The most astonishing part of all is that I went there to take a temporary job **as** a waiter over the winter break. After that, it was nothing but sheer luck!

One night, as I was serving customers in the capital city, St. George's, I couldn't help but overhear the word "sailboat" in a conversation. Of course, my ears pricked up immediately, and I got up the courage to introduce myself. Lo and behold, it turned out that a young couple from Grenville, the island's second largest city, was looking for someone to take care of their boat **as** they were going to be abroad for a year. They explained that they needed an experienced "captain," who could also handle repairs. I wasn't a certified captain, and I was all but certain I had no chance at the job. Still, I couldn't let this marvelous opportunity pass, so instead of meeting friends when my shift ended, I did some research and enrolled in a sailing exam-preparation course.

I had a lot of work ahead of me, and for two months, I did nothing but study. In the end, though, I passed the test with flying colors. I had to refresh my knowledge of astronomy and meteorology. But now it's over, and I can do nautical calculations using the sun and stars **as** a reference. At the beginning of May, I moved … into their sailboat! My new home is a little small, and my parents are a little disappointed that I haven't gone back to school, but I've never been happier.

My friends always told me to follow my dreams, and at first, I was a little skeptical. Now I couldn't agree with them more!

Common mistake

I had the experience of a lifetime. ~~I've~~ *I'd* never felt that way before.

Remember to maintain tense consistency in your writing.

15

2 What would you change about your lifestyle?

1 Listening

A ▶ 2.1 Look at the "vision board." Guess what it is and what it's used for. Listen to the start of Luke and Julia's conversation to check. How close were you? Do you like the idea?

> It might have something to do with lifestyles.

> I wonder if it's an app.

B ▶ 2.2 Listen to the second part. Infer Luke's two main objections. Do you agree?
Luke thinks "vision boards" are …

☐ boring.   ☐ illogical.   ☐ time-consuming.   ☐ unscientific.

C ▶ 2.3 Listen to the end. Circle the photos in **A** Julia talks about. Which goal(s) is she definitely going to pursue?

D Make it personal Talk about your own "vision board."

1 ▶ 2.4 **How to say it** Complete the chart. Listen to check.

Decision-making	
What they said	What they meant
1 I'm _____ (to get it published).	I'm definitely going to …
2 My _____'s made up.	I'm convinced.
3 I'm _____ between (an MA in literature) and (an MBA).	I can't decide between …
4 There's a lot at _____.	There's a lot that could be lost.
5 I need to give it some more _____.	I need to think about it some more.
6 I've been _____ with the idea of (selling this house).	I've slowly been considering …

2 Think of at least four personal goals and note them down for these categories:
   a short-term (definitely)   b short-term (maybe)   c long-term (definitely)   d long-term (maybe)
3 Compare your ideas in pairs. Use *How to say it* expressions. Anything in common?

> I'm determined to take a trip abroad next year. My mind's made up! I want a freer lifestyle.

> Where will you get the money?

What would you change about your lifestyle? 2.1

Lesson Aims: Sts learn language for expressing life goals and discuss ways of achieving them.

Skills	Language	Vocabulary	Grammar
Listening to a conversation about life goals	Talking about making decisions, e.g. *I'm torn between ...*, *to give something some thought*, *to toy with ...*	Expressing goals: *go the extra mile*, *work toward*, *meet your goals*, *put your mind to something*, *far-fetched*, *fall into your lap*, *unattainable*	Review of future tenses including *going to*, *might*, and *will*

Warm-up

Focus on the lesson title question: *What would you change about your lifestyle?* Elicit a few ideas from sts, e.g. *I'd like to get in shape, I'd like to eat more healthily, I'd like to spend more time with my friends, I would like to spend less time working.* Ask: *Do you often set yourself goals? How do you go about trying to meet your goals?*

1 Listening

A ▶ 2.1 Focus on the photos and quotes. Ask: *What can you see? Which of the quotes do you like best / is most useful?*

Ask: *What do you think a "vision board" is? Do you have one or do you know anyone who uses them?* Play the audio for sts to listen and check. Paircheck and listen again if necessary to doublecheck. Discuss with the class whether they think it is a good idea or not.

> **Answer**
>
> A vision board is somewhere to display things (e.g. photos, quotes, sayings) that represent whatever you want to be / do / achieve. Vision boards can help motivate and inspire you, and to clarify and maintain focus on specific life goals.

» See Teacher's Book p.313 for Audio script 2.1.

B ▶ 2.2 Before sts listen, ask: *Do you think vision boards are boring / illogical / time-consuming / unscientific?* Have them listen and find out what Luke thinks. Class check, and ask who agreed with Luke.

> **Answers**
>
> illogical, unscientific

» See Teacher's Book p.313 for Audio script 2.2.

C ▶ 2.3 Tell sts that in the last part of the audio they are going to hear Julia talking about three of her goals. Play the audio. Sts circle the photos Julia refers to, and make a note of the goal she is definitely going to pursue.

Classcheck, and ask how they figured out the answer. (She says she is "**determined** to get [her book] published," but she is less certain about doing an online course, saying she "**might** take an online course," and, referring to her third goal, she says she is "**toying with** the idea of moving," which means she is thinking about it.)

> **Answers**
>
> photo of the office (top left), photo of someone writing (bottom right), photo of studio (top right)
> Julia is definitely going to pursue getting her book published.

» See Teacher's Book p.313 for Audio script 2.3.

» Song lyric: See Teacher's Book p.342 for notes about the song and an accompanying activity to do with the class.

D Make it personal

1 ▶ 2.4 **How to say it** Go through the expressions in the chart, and ask sts to complete them from memory. Play the audio for them to check.

Stronger classes: Ask sts to cover up the expressions in the "What they said" column, and say: Listen to the audio again and try to listen out for expressions which mean: *I'm definitely going to ..., I'm convinced ..., I can't decide between ...*, etc.

> **Answers**
>
> 1 determined 2 mind 3 torn 4 stake 5 thought
> 6 toying

2 Have sts think of their own personal goals and note them down. If helpful, agree on the time scales, e.g. short-term = this year / within two years.

3 Put sts in pairs to discuss their ideas. Monitor and encourage them to use the expressions in the **How to say it** chart.

Weaker classes: Elicit phrases for sts to use to talk about their plans, and remind them that we use the *going to* future for definite plans and *will* future with *maybe* if they are less sure, e.g. *I'm going to ..., I'd love / like to ..., I'm planning to ..., I might ..., Maybe I'll.*

Class feedback. Ask individual sts to report back to the class what they learned about their partner. Ask: *Did you and your partner have any goals in common? Do you think your partner's goals are attainable / far-fetched?*

Tip

Encourage sts to ask follow-up questions to get more information, e.g. *Where did you get the idea for that? When do you think you'll do it? Why is it important to you?*

» 2.1

2 Vocabulary: Expressing goals

Tip

To get good mileage out of any focus, try this: Books closed. Ask sts in pairs to remember all they can about the two people in the photo (as they will have been half-looking at it already) and speculate about what they might be thinking/saying. Books open to check. Any surprises?

A Sts read and complete the extract. Have them check the audio script on page 162 of the Student's Book or, alternatively, play the audio for them to check. Classcheck, and ask sts who is more like Luke / Julia.

For pronunciation practice, play the audio and pause after each expression for them to repeat. Highlight the stress on far-FETCHed and unatTAINable.

> **Answers**
> 1 meet your goals   2 far-fetched   3 fall into your lap
> 4 put your mind to something   5 go the extra mile
> 6 work towards your goal   7 unattainable

B Focus on the memes in 1A. Elicit the meaning of meme (= an idea or piece of information that spreads very quickly on the internet). Put sts in groups. Have them discuss the memes and explain what they mean, and then use the phrases in 2B to say if they agree with the memes and how achievable they are. Give an example to start sts off, e.g. Say: *Simplicity is the key to happiness. I think this is saying try to enjoy the simple things in life, and that happiness can be obtained easily from very little, e.g. having coffee with a friend or watching a sunset. I think, if you put your mind to it, this is attainable. You just need to slow down, and enjoy the moment.*

Class feedback and find out which is the most popular meme. Ask: *Which of the goals would you like to work toward? How are you going to meet this goal?*

Optional activity

As a follow up, ask sts to find other memes online which express the same ideas, then show them to their partners. In feedback, elicit some examples to share with the class.

C ▶ 2.5 Focus on the collocation mind maps and do the first one with the class as an example. Ask sts to complete the other collocations, then play the audio for them to check.

Ask sts which of these collocations they already knew. Have them write their own true personalized sentences with some of the collocations, e.g. *My brother told me a very far-fetched story the other day. I'm worried that I won't meet my parents' expectations.*

> **Answers**
> 1 far-fetched   2 unattainable   3 meet   4 work toward

» See Teacher's Book p.313 for Audio script 2.5.

D Make it personal Read through the instructions, and check sts understand what they have to do. Focus on the example in the speech bubble. Elicit a further example from one of the stronger sts, e.g. *My teacher is always annoyed with me because my homework is always late. I am not very good at (meeting deadlines).*

Weaker classes: Have sts write down their sentences. Tell them to blank out the missing the collocation, and exchange their sentences with their partner. They then complete the missing words in their partners' sentences.

Have sts feedback some of their favorite examples to the rest of the class.

» Workbook p.8.

♪ You say you want a leader, But you can't seem to make up your mind. I think you better close it, And let me guide you to the purple rain

2 Vocabulary: Expressing goals

A Complete the extract from the dialogue with a–g. Check in **AS** 2.2 on p.162. Are you more like Luke or Julia?

LUKE: In other words, you're saying that a vision board really can help you [1]_____?

JULIA: Exactly.

LUKE: The whole idea seems so [2]_____! You can stare at a picture of a new car till you're blue in the face, but it won't just [3]_____. It's not enough just to [4]_____. You've got to do your part and [5]_____ – you know, save money for a long time, if necessary.

JULIA: Yes, of course, you've got to [6]_____ your goals, even if they seem [7]_____. But our minds help us do that.

a **go** the extra mile: make a special effort
b **work toward**: move gradually toward your objectives
c **meet** your goals: achieve your objectives
d **put** your mind to something: be determined to achieve something
e **far-fetched**: (adj) unlikely (e.g. an idea)
f **fall into your lap**: happen without any effort
g **unattainable**: (adj) cannot be reached or achieved (e.g. a goal)

B In groups, describe the memes in **1A** using the vocabulary from **A**. What's your (least) favorite one? Why?

> Let's see. "Goals: keep your eye on the prize." It's saying if you really work toward something, you can achieve it.

> I think that's pretty obvious.

C ▶ 2.5 Complete collocations 1–4 with words in red from **A**. Then listen to check. How many collocations were you familiar with?

1
story   explanation
a(n) _____
example

2
objective   wish
a(n) _____
(sales) target

3
a (tight) deadline   the requirements
_____
someone's expectations

4
a (law) degree   a solution (to a problem)
_____
a career in (journalism)

D Make it personal Choose a collocation from **C** and a topic below. Then tell your partner something about yourself. Stop before the collocation. Can he/she guess what you had in mind?

a degree   a job problem   a personal goal   a news item   a teacher   your boss

> My boss is incredibly demanding. It's nearly impossible to meet …

> Meet her expectations?

> Exactly. Can you believe she …

» 2.2 What's the biggest house you've ever been to?

3 Language in use

A ▶ 2.6 Barry and Crystal have just moved into a new place. Listen and choose the right photo. Which one do you like better?

> I grew up in a small apartment, so I don't actually know what a big house would be like.

B ▶ 2.6 Listen again. What can you infer about Barry and Crystal? Do they remind you of anyone you know?
1. ☐ They've always lived in relatively small spaces.
2. ☐ He's probably more open to change than she is.
3. ☐ They don't work anymore.
4. ☐ Most of Crystal's friends are about her age.

C ▶ 2.7 Listen to the rest. Order Crystal's arguments about small homes 1–3. There's one extra. Do you think she convinced him?
1. ☐ more affordable
2. ☐ emotionally freeing
3. ☐ cozier
4. ☐ easier to maintain

D ▶ 2.8 Read *Plural-only nouns*. Then complete excerpts 1–4. Listen to check.

> **Plural-only nouns**
>
> Some nouns are only used in the plural. They include articles of clothing and tools / instruments that have two sides or pieces:
> jeans, pants, pajamas, shorts, glasses, earphones, scissors
>
> Other plural nouns include:
> congratulations, likes and dislikes, possessions, savings, stairs, surroundings

1. CRYSTAL: The one we kept near the _____? I threw it out.
   BARRY: You what?! I loved that painting. You did, too.
2. BARRY: I have to admit I like the _____, especially these tree-lined streets.
   CRYSTAL: I knew you would!
3. BARRY: Well, I suppose we can downsize. Especially now that we're living off our pension and _____!
   CRYSTAL: It's a new phase of life.
4. BARRY: Some of our _____ won't fit in this apartment.
   CRYSTAL: I'm sure most of them will.

E Make it personal In groups, answer 1–4. Any big surprises?
1. What would be your top priority when choosing a new home?
   > price   size   surroundings   space for your possessions   noise   parking
2. How easy would it be for you to get used to living in a smaller space?
3. If you had one extra closet, what would you put in it?
4. Is the saying, "Less is more" always, sometimes, or never true? Why?

> Size is definitely number 1 for me. I've got tons of possessions!

> I'm not so sure. I'd put ... first.

What's the biggest house you've ever been to? 2.2

Lesson Aims: Sts listen to a couple who are downsizing and learn how to avoid repetition using auxiliaries and modals.

Skills	Language	Vocabulary	Grammar
Listening to a conversation between a couple who have just moved to a new house Role-play with a future roommate	Making suggestions, e.g. *Why don't you give them away? You could always ...*	Plural-only nouns, e.g. *jeans, pants, pajamas, glasses, scissors throw out, get rid of, give away*	Avoiding repetition (affirmative and negative statements) using auxiliary or modal verbs

Warm-up

Focus on the lesson title question. Ask: *How many bedrooms did it have? What are the advantages / disadvantages of living in a big house?* Have sts work in groups and think of as many as they can. If they need prompting, ask them to think about: housework, cost, upkeep, storage space. Class feedback.

» Song lyric: See Teacher's Book p.342 for notes about the song and an accompanying activity to do with the class.

3 Language in use

A ▶ 2.6 Focus on the photos. Ask: *What types of houses are these?* Elicit *single family, townhouse*.

Play the audio and ask sts to say which of the two houses Barry and Crystal have just moved into. Check answers. Ask: *Are Barry and Crystal's neighbors older or younger than them?*

Answer

2

» See Teacher's Book p.314 for Audio script 2.6.

B ▶ 2.6 Have sts read through the statements about Barry and Crystal. Re-play the audio. Sts choose which ones they think are true. Classcheck, and ask them to explain how they arrived at their answers, e.g. They know Barry and Crystal don't work anymore because they mention they are living off their pensions.

Answers

3 and 4

Optional activity

Weaker classes: If you think sts will have difficulty inferring, board the following extract:

Barry: ... it feels kind of claustrophobic, don't you think?
Crystal: Well, compared to our old place, yes.

Look at the first statement in **B**, and elicit which two parts of the extract give us the answer (*claustrophobic; compared to our old place*). Sts then continue with the exercise.

C ▶ 2.7 Tell sts they are going to listen to Crystal trying to convince Barry that a smaller place will be better for them. Have them read through the arguments and ask them which they think Crystal will mention. Play the audio for them to check. Classcheck. Elicit that Barry is not convinced by Crystal's arguments.

Answers

1 easier to maintain
2 more affordable
3 emotionally freeing
Barry is not convinced.

» See Teacher's Book p.314 for Audio script 2.7.

Tip

Before doing a listening exercise, exploit the information given as much as possible by going through each option and asking sts to predict the answers. Even if they can't at this stage, it will help focus them on what information to listen out for when they listen to the recording.

D ▶ 2.8 Go through **Plural-only nouns** with the class. Ask sts to translate the words into their own language. In pairs, have them think of other plural-only nouns they know, e.g. *clothes, refreshments, sunglasses, underpants, binoculars*. Tell sts or elicit that we do not usually use numbers in front of these nouns. You can, however, use some determiners, such as *some* or *many*, e.g. *He gave them some refreshments*. With the nouns which have two sides or pieces, we use *a pair of*, e.g. *a pair of sunglasses / two pairs of pants*.

Sts complete excerpts 1–4, then listen to check. Classcheck.

Answers

1 stairs 2 surroundings 3 savings 4 possessions

E Make it personal Put sts in groups, and ask them to answer 1–4. For question 1, have them rank the factors in order of priority 1-5 (1 = most important) and see if they can think of any others. Monitor, help, and feed in any language they need. Invite a spokesperson from each group to report back their answers to the rest of the class. Class feedback. Do sts mostly agree / disagree?

2.2

4 Grammar: Avoiding repetition

A Focus on repetition. Elicit its root (*repeat*), the adjective *repetitive*, some synonyms (*boring, mechanical, monotonous, routine, tedious, uninteresting*) and what it makes them think of. (e.g. dull tasks like doing the dishes, traveling to work). Use this as a cue to move into the importance of avoiding repetition in speech.

Read the grammar box with the class. Check they understand the example sentences. Ask sts how they would say these sentences in their language. Sts check the correct rules. Classcheck.

Ask sts to identify the sentences in which the two parts refer to a different time period (*I haven't started looking for an apartment, but I think I might soon. I didn't rent an apartment, and I really should have. I'd love to have more space, but I may never be able to.*)

> **Answers**
> 1 an auxiliary or modal verb   2 second   3 sometimes
> 4 can't

Refer sts back to **3D** on page 18. Have them work on their own and underline the parts of the excerpts that avoid repetition. Classcheck.

> **Answers**
> You did too. (Missing words – *loved that painting*)
> I knew you would (Missing words – *like the tree-lined streets*)
> I'm sure most of them will. (Missing words – *fit in this apartment*)

» Refer sts to the **Grammar expansion** on p.140.

Focus on the **Common mistake**. Point out that we use *does* in this case because *I have an MBA* is in the simple present. To clarify, board the following sentence for sts to compare: *I've done an MBA, and my sister has too.*

B ▶ 2.9   Ask sts: *Do you still listen to CDs? Do you use Spotify?* Focus on the photo of Holly. Ask sts what she is doing (looking through CDs). Have sts read through the dialog quickly ignoring the blanks. Check they understand the meaning of *to be able to bring yourself to* (to force, make, or persuade oneself to do something). Elicit other example sentences using the phrase, e.g. *He couldn't bring himself to speak to her. He was so annoyed.*

Ask sts to read through the first part crossing out the unnecessary words as in example 1. Then they complete blanks 5–8 with the correct auxiliary or a modal verb. Peercheck. Classcheck by playing the audio. Ask sts if they think Tom will get rid of any of his CDs.

You could put sts in pairs and have them read the dialog for pronunciation practice. When they speak, to help them pronounce well, encourage them not just to read it aloud but to really deliver it, looking up, making eye contact, and speaking from memory, feeling the words and their meaning.

> **Answers**
> 2 ~~listen to them~~   3 ~~on Spotify~~   4 ~~give them away~~
> 5 do   6 did   7 isn't   8 could

Optional activity

For further practice, arrange the sts in groups of three or four. Board the following auxiliaries, spaced out:

do, does, have, has, doesn't, haven't, is, aren't

Give each group a team name and write them down the side of the board. In turn, read out one of the following sentence starters:

1 *I have a pet dog, but my cousin ...* (doesn't)
2 *I'm not very good at languages, but my brother ...* (is)
3 *I've never lived on my own, but my girlfriend ...* (has)
4 *We don't have a test this week, but the students in the other class ...* (do)
5 *I've never bought a house, but most of my friends ...* (have)
6 *I'm really happy here, but it seems you ...* (aren't)

Every time you read out a sentence starter, one st from each group comes to the board and touches the correct auxiliary. The first st to do so correctly wins a point for their team. The team with the most points at the end wins.

C Make it personal   Go through the instructions and check sts understand what they have to do. Brainstorm useful phrases they can use in their role-plays and board them, e.g. *Why don't you give away ...? You could always ... I can't bring myself to ... It brings / They bring back memories.*

Weaker classes: Have sts note down some key prompt words to help them remember each of their lines, so they can act it out without just reading aloud.

In pairs, sts practice their role plays. Ask one or two volunteers to act them out for the class. Class feedback. Ask: *How did you perform in the role-play?* Ask sts to give themselves a score between 1–5 for fluency.

Optional activity

When they have practiced their role-plays, you could ask sts to film themselves, then watch them after.

» Workbook p.9.

♪ Home where my thought's escaping. Home where my music's playing. Home where my love lies waiting, silently for me

2.2

4 Grammar: Avoiding repetition

A Read the grammar box and check (✔) the correct rules (1–4). Then underline the parts of the sentences in 3D that avoid repetition. What words are missing?

Avoiding repetition: affirmative and negative statements	
I'm worried about finding a place to live,	but my friends **aren't**.
I've never lived in a house,	but my boyfriend **has**.
I haven't started looking for an apartment,	but I think I **might** soon.
I didn't rent an apartment of my own,	and I really **should have**.
I'd love to have more space,	but I may never be able **to**.
I love this neighborhood,	and my sister **does, too**.
I've never lived on my own,	and my girlfriend **hasn't, either**.

1 To avoid repetition, use ☐ a main verb ☐ an auxiliary or modal verb.
2 The missing words are in the ☐ first ☐ second part of the sentence.
3 The verbs in both parts ☐ always ☐ sometimes refer to the same time period.
4 You ☐ can ☐ can't use a contracted form when the final verb is affirmative.

» Grammar expansion p.140

B ▶ 2.9 Cross out the unnecessary words in 1–4 and complete 5–8 with an auxiliary or modal verb. Listen to check.

Common mistake
I have an MBA, and my sister ~~has~~ *does*, too.

HOLLY: I didn't know you had so many CDs!
TOM: Yeah. Some are mine, and some I inherited from my brother when he went off to college.
HOLLY: Do you still listen to them?
TOM: ¹**No, I haven't** ~~listened to them~~ **in years**, ²**but I might listen to them one day**. Who knows?
HOLLY: Why would you? I mean, you're on Spotify, right?
TOM: ³**I am on Spotify**.
HOLLY: So, why don't you give them away?
TOM: ⁴**I can't bring myself to give them away**.
HOLLY: Why not? Do they bring back memories or something?
TOM: Some of them ⁵_____, yeah. This one was a gift from my grandmother.
HOLLY: One Direction? Do you actually like them?
TOM: I ⁶_____ when I was younger. But, you see, it's not about the music.
HOLLY: It ⁷_____?
TOM: No. It's the memory that counts! I mean, look at Grandma's note on this one.
HOLLY: Well, you could always pick the ones that mean something special and get rid of the rest.
TOM: Yeah, I guess I ⁸_____ if my brother was OK with that, too.

C Make it personal Your prized possessions! Role-play a conversation with a future roommate.

1 You're about to rent a very small apartment. Make a list of things you can't do without.

> books   music   art / photos   clothes / shoes   appliances / devices of my own   sentimental objects

2 Decide on at least two things you will each throw out to save space. Which one was most difficult?

> I have no idea where to start.

3 Role-play the conversation again with a new partner. Be sure to avoid repetition where possible.

> Of course you do! What big appliances do you have?

19

2.3 Do you like to spend time alone?

5 Reading

A ▶ 2.10 Read and listen to the article. Circle the correct answer.
Its main aim is to [**describe** / **question** / **argue against**] a trend.

Going it alone: more popular than ever

Travelers to the United States are sometimes struck by a phenomenon they don't see frequently at home – or, at least, one they don't think they see – the sheer number of people dining alone in restaurants. They are wrong to think this trend is limited to the U.S. In fact, it's spreading and becoming harder to miss – wherever one goes. A "single" in Amsterdam can even enjoy dining at Eenmaal, a restaurant featuring tables for one. What's more, solo dining has become common in upscale locations, as well. Long gone are the days when a diner stating "one, please" might have been ushered out of the way and into an empty room. These days, solo dining is good for business. In fact, Open Table reports that between 2013 and 2015 alone, the number of single reservations rose by 62 percent. It looks as if the solo diner is becoming more and more ubiquitous.

Another increasingly familiar presence is the solo traveler. Tour companies have gone out of their way to convey a clear message that single customers are welcome, and the success rate for their efforts is high. Among those 45 and older, according to the American Association for Retired People (AARP), more than 80 percent of those who have taken a solo trip plan to do it again.

What could possibly account for these trends? For one thing, it turns out that the number of people living alone has grown exponentially. To cite just a few examples, more than half of all homes in New York City are occupied by just one person; in London, a third; in Paris, more than half; and in Stockholm, 60 percent. As of 2012, one in five U.S. adults over the age of 25 had never been married, as opposed to one in ten in 1960. No longer a last resort, living alone has become a coveted choice for many who savor their solitude. While some singles may be avid chefs, many would rather "people gaze" than cook for just one person. As solo living has become more prevalent, solo dining has spread. And for those with a bit more disposable income, it's a short hop, skip, and jump to solo travel.

Companies planning solo tours don't only cater to those who are single, however. Increasingly, solo travelers may be half of a couple whose vacation schedules clash, or anyone who wants a taste of independence and craves new experiences. A solo vacation is, in many cases, a ticket to a week of freedom.

Where has this desire for freedom come from? Some say it may have arisen in childhood. As more children have their own rooms and spend time alone after school, they have become increasingly comfortable with a solo existence. Today, colleges are inundated with requests for single rooms. At Montclair State College in New Jersey, for example, a full 1,500 dorm rooms out of 5,000 are single rooms. Of course, it can be argued that with social media always available, students are never very far away from those they are closest to. Dining, traveling, or living on our own, it is easy enough to "reach out and touch someone," just as the phone company commercials once suggested.

B Sentences 1–4 are true, according to the writer. Find the evidence in the article. Do any surprise you?

1 Solo diners have become not only commonplace, but an identifiable market.
2 Children who grow up alone have less of a need for company.
3 Living alone can be a positive lifestyle choice.
4 Solo travelers are not necessarily single.

Do you like to spend time alone? 2.3

Lesson Aims: Sts learn language to talk about lifestyle changes, and read about the growing trend of "going it alone."

Skills	Language	Vocabulary
Reading an article about dining / traveling and living alone	Talking about trends: *This trend is spreading. Increasingly. The number of people living alone has grown.*	Metaphors, e.g. *a taste of independence, a ticket to freedom* Common verb/adjective + noun collocations with *convey, crave, ubiquitous, cater to,* and *upscale*

Warm-up

Focus on the lesson title question. Ask: *Do you like to spend time alone? How much time? When? How often are you completely alone, offline and isolated from the rest of the world? Do you feel lonely when you're alone? Have you ever eaten in a restaurant alone / been on vacation alone? How did you feel?* Ask sts to tell their partner. Classcheck to share their best answers.

5 Reading

A ▶ 2.10 Refer sts to the photo. Ask them what they can say about it. Focus on the title of the article and ask sts to guess what might be mentioned in it. Have them read the article quickly for gist to check whether they guessed correctly, and then circle the main aim.

Then play the audio for sts to listen and re-read it, this time asking them to remember both the pronunciation of the pinked words and the evidence for their answer. Classcheck.

Answer
describe

Weaker classes: To help sts get a more detailed understanding of the text, ask them to do this comprehension activity:

Sts read the text and choose the most appropriate option, according to the text.
1 Eating alone has become very common *in the United States / all over the world.*
2 Most people over 45 who travel alone say they *never want to do it again / would do it again.*
3 Less than 50% of people live alone in *New York / London.*
4 Solo travelers *have to / don't have to* be single.
5 *More people / Fewer people* are requesting single rooms at colleges.

Tip
The reading texts are all recorded and available for sts to listen to. Sometimes it's better to allow sts to read alone first at their own pace, especially when reading for gist, then listen and read a second time so they can focus on pronunciation.

B Read through the statements with the class, and check understanding. Sts find the evidence in the article and underline it. Classcheck.

As follow-up, ask: *Are you surprised by any of the statements? Do you feel comfortable dining alone / traveling alone? How do you feel about living alone? What are the advantages / disadvantages? How do you think the advent of social media has made it easier to do things alone?*

Answers
1 A "single" in Amsterdam can even enjoy dining at Eenmaal restaurant featuring tables for one.
2 As more children have their own rooms and spend time alone after school, they have become increasingly comfortable with a solo existence.
3 Living alone has become a coveted choice for many who savor their solitude.
4 Solo travelers may be half of a couple.

Optional activity

Stronger classes: Ask sts to go through the article and make a note of all the expressions used to describe a trend, e.g. *this trend is spreading, ... has become more common, the number ... rose by 62%, Another increasingly, ... More than 80%, The number of ... has grown exponentially, ... has become a coveted choice, ... has become more prevalent, Increasingly ..., ... have become increasingly ...*

Ask sts to write about a trend they have become aware of, using these phrases. This can be related to lifestyle (e.g. more people working from home, more people retiring early) or they can choose a different type of trend if they prefer, (e.g. the increasing use of technology in the classroom, fewer people speaking on the phone). They can research some ideas on the Internet.

Tip
Remember to focus your Reading activities on the skill of Reading, not just new vocabulary and grammar. At the end of any of longer text, try to elicit their overall reaction to it, e.g. how they felt reading it, if they were happy with the speed they read it at and how they might read faster, how much easier it got the second time, what they learned from the text, if it's the kind of thing they'd enjoy reading in their own language.

▶▶ Song lyric: See Teacher's Book p.343 for notes about the song and an accompanying activity to do with the class.

2.3

C Read **Understanding metaphor** and the example in the speech bubble with the class. Put sts in pairs to try to figure out the meanings of the metaphors. They can use a dictionary if necessary to help them. Classcheck. Ask sts if there are similar metaphors that can be used in these contexts in their own language.

For homework, ask sts to look through English texts they might have at home or find some on the Internet and find five more examples of metaphors. Tell them to bring them to the next lesson. Have a few sts explain their metaphors to the class.

> **Answers**
>
> *savor their solitude* – the verb *savor* is usually referred to food meaning to enjoy the taste of something. Here, it means to relish or enjoy.
> *wants a taste of independence* – the noun *taste* usually refers to food and the sensation of flavors that it produces; the metaphoric meaning in this context is a brief experience of something.
> *a ticket to a week of freedom* – in this case a solo vacation is referred to as a "ticket," because it gains a person access to something (i.e. a week of freedom) in the same way that a ticket does (e.g. bus ticket or movie ticket).
> *colleges are inundated with requests* – *inundated* normally means flooded. Here, it means to be overwhelmed (by requests) as in a flood

Optional activity

Ask sts to choose one of the metaphors and draw a simple picture to illustrate it, e.g. a building being flooded with emails with questions on them (*be inundated with requests*). They then show their picture to other sts to guess the metaphors. If sts are happy to do so, you could display the best ones around the class.

D Make it personal Go through the list of experiences with the class and ask: *Have you experienced any of these?* Ask sts to note down the advantages and disadvantages of each one. If you have a younger class, you could add *playing an individual sport, home schooling* to make the task more relevant.

Highlight the example in speech bubbles and encourage them to use this phrase. In groups, sts discuss the pros and cons of each of the experiences. Class feedback. Ask: *Did you all agree / disagree?*

6 Vocabulary: Common verb / adjective + noun collocations

A ▶ 2.11 Sts complete the chart. Play the audio for them to check. Classcheck. Ask: *Do you enjoy having things explained by a "cyber teacher"? Do you think language teaching in the future will be even more like this?*

Stronger classes: Ask sts to write their own personalized sentences containing each of the new words in column 1.

> **Answers**
>
> 1 convey   2 crave   3 ubiquitous   4 cater to   5 upscale

» See Teacher's Book p.314 for Audio script 2.11.

B Focus on the photo and ask: *Have you ever been to a city like this/São Paulo?* (the third biggest after Tokyo and Mexico).

Have sts read the text quickly, ignoring the blanks. Sts complete 1–4 with the collocations from **A** after doing the first one together as an example. Peercheck. Classcheck.

Ask sts to change two of the sentences so they are true for them. Alternatively, ask them to write two true sentences and two false sentences. They read their sentences to their partner who has to guess which are the true sentences.

> **Answers**
>
> 1 craved, excitement
> 2 conveys, sense, ubiquitous presence
> 3 upscale restaurants
> 4 caters to, interests

C Make it personal Brainstorm a few ideas with the class before they start, e.g. reasons for ditching social media – 1) you wouldn't get unwanted interruptions, 2) you'd have more time to do other things, 3) you'd spend more time with your friends really talking instead of messaging, 4) you'd probably do more exercise.

Sts choose one of the lifestyle changes and create their posters, using pictures if they like, as on the vision board on p.16. Tell sts to write at the top of their posters: *Four reasons why you should ...* Encourage them to use collocations from **A** if appropriate. When they have finished, invite sts to present their posters, e.g. *Four reasons why you should work from home. First, you'd get more work done, Secondly you wouldn't waste time traveling, Third, you wouldn't have unwanted interruptions, and Finally, you wouldn't have to put up with annoying colleagues!!*

Have sts discuss in pairs which is the most convincing poster. Refer them to the models in the speech bubbles. Class feedback. *Which lifestyle change would you most like to make?*

» Workbook p.10.

♪ What doesn't kill you makes you stronger. Stand a little taller. Doesn't mean I'm lonely when I'm alone

2.3

C Read *Understanding metaphor*. Then identify the metaphors in the underlined phrases in the article. In pairs, explain their meaning in that context.

> **Understanding metaphor**
>
> Authentic texts often include metaphors, where non-literal meanings are used to add power and imagery. For example: A diner might have been **ushered** into an empty room.

> Doesn't *usher*, as a verb, usually mean "to show someone to a seat," like in a theater? So here the meaning is extended to a restaurant.

D Make it personal In groups, what are the pros and cons of these experiences? Any disagreements?

having your own room as a child   having a roommate in college
living alone as an adult   living separately from your partner / spouse

> I can't see any advantages to couples living separately. He or she might meet someone else!

6 Vocabulary: Common verb / adjective + noun collocations

A ▶ 2.11 Complete the chart with the highlighted words in the article. Listen to check.

	Word	Meaning	Examples of common collocations
1	_____	make known, communicate	an idea, a sense of (freedom), an impression
2	_____	long for, want greatly	excitement, attention, peace and quiet
3	_____	widespread	influence, presence, fashion
4	_____	supply what a specific audience desires or requires	a (young) audience, (students') needs, (different) interests / tastes
5	_____	appealing to those with money	neighborhood, restaurant, market

B Complete 1–4 with collocations from **A**, changing the forms of the words as needed. Which sentences might be true for you?

> **City vs. country life: Four reasons why I went back to São Paulo!**
>
> 1. I'm not cut out for country life. When I lived in Itu, I missed São Paulo and _____ the _____ of a big city.
> 2. *Avenida Paulista*. It _____ a unique _____ of energy and freedom that's hard to put into words. Not to mention the _____ _____ of street musicians on every other corner!
> 3. How I missed the food! Not the _____ _____, but the small, affordable ones, which are just as good – and sometimes even better.
> 4. Oh, and the nightlife! It _____ everyone's tastes and _____, tourists and locals alike.

C Make it personal In groups, create a poster with four reasons for making one of the lifestyle changes below. Use collocations from **A**. Whose is the most convincing?

ditch social media   do yoga   never get married   save money instead of taking vacations   work from home

> I crave peace and quiet, so it would be great to work from home.

> OK, so number 1: If you crave peace and quiet, you'll never have unwanted interruptions.

21

2.4 Are you more of a morning or an evening person?

7 Language in use

A ▶ 2.12 Listen to the start of a conversation with a sleep expert. What's it about?

☐ insomnia ☐ sleep patterns ☐ morning routines

B ▶ 2.13 In pairs, are 1–3 good ways to start your morning? Listen to the rest to check. Were you right?

1 drinking coffee as soon as you get up
2 making your bed first thing, before taking a shower
3 checking email on your phone right after you wake up

> I see nothing wrong with drinking coffee. Do you?

C ▶ 2.13 Listen again. True (T) or false (F)? Correct the false statements.

1 It's not very important how you start your morning.
2 Postpone coffee because cortisol provides natural energy.
3 Your first task should be something achievable.
4 It's sometimes OK to skip breakfast.
5 A good time to answer email is when you first get up because you're alert.

D Complete what the participants said with the correct form of a word or expression from the box. Which person is most like you?

| boost (n) | drag (v) | drowsy | hectic | not sleep a wink |

I was such a night owl that I wrote most of my assignments between 1:00 and 4:00 a.m. Sometimes, I ¹_____ before exams! I looked like a zombie, but it was so much easier to study at night!

I looked for studies on sleep habits, but there were so few that it was hard to figure out how morning habits could ruin your day – you know, when time ²_____ and you can't think straight.

If you drink coffee as soon as you wake up, you end up with so much energy that you run out of stamina faster. But if you drink it later in the day, you get an extra energy ³_____. It's such useful advice.

You see, my mornings are so ⁴_____ I have to skip breakfast sometimes. There's just no time. In fact, there's so little I have to run for the bus.

All too often I have so little time and so many urgent messages, it's hard to put them on hold, even though I know it's not a good idea to handle email when I'm still ⁵_____.

E Make it personal In pairs, what's your typical morning routine? Does it affect the rest of your day?

> In my case, I usually sleep the morning away because I'm a night owl.

> But aren't you drowsy if you have to be somewhere early?

22

Are you more of a morning or an evening person? 2.4

Lesson Aims: Sts learn vocabulary to talk about productivity and listen to some young people talking about their morning routines.

Skills	Language	Vocabulary	Grammar
Listening to some young people taking part in research in a sleep clinic	Reacting to opinions, e.g. *That is so true! It's a no-brainer! There's so little truth in that.*	boost, drag, drowsy, hectic, not sleep a wink, yawn	*so, so much, so little, so many, so few, such* and *such a (an)*

Warm-up

Focus on the lesson title question. Encourage sts to answer with *I'm more of (a morning/ evening person)* and teach "a night owl." Board the following survey questions: *When are you most productive? Do you prefer to do difficult tasks in the morning, evening, or at night? Do you like getting up early? Do you enjoying staying out late?* Have sts ask and answer in pairs, and decide if their partner really is a morning or evening person.

Ask sts: *What time do you go to bed / get up? How many hours sleep do you usually get? Are you tired when you wake up in the morning? Have you ever suffered from insomnia?*

7 Language in use

Weaker classes: Check understanding of the expressions in **A** by reading out the following descriptions and eliciting which each one refers to:
1 First I get up, usually at 6:15. After that I take a shower and brush my teeth. (morning routines)
2 I often find myself awake at 2 am, even though I'm really tired. (insomnia)
3 I know I dream every night, but I never remember my dreams. (sleep patterns)

A ▶ 2.12 Explain that sts are going to listen to a conversation taking place between a sleep expert and some 20 year olds who are participating in some research. Play the audio. Classcheck.

Answer

sleep patterns

» See Teacher's Book p.314 for Audio script 2.12.

B ▶ 2.13 Focus on the statements and elicit sts' opinions. Then play the audio for them to check their ideas.

Answers

1 no   2 yes   3 no

» See Teacher's Book p. 314 for Audio script 2.13.

C ▶ 2.13 Have sts read the statements, and try to answer T or F from memory. Re-play the audio for them to check. Classcheck. Ask sts how many of them start the day by checking their cell phones.

Answers

1 F   2 T   3 T   4 F   5 F

D Go through the words in the box with the class, and check pronunciation, especially *drowsy* /draʊzi/. Focus on the photos and ask sts to cover the texts below them. Ask them what they can remember from the audio using the photos to prompt them, e.g. photo 1: *One of the participants said he wrote his assignments really late at night*. Sts uncover the texts and do the completion task, then listen and check. Classcheck. Ask: *Which of the participants do you have the most in common with?*

Answers

1 didn't sleep a wink   2 drags   3 boost   4 hectic
5 drowsy

E Make it personal Focus on the questions. Ask: *What's your typical morning routine? Does it affect the rest of your day?* Tell them your own routine first, going into as much detail as you can, the exact order you tend to do things in, and inviting questions to illustrate just how much they can say. Elicit a few answers from volunteers. You could also ask: *Does your morning routine vary much on weekends?* Put sts in pairs to discuss the questions. Class feedback. Have sts report back to the class what they learned about their partner's morning routine.

Optional activities

- Board the following questions for sts to discuss: *When your alarm goes off, do you get up immediately or hit snooze? How many cups of coffee do you drink in the morning? What do you do while you're eating breakfast? How soon after waking up do you go online? What's the first website you look at every day?*

- Have sts carry out a class survey. In pairs, sts first think of and write five questions about morning routines. Then they walk around the class asking other sts their questions.

2.4

> Song lyric: See Teacher's Book p.343 for notes about the song and an accompanying activity to do with the class.

8 Grammar: Using *so* and *such*

A First, cover the grammar box and put sts in pairs to brainstorm all the rules they know for *so* and *such*, and produce their own examples, e.g. from song lines. Elicit answers, then use the box to check. Go through the examples and rules in the grammar box. Check sts know that we also use *such* before countable plural nouns, e.g. *We have such difficult exams.* Ask sts to check the correct rules, and then find examples of the rules in 7D. Peercheck. Classcheck.

Stronger classes: Elicit sts' own examples, e.g. *It's so noisy living near an airport. It's such important news.*

Refer sts to **Common mistakes**. Ask: *Which of these mistakes have you made?*

> **Answers**
> 1 Use *such* before non-count nouns
> 2 Use *so many / so few* with count nouns, and *so much / so little* with non-count nouns
> 3 Use *so much* before a comparative
> 4 You can delete the noun after *so much, many*, etc. when it is in the sentence or understood
> Examples from 7D: *such a night owl, so much easier, so few (studies), so much energy, such useful advice, so little (time), so many urgent messages*

> Refer sts to the **Grammar expansion** on p.140.

Tip

In expressions with *so* and *such*, these words are usually stressed to provide emphasis. Drill the expressions in the chart with the class, making sure they stress them naturally.

B Before sts read the text, focus on the title and have the class brainstorm possible suggestions for inclusions. Ask sts to read the text quickly for gist, ignoring the blanks, then in pairs remember all that they can. Ask: *Are you very productive at work / in your studies? Do you waste a lot of time?* Have them complete sentences 1–3 and join underlined sentences in 4–5, following the instructions in the Student's Book. Peercheck. Classcheck. Ask: *Which of these do you think are good / bad ideas? Do you think any of them would help you?*

> **Answers**
> 1 so little 2 so many 3 such a
> 4 There are so many distractions invading our lives that they're changing the way our brains work.
> 5 Long meetings are such a waste of time that some companies have switched to stand-up meetings.

C Make it personal

1 Go through the expressions, and have sts complete them. Explain the meaning of *no-brainer* (something such as a decision that is very easy or obvious).

Put sts in groups of three or four to discuss the ideas in B. Encourage them to use the expressions in the box. Teach or elicit others such as: *That's such an obvious thing to do. That would save so much time. That would be so difficult.*

> **Answers**
> 1 so 2 such 3 such 4 so little 5 such

Optional activity

After they've completed the expressions, ask sts in pairs to rank the tips in B, from 1=least effective to 8=most effective. When they have finished, combine the pairs into groups of four to compare answers.

2 Have sts discuss question 2: *When are you the most / least productive during the week / day?* Ask also: *What about other members of your family, e.g. your parents? Who is the most productive person in your family?* Class feedback. Ask: *Are there similarities or big differences within your group?*

3 In their groups, have sts suggest to each other how they could be more productive. Have them report back to the rest of the class, e.g. *I think X should get up earlier and do more work in the morning. If he tried going to bed earlier, it would be easier.*

> Workbook p.11.

🎵 *So many tears I've cried. So much pain inside. But baby it ain't over 'til it's over*

2.4

8 Grammar: Using *so* and *such*

A Read the grammar box and check (✔) the correct rules (1–4). Then find examples of the rules in 7D.

so, so much, so little, so many, so few, such and *such a(n)*		
It's	**so** comfortable	sleeping in this bed.
It's	**such** useful information	(that) I always remember it.
It makes	**such a** big difference	to wake up early.
It's	**so much** better	than staying up late.
I have	**so many** things to do	I don't know where to start.
There are	**so few** ways	to get a good energy boost.
They're charging	**so much** (money)	I can't even consider it.
As for free time, I have	**so little** (time)	I can barely have lunch.

1. Use ☐ **such** ☐ **such a** before non-count nouns.
2. Use **so many / so few** with ☐ **count** ☐ **non-count** nouns, and **so much / so little** with ☐ **count** ☐ **non-count** nouns.
3. Use ☐ **so** ☐ **so much** before a comparative.
4. You can delete the noun after *so much, many,* etc.
   ☐ When it is in the sentence or understood
   ☐ only when it is in the sentence.

» Grammar expansion p.140

Common mistakes

This article has such ~~a~~ useful **information** / **advice**.

I have such ~~a~~ strange **dreams** that I'm always scared.

B Complete 1–3 using the blue words in the grammar box. Then join the underlined sentences in 4–5 using the bold words and *that*.

FIVE WAYS TO BECOME MORE PRODUCTIVE!

1. Drink more water. If you're dehydrated, you'll have _____ energy you'll barely make it through the day.
2. Use your commuting time to do something productive. There are _____ good audio books on Amazon and iTunes! You can even learn a new language while you're stuck in traffic.
3. Make yourself unavailable for a few hours, and turn off your devices, so you can work in _____ way that there are as few interruptions as possible.
4. Stop multi-tasking. Research shows <u>there are a lot of distractions invading our lives. They're changing the way our brains work.</u>
5. Have fewer and shorter meetings. <u>Long meetings waste a lot of time. Some companies have switched to stand-up meetings.</u>

C Make it personal In groups, share opinions on productivity.

1 What's your immediate reaction to the tips in **B**? Why? Use some of these expressions with words from **A**.

Number ___ is [1]_____ true!	Number ___ is [2]_____ nonsense!
Number ___ is [3]_____ a misconception!	There's [4]_____ truth to number ___ .
Number ___ is [5]_____ a no-brainer!	

> Number 4 is such nonsense! Multi-tasking is a great way to get more done.

> Yes, but if you tried doing one task at a time, you might find …

2 When are you most / least productive during the week / day?
3 Are you as productive as you could be? If not, what would you need to change in your lifestyle?

23

2.5 Can an apartment be too small?

9 Listening

A ▶ 2.14 In pairs, brainstorm some ways your city (or one you know) has changed in recent years. Then listen to / watch (to 1:12) Shawn Groff talking about his micro apartment. Answer the questions.

1 Where does Shawn live?
2 Why has he chosen to live in a micro apartment?

> Here in ... there are a lot more people than there used to be!

B ▶ 2.14 Listen to / watch the second part (1:12 to 3:22). Number the reasons for micro apartments in the order mentioned. There's one extra.

a ☐ Life expectancy has increased.
b ☐ Cities are growing in size.
c ☐ More people are living alone.
d ☐ People spend less time at home than they used to.
e ☐ There is an inadequate amount of housing.
f ☐ People are marrying later and divorcing more often.

C ▶ 2.14 Complete 1–6 with words from the box. Listen to / watch the third part (3:22 to the end) to check.

| addressing | backlash | geared | higher | priced out | target | voiced |

1 Recent college graduates ... might otherwise be _____ of the city.
2 There has been _____. In Seattle, community groups have _____ concerns.
3 [The apartments] are really _____ toward young, high-income people.
4 [The apartments] aren't _____ the needs of lower-middle income workers.
5 A lot of these pilots that are happening in cities are definitely on the _____ end.
6 And you can _____ different populations [with micro apartments].

D ▶ 2.14 Listen to / watch again (3:22 to end). In pairs, summarize two key criticisms of micro apartments. What answers to the criticisms are given? Use expressions from C.

> I think a reason there's been backlash is that ...

10 Keep talking

A Watch to 1.12 again with the sound off. Note down the features of the apartments that appeal to you most.

B In groups, discuss which statements in 9B are true where you live. Would micro apartments be a good solution? Which features from A might be most appealing?

> There's definitely overcrowding here, but on the other hand, I think there would be backlash if we ...

C Search on "innovative solutions to city problems." Share one in groups. Be sure to present the pros and cons of each solution.

> I read that in Japan, they're addressing overcrowding in Tokyo by moving jobs elsewhere.

> Yes, but what about leaving your friends and family? I think it's better to ...

24

Can an apartment be too small? 2.5

Lesson Aims: Sts learn about solutions to housing problems and write an email comparing and contrasting.

Skills	Language	Vocabulary
Writing a compare-and-contrast email Discussing how cities are changing and any associated problems	Comparing and contrasting, e.g. *but on the other hand, each has its pros and cons, the main difference between them is …*	address, backlash, gear (stg.) toward, price out, target, voice (v)

Warm-up

Board the lesson title question, plus others: *What's the smallest place you've lived in? What are the problems / advantages of living in a small space?* In pairs, then as a class, elicit their answers.

9 Listening

A ▶ 2.14 Put sts in pairs to discuss changes in their city. Refer them to the example in the speech bubble, and highlight the use of *used to*.

Weaker classes: Help sts by boarding the following questions: *Is the city busier? Is it difficult to find somewhere to live? Has there been an increase in new houses / apartments? Do more people live alone?*

Focus on the photo. Ask sts to describe Shawn's apartment. Ask: *Do you like it?* Have sts read the questions and guess the answers before playing the video. Play the video, then check answers.

Tip

Play the video sound off first for them to guess what he might be saying.

Answers

1 Vancouver
2 He doesn't need much space because he doesn't own much and he isn't at home much.

» See Teacher's Book p.315 for Video script 2.14.

B ▶ 2.14 Have sts read through the reasons and check understanding. Play just the second part of the video (1.12 to 3.22) and have sts number the reasons in the order they hear them. Check answers.

Answers

1 More people are living alone.
2 People are marrying later and divorcing more often.
3 Life expectancy has increased.
4 There is an inadequate amount of housing.
5 Cities are growing in size.

C ▶ 2.14 Check sts' understanding of the words in the box. Have them check meanings in a dictionary if necessary. Ask them to try and complete sentences 1–6. Then play the third part of the video for them to check.

Answers

1 priced out   2 backlash, voiced   3 geared
4 addressing   5 higher   6 target

Optional activity

Ask sts to close their books. Board one of the words you think they won't know, and have them race to use their mobile devices to find its meaning. Repeat for the other words. Sts then do the activity.

D ▶ 2.14 Play the last part of the video, and ask sts to listen for the two main criticisms of micro apartments. Check answers. Ask: *Would you like to live in one of these apartments? Why / why not?*

Answers

Community groups have voiced concerns that these units crowd too many people together and that they make neighborhoods less stable as young people come and go. Critics worry that micro-apartments will replace housing for the poor.
Answers to the criticisms: you can target different populations, micro-apartments make sense for the way many people live

10 Keep talking

A ▶ 2.14 Sts work individually to note down the features they liked. In feedback, elicit adjectives they can use to describe the apartment, e.g. *multi-functional, compact, practical, easy to clean*. You could ask sts what they don't like about the apartments, e.g. *cramped, lack of storage space, unsociable*.

B Put sts in groups of three or four. Tell them they are going to discuss the questions together. If they need to, they can research some of the information on the Internet, e.g. what the life expectancy is in their area, how many people are living alone, if there is a housing shortage.

Class feedback. Invite a volunteer from each group to report back their views to the rest of the class.

C You could set this research for homework, then have sts discuss their findings in the next lesson. Ask groups to agree on the best solution, and present it to the rest of the class. Have a class vote on the best solution.

2.5

> Song lyric: See Teacher's Book p.343 for notes about the song and an accompanying activity to do with the class.

11 Writing: A compare-and-contrast email

A Focus on the title. Ask the class to give an example of what a compare-and-contrast email might be about.

Have sts read the email quickly. Ask: *What's Marta trying to decide? Which apartment do you think she should choose? Why? Do you think she knows Ann well?* Highlight the binomial *pros and cons*. Remind sts that the words in this type of expression are always in the same order, i.e. you can't say ~~cons and pros~~. Elicit other binomials they know, e.g. *ups and downs, now and then*.

Sts read the email again and write the numbers of the paragraphs. Peercheck. Classcheck.

> **Answers**
> a 4   b 1   c 3   d 2

Optional activity

Put sts in A/B pairs. Ask As to read the first two paragraphs of the email and Bs to read the last two paragraphs, and find which of the statements a–d corresponds to their paragraphs. Sts then summarize the paragraphs they read to their partner and check answers together before checking with the whole class.

B Read **Write it right!** with the class. Have sts find more words or expressions in the email as examples of the three categories. Classcheck.

Elicit other examples sts might know, e.g. Category 1 – *each one, both of them*; Category 2 – *furthermore, on top of that, besides, what is more, also*; Category 3 – *but on the positive / negative side, even though*.

> **Answers**
> 1 The two apartments are (more or less identical in price); Both apartments are (good deals)
> 2 moreover, finally, not to mention
> 3 although, however, but, the main difference between them

C Have sts find the examples of speculation with *may* and *might* in the email. Classcheck.

Ask sts to find other examples in the email where Marta is asking for Ann's opinion / reaction, e.g. *I wondered if you wouldn't mind giving me your opinion ...; So, what do you think? Where do you think I'd be the happiest?*

> **Answers**
> You may not want the responsibility of answering this question, but where do you think I'd be the happiest? You might say it's no contest, right?

Tip

Before going into the writing, remember to extract as much as you can from having read the email. Ask the class: *What do you know about Ana and Marta? Which of them do you think is older? Why? What do you think the result of the email might be? Have any of you had a decision to make like this? How did you decide what to do and did you make the right decision?*

D Your turn!

Read through the instructions and ask sts to think back to the solutions they researched or heard about in 10C. Tell them they are going to write an email comparing the pros and cons of two of the solutions. You could write the first paragraph together because this will be different from the email in 11A, e.g.

Dear Sam,

How are you? Have you been busy? I'm apartment hunting right now. It's so difficult to find somewhere to live here. I've been reading about housing problems in other places, and possible solutions. There were a couple of really interesting ones. I just wondered what you thought about it, since you live in a big city yourself.

The first solution, which apparently they have tested out in Japan, is ...

Weaker classes: Tell sts they are trying to decide whether to move into a large shared house with four other people, or live on their own in a small micro-apartment. Ask them to write a similar email to the one in A, asking a friend for advice. Tell them to include advantages / disadvantages of living alone vs. the advantages / disadvantages of having more or less space.

When sts have finished their emails, have them exchange them with a partner, and give each other feedback. For homework, you could ask them to write a reply to their partner's email.

Class feedback. Ask: *What types of mistakes were the most common? Did you manage to include some of the expressions from B?*

> Workbook p.12.

♪ There are places I remember all my life, though some have changed

2.5

11 Writing: A compare-and-contrast email

A Read Marta's email to her friend Ann. Write the numbers of the paragraphs.

In paragraph …
a ☐ , she compares the two apartments to others available.
b ☐ , Marta first establishes that she's asking for something.
c ☐ , she mainly compares good and bad points of one apartment, but mentions a similarity for both.
d ☐ , she only compares good and bad points of one apartment.

Ann Johnson (ann.johnson@allmail.com)
Help me decide!

1   Hey there Ann,
Hope everything has been going well. It's been a while, hasn't it? Some big news from my end: I'm just about to rent my first apartment, and I wondered if you wouldn't mind giving me your opinion. I mean, there's so much at stake! And you always have such good practical advice!

2   I've seen two apartments. Each has its pros and cons, so my mind isn't totally made up. The first one is right in the center of town, only a ten-minute walk from my job, and the price is reasonable, too. In addition, the neighbors I've met were all very friendly. However, while the neighborhood has many amenities, including lots of stores and even a movie theater, this apartment also has some key drawbacks. For one thing, it's small and dark. Even in the morning, I'd have to keep the lights on, which would inevitably raise my electricity bill. Moreover, it's a studio apartment with tiny closets. Although there's a separate kitchen, the stove has only two burners, and there's no oven. Finally – get this (!) – one of the neighbors said he had mice last year, even though he assured me the problem has been solved!

3   The second apartment, on the other hand, is modern, light, and spacious, with a stunning view of the park. It's in an upscale neighborhood. It's also a one bedroom with fairly large closets and, of course, a full kitchen. You might say it's no contest, right? If only it were that simple. The two apartments are more or less identical in price, but the commute from the second one is horrendous. I'd have to switch trains every morning, not to mention take a bus just to get to the train. I estimate my commute would take a good hour and a half. Even so, in spite of these disadvantages, I'm thinking about it seriously. Yet it worries me that I may find I don't have much of a social life as there's very little to do in the neighborhood.

4   So what do you think? Both apartments are good deals compared to others that are available, so I'm really torn. The main difference between them would be one of lifestyle. You know me really well. You may not want the responsibility of answering this question, but where do you think I'd be happiest?

Looking forward to hearing from you. I have to leave a downpayment tomorrow!

Love,
Marta

B Read *Write it right!* Then match the underlined words or expressions in the email to 1, 2, or 3.

Write it right!

Words and expressions used to compare and contrast fall into three categories:
1 Considering two things together: *Each has its pros and cons.*
2 Adding additional supporting points: *In addition*, the neighbors I've met were all very friendly.
3 Offering a contrast: The second apartment, *on the other hand*, is modern, light, and spacious.

C The modal verbs *may* and *might* can be used to speculate about the reader's reaction. Find two examples in the email.

D Your turn! Write a four-paragraph compare-and-contrast email (250 words) on one of the topics discussed in 10C.

Before
Note down the pros and cons of both options, and decide which you will cover together in the same paragraph.

While
Write four paragraphs following the model in A, making sure to include a summary paragraph. Use expressions to compare and contrast, and at least one example of *may* or *might* to speculate.

After
Post your email online and read your classmates' work. Whose presents a contrast more clearly?

25

Review 1
Units 1-2

1 Speaking

A Look at the vision board on p.16.

1 In pairs, share everything you can remember about it, using these expressions.

> fall into your lap   far-fetched   go the extra mile   meet your goals   put your mind to something
> meet someone else's expectations   work toward   unattainable

2 In groups, share highlights of what you learned from your own vision boards.

> I learned I really didn't want to have to meet someone else's expectations.

3 Summarize your discussion for the class, using some of these expressions.

> a lot of us   some of us   a few of us   only one of us   no one in our group   some of us

> No one in our group has unattainable goals. ...

B **Make it personal** Choose three question titles from Units 1 and 2 to ask a partner. Ask at least three follow-up questions for each. What did you learn about each other?

> What are your earliest memories of school?

> I have a vague recollection of not wanting to play with anyone.

C 🌐 Search on "first day of school" and, in groups, make a list of the best advice.

If you want to pull off having a totally new image, don't wear last year's clothes.

2 Listening

A ▶R1.1 Listen to the beginning of a lecture on fashion and lifestyle. Choose the correct answer.
The main purpose of the teacher's lecture is to …
a describe new fashion trends in China.
b illustrate the meaning of "lifestyle."
c compare East and West.

B ▶R1.2 Listen to the whole lecture and take notes on 1–2.
1 Why is fashion important?
2 In what other areas of life might fashion trends in China lead to a more open lifestyle?

C **Make it personal** With a partner, share your answers to B. What does the way you dress say about your own personal lifestyle?

> Fashion is important because it ...

> I've never thought about that before, but it's true. For example, the fact that I wear ... shows that ...

26

Review 1 (Units 1–2) R1

Warm-up

In pairs, sts ask and answer the lesson title questions from Units 1 and 2 in random order, plus follow-up questions.

Board the incorrect sentences from the **Common mistakes** boxes for sts to correct.

Ask sts to find five phrasal verbs from Units 1 and 2, and write their own personalized sentences using them. Have sts copy the sentences out, blanking the phrasal verbs, then exchange the blanked sentences with a classmate to complete.

1 Speaking

A Ask: *What is the purpose of a vision board? Do you remember?* (It focuses you on your goals.)

1 Focus on the expressions in the box. Have sts look back at 2A on p.17, if necessary, to review what they mean. Individually, sts make notes about the vision board using the expressions. Peercheck. Classcheck.

Suggested answers

A vision board can help you meet your goals.
However long you stare at a picture of something it won't just fall into your lap.
The idea of a vision board helping you meet your goals seems far-fetched.
If you want to meet your goals, you've got to go the extra mile.
It's not enough to put your mind to something.
You've got to work towards your goals even if they seem unattainable.

Optional activity

To review the meanings of the expressions, put sts into "teams." Each turn, read out a description of the meaning of each phrase. Award a point to the team that calls out the phrase first and board it.

2 In groups, sts share what they learned from their vision boards. Focus on the model in the speech bubble. Monitor and note any common errors for class feedback.

3 Elect a spokesperson for each group to report back to the class, using the expressions in the box. Check they know which verb form to use after each expression. Quickly check by saying the expressions, and have sts respond with *has* or *have*, e.g. Teacher: *a lot of us* Sts: *have.*

Have them refer back to Grammar box 5A on p.9, if necessary.

B Make it personal Sts choose three lesson title questions. Put sts in pairs to ask and answer the questions. Encourage them to ask at least three follow-up questions each, e.g. *How old were you? Did you use to live life far from school? Do you remember your teacher's name?*

Monitor and help with vocabulary.
Classcheck by asking two pairs to act out their exchanges.

Optional activity

Tell sts that when they are answering their partner's questions, they should tell one small lie. When finished, the st who was asking the questions has to guess the lie.

2 Listening

A ▶ R1.1 Focus on the photo. Ask: *What's happening?* (It's a lecture) *How old are the students?* (around 19/20). Have sts listen to the start of the lecture and choose the correct option. Classcheck.

Answer

a

▶▶ See Teacher's Book p.315 for Audio script R1.1.

B ▶ R1.2 As a pre-listening activity to spark sts' interest, elicit five things sts would like to know about fashion in China, e.g. *What are the most popular brands? Do they follow Western fashion?* Play the audio and find out if any of their questions are answered. It may be that none of them are, but they are probably curious now about the topic.

After the lesson, have sts research answers to the questions which were not answered on the audio.

Focus on questions 1 and 2. Re-play audio and have sts listen and make notes on them. Classcheck.

Answers

1 It encompasses the areas of psychology (personal style meets our need for individuality), sociology (imitating a clothing style demonstrates our need to belong to a group), and economics (the clothes we wear convey our level of prosperity).
2 Since they merge East and West, they lead to openness in other areas, like food, movies, or travel.

▶▶ See Teacher's Book p.316 for Audio script R1.2.

C Make it personal Ask sts what their views on questions 1 and 2 in **B** are. Put them in pairs, and have them share their ideas. Ask the question in the Student's Book: *What does the way you dress say about your own personal lifestyle?* Encourage follow-up discussion by asking: *Do you choose clothes to make a statement or because they are practical? Do you care what brands you wear?*

R1

3 Grammar

A If necessary, refer sts back to 5A and B on p.9 first. Do the first one as an example. Sts find and correct the mistakes in the remaining sentences.

Answers
1 Some of this book's grammar exercises **are** a little difficult.
2 Two hundred dollars really **is** a lot for a hotel room.
3 [✓]
4 Only one person in my family **lives** alone.
5 Being organized **requires** lots of planning.
6 [✓]
7 Having new experiences, as well as learning from them, **is** a sign of maturity.
8 In general, most people **are** very impatient in stores.

B **Make it personal** Sts compare their answers to A and explain the incorrect ones. Focus on the speech bubbles as a model. Classcheck and ask: *Are you confident about subject-verb agreements now? Or do you need more practice?*

Ask sts to make the sentences true for them. Elicit examples for the first one, e.g. *A few of this book's grammar exercises are a little easy*. In pairs, sts share their sentences.

4 Writing

Ask sts if they can remember a "first experience" a classmate shared in Lesson 1. If they need reminding, have them mingle and ask questions to jog their memory.

Before writing, read through 1 and 2, and ask them to look back at **Write it right!** on p.15, and review functions of *as*.

When sts have written their paragraphs, make sure they proofread them.

Classcheck, by asking a few sts to read them out to the class. Ask other classmates to correct any errors they hear. Collect and correct them for the next lesson.

5 Self-test

Tell sts that the aim of these sections is not only to help them review and consolidate vocabulary and grammar, but also to help them practice their proofreading skills.

Sts do the test individually, then paircheck. Encourage them to look back through Units 1 and 2 if they're unsure about any of the sentences. If sts score less than 15 out of 20, suggest they re-do the exercise in a few days, to see if they get a better score. If they do really well, they could also repeat the exercise later, but without referring to Units 1 and 2 this time.

Answers
1 I can still picture that party like it **was** yesterday.
2 My fatigue hasn't **worn** off, and, in fact, I **dozed** off in class this morning.
3 **I've seen** some great movies lately and I **went** to a really good one last weekend.
4 Most people today **have stopped** using their landline phones and **have now been** using a cell phone exclusively.
5 **As** we both didn't study enough, we thought the test **was** awful.
6 Your dream of being a chef won't seem **unattainable** if you really put your **mind** to it.
7 I wasn't familiar with my new **surroundings**, and I fell going down the **stairs**.
8 I didn't take the apartment, but I think I **should have** because now I'm having trouble finding a place, and my roommate is too.
9 This TV show has **such useful** information and so **many** suggestions.
10 There are so few ways to tell the twins apart, but the main difference **between** them is their eyebrows.

Optional activity

Divide the class in two halves. Have half the class correct sentences 1–5, and the other half correct sentences 6–10. When they have finished, go through the answers with each group. Put sts in pairs with one person from each of the groups and ask them to test each other, reading out their sentences for their partner to correct.

6 Point of view

Go through topics a–d with the class, and brainstorm a few ideas for each one. Individually, sts choose one of them and make some preparatory notes. Tell them to make brief notes (prompts), just enough to make them feel confident enough to be able to speak for about 80 seconds on the topic.

Review expressions for a) giving opinions, e.g. *In my view / opinion … , It seems to me that …, It seems that …, I think / believe that …, In my mind …, As far as I'm concerned …,* and b) supporting them, e.g. *because, thanks to …, owing to …, the reason is …, the facts suggest …*

Weaker classes: Sts can write out their argument in full, but get them to rehearse it before they record it, so they don't have to read directly from their notes.

Group together sts who chose the same topic so that they can compare, share, expand on, and improve their ideas. Monitor and correct as much as you can.

If possible, sts record their opinion in class using a cell phone. Allow them to re-record if they aren't happy. It's all good practice and everybody wants the best possible end product. Encourage sts to swap recordings with a partner and give each other feedback.

3 Grammar

A Check (✔) the correct sentences, and correct the mistake in the incorrect ones.

1. Some of this book's grammar exercises is a little difficult.
2. Two hundred dollars really are a lot for a hotel room.
3. Everyone in our class has unusual "first" experiences.
4. Only one person in my family live alone.
5. Being organized require lots of planning.
6. A few of the apps on my phone are really innovative and unusual.
7. Having new experiences, as well as learning from them, are a sign of maturity.
8. In general, most people is very impatient in stores.

B **Make it personal** In pairs, share your answers and explain the incorrect ones. Then make the sentences true for you.

> The first sentence should be "are": "Some of this book's grammar exercises are a little difficult."

> Actually, I think some of this book's grammar exercises are a little easy. But then I really love grammar!

4 Writing

Write a paragraph about a "first" experience a classmate told you. How much do you remember about him / her?

1. Use a range of tenses to give background information, describe the events, and bring the reader up to the present.
2. Use at least two different meanings of the word *as*.

5 Self-test

Correct the two mistakes in each sentence. Check your answers in Units 1 and 2. What's your score, 1–20?

1. I can picture that party yet like it were yesterday.
2. My fatigue hasn't gone off, and, in fact, I slept off in class this morning.
3. I saw some great movies lately and I've gone to a really good one last weekend.
4. Today most people stopped using their landline phones and had been using a cell phone exclusively.
5. Like we both didn't study enough, we thought the test went awful.
6. Your dream of being a chef won't seem inattainable if you really put your head to it.
7. I wasn't familiar with my new surrounding, and I fell going down the stair.
8. I didn't take the apartment, but I think I should have taken because now I'm having trouble finding a place, and my roommate has too.
9. This TV program has such a useful information and so much suggestions.
10. There are so little ways to tell the twins apart, but the main difference from them is their eyebrows.

6 Point of view

Choose a topic. Then support your opinion in 100–150 words, and record your answer. Ask a partner for feedback. How can you be more convincing?

a. You thought the 2000s were a really innovative decade until the 2010s came along. OR
   You think the 2000s definitely had more "firsts."
b. You think deep down people are the same regardless of where they live. OR
   You think cross-cultural relationships can be really challenging.
c. You think never getting married is a valid lifestyle choice. OR
   You can't imagine living and traveling alone and think marriage is a wonderful way of commiting to someone.
d. You think choice of neighborhood is far more important than the size of your apartment. OR
   You think a very small apartment is never worth it, even if the neighborhood is exciting.

3

What language would you least like to learn?

1 Listening

A Which way of learning a foreign language (photos a–d) have you found most effective / enjoyable? Why?

> Well, I'm really into American sitcoms, but I'm not sure I've learned a lot of English from TV.

a ☐ b ☐

c ☐ d ☐

B ▶ 3.1 Listen to part of an English class. Which photo (a–d) best illustrates the way Hugo learned French?

> **Common mistake**
> ~~don't think~~   *is*
> I think learning grammar rules isn't effective.

C ▶ 3.2 Listen to the second part. What can you infer about Hugo, María, and the teacher? Complete 1–5 with the correct names. Check in **AS** 3.2 on p.162. What sentences made you decide?

1 _____ doesn't read a lot in a foreign language.
2 _____ finds language learning a challenge.
3 _____ and _____ feel hard work is essential for language learning.
4 _____ connects emotionally to English online.
5 _____ thinks living abroad makes you almost feel like a native.

D **Make it personal** In pairs, discuss 1–4. How much do you have in common?

1 Which phrase best describes your experience learning English? Why?

    a bumpy ride   a necessary evil   a whole new world   Fun, fun, fun!

2 Are you more like Hugo or María? How much English have you learned through interaction? How about reading / listening for pleasure?
3 How much progress have you made in the past year in listening and speaking? Do you have any useful tips?
4 When did you first realize you could really speak English?

> Well, at first I thought English was just a necessary evil. But now it's a whole new world.

> I agree. As soon as I started understanding song lyrics, I was hooked!

28

What language would you least like to learn? 3.1

Lesson Aims: Sts learn language to talk about their learning experiences.

Skills	Language	Vocabulary
Listening to a conversation between teacher and sts in an English class	Describing learning experiences, e.g. *I picked it up naturally. My French is a bit rusty.*	Learning expressions: *improve by leaps and bounds, pick something up, put a lot of effort into ..., rusty, out of your depth, get by, debatable* Homographs, e.g. *record, command, suspect, progress*

Warm-up

Board this question: *What are the eight languages most spoken in the world?* for sts to answer in pairs. Monitor and help with pronunciation. Classcheck. (Answers: English, Mandarin, Spanish, Hindi, Arabic, Portuguese, Russian, Japanese)

Ask sts the lesson title question: *What language would you least like to learn? Why?* Ask: *What languages have you tried to learn in the past? Which did you find easiest / most difficult? What language would you most like to learn? Why?* Have sts discuss the questions in pairs. Class feedback.

» Song lyric: See Teacher's Book p.343 for notes about the song and an accompanying activity to do with the class.

1 Listening

A Focus on the photos. Ask sts how the people in the photos are learning. Try to elicit: a) studying alone, b) talking to native speakers / visiting the country, c) taking a course, d) watching TV shows in English. Ask: *Which ways have you tried? Which were the most effective / enjoyable?* Focus on the model in the speech bubble. Elicit other ways of learning a foreign language, e.g. reading newspapers / magazines, watching movies / videos, downloading apps, studying grammar books, listening to songs.

B ▶ 3.1 Tell sts they are going to hear Hugo talking to his English teacher. Ask: *Which photo shows Hugo?* Play the audio, then peercheck, getting pairs to share all they understood. Ask: *How did Hugo learn French?* Elicit that Hugo spent a year in Paris working as an au pair, and learned French by speaking with native speakers. Ask: *What other language does he speak?* (Portuguese)

Class feedback. Ask sts if any of them have ever spent a long time in a foreign country. Ask: *Did you learn much of the language of that country? What were the most useful phrases?*

Answer

b

» See Teacher's Book p.316 for Audio script 3.1.

Refer sts to the **Common mistake**. Ask sts how they would say this sentence in their own language. Then make it personal. Ask: *Do you agree with it?* Modify the sentence so it becomes true for you, e.g. *I don't think learning grammar rules is the most important aspect of learning a language. For me, it's listening and speaking.*

C ▶ 3.2 Have sts read sentences 1–5 before they listen. Play the second part of the audio. Sts fill in the blanks. Highlight the adjective *rusty*. Elicit or teach the meaning (not as good as it used to be because of lack of practice). Class feedback. Ask sts: *Which of the statements is true for you?* Have them change the other sentences so they are true, e.g. *No 1 isn't true for me. I read a lot in English.*

Answers

1 Hugo 2 Maria 3 The teacher and Maria
4 Maria Hugo

» See Teacher's Book p.316 for Audio script 3.2.

D Make it personal Go through the phrases and elicit or teach the meanings (*necessary evil* is something you don't like that can't be avoided). Ask sts if there are similar expressions in their language. Elicit the opposite of *bumpy ride* (smooth road). In pairs, sts discuss questions 1–4. Focus on the models in the speech bubbles. Have sts swap partners and ask and answer the questions with their new partner.

Invite sts to report back to the rest of the class what they have learned about their classmates' experiences of learning English, and what they have in common, e.g. *Erica says that learning English for her has been fun. We both love reading English novels.*

Optional activity

After sts discuss the questions in D, ask them to note down their five top tips for learning English. Put sts in pairs to share their ideas and agree on the five best tips. Put pairs into groups of four to repeat the process. Tell sts to imagine they are going to give a presentation to new learners of English to present their five tips. Sts present their ideas to the class.

3.1

2 Pronunciation: Stress in noun / verb homographs

A ▶ 3.3 Board the following words, and ask sts to write down two different meanings and pronunciations for each word: *close, house, lead, live, minute, read, row, tear, use, wind*. They can use a dictionary if necessary, e.g. *close* /kloʊs/ (adj) = near, *to close* /kloʊz/ (v) = shut; *house* /haʊs/ (n) = building you live in, *to house* /haʊz/ (v) = to find a house for someone. Tell sts these words are called homographs; words which have the same spelling but different meanings and different pronunciation.

Tell sts that homographs (of two syllables or more) may have different stress patterns. Play the audio and have sts follow the rules and examples in their books. Have sts practice the pronunciation of the example words. Elicit other homographs which sts know.

Tip

When drilling words/phrases for pronunciation, as well as using the model on the audio, make sure you give sts a clear model yourself for them to repeat, and physically beat the stress with your hands or feet. This will allow them to see, as well as hear, how you are stressing the words.

B ▶ 3.4 Check understanding of the statements. Elicit the meaning of *go the extra mile* (make a special effort to achieve something). Ask them to mark the stress on the correct syllable (with a blob or underlining). Play the audio for them to check, then practice pronouncing the sentences in pairs.

You could play the audio again and ask sts to notice the schwa sounds, e.g. *I think you need to spend some time in an English-speaking country to have a really good command of the language.* Have sts practice saying the complete sentences, paying particular attention to the correct stress and the schwa sounds.

Ask sts which of the statements they agree / disagree with. Encourage them to justify their opinions. Refer them to the model in the speech bubble, as an example.

Answers

1 com**mand**   2 su**spect**   3 **prog**ress   4 **ac**cess
5 **in**crease

Tip

Before sts discuss which statements they agree / disagree with, give them some time alone to think about their reasons, and make notes if they want to. This will ensure they're more confident when they have the discussion and have more to say.

3 Vocabulary: Learning expressions

A ▶ 3.5 Go through teacher's responses a–g with the class. Elicit the meanings of the expressions highlighted in yellow. Encourage sts to try and guess those they don't know from the context.

Tell sts they are going to hear again some of things Maria and Hugo said in 1B and 1C. After hearing each one, they have to match them with one of the teacher's responses a–g. Play the audio. Check answers with the class.

Answers

1 f   2 b   3 d   4 a   5 e   6 c

▶ See Teacher's Book p.316 for Audio script 3.5.

B Make it personal

1 Focus on the photos. Ask sts: *Which of these activities do you do?* Elicit *flute, easel, paint, spelling competition, play in an orchestra*. Tell sts they are going to role-play conversations with the people in the photos. Put sts in pairs. They can write out their role-plays together. Encourage them to use the expressions in A.

Weaker classes: Start sts off by writing the opening together, e.g.

A: *I had a great tennis lesson today. My serve is getting much better.*

B: *That's great. How long have you been playing?*

A: *I played when I was young, but haven't played for ages. I'm really rusty.*

B: *Are you enjoying it?*

A: *Yes, now I've joined the rusty rackets class, and I'm improving by leaps and bounds …*

Sts read out their role-plays taking turns playing each role. Invite a few pairs to read out their role-plays to the rest of the class.

Optional activity

Tell sts that they should avoid naming the situation when they prepare their role-plays. When they are ready, sts perform their role-plays for the class, who guess which situation they are talking about.

2 Put sts in new pairs. Have them choose two subjects they have had experience of learning. Focus them on the models in the speech bubbles.

Have them share information about their learning experiences. Encourage them to use the expressions in A. Invite some sts to report back to the class anything interesting or surprising they learned about their partner.

▶ Workbook p.13.

♪ Jigeumbuteo gal dekkaji gabolkka, Oppa Gangnam Style. Gangnam Style

3.1

2 Pronunciation: Stress in noun / verb homographs

A ▶ 3.3 Read and listen to the rules and examples. Can you think of any other homographs?

> Homographs are words that have the same spelling, but may be different in meaning or pronunciation. When the pronunciation isn't the same, nouns are stressed on the first syllable and verbs on the second:
> I like to **record** (v) myself speaking English. My **record** (n) is a two-hour video!
> But many nouns and verbs are pronounced the same:
> My teacher **comments** (v) on my written work every week. Her **comments** (n) are very helpful.

B ▶ 3.4 Do you remember the stressed syllable in the bold words (1–5)? Listen to check. Which do you agree with?

1 I think you need to spend some time in an English-speaking country to have a really good **command** of the language.
2 I **suspect** you learn a language more easily when you're an extrovert.
3 If you're willing to go the extra mile, you can make a lot of **progress**, whether or not you're naturally good at languages.
4 Why do you need to live abroad when you can **access** the Internet and immerse yourself in a foreign language without leaving your home?
5 Reading for pleasure is the only way to **increase** your vocabulary.

> I disagree with the first one. Remember how our teacher told us she'd never lived abroad.

3 Vocabulary: Learning expressions

A ▶ 3.5 Listen to six conversation excerpts from 1B and 1C. After you hear a "beep", match each one to the teacher's response (a–g). There's one extra. Continue listening to check your answers.

a ☐ Yes, it's improved by leaps and bounds!
b ☐ You mean you picked it up naturally by talking to native speakers?
c ☐ Yes, I know you have! You've put a lot of effort into your work!
d ☐ So your French is a bit rusty …
e ☐ Well, it's natural to feel out of your depth sometimes.
f ☐ You mean you could get by?
g ☐ That's debatable.

B **Make it personal** Learning can be a bumpy ride!

1 In pairs, role-play conversations about these other learning experiences. Use learning expressions from A.

1. My serve is getting much better.
2. I really struggled when I first joined the orchestra.
3. I used to depend on my spell checker till I joined the spelling club.
4. I've worked very hard on this painting.

2 Choose at least two topics. Share true information. End by answering question 1 in 1D.

art   math   music   spelling   sports

> I've started playing the violin again. I was really rusty, but I've been putting a lot of effort into my technique.

> That's fantastic! Are you enjoying it?

> In a way I am. It's a whole new world.

29

3.2 Are you into tweeting?

4 Language in use

A ▶3.6 What are the blue words in the tweets called? How can they help you search for information? Listen to the start of a talk on digital literacy and check your answers.

> I think you can search by typing ..., both in Twitter and other applications like ...

1. Having lunch at Au Bon Pain. Love this place! #lunch

2. Very interesting article on global warming: www.globalwarming_whatweknow #climatechangeisrealandweshouldactnow

3. Wonder if Rihanna thinks of Pinocchio when she sings "I love the way you lie." #funny

B ▶3.7 Listen to the second part. Complete a student's notes.

> Reasons to use hashtags:
> - Stronger messages, which reflect your ¹_____ and ²_____ identity.
> - Gives your message a humorous ³_____
> - Easier to express non-verbal ⁴_____.
> - Political and ⁵_____ significance.
> - A clearer sense of belonging to a larger ⁶_____.

C ▶3.8 Guess the problems (a–c) for the hashtags (1–3) in A. Listen to check.

a ☐ It's hard to read.   b ☐ It doesn't offer new information.   c ☐ It assumes you agree.

D Make it personal What do you think of hashtags?

1 ▶3.9 **How to say it** Complete 1–6 with the words in the box. Listen to check.

> extent   mildly   respects   say   speak   will

Making your attitude clear		
What they said		**What they meant**
1	Hashtags let you search by topic, which, to a certain _____, filters out some of the less relevant results.	This is only partially true.
2	Hashtags are an integral part of online communication – and, in some _____, of our culture at large.	
3	What a hashtag can do is give your text more color and depth – like a clever punchline, if you _____.	I'm speaking figuratively.
4	They're just noise so to _____, and, honestly, why people use them is beyond me.	
5	This hashtag is confusing to _____ the least, and how it can help the reader isn't clear.	It's worse than I'm suggesting.
6	Personally, I find that tweet a bit lame – to put it _____ – but that's beside the point.	

2 In groups, discuss a–d.

a Do you find hashtags helpful? How often do you use them?
b How would you improve the hashtags (1–3) in A?
c How important is it for you to get lots of likes and retweets?
d What point is the cartoon trying to make? Do you agree?

> I think the people in the building are all trying to pass the responsibility to someone else!

> I don't really agree. In the digital age ...

Are you into tweeting? 3.2

Lesson Aims: Sts learn language to talk about types of communication through social media.

Skills	Language	Vocabulary	Grammar
Listening to a professor talking about hashtags Reading a text about slang terms	Making your attitude clear, e.g. *This hashtag is confusing to say the least.*	Slang words and expressions, e.g. *doll up, dough, swanky, What's eating you?* Expressions for making your attitude clear: *to a certain extent, in some respects, if you will, so to speak, to say the least, to put it mildly*	Information-focus clauses, e.g. *How often people post increases their influence.*

Warm-up

Ask the lesson title question and sts to raise their hands if they have a Twitter account. Ask: *If you tweet, what topics do you tweet about? How many followers do you have? How many people do you follow on Twitter? How much time do you spend a day tweeting or following other people's tweets? Do you think it is a useful form of social media? Why / why not?* Have sts discuss these questions in pairs, then open up to a class discussion.

4 Language in use

A ▶ 3.6 Focus on the tweets. Elicit the significance of the reference to Pinocchio in the 3rd tweet (he was a wooden puppet in a children's novel whose nose grew longer every time he lied). Ask: *Do you think the tweets are funny / interesting?*

Elicit the answers to the questions in the Student's Book: *What are the blue words called? How do they help you search for information?*

Answers

Hashtags. They let you search by topic, which helps filter out some of the less relevant results.

» See Teacher's Book p.317 for Audio script 3.6.

Optional activities

- Before class, look up some common hashtags and find an example of a tweet for each. Board the hashtags and read out the tweets in a different order. Ask sts to guess which hashtags were used with each tweet.
- Ask sts to use their mobile devices to look up some common hashtags, and share them in small groups.

B ▶ 3.7 Focus on the title of the notes. Elicit reasons why we use hashtags. Ask sts to read the notes. Can they guess any of the missing words? Play the audio for them to check. Classcheck.

Answers

1 personal 2 professional 3 twist 4 emotions
5 social 6 community

» See Teacher's Book p.317 for Audio script 3.7.

Tip

This type of exercise is common in many exams. A good way to help sts prepare for it is to ask them to predict not only *what* information they expect to hear in each blank, but what *kind* of information they expect to hear, e.g. in 1 and 2, we'd expect to hear an adjective. Go through the blanks in this way before sts listen and elicit what kind of information they expect to hear.

C ▶ 3.8 Sts match the problems a–c with the hashtags in A. Classcheck.

Stronger classes: Ask sts to think of their own hashtags for the tweets in 4A. In pairs, ask them to compare their hashtags. Class feedback. Have sts vote on the best hashtags.

Answers

a 2 b 1 c 3

» See Teacher's Book p.317 for Audio script 3.8.

D Make it personal

1 ▶ 3.9 Have sts read the text in the "What they said" column and complete the highlighted expressions. Play the audio for sts to check their answers. Classcheck.

For pronunciation practice, you could play the audio again pausing after each expression, and ask sts to repeat, paying particular attention to the stress patterns.

Stronger classes: Cover the "What they meant" column, and ask sts to write their own definitions.

Answers

1 extent 2 respects 3 will 4 speak 5 say 6 mildly

2 Put sts in groups of three or four to discuss the questions. Before they start, elicit what "likes" and "retweets" are. Give sts five minutes to discuss the questions. Classcheck by asking a spokesperson for each group to summarize their conclusions. Class feedback. Ask: *Did you mostly agree / disagree?* Focus on the cartoon. *Do they think it's funny/common/sad?* Ask: *Has anyone had any similar experiences?*

3.2

5 Grammar: Information-focus clauses

A Explain that we use information-focus clauses when it is difficult to refer to something by using a noun group. The clause begins with a question word and can be used as a subject or object. Have sts read the grammar box. Check they understand the example sentences. Sts check the correct rules. Refer them to 4D and elicit three more examples. Ask sts: *Does this work in a similar way in your language?*

> **Answers**
> 1 active or passive 2 singular or plural
> Examples from 4D
> What a hashtag can do is give your text more color and depth …
> … why people use them is beyond me.
> … how it can help the reader isn't clear.

Stronger classes: Ask sts to think of, and write, a further example sentence for each type in the box.

» Refer sts to the **Grammar expansion** on p.142.

B Ask: *Do you use emoticons? How often?* For fun, ask sts to draw as many emoticons as they can in 60 seconds, with the adjective it portrays next to it, e.g. ☹ sad. Ask: *Who has drawn the most emoticons? Who has the most unusual one?*

Refer sts to the emoticons in the text in **B**. Ask: *What do you think these mean?* Sts read the text and correct the errors. Peercheck. Classcheck.

> **Answers**
> … but what **it is** meant to be **is** a sweat drop
> Why they **decided** to make it look like an angry bull **remains** a mystery

Refer sts to **Common mistakes**. Ask: *Are these and the ones in the text the types of mistakes you have made?* Have them rephrase the sentences to make them true about people they know, e.g. *How my grandmother managed to bring up six children, I'll never know!*

Stronger classes: Books closed. Board the incorrect sentences and ask sts to correct them.

C Elicit the meaning of *old-fashioned* (the opposite of modern / contemporary) and drill it, plus *make a comeback* (return) and slang (words or expressions that are very informal). Exemplify all three by asking: *Who has made a comeback recently? What slang words do you know in English?* (e.g. an "emo" is a drama queen, "my bad" means I was wrong, "frenemy" is a combination of friend and enemy, someone who appears to be your friend but is also antagonistic towards you).

Sts do the rest of the exercise on their own. Peercheck. Classcheck. Ask: *What old-fashioned slang terms do you like in your language?*

> **Answers**
> 1 how long it will last no one knows.
> 2 what it means is to "get dressed up."
> 3 how friends would react if I said this is a mystery
> 4 When it originated might / will surprise you
> 5 whether it really is people can / will / should decide for themselves
> 6 Where exactly I heard this for the first time I can't / don't remember

» Song lyric: See Teacher's Book p.344 for notes about the song and an accompanying activity to do with the class.

D Make it personal Have sts read through the questions. Put them in groups of three or four to discuss. You could ask them to make a list of the 10 most frequently-used slang words within their group.

Class feedback. Ask: *Does your group use slang a lot? What are your group's most frequently-used slang words?* Discuss where sts think new slang expressions come from and how long they last.

For homework or in class, ask sts to search online for the latest English slang expressions, e.g. *to be bent on doing something* (to be determined to do something). In the next lesson, have them share their favorites.

Tip

A common error is to use the word *slang* in the plural e.g. ~~I don't use many slangs~~. Make sure sts know that *slang* is uncountable, e.g. *I don't use much slang*. To make it countable, we can say *slang words* or *slang expressions*.

» Workbook p.14.

♪ I'm gonna raise a fuss, I'm gonna raise a holler. About a workin' all summer just to try to earn a dollar

3.2

5 Grammar: Information-focus clauses

A Read the grammar box and check (✓) the correct rules. Then underline three more examples in 4D.

Information focus: subject and object clauses		
To prepare the listener for new information, we sometimes use a subject clause:		
Subject	**How often** people post	increases their influence.
	What she did to simplify her life	was (to) unfollow lots of people.
To explain something further, we can use an object clause:		
Object	**Why** my writing is unclear	I'm not really sure.
	Whether slang should be used	we think is a question of personal style.
1 The verb in the information-focus clause can be ☐ active ☐ passive ☐ active or passive.		
2 The verb starting the main clause is ☐ singular ☐ plural ☐ singular or plural.		

» Grammar expansion p.142

B Correct two errors in each sentence. Can you think of any other ambiguous emoticons?

TWO POPULAR EMOTICONS YOU MIGHT BE USING WRONG!

Many people assume this is a tear drop, but what is it meant to be are a sweat drop that shows you're stressed out. I spent years misusing this one!

This one's used to convey triumph rather than anger. Why did they decide to make it look like an angry bull remain a mystery!

Common mistakes

How ~~does~~ *manages* my sister ~~manage~~ to be so funny I'll never understand!

Why Bob has so many followers ~~remain~~ *remains* a mystery.

C Write sentences with information-focus clauses using the prompts 1–6. Use the correct tense and verb form, and add words, as needed.

4 old-fashioned slang terms I wish would make a comeback!

The thing about slang is that it's unpredictable. A new word or expression may catch on quickly, but ¹[how long / last / no one / know]. It may disappear in a year or two or stick around for decades. Here are four old-fashioned slang terms you might still hear:

1 DOLL UP: I love this one! You might think it has to do with dolls, but ²[what / mean / be / "get dressed up"], as in "I got all dolled up for the party." Now, ³[how / friends / react / if / say this / mystery!]

2 DOUGH: Slang words for "money" come and go, but "dough" is my favorite. ⁴[When / originate / surprise you]: The first printed records date back to the mid 1800s!

3 SWANKY: If you describe something as swanky, you're saying it's expensive and fashionable. ⁵[Whether / really / be / people / decide / for themselves].

4 WHAT'S EATING YOU? This one means "What's bothering you?" ⁶[Where exactly / hear / first time / not / remember]. It might have been in a movie. Or maybe my grandfather used it.

D **Make it personal** In groups, discuss 1–3.
1 What are the most popular slang terms right now where you live?
2 How much slang do you use? When? Where? Why?
3 Do your parents / grandparents / children ever use slang you don't recognize?

Have you heard the expression ...?

3.3 Can someone learn to be a good speaker?

6 Reading

A In pairs, how do you feel when you have to speak in front of a group of people?

> I feel kind of self-conscious, but I never panic.

> Lucky you! I usually start to sweat and forget what I was about to say.

B Read the first paragraph. Predict at least three strategies the article might give for overcoming nervousness when speaking to a group. Continue reading to check. Were your ideas mentioned?

Better Public Speaking:
Becoming a Confident, Compelling Speaker
BY MINDTOOLS.COM

1. Whether we're talking in a team meeting or presenting in front of an audience, we all have to speak in public from time to time. We can do this well or we can do this badly, and the outcome strongly affects the way that people think about us. The good news is that, with thorough preparation and practice, you can overcome your nervousness and perform exceptionally well. This article explains how!

2. **Plan appropriately:** Think about how important a book's first paragraph is; if it doesn't grab you, you're likely going to put it down. The same principle goes for your speech: from the beginning, you need to intrigue your audience. For example, you could start with an interesting statistic, headline, or fact that pertains to what you're talking about and resonates with your audience. You can also use story telling as a powerful opener.

3. **Practice:** There's a good reason that we say, "Practice makes perfect!" You simply cannot be a confident, compelling speaker without practice. If you're going to be delivering a presentation or prepared speech, create it as early as possible. The earlier you put it together, the more time you'll have to practice. Practice it plenty of times alone, using the resources you'll rely on at the event, and, as you practice, tweak your words until they flow smoothly and easily.

4. **Engage with your audience:** When you speak, try to engage your audience. This makes you feel less isolated as a speaker and keeps everyone involved with your message. If appropriate, ask leading questions targeted to individuals or groups, and encourage people to participate and ask questions. Also, pay attention to how you're speaking. If you're nervous, you might talk quickly. This increases the chances that you'll trip over your words, or say something you don't mean. Force yourself to slow down by breathing deeply. Don't be afraid to gather your thoughts; pauses are an important part of conversation, and they make you sound confident, natural, and authentic.

5. **Cope with nerves:** How often have you listened to or watched a speaker who really messed up? Chances are, the answer is "not very often." Crowds are more intimidating than individuals, so think of your speech as a conversation that you're having with one person. Although your audience may be 100 people, focus on one friendly face at a time, and talk to that person as if he or she is the only one in the room.

6. **Watch recordings of your speeches:** Whenever possible, record your presentations and speeches. You can improve your speaking skills dramatically by watching yourself later, and then working on improving in areas that didn't go well. Are you looking at the audience? Did you smile? Did you speak clearly at all times? Pay attention to your gestures. Do they appear natural or forced? Make sure that people can see them, especially if you're standing behind a podium.

7. If you speak well in public, it can help you get a job or promotion, raise awareness for your team or organization, and educate others. The more you push yourself to speak in front of others, the better you'll become, and the more confidence you'll have.

© Mind Tools Ltd, 1996–2016. All rights reserved. "Mind Tools" is a registered trademark of Mind Tools Ltd. Reproduced with permission: https://www.mindtools.com/CommSkll/PublicSpeaking.htm

Can someone learn to be a good speaker? 3.3

Lesson Aims: Sts learn vocabulary to talk about speaking in public, and read about how to become a better public speaker.

Skills	Language.	Vocabulary
Reading an article about becoming a better speaker	Talking about how you feel, e.g. *I feel kind of self-conscious. I start to sweat.*	Expressions with *word*: *word of mouth, keep your word, spread the word, take back your words, get a word in edgewise, have the final word.*

Warm-up

Ask: *When did you last get really nervous? What did you do to try to calm your nerves? Did it work?* Then give sts in pairs five minutes to prepare a two-minute presentation on "Learning a foreign language." Ask four or five sts to give their presentations to the class. Ask: *How did you feel?* Ask the rest of the class: *Did they look nervous / confident? What did you notice about their body language?*

Focus on the lesson title question. Ask sts to discuss the question and explain their opinion. Class feedback.

6 Reading

A Refer sts to the photo and get them to speculate about her: her age, nationality, where she might be, etc. Ask: *What is the girl doing? How do you think she feels? Does she seem nervous / confident? How can you tell?* Ask sts to discuss in pairs how they feel when they speak in front of a group. Focus on the examples in the speech bubbles. Elicit or teach the meaning of self-conscious.

Weaker classes: Elicit adjectives sts can use and board them, e.g. *anxious, panicky, stressed, apprehensive, tense, embarrassed, uncomfortable*.

Optional activity

Search online for a video of a good public speaker. Ask sts to watch it and, in pairs, discuss their body language. You could tell them to turn the sound off to make them focus more on the body language. Have them write five tips on "good body language," and what body language to avoid when doing a presentation.

B Refer sts to the title of the article and the first paragraph. Ask them to predict three strategies they think will be mentioned. Sts read quickly to see if they guessed correctly. The aim of this task is to get sts to read for gist, so give them a time limit. Encourage them not to stop for words they don't know.

Highlight the following new words and elicit or teach the meanings: *pertains* (is related to), *tweak* (change slightly), *engage* (capture the attention of), *leading questions* (questions which prompt the answers wanted), *messed up* (failed or did something really badly).

Tip

With longer texts like this one, it's important to set time limits so sts don't read too slowly, and to break it up, both to check comprehension and make the class far more interactive, but also to lessen the differential between stronger sts – who will get to the end faster – and weaker sts, who won't. A great activity requiring no preparation is to cover the text with a sheet of paper and have sts uncover and read it one line at a time in pairs. When they reach the end of the first line, they predict the first word / phrase in the next line, then carefully uncover it so they see only the next line to check. They can repeat this procedure for the whole of the first paragraph, or even the whole text, either as a first or second read activity, or for review another day. You can even have sts award themselves a point for each correct guess, then feedback their scores afterwards!

3.3

C ▶ 3.10 Have sts read sentences 1–5 carefully before they listen. Play the audio while sts follow the text in their books. Pause after each paragraph to break it up and for sts to work in pairs rather than alone. This way, they say much more and you get more feedback as to how much each of them has understood. Sts answer T or F, and underline the evidence in the text. Classcheck, have them repeat the words with pink stress, then play the next paragraph. Elicit their reactions both to the text and the activity to find out if they enjoyed reading it, how difficult / interesting it was, etc.

> **Answers**
>
> 1 T (The same principle goes for your speech: from the beginning, you need to intrigue your audience.)
> 2 T (There's a good reason that we say, "Practice makes perfect!" / Practice it plenty of times alone)
> 3 F (When you speak, try to engage your audience. This makes you feel less isolated as a speaker and keeps everyone involved with your message.)
> 4 F (...focus on one friendly face at a time, and talk to that person as if he or she is the only one in the room)
> 5 T (You can improve your speaking skills dramatically by watching yourself later, and then working on improving in areas that didn't go well.)

D Sts scan the text to find words 1–5. Peercheck. Classcheck.

For further vocabulary practice, ask sts each to find three more new words in the text. Have them look up the words in a dictionary and find a synonym for each.

> **Answers**
>
> 1 outcome 2 thorough 3 grab 4 compelling 5 gather

Optional activity

Before sts scan to find the words, ask them to go online and find possible synonyms for each word. Elicit their answers and board them. After they have found the words in the text, check off any that were on the board, and discuss which of the other words on the board could be used in the text instead.

E Make it personal Ask: *What type of people do you see speaking in public?* Prompt them if necessary (sports people, e.g. soccer managers, politicians, professors, teachers, grooms at a wedding). *When did you last see someone speak in public? Where was it? What was the occasion?*

Have sts discuss the questions in groups of three or four. For question 1 they could also include other public speakers they see (not just on TV). Ask: *Which foreigners sound good / awful speaking in your language?* (e.g. soccer players!) Class feedback.

7 Vocabulary: Expressions with *word*

A For fun, do this as a race. Ask sts to find the word as quickly as they can and raise their hand. Elicit the literal meaning of *trip over* (to fall over something), and elicit a sentence, e.g. *I tripped over someone's suitcase at the airport, and twisted my ankle.*

> **Answer**
>
> trip over your words

▶ Song lyric: See Teacher's Book p.344 for notes about the song and an accompanying activity to do with the class.

B Focus on the cartoon. Ask: *What's the message? What does "get a word in edgewise" mean?* (meaning find it hard to contribute to a conversation because the other speaker talks incessantly). *Do you find it funny? Does it remind you of anyone you know?*

Ask sts to look first at the authors of the quotes. Have they heard of any of them? They may at least know Martin Luther King, Jr. (African-American Civil Rights leader assassinated in Memphis in 1968).

Then sts read the quotes. Ask them to figure out the meanings of the highlighted expressions from the context. Peercheck or have them check in a dictionary. Classcheck. Ask sts if there are similar expressions in their own language. Elicit other expressions with *word*, e.g. *give your word, not breathe a word, be at a loss for words, eat one's words, hang on s.o.'s every word*.

> **Answers**
>
> 1 *by word of mouth* just means "by talking."
> 2 *Keep your word* means to always do what you promised.
> 3 *Spread the word* means to communicate the message to a lot of people.
> 4 *take back your words* means to change your mind about what you said.
> 5 *get a word in edgewise* means to be able to contribute to a conversation when the other person is speaking incessantly
> 6 *to have the final word* means to win the argument or make the final decision so this means that these will be the most important factors

Optional activity

To check understanding of the quotes, ask sts to rewrite them in their own words, paraphrasing where possible. Sts then read out their sentences in random order to a partner, who guesses the original quote.

C Make it personal Ask sts which quotes they agree with. For homework, ask sts to search online and try to find other quotes containing expressions with *word*. Have them share them with the class in the next lesson.

▶ Workbook p.15.

♪ Drench yourself in words unspoken. Live your life with arms wide open. Today is where your book begins. The rest is still unwritten

3.3

C ▶ 3.10 Re-read and listen to the article. T (true) or F (false)? Underline the evidence.
1. First impressions are critical.
2. There's no such thing as too much rehearsal.
3. Audience participation can be distracting.
4. Eye contact should be random, and it's best not to look at people.
5. You can recognize and correct your own mistakes.

D Scan paragraphs 1–4. Find words that mean …
1. result (n): _____ (paragraph 1)
2. complete (adj): _____ (paragraph 1)
3. appeal to: _____ (paragraph 2)
4. persuasive: _____ (paragraph 3)
5. collect: _____ (paragraph 4)

E Make it personal In groups, discuss 1–3.
1. Who's the best / worst public speaker you see on TV? Why?
2. Which advice in the article seems most useful? Have you ever tried any of it?
3. What additional problems do people face when speaking in public in a foreign language? What can they do to cope?

> In a foreign language, you could forget words or make grammar mistakes.

> Yes, and if you have a strong accent, your audience might not understand you!

7 Vocabulary: Expressions with *word*

A Read paragraph 4 again. Underline an expression that means "to stumble" or "have trouble saying" your words.

B Read the quotes. Can you figure out what the highlighted expressions mean?
1. "They say 90% of the promotion of a book comes **by word of mouth**. But you've somehow got to get your book into the hands of those mouths first!." (Abraham Cahan)
2. "**Keep your word**. It creates a life of never having to explain who you are." (Cleo Wade)
3. "Happiness is a choice, not a destination. **Spread the word**." (Unknown quote)
4. "No, you can't **take back your words**. Because once you've said them, there's no refund." (Francine Chiar)
5. "I got well by talking. Death could not **get a word in edgewise**, grew discouraged, and traveled on." (Louise Erdrich)
6. "I believe that unarmed truth and unconditional love will **have the final word** in reality." (Martin Luther King, Jr.)

> I think *by word of mouth* just means "by talking." So, number 1 means you have to read the book first to be able to talk about it.

C Make it personal Which quotes do you agree with? How many similar opinions?

> I agree with the first. Most of the books I've read recently have been recommendations from friends.

Common mistakes
I couldn't get ~~the~~ *a* word in edgewise.
It spread by ~~the~~ word of mouth.
He was at a loss for ~~the~~ words.

33

3.4 What's the ideal age to learn a language?

8 Listening

A In pairs, what advantages can you imagine to growing up bilingual?

> Well, a big plus, is that you can communicate with more people.

B ⏺ 3.11 Guess the true statements. Then listen to / watch speech pathologist Caroline Erdos to check.

1. Bilingual children solve problems more easily.
2. Later in life, bilinguals are less likely to develop Alzheimer's disease.
3. There must be only one language at home and one at school.
4. It's natural for children to mix languages, even when the parent doesn't understand both.
5. Bilingual children learn to speak a little later than monolingual children.
6. Special-needs children with language difficulties should remain monolingual.
7. To become bilingual, children need to be exposed to proficient speakers, at least 30% of the time.

Caroline Erdos

C ⏺ 3.11 Listen / Watch again. In pairs, correct the false statements in B. Any surprises? Which facts seem the most logical?

> I was really surprised by number … because I thought …

9 Language in use

A ▶ 3.12 Read the discussion forum for people raised bilingual, and put 1–4 back into the posts. Listen to check. There's one extra sentence.

1. Having studied Italian informally, I've now learned the grammar
2. Taught in both languages, I felt I was always in close contact with my roots
3. Living in a city like Rio, though, I still use my German every now and then, too
4. Maybe that's why, when talking to my mom, I find it hard to discuss very abstract ideas

B Make it personal In pairs, answer 1–4. Any interesting stories?

1. Do you know anyone who grew up bilingual?
2. If you know bilingual people, do they mix languages? Do they switch easily from one to the other?
3. Do you think bilinguals have a favorite language? Do they think mainly in one?
4. Do you agree with the video that bilingualism has only advantages?

> I'm not sure I agree with number 4. I knew this guy who couldn't speak either language well.

> But did he have enough input? Remember the video said that …

Anita: Having been raised in Brazil by an Australian mother and German father, I learned how to navigate between languages comfortably from a very early age. Today, I use both Portuguese and English at work. _____, even if it's only to help tourists with directions and things like that.

Fred: I grew up in Chicago, speaking English with my dad and Italian with my mom, almost exclusively. When I went to school, my English surpassed my Italian, of course. _____ My conversations with Dad, on the other hand, tend to be more profound – unless, of course, I switch to English with Mom.

Marco: Growing up in a multicultural home in Buenos Aires, I've always cherished my heritage. My mother is Argentinean, and my dad is American. We spoke both English and Spanish at home, and when I was six, my parents enrolled me in a bilingual school. Looking back, it was the best thing they could have done. _____

34

What's the ideal age to learn a language? 3.4

Lesson Aims: Students learn how to use participle clauses to express result, time, and reason, and perfect participles.

Skills	Language	Vocabulary	Grammar
Listening to speech language expert talking about bilingualism Discussing sts' own learning experiences	Expressing reasons in the past, e.g. *Knowing some English, I never have trouble getting by.*	bilingual, monolingual, proficient, input	Using participle clauses, e.g. *When driving to work, I used to listen to audio books.* Perfect participles, e.g. *Having played the trombone when I was younger, I already knew ...*

Warm-up

Ask sts the lesson title question: *What's the ideal age to learn a language?* Ask: *When did you start learning English? Do you think it is easier to learn a second language when you are older or younger? What do you think most influences second language learning? Do you think some people find it easier than others to learn a language?* Have sts discuss these questions in groups.

8 Listening

A Ask: *Do you know anyone who is bilingual? Which languages do they speak? Which language do they speak at home / with their parents / with their siblings?*

In pairs, sts discuss the advantages of being bilingual. Class feedback. Ask: *Do you think there are any disadvantages?*

Optional activity

As an alternative, before class, board the following statements in random order:

- I have developed better cognitive abilities.
- I will delay dementia in old age.
- I find it easier to learn other languages.
- It can be difficult to express myself in only one language.
- I sometimes have issues with identity
- I'm never sure which team to root for in the Olympics.
- I make up words and expressions.

Put sts in pairs and ask them to decide if each one is an advantage or disadvantage of being bilingual, and also if they agree / disagree with the statement.

B ▶ 3.11 Have sts read the statements carefully. Ask them which they think are true. Play the video for them to check their guesses.

Answers

1 T 2 F 3 F 4 T 5 F 6 F 7 T

» See Teacher's Book p.317 for Video script 3.11.

C ▶ 3.11 Play the video a second time and have sts correct the false statements. Classcheck. Ask: *Which of the statements do you find surprising / most interesting?*

Answers

2 They will develop Alzheimer's disease later than those who are monolingual.
3 One can choose the formula one wants ...
5 Bilingual children learn to speak around the same time / age as monolingual children.
6 Bilingualism does not further exacerbate any language difficulties a special-needs child has.

9 Language in use

A ▶ 3.12 Before sts do the reading task, ask them to skim the texts and write down which languages Anita, Fred, and Marco speak. Ask: *How many languages do they speak between them?*

Tell them to re-read the texts, and put the sentences in the correct blanks. Play the audio for them to check. Highlight the words *surpassed, profound, heritage,* and *enrolled,* and model and drill pronunciation.

Answers

Anita: 3 Fred: 4 Marco: 2

Stronger classes: Ask sts to cover up sentences 1–4. Ask them to read the paragraphs and think about the missing information, then listen to the recording and write the missing sentences.

B Make it personal Refer sts to the example in the speech bubble. Have them discuss questions 1–4 in pairs, then open up to a class discussion. Ask: *If you could be bilingual, which languages would you choose? Why?*

In the video, Caroline Erdos says, "Worldwide there are more individuals who are bilingual than monolingual." Ask sts if they are surprised by this. Discuss which parts of the world have a lot of bilingual speakers, e.g. Switzerland has four official national languages (German, French, Italian, and Romansh), and many Swiss people speak a combination of two of these. Ask sts to research other multilingual countries, and find out which countries have most bilingual speakers, either in class or for homework. Have sts pool their information in groups, and report back their findings to the rest of the class.

3.4

10 Grammar: Using participle clauses

Tip

Try to begin with and link the grammar box to a participle clause song line they may know, e.g. Abba's *Knowing me, knowing you, ah-ha, there is nothing we can do*, and its use (reason). This ought to help them remember it, as they know it already!

A Go through examples 1–4 in the grammar box with the class. Have sts translate the sentences into their language. Ask: *What are the similarities / differences between your language and English?* Sts check the correct rules. Peercheck. Classcheck.

Answers

a present or past   b subject   c either active or passive

>> Refer sts to the **Grammar expansion** on p.142.

B Do the first one together as an example. Ask sts to choose the correct meanings for b, c, and d. Peercheck. Classcheck. Sts then rephrase the participle clauses in 9A.

Weaker classes: Rephrase the participle clauses 1–3 together on the board. Note that there may be more than one possible answer.

Focus on the **Common mistake**. Ask sts to explain the error (*my time* is not the subject of the participle clause). Ask: *Is this a mistake you might make if you translated from your language?*

Answers

1 know   2 grew up   3 drove   4 is

Possible answers

1 Because I studied Italian informally, …
2 I was taught in both languages, so I felt …
3 As I live in a city like Rio, though, I …

>> Song lyric: See Teacher's Book p.344 for notes about the song and an accompanying activity to do with the class.

C Focus on the text. Discuss the meaning of the title: *The apple doesn't fall far from the tree*. Explain that this is an idiom meaning kids are like their parents. Ask them if there is a similar idiom in their language. You could also teach them *He / She's a chip off the old block*, another idiom, meaning he or she is similar in character to their parents.

Ask: *Which of these musicians have you heard of? Do you know any songs by them?*

Have sts complete 1–5. Remind them that the participle clause can be passive or active. Elicit the meaning of *crooner* (typically a male singer who sings sentimental songs in a soft, low voice). Peercheck. Classcheck. Ask: *Which of the facts do you find most interesting?*

Weaker classes: Before sts do the task, check they know the past participles of the verbs in the box.

Answers

1 Watching   2 Inspired   3 Beginning   4 Winning
5 Educated

D Read **Perfect participles** with the class. Point out that the verb in the second clause is always in the past simple. Sts do the task individually. Peercheck. Classcheck.

Tip

Perfect participles are more common in written English than spoken English.

Answers

1 (After) Having watched   2 (After) Having been inspired
3 (After) Having begun   4 (After) Having won
5 (After) Having been educated

E Make it personal Give sts a few minutes to read the questions and make notes of the answers. Put them in groups of three and have them share their answers. Refer them to the model in the speech bubble. Encourage them to use participle clauses.

Classcheck by asking sts to report back something interesting they learned about their classmates.

Optional activity

Ask sts to imagine they are in their 80s, looking back on their lives. Sts write a paragraph describing their (fictional) achievements, and where they picked them up from. Encourage them to be as imaginative as possible! When they have finished, display their texts around the class, and ask sts to walk around and read them, then choose their favorite.

>> Workbook p.16.

♪ And promise you kid that I'll give so much more than I get. I just haven't met you yet

10 Grammar: Using participle clauses

A Read the grammar box and check (✔) the correct rules (a–c).

Participle clauses to express result, time, and reason	
1 **Knowing** some English,	I never have trouble getting by.
2 **Growing up** in a family of artists,	Gwen eventually became an actress.
3 **When driving** to work,	I used to listen to audio books.
4 **Supported** by his parents,	Ben is in no hurry to find a job.

Participle clauses, which are very common in written English ...
a describe the ☐ past ☐ present or past.
b refer to the ☐ subject ☐ object of the main sentence.
c are ☐ always active ☐ either active or passive.

» Grammar expansion p.142

B Choose the correct meaning (a–d) for the example sentences (1–4) in the grammar box. Then rephrase the participle clauses 1–3 in 9A beginning with a conjunction, too.

a As I [**know / knew**] some English, I ...
b She [**grew up / is growing up**] in a family of artists, so ...
c When I [**drive / drove**] to work, I ...
d Because he [**is / was**] supported by his parents, he ...

Common mistake

I spent a lot of time writing
Growing up as only child, ~~my time was spent writing~~.

Participle clauses must have a clear subject: Your time didn't grow up – you did.

C Complete 1–5 with participle clauses, using the verbs in the box.

| begin | educate | inspire | watch | win |

The apple doesn't fall far from the tree

1 _____ her mother perform across the globe for decades, singer and actress **Liza Minnelli** went on to become one of the world's most successful entertainers.

2 _____ by his grandfather's collection of jazz records, crooner **Michael Bublé** decided he wanted to become a singer at a very early age.

3 _____ his musical career at the age of five with a story on Yoko Ono's 1981 album, *Season of Glass*, **Sean Lennon** went on to become a musician and singer in his own right.

4 **Laila Ali**, daughter of world champion Muhammad Ali, became a professional boxer at age 18. _____ all the fights she ever took part in, **Laila Ali** retired from the ring in 2007.

5 _____ in Miami from the age of seven, **Enrique Iglesias**, son of Spanish singer Julio Iglesias, sings in both Spanish and English.

D Read *Perfect participles*. Then rephrase 1–5 in C.

Perfect participles

You may use a perfect participle to emphasize that an action happened before another one:
Having played the trombone when I was younger, I already knew how to read music.
After having graduated, I started looking for a job in my field.

E **Make it personal** In groups, answer 1–3. Any interesting stories?
1 List a few of your special skills, talents, and accomplishments.
2 Which did you pick up mostly from your (a) family, (b) friends, (c) teachers?
3 Do you know anyone with a special talent that became clear early in life?

Yes, my nephew started writing music when he was just 12. Growing up in a musical family, he was exposed to music all the time.

35

3.5 What can't you learn through practice?

11 Listening

A ▶ 3.13 Listen to part one of a conversation between two friends, David and Paula. In pairs, answer 1–2.
1 What did the musician do during the concert?
2 Why did he do it?

B ▶ 3.14 Listen to part two. Then check (✔) Paula's advice, a or b. Do you agree with her reasons?
1 a ☐ Think about your audience during a performance. You need to be concerned with people's reactions.
   b ☐ Don't worry too much about your audience. People tend to be more accepting than we give them credit for.
2 a ☐ Don't try too hard. It will just make you nervous.
   b ☐ Try to do the best you can. It's important to be good, but within reasonable limits.
3 a ☐ Don't focus on talent. Learning is mainly motivation and practice.
   b ☐ Consider if you have talent. If not, choose something else to learn.

C ▶ 3.15 Fill in the missing words in these expressions. Listen to check.
1 Practice makes _____, remember?
2 I really have my _____ about my playing! I can't even _____ to imagine giving a concert.
3 You're setting yourself impossibly high _____.
4 Don't go to the other _____. You need to hit a middle _____.
5 Do your very _____, but don't worry about being perfect.
6 Do you think I could learn to ski if I put my _____ to it?
7 Yeah, I do. Why not give it a _____?

12 Keep talking

A Choose or invent something you've been <u>unable</u> to learn. Think about these questions:
1 Why did you have trouble learning it?
2 How often / hard did you try?
3 Might you give it another shot in the future?
4 What would you do differently?

B In groups, take turns presenting your problem for the others to offer advice. Use the expressions in 11C and those below.

> In addition to ..., you might want to ... Have you thought about ...?
> You might not ..., but you can still ...

> I've been unable to learn how to swim! I can't even begin to imagine being in the deep end of the pool. Maybe you can give me some advice.

> Have you thought about relaxation techniques? Maybe you're scared.

"I CAN'T READ BUT I HAVE EXCELLENT TV VIEWING SKILLS."

What can't you learn through practice? 3.5

Lesson Aims: Sts listen to some friends discussing the pressure of performing, and learn to write an expository essay.

Skills	Language	Vocabulary	Grammar
Listening to friends talking about performing before an audience Writing an expository essay using participle clauses and linking time words	Talking about practice and setting goals, e.g. *I could learn to ski if I put my mind to it. Why not give it a shot?*	do your best, put your mind to it, give it a shot, practice makes perfect, have your doubts, not begin to ..., set (high) standards	Using participle clauses in an essay

Warm-up

Ask sts the lesson title question: *What can't you learn through practice?* To help them answer this question, ask sts to write a list of ten skills which require a lot of practice, e.g. tennis, learning to drive. In pairs, have them rank the skills 1–10 in order (1 = requiring most practice.) This should lead to some interesting discussion and disagreement!

» Song lyric: See Teacher's Book p.344 for notes about the song and an accompanying activity to do with the class.

11 Listening

A ▶ 3.13 Focus on the photo. Ask: *What can you see?* (A male violinist playing in an orchestra at a concert, and below it, a violin and music score.) Ask: *Can any of you read music?* Ask sts to read the questions in the SB. Play the audio, sts answer, then classcheck.

Weaker classes: Ask the following listening comprehension task to check sts' understanding.
1 What's Paula going to practice?
2 Where did Paula go the other night?
3 What did she think of the concert?
4 Why did the violinist not want to play anymore?
5 Was he an experienced performer?

Answers
1 The violinist got up and left mid-concert.
2 He decided he didn't want to continue.

» See Teacher's Book p.318 for Audio script 3.13.

B ▶ 3.14 Have sts read the advice before they listen. Play the audio and sts check advice a or b. Classcheck. Ask: *Do you think the advice is good?* Highlight the expression *be gifted* (to have talent).

Answers
1 b 2 b 3 a

» See Teacher's Book p.318 for Audio script 3.14.

C ▶ 3.15 Encourage sts to fill in the missing words from memory before they listen. Play the audio for them to check. Classcheck. Re-play it pausing after each of the expressions, and have sts mark the stress. Sts practice saying the expressions in pairs.

Answers
1 perfect 2 doubts, begin 3 standards
4 extreme, ground 5 best 6 mind 7 shot

Optional activity

Before sts listen again, put them in two large groups, and give a board pen to each group. Ask them to close their books. Each round, read out one of the expressions in C but don't say the missing word. One st from each group comes to the board and writes the missing word. The first group to write it correctly wins a point. If neither team guesses, leave it and move on to the next one. The team with the most points at the end wins. When you have finished, do exercise C as in the book.

12 Keep talking

A Focus on the cartoon and see if they find it funny. Read the rubric to the class, then give a personal example yourself first to exemplify. Get sts to ask you questions 1–4.

Give sts a few minutes to choose a skill they have had problems learning, and make a few notes. Put them in pairs, and have them take turns asking each other the questions. Ask: *Did you and your partner share any similar experiences?*

B Put sts in groups. In turns, sts tell the rest of the group about their learning experience, and the problems they had learning the skill. The rest of the group listens carefully, then offers advice. Encourage sts to use the expressions in 11C. Before sts begin, focus on the expressions in the box, and elicit some sentences using them, e.g. *Have you thought about changing your teacher? You might not be the best tennis player, but you can still have fun and keep in shape.* Refer them also to the models in the speech bubbles.

Weaker classes: You could have sts do this in pairs rather than groups.

Optional activity

While sts are doing the activity, ask them to note down any useful advice they hear. After the exercise, sts write a short paragraph of advice for their chosen activity.

3.5

13 Writing: An expository essay

A Have sts read the essay title. Tell them the essay is written by a language learner, Zak, for a website for language learners. Give them two minutes to read it quickly for gist then, in pairs, share what they remember and say what they can infer about Zak and his personality. (He's clearly a fluent English speaker who's obviously into languages.)

Sts read the essay again and find examples of 1–3. Classcheck.

> **Answers**
> 1 We've all seen announcements from language programs that promise we can learn English (or another language) in "twenty easy lessons."
>   But you might well be wondering what exactly the best way to learn a language really is.
> 2 Just as there are multiple kinds of intelligences, there are multiple ways of learning a foreign language.
> 3 listening to music, watching movies with subtitles, reading

Stronger classes: Ask sts to cover up topic sentences 1–3. Sts read, then write their own topic sentence, and peercheck. Elicit ideas from the class. Sts then choose the best topic sentence from 1–3.

B Sts find the seven time words. Classcheck. Elicit other time words they might know, e.g. *initially, eventually, suddenly, after a long time*.

> **Answers**
> Para 3: First, Then, Over time
> Para 4: Then, In the beginning, in no time at all
> Para 5: after a while, In a matter of weeks

C Go through **Write it right!** with the class, then ask sts to find three more participle clauses. Refer them back to the Grammar box on page 35, if necessary.

> **Answers**
> Then listening to the songs over and over, I would compare the lyrics with the English translation I had also downloaded.   Subject = I (Zac)
> As well as focusing on music, I thought TV could be useful for language learning.   Subject = I (Zac)
> So, after a while, in addition to listening to music and watching TV, I decided to read novels to improve my grammar.   Subject = I (Zac)

D Go through the example together. Point out that the participle clause sometimes comes at the end of the sentence, not always at the beginning. Sts work individually to do 2–5. Peercheck. Classcheck.

> **Answers**
> 1 In addition to being motivated, you need to go the extra mile.
> 2 My friends tell me I can improve my English by listening to music.
> 3 Having bought some new albums, I started to listen to them every day.
> 4 Imagining visual scenes as I listened, I felt as if I was in the U.S.
> 5 Having learned a lot more colloquial language, I've improved my listening skills.

Tip

Good essays always contain a range of structures. When sts have written an essay, ask them to go back and look for places where they could experiment with more complex structures, using those they've studied in the book so far.

E **Your turn!** Read through the instructions with the class and check that everyone understands what they have to do. Alternatively, sts could choose a skill they have successfully learned and give advice related to that.

Sts could do this for homework. In this case, assign each st a partner to email their essay to for peer correction, e.g. by underlining any mistakes they think they have found in each other's work then sending it back again. Sts can try to improve their own work before sending it to you. This should reduce your marking load. You could then use a code like the one below, and return it back to them once more afterwards. Remember the essence of written correction should be a focus on improving, not on you being their editor or correction machine!

Tip

When correcting sts' writing, use a correction code leaving sts to correct their own mistakes, rather than making the corrections for them, e.g.

G = grammar mistake   WO = word order
Sp = spelling   M = missing word
P = punctuation   ? = not clear
T = tense   ! = silly mistake

Display the correction code on the classroom wall and use it consistently so that sts instantly recognize the correction.

» Workbook p.17.

♪ There's nothing you can do that can't be done … It's easy. All you need is love

3.5

13 Writing: An expository essay

A Read the essay on an online site for language learners. Find …
1 a sentence that creates initial interest.
2 the topic sentence.
3 three concrete techniques the essay offers.

B A good expository essay maintains the theme in a paragraph. In paragraphs 3–5 underline seven time words and expressions that help link ideas.

C Read *Write it right!* Then find three more participle clauses that the writer uses to link ideas. What is the subject of each one?

> **Write it right!**
> Expository essays use a variety of structures to create interest. Participle clauses with *-ing* are one way to link ideas or create suspense.
> **Before downloading** a full album, I would look at the lyrics to see if the language seemed "useful."

D Combine 1–5 with participle clauses. Check all sentences to be sure the subject is clear!
1 You need to be motivated. In addition, you need to go the extra mile.
   In addition to being motivated, you need to go the extra mile.
2 I love listening to music. My friends tell me I can improve my English that way.
3 I bought some new albums. I started to listen to them every day.
4 I imagined visual scenes as I listened. I felt as if I was in the U.S.
5 I've learned a lot more colloquial language. My listening skills have improved.

E Your turn! Choose a topic you role-played in 12 and write an essay giving three pieces of advice in about 280 words.

Before
Choose three pieces of advice. Note down details to support your arguments.

While
Write six paragraphs following the model in **A**. Use at least two participle clauses and two other linking words or expressions.

After
Post your essay online and read your classmates' work. Who had the best advice?

What worked for me when I was studying Russian

1 We've all seen announcements from language programs that promise we can learn English (or another language) in "twenty easy lessons." Naturally, that's false. But you might well be wondering what exactly the best way to learn a language really is.

2 Just as there are multiple kinds of intelligences, there are multiple ways of learning a foreign language. Your personal techniques have a lot to do with your personality and your learning style. What you need is lots of patience – and, of course, motivation. These three techniques helped me tremendously with Russian, my college major.

3 I'm the kind of person who likes to listen. In fact, my friends tell me I'm a good listener, and they often choose me when confiding their problems. So, I decided to apply my listening skills to learning Russian. <u>First</u>, I had some Russian friends recommend popular music to me. Before downloading a full album, I would look at the lyrics to see if the language seemed "useful." Then listening to the songs over and over, I would compare the lyrics with the English translation I had also downloaded. Over time, I started to pick up new words and expressions, and what's more, I even heard them used when I had a chance to practice my Russian with native speakers.

4 As well as focusing on music, I thought TV could be useful for language learning. So even though I don't really like TV, I decided to pay extra to have access to the local Russian channel, too. Then I began to watch movies with the English subtitles on. In the beginning, I understood very little. The actors talked so fast! But in no time at all, I started to follow the dialogue because my favorite soap opera had a predictable plot.

5 There was no way I was going to do grammar exercises in my free time, but I love to read. So, after a while, in addition to listening to music and watching TV, I decided to read novels to improve my grammar. I would look closely to see if I could recognize the structures taught in class, and sometimes made a mental note to use parts of sentences myself in conversation. In a matter of weeks, I was trying out new expressions! You could try this technique, too. But be careful! It only works with modern novels. If you read Tolstoy or Dostoyevsky, you may start sounding as if you were born in the 1820s!

6 These are just a few fun and useful ways you can improve your language skills in any language. You might want to try them, too!

37

4. How often do you remember your dreams?

1 Listening

A ▶ 4.1 Listen to the start of a radio show with a psychologist. Circle the correct answer.

Scientists [**are fairly sure** / **only suspect**] that some dreams may reveal certain things about our personalities.

B ▶ 4.2 Guess what dreams 1–3 represent. Listen to the second part and write the numbers. There's one extra choice. Any surprises?

- ☐ anger
- ☐ anxiety or guilt
- ☐ perfectionism in your work
- ☐ unassertiveness

C ▶ 4.2 Listen again and complete the chart.

In which conversation(s) does Dr. Wallace …	1	2	3
1 reassure the caller things will be OK?			
2 offer two different interpretations of the same dream?			
3 ask for further details about the dream?			
4 avoid committing to a point of view?			
5 seem to have trouble convincing the caller?			

D ▶ 4.3 Listen to the end of the show. Summarize Dr. Wallace's last point in one sentence.

E Make it personal In pairs, discuss these questions.
1. Have you ever had a dream that came true? What happened?
2. Have you recently dreamed about …?

fire   water   flying   falling   being trapped
being unable to move   missing a plane/train   failing in school

3. 🌐 Search online for an interpretation. Does it make sense?

> **Common mistake**
> *about*
> I dreamed ~~with~~ falling last night.

> I've had dreams about falling, but I don't feel insecure and anxious like the website says.

> It can mean other things, too. Maybe you were afraid of failing at love.

38

How often do you remember your dreams? 4.1

Lesson Aims: Sts listen to an expert talking about interpreting dreams.

Skills	Language	Vocabulary
Listening to a radio interview with an expert on dreams Talking about dreams and dreams that have come true	Committing to a point of view, e.g. *I wouldn't go so far as to call it a masterpiece. There's no doubt in my mind. Without a shadow of a doubt.*	Productive suffixes: *-friendly, -conscious, -oriented, (-)like, -related, worthy*

Warm-up

Focus on the the lesson title question: *How often do you remember your dreams?*

Ask: *How often do you dream? Do you dream in color or black and white? Are you always in your dreams? What affects whether you dream or not? Do you dream more when you … go to bed late / drink alcohol / eat spicy food / eat cheese?* Have sts discuss the questions in pairs. Feedback one interesting discovery from each pair.

1 Listening

A ▶ 4.1 Focus on the photo. Ask: *What can you say about the people? What are they doing?* Explain that sts are going to hear an interview with Dr. Emilia Wallace, who has written a book called *Dream On: What we can learn about ourselves at night.*

Weaker classes: Pre-teach *research, in the light of … random neural signals, to matter, outside stimuli, fire-engine siren, beneath.*

Have sts read the statement and guess the correct answer. Play the audio for them to check. Check answers. Ask: *Does this surprise you?*

If sts have difficulty with the task, play the last part of the audio again and pause after the answer *The general consensus seems to be that some …*

> **Answer**
> are fairly sure

» See Teacher's Book p.318 for Audio script 4.1.

B ▶ 4.2 Ask sts: *Do you have recurring dreams? What are they about?* Focus on the pictures. Ask: *What do you think these dreams are about?* Try to elicit that in picture 1 the car is crashing into a tree; in picture 2 a man is being followed; and in picture 3 a woman is losing her teeth. Before sts listen, discuss what they think the dreams symbolize. Play the audio for them to check, pausing after each one to peercheck and play that part again if necessary. Ask: *Have you ever had similar dreams to these?*

> **Answers**
> 1 perfectionism in your work   2 anxiety or guilt
> 3 unassertiveness

» See Teacher's Book p.319 for Audio script 4.2.

C ▶ 4.2 Go through the chart with the class. Have sts try to complete some of the chart from memory. Play the audio for them to complete the rest. Check answers.

In pairs, have sts discuss any recurring dreams they have. Sts take turns trying to interpret their partner's dream. Ask: *Is your partner's interpretation convincing?*

> **Answers**
> 1 Conversations 1 and 2   2 Conversations 2 and 3
> 3 Conversation 2   4 Conversation 1   5 Conversation 3

D ▶ 4.3 Play the audio, and elicit some suggested summaries. Agree on the best summary with the class.

Weaker classes: Allow sts to read the audio script before summarizing.

Highlight the expression used by the interviewer *take something with a grain of salt* (to consider something to be not completely true / to view with skepticism). Ask sts: *How convincing is Dr. Wallace? Do you believe that dreams can be interpreted?*

> **Suggested answer**
> Dreams do not have a universal meaning – they need a context in which to be interpreted.

» See Teacher's Book p.319 for Audio script 4.3.

E Make it personal Before you put sts in pairs, elicit a few answers to question 1, or tell the sts about a dream you have had yourself.

Put sts in pairs, and have them discuss the questions. If sts have dreamed about any of the subjects in 2, ask them to describe their dream to their partner. In turns, they can try and interpret their partner's dream.

Sts then search online for an interpretation. Ask: *How close was it to your partner's interpretation?*

Optional activity

Ask sts to remember a dream they had, either recently or at some time in the past, then record / write a paragraph describing it in as much detail as possible. Sts swap recordings / texts with a partner, and try to interpret them. In feedback, ask sts if they agree with their partner's interpretation.

» Song lyric: See Teacher's Book p.345 for notes about the song and an accompanying activity to do with the class.

4.1

2 Vocabulary: Productive suffixes

A ▶ 4.4 Read about productive suffixes with the class. Go through the examples and check understanding. Sts complete 1–6, then play the audio for them to check. Elicit that the stress is on the first word, not on the suffix. Drill pronunciation and have sts practice in pairs.

Re-play the audio and ask sts to pay attention to the pronunciation of /th/ in *thoroughly*, *through*, and *worthy*. Ask: *How is it different?* (/th/ is unvoiced in *thoroughly* and *through* and voiced in *worthy*).

> **Answers**
> 1 friendly   2 worthy   3 oriented   4 related   5 like
> 6 conscious

Tip

Vary the way you have sts practice pronunciation in pairs, e.g. they can …

– alternate: one points at a word / phrase, the other says it, then swap roles.
– one says them all to the other, who listens and suggests any improvements, swap roles.
– one says a suffix, the other remembers the word / phrase
– mouth a word / phrase silently for their partner to guess which one it is.

As ever, and especially at this level, try to work at a phrase level, not just words alone, e.g. here have them work with the examples in column 3, not just the adjectives alone.

Optional activity

For further practice, put sts in pairs. Ask one st to close his / her book, and the other st to read out a word. The partner responds with the correct suffix, and then the full example phrase as quickly as possible.

B Focus on the examples in the speech bubbles, and elicit a few example sentences to get sts started. Have sts write down their sentences, then share them in pairs. Remind them that the suffix *like* does not always have a hyphen and *worthy* never has a hyphen (refer them back to the table in A). Classcheck by asking some sts to read out their sentences to the class.

Optional activity

Ask sts to go online and use a search engine to find more words that can be used with each suffix. Sts compare their answers in pairs, then elicit what they found as a class and board the new words.

C Sts reword the phrases in italics. Peercheck. Classcheck. Board the following list of words, and ask sts to guess the meanings: *stress-related, eco-friendly, childlike, noteworthy, seaworthy, self-conscious*. Elicit other words sts know with the productive suffixes.

> **Answers**
> 1 Health-conscious people   2 A trustworthy leader
> 3 Exam-oriented teaching   4 Family-friendly entertainment
> 5 School-related programs

D Make it personal

1 ▶ 4.5 **How to say it** Go through **Committing to a point of view** with the class. Ask sts if they remember who made the comments in the *What they said* column. (1–4 Dr. Wallace, 5 – radio presenter). Have sts try to complete the chart from memory before they listen and check. Re-play the audio so sts can listen and repeat. Go through the meanings.

> **Answers**
> 1 far   2 jury   3 doubt   4 shadow   5 salt

2 Sts go through the statements in 2C and think about which they agree / disagree with. Then they write them in two columns, *"I'm convinced that …" / "I'm not entirely convinced that …"*.

3 Sts share their ideas in groups, going through the statements one by one.

Classcheck by asking sts: *Did you mostly agree / disagree? Did you use many of the How to say it expressions?*

Tip

To encourage sts to use the expressions in the box, appoint one group member as a "secretary." Ask them to monitor the conversation, and check every time one of the expressions is used. In feedback, ask the secretary to share which phrases were used in the conversation, and how each one was used.

» Workbook p.18.

♪ Never forget where you've come here from. Never pretend that it's all real. Someday soon this will all be someone else's dream

2 Vocabulary: Productive suffixes

A ▶4.4 Read about productive suffixes. Then complete 1–6 with the correct suffixes. Listen to check. Where does the stress fall?

Unlike suffixes such as *-ment*, *-ous*, *-al*, which usually change word class (for example, *enjoy*, *enjoyment*), productive suffixes can be used to create brand new words:

Suffix	Definition	Example
___-friendly	helpful or safe	a user-friendly interface
___-conscious	concerned about	a politically-conscious artist
___-oriented	directed at, focused on	a consumer-oriented company
___(-)like	similar to	a lifelike portrait
___-related	connected with	an age-related disease
___worthy	deserving of something	a newsworthy event

1 The book is thoroughly researched and very reader-_____ at the same time.
2 Your review of the current literature on dreams is especially praise _____ .
3 Highly competitive, results-_____ individuals often have this sort of dream.
4 It really sounds as if your nightmare is stress-_____ .
5 I have a recurring dream of being chased through the woods by a tall, ghost-_____ figure.
6 The more image-_____ we are, the worse it gets.

B In pairs, take turns thinking of an example for each item in column 3. Share opinions.

> I think the iPhone has a very user-friendly interface.

C Reword the phrases in italics with a suffix from A.

> I'm not sure. I think Androids are slightly more user-friendly.

1 *People who are concerned about their health* aren't fun to hang out with.
2 *A leader that you can trust* is almost impossible to find these days.
3 *Teaching that is directed at exams* does students more harm than good.
4 *Entertainment that's safe for the whole family* is almost impossible to find these days.
5 *Programs connected with school* are a great way for kids to develop independence.

D **Make it personal** Are you set in your ways? What fixed opinions do you have?

1 ▶4.5 **How to say it** Complete the chart. Listen to check.

Committing to a point of view	
What they said	What they meant
1 I wouldn't go so _____ as to (call it a masterpiece).	I wouldn't go to the extent of …
2 The _____ is still out on (whether that's true).	There's no agreement that …
3 There's no _____ in my mind that (they will).	I'm absolutely sure that …
4 Oh, yes, without a _____ of a doubt.	I'm positive.
5 We should take (these claims) with a grain of _____ .	We should be skeptical of …

2 Choose two statements from **2C** you feel strongly about. Note down a few ideas under "I'm convinced that …"/ "I'm not entirely convinced that …"
3 In groups, share your ideas. Use *How to say it* expressions. Any major disagreements?

> OK, number 1: "Health-conscious people aren't fun to hang out with" … Hmm, I wouldn't go so far as to call them boring, though.

> Well, not unless they try to change your eating habits.

39

» 4.2 Do you believe everything you're told?

3 Language in use

A ▶ 4.6 Use the photos and speech bubbles to guess what happened. Listen to check. Then choose the correct option in the heading.

The greatest [prank / misunderstanding] of all time!

Little did he know it would scare millions of people.

Not only did the creatures look hideous, they were evil, too.

Never before had a radio show caused so much panic.

Only when he realized the seriousness of the situation, did he interrupt the show.

Didn't The War of the Worlds begin as a radio show?

Yes, with actor Orson Welles. I think it might have been about …

B ▶ 4.6 Number the events in order (1–5). Listen again to check. Then look in AS 4.6 on p.162. Underline phrases that helped you decide.

☐ People tried to escape from their homes.
☐ Listeners discovered the truth and relaxed.
☐ The radio station learned about the impact of the show.
☐ The show was heavily criticized.
☐ News of the killer aliens scared listeners.

C ▶ 4.7 Match each verb (1–5) with an object (a–e). What does each phrase mean? Listen to check. Which two verbs are used figuratively?

1 throw   a ☐ a sigh of relief
2 clog   b ☐ havoc
3 flee   c ☐ someone into a frenzy
4 breathe   d ☐ the attack
5 wreak   e ☐ the highways

D In pairs, take turns telling the story from memory. Use expressions from C, making sure you know the past forms, too.

E Make it personal Have you, or has anyone you know, ever believed a science-fiction story about one of these topics? What happened as the result?

mythical creatures   the end of the world
natural disasters   transportation

When I was a kid, I believed a dragon could fly in our window. I really thought I might have to flee an attack!

Do you believe everything you're told? 4.2

Lesson Aims: Sts discuss pranks and learn how to use emphatic inversion.

Skills	Language	Vocabulary	Grammar
Listening to a radio presenter talk about a famous radio prank Discussing science-fiction stories and practical jokes	Being emphatic, e.g. *Only when you watch this movie will you fully appreciate it. Rarely have critics voted a movie "the greatest film of all time."*	prank, martian, breathe a sigh of relief, flee, wreak havoc, clog, throw someone into a frenzy	Emphatic inversion: inverted subject and verb, e.g. *Rarely do we find ... , Little did they know ... , Nowhere could they find*

Warm-up

Focus on the lesson title question and answer it yourself as an example. Sts then answer it in small groups. Board two follow-up questions for groups to add to their conversations: *Has anyone ever played a practical joke on you, or have you on someone else?* Have groups share their best answers.

3 Language in use

A ▶ 4.6 Focus on the photos and elicit all you can. Who's the man? (Orson Welles). What do you know about H.G. Wells? (English writer best known for science fiction novels, including *The Time Machine* (1895) and this one (1898). Ask: *Have you read the novel "The War of the Worlds"? What was it about?* Teach the word martian.

Focus on the speech bubbles. Ask sts to try and figure out what happened on October 30. Have them share their ideas with the class, then board their guesses, e.g. *It was a radio program, It was about War of the Worlds.* Play the audio for sts to check. Go back to sts' guesses on the board and check the ones that were correct.

Answer

A dramatized version of The War of the Worlds caused panic among many Americans who believed the events were actually happening.

» See Teacher's Book p.319 for Audio script 4.6.

B ▶ 4.6 Sts try to order the events. Play the audio for them to check. Have them look at the audio (see Student's Book p.162) and underline the relevant parts which gave them the answers. Classcheck.

Ask sts if they have heard anything like this on the radio. Ask: *What happens on April Fools' Day? Have you ever heard any April Fools' jokes / pranks on the radio? Can you imagine anything like this happening today?*

Weaker classes: Board the phrases from the audio script first, and ask sts to match them to the events. Sts then listen and put them in order.

Answers

1 News of the killer aliens scared listeners.
2 People tried to escape from their homes.
3 The radio station learned about the impact of the show.
4 Listeners discovered the truth and relaxed.
5 The show was heavily criticized.

C ▶ 4.7 Focus on verbs 1–5 and check the meanings as stand alone verbs. Have sts match them with the correct objects. Play the audio for them to check. Check pronunciation of the expressions. Re-play it and ask sts to note down the definition the cyber teacher gives for each one. Peercheck. Classcheck.

Answers

1 c 2 e 3 d 4 a 5 b
clog and breathe are used figuratively

» See Teacher's Book p.319 for Audio script 4.7.

D Before sts get into their pairs, elicit the past forms of the verbs (*threw, clogged, flew, breathed, wreaked*). In pairs, sts re-tell the story. Encourage them to prompt each other if they get stuck. You could ask each st to tell half the story.

Weaker classes: Let sts refer to the audio script.

Optional activity

Put sts in pairs, and ask them to reconstruct the story together, but add one small piece of false information. Combine pairs into groups, and ask each pair to share their version of the story with the other pair, who listens and tries to guess the false piece of information.

E Make it personal Ask: *Are you interested in science-fiction? Do you read science fiction? Were you scared of anything as a child?*

If sts have not heard any stories, then have them research some recent science fiction news stories on the Internet, e.g. sightings of UFOs or strange animals.

Put sts in pairs for a role-play. Tell sts to imagine they are on a radio program entitled "I don't believe it!" One st is the presenter, and the other st is a listener who has called in to tell an "unbelievable" story, and what happened when they were "taken in" by it.

Class feedback by asking one or two pairs to do the role play for the class. Ask: *How believable was the story? Would you have believed it?*

4.2

>> Song lyric: See Teacher's Book p.345 for notes about the song and an accompanying activity to do with the class.

4 Grammar: Emphatic inversion

A Board the word *emphatic* and elicit
- the stress on the second syllable
- the meaning (expressed with force and clarity)
- synonyms (*assertive, forceful*),
- the noun and verb with their stress on the first syllable (*emphasis, emphasise*).

Ask sts to mime inversion and elicit the meaning (*the other way around, upside down*). Then focus on the **Common Mistakes** as a way into the grammar. Ask: *Were you aware of this aspect of grammar / these mistakes? Have you made them?*

Have sts read through the grammar box. Check they understand the example sentences. Point out the use of the auxiliary (*do* and *did*). This is because the inverted question word order is used. Ask sts if they have a similar structure in their own language.

Sts check the correct rules. With regards to rule 4, clarify that, in some cases, the adverbials are really negatives, e.g. *Little did they know …* means *They didn't know*, whereas some adverbials limit the time frame, e.g. *Only when* and *not since*.

> **Answers**
>
> 1 emphasize   2 topic   3 second
> 4 negative, or in some cases, limited

>> Refer sts to the **Grammar expansion** on p.144.

B Board *Citizen Kane* and elicit all you can about the movie (a 1941 mystery drama by and starring Orson Welles, hence the link. Based loosely on the life of U.S. newspaper magnate William Randolph Hearst, it's often considered the best movie of all time.) Ask: *Have any of you heard of it / seen it? If so, what did you think of it?*

Ask sts to read the reviews of *Citizen Kane*, and circle the correct answers in column B.

Board *Little did he know it would scare millions of people* from 3A and rephrase this together. Ask sts to work through the other speech bubbles doing the same thing. Peercheck. Classcheck.

> **Answers**
>
> 1 will there be
> 2 you watch, will you
> 3 have critics voted
> 4 came out, has there been
>
> 1 He didn't know it would scare millions of people.
> 2 The creatures looked hideous and they were evil.
> 3 A radio show had never caused so much panic before.
> 4 Welles only interrupted the show when he realized the seriousness of the situation.

Optional activity

For further practice, write the following prompts at the top of a piece of paper (one prompt on each piece of paper):

Rarely do I …
Only after I've gotten home …
Little does the teacher know …
Never again will I …
Not since …

Display the pieces of paper on the walls around the classroom. Ask sts to walk around the class and complete each sentence however they want to, writing on the paper. When they have finished, put the sts into five groups and give each group one of the pieces of paper. Ask them to read the responses and correct any errors. Monitor and help where necessary. When they have finished, ask each group to choose their three favorite responses and share them with the class.

C Ask sts to read the title of the text. To teach the word prank, use the photo and speech bubble beside 4D. Ask *What's happened? What's a prank?* (a practical joke or mischievous act). Ask: *What is the best April Fools' joke anyone has played on you?* Have sts discuss in pairs. Ask: *Have you ever played an April Fools' joke on anyone else?* Have sts report back any good jokes to the class.

Have sts rewrite 1–4. Peercheck. Classcheck. Ask: *What was your favorite prank?*

> **Answers**
>
> 1 No longer would train travel be sedentary.
> 2 Only after the plane had landed did they realize it was a prank.
> 3 Not only were people shocked, but they were also outraged.
> 4 Not since the invention of TV had there been such a creative prank.

D Make it personal Sts can do their research in class or for homework. After sts have shared their pranks in groups, have each group vote for the best one. Ask a spokesperson for each group to relate it to the rest of the class. Have a class vote.

As follow-up, in pairs, ask sts to imagine they are going to play an April Fool's prank on the head of the school. Ask them to plan it together. Have sts share their ideas with the class. Ask: *Which do you think would be the best? How do you think the head would react?*

>> Workbook p.19.

♪ Never in my wildest dreams, Did I think someone could care about me

4 Grammar: Emphatic inversion

A Read the grammar box and check (✔) the correct rules.

Emphatic inversion: Inverted subject and verb	
Rarely **do we find**	such realistic sound effects.
Little **did they know**	what the show would cause.
Nowhere **could they find**	the cause of the panic.
Only after the scandal had blown over,	**was he** asked to direct *Citizen Kane*.
Not since CBS aired the show,	**has there been** so much excitement.

1. Inversion is used with adverbs and adverbial expressions to ☐ emphasize ☐ de-emphasize what you are saying. It is especially common in writing.
2. Whether inversion is possible is determined by the ☐ topic ☐ adverb or adverbial expression.
3. With *only after / when, not since,* etc., inversion is always in the ☐ first ☐ second clause.
4. The adverbials in italics have a ☐ positive ☐ negative or, in some cases, limiting meaning.

>> Grammar expansion p.144

Common mistakes
I watched
Only when ~~did I watch~~ the movie, did I appreciate it.
did I watch
Not only ~~I watched~~ it six times, but I memorized the script.

B Circle the correct answers in column B. Then rephrase the sentences from 3A so they are neutral.

Orson Welles' *Citizen Kane:* **What the reviewers have said**

A: Neutral	B: Emphatic
1 There'll never be such an excellent script again!	Never again [will there be / there will be] such an excellent script.
2 You'll only fully appreciate this movie when you watch it.	Only when [you watch / do you watch] this movie, [you will / will you] fully appreciate it.
3 Critics have rarely voted a film "the greatest film of all time."	Rarely [have critics voted / critics have voted] a film "the greatest film of all time."
4 There hasn't been such a critical success since the movie came out.	Not since the movie [did come out / came out] [has there been / there has been] such a critical success.

C Rewrite 1–4 starting with the adverbials in parentheses. What was your favorite prank?

The most epic April Fools' day pranks of all time!

2015: A train company announced that it had plans to replace conventional seats with state-of-the-art gym equipment. (1) *Train travel would no longer be sedentary* (no longer)!

1992: Passengers approaching Los Angeles airport were shocked to see a huge banner welcoming them to Chicago! (2) *They only realized it was a prank after the plane had landed.* (only after)

1980: A TV station reported that London's iconic Big Ben was going to be turned into a digital clock. (3) *People were not only shocked, but they were also outraged.* (not only)

1957: A news program had convinced viewers that spaghetti could grow on trees. (4) *There had not been such a creative prank since the invention of TV.* (not since)

D 🌐 **Make it personal** Search on "April Fools' pranks" and share your best two in groups. Which one was funniest?

This guy bought colored post-it notes and covered his friend's car. So not only did she not recognize her own car, but she also thought it was a wedding decoration.

4.3 When did you last hear something illogical?

5 Vocabulary: Nouns and adjectives from phrasal verbs

A Read *Synonyms for nouns and adjectives from phrasal verbs*. Then circle five more examples in the headlines below and draw an arrow connecting them to their synonyms.

> **Synonyms for nouns and adjectives from phrasal verbs**
>
> Nouns and adjectives formed from phrasal verbs often have neutral or slightly more formal one-word synonyms:
> We've had two burglaries this year. I'm of tired of these **break-ins** (n). We need to beef up security. (= Someone **broke in**.)
> Even computers can be disposable. Most companies these days are producing **throwaway** laptops with cheap plastic bodies. (= That we **throw away**.)
>
> Remember: Some words formed from phrasal verbs are hyphenated, and some are one word. The stress is on the first syllable.

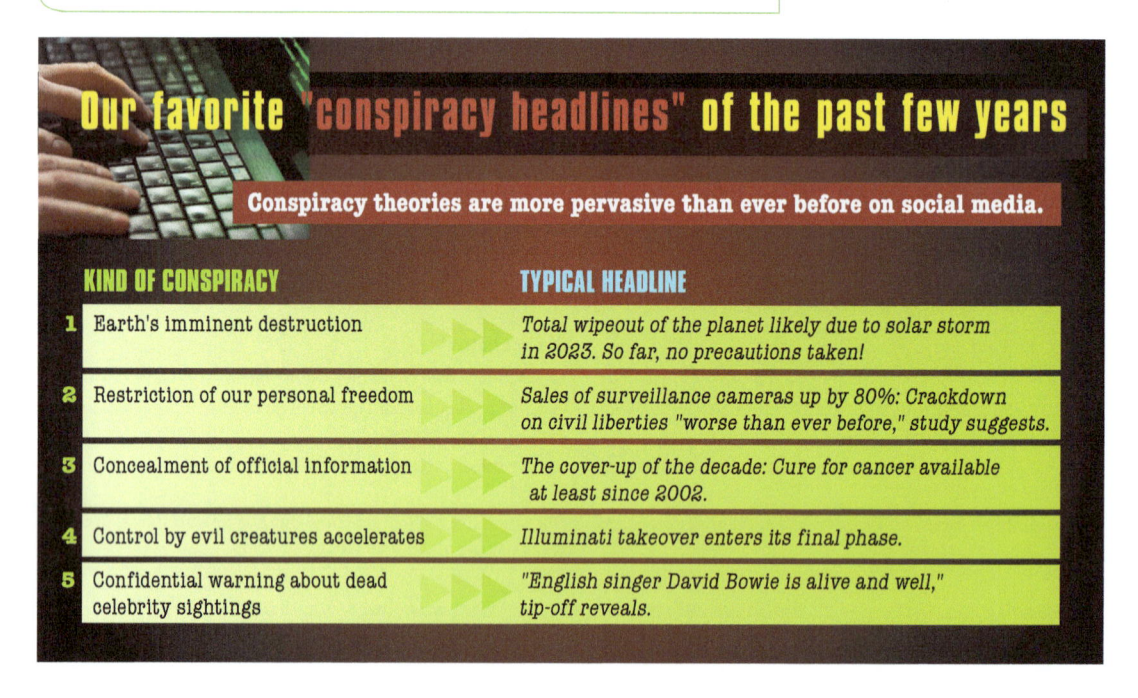

Our favorite "conspiracy headlines" of the past few years

Conspiracy theories are more pervasive than ever before on social media.

	KIND OF CONSPIRACY	TYPICAL HEADLINE
1	Earth's imminent destruction	Total wipeout of the planet likely due to solar storm in 2023. So far, no precautions taken!
2	Restriction of our personal freedom	Sales of surveillance cameras up by 80%: Crackdown on civil liberties "worse than ever before," study suggests.
3	Concealment of official information	The cover-up of the decade: Cure for cancer available at least since 2002.
4	Control by evil creatures accelerates	Illuminati takeover enters its final phase.
5	Confidential warning about dead celebrity sightings	"English singer David Bowie is alive and well," tip-off reveals.

B Complete 1–5 with the phrasal verb form of the words you circled in the headlines in **A**. Then change the sentences, if necessary, so they're true for you.

1 Where I live, if you witness a crime, it's easy to _____ _____ the police anonymously.
2 The police should _____ _____ on graffiti artists. Enough is enough!
3 I suspect the truth behind the side effects of many drugs has been _____ _____ by drug companies.
4 I'm not entirely convinced dinosaurs were _____ _____ by an asteroid.
5 I'm sure tech companies are trying to _____ _____ the world.

> I doubt tech companies are trying to take over the world. They're only offering products we want.

C **Make it personal** In pairs, answer 1–3. Who's more skeptical of conspiracy theories?

1 Which conspiracy theories from **3** are you familiar with? Which are the most outlandish / plausible?
2 🌐 Search online for conspiracy theories. Share your favorite ones.
3 Why are some people attracted to these theories?

> I think some people are suspicious by nature, and so they love these kinds of theories.

When did you last hear something illogical? 4.3

Lesson Aims: Sts discuss conspiracy theories using tentative language and read about cognitive bias.

Skills	Language	Vocabulary
Reading an article about cognitive bias	Using tentative language in academic writing, e.g. *Most writers tend to avoid making generalizations. You are more likely to believe that …*	Nouns and adjectives from phrasal verbs, e.g. *break-in, throwaway*

Warm-up

Board the word *illogical* and elicit pronunciation, meaning, and synonyms: lacking sense or clear reasoning, unreasonable, unjustified. Board the lesson title question and answer it yourself with a locally relevant example to help sts prepare, e.g. something the government has said which is hard to believe. Put sts in pairs to share their own answers, adding more questions: *Do you accept everything you hear / read? Are you very skeptical?* If sts get stuck for ideas, ask if they know the conspiracy theories surrounding the deaths of, e.g. JFK, Princess Diana. If interested, they can research them on the internet.

Background information

Theories surrounding **Lady Di**'s death in 1997 include a plot by MI6 to kill her because she was a threat to the throne, and faking her own death to escape media attention, and retreat into an anonymous life.

Amongst those accused of carrying out **J.F. Kennedy**'s murder in 1963 are the Russian president, JFK's driver, the Mafia, his bodyguard, and even his wife.

» Song lyric: See Teacher's Book p.345 for notes about the song and an accompanying activity to do with the class.

5 Vocabulary: Nouns and adjectives from phrasal verbs

A As a warm-up, board these nouns and adjectives: *backup* (n), *breakdown* (n), *giveaway* (adj), *takeaway* (adj), *sleepover* (n), *check-in* (adj). Ask sts to guess the meanings or look them up in a dictionary. Elicit nouns to go with the adjectives (takeaway food, giveaway services, check-in desk).

Read **Synonyms for nouns and adjectives from phrasal verbs** together with the class and check understanding. Model pronunciation and highlight the stress BREAK-in, THROWaway.

Have sts read the title of the text and discuss the meaning of *pervasive* (spreading throughout something to become an obvious feature of it, usually negative).

Ask sts to find examples of phrasal nouns and adjectives, and match them with their synonyms. Peercheck. Classcheck.

Elicit other phrasal nouns and adjectives that sts might know, e.g. *check-up* (n), *walkout* (n), *break through* (n), *cover-up, wake-up* (call), *wind up* (clock).

For fun, have sts read out the headlines in the voice of a newsreader. Encourage them to be dramatic. If possible, have them record them.

Answers
1 wipeout (destruction)   2 crackdown (restriction)
3 cover-up (concealment)   2 takeover (control)
5 tip-off (warning)

B Have sts read sentences 1–5. Check they understand the meaning of *witness* in 1 (= see an event, typically a crime or accident) and *side effects* in 3 (secondary, typically undesirable, effect of a drug).

Sts complete the sentences. Point out that they may need to change the form of the verb. Ask sts to change the sentences so they are true for them. Focus on the model in the speech bubble, and elicit a few answers to 1 as examples, e.g. *Where I live, it isn't easy to tip off the police. Where I live it's also easy to tip off the police.* Classcheck.

Answers
1 tip off   2 crack down   3 covered up   4 wiped out
5 take over

C Make it personal Ask: *Why do you think conspiracy headlines are more common these days?* Discuss the influence of social media and the increase in news sources, many unofficial, and the need to grab headlines, sometimes for political gains.

Check understanding of *outlandish* (weird or odd) and *plausible* (credible). The best way to do this is by establishing their opposites (normal, unbelievable). Put sts in pairs to discuss the questions.

Optional activity

Put sts in pairs, and ask them to choose one of the conspiracy theories they researched online and prepare a short presentation, arguing the case for the conspiracy theory. Each pair then presents the case to the class, who ask questions to find out more information. After each presentation, hold a class vote to see how many people believe the conspiracy theory.

4.3

6 Reading

A Focus on the title of the text. Ask: *Are you more likely or less likely to believe in conspiracy theories? What do you think makes people believe in them?*

Sts re-read question 3 in 5C, read the first paragraph and check the correct option.

> **Answer**
>
> Because they have a natural tendency to look for meaning in random events

Tip

Before reading on, have the class predict first in pairs, then as a group what the rest of the text might say. This will give check their comprehension of the first paragraph and give an idea of their enthusiasm for the text / topic. Then, rather than read it all, assign the remaining four paragraphs, one each, to sts in groups of four, numbered Student A, B, C, and D. Each of them reads their paragraph and reports its contents back to the rest of the group. Monitor to see how much they have understood and can say after this first reading, but resist explaining new vocabulary for now. Remind sts they're unlikely ever to understand every word in an authentic text like this.

B ▶ 4.8 Read the instructions to the class and ensure sts understand the task they have to do (to identify which of the remaining five paragraphs mention each type of cognitive bias; the answer is para 2, 3, and 4). Get them to cover quotes 1–3 for now.

Elicit meaning and pronunciation of *bias* (partiality, prejudice for one group over another). Sts will almost certainly seek a translation, so help them to do so, e.g. letting them look the word up. Ask: *Any ideas what terms a, b, and c mean?* Encourage sts to guess / try to explain before they read.

Sts read and listen to the whole article to find the meanings of terms a–c. As a secondary task, tell them to remember the pronunciation and stress on the words highlighted in pink.

Uncover the quotes. In pairs, sts do the matching task. Monitor and help any weaker sts who may be struggling with the complexity of the language and ideas. Classcheck. Seek feedback and personalize the quotes. Ask: *How hard was that? What did you learn? What do you think about the ideas expressed in the text? Are the psychologist's arguments persuasive? Do you agree with quote 1? Did you like Bowie's music? When did he "die"?* (January 10th, 2016, of liver cancer) *Do you think cell phones are bad for your health? Can you think of any examples where you have seen this bias come into play? Or have you experienced any of these types of bias yourself?*

> **Answers**
>
> 1 c   2 b   3 a

Optional activity

Sts think of their own examples for each type of cognitive bias. They then read out their examples to a partner for them to guess which type of bias it exemplifies.

C Read through **Tentative language** with the class. Check understanding. Elicit other examples of "tentative language," e.g. *perhaps, maybe, to some extent, to a large degree, probably, is / are inclined to, be liable to*. Ask sts what equivalent words there are in their language. Have sts go through and underline examples in the text. Classcheck.

> **Answers**
>
> Paragraph 1: conspiracy beliefs <u>can occasionally</u> be based on / <u>most</u> of the time they are not / We <u>sometimes</u>, however, see patterns
>
> Paragraph 2: The attractiveness of conspiracy theories <u>may</u> arise / the subject of conspiracy theories <u>tend to</u> be intrinsically complex / The real-world events that often / Early reports <u>may</u> contain errors
>
> Paragraph 3: <u>may</u> also explain our <u>tendency</u> to accept conspiracies / This is one reason <u>many</u> people
>
> Paragraph 4: People who endorse conspiracy theories may be more <u>likely</u> to engage / it <u>may</u> seem natural / more <u>likely</u> to endorse mutually contradictory theories / you are also more <u>likely</u> to believe that he is still alive.
>
> Paragraph 5: None of the above <u>should</u> indicate / <u>Some may</u> indeed turn out to be true / The point is that <u>some</u> individuals may have a <u>tendency</u> to find such theories attractive

D Make it personal Read through the instructions, and check sts understand what to do. You could add a few more words to the list, e.g. *Rihanna, beards, miniskirts, political correctness, smoking*. Go through the models in the speech bubbles. Highlight the use of the verb form (*be biased*). Tell sts they can also use *unfair, one-sided, unreasonable*.

Board the following expressions sts can also use in their discussions:

In my mind ... is associated with ..., Whenever I hear ..., ... comes to mind ...

Elicit a few examples using these expressions, e.g. *In my mind beards are associated with the hippy era.*

Monitor and collect examples of good and erroneous language use to give them some feedback at the end. Classcheck each group's conclusions about each other's biases! Who has the most prejudices?

» Workbook p.20.

> ♪ But then they sent me away to teach me how to be sensible. Logical, responsible, practical

6 Reading

A Read paragraph 1 of the article. How would the author answer question 3 in 5C?

- [ ] Because they have a natural tendency to look for meaning in random events.
- [ ] Because the evidence the theories are based on can be misleading.

Why Do Some People Believe in Conspiracy Theories?

Christopher French, a professor of psychology at Goldsmiths, University of London, explains:

Although conspiracy beliefs can occasionally be based on a rational analysis of the evidence, most of the time they are not. As a species, one of our greatest strengths is our ability to find meaningful patterns in the world around us and to make causal inferences. We sometimes, however, see patterns and causal connections that are not there, especially when we feel that events are beyond our control.

The attractiveness of conspiracy theories may arise from a number of cognitive biases that characterize the way we process information. "Confirmation bias" is the most pervasive cognitive bias and a powerful driver of belief in conspiracies. We all have a natural inclination to give more weight to evidence that supports what we already believe and ignore evidence that contradicts our beliefs. The real-world events that often become the subject of conspiracy theories tend to be intrinsically complex and unclear. Early reports may contain errors, contradictions and ambiguities, and those wishing to find evidence of a cover-up will focus on such inconsistencies to bolster their claims.

"Proportionality bias," our innate tendency to assume that big events have big causes, may also explain our tendency to accept conspiracies. This is one reason many people were uncomfortable with the idea that President John F. Kennedy was the victim of a deranged lone gunman and found it easier to accept the theory that he was the victim of a large-scale conspiracy.

Another relevant cognitive bias is "projection." People who endorse conspiracy theories may be more likely to engage in conspiratorial behaviors themselves, such as spreading rumors or tending to be suspicious of others' motives. If you would engage in such behavior, it may seem natural that other people would as well, making conspiracies appear more plausible and widespread. Furthermore, people who are strongly inclined toward conspiratorial thinking will be more likely to endorse mutually contradictory theories. For example, if you believe that Osama bin Laden was killed many years before the American government officially announced his death, you are also more likely to believe that he is still alive.

None of the above should indicate that all conspiracy theories are false. Some may indeed turn out to be true. The point is that some individuals may have a tendency to find such theories attractive. The crux of the matter is that conspiracists are not really sure what the true explanation of an event is – they are simply certain that the "official story" is a cover-up.

B ▶ 4.8 A *cognitive bias* is a tendency to confuse our subjective perceptions with reality. Listen to and read the article. Match the quotes (1–3) to the types of cognitive bias in the article (a–c).

| a confirmation bias | b proportionality bias | c projection |

1. [ ] "I'm sure our politicians are spying on us. If I were in charge, I'm sure I would do the same."
2. [ ] "A legend like David Bowie couldn't have died just like that without our knowing he was sick. Something smells fishy."
3. [ ] "I get severe headaches whenever I use my phone a lot. I've always believed in the the dangers of radiation."

C Read *Tentative language*. Underline two examples in each paragraph in the article.

> **Tentative language**
>
> Academic writing is **often** based on hypotheses and interpretation. Therefore, **most** writers **tend** to avoid making generalizations and being too assertive, which **might** put readers off. The words in bold (e.g. modals, adverbs, quantifiers) are examples of how writers use tentative language to show they aren't 100% certain.

D Make it personal What are *your* biases?

1. In groups, read each word in turn and say <u>the very first word</u> that comes to mind.

   cooking   fitness   Hollywood   smartphones
   Lady Gaga   politics   soccer   taxi drivers

2. Which words, if any, reveal(s) a hidden bias?

> Taxi drivers conjure up images of speeding!

> I think that's biased. Some drive very carefully.

4.4 How would you describe your personality?

7 Language in use

A 🌐 Look at the eyes and pick the one you're immediately drawn to. Then search on "eye personality test" and read the results on one of the sites you find. Are they accurate for you?

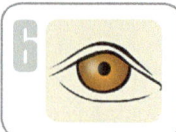

1. 2. 3. 4. 5. 6. 7. 8. 9.

> I chose the first one. It says I'm an open, kind spirit who welcomes everyone into my life.

B ▶ 4.9 Listen to the start of an interview with a psychologist. How does he feel about the test in A? Do you agree?

C ▶ 4.10 Listen to the rest. Why is he skeptical of personality tests? Check (✔) the points he makes.

1 People's personalities …
a ☐ are sometimes contradictory.
b ☐ are influenced by life events.
c ☐ can be captured better in interviews than tests.

2 Employee personality tests …
a ☐ haven't been updated in years.
b ☐ may be used inappropriately.
c ☐ can't predict performance accurately.

D ▶ 4.11 Read *Pronouncing the letter s*. Then write /s/ or /z/ next to the highlighted letters in 1–4. Listen to check.

> **Pronouncing the letter *s***
>
> The letter *s* is tricky. We say *a**ss**ume* /s/, but *po**ss**ess* /z/; *ba**s**e* /s/, but *pha**s**e* /z/. These simple rules will help you. Say …
> • /s/ in the suffix *sis*: *ba**sis*** and in the prefix *dis*: *dis**advantage*.
> • /z/ in the suffix *sm*: *sarca**sm***.
> • /z/ for a verb (*u**s**e a pen*) and /s/ for a noun or adjective (*make u**s**e of it*) in homographs.

1 It depends on the kind of research on which the test was ba**s**ed ☐ and on the subsequent data analy**s**is ☐.
2 The web is full of amateur tests, all of which have come in for a lot of critici**s**m ☐ in recent years.
3 These tests provide vague personality descriptions, with which it's hard to di**s**agree ☐.
4 I interviewed over a hundred recruiting managers, some of whom admitted to using test results as an excu**s**e ☐ not to hire or promote someone.

E **Make it personal** In pairs, how do you feel about …? Be sure to pronounce the bold words correctly.

fad diets   faith-healing   fortune-telling   horoscopes   self-help books   telepathy

> I (don't) think … make(s) sense. I can('t) understand people's **skepticism**!
> Once I … and I was(n't) **disappointed**. What happened was …
> Most of my friends would **disagree** with me, but …
> The **hypothesis** that … sounds … to me. For one thing …
> I don't think you can **use** … to …

> Most of my friends would disagree with me, but I don't think you can use the argument that fad diets are better than no diet.

44

How would you describe your personality? 4.4

Lesson Aims: Sts learn vocabulary to talk about personality and discuss the reliability of personality tests.

Skills	Vocabulary	Grammar
Reading a short text about classifying personalities Discussing which qualities and characteristics they most value	Personality adjectives, e.g. *imaginative, adventurous, reliable, thorough, self-disciplined, kind, cooperative, sympathetic, anxious*	Formal relative clauses, e.g. *I prefer to read books and articles **from which** I can derive new insights.*

Warm-up

Board as a two-column heading *Adjectives to describe personality, Positive and Negative*. In pairs, sts brainstorm as many as they can for each column. Feedback their answers, adding in *unreasonable, obnoxious, bossy, inconsiderate, selfish, controlling, opinionated, childish, arrogant, temperamental, rude* with stress-marked, to review / pre-teach them. The best way to do this is by asking for opposites and synonyms.

Then ask the lesson title question: *How would you describe your personality?* In pairs, they tell each other. Classcheck any fun answers.

7 Language in use

A When sts have chosen their eyes, board the following adjectives: *open, mysterious, conscientious, philosophical, fiery, tortured, sensitive, eccentric, intuitive*. Discuss the meanings. Ask: *Which of these adjectives would you use to describe yourself?* Sts search online for the results of the personality test, and check if they were right. Have them compare the results with their partner. Class feedback. Ask: *Do you think the test is accurate?*

B ▶ 4.9 Play the audio, and elicit that the psychologist is skeptical / dismissive. Have sts say whether they agree or disagree with this point of view.

Answer

The psychologist is dismissive.

▶ See Teacher's Book p.320 for Audio script 4.9.

Background information

The psychologist refers to the *Myers-Briggs Type Indicator* (MBTI) – a personality test designed by Katharine Cook Briggs and Isabel Briggs Myers, based on a theory proposed by Carl Jung. It assumes that there are different ways in which humans experience the world, and that one of these is dominant for certain types of personalities most of the time. Its use is popular with employers, though it has shortcomings in terms of reliability and validity.

C ▶ 4.10 Read through the two lists of points made by the psychologist, and check understanding. Pre-teach *rigorous* (extremely thorough and careful) and *recruiting manager* (person in charge of finding new staff).

Play the audio and ask sts to check the points the psychologist makes. Classcheck.

Class feedback. Ask sts: *Have you ever done a personality test for a job or school place? Do you think they have any value?*

Answers

1 a and b   2 b and c

▶ See Teacher's Book p.320 for audio script 4.10.

▶ Song lyric: See Teacher's Book p.345 for notes about the song and an accompanying activity to do with the class.

D ▶ 4.11 Read through **Pronouncing the letter s** with the sts. Sts write /s/ or /z/ next to the highlighted letters in 1–4 based on the rules in the box. Play the audio for them to check. Check answers. Drill the pronunciation of the highlighted words, by pausing after each word in the audio, and having sts repeat.

Point out that when we use *excuse* as a verb, we pronounce the *s* as /z/, e.g. *He excused me for being late.*

Stronger classes: Ask sts to list other words with /s/ and /z/ sounds, checking in a dictionary if they aren't sure.

Answers

1 s, s   2 z   3 s   4 s

Optional activity

For further practice, put sts in small groups, and assign the /s/ sound to half the groups, and the /z/ sound to the other half. Give them two minutes to think of as many words with these sounds as they can. Put pairs into groups to share their words.

E **Make it personal** Brainstorm a few ideas together with the class. Ask sts: *Have you ever been to a faith-healer or fortune teller? Do you read horoscopes / self-help books? Do you believe in telepathy?* Have sts discuss each of the topics in pairs. Encourage them to use the language in the box, and refer them to the model in the speech bubble as an example.

Class feedback. Invite some sts to report back to their class what they learned about their partner's views.

4.4

8 Grammar: Formal relative clauses

A Go through the grammar box with the class. Check understanding. Sts complete the rules. Clarify the meaning of *non-restrictive clause* in rule 3 (The clause is adding extra information about the noun, Dr. Cooper, i.e. the sentence makes sense without it. In the other examples the clause is necessary to define the noun.)

Refer sts back to **7D**, and ask them to underline the relative pronoun in each sentence. Then say which noun it refers to. Classcheck.

> **Answers**
> 1 before   2 whom, which   3 comma
> From **7D**:
> 1 on which refers to "the kind of research"
> 2 all of which refers to "amateur tests"
> 3 with which refers to "vague personality descriptions"
> 4 some of which refers to "over a hundred recruiting managers"

» Refer sts to the **Grammar expansion** on p.144.

Tip

A good way to help sts to remember these complex terms / ideas is to explore the name, e.g. Ask: *What do you associate with the word "relative"?* (a person connected by blood or marriage). *What does it mean in grammar terms?* (a pronoun, determiner, or adverb connected / referring to something already expressed or implicit) *What does restrictive mean?* (limiting) *And non-restrictive?* (no limit, non-specific). Use the **Common mistake** to highlight the degrees of formality.

B Focus on the title of the text. Ask sts what they think the "Big 5" refers to. Ask: *What does the image make you think of?* to help them brainstorm ideas.

Before doing the unscrambling task, have them quickly read through the whole text to get the gist. Sts work individually to unscramble the words in parentheses. Peercheck. Classcheck.

Check the meaning of any unknown words in the text, and elicit the adjectival forms and pronunciation of *reliability, thoroughness, self-discipline, anxiety, anger,* and *depression* (*reliable, thorough, self-disciplined, anxious, angry,* and *depressed*). Ask: *Which two categories do you think you fit into best?*

Weaker classes: You could tell sts what the extra words are before they do the unscrambling task to make it easier.

> **Answers**
> 1 into which our personalities can be classified (extra word – that)
> 2 to which someone is curious (extra word – what)
> 3 with which conscientiousness is often associated (extra word – whom)
> 4 with whom they can exchange ideas (extra word – who)
> 5 on whom we can usually count (extra word – which)
> 6 with which an individual experiences (extra word – that)

C Have sts do the completion task. Classcheck. Model and drill the stress and pronunciation of *kindness, ethics, empathy,* and *approach*.

Ask sts to rank the values themselves (1 = most important, 5 = least important), then compare with a partner. Ask: *Do you and your partner share the same values? How similar are your answers to the survey results?*

> **Answers**
> 1 with which   2 with which   3 with whom   4 on which
> 5 to / towards whom

Optional activities

- Have sts design their own "personality test" in pairs. Ask them to first decide on four personality types, then decide which things might represent each type, e.g. eye color, what they do to relax, favorite food, etc. Stress that it's lighthearted so doesn't need to be accurate. Get them to write a sentence for each personality type using the language in **A**, and the sentences in **C** as a model. Monitor and help where necessary. When they have finished, combine pairs into groups of four, and have them try out their tests on each other.

- A simple game to play at any time to review adjectives of personality is to ask sts to write down the first three they can think of. Then tell them it was a Personality test! The first one they wrote was *How they see themselves*, the second *How others see them*, and the third the truth, *How they really are!*

D Make it personal Focus on the list. Ask: *Which of these items have you had to choose recently? How did you decide? Why did you decide to come to this school?*

Put sts in groups to discuss the question *What do you value the most when choosing a ...?*

Weaker classes: You could allow sts to write down their sentences before they get together in groups.

Monitor around the class and encourage sts to use formal relative clauses where appropriate. Classcheck by inviting sts to share their opinions with the rest of the class. Ask: *Were there any disagreements?*

» Workbook p.21.

♪ I don't wanna close my eyes, I don't want to fall asleep. 'Cause I'd miss you baby and I don't want to miss a thing

4.4

8 Grammar: Formal relative clauses

A Read the grammar box and complete rules 1–3. Then look at 1–4 in **7D** and say which nouns *which* and *whom* refer to.

> **Formal relative clauses with *which* and *whom***
>
> | A hundred **people** were surveyed, | **most of whom** regularly take personality tests. |
> | Most tests are based on **theories** | **about which** very little is known. |
> | I'd like to thank **Dr. Cooper**, | **without whom** this study wouldn't have been possible. |
> | I prefer to read **books** and **articles** | **from which** I can derive new insights. |
>
> In formal relative clauses …
> 1 the preposition goes _____ the relative pronoun.
> 2 we use the pronoun _____ for people and _____ for things.
> 3 a non-restrictive clause is preceded by a _____.

» Grammar expansion p.144

B Unscramble the bold words in 1–6 using formal relative clauses. There's one extra word in each group.

> **Common mistake**
> ✓ (that) the movie is based **on**. (neutral)
> ✓ **on which** the movie is based. (more formal)
> This is the book ~~(that)~~ the movie is based.

The "Big 5"

The Five Factor Model is based on the idea that there are five broad domains ¹[which / our / can / personalities / that / into / be / classified]:

1 Openness to experience: This describes the extent ²[which / to / what / someone / curious / is], imaginative, and adventurous. Can he or she "think outside the box?"

2 Conscientiousness: Reliability, thoroughness, and self-discipline are traits ³[whom / with / often / is / conscientiousness / which / associated].

3 Extroversion: Extroverts thrive on social interaction and seek the company of people ⁴[who / exchange / can / they / with / ideas / whom].

4 Agreeableness: These individuals, ⁵[on / which / we / count / usually / whom / can] in times of trouble, tend to be kind, cooperative, and sympathetic.

5 Neuroticism: This trait refers to the frequency ⁶[that / with / an / which / experiences / individual] negative emotions. e.g anxiety, anger, or depression.

C Complete the survey results with *which*, *whom*, and a preposition. How would *you* personally rank 1–5?

> **What do you value the most when choosing a boyfriend / girlfriend? Our survey results:**
>
> | | Number 1 for % of responses |
> |---|---|
> | 1 The kindness _____ _____ they treat pets. | 15 |
> | 2 The creativity _____ _____ they approach their job. | 25 |
> | 3 The friends _____ _____ they surround themselves. | 55 |
> | 4 The sense of ethics _____ _____ they base their lives. | 75 |
> | 5 The people _____ _____ they show empathy. | 90 |

D Make it personal In groups, answer the question and list at least three qualities or characteristics. Use formal relative clauses where possible. Similar opinions?

What do you value the most when choosing a(n) …?

> Doctors? I value the empathy with which they treat their patients.

airline   bank   doctor / dentist   friend   language school   roommate   vacation spot

45

4.5 Would you ever hire a former criminal?

9 Listening

A ▶ 4.12 In pairs, guess two reasons for 1–2. Then listen to the first part of a conversation between Julie and Seth to check.

> Should an employer have a right to know if an applicant has a criminal record?
> 1 Yes, because … 2 No, because …

B ▶ 4.13 Listen to the rest. Match topics 1–4 with arguments in favor of censorship a–e. There's one extra argument.

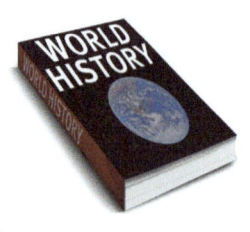

1 sensitive government information
2 Internet sites
3 books
4 history

a ☐ Too many details might erode trust.
b ☐ Too much can make you nervous.
c ☐ The more control, the better.
d ☐ They might be too upsetting.
e ☐ Kids lack the maturity to evaluate them.

C In pairs, can you remember Seth's four arguments <u>against</u> censorship? Check in AS 4.13 on p.162 and underline them.

D ▶ 4.14 Match the sentence halves. Listen to check. Which of the highlighted expressions did you know?

1 You should be up front about
2 The truth always comes out when your
3 A company has to hire you
4 We have no need to see
5 I want to know what my government
6 If we conceal information,
7 Shouldn't some novels be banned from

a ☐ sensitive government documents.
b ☐ boss starts to wonder why you're secretive.
c ☐ kids will be suspicious.
d ☐ a prior conviction.
e ☐ with all the information on the table.
f ☐ is up to.
g ☐ school?

10 Keep talking

A Choose a topic from 9A or B, and decide if you are for or against censorship. Note down at least three arguments to support your position.

B **Make it personal** In groups, present your arguments using the expressions below and in 9D. Whose are the most convincing?

> Rarely do we … That may be, but … That's my whole point.
> There's no such thing as … I'm 100% opposed to … At the very least, it can …

> Schools shouldn't censor what students read. Rarely do kids suffer from overexposure to ideas!

> That may be, but teachers might still have to conceal some information.

46

Would you ever hire a former criminal? 4.5

Lesson Aims: Sts talk about censorship, and the rights of employers to be told about potential employees' past convictions.

Skills	Language	Vocabulary
Listening to two friends having a discussion about censorship Writing a letter to the editor of a newspaper presenting an argument	Phrases for presenting an argument verbally, e.g. *Rarely do we ..., That may be, but ..., That's my whole point, There's no such thing as ... I'm 100% opposed to ..., At the very least, it can ...* Phrases for supporting an argument in writing, e.g. *Contrary to popular belief ..., There is some debate as to whether ...*	be up front, conceal information, censorship, openness

Warm-up

Board six crimes, e.g. burglary, piracy, kidnapping, theft, smuggling, and corruption and get sts in pairs to put them in order of seriousness, from 1–6. Classcheck. Ask: *Which ones are worthy of prison? If so, for how long?* and discuss opinions. Then ask the lesson title question for them to discuss further. For fun, ban them from saying "It depends," so they have to give more concrete examples!

» Song lyric: See Teacher's Book p.346 for notes about the song and an accompanying activity to do with the class.

9 Listening

A ▶ 4.12 Ask: *Do you think ex-convicts should be required by law to reveal their past crime(s)? In what circumstances? Should it always depend on the conviction? How would you feel if a friend of yours revealed they had a past conviction that you had not previously known about?* Have sts discuss in pairs.

Focus on the question in the box. Elicit sts' opinions. Explain that they will hear Julie and Seth discussing a survey they are doing which includes the question in the box. Play the audio, and ask sts to find out which of them answers Yes (Seth), and which answers No (Julie). Re-play the audio and have sts listen out for the reasons they give. Check answers. Ask: *Who do you agree with?*

Answers

1 Yes, because an employer needs to have all the facts with which to make a decision.
2 No, because once you've served your time, you're not a criminal any longer.

» See Teacher's Book p.320 for Audio script 4.12.

B ▶ 4.13 Focus on the photos. Ask sts: *How do you think they are related to censorship?* Encourage sts to guess. Before listening, have sts read through the reasons a–e. Check the meaning of *erode* (gradually destroy). Ask: *What do you think these reasons refer to?* Play the audio for sts to check. Classcheck and play it again, if necessary.

Answers

1 b 2 e 3 d 4 a

» See Teacher's Book p.320 for Audio script 4.13.

C Have sts try to remember the four arguments, then refer them to the Audio script to check (see Student's Book p.162). Peercheck. Classcheck.

Class feedback. Ask: *Do you agree / disagree with his arguments? Why? Are there any other areas where you think that censorship is justified, e.g. TV or movies?*

Answers

1 I want to know what my government is up to. I'm not in favor of Big Brother!
2 Seldom do kids not respond well when their parents trust them.
3 Kids will be more resilient if they know what the real world is like!
4 If we conceal information, kids will be suspicious as soon as they find out.

D ▶ 4.14 Sts match the sentence halves. Encourage them to do this from memory, and also by considering which halves go together grammatically. Play the audio for sts to check their answers.

Answers

1 d 2 b 3 e 4 a 5 f 6 c 7 g

10 Keep talking

A Have sts choose two topics from: criminal records, sensitive government information, internet sites, books and history. Tell them to think about whether they are for or against censorship of these things. Encourage them to choose one for and one against if possible. Sts note down their reasons.

Optional activity

If sts are having difficulty thinking of ideas, give them a few minutes to search online using their mobile devices to find possible reasons for and against.

B Make it personal Go through the phrases in the box and the models in the speech bubbles. Put sts into groups to present their ideas. Monitor and give help where necessary. When they have finished, ask one or two sts to present their ideas to the whole class. Class feedback. Ask: *Do you mostly agree / disagree with your classmates? Are most people in this class for or against censorship?* You could carry out a class survey, and have sts vote For or Against for each of the topics.

4.5

11 Writing: A letter to the editor

A As a warm-up, ask: *Have you (or has anyone you know) ever posted a comment on a newspaper website, or tweeted? Or an email? Or even a letter to an editor of a newspaper? What was it about?* Then tell them that this is their chance!

Give students two minutes to quickly read the letter, then in pairs share all they remember about Julie and her point of view.

Ask: *What is the purpose of a thesis statement?* (It presents the main idea of a writing assignment and, at the same time, should reflect the opinion of the writer).

Then let them re-read the letter and answer questions 1–3.

Weaker classes: Allow sts to do this in pairs.

Peercheck. Classcheck. Ask: *What do they think of Julie, the tone of the letter, her point of view, and the way she expressed it? Have you ever written such a formal letter?*

> **Answers**
> 1 I strongly believe that a job candidate should never be required to reveal a prior conviction for a crime.
> 2 While there is certainly no denying that companies need to keep their employees safe, there are compelling reasons to eliminate background checks.
> 3 Para 3: The conviction might be unrelated to the job and therefore irrelevant.
> Para 4: Those who cannot find work may return to crime.
> Para 5: Background checks have been found to sometimes contain errors.

B Read through **Write it right!** with the class.

Before sts do the task, ask them to explain / paraphrase the meaning of the highlighted expressions, e.g. (Possible answers) 1 I'm totally convinced that … 2 A lot of people would say that … 3 Of course it's true that … 4 Despite the common perception … 5 It's unclear if … 6 Regardless of … 7 Although some people think the opposite …

Ask them to read opinions 1–4, and circle the correct option. Classcheck.

> **Answers**
> 1 Many would argue that
> 2 There is some debate as to whether
> 3 Irrespective of the seriousness of the crime
> 4 I believe strongly that

Optional activity

Stronger classes: Point out that certain structures are very common in formal writing. Ask them to find …

1 a passive sentence when the person doing the action is understood.
2 two subject-verb inversions in the first clause for emphasis.
3 a participle clause.
4 two formal relative clauses.

Answers

1 And shockingly, even those falsely arrested in cases of mistaken identity may be denied jobs.
2 And nowhere are our imaginations more active than in imagining the flawed characters of those once convicted of crimes.
Second, in no way is public safety undermined more than by having large numbers of unemployed people on the streets.
3 Facing a lifetime of social and economic disadvantage, those with prior convictions who cannot find work have little motivation not to fall prey to negative influences.
4 An enormous pool of potential workers, many of whom have long ago served their sentences, are never given an opportunity to prove their worth.
… studies have shown that background checks may contain errors, all of which are a potential tool for discrimination.

C Your turn! Focus on the **Common mistake** and ask sts to find examples of this rule in the letter, e.g. *openness is unlikely to have a positive outcome, employers have a responsibility to their staff, safety is of utmost importance.*

Read through the instructions and ask sts to think back to their discussions in 10B. Tell them to choose a topic they felt strongly about. They can argue For or Against censorship.

Encourage sts to use the paragraph starters from the model letter: *First, Second, Finally, For all the reasons above.* Ask sts to post their letter online and read their classmates' letters. Ask: *Whose is the most convincing? Which would you publish in the newspaper?*

Weaker classes: You could put sts in groups and have them choose one of the topics in 10B. Then they can brainstorm ideas together and plan their letters before writing them up individually.

Optional activity

Put sts in pairs/groups who have chosen the same topic. Ask them to write three arguments (for or against, whichever they've chosen) on a piece of paper. They then hand this to another st, who adds a supporting argument for each one. The st who wrote the original arguments can then decide whether to use this or their own ideas.

>> Workbook p.22.

♪ (Freedom!) I won't let you down. (Freedom!) I will not give you up

11 Writing: A letter to the editor

A Read Julie's letter to the editor. Answer 1–3.
1. Identify the thesis statement in paragraph 1.
2. Identify the opposing argument in paragraph 2.
3. Summarize the main arguments in paragraphs 3–5.

B Read *Write it right!* Look at the highlighted expressions (1–7) in context. Then circle the options in 1–4 below that logically reflect Julie's most likely point of view.

> **Write it right!**
>
> In formal writing, writers support their arguments with fixed expressions that add clarity to their message:
> **Contrary to popular belief, I strongly believe that** a job candidate should never be required to reveal a prior conviction.
> **There is some debate as to whether** a prior conviction is an accurate predictor of job performance.

1. [**Many would argue that** / **There's certainly no denying that**] "once a criminal, always a criminal."
2. [**There is some debate as to whether** / **I strongly believe that**] personality tests can reveal a criminal mind.
3. [**Irrespective of the seriousness of the crime,** / **There is some debate as to whether**] criminals often serve a lifelong "sentence."
4. [**Despite claims to the contrary,** / **I believe strongly that**] everyone deserves a second chance.

C *Your turn!* Choose a topic from **10B** and write a five to six-paragraph letter to the editor in about 280 words.

Before
Decide whether you are for or against, and note down three arguments with supporting details. Also note down an opposing argument.

While
Write the letter, following the model. Include expressions from **B** to support your argument in three paragraphs. Introduce your thesis in paragraph 1 and summarize it at the end.

After
Post your letter online and read your classmates' work. Whose is most convincing?

> **Common mistake**
>
> *unemployment*
> ~~The~~ unemployment also erodes confidence.
> Remember: Non-count and plural nouns used to make generalizations have no article.

By Julie Montague

Many letters in this column have praised the benefits of openness, transparency, and a lack of censorship. However, there's one area where openness is unlikely to have a positive outcome. ¹**I strongly believe that** a job candidate should never be required to reveal a prior conviction for a crime. In fact, it should be illegal for employers to gain access to information on crimes that occurred more than 10 years ago.

²**Many would argue** that employers have a responsibility to their staff, and that safety is of utmost importance. While ³**there is certainly no denying that** companies need to keep their employees safe, there are compelling reasons to eliminate background checks.

First, ⁴**contrary to popular belief,** ⁵**there is some debate as to whether** a prior conviction is an accurate predictor of job performance. The conviction may have been for a minor offense and in an area that has no relevance to the job in question. Moreover, background checks do not provide contextual information or information on mitigating circumstances. They do, however, create an image. And nowhere are our imaginations more active than in imagining the flawed characters of those once convicted of crimes. An enormous pool of potential workers, many of whom have long ago served their sentences, are never given an opportunity to prove their worth. In fact, many never even get so far as an interview.

Second, in no way is public safety undermined more than by having large numbers of unemployed people on the streets. Unemployment also erodes confidence, which, in turn, might encourage a return to crime. Facing a lifetime of social and economic disadvantage, those with prior convictions who cannot find work have little motivation not to fall prey to negative influences. In addition, our economy needs workers willing to take entry-level jobs. ⁶**Irrespective of** our personal prejudices, employment for all means improvement in our economy, and a rising standard of living across the board actually improves safety.

Finally, ⁷**despite claims to the contrary**, studies have shown that background checks may contain errors, all of which are a potential tool for discrimination. The information may be out of date, offered by obsolete computer systems. It may not show that an arrest never led to a conviction. And shockingly, even those falsely arrested in cases of mistaken identity may be denied jobs.

For all of the reasons above, I strongly recommend a rethinking of our current policies. Withholding information, as opposed to offering it, may be the best way to offer productive employment to all. Let's not ask a percentage of our population to serve a second, lifetime sentence.

Review 2
Units 3–4

1 Speaking

A Look at the photos on p.28.

1 Note down three language-learning techniques you think work well, using these words and expressions.

> access (n,v)   command (n)   get by   improve by leaps and bounds   increase (n,v)
> out of my depth   pick it up   progress (n,v)   put a lot of effort into   rusty

2 In groups, share your reasons. Any original ideas?

> Your vocabulary can improve by leaps and bounds if you listen to music more.

> Really? Have you ever tried that?

B Make it personal Language-learning problems!

1 Note down two areas where you're still having trouble. Use participle clauses.

When speaking to new people, I often feel very shy.

2 Share your problems with a partner, who will give you advice. Use some of these expressions.

> Problem: I can't even begin to imagine …   I have my doubts about …   to say the least
> … if you ask me   to put it mildly   to a certain extent   so to speak

> Advice: practice makes perfect.   set yourself impossibly high standards   give it a try
> go to the other extreme   hit a middle ground   put your mind to it

> When speaking to new people, I often feel very shy. I have my doubts about whether I seem interesting.

> Maybe you're setting yourself impossibly high standards.

2 Grammar

A Rewrite Lucille's story about dreams, changing the underlined phrases (1–7) so there is an emphatic inversion using the words in parentheses.

> When I woke up in a cold sweat during the night, ¹I didn't know (little) I'd had a fairly common dream. ²When I read an article on the subject, I found out (only when) dreams of being chased were common. ³And they're not only (not only) common, but they usually mean the person is feeling vulnerable. I was feeling that way because I'd broken up with my boyfriend after five years, and ⁴I'd never felt so guilty before (never before). ⁵After I learned that guilt could lead to such dreams, I started to relax (only after) little by little. I'm a lot more aware of my dreams now, and ⁶I haven't had a similar dream since then (not since). Before this happened, ⁷I hardly ever thought (rarely) about the significance of dreams, but now I'm fascinated by the topic.

B Make it personal In pairs, share a story about something you learned about yourself from a dream. Use emphatic inversion and formal relative clauses.

> Rarely had I had recurring dreams until I changed schools …

48

Warm-up

See p.61 of the Teacher's Book for warm-up ideas.
In addition, sts can

- look for links between the song lines and the lessons, e.g. *Gangnam style* in 3.1 is there because of the topic, which is learning a foreign language
- check through the Phrasal verbs list on p.164 to see how many they can remember and are using. Remember the key thing with Phrasal verbs is to force them into your English, so encourage sts to try to use them as much as possible in class, so they can get feedback until the verbs become "friends"
- choose a picture from an earlier unit and dictate for a partner to draw
- choose a listening, e.g. to one of the reading texts, that they would like to hear again, or one from the test platform, as there is no listening in this Review
- do one of the tasks from the platform that they haven't yet had time for

1 Speaking

A Sts look back at the photos on p.28. Elicit the language-learning techniques shown, and a detailed description of each photo. Ask if sts remember any other learning techniques from the audio in Lesson 3 (spending time in the country, talking to native speakers, reading to increase vocabulary, downloading apps with grammar and vocab exercises, accessing the Internet and watching videos in the language you are learning). Brainstorm others.

Go through the expressions in the box and review the meanings. Sts can refer to 3A on p.29.

2 Put sts in groups to share their ideas. Focus on the models in the speech bubbles. Monitor and make a note of any common errors for class feedback later. Have a class vote on their top three techniques.

B Make it personal

1 Refer sts to 10A on p.35 to remind them of the rules for participle clauses. Focus on the example, and elicit others, e.g. *When watching non-subtitled videos, I often find it difficult to know what's going on*. Have sts note down two problems they have.
2 Put sts in pairs to share their problems. Go through the expressions in the boxes and review what they mean. Refer sts to 4D on p.30 to see examples in context.

Focus on the models in the speech bubbles, and have two sts read them out with correct stress and intonation, and try to continue the conversation. Sts tell each other their problems and give each other advice, using the expressions in the advice box if possible.

Monitor while sts are in their pairs, and help with vocabulary where necessary.

Classcheck by asking one or two pairs to act out their exchanges in front of the class. Summarize for them what you heard to be the main on-going problems they have and elicit their best solutions, plus any of your own.

Optional activity

Put sts in groups to make a poster with useful advice for advanced learners like themselves trying to refine and polish their English. Encourage them to use the expressions in A. When they have finished, display the posters around the classroom and ask other sts to walk around and choose their favorite one.

2 Grammar

A Cover the text and focus on the photo. Ask: *What's happening?* Then tell sts it's a sequence from a dream. *What might she be thinking?* Ask: *Do you ever have recurring dreams or nightmares? What are they normally about?* In trios, sts share their experiences. Classcheck.

Have sts read the text quickly for gist and find out what Lucille's dream was about (being chased). Peercheck. What else can they remember or did they think?

Sts re-read the text, re-wording the underlined phrases. Do the first one together as an example. Refer them to 4A on p.41 if they need reminding of the rules. Peercheck. Classcheck. Any final reactions?

Answers

1 little did I know
2 Only when I read an article on the subject did I find out
3 And not only are they
4 never before had I felt so guilty
5 Only after I learned that guilt could lead to such dreams did I start to relax
6 not since then have I had a similar dream
7 rarely did I think

Tip

With weaker classes, rewrite the first one or two together on the board as examples. Point out that the adverbial goes first, and remind them to invert the subject and the auxiliary.

B Make it personal Ask sts if they can remember any of the interpretations of dreams from Lesson 4. Re-play the audio 4.2 if possible. Elicit the following: snakes = your feelings towards your boss or mother-in-law; losing control in a car = you're pushing yourself too hard; being chased = feeling vulnerable or guilty; teeth falling out = anxiety about how people perceive us.

Put sts in pairs to discuss their own dreams. Sts tell their partner what they have learned about themselves from the dream. Ask sts to suggest alternative interpretations of their partner's dreams, if appropriate.

Classcheck, by asking sts to tell the class what they learned about their partner.

R2

3 Reading

A Books closed. Ask: *What do you know about Martin Luther King, Jr.?* Brainstorm as much information as possible. Do they have any idea why his speeches were so powerful or his legacy so strong?

Books open. Tell sts to read the article and find three reasons why he was a great public speaker.

Check answers. Elicit the meaning of *cadence* (rhythm or tempo).

Answers

1 He was authentic.
2 He used tone and cadence, starting slowly and quietly and building up to a rapid delivery with increased volume.
3 He used repetition to reinforce his message.

Background information

Martin Luther King, Jr. (1929–1968) was an American Baptist minister and campaigner for civil rights for African Americans in the 1960s. He preached non-violence, led many successful protests, and received the Nobel Peace Prize in 1964. He was assassinated in Memphis in 1968, when he was 39 years old.

B Make it personal Ask sts to research the speech, and listen to it if possible. Elicit other qualities which make a good speech. Sts may be able to suggest other videos of great speakers.

As follow-up, have sts choose a couple of paragraphs to learn and deliver as a speech. Tell them to speak with meaning, and to start slowly and build up pace, as Martin Luther King did! Tell them to write key words on cards to prompt them. Have them practice their speech with a partner, then ask a few volunteers to deliver it to the class.

Possible answers

Keep sentences short and simple.
Make sure you start with something interesting or funny to get people's attention.
Wait for a few seconds before you start your speech to get everyone's attention, and create a feeling of anticipation.
Use cue cards, but try not to rely on them too much.
Make eye contact with your audience.
Speak slowly and deliberately, pausing after making key points.

4 Self-test

Remind sts these sections help them both to review and consolidate vocabulary and grammar, and practice proofreading.

Sts do the test individually, then paircheck. Encourage them to look back through Units 3 and 4 if they're unsure about any of the sentences. If sts score less than 15 out of 20, suggest they re-do the exercise in a few days, to see if they get a better score. If they do really well, they could also repeat the exercise later, but without referring to Units 3 and 4 this time.

Answers

1 I used to feel really out of **my** depth at college, even though I could more or less get **by**.
2 You're **setting** yourself very high standards and need to hit a middle **ground**.
3 **Why I still** have an accent is a mystery, but an article I read recently said **practice** makes perfect.
4 How often people **use** hashtags **differs** from one location to another.
5 At first, I couldn't get **a** word in edgewise, but later on, I was actually at a loss **for words**.
6 I wouldn't go **so** far as to say it's an **age-related** illness.
7 **I not only watched** the guy break in to the apartment, but I also tipped **off** the cops.
8 It's the movie which the show is based **on** and about **which** I wrote a review.
9 So many people suffer from **stress-related** problems, most of **whom** don't know it.
10 I read lots of blogs from **which** I get ideas, **irrespective** of the author.

5 Point of view

Go through topics a–b with the class, and brainstorm a few ideas for each one. Individually, sts choose one of them and make some preparatory notes. Tell them to make only brief notes (prompts), just enough to make them feel confident enough to be able to speak for about 80 seconds on the topic.

Review expressions for a) giving opinions, e.g. *In my view / opinion…, It seems to me that …, It seems that …, I think / believe that …, In my mind, As far as I'm concerned …,* and b) supporting them, e.g. *because, thanks to …, owing to …, the reason is …, the facts suggest …*

Weaker classes: Sts can write out their argument in full, but get them to rehearse it before they record it, so they don't have to read directly from their notes.

Monitor and correct as much as you can. If possible, sts record their opinion in class using a cell phone. Allow them to re-record if they aren't happy. It's all good practice and everybody wants the best possible end product. Encourage sts to listen to each other's recordings and give each other feedback.

Stronger classes: For fun, you could hold a debate on one of the topics. Choose one and divide the class into four groups. Tell two groups to argue "For" and two to argue "Against." In their groups, sts brainstorm and note their ideas. Groups take turns presenting arguments to the class. Sts elect a spokesperson or take turns speaking. Encourage them to explain and justify their points of view. After each group has presented, allow the other sts to ask questions and challenge the ideas presented. When all groups have spoken, have a class vote on the most convincing group (they can't vote for themselves!).

3 Reading

A Read the article about Martin Luther King, Jr. In pairs, recall three reasons he was a great public speaker.

> One of the greatest orators of all time was Martin Luther King, Jr. Only 34 years old when he delivered his famous "I have a dream" speech in 1963, he changed the course of history. However, rarely have people stopped to consider the qualities that made King such a powerful speaker. Let me point out just a few.
>
> First, really convincing speakers are authentic. They have a message to deliver, which they themselves fully embody, and King's life and words were harmonious. By the time he delivered his famous speech, he had already established himself as a committed civil rights leader.
>
> Listen carefully, and you'll also notice King's tone and cadence. He usually began his speeches slowly before building up to a powerful, more rapid delivery. As he increased his pace and volume, he captivated his listeners. Not only did he create a powerful connection in this way, but he also reinforced his message through repetition. The repetition of the words "I have a dream" comes through again and again in his speech.
>
> Finally, while King may have improvised his famous speech, delivered without notes, what is less well-known is that not only had he been practicing parts of it for years, he also had been preaching about dreams since 1960. Rehearsing his message over and over, King was able to evaluate its impact on smaller audiences to whom he had delivered it. Fully aware that "practice makes perfect," he honed his talents. It is no wonder that "I have a dream" was ranked the top speech of the 20th century in a 1999 poll.

B **Make it personal** Search on "I have a dream," and read or listen to the speech. What other qualities do you feel make a good public speaker?

> He mentions history a lot, so listeners can feel part of something greater.

4 Self-test

Correct the two mistakes in each sentence. Check your answers in Units 3 and 4. What's your score, 1–20?

1. I used to feel really out of the depth at college, even though I could more or less get through.
2. You're putting yourself very high standards and need to hit a middle road.
3. Why do I still have an accent is a mystery, but an article I read recently said speaking makes perfect.
4. How often people uses hashtags differ from one location to another.
5. At first, I couldn't get the word in edgewise, but later on, I was actually at a loss for the words.
6. I wouldn't go too far as to say it's an agerelated illness.
7. Not only I watched the guy break in to the apartment, but I also tipped up the cops.
8. It's the movie which the show is based and about that I wrote a review.
9. So many people suffer from stress-oriented problems, most of who don't know it.
10. I read lots of blogs from that I get ideas, unrespective of the author.

5 Point of view

Choose a topic. Then support your opinion in 100–150 words, and record your answer. Ask a partner for feedback. How can you be more convincing?

a. You feel most people have serious hidden biases. OR
   You feel only a small percentage do, just like a small percentage believes in conspiracy theories.
b. You think parents need to monitor what their children read. OR
   You think any kind of censorship is inappropriate and kids need to be exposed to the real world.

49

5 ›› Why do good plans sometimes fail?

1 Listening

A ▶ 5.1 In pairs, use the photo and excerpts from a radio show (1–4) about a publicity stunt to guess what happened. Listen to check. How close were you?

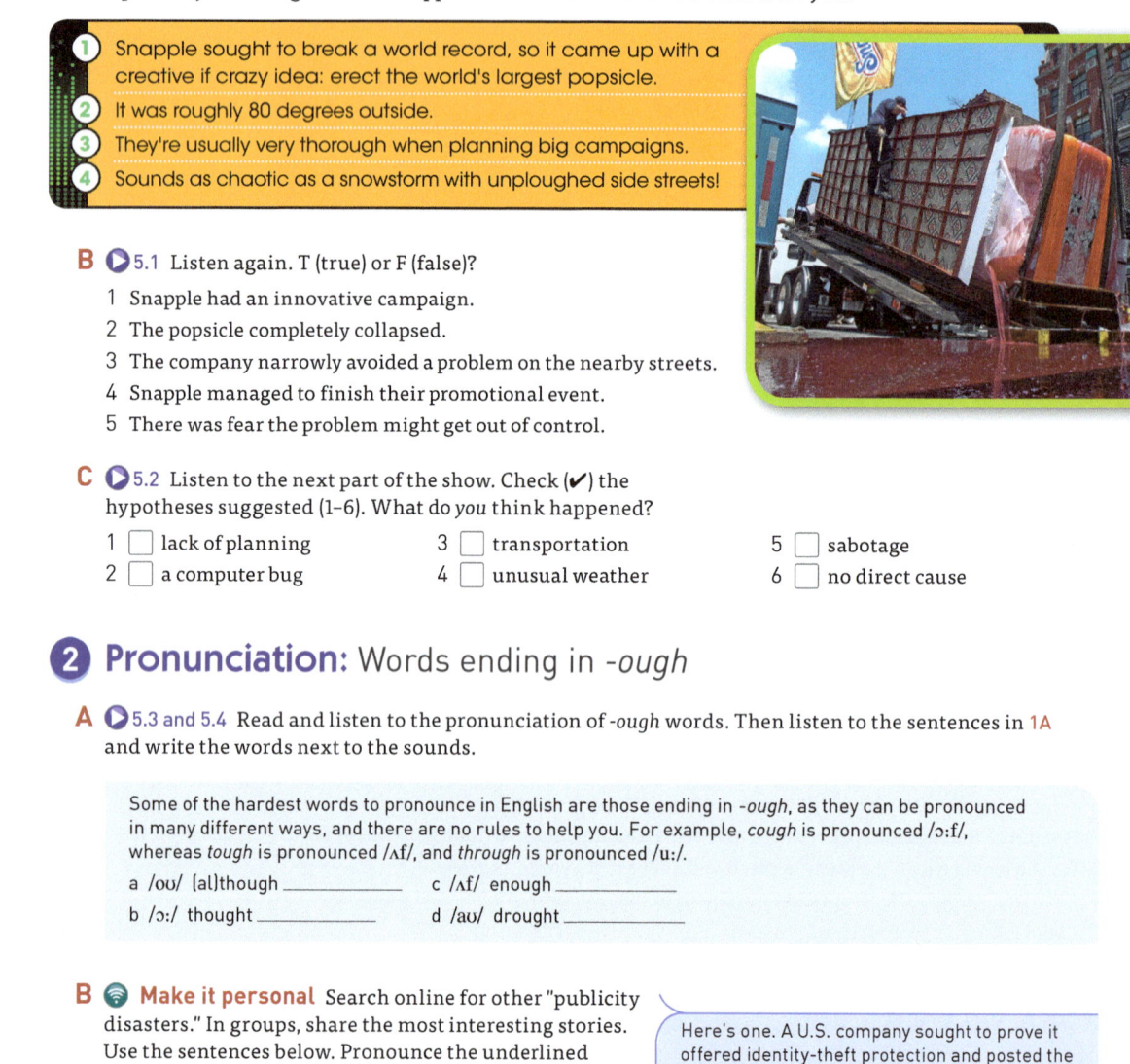

1. Snapple sought to break a world record, so it came up with a creative if crazy idea: erect the world's largest popsicle.
2. It was roughly 80 degrees outside.
3. They're usually very thorough when planning big campaigns.
4. Sounds as chaotic as a snowstorm with unploughed side streets!

B ▶ 5.1 Listen again. T (true) or F (false)?
1. Snapple had an innovative campaign.
2. The popsicle completely collapsed.
3. The company narrowly avoided a problem on the nearby streets.
4. Snapple managed to finish their promotional event.
5. There was fear the problem might get out of control.

C ▶ 5.2 Listen to the next part of the show. Check (✔) the hypotheses suggested (1–6). What do *you* think happened?
1. ☐ lack of planning
2. ☐ a computer bug
3. ☐ transportation
4. ☐ unusual weather
5. ☐ sabotage
6. ☐ no direct cause

2 Pronunciation: Words ending in *-ough*

A ▶ 5.3 and 5.4 Read and listen to the pronunciation of *-ough* words. Then listen to the sentences in 1A and write the words next to the sounds.

> Some of the hardest words to pronounce in English are those ending in *-ough*, as they can be pronounced in many different ways, and there are no rules to help you. For example, *cough* is pronounced /ɔːf/, whereas *tough* is pronounced /ʌf/, and *through* is pronounced /uː/.
>
> a /oʊ/ (al)though _____   c /ʌf/ enough _____
> b /ɔː/ thought _____   d /aʊ/ drought _____

B 🌐 **Make it personal** Search online for other "publicity disasters." In groups, share the most interesting stories. Use the sentences below. Pronounce the underlined words correctly.

| [Company] <u>sought</u> to _____ , but it didn't work. |
| They must have _____ <u>thoroughly</u>, but it was a fiasco. |
| Things got a bit (really) <u>rough</u> when _____ . |
| It must have been <u>tough</u> for them (not) to _____ . |

> Here's one. A U.S. company sought to prove it offered identity-theft protection and posted the CEO's personal information. Can you believe it?

> Was he hacked?

> He sure was! And things got really rough when he was also fined for deceptive advertising!

50

Why do good plans sometimes fail? 5.1

Lesson Aims: Sts learn vocabulary to talk about plans which fell through, and listen to a story about a failed publicity campaign.

Skills	Language	Vocabulary
Listening to a radio presenter describing a failed publicity stunt Acting out a role-play	Talking about your disappointments, e.g. *I fell flat on my face. Things got out of hand. It was back to square one.*	Expressions for talking about failed plans, e.g. *fall through, call (stg.) off, oversight, high-stakes, glitch, on the verge of*

Warm-up

Focus on the lesson title question: *Why do good plans sometimes fail?* Ask sts to tell of a time when something went wrong for them despite all their attempts to prepare for the event. You may like to start with a personal anecdote of your own, e.g. a job interview or disastrous first date, and ask students to suggest the reasons why it went wrong.

1 Listening

A ▶5.1 Books closed. Refer sts to the photo and ask: *Where is this? What do you think is happening? What's on the truck? What do you think they are trying to do?* Elicit the meaning of publicity stunt (a planned event to attract attention). Have sts read the radio excerpts 1–4, and see if they can guess more about what happened. Monitor, but don't confirm yet.

Have sts re-read the instructions, then listen to the radio show about one of Snapple's campaigns to find out if they guessed correctly. Peercheck. Play it again if necessary. Classcheck.

Answers

Snapple, the New York-based beverage company tried to raise awareness of their range of frozen treats and break a world record at the same time by erecting the world's largest popsicle in Manhattan. The plan backfired, however, as it started to melt in the 80 degree temperatures.

≫ See Teacher's Book p.320 for Audio script 5.1.

Background information

Snapple is a U.S. soft drink manufacturer owned by the *Dr. Pepper Snapple Group*, which was established in 1972. Famous for its range of interesting flavors and iced tea drinks, which are usually sold in small glass bottles.

B ▶5.1 Before sts listen, have them read the sentences carefully. Check any unknown words. Play the audio for sts to answer true or false. Classcheck. Re-play the audio if necessary, pausing at the relevant parts. Ask: *Do you think the campaign was a good idea?*

Answers

1 T 2 F 3 F 4 F 5 T

C ▶5.2 Tell sts that they are going to hear the two radio presenters speculate about causes of the failed campaign. Play the audio. Sts check the hypotheses they hear suggested.

Ask: *Do they really know what happened? (No) What do you think is the most likely reason? Do you think they planned to fail and it was all just a publicity stunt?*

Answers

Checked: 2, 3, 5, and 6

≫ See Teacher's Book p.321 for Audio script 5.2

2 Pronunciation: Words ending in *-ough*

A ▶5.3 and 5.4 Refer sts to the pronunciation box. Play the audio 5.3 while they follow in their books. Re-play the audio pausing so that sts can repeat the *-ough* words.

Refer sts to sentences 1–4 in 1A to guess how the words are pronounced. Play audio 5.4 for them to check. Sts write the words next to a–d.

Answers

a thorough b sought c roughly d unploughed

Tip

Given the notoriety of English spelling, it's a good idea, whenever possible, to introduce new words / phrases orally, so that sts get a feel for what they sound like and how they're pronounced, before they see how they're spelled. When you introduce new lexis, drill it around the class a few times before boarding it.

B Make it personal Ask: *Do you remember any similar publicity disasters?*

Have sts discuss any they can remember, and search for others on the Internet. Before they do, go over the language in the box, and the models in the speech bubbles with the class.

Class feedback. Invite sts to share their stories with the class.

Ask: *Do you think publicity disasters can be a good thing? Do you believe that "Any publicity is good publicity"? Can you think of examples?*

5.1

3 Vocabulary: Failed plans

A ▶ 5.5 Tell sts the sentence halves come from audio 5.1. Sts do the matching, then compare their answers with a partner. Play the audio for them to check.

Stronger classes: Sts test each other in pairs. One covers sentence halves 1–6, and their partner reads out an ending, a–f. They need to remember and say the first half of the sentence, then swap roles.

Classcheck and drill pronunciation of the highlighted expressions.

> **Answers**
> 1 b   2 d   3 a   4 e   5 c   6 f

Optional activity

Sts test each other in pairs. One st covers sentence halves 1–6, and their partner reads out one of the endings a–f. They need to remember and say the first half of the sentence. Sts take turns testing each other.

B Sts choose the correct meanings. Peercheck. Classcheck. Elicit other synonyms sts might know for *glitch*, e.g. *blip, come to nothing, blunder*.

Stronger classes: Cover up B, and ask sts to write their own definitions of the highlighted expressions. Have them look at B and compare.

As follow up, ask sts to write their own sentences using the expressions, e.g. *I was on the verge of tears when my phone was stolen.*

> **Answers**
> 1 a   2 b   3 a   4 b   5 a   6 a

C Explain that sts are going to do a role-play. Have them choose which role they would like to play, journalist, or the owner of Snapple. If they choose journalist, then sts should take turns doing the TV report, or they can present the news item together. If they choose owner of Snapple, they should take turns being both the owner, and then the campaign planner.

In either case, sts should plan and map out their dialogs together before they act them out. Brainstorm a few ideas to help them. Ask: *How do you think the owner felt?* Elicit *angry at the campaign planner*. Elicit a few phrases they might use to express their anger, and board them, e.g. *Why didn't you ...? You should have ...*

Monitor while they act out their role plays. Invite one or two pairs to act them out for the class.

Weaker classes: Suggest they play the role of the journalist. Allow them to use audio script 5.1 on page 320 of the Teacher's Book to help them.

D ▶ 5.6 Ask sts: *Have you done a PhD or do you know someone who has?* Explain or elicit that after you have written your PhD thesis, you normally have an oral examination on it, which is called "defending your thesis." Ask sts if anyone has done this or knows someone who has. Ask: *What was it like?*

Explain that they are going to hear the two presenters from 1A talking off air about when one of them was defending their thesis.

Tell sts to listen and make notes, then write a summary of the story using expressions from A. Ask sts to exchange their summaries with a partner, and to correct them. Classcheck by asking volunteers to read out their stories to the class.

Ask: *Has anyone had a similar experience with failing technology?*

» See Teacher's Book p.321 for Audio script 5.6.

E Make it personal

1 ▶ 5.7 **How to say it** Ask sts to try to complete 1–5 from memory. Play the audio for them to listen and check. Re-play the audio and ask sts to pay attention to the stress and pronunciation. Have them practice in pairs. Ask sts if there are similar expression in their language.

> **Answers**
> 1 face   2 hand   3 pull   4 back   5 close

Focus on the **Common mistake**. Teach or elicit the meaning of *come close to* (to nearly do something).

2 Have sts think of an occasion when something they had planned fell through or went wrong. They can choose from the list or add their own ideas, e.g. an interview. Tell them to make notes using the question words as prompts, e.g. *What happened? When did it happen? Where did it happen?*

3 Put sts in pairs. Have them take turns telling their stories. Encourage the "listener" to react where appropriately and ask for further explanation where needed. Board the following to help: *What happened then? Sounds awful! Oh no, Really? A nightmare! What do you mean?*

Optional activity

Sts write up their stories from exercise E as a short paragraph, either in class or for homework.

» Song lyric: See Teacher's Book p.346 for notes about the song and an accompanying activity to do with the class.

» Workbook p.23.

> ♪ Yeah, I know that I let you down. Is it too late to say I'm sorry now?

5.1

3 Vocabulary: Failed plans

A ▶ 5.5 Match the two sentence halves. Listen to check.
1. They were **on the verge of** something big,
2. Their plans **fell through** and the whole thing
3. The company decided to **call** the whole thing **off**
4. But was it an **oversight**?
5. It was a **high-stakes** operation, meaning that
6. It might have been a **glitch** or something, maybe

a ☐ and stopped raising the popsicle.
b ☐ but the campaign never materialized.
c ☐ if it failed, it would be a disaster.
d ☐ ended in a sticky mess.
e ☐ I mean, didn't they see it coming?
f ☐ software related.

B Choose the most likely meaning (a or b) for the **highlighted** expressions (1–6) in **A**.
1. a ☐ about to experience something — b ☐ at the end of a difficult process
2. a ☐ took a long time to succeed — b ☐ failed
3. a ☐ cancel — b ☐ delay
4. a ☐ a deliberate mistake — b ☐ an unanticipated mistake
5. a ☐ important and risky — b ☐ important and relatively risk-free
6. a ☐ an unexpected, but minor problem — b ☐ a lack of attention to detail

C In pairs, role-play retelling the popsicle fiasco as: 1) a journalist reporting it on TV or 2) the owner of Snapple talking to the campaign planner. Use the new expressions in **A**.

> Snapple planned a really high-stakes promotion event, and ...

D ▶ 5.6 Listen to the DJ's story and take notes. Then summarize it using expressions from **A**.

E Make it personal Can you remember a plan or goal that fell through?
1. ▶ 5.7 **How to say it** Complete the chart. Listen to check.

Talking about disappointments	
What they said	What they meant
1 I fell flat on my _____.	I failed completely.
2 Things got out of _____.	Things got out of control.
3 It took me a while to _____ myself together.	It took me a while to recover.
4 It was _____ to square one!	I had to start from scratch.
5 I came this _____ to (having a nervous breakdown)!	I almost (had a nervous breakdown).

2. Choose a topic and note down a few details. Ask yourself:
   What / When / Where / Why / How ...?

   a date   a do-it-yourself project   a job application   a party   travel plans

3. In pairs, share your stories. Use expressions from **A** and **E**. Any comic moments?

> I once invited 20 people to a party and at the last minute, I dropped all the food on the floor.

> You're kidding!

> I came this close to having a nervous breakdown. I wasn't sure whether to call the whole thing off ...

Common mistake
I came close to ~~lose~~ *losing* my job.

» 5.2 Do you ever make resolutions?

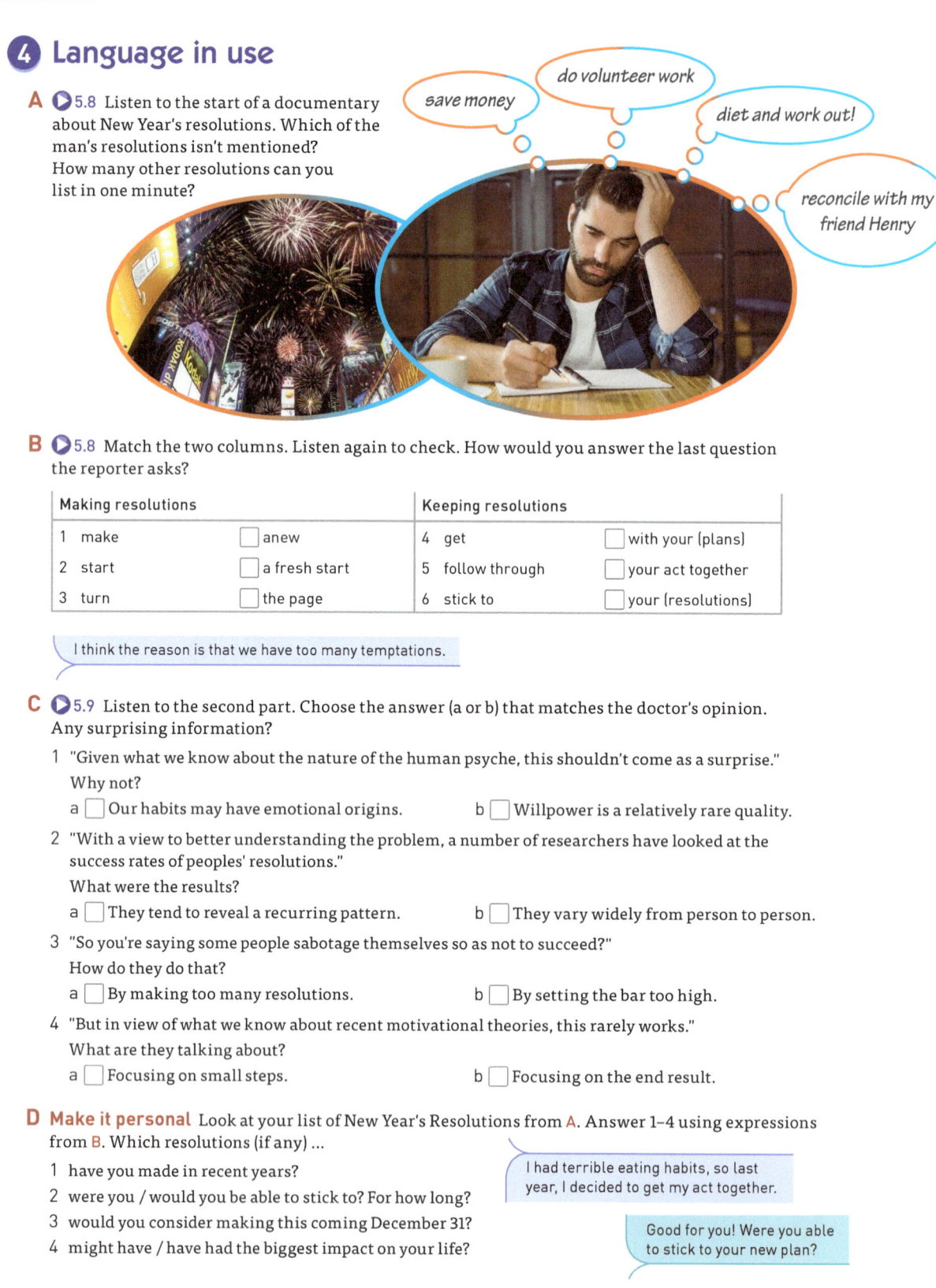

4 Language in use

A ▶ 5.8 Listen to the start of a documentary about New Year's resolutions. Which of the man's resolutions isn't mentioned? How many other resolutions can you list in one minute?

- save money
- do volunteer work
- diet and work out!
- reconcile with my friend Henry

B ▶ 5.8 Match the two columns. Listen again to check. How would you answer the last question the reporter asks?

Making resolutions		Keeping resolutions	
1 make	☐ anew	4 get	☐ with your (plans)
2 start	☐ a fresh start	5 follow through	☐ your act together
3 turn	☐ the page	6 stick to	☐ your (resolutions)

> I think the reason is that we have too many temptations.

C ▶ 5.9 Listen to the second part. Choose the answer (a or b) that matches the doctor's opinion. Any surprising information?

1 "Given what we know about the nature of the human psyche, this shouldn't come as a surprise."
   Why not?
   a ☐ Our habits may have emotional origins.   b ☐ Willpower is a relatively rare quality.

2 "With a view to better understanding the problem, a number of researchers have looked at the success rates of peoples' resolutions."
   What were the results?
   a ☐ They tend to reveal a recurring pattern.   b ☐ They vary widely from person to person.

3 "So you're saying some people sabotage themselves so as not to succeed?"
   How do they do that?
   a ☐ By making too many resolutions.   b ☐ By setting the bar too high.

4 "But in view of what we know about recent motivational theories, this rarely works."
   What are they talking about?
   a ☐ Focusing on small steps.   b ☐ Focusing on the end result.

D **Make it personal** Look at your list of New Year's Resolutions from A. Answer 1–4 using expressions from B. Which resolutions (if any) …

1 have you made in recent years?
2 were you / would you be able to stick to? For how long?
3 would you consider making this coming December 31?
4 might have / have had the biggest impact on your life?

> I had terrible eating habits, so last year, I decided to get my act together.

> Good for you! Were you able to stick to your new plan?

52

Do you ever make resolutions? 5.2

Lesson Aims: Sts learn language to talk about making and keeping New Year's resolutions.

Skills	Language	Vocabulary	Grammar
Listening to a documentary about New Year's Resolutions	Explaining quotes using formal conjunctions, e.g. *Given that people keep repeating the same patterns, their destiny may actually be some sort of emotional problem.*	Making and keeping resolutions: *make a fresh start, start anew, turn the page, get your act together, follow through with your* (plans), *stick to your* (resolutions)	Formal conjunctions and prepositions, e.g. *In an effort to ..., In view of ..., With the aim of ...*

Warm-up

Focus on the lesson title question: *Do you ever make resolutions?* Ask: *Did you make a New Year's Resolution this year? Have you broken it yet? How long did you keep it? What do most people make resolutions about?* Have sts discuss in pairs.

>> Song lyric: See Teacher's Book p.346 for notes about the song and an accompanying activity to do with the class.

4 Language in use

A ▶ 5.8 Focus on the photos. Ask: *What can you see in the photos?* (Fireworks / New Year's celebrations) *What is the man doing?* (making New Year's Resolutions). Have sts read the resolutions in the speech bubbles. Ask: *Have you ever made any of these resolutions?*

Play the audio and have sts say which resolution is not mentioned. Classcheck.

Put sts in pairs to list as many resolutions as they can in one minute. These can be resolutions they have made themselves in the past or ones they have heard other people make, e.g. *give up drinking fizzy drinks, go to bed early*. Class feedback. Ask: *Who has the most resolutions?*

Answer

do volunteer work

>> See Teacher's Book p.321 for Audio script 5.8.

B ▶ 5.8 Explain that the phrases in the table are all used by the reporter in the audio they heard in **A**. Have them match the columns. Play the audio for them to check. Peercheck. Classcheck.

Answers

1 make a fresh start   2 start anew   3 turn the page
4 get your act together   5 follow through with your plans
6 stick to your resolutions

Ask sts to write a true sentence about themselves using one or two of the phrases, e.g. *I always start anew at New Year, but I never stick to my resolutions*.

Ask: *Do you remember what question the reporter asks at the end?* (Why is it so hard to stick to your resolutions?) Focus on the example in the speech bubble. Ask: *Do you agree with this?* Elicit other reasons.

C ▶ 5.9 Explain that sts are going to hear the continuation of the radio program from **B** with the same presenter who is joined by a psychologist, plus two guests. They are going to talk about why we so often break resolutions. Before they listen, have them read the doctor's opinions, and the two options a and b.

Play the audio and have them choose the correct answer a or b.

Check answers. Ask: *Are you surprised by anything the psychologist said?*

Answers

1 a   2 a   3 b   4 b

>> See Teacher's Book p.321 for Audio script 5.9.

Optional activity

Before sts listen again, board the numbers 1– 4. Have a class vote for each sentence, as to whether the correct answer is a or b. Board the most popular letter next to the number. Sts listen and peercheck, then go through the answers on the board and check which are correct and why.

D **Make it personal** Go through the questions with the class. Have sts refer to the lists of resolutions they made in **A**, and have them ask and answer the questions in pairs. Classcheck by asking sts to report back to the class something interesting they learned about their partner. Class feedback.

For fun, carry out a quick survey. Ask: *Who made a resolution at the beginning of the year?* (Ask sts to raise their hands if they did.) Ask: *Who kept their resolution?* Board the numbers, and figure out the percentage of sts who kept / broke their resolutions. Ask: *Does this figure support the psychologists's opinions?*

Optional activity

Ask each st to write three "resolutions" for that week, related to different things in their lives, e.g. learning English, free time, exercise, spending time with family. Monitor and help where necessary. When sts have finished, ask them to show their resolutions to two other sts, and have them sign their paper as "witnesses." Revisit the activity next week and find out how many sts stuck to their resolutions.

5.2

5 Grammar: Formal conjunctions and prepositions

A Have sts read through the grammar box. Check they understand the example sentences. Ask sts what the equivalent is for the bold phrases in their language. Have them complete rules 1–3. Focus on the quotes 1–4 in 4C, and rephrase the first one together with the class as an example. Ask sts to rephrase 2–4. Peercheck. Classcheck.

> **Answers**
> 1 in view of, given, thanks to
> 2 with the aim of, with a view to, so as to, in an effort to
> 3 -ing, infinitive
>
> Reworded quotes:
> 1 Because of what we know about the nature of the human psyche
> 2 To better understand the problem
> 3 ... sabotage themselves to not succeed
> 4 Because of what we know about recent

» Refer sts to the **Grammar expansion** on p.146.

B Focus on the title of the blog. Check sts know the meaning of *deadline* (latest time or date to complete something). Ask: *Are you good at keeping deadlines? Are you good at sticking to resolutions? Are you good at meeting goals?* Board the collocations (*keep deadlines, stick to resolutions, meet goals*). Ask sts if they know any other collocations, e.g. *set goals, meet deadlines, adhere to deadlines, keep a resolution, break a resolution, miss a deadline, fulfill a goal*.

Ask sts to read the blog post and circle the correct alternatives. Peercheck. Classcheck.

Ask: *Had you heard of mindfulness? Have you tried it? What do you think about the idea?*

> **Answers**
> 1 given   2 in view of   3 so as to   4 with the aim of
> 5 in an effort to

C Sts read the rest of the text and rephrase sentences 1–5. Do the first one together as an example. Have sts do 1–4 individually. Peercheck. Classcheck. Ask: *Do you think this is good advice?*

Focus on the **Common mistake**. Ask sts to write their own sentences using *given* and *in view of*.

> **Answers**
> 1 We live in the future in view of the endless possibilities it offers.
> 2 Given (the fact) that we feel dissatisfied in the present, we take refuge in the future.
> 3 We fantasize about our future successes in an effort to escape our current misery / In an effort to escape our current misery, we fantasize about our future successes.
> 4 Accept the fact that there are things you can't control so as to find peace.
> 5 Learn how to do one thing at a time with a view to giving it your full attention.

D Make it personal

1 Ask sts to read the quotes. Ask: *What do you know about the authors of the quotes?* (in parentheses). Teach or elicit the meaning of *to duck behind* (to hide behind). Have sts discuss the meanings of the quotes in pairs. Refer sts to the model in the speech bubble. In class feedback have sts compare ideas with their classmates. Do they agree about the meaning of the quotes?

Ask: *Which quotes do you agree / disagree with?*

2 Sts choose their favorite one. Ask sts to tell the class which one they have chosen and why.

Stronger classes: Ask sts to search online for or even write their own quote relating to "controlling our destiny." Have sts share them with the class and vote for the best one.

Tip

While sts are discussing which quotes they agree / disagree with and why, ask them to think of examples in their own lives which support their view. Give them a few minutes to prepare on their own before starting the discussion.

Background information

John Lennon (1940–1980) was a singer, songwriter, and co-founder of the Beatles.

Diana Trilling (1905–1996) was an American literary critic and author.

Sarah Jessica Parker (b. 1965) is an actor, producer, and designer.

Henry Moore (1898–1986) was an English sculptor and artist.

Alan Cohen (b. 1950) is an American writer of self-help books.

Jodie Foster (b. 1962) is an American actor, director, and producer.

» Workbook p.24.

♪ All is quiet on New Year's Day. A world in white gets underway. I want to be with you, Be with you night and day

5.2

5 Grammar: Formal conjunctions and prepositions

A Read the grammar box and complete rules 1–3. Then rephrase the quotes in **4C** using *to* or *because of*.

Formal conjunctions and prepositions for reason and purpose

In view of Given Thanks to	the increase in stress levels, the fact that life is so busy, good promotion,	more and more people are doing yoga.
With the aim of With a view to	studying people's resolutions,	a number of studies were conducted.
So as to In an effort to	save money,	I moved back in with my parents.

1 _____ , _____ , and _____ mean "because of."
2 _____ , _____ , _____ , and _____ mean "(in order) to."
3 *With a view to* is followed by the _____ form. *So as to* is followed by the _____ form.

» **Grammar expansion p.146**

B Read the blog post and circle the correct alternatives (1–5).

Resolutions, goals, deadlines …

¹[**Given** / **With a view to**] our hectic lifestyles, our days sometimes pass us by while our minds are elsewhere, either dwelling in the past or making plans. I work for a major finance company and ²[**with the aim of** / **in view of**] the long hours I had to work, I kept trying new relaxation techniques ³[**so as to** / **with a view to**] reduce the toll on my physical and mental well-being. That was when a friend suggested mindfulness, and it's changed my life. Mindfulness means being aware of your senses, actions, and thoughts. It's living in the present moment ⁴[**with the aim of** / **thanks to**] feeling more relaxed and fulfilled. I started to practice it throughout the day ⁵[**with a view to** / **in an effort to**] defeat anxiety, and I couldn't be happier.

C Rephrase 1–5 using the words in parentheses.

So … Why do we live in the future? ¹We live in the future because it offers endless possibilities. (in view of) ²We feel dissatisfied in the present, so we take refuge in the future. (given) ³We fantasize about our future successes because we want to escape our current misery. (in an effort to) How can we live in the present moment? ⁴Accept the fact that there are things you can't control if you want to find peace. (so as to) ⁵Learn how to do one thing at a time so that you can give it your full attention. (with a view to)

Common mistake

in view of the fact that / given (the fact that)
I decided to resign ~~in view of~~ there were no fringe benefits.

"the fact that" is optional after *given*, but obligatory after *in view of*.

D **Make it personal** Are we in control of our destiny?

1 Explain the idea behind each quote (a–f). Use some of the formal conjunctions and prepositions in **A**.

   a "Life is what happens to you while you're busy making other plans." (performed by John Lennon; attributed to Allen Saunders)
   b "There's so much to be said for challenging fate instead of ducking behind it." (Diana Trilling)
   c "Maybe our mistakes are what make our fate." (Sarah Jessica Parker)
   d "I think in terms of the day's resolutions, not the year's." (Henry Moore)
   e "Our history is not our destiny." (Alan Cohen)
   f "I think destiny is just a fancy word for a psychological problem." (Jodie Foster)

2 Choose your favorite one. Why do you like it?

> I think the last one means that given that people keep repeating the same patterns, their destiny may actually be some sort of emotional problem.

53

» 5.3   How well do you deal with failure?

6 Reading

A Read the introduction. In one minute, list all the parts of life people commonly fail at that you can think of. Then in pairs, suggest an answer for the last question.

> Well, for one thing, most people fail in their relationships from time to time …

Coming to terms with failure

Can you think of even one person who doesn't dread failure and go to great lengths to avoid it? Who in their right mind would want to experience all the negative emotions that come from failing to accomplish an important goal? Obviously the answer is no one. However, failure is an inherent part of life, so our best bet is to keep it in perspective. Why is that so very difficult?

"Well, there's nowhere to go but up."

Below are five strategies designed to help you make it through unscathed:

1 **Be upset!** Yes, that's right. Give in to your emotions. Simultaneously, reject the temptation to take failure personally. Even though your relationship or job didn't pan out, you are still a successful person. Separate your failure from your self-esteem. You'll go far. And the proof: Lady Gaga was fired from her record label after only three months. Ang Lee failed Taiwan's college entrance examinations and couldn't get into acting because his English "wasn't good enough." Look where they are today. Lady Gaga may have "cried so hard she couldn't talk," but we know she succeeded in putting her failure behind her.

2 **Snap out of it!** After you've had a good cry, then it's time to move on. The longer you dwell on your failure, the more miserable you'll be. The Irish writer Oscar Wilde died young and faced many obstacles in his lifetime. But you'd do well to heed his advice, "Life is too important a thing ever to talk seriously about." It's critical not to obsess about what might have been because you'll only sink deeper into depression.

3 **Make a right turn.** Think of your failure as you would a road blocked by construction and evaluate it logically. First you take stock of the situation, and then you act. And fairly quickly. The same can be said for failure. You need to keep moving, but just in a slightly different direction. Oh, "come on," you might say. That analogy doesn't hold water. The evidence, however, shows it does. A case in point is Theodore Seuss Geisel, known as Dr. Seuss – author of *The cat in the hat* and many other children's books that have delighted young readers the world over. He had his first book rejected by 27 publishers! Just as he was on the verge of burning the manuscript, he ran into an old classmate who helped him get it published at Vanguard Press. You may not know that until this point, Geisel had supported himself entirely through drawing cartoons.

4 **Reject others' opinions.** If you hold on to someone else's negative opinion of you, it will be hard to move forward, so be careful to avoid that trap! Never forget that what someone thinks is true about you may actually be false. Terry Gross of National Public Radio felt she "couldn't do anything" when she failed at her first teaching job and was fired after only six weeks. That was before she discovered radio. Her program "Fresh Air" now reaches over five million listeners.

5 **Focus on the positive!** It may seem obvious, but your attitude may be the only thing separating you from those who have achieved greatness. It's so tempting to let a negative voice take over, and give way to anger and despair. However, Confucius certainly had it right when he proclaimed, "Our greatest glory is not in never falling, but in rising every time we fall."

How well do you deal with failure? 5.3

Lesson Aims: Sts learn language to talk about dealing with failure.

Skills	Language	Vocabulary
Reading a text on coming to terms with failure	Giving advice: *Focus on the positive. Snap out of it! Reject others' opinions.*	Phrases for evaluating success, e.g. *put stg. behind you, dwell on, keep stg. in perspective, go to great lengths, take stock, hold onto*

Warm-up

Ask the lesson title question: *How well do you deal with failure? Have you had any failures recently? Have you failed an exam / a driving test? Have you failed to get a job you wanted? How did you feel afterwards? Did you blame yourself? Did it make you more determined to succeed?* Have sts discuss the questions in pairs.

Ask: *What's your idea of success? Have you experienced success at something recently? How did it make you feel?*

6 Reading

A Refer sts to the cartoon. Ask: *What can you see?* (Five colleagues in a business meeting.) *What do you think they are discussing?* (Sales falling or not increasing.)

Sts read the title of the article and the first paragraph. Ask: *What do you think "coming to terms with" means?* (to gradually accept a situation, usually a sad one). *What else can you come to terms with?* (a death, a critical illness, or crippling injury).

Brainstorm areas of life people often fail in, e.g. *relationships with family / partners, jobs, studies, not saving money, getting fired, failing an exam.*

Ask: *What is meant by keeping failure in perspective?* (seeing it from an objective point of view). Ask sts to give you an example, e.g. a young person may be emotionally devastated by a breakup with a boyfriend or girlfriend, and think it is the end of the world, but if they try to see the relationship in the context of their whole life, it will help them get over it.

Ask sts to discuss the last question in pairs. Have sts share their views with the rest of the class.

Tip

The key reading skill is prediction. So, ask sts to take three minutes to scan the text to find ten famous names and say why they are mentioned here (because they all experienced some type of failure). Then ask them to try to predict what the text will say about each of them, to incentivize them to read on and see if they were right.

5.3

B ▶ 5.10 Ask sts to read the sentence starters 1–5. Tell them they correspond to paragraphs 1–5. Sts read each paragraph one at a time then complete the corresponding sentence so that it summarizes the paragraph. You can play the audio so they can listen and read at the same time (pausing after each paragraph), or play the entire audio at the end. Paircheck. Classcheck.

Weaker classes: Before sts do this task, put them into five groups. Allocate one paragraph to each group. Have them read their paragraph for one minute, and then try to summarize it. Elect a spokesperson for each group to summarize the paragraph for the rest of the class.

Tip

Vary the way you pick up on and exploit the pink stress words, e.g. ask sts to go back and, in pairs, pronounce them all. Monitor for any they find hard. Then drill these ones with the class in fun ways, e.g.

- all the males, then all the females
- left half, then right half of the class, pair by pair, or St As then st Bs, or in teams
- loudly, whispering, silently mouthing, singing …
- normal speed, fast, slowly, very slowly sy-lla-ble by sy-lla-ble
- backchaining (starting from the end & building syllable by syllable)

Weaker classes: Board the answers (the sentence endings) in random order. Sts read the rest of the text and match them to the sentence halves in the book.

Answers

1 take failure personally
2 it won't change the outcome and it will make you feel worse about the failure
3 figure out why it / you failed and what you could do better next time
4 it can undermine your confidence and affect your ability to succeed
5 believe you can succeed

C Sts find the underlined words in the article and read the whole sentence which contains them. Have them choose the correct definition. Classcheck. Drill pronunciation of the words.

For extra vocabulary practice, have sts re-read the text and underline the words which are similar in their language (cognates). They can check in a dictionary whether they have a similar meaning or are a "false friend."

Answers

1 feel afraid of 2 unharmed emotionally 3 accept
4 succeed 5 pay attention to 6 seem logical

▶ Song lyric: See Teacher's Book p.346 for notes about the song and an accompanying activity to do with the class.

D Make it personal Have sts choose a statement from B, then think of a story to back it up. Encourage sts to draw on personal experience if they have experienced failure of any type, or they can talk about someone they know. Elicit an example, e.g. *I played in a soccer game recently, and we were playing a team who were top of the league, but our coach told us to believe in ourselves and think positively, and we won!*

7 Vocabulary: Evaluating success

A Have sts read the title of the text. Discuss the meaning of *go to your head* (make you too proud). Tell them to read the whole text quickly to get the gist, ignoring the blanks.

Focus on the highlighted words in the article. Have sts try to do the fill-in-the-blank activity in pairs, without explaining the meaning or looking them up.

Weaker classes: Elicit or give the meanings first.

Pairs peercheck with the sts on either side of them, then classcheck. Ask: *What do you think the green arrow image beside the text represents?* (the speed and zigzags of success). *What's your favorite tip?* Elicit other tips to add to the list.

Answers

1 go to great lengths
2 keep fame and fortune in perspective
3 take stock
4 put them behind you
5 hold on to
6 dwelling on

B Make it personal Discuss the life events in the box. Ask sts: *Have you experienced any of these? Have did you feel? Do you think it changed you as a person?*

1 Sts discuss in pairs people they know who did change after one of these events. These can be people they know or famous people.
2 Have them tell each other what happened, using expressions from A where possible.

Classcheck by asking some sts to tell the rest of the class.

Tip

If sts aren't comfortable talking in this way about people they know, or they think other sts might know the person, ask them to change the name / some of the details before they share their ideas.

▶ Workbook p.25.

♪ When you try your best, but you don't succeed. When you get what you want, but not what you need

B ▶ **5.10** Listen to and read the whole article. In pairs, complete each sentence so that it captures the essence of each section in the article.
1 Even if you've failed, it's OK to be upset, but important not to _take failure personally_.
2 Stop obsessing about your failure because _____.
3 Look at failure analytically, which means _____.
4 It's dangerous to give too much power to others' opinions because _____.
5 It's important to think positively and _____.

C Find the underlined words in the article. Circle the word or expression with the same meaning in context.
1 dread: [**feel afraid of** / **feel reluctant about**] failure
2 unscathed: [**uninjured physically** / **unharmed emotionally**]
3 give in to: [**accept** / **hand over**]
4 pan out: [**succeed** / **take place**]
5 heed: [**read** / **pay attention to**]
6 hold water: [**seem factual** / **seem logical**]

D **Make it personal** Choose a statement from **B** you agree with. Do you have a story to back it up?

> I totally agree with number 1. Let me tell you about what happened to me at my old school ...

7 Vocabulary: Evaluating success

A Complete 1–6 with six of the highlighted expressions from the article. What's your favorite tip? Can you think of any others?

Success: Don't let it go to your head!

Some people ¹_____ to achieve success in life, but don't always know what to do with it. Here are four tips to help you ²_____ fame and fortune _____.

– Keep your feet on the ground. Before making major decisions, stop and ³_____ of your values, goals, and interests.
– Fame doesn't erase your own failures, so be empathetic! You've just ⁴_____ them _____ you successfully and moved on.
– Keep in mind that success may not last forever, however hard you may try to ⁵_____ it.
– If you find your new-found fortune slips away, there's no point ⁶_____ what might have been. Remember, you're still you!

B **Make it personal** In pairs, discuss 1–2.
1 Do you know anyone who changed after he / she got ...

a new job   famous   into college   married   promoted   rich

2 What happened? Use expressions from **A**.

> My brother went to great lengths to find a new job. But then ...

5.4 Have you ever had a wrong first impression?

8 Language in use

A ▶ 5.11 Listen and match six conversations to pictures a–f. In pairs, what character trait was the surprise in each case?

> In the first one, the guy was actually irresponsible.

B ▶ 5.12 Read the conversation excerpts and guess whether the speakers are those in A or new people. Listen to check.

1 I resent him expecting me to do everything! I thought I could count on his help, but I can't. It looks as if I'll have to team up with someone else.

2 I heard about you breaking up and that you couldn't work things out. I can see why you didn't want to stay with him!

3 Bill and I have some legitimate concerns about your not sticking to the deadline. I know that might strike you as heartless.

4 The principal is appalled at the boy's cheating and plans to take the matter up with his parents.

5 She appreciated us inviting her, even though it didn't come off that way ... We might wind up being good friends.

6 The police officer insisted on our coming to the station. At first, I thought he'd let us off.

C ▶ 5.12 Listen again. Complete the misleading behaviors. Which one is the worst?
1 Roger misled Barbara by taking _____ and asking _____.
2 At first John would ask about Ann's _____ and cook a wonderful _____ .
3 Bill used to stop by Susan's _____ often and ask about her _____ .
4 Simon would talk about _____ and _____ in classes on social issues.
5 Georgina didn't know Amy was _____ because she always offered to give _____ .
6 The officer had good _____ and a _____ accent.

> **Common mistake**
> I'm really counting ~~with~~ *on* you.

D Write the highlighted phrasal verbs in B next to their meanings in context.
1 _____ solve
2 _____ depend on
3 _____ not punish
4 _____ work with
5 _____ stay with
6 _____ end up
7 _____ discuss
8 _____ seem, appear

E Make it personal Has your first impression of anyone ever been really wrong? How did you find out? Share your stories in groups, using phrasal verbs from C. Whose was the most unusual?

> I had a neighbor who came off as really easygoing at first. He smiled a lot and told jokes. But then one day, he showed his true colors!

Have you ever had a wrong first impression? 5.4

Lesson Aims: Sts listen to people talking about first impressions which proved to be wrong, and talk about getting the wrong first impression of someone.

Skills	Language	Vocabulary	Grammar
Listening to short conversations in which people are disappointed by someone's behavior	Sharing your reactions: *I'm (not) in favor of …, I'm against …, I'm concerned about …, I'm skeptical of …*	Phrasal verbs: *count on, team up with, work out stg., stick to, take up, come off, wind up, let off*	Nouns, object pronouns, and possessive adjectives + *ing* form, e.g. *I'm sick of my mom yelling at me.*

Warm-up

Ask the lesson title question: *Have you ever had a wrong first impression? What did you get right / wrong about this person?*

Ask sts to brainstorm situations in which it's very important to make a good first impression, e.g. meeting a partner's parents for the first time, job / college interview. Ask: *How would you dress / behave if you wanted to make a good first impression? How do you avoid making the wrong impression?*

8 Language in use

A ▶5.11 Focus on the pictures. Ask: *What can you say about the people? What are they doing? What do you think the relationship between them is? How do you think they are feeling? What type of conversation are they having?*

Play the audio and have sts match the conversations with a–f. Re-play the audio and say what character trait was the surprise in each case. Classcheck.

As follow-up, elicit the opposite adjectives (1 responsible, 2 mature, 3 sympathetic, 4 honest, 5 outgoing, 6 understanding), then have sts formulate sentences about each of the people using both adjectives, e.g. *Barbara had always thought Roger was responsible, but he turned out to be lazy and irresponsible.*

> **Answers**
> 1 d Roger turned out to be lazy and irresponsible.
> 2 f John was selfish and immature.
> 3 b Bill was insensitive (and unfailing).
> 4 e Simon was dishonest.
> 5 a Amy was shy.
> 6 c The officer was mean (or tough).

» See Teacher's Book p.322 for Audio script 5.11.

B ▶5.12 Ask sts to read the excerpts quickly. Elicit the meaning from context of *resent* (angry), *appalled* (very angry), and *wind up* (finish). Ask: *Which of the situations seem familiar from* A? *Which of the speakers did they hear? Which are new situations?*

Explain that sts are going to hear six conversations, in three of them they will hear the speakers from A talking to friends about the conversations they had in A, in the other three, they will hear new speakers. Play the audio and ask them to check which speakers they heard in A. Classcheck.

Weaker classes: To check comprehension, board the following character traits: a) only thinks about himself, b) capable of cheating, c) cold and unfeeling. Ask sts to listen again to audio 5.12 and say in which conversations these were mentioned (2a, 3c, and 4b).

> **Answers**
> In A: 1, 5, 6   New: 2, 3, 4

» See Teacher's Book p.322 for Audio script 5.12.

» Song lyric: See Teacher's Book p.347 for notes about the song and an accompanying activity to do with the class.

C ▶5.12 Have sts read the sentences, and complete them from memory if they can. Then play the audio for them to check and complete the rest. Classcheck.

Focus on the **Common mistake**. Elicit the meaning / synonyms from the context in B (depending, relying) and highlight the error of preposition.

> **Answers**
> 1 notes, questions   2 day, dinner   3 office, work
> 4 values, ethics   5 shy, presentations   6 manners, soft

D Ask sts to find the phrasal verbs in the texts in B and write them next to their meanings 1–8. Ask sts: *Which of these phrasal verbs did you already know?* Classcheck.

> **Answers**
> 1 work out   2 count on   3 let off   4 team up with
> 5 stick to   6 end up   7 take up   8 come off

Tip

Sts can record phrasal verbs e.g. by verb or by particle but, in terms of retention and recall, it's usually best to record them by topic.

E Make it personal Ask: *Have you ever formed a completely wrong impression of someone? What happened to make you realize you were wrong?* Have sts discuss in groups. Encourage them to use the phrasal verbs in C. Have a few sts report back to the rest of the class.

5.4

9 Grammar: Nouns, object pronouns, and possessive adjectives + -ing form

A Go through the grammar box with the class. Check sts understand the example sentences. Ask them how they would say them in their language.

Tip

Especially with Romance language speakers, ask sts to go through the sentences in pairs, translating each of them and highlighting the differences in form from the equivalents in their language, e.g. where they would use an infinitive rather than a gerund. Classcheck any interesting findings. This can be a useful strategy with any new grammar point to help prevent errors, just like our **Common mistake** feature.

Weaker classes: Check spelling rules for *-ing* form. Review the rules for singular possession ('s) and plural possession (s') too.

Sts check the correct rules. Peercheck. Classcheck.

> **Answers**
>
> 1 object pronoun, possessive adjective   2 his, more
> 3 always, always   4 possessive

Weaker classes: Before they do exercise A, board the following words: *our, you, my dad, my dad's, him, her, his, hers*. Ask sts to identify which are *object pronouns* and which are *possessive adjectives* (object pronouns: *you, my dad, him, her*; possessive adjectives: *our, my dad's, his, hers*)

» Refer sts to the **Grammar expansion** on p.146.

B Sts find six examples in 8B and write I or N next to them. Do the first one together with the class as an example. Classcheck.

> **Answers**
>
> 1 I resent him expecting – I
> 2 I heard about you breaking up – I
> 3 … about your not sticking to the deadline – N
> 4 The principal is appalled at the boy's cheating – N
> 5 She appreciated us inviting her – I
> 6 The police officer insisted on our coming – N

C For fun, first cover the text, look at the list heading and get sts to guess what the seven complaints might be. If time, board their suggestions exactly as they say them, then do the exercise.

Have sts do this individually. Classcheck by inviting sts to board the sentences one by one. Elicit any errors from the class, and correct the sentences on the board. Ask: *Do you identify with any of the complaints? Can you add any others now, too?*

Stronger classes: Have sts make the sentences true for them, e.g. 1 *I'm tired of my teacher constantly criticizing my work.* 2 *I'm not comfortable with my sisters borrowing my clothes.*

> **Answers**
>
> 1 I'm tired of her constantly criticizing me.
> 2 I'm not comfortable with his parents dropping by unexpectedly.
> 3 I'm tired of you snoring.
> 4 I resent Jim being Facebook friends with his ex.
> 5 I'll never get used to him giving me the silent treatment when he's angry.
> 6 He can't stand me taking a long time to answer his texts.
> 7 I'm not happy with us wanting different things.

D Make it personal Ask sts to read through the headlines. Have individual sts explain the stories in their own words to the rest of the class. After each story, ask: *Does the story make you angry or happy?* Ask sts to say what they think using the phrases in the box, and a noun / object pronoun before an *-ing* form. Focus sts on the examples in the speech bubbles. Have sts share their reactions in groups.

Classcheck by asking individual sts what the other members of their group think. Ask: *Were there any big differences of opinion?*

Optional activities

- As an extension, ask sts to search online and find other interesting / controversial headlines. Sts then share these in groups and discuss their reactions, using the phrases in the box.

- As a fun finish to the class, or a warm-up for the next, have pairs cover the seven complaints in 9C and try to remember them together. They can unveil them a word at a time until they get them exactly right.

» Workbook p.26.

♪ You and I should ride the coast and wind up in our favorite coats just miles away

5.4

9 Grammar: Nouns, object pronouns, and possessive adjectives + -ing form

A Read the grammar box and check (✔) the correct rules.

Levels of formality in nouns, object pronouns, and possessive adjectives + -ing form			
Informal	I'm sick of	**my mom**	yelling at me.
	Roger was counting on	**me**	helping him with the project.
	I resent	**you**	not doing your fair share.
	The officer insisted on	**them**	going to the station.
Neutral to formal	I'm against	**our school's**	giving so many exams.
	My boss showed concern about	**my**	not turning in the report.
	He wasn't very supportive of	**your**	being sick.
	I'm uncomfortable with	**their**	not giving me an honest answer.

1 Informal sentences have a(n) ☐ **object pronoun** ☐ **possessive adjective** before the verb, and more formal sentences have a(n) ☐ **object pronoun** ☐ **possessive adjective.**
2 Therefore, when talking to your boss, say "I appreciate ☐ **him** ☐ **his** calling me" because it is ☐ **more** ☐ **less** formal.
3 The form of the verb is ☐ **sometimes** ☐ **always** an -ing form, and the form of the negative is ☐ **sometimes** ☐ **always** not.
4 When there is a noun before a verb, the more formal form is ☐ **possessive** ☐ **plural**.

B Find the six undelined examples in **8B** of nouns, pronouns, or possessive adjectives before -ing forms. Write *I* next to the informal forms and *N* next to the neutral to formal ones.

» Grammar expansion p.146

C Rewrite 1–7 informally with nouns or object pronouns. Do you identify with any of the complaints? Can you think of any others?

> ### Top seven relationship complaints
> 1 "She's constantly criticizing me. I'm tired of that."
> 2 "His parents drop by unexpectedly. I'm not comfortable with that."
> 3 "You snore. I'm tired of that."
> 4 "Jim is Facebook friends with his ex. I resent that."
> 5 "He gives me the silent treatment when he's angry. I'll never get used to that."
> 6 "I take a long time to answer his texts. He can't stand that."
> 7 "We want different things. I'm not happy with that."

I'm tired of her constantly criticizing me.

D Make it personal Do you approve? In groups, read the headlines and share your reactions. Use nouns or object pronouns before -ing forms, where possible. Any big differences?

I'm (not) in favor of … I'm against … I'm concerned about … I'm skeptical of …

1 **A bittersweet ending: Japanese train station closes after lone passenger, picked up every day at 7:04 a.m. and brought back at 5:08 p.m., graduates from high school**
2 **Undercover officer dressed as homeless man catches drivers using phones**
3 **Vice-principal greets students with singing, dancing every morning**
4 **Table manners rewarded: restaurant offers diners 5% off to drop their devices**

> I'm not in favor of trains operating with just one passenger. What a waste of money!

> I disagree. This station stayed open to support education.

57

5.5 How bad are drivers where you live?

10 Listening

A ▶ 5.13 Listen to a conversation between Monica and Ed about bad drivers. In pairs, answer 1–2.
1. What dangers do pedestrians face in their city?
2. What does Ed think can be done about it?

B ▶ 5.14 Listen to a second conversation. Note down …
1. two problems with Ed's proposal for a test based on the London exam.
2. one problem with Monica's proposal for speed bumps.

C ▶ 5.15 Listen to a third conversation. Check (✔) the aspects of driver psychology mentioned.
1. ☐ future ability to stay focused 2. ☐ driver sociability 3. ☐ current degree of concentration

D **Make it personal** In pairs, would Monica and Ed's proposal work in your city? Is the revised proposal an improvement?

> I think it's still impractical. What if a driver can only afford one driving test?

11 Keep talking

A ▶ 5.16 Read *Proposal language*. Then complete 1–5 using a form of the words or expressions in the box. There's one extra. Listen to check.

> **Proposal language**
>
> Specific expressions are used to talk about proposals. For example, we *make* or *put together* a proposal, and a proposal has a *rationale* behind it, or central reason for existing.

| airtight | entail | put together | rationale | redo | spell out | steps | turn down |

1. I'm going to _____ a proposal anyway. And maybe I can submit it next week.
2. They _____ my proposal. Guess it's back to square 1.
3. What did your proposal _____ ? What was the general idea?
4. The _____ was that there would be a special exam for city drivers.
5. It [the proposal]'s got to be _____ this time. It has to _____ all the different _____ and show how to get from point A to point B.

B In groups, choose a topic below and develop a proposal. Make certain it has a clear rationale and list at least four features as bullet points. Use proposal language from **A** and the expressions below. Share it with the class. Whose is most convincing?

How to …
evaluate students who aren't good at exams   develop new parking rules in your city
make your neighborhood cleaner or safer   offer scholarships to needy students
earn money if you can't find a good job

| I think you're on to something.   Why not focus on …?   Suppose you only …   You've got a point. |

> OK, exams. My proposal is to eliminate the final exam.

> I think you're on to something. First, let's go over the rationale.

58

How bad are drivers where you live? 5.5

Lesson Aims: Sts listen to a proposal to improve driving standards, and learn language to write their own proposal.

Skills	Language	Vocabulary
Listening to two friends talking about the problems of bad driving Writing a proposal	Talking about proposals, e.g. *We're going to put together a proposal. The proposal has been turned down. The rationale behind the proposal ...*	Making proposals: *airtight, entail, put together, rationale, redo, spell out, steps, turn down* Adverbs: *admittedly, broadly speaking, frankly, essentially, incidentally, clearly, obviously*

Warm-up

Board the lesson question title plus follow-up questions for st to answer in pairs: *Do people drive too quickly? What measures are there in place to reduce drivers' speed?* Try to elicit *speed bumps, speed limits, road signs warning drivers that they are driving over the speed limit, speed cameras*.

» Song lyric: See Teacher's Book p.347 for notes about the song and an accompanying activity to do with the class.

10 Listening

A ▶ 5.13 Focus on the photo. Tell sts they are going to hear Monica and Ed, two friends, talking about the traffic. Play the audio for sts to answer the questions. Classcheck. Ask: *Can you guess what the London taxi exam involves?*

Answers
1. Being killed by distracted / dangerous / speeding drivers
2. Introducing a new style of driving test based on the London taxi exam

» See Teacher's Book p.322 for Audio script 5.13.

B ▶ 5.14 Tell sts they are going to listen to Ed and Monica discussing other solutions to bad driving. Refer them to 1 and 2. Ask what the problems might be. Have them listen again and make notes. Classcheck. Ask: *Were you right? What other idea did Monica have?*

Answers
1. It's unrealistic to ask drivers to spend years learning all the streets in their city (particularly if they work / live in one area only), and learning the streets won't make them slow down
2. They would be too expensive to install (and it would be like driving on a roller-coaster)

» See Teacher's Book p.322 for Audio script 5.14.

C ▶ 5.15 Tell sts Monica and Ed are now discussing a proposal for new driving tests, which involve driver psychology. Play the audio for sts to check the aspects mentioned 1, 2, or 3. Ask: *How many tests are they proposing?* (three)

Weaker classes: Play the audio pausing after the relevant parts which give the answer.

Answers
1 and 3

» See Teacher's Book p.323 for Audio script 5.15.

D Make it personal Sts discuss Monica and Ed's proposal and decide whether they think it would improve road safety in their city. Ask: *What are the problems with the proposal?* Ask sts how they would improve road safety in their town. In pairs, ask them to come up with their own proposal. This could be a new driving test, speed restrictions, road signs, driving ages.

11 Keep talking

A ▶ 5.16 Ask: *Have you ever had to make a proposal? When? Why?* Make sure sts don't confuse this with *to propose marriage!* Read **Proposal language** together with the class. Go through the words in the box and check the meanings. Sts complete 1–5. Play the audio for them to check answers.

Stronger classes: Ask sts to write their own sentences using some of the words in the box.

Answers
1 put together   2 turned down   3 entail   4 rationale
5 airtight, spell out, steps

B Go through the topics with the class and brainstorm ideas. Put sts in groups to develop a proposal about one of the topics. Elicit an example of a rationale and bullet point and board them, e.g. *Proposal to make the downtown area cleaner. Bullet point 1: Petty criminals to do community service which involves cleaning the streets.*

Have sts present their proposal to the rest of the class using the language in A, e.g. *The rationale of our proposal is to make the downtown area cleaner.* Class feedback. Ask: *Which is the best proposal?*

Tip

When sts are presenting to the class, make sure other sts pay attention by giving them a task while they listen. This could be a language task, e.g. check off the phrases as and when the presenters use them, or a comprehension task e.g. think of two questions you'd like to ask at the end of the presentation.

5.5

12 Writing: A proposal

A Focus on the email. Ask: *Who is the email from?* (President of the School Council) *Who is it to?* (Probably the head of governors or the principal of a school). Then give sts two minutes to read it quickly for gist and remember as much as they can.

Focus on questions 1–3. Ask pairs: Which ones can you answer from memory? Monitor how they do. Then, after a couple of minutes, have sts scan the proposal to check / complete their answers and highlight the relevant parts. Classcheck. Ask: *What do you think of his proposal? Do you think they will accept? Why (not)?*

Tip

When checking answers to **A**, ask sts to reformulate each of the supporting arguments in their own words, in order to check comprehension.

Answers

1 I'd now like to propose the following in an effort to submit a plan that is more practical.
2 Suggested answers:
Goal 1: with the acute needs of our global economy at stake, we simply cannot afford to have segments of society who are left without access to continuing education
Goal 2: We owe it to our students to enable them to experience the richness of different cultures and sub-cultures
Goal 3: Poor students, quite obviously, face enough obstacles and prejudice
3 Regarding our next step, we would be happy to meet with you at your convenience to discuss the specifics

B Read through **Write it right!** with the class. Ask sts to find the highlighted adverbs in the email, and if they don't know the meaning, try to figure it out from the context. Ask them to think of synonyms (*incidentally* = by chance / by the way, *frankly* = to be honest, *essentially* = in essence, *apparently* = it seems that, *obviously* = of course, *broadly speaking* = generally). Sts choose the correct options in sentences 1–4. Classcheck. Ask: *Which of these adverbs are cognates in your language?*

Answers

1 Admittedly 2 Essentially 3 Apparently
4 Broadly speaking

C Read through **Formulaic expressions (1)** with the class. Have sts find the underlined sentences in the email, and pick out the formulaic expressions. Classcheck. Check they understand what they mean.

Board the following incorrect sentence: *We were disappointed, however, we understand the limited budget.* Ask sts to find the word *However* in the first paragraph, and correct the mistake. (*We were disappointed. However, we understand the limited budget.*) Tell sts we can also use a semi-colon *We were disappointed; however, we understand ...*

Answers

The importance of ... cannot be overemphasized.
Please allow me to ...
We would be happy to ...
at your convenience
We will do our best to ...

D **Your turn!** Read through the instructions and check sts know what they have to do.

Weaker classes: Plan the opening paragraph together and board it, e.g.

Dear ...

We are very concerned about the increase of litter in our neighborhood. Frankly, it is not acceptable. We are a group of students who care about where we live and want to be proud of it, so we have come together to try to do something about it. We would like to make the following proposal:

When sts have finished, you can have them post their emails online or present them verbally to the rest of the class. Encourage sts to ask questions about their classmates' proposals and say whether they are practical or not.

Class feedback. Have sts vote on the most convincing proposal.

Tip

It's often a good idea to tell sts you will only correct their major pieces of written work if they have shown them to a partner first for some peer evaluation, and hopefully, some correction. Get their partner to initial and write a comment to prove that they have read it. That way, not only should sts get more used to helping each other but you might have less marking to do yourself!

» Workbook p.27.

🎵 It's all over the front page. You give me road rage

12 Writing: A proposal

A Read the proposal and find ...
1 the purpose of the email.
2 one supporting argument for each of the goals in paragraphs 4, 5, and 6.
3 the next step in the proposal.

B Read *Write it right!* Then read 1–4 and choose the most logical answers.

> **Write it right!**
>
> In many kinds of writing, adverbs and adverbial expressions not only help to link ideas, but they also signal what the sentence or next point will be about:
>
> **Admittedly** [= I concede it's true that] our school is not a charity.

1 [**Admittedly** / **Incidentally**] we have an ambitious plan, but we still think there are ways to achieve it.
2 [**Frankly** / **Essentially**], our proposal can be summarized in one sentence.
3 [**Apparently** / **Obviously**], it seems two other schools have tried something similar from what I've heard.
4 [**Obviously** / **Broadly speaking**], our proposal has three parts.

C Read *Formulaic expressions (1)*. Circle five more fixed expressions in the underlined sentences in the proposal.

> **Formulaic expressions (1)**
>
> Formal letters and emails often contain formulaic expressions, where the wording is fixed. They facilitate written communication by offering standard openings, closings, and other useful language.
>
> Thank you (very much) for your response to our proposal of February 15 (date).

D Your turn! Choose a proposal you discussed in **11B** and write a formal email to present it in about 280 words.

Before
Plan three arguments for your proposal and note down supporting details.

While
Write five to six paragraphs to support your proposal, following the model in **A**. Use a variety of adverbs and at least one formulaic sentence.

After
Post your essay online and read your classmates' work. Whose proposal is most convincing?

Dear Ms. Harbinger:

Thank you very much for your response to our proposal of February 15. We were quite disappointed that our project wasn't accepted, as I'm sure you can understand. However, we understand that the budget was insufficient. With the aim of finding an acceptable solution, we've rethought some aspects of our strategy. I'd now like to propose the following in an effort to submit a plan that is more practical:

1. Our school would offer a scholarship each semester to 50 qualifying students, rather than a full scholarship.
2. The remaining tuition costs would be covered in three potential ways:
   a) Through work-study programs at our school.
   b) By offering loans, which would be repaid within ten years of graduation.
   c) By offering part-time degree programs, thereby allowing students to pay half tuition and take jobs in the community.

Broadly speaking, we have three goals: (1) to give needy students a chance at upward mobility, (2) to expand our student base and make it more diverse, and most importantly, (3) to reward academic effort and achievement. The importance of these objectives cannot be overemphasized, so please allow me to elaborate.

Admittedly, our school is not a charity. Nevertheless, our long-term goal should be a more egalitarian society with opportunities for all. Frankly, in the 21st century, with the acute needs of our global economy at stake, we simply cannot afford to have segments of society who are left without access to continuing education. Upward mobility must be a dream within the reach of all of us.

Exposing students to diversity is also important if we hope to create a society free of conflict, and essentially, our school has attracted students from only one social and economic background. Apparently, as we've learned from a survey we conducted in one of the communities we have in mind, promotion is not reaching students from across the city. In view of this, we feel we need to try harder. We owe it to our students to enable them to experience the richness of different cultures and sub-cultures. Incidentally, a brief survey here at Fourth District College shows that our own students find this goal important, as well.

Clearly, in a just society, academic achievement must be rewarded also. Poor students, quite obviously, face enough obstacles and prejudice. This last goal doesn't seem to require amplification.

I hope I have managed to provide a convincing rationale. Regarding our next step, we would be happy to meet with you at your convenience to discuss the specifics. We will do our best to answer any questions you may have.

Sincerely,
Ricardo Ortega
Student Council President

6

Do you still read paper books?

1 Listening

A ▶6.1 Listen to the start of an interview with Dr. Soars. Then in pairs, look at photos 1–2 and compare your understanding of "the digital apocalypse never came."

B ▶6.2 Guess whether the features (1–6) are E (e-book), P (paper book), or NI (no information)? Listen to the next part to check.

1. convenient
2. affordable
3. prone to damage
4. environmentally friendly
5. sensory-rich
6. reader friendly

C ▶6.2 Listen again. Match the opinions (1–6) to their responses (a–e). Then give your own responses.

1. Paper books aren't going anywhere in the foreseeable future.
2. Reading is essentially an abstract activity, right?
3. You see, reading involves a certain degree of physicality.
4. So … e-books fail to recreate this sort of hands-on experience?
5. Some people find it easier to take notes using a pen or pencil.

a ☐ "You've lost me there."
b ☐ "But how can that be?"
c ☐ "Well, guilty as charged."
d ☐ "Well, yes and no."
e ☐ "To some extent, yes."

> Paper books aren't going anywhere in the foreseeable future.

> I completely disagree. Actually, I just read today that …

D ▶6.3 Listen to the end of the interview. How does Dr. Soars feel about phone reading? Do you agree?

E ▶6.3 Match the two columns. Listen again to check. Which phrases do you associate with fast reading?

1 skip	a ☐ it past the first paragraph
2 (not) make	b ☐ your eyes over a text
3 run	c ☐ over whole sentences

4 get	a ☐ over a challenging text
5 pore	b ☐ the gist of a text
6 read	c ☐ between the lines

F Make it personal In groups, discuss 1–2.

1. Do you think paper books will have a future similar to CDs? Why (not)?
2. How do you usually read these items? Use expressions from E.

books by (Stephen King)   (Facebook) posts   (computer) instruction manuals
news about (politics)   (physics) textbooks   (rental) contracts

> I almost always read Facebook posts on my phone. They're usually short, so I can get the gist right away.

> I like to read them on my laptop so I don't just skip over the comments.

60

Do you still read paper books? 6.1

Lesson Aims: Sts learn language to talk about reading habits, and listen to an author talking about e-books vs. paper books.

Skills	Language	Vocabulary
Listening to an interview with an author about the advantages of paper books. Talking about reading habits	Talking about reading habits: *I always read Facebook posts on my phone. I can get the gist straight away. I skip over a lot of sentences when I read the news.*	Phrasal verbs with *out*: *pick out, wear out, bring out, cross out, point out, work out*

Warm-up

Brainstorm and board a list of all the items sts have read this week, e.g. *recipes, signposts, subtitles,* and underline those which still involve paper. Then ask the lesson title question, plus board prompts for sts to ask each other in pairs, e.g. *What type / books? How often? How many / a year?* Classcheck their most interesting answers.

1 Listening

A ▶ 6.1 Explain they are going to hear a radio show host introducing a guest. Ask sts to listen and find out why he's on the show (to talk about the resilience of paper books).

Board the quote "the digital apocalypse never came" and have sts discuss it in pairs. Classcheck.

> **Suggested answer**
> That the digital industry (e.g. e-books) didn't in fact kill off the print industry as people had thought it would, and that paper books are still popular.

» See Teacher's Book p.323 for Audio script 6.1.

B ▶ 6.2 Go through adjectives 1–6 and check the meanings. Tell sts they will hear Dr. Soars talking about some of these features. Tell them to listen and say whether he uses them to describe e-books or paper books or whether he doesn't mention them at all. Classcheck.

> **Answers**
> 1 E 2 NI 3 P 4 NI 5 P 6 P

» See Teacher's Book p.323 for Audio script 6.2.

C ▶ 6.2 Before sts listen, have them read opinions 1–5. Sts match them with the responses a–e. Play the audio for sts to check. Ask: *Do you agree / disagree with opinions 1–5?*

> **Answers**
> 1 b 2 d 3 a 4 e 5 c

Optional activity

Sts work in pairs and think of another opinion for each of the responses a–e.

D ▶ 6.3 Ask: *How is reading things on your phone different from reading books or from an e-reader?* Read the question: *How does Dr. Soars feel about phone reading?* Play the audio for sts to find out. Classcheck. Ask: *Do you agree?*

> **Answers**
> He feels that reading a text on a phone is adequate for getting the gist but that it's not suitable for careful reading where you need to analyze text and read between the lines – you need a paper book or an e-book to do that

» See Teacher's Book p.323 for Audio script 6.3.

E ▶ 6.3 Sts match the two columns, then listen to check. Classcheck. Ask sts to explain the meaning of *to read between the lines* (to look for or discover a meaning which is implied rather than stated). Ask sts which of these phrases they already knew.

Ask: *Which of these actions do you do when reading quickly? For example, do you skip over whole sentences?*

> **Answers**
> 1 c skip over whole sentences
> 2 a (not) make it past the first paragraph
> 3 b run your eyes over a text
> 4 b get the gist of a text
> 5 a pore over a challenging text
> 6 c read between the lines
> Fast reading: 1, 3, 4

F Make it personal Ask: *Do you buy CDs? Why / Why not? Do you buy paper books? Why / Why not?* Discuss whether their reasons for not buying CDs / books are the same. Read question 1 and have sts discuss in groups or discuss together with the class.

Focus on the list of items in question 2. Ask: *Which of these items do you read regularly?* Read the question. Elicit a few answers as examples, e.g. *I always skip over whole sentences when I'm reading news.*

Put sts in groups of three or four to talk about the other items. You could add tweets and text messages to the list.

» Song lyric: See Teacher's Book p.347 for notes about the song and an accompanying activity to do with the class.

6.1

2 Vocabulary: Phrasal verbs with *out*

A ▶ 6.4 Quickly drill the words in the box. Check the meaning of *titles* by asking: *What's the title of your favorite book now / when you were a kid?* Ask sts to read the quotes about e-books and paper books, and fill in the blanks. Elicit the meaning via mimes of both *browse* and *shortcuts*.

Tip

Check pronunciation by asking: *What does "browse" rhyme with?* (*cows, drowse, eyebrows,* not *house* or *mouse*). Rhyme is often a good way to check both pronunciation and spelling patterns, as well as building the obvious memory links between words.

Play the audio for sts to check. Ask: *Which can you imagine saying yourself?*

Stronger classes: Ask sts to write their own sentences with each of the phrasal verbs.

Elicit other verbs sts know with *out*, e.g. *die out, watch out, break out, come out, drop out, fall out, go out, run out, start out, walk out.* For each one they volunteer, ensure they produce an appropriate example to show they know its meaning, otherwise they might just be calling out random guesses!

> **Answers**
> 1 titles 2 e-books 3 nature 4 sentences
> 5 studies 6 meaning

B Go through the words on the mind maps. Check the meaning of *battery*.

Sts complete the mind maps with the phrasal verbs in **A**.

Put sts in pairs to ask and answer questions using the prompts in the box. Refer sts to the examples in the speech bubbles and elicit a few other examples, e.g. *Who in your family brings out the best in you? What do you do to bring out the flavor of meat?*

Class feedback. Ask: *Did you find out anything surprising? Do you have anything new in common? What was the funniest question / answer?*

> **Answers**
> 1 wear out 2 bring out 3 work out

C Make it personal Ask: *How do you feel about reading? How would you describe your reading habits nowadays? Have they changed much over the years? Do / Did you have shelves of books like the ones in the photo at home? Do you read more online or off? More from a screen or from paper? When are you most likely to read a novel? What would make you read more?*

1 Ask sts to read the quotes. Ask: *What do you know about the authors of the quotes?* (names in parentheses). Have sts discuss the meanings of the quotes in pairs. Refer them to the model in the speech bubble. Ask them to choose their three favorites.

Have them tell the class which one they have chosen and why.

Stronger classes: Ask students to add more quotes of their own, e.g. "Reading is to the mind what exercise is to the body." (Joseph Addison). Ask sts to search and find others or even write their own quote too about reading, then share them for the class to vote for the best one.

2 In their pairs, sts discuss what or who the quotes remind them of. Elicit an example from one of the stronger sts, e.g. *This reminds me of my younger brother. He hated reading until he found a book called Varjak Paw when he was about ten. Once he discovered that book, he never stopped reading.*

Background information

Mark Twain was an American writer who lived in the 19th Century. His most famous books were *The Adventures of Tom Sawyer* and *Adventures of Huckleberry Finn*.

Fran Lebowitz is an American author and public speaker. She is known for her social commentary on American (particularly New York City) life.

Stephen Fry is an English comedian, actor, writer, and activist for social causes.

Ambeth R. Ocampo is a Filipino author and historian. He writes a bi-weekly editorial column in the *Philippine Daily Inquirer*.

Edmund Wilson was an American writer who lived in the 20th Century. He is said to have influenced many other famous writers, including F. Scott Fitzgerald.

Margaret Fuller was an American journalist and women's rights activist who lived in the 19th Century. Her book *Woman in the Nineteenth Century* is thought to be the first feminist work in the U.S.

Lisa See is an American novelist, whose books have earned literary acclaim all over the world.

J. K. Rowling is a British novelist and screenwriter, most famous for writing the Harry Potter series. She also writes under the pen name Robert Galbraith.

» Workbook p.28.

> ♪ I got a shelf full of books and most of my teeth. A few pairs of socks and a door with a lock

6.1

2 Vocabulary: Phrasal verbs with *out*

A ▶ 6.4 Complete 1–6 with the nouns in the box. Listen to check.

| e-books | meaning | nature | sentences | studies | titles |

1 It's so much easier to browse an online store, **pick out** (= select from a group) your favorite _____ and download them.
2 You can't **wear out** (= damage from too much use) or accidentally tear _____.
3 A paper book has an easily indentifiable size, shape, and weight, which **brings out** (= reveals) its more concrete _____.
4 Some people find it easier to take notes, highlight, or even **cross out** (= draw a line through) _____ in a paper book.
5 Some _____ **point out** (= mention) that people reading on their phones take lots of shortcuts.
6 They're also more likely to ignore unknown words rather than **work out** (= try to discover) their _____ in context or look them up.

B Complete the mind maps with **highlighted** phrasal verbs from **A**. Then, in pairs, use the prompts to find out more about each other.

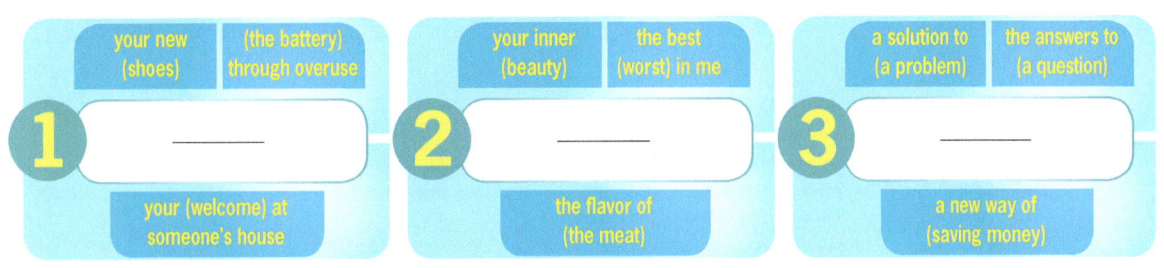

1 _____
- your new (shoes)
- (the battery) through overuse
- your (welcome) at someone's house

2 _____
- your inner (beauty)
- the best (worst) in me
- the flavor of (the meat)

3 _____
- a solution to (a problem)
- the answers to (a question)
- a new way of (saving money)

> Do / Have you ever ...?   When did you last ...?   Who in your (family) ...?   What do you do to / when ...?
> What's the best way to ...?   What would you do if ...?

> Have you ever ... your welcome at someone's house?

> Not as far as I know! I hope not.

C Make it personal How do you feel about reading?

1 Choose your three favorite quotes from those below. In pairs, explain what they mean.

a "'Classic' — a book which people praise and don't read." (Mark Twain)
b "Think before you speak. Read before you think." (Fran Lebowitz)
c "Books are no more threatened by Kindle than stairs by elevators." (Stephen Fry)
d "School made us 'literate' but did not teach us to read for pleasure." (Ambeth R. Ocampo)
e "No two persons ever read the same book." (Edmund Wilson)
f "Today a reader, tomorrow a leader." (Margaret Fuller)
g "Read a thousand books, and your words will flow like a river." (Lisa See)
h "If you don't like to read, you haven't found the right book." (J.K. Rowling)

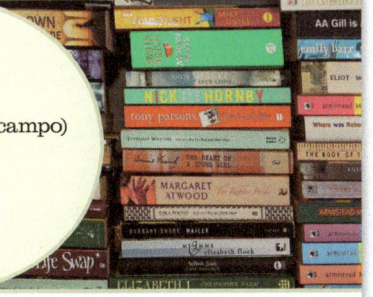

> I really like b. The first part is pretty obvious. But the second part means that books help us think in new ways. They bring out our creativity.

2 Do the quotes remind you of anyone or anything? Share your ideas, using phrasal verbs from **A** where possible.

61

6.2 Do you ever watch dubbed movies?

3 Language in use

A ▶6.5 Listen to two friends, Grace and Noah, talking about the movie *La Vie en Rose*. Complete 1–5 with short phrases.

1 Grace really enjoyed watching the movie, while Noah _____ .
2 He's not used to _____ .
3 In Germany, most TV shows and movies _____ .
4 Grace seems surprised, given _____ .
5 Countries that avoid subtitles include _____ .

B ▶6.6 Guess the speaker's main arguments. Then listen to check. Can you think of any others?

Noah doesn't like subtitles because …
1 he misses _____ .
2 it's hard for him not to _____ .

Grace doesn't like dubbed movies because …
3 the voices don't _____ .
4 actors can't _____ as well.

C ▶6.7 Read *Using out of*. Then write the use of *out of* (1–4) next to the bold phrases below. Listen to check. Notice the /ə/ sound in *of*.

> **Using *out of***
>
> *Out of* is a very common prepositional phrase. Here are four uses:
> 1 movement from within outwards: *We walked **out of the room**.*
> 2 caused or motivated by: *I watched the Oscars last night, more **out of curiosity** than interest.*
> 3 not having: *The theater company is **out of money** and can't produce a new play this year. Lots of record stores went **out of business** in the 2010s.*
> 4 selection from a group: *Ask anyone who the greatest American actress is, and at least **three out of five** people will say Meryl Streep.*

1 In Germany, nearly every foreign TV show is dubbed. I mean, like **8 out of 10** ☐, unless it's pay per view or something.
2 I end up reading the subtitles whether or not I understand what's being said. I guess I do it **out of** sheer **habit** ☐ – just in case I might have missed something.
3 It annoys me how the actors' lips and their voices are always a little **out of sync** ☐, even if the dubbing is done well.
4 Sometimes I just feel like getting up and walking **out of the theater** ☐.
5 I don't mind the occasional subtitle as long as there's not too much text to process. Otherwise, I find I'm **out of patience** ☐ pretty quickly.

D Make it personal In groups, answer 1–3.

1 Modify 1–5 in **C** so that they're true for you.
2 Are most foreign movies dubbed or subtitled where you live?
3 🔍 Search on a recent movie in English that you've seen or would like to see and watch the original trailer (name of movie + "original trailer"). Then search again for a dubbed trailer in your own language (name of movie in your language + "trailer" + name of language) and compare.

> I just watched the trailer for the movie *Brooklyn* in English and Spanish. I couldn't stand the dubbed version!

> What was wrong with it?

> Well, for one thing, the accents, one of the most appealing parts of the movie, were completely lost. The Irish accent, the Italian-American accent: they're all gone!

Do you ever watch dubbed movies? 6.2

Lesson Aims: Sts learn to use adverb clauses of condition and phrasal verbs with *out of*.

Skills	Language	Vocabulary	Grammar
Listening to two friends talking about watching dubbed movies vs. original version movies	Talking about trends, e.g. *More people my age are breaking up.*	Phrases with *out of*: *out of sheer habit, walk out of the room, out of sync, be out of patience*	Adverb clauses of condition: *as long as, whether or not, in case, unless*, and *even if*, e.g. *I don't mind dubbed movies as long as the voices are good.*

Warm-up

If possible, begin with a videoclip which is dubbed then show the same clip, subtitled, ideally from *La Vie en Rose*. Ask: *Which do you prefer and why?*

Expand into the lesson title question plus board more for sts to answer in pairs, e.g. *Do any local movie theaters show foreign movies in the original language? Do you generally prefer to watch dubbed or subtitled movies? Why? Do you watch foreign language movies on TV? Are they subtitled or dubbed?* Feedback their most interesting answers.

4 Language in use

A ▶ 6.5 Focus on the photo. Ask sts: *Have you seen this movie? What's it about?* (The life of Edith Piaf, who wrote the lyrics). *What does "la vie en rose" mean?* (Literally *Life in pink*, but better as *life through rose-tinted glasses* as it celebrates finding love after a bad period, in this case World War 2.) *Did you like it? Why / why not?* Have sts read the sentences. Then play the audio and have them complete them. Classcheck.

> **Answers**
> 1 didn't 2 subtitles 3 are dubbed
> 4 the movie is a classic 5 German, Austria, Italy, and Spain

>> See Teacher's Book p.323 for Audio script 6.5.

B ▶ 6.6 Tell sts they are going to hear Grace and Noah discussing why they prefer subtitles / dubbed movies. Ask them to guess what their arguments might be.

Optional activity

Before sts listen, divide the class in half. Ask one half to work in pairs and think of reasons why someone might not like subtitles, and the other half to work in pairs and do the same for dubbed movies. When finished, pair sts from each half of the class to share their ideas. In feedback, board their reasons. After exercise B, go back to the reasons on the board and check off any which were mentioned in the recording.

Play the audio for them to check and complete their arguments. Classcheck. Ask: *Who do you agree with?*

> **Answers**
> 1 out on all sorts of nuances in the actors' expressions
> 2 read the subtitles even if he understands what they are saying
> 3 match the actors' lips moving
> 4 convey emotion

>> See Teacher's Book p.324 for Audio script 6.6.

C ▶ 6.7 Read **Using out of** with the whole class. Check understanding of the example sentences. Ask sts to compare how they would say the expression *out of* in their language in each example. Ask: *What similarities / differences are there?*

Sts read through sentences 1–5. Ask: *Do you remember who said these things, Grace or Noah?*

Have sts match the bold phrases in 1–5 with the uses 1–4. Play the audio for them to check. Drill pronunciation of the /e/ sound in the *out of* expressions, e.g. /aʊt e/.

> **Answers**
> 1 Use 4 2 Use 2 3 Use 3 4 Use 1 5 Use 3

>> Song lyric: See Teacher's Book p.347 for notes about the song and an accompanying activity to do with the class.

D Make it personal Put sts in groups of three or four.

1 Sts write out 1–5 making the sentences true for them. Elicit a couple of examples, e.g. *In Spain, where I was on vacation, most TV shows have subtitles. I never read the subtitles if it's a language I understand, because it helps me improve.*

2 Sts can discuss movies at the theater or on TV. Ask: *Do you think this is a good thing? If not, how would you improve the situation?*

3 Check sts understand *trailer* (an extract from a movie used for publicity). Have sts watch the trailers in the classroom if possible. (You could show the whole class a trailer that you have chosen to begin with and discuss as a class). If not, they can do this for homework. Class feedback. Invite sts to share their opinions about the trailers they watched. Focus them on the speech bubbles as models, and check the meaning of *not be able to stand* (to hate).

Monitor as they do 1–3, prompt, correct, and collect some useful feedback to give them at the end, including *Congratulations!*

6.2

4 Grammar: Adverb clauses of condition

A Have sts read through the grammar box. Check they understand the conjunctions in bold (as *long as* = provided that, *whether or not* = no matter if / regardless of whether, *in case* = as a precaution, *unless* = if I don't, *even if* = whether or not.) Sts check the rules. Check answers.

Read through sentences 1–5 and ask sts if they mean the same as sentences a–e. Peercheck. Classcheck. Be careful with pronunciation of *I don't object*.

> **Answers**
> Rules: 1 present   2 don't use
> Sentences: 1 S   2 D   3 S   4 S   5 D

Tip

Whenever you can, personalize grammar box sentences, for example here, ask: *Who do you think is saying each of these sentences? To who? When? Which ones can / can't you imagine yourself saying? How would you have to modify each one to make it a sentence of your own?* Do the same thing with the **Common mistake** below too. Many teachers rely a lot on photocopies / worksheets, but working along these lines can save a lot of time / paper and produce much more personalized practice sooner.

Refer sts to the **Common mistake**. Explain that *even if* and *even though* are not interchangeable. *Even though* = despite the fact that. *Even if* = whether or not. Board the following sentences for sts to compare:

Even if I spent two hours shopping, I wouldn't find a suit I liked. (Unreal situation)

Even though I spent two hours shopping, I couldn't find a suit I liked. (Real situation)

» Refer sts to the **Grammar expansion** on p.148.

B Books closed. Ask: *Do you often go out to the movies or do you prefer to watch them at home? Why do you think some people are choosing not to go to the movies these days?*

Books open. Have sts read the text quickly and see if they guessed correctly. Sts re-read the text and choose the correct options. Peercheck. Classcheck.

Class feedback. Ask: *Do you agree with the text? Do you think people are going to the movies less? What are the advantages / disadvantages of watching movies at home / at the movie theater?*

> **Answers**
> 1 unless   2 whether or not   3 as long as   4 even if
> 5 in case

Tip

To check answers, read the text aloud as fast as you would naturally say it. Ask sts to listen and check but also to notice anything they can about word and sentence stress, links, elision, etc. Take their feedback then for fun, have them imitate you, reading the text aloud as fast as they can in pairs, but simultaneously, pausing and correcting each other if one pronounces something too differently from the way you said it.

Optional activity

- **Stronger classes:** Have sts write a similar article entitled, *Three reasons why people still prefer the movies*. If they need help, tell them to consider: quality of sound / vision, big screen, shared experience, latest movies, poor choice on TV.

- Divide the class in half and give a board pen to each group. Each turn, read out one of these sentence beginnings:

  Whether or not you like English grammar,

  Unless I go to bed early tonight,

  Even if I'm watching a movie I don't like,

  As long as I'm not tired when I get home tonight,

  In case it rains this weekend,

  Each time you read out a sentence half, sts come to the board to write an appropriate ending. The first team to write an ending correctly wins a point. The team with the most points at the end wins.

C Make it personal Ask: *When did you last buy a newspaper / go to a museum / buy a DVD?* Have them read through the list of trends in the box.

1 Put sts in groups of four or five. Have them discuss all the trends, and write M or F next to each one. Fast finishers can add more ideas to each category, e.g. magazines, a candy store, DVDs. Class feedback. Ask each group for their answers, and board them. Did all the groups agree?

2 Have sts choose two of the trends, and in their groups, discuss the reasons for them. Classcheck. Invite a spokesperson from each group to share their reasons with the class. Ask: *Do you mostly agree / disagree?*

   Stronger classes: Have sts write a short article like the one in B about one of the trends they have chosen.

» Workbook p.29.

♪ I'm out of touch, I'm out of luck, I'll pick you up when you're getting down

6.2

4 Grammar: Adverb clauses of condition

A Read the grammar box and check (✔) the correct rules (1–2). Do 1–5 below mean the same as a–e? Write S (same) or D (different).

Adverb clauses of condition: *as long as*, *whether or not*, *in case*, *unless*, and *even if*	
a I don't mind dubbed films	**as long as** the voices are good.
b **Whether or not** you speak Spanish,	you should try to watch the original versions.
c I think I should turn on the subtitles	**in case** I miss something.
d **Unless** I stop watching dubbed movies,	my listening won't improve.
e I don't miss a single episode of *The Simpsons*	**even if** it's the dubbed version.
1 In the clause expressing condition, the verb is always in the ☐ present ☐ future.	
2 We ☐ use ☐ don't use a comma when the main clause comes first.	

Remember: *Even though* expresses contrast, not condition:
Even though I don't like Quentin Tarantino that much, I enjoyed his latest movie.
I rarely watch Hollywood blockbusters, **even if** the reviews are good.

» Grammar expansion p.148

1 I don't object to dubbed films, but only if the voices are good.
2 You should try to watch the original versions, especially if you speak Spanish.
3 There's a chance I might miss something. I think I ought to turn on the subtitles.
4 My listening won't get better if I don't stop watching dubbed movies.
5 I don't watch *The Simpsons* if it's dubbed.

Common mistake
We're going away for the weekend ~~even though~~ *even if* it rains. Nothing's going to stop us!

B Circle the correct answers. Can you think of any other reasons?

Three reasons people aren't going to the movies anymore

1 **Ticket prices**
Ticket prices are on the rise, especially now with IMAX and 3D. This might put some viewers off, ¹[**as long as** / **unless**] they have the extra money to spare, of course. Not to mention the popcorn, which we're mysteriously compelled to buy, ²[**even if** / **whether or not**] we're actually hungry!

2 **Streaming**
Who needs to leave home on Saturday night when there's Netflix? ³[**As long as** / **Even if**] you have an Internet connection – ⁴[**even if** / **even though**] it's a relatively slow one – you can watch thousands of movies from the comfort of your couch.

3 **Better quality TV**
⁵[**In case** / **Unless**] you haven't noticed, we might be experiencing the golden age of television. Because of shows such as *Game of Thrones*, people don't need to go to the movies anymore.

C Make it personal In groups, discuss which trends are popular.

1 Among people your age, are more or fewer people doing these things compared to five years ago? Write M (more) or F (fewer).

Arts, news, and entertainment	Shopping	Relationships
reading paper newspapers	buying bigger cars	sticking to relationships
going to museums / galleries	avoiding brand names	interacting face to face
downloading / streaming music	choosing more casual clothes	breaking up by text message

2 Choose two trends. Give three reasons that might explain each one. Use expressions from A and 3C.

> More people my age are definitely breaking up by text message unless they were very serious.

> How awful! Why do you think that is?

6.3 Who are your favorite authors?

5 Reading

A Roald Dahl (1916–1990) was a British writer. His short story *The way up to heaven* was published in 1954. Read the first two paragraphs of the excerpt. What is unusual about Mrs. Foster?

B Read the rest. Underline a sentence that shows …
1 Mrs. Foster was probably a traditional wife.
2 the Fosters were most likely wealthy.

The Way Up To Heaven
By Roald Dahl

All her life, Mrs Foster had had an almost pathological fear of missing a train, a plane, a boat, or even a theatre curtain. In other respects, she was not a particularly nervous woman, but the mere thought of being late on occasions like these would throw her into such a state of nerves that she would begin to twitch.

It was really extraordinary how in certain people a simple apprehension about a thing like catching a train can grow into a serious obsession. At least half an hour before it was time to leave the house for the station, Mrs Foster would step out of the elevator all ready to go, with hat and coat and gloves, and then, being quite unable to sit down, she would flutter and fidget about from room to room until her husband, who must have been well aware of her state, finally emerged from his privacy and suggested in a cool dry voice that perhaps they had better be going now, had they not? Mr Foster may possibly have had a right to be irritated by this foolishness of his wife's, but he could have had no excuse for increasing her misery by keeping her waiting unnecessarily.

Mind you, it is by no means certain that this is what he did, yet whenever they were to go somewhere, his timing was so accurate – just a minute or two late, you understand – and his manner so bland that it was hard to believe he wasn't purposely inflicting a nasty private little torture of his own on the unhappy lady. And one thing he must have known – that she would never dare to call out and tell him to hurry. He had disciplined her too well for that. He must also have known that if he was prepared to wait even beyond the last moment of safety, he could drive her nearly into hysterics. On one or two special occasions in the later years of their married life, it seemed almost as though he had wanted to miss the train simply in order to intensify the poor woman's suffering.

Assuming (though one cannot be sure) that the husband was guilty, what made his attitude doubly unreasonable was the fact that, with the exception of this one small irrepressible foible, Mrs Foster was and always had been a good and loving wife. For over thirty years, she had served him loyally and well. There was no doubt about this. Even she, a very modest woman, was aware of it, and although she had for years refused to let herself believe that Mr Foster would ever consciously torment her, there had been times recently when she had caught herself beginning to wonder.

Mr Eugene Foster, who was nearly seventy years old, lived with his wife in a large six-storey house in New York City, on East Sixty-second Street, and they had four servants. It was a gloomy place, and few people came to visit them. But on this particular morning in January, the house had come alive and there was a great deal of bustling about. One maid was distributing bundles of dust sheets to every room, while another was draping them over the furniture. The butler was bringing down suitcases and putting them in the hall. The cook kept popping up from the kitchen to have a word with the butler, and Mrs Foster herself, in an old-fashioned fur coat and with a black hat on the top of her head, was flying from room to room and pretending to supervise these operations. Actually, she was thinking of nothing at all except that she was going to miss her plane if her husband didn't come out of his study soon and get ready.

'Walker, what time is it?' 'Twenty-two minutes past, Madam.'

As he spoke, a door opened and Mr Foster came into the hall.

'Well,' he said, 'I suppose perhaps we'd better get going fairly soon if you want to catch that plane.'

'Yes, dear – yes! Everything's ready. The car's waiting.' 'That's good,' he said.

64

Who are your favorite authors? 6.3

Lesson Aims: Sts read part of a short story by Roald Dahl and pick out evocative vocabulary from the text.

Skills	Language	Vocabulary
Reading part of a short story	Creating images using evocative language, e.g. *He had a peculiar way of cocking his head. He sniffed the cold morning air.*	Evocative language: *twitch, flutter, fidget, bustle about, clasp, cock (v), sniff*

Warm-up

Ask the lesson title question: *Who are your favorite authors? What type of books do you like (mystery, romance, thrillers, science fiction, comics, joke books, coffee table books, "How to" type manuals, dictionaries, grammar books)?* If time, board some genres they don't come up with to show just how many types there are that they might enjoy browsing, even if they don't read from cover to cover. *What was the last book you read? Did you enjoy it? Why / Why not?*

5 Reading

A Ask: *Have you heard of Roald Dahl? Have you read the book in the photo? Do you know any other books by Roald Dahl?* (e.g. *Matilda, Charlie and the Chocolate Factory, BFG*) Elicit what they know about him.

Note: If they know the story, or suddenly remember it halfway through the reading, ask them not to give away the ending at this stage!

Ask: *Do you like to be punctual or are you often late? Do you get anxious if you think you are going to be late?* Focus on the title of the story and the book cover. Have sts describe the woman's appearance in detail and guess her age, personality, social status, etc. Ask sts what they think the title means.

Tell sts that today's lesson is a little different. They're going to enjoy reading a long, authentic text together, then talk about the experience. Set a reasonable (three-minute) time limit for sts to read the first two paragraphs to find out what's unusual about Mrs. Foster. Don't rush them, as the aim is for them to enjoy extensively reading a longer, authentic text. Tell them to try to ignore new lexis for now. Peercheck then classcheck their ideas. Ask: *Do you know anyone like this? What do you think is going to happen next?* Sts guess in pairs.

Answers

Although she was a calm woman, Mrs. Foster got very agitated about being late and missing planes or trains or the start of a play. She used to get so nervous she would twitch.

Tip

Monitor their guesses as closely as you can but don't take their feed back yet in case anyone gives the game away.

Background information

Roald Dahl was a British author and poet, most famous for his children's stories, who lived in the 19th Century. Before becoming an author, he had a variety of interesting careers, including a fighter pilot, diplomat, and intelligence officer. In his later years he used to write in a shed at the bottom of his garden. His books have sold more than 250 million copies around the world, and in 2008, The Times named him as one of the 50 greatest British writers since 1945.

B Give sts plenty of time to read the story.

Stronger classes: Alternatively, you might like to read the story aloud together, choosing a different st to read every two or three lines. Remember however, that they will go slowly and struggle with pronunciation, so decide first how much reformulatory-type correction you're going to give, if any at all, especially of the new words which they will be studying and hearing later, or you might end up over-correcting and taking away some of their pleasure in simply reading silently and extensively for once.

Sts underline sentences which show 1 and 2.

Explore their reading experience. Ask: *Did you enjoy that? How easy was it to understand most of it? How often did you get lost / have to re-read parts / give up and move on? Are you intrigued to know the ending?*

Answers

1 For over thirty years, she had served him loyally and well.
2 Mr. Eugene Foster, who was nearly seventy years old, lived with his wife in a large six-storey house in New York City, on East Sixty-second Street, and they had four servants.

Tip

Encourage sts to take their time while reading the extract, and read it for pleasure. Consider playing some gentle, non-distracting music to change the atmosphere and show them this is a different type of reading activity, e.g. something 1950s-esque.

≫ Song lyric: See Teacher's Book p.348 for notes about the song and an accompanying activity to do with the class.

6.3

C ▶6.8 Have sts read the statements. They answer those they can from memory, paircheck, then re-read the text to answer the others. This time, play the audio and have them follow the text in their books. Hearing the words well-delivered should heighten the experience and their comprehension.

Ask them to underline the evidence in the text, and correct the false sentences. Paircheck, then classcheck. Drill pronunciation of the words highlighted in pink.

Ask sts to write four more True / False statements about the story, then exchange them with a partner, for them to answer T or F.

Ask: *Do you think Mr. Foster deliberately tried to agitate Mrs. Foster? Do you think he enjoyed seeing her suffer? What do you think the author thinks? Would you like to know the ending?*

> **Answers**
>
> 1 F   2 T   3 F   4 T

D Make it personal Ask: *Do you think the Fosters were a happy couple? What evidence is there in the text to suggest that the story took place in the 1950s? Do you feel sorry for Mrs. Foster?*

Put sts in small groups and have them discuss questions 1 and 2. Class feedback. Then students search online for the ending, and discuss question 3.

Ask: *Do you like the ending? Was it surprising? Do you have any thoughts about the title of the story? Do you think it is a good title? Why / why not?*

Stronger classes: Ask sts to write the ending of the story in their own words.

> **Suggested answer**
>
> 1 Mrs. Foster seems afraid of Mr. Foster. He shows no empathy towards her, and seems to enjoy making her suffer. They do not seem to show each other much affection, and do not communicate very much. They seem to have very separate lives.
> 2 Their relationship is probably quite typical of the day. Today couples are far more equal. They communicate more, and wives would not tolerate such insensitivity on the part of their husband.
> 3 After Mr. Foster deliberately tries to delay Mrs. Foster on a trip to Paris to see her daughter, she leaves for the airport on her own, leaving her husband in the house searching for something he has forgotten. She is in Paris for six weeks, and when she returns she finds no sign of her husband, but there is a very strange smell and the elevator is broken. The implication is that her husband has been stuck in the broken-down elevator for six weeks and is dead.

Optional activity

Ask sts to work in pairs and think of what they would like to happen next. Sts then act out the extract plus their chosen ending in pairs. Ask volunteers to act it out for the class, who can vote on the best ending.

6 Vocabulary: Evocative language

A Before sts read **Evocative language**, ask: *What do we mean by evocative language?* Read through the box together. Focus on the highlighted words in the text. Drill pronunciation and check meanings. Have sts try and guess the meanings from the context. Then ask them to complete sentences 1–6. Peercheck. Classcheck. Perhaps ask: *Which ones are onomatopoeic?* (sounding like the noise they represent) *What other onomatopoeic words have we seen?* (e.g. *snap, bang*)

> **Answers**
>
> 1 twitched   2 fluttered   3 cocks   4 clasped
> 5 bustling about   6 fidgeting

Optional activity

Sts take turns acting out the verbs for their partner to guess which verb it is.

B Make it personal Ask sts: *What happens when you are nervous? Do you start fidgeting / sweating? What kinds of things make you nervous?*

Focus on the questions in the rubric and the model in the speech bubbles. Have sts discuss the questions in pairs.

In groups, invite sts to share stories about when they were late for a plane or train, or an important appointment. Class feedback. Ask sts to share their stories with the class. Ask: *How did you feel? Was anyone with you? How did they feel?*

» Workbook p.30.

♪ And baby, you're all that I want, When you're lyin' here in my arms. I'm findin' it hard to believe, We're in heaven

With his head over to one side, he was watching her closely. He had a peculiar way of <mark>cocking</mark> the head and then moving it in a series of small, rapid jerks. Because of this and because he was <mark>clasping</mark> his hands up high in front of him, near the chest, he was somehow like a squirrel standing there – a quick clever old squirrel from the Park.

'Here's Walker with your coat, dear. Put it on.'

'I'll be with you in a moment,' he said. 'I'm just going to wash my hands.' She waited for him, and the tall butler stood beside her, holding the coat and the hat. 'Walker, will I miss it?' 'No, Madam,' the butler said. 'I think you'll make it all right.'

Then Mr Foster appeared again, and the butler helped him on with his coat. Mrs Foster hurried outside and got into the hired Cadillac. Her husband came after her, but he walked down the steps of the house slowly, pausing halfway to observe the sky and to <mark>sniff</mark> the cold morning air.

'It looks a bit foggy,' he said as he sat down beside her in the car. 'And it's always worse out there at the airport. I shouldn't be surprised if the flight's cancelled already.'

'Don't say that, dear – please.' They didn't speak again until the car had crossed over the river to Long Island.

C ▶ 6.8 Listen to and re-read the excerpt. T (true) or F (false)?

1 In many areas of her life, Mrs. Foster wasn't a calm person.
2 Mr. Foster may have enjoyed seeing Mrs. Foster suffer.
3 Mrs. Foster was sure Mr. Foster could be deliberately cruel.
4 The writer feels Mr. Foster is controlling and potentially mean.

D Make it personal In groups, discuss 1–3.

1 Why were(n't) the Fosters probably a happy couple?
2 How typical are the Fosters of couples who have been married for decades? Are things the same / different today?
3 🌐 Guess how the story will end. Then search on "The Way Up To Heaven" and find a plot summary. How surprised are you by the ending?

6 Vocabulary: Evocative language

A Read *Evocative language*. Then complete the sentences (1–6) with a form of the <mark>highlighted</mark> words in the excerpt. There's one extra.

> **Evocative language**
>
> Meaning can often be guessed from context. Writers often use vivid verbs to create an image, whose rough meaning you can guess if you try to visualize the situation:
> Her husband *sniffed* the cold morning air. (= smelled)

1 Her eye _____ when she was anxious.
2 Her eyelashes _____ when he looked at her.
3 My dog _____ his head to one side whenever I open the door.
4 She _____ her hands behind her back.
5 In the market, tons of workers were _____ .
6 My children are always _____ and can't sit still.

B Make it personal How nervous do you get when you think you might be late to class or for an important appointment? Do you know anyone with nervous habits like Mrs. Foster? Use words from A.

> I look at my watch constantly, and my eye sometimes starts twitching ...

6.4 What do you think of graffiti art?

7 Language in use

A ▶6.9 Look at the photos. Do you know which countries the artists are from? Listen to two friends, Donna and Jason, to check.

Maya Hayuk • *Os Gêmeos* • *Olek* • *Inti* • *Kashink* • *El Bocho*

B ▶6.9 Match the extracts with the photos Donna and Jason were talking about at the time. Listen again to check.

1 It does look original, doesn't it? I wish I could buy one!	3 I have seen some women graffiti artists.	5 But his name does sound Mexican. Let me look it up.
2 I did like it. It's just that I really like graffiti with a message.	4 I had realized. But still, I always thought graffiti was mainly done on buildings.	6 The mural does seem very South American, doesn't it?

C ▶6.10 and 6.11 Listen and read about falling intonation on question tags. Then listen to 1–4 and mark the intonation ↗ or ↘.

> Sometimes tag questions are not true questions, but are opinions. In that case the intonation falls, rather than rises. Compare:
>
> ↗   ↘
> The mural seems South American, doesn't it?   It looks original, doesn't it?

1 You can't call that art, can you?
2 You liked this painting, didn't you?
3 She really has talent, doesn't she?
4 He's really awful, isn't he?

D Make it personal In pairs, which is your favorite piece of graffiti in **A**? Your least favorite? Use some of these words and tag questions to give opinions. Then take a class vote.

amazing   bizarre   colorful   creative   dull   (un)imaginative
(un)inspiring   (un)original   thought-provoking   vibrant

> The Os Gêmeos piece is amazing.

> Yes, it's so original, isn't it? I can't take my eyes off it!

What do you think of graffiti art? | 6.4

Lesson Aims: Sts learn to use auxiliaries as rejoinders and talk about graffiti art.

Skills	Language	Vocabulary	Grammar
Listening to two friends talking about graffiti art	Making rejoinders, e.g. *I **have** been listening to you! I **do not have** other priorities!* Describing pieces of art, e.g. *It leaves me cold. They use vibrant colors.*	Describing art: *cute, leave me cold, vibrant, unusual, mural, piece (of art), amazing, bizarre, colorful, creative, dull, imaginative, inspiring, original, thought-provoking*	Using auxiliaries as rejoinders, e.g. *It **does** seem kind of dull, doesn't it?*

Warm-up:

Focus on the lesson title question: *What do you think of graffiti art?* Ask: *Have you ever seen any real graffiti art? Where? Where do you normally find graffiti art?* Try to elicit *in the street, on the sides of buildings, on walls.* Ask: *Have you ever seen a street art installation?* Street artists often like to remain anonymous. Ask: *Why do you think this is?* Have sts discuss in pairs.

7 Language in use

A ▶ 6.9 Focus on the photos. Ask: *Have you heard of any of these graffiti artists? Have you seen pictures of any of this street art before? Where is the art?* (on an advertising hoarding, outside of an airplane, on a bicycle, on the side of an apartment building, on the side of a building, on a wall). Have sts guess which countries the artists are from and whether they are male or female.

Tell sts they are going to hear two friends, Donna and Jason, discussing an article about graffiti art. Play the audio for sts to check the artists' nationalities. Elicit that Olek, Hayuk, and Kashink are women.

Ask: *Were you right about the nationalities?*

> **Answers**
> 1 Maya Hayuk – American, from Baltimore, lives in Brooklyn, New York
> 2 Os gêmeos (Otávio and Gustavo Pandolfo) – Brazilian twins, from São Paulo
> 3 Inti – from Valparaíso, Chile
> 4 Olek – originally from Poland, lives in New York
> 5 Kashink – from Paris (France)
> 6 El Bocho – originally from Spain, settled in Berlin (Germany)

» See Teacher's Book p.324 for Audio script 6.9.

B ▶ 6.9 Sts read the extracts. Elicit the meaning of *mural* (a painting on a wall). Ask them which photos Donna and Jason were talking about when they made these comments. Re-play the audio if necessary for sts to check.

Ask sts if they can remember two interesting facts about Kashink and Olek (Kashink has been drawing a thin mustache on her upper lip every day for a few years; Olek was homeless until her art was discovered.)

> **Answers**
> 1 Olek 2 Hayuk 3 Os gêmeos 4 Kashink 5 El Bocho 6 Inti

C ▶ 6.10 and 6.11 Focus on sentences 1–4, and ask sts to underline the tag questions. Sts listen and read the information about falling intonation on tag questions. Ask them which of the sentences 1–4 are opinions. Have them mark the intonation then listen to check.

> **Answers**
> 1 ↘ (falling) 2 ↗ (rising) 3 ↗ (rising) 4 ↘ (falling)

Tip

Explain to sts that when we use intonation to express ourselves in this way, the most important pitch change occurs at the end of the phrase, not the beginning. So in the second example, our intonation may actually rise at the beginning, but falls at the end.

D Make it personal Check the meanings and drill pronunciation of the adjectives in the box. Ask which they would use to describe the photos in A. Ask sts which their favorite / least favorite piece of graffiti art is.

Focus on the models in the speech bubbles. Have sts tell their partner and discuss their choices using the adjectives and tag questions in similar ways. Have a class vote. Which is the class' favorite? Ask: *What do you think of graffiti and street art? Are you for or against? Can it help society to improve or is it dangerous (e.g. as a trigger to social protest)?* Have a class vote.

Optional activity

Ask sts to research other graffiti artists in their local area. In groups, sts compare what they've found, look at some of their work, and discuss which they like best.

6.4

> Song lyric: See Teacher's Book p.348 for notes about the song and an accompanying activity to do with the class.

8 Grammar: Using auxiliaries as rejoinders

A ▶ 6.12 Play the audio and tell sts to follow the text in the grammar box. Tell them to listen out for the stress and circle the correct words. Have sts say the sentences themselves stressing the correct words.

Sts check the correct rules. Classcheck. Ask sts how they express similar emphasis in their language. Ask sts to write out the example sentences with no emphasis to highlight the difference, e.g. *I'm open to appreciating graffiti, It seems kind of dull, doesn't it? I really liked the play, even though the acting was bad.*

Board the following common mistake: *We did loved the movie.* Ask sts to correct it. (*We did love the movie.*)

> **Answers**
>
> Main stress on: am, does, did, have, haven't, not
> Rules: 1 auxiliary, don't contract   2 do   3 not   4 can

> Refer sts to the **Grammar expansion** on p.148.

B Refer sts to the Audio Script 6.9 on p.324. Have them circle six examples of auxiliaries for emotion or emphasis, and underline the six comments they are made in riposte to. Peercheck. Classcheck.

> **Answers**
>
> 1 But his name **does** sound Mexican. (He's from Spain originally)
> 2 I **have** seen some women graffiti artists. (Personally, I've never seen graffiti done by a woman)
> 3 I **did** like it. (Sounds as if you didn't really like it.)
> 4 The mural **does** seem very South American, doesn't it? (His name comes from the Incan sun god and the Quechua word for "sun.")
> 5 It **does** look original, doesn't it? (I love the bicycle.)
> 6 Well, I **had** realized. (I bet you hadn't realized how creative graffiti could be.)

C Ask sts to read through the conversations. Check the meaning of *cute* (pretty or attractive), *leave me cold* (not interest me), *crochet yarn* (wool used for crocheting which is a kind of knitting with one hooked needle). Highlight the use of the word *piece*, which means, in this context, a written, musical, or artistic creation. Tell them we also say a *piece of music* or a *piece of writing*.

Sts complete the exchanges 1–4. Peercheck. Classcheck. Have sts practice the exchanges in pairs. Ask sts which comments they agreed with, e.g. *I agreed with comment 1B. I loved the yellow head. / I don't agree with 2B. I find the El bocho piece really interesting.*

> **Answers**
>
> 1 did like   2 have looked at   3 do see   4 doesn't use

Optional activity
Board the following sentences:
You don't like my hairstyle, do you?
All graffiti looks the same.
You haven't been listening to me, have you?
I think this topic is interesting.
In pairs, sts practice saying the sentences and responding using auxiliaries as rejoinders.

D Ask sts to complete the conversations in a different way. Focus on the model, and elicit other phrases sts could use: *That's not true, Well I wouldn't say that, That's not what I said, Yes, I did. I loved it, That's nonsense.*

Have sts role play their conversations in pairs.

Stronger classes: In pairs, ask sts to make their own comments about the pieces of art, and reply to each other using either auxiliaries for emphasis or other phrases, e.g.

A: *You don't like the bike, do you?*
B: *I do like it. It's really beautiful.*
A: *You think that the El bocho piece is weird, don't you?*
B: *I don't think it's weird. I think it's really interesting.*

Monitor to check sts are stressing the auxiliaries.

> **Suggested answers**
>
> 1 That's not what I said. I actually think it's cute.
> 2 That's not true. I just didn't really like it.
> 3 Well, I wouldn't say that. I actually love the expression on her face.
> 4 That's nonsense. That's just typical crochet yarn!

E Make it personal Ask: *Is there any graffiti in your town or city? Have you ever seen any famous graffiti art?* Put sts in groups of three or four to discuss questions 1–3. Refer sts to the examples in the speech bubbles.

Class feedback. Ask sts to report back any interesting ideas they noted.

As follow-up, board the following graffiti quote: *Winners are not those who never fail, but those who never quit!* (Banksy) Ask sts if they have heard of Banksy. Ask: *What do you think of the quote? Do you know any other famous graffiti quotes?*

Ask sts to search for graffiti quotes online, and share them with the class. Ask: *Are there any you really like*?

For homework, perhaps ask sts to produce their own piece of graffiti with a message. Next lesson, have sts show them to the class, who then comments and tries to guess the message.

> Workbook p.31.

🎵 Near, far, wherever you are. I believe that the heart does go on

6.4

8 Grammar: Using auxiliaries as rejoinders

A ▶ 6.12 Read and listen to the sentences in the grammar box and circle the word with the main stress. Then check (✔) he correct rules (1–4).

Using auxiliaries to express emotions and emphasis

I	am	open to appreciating graffiti.
It	does seem	kind of dull, doesn't it?
I really	did like	the play, even though the acting was bad.
I	have been	listening to you!
I	haven't been	looking at my phone!
I	do not have	other priorities!

1 To express emphasis or emotion, stress the ☐ auxiliary ☐ main verb and, in affirmative sentences, ☐ contract ☐ don't contract the auxiliary.
2 Add a form of ☐ do ☐ have before an affirmative verb in the simple present.
3 When a negative sentence isn't contracted, the stress is on ☐ the auxiliary ☐ not.
4 Tag questions ☐ can ☐ can't be used in sentences where an auxiliary expresses emotion or emphasis.

» **Grammar expansion p.148**

B Look at **AS** 6.9 on p.163. Circle six examples of auxiliaries for emotion or emphasis. Then underline the six sentences that the examples are in response to.

C Complete the conversations (1–4) about the artists from **7A** with appropriate auxiliaries and verbs to express emotion or emphasis. How many opinions matched yours?

1 A: You didn't like the yellow head in the Os Gêmeos piece, did you?
   B: I _____ it! It's actually cute.
2 A: You haven't looked at the El Bocho piece yet.
   B: I _____ it! I just didn't like it. In fact, it leaves me cold!
3 A: You don't see what's so unusual about Inti.
   B: I _____ what's unusual! Just look at the expression. She represents all of us.
4 A: Maya Hayuk, Kashnick, and Olek all use vibrant colors.
   B: Olek _____ vibrant colors. That's just typical crochet yarn!

D Complete the conversations again in a different way, this time avoiding auxiliaries for emphasis.

> You didn't like the yellow head in the Os gêmeos piece, did you?

> I never said I didn't like it! It's actually cute.

E **Make it personal** In groups, discuss 1–3.
1 Does graffiti always need to have a message? Which in **7A** have one?
2 How effective is graffiti in influencing people's ideas?
3 Should the government encourage graffiti as a means of expression?

> Graffiti should have a message. The Olek bicycle is colorful, but it doesn't say anything.

> It does say something. To me the message is that even everyday objects have beauty.

67

6.5 Are musicals popular where you live?

9 Listening

A Look at the photos. In pairs, discuss 1–2.
1. Do you ever go to musicals? What do(n't) you like about them?
2. Are you familiar with any of these musicals? Which others do you know?

B ▶ 6.13 Listen to the first part of a conversation between two friends, Stan and Kenna. T (true), F (false), or NI (no information)? Correct the false statements.
1. The name of the book is *The secret life of the American musical: How Broadway shows its guilt*.
2. The book is written for the general public.
3. One of the musicals talked about is *Mamma Mia*.
4. The book compares different musicals, which can be boring for more knowledgeable readers.
5. Millennials may not know that much about musicals.

C ▶ 6.14 Listen to the second part. Check (✔) the best description (1–3) for the first part of the book.
1. ☐ From *Oklahoma* to *Hamilton*: a complete chronology of the American musical
2. ☐ A common core and then "an eleven o'clock number": how the typical musical is structured
3. ☐ An experience for all, even those with limited English

D ▶ 6.15 Listen to the third part. Does Stan imply the book fully covers the musical of the future? Is it important for the book to cover this topic?

10 Keep talking

A ▶ 6.16 **How to say it** Complete the chart. Listen to check.

Recommending books	
What they said	What they meant
1 (This book is) a really good _____.	I really liked it.
2 It's written with a _____ audience in mind.	It's written for all audiences.
3 This book will _____ you _____ on lots of interesting facts.	This book will explain lots of interesting facts.
4 So what else does this book _____ _____ ?	So what else does this book cover?
5 What's really _____ about the book is that it (captures what musicals have in common).	What's special and noteworthy about this book is that it ...

B 🌐 Choose a book you've recently read or research one you'd like to recommend.
1. If it's fiction, note down the setting, characters, and plot, but not the ending!
2. If it's non-fiction, note down the organization, main themes, and at least three details.

C In pairs, make your recommendation! Use *How to say it* expressions.
1. Convince your partner to read the book. Make sure your reasons are persuasive.
2. Add in any criticisms you can think of, but make it clear you still feel the book is worthwhile.

Are musicals popular where you live? 6.5

Lesson Aims: Sts learn vocabulary to discuss musicals and then write a book review.

Skills	Language	Vocabulary
Writing a book review	Recommending books, e.g. *This book is a good read. It's written with a broad audience in mind. What's really unique about this book is …*	plot, characters, depiction, unfold, spoil, put down (book), page-turner, cover (v), setting

Warm-up

Ask the lesson title question, plus *Have you ever seen a musical live on the stage? Where? What was the last musical you saw? Do you know anyone who is a fan of musicals?*

9 Listening

A Focus on the posters. Ask: *What type of movie are they advertising?* (musicals) *Have you seen any of these musicals? What are they about? Which actors starred in them?* Ask: *Who is Hamilton?* (Elicit that he is Alexander Hamilton, one of the founding fathers of the U.S.) *Do the posters make you want to go and see the musicals?*

Put sts in pairs to discuss questions 1 and 2 in the Student's book. Class feedback.

B ▶ 6.13 Tell sts that Stan and Kenna are discussing a book Stan is reading about musicals. Have sts read statements 1–5 about the book. Play the audio. Sts listen and answer T, F, or NI. Check answers. Ask: *Do Stan and Kenna know much about musicals?*

Answers

1 F 2 T 3 NI 4 F 5 T

» See Teacher's Book p.324 for Audio script 6.13.

C ▶ 6.14 Tell sts that they will hear Stan telling Kenna a little more about what the book is about. Elicit or teach the meaning of *show-stopping* (a performance that wins so much applause the show is temporarily interrupted). Play the audio and have them check the best description 1–3. Check answers.

Answers

1 From Oklahoma to Hamilton: a complete chronology of the American musical

» See Teacher's Book p.325 for Audio script 6.14.

D ▶ 6.15 Play the audio then discuss the questions in the Student's Book together. As follow-up, ask: *What does Kenna think will affect the future of the musical?* (technology and immigration). *How do you think these things will affect the musical? How do you think the musical will evolve over the next ten years? Will it gain or lose popularity?*

Answers

1 No 2 Sts' own answers

» See Teacher's Book p.325 for Audio script 6.15.

» Song lyric: See Teacher's Book p.348 for notes about the song and an accompanying activity to do with the class.

10 Keep talking

A ▶ 6.16 **How to say it** Have sts try to complete the sentences from memory, then play the audio for them to check. Classcheck. Ask sts to practice the sentences in pairs. Monitor and check pronunciation and stress.

Elicit other adjectives which you could use in 2, e.g. *wide, young, limited, narrow.* (*It's written with a young audience in mind.*)

Board the following common mistake: *The book discusses about musicals.* Ask sts to correct the sentence (*The book talks about musicals.*)

Answers

1 read 2 broad 3 fill, in 4 go, into 5 unique

B Ask: *Do you read more fiction or non-fiction books? Have you read any really good books recently?* Sts choose a book. Give them time to make notes about it. If they haven't read any books recently, they can research one on the Internet.

C **Make it personal** Put sts into pairs to recommend their books. Encourage sts who are listening to ask for clarification or more information from their partner, where necessary, using the language in the *How to say it* box, e.g. *So what else does this book go into?*

Weaker classes: Board other questions to help sts, e.g. *In what way does the book …? What kind of stuff do you learn? Who is the book written for? What's unique about the book?*

Ask sts to present their books to the whole class. Have them choose one book they would like to read based on their classmates' recommendations.

Tip

Demonstrate the activity first by talking about a book you'd like to read, giving the information outlined in exercise B.

6.5

11 Writing: A book review

A Have sts look at the picture and the title of the book review. Ask: *Have you read this book? Do you know the author? Have you seen the movie?* (which is based on the book) Ask: *Where can you find book reviews like this?* (newspapers, online, magazines)

Tip

As ever, give sts an initial reading task for these writing models, e.g. set sts two minutes to gist read the review then share in pairs all they remember, and / or read the six paragraphs in pairs, with St. A reading paragraph 1, St. B reading paragraph 2, then pause and share all they understood. Repeat the procedure for paragraphs 3 and 4 and finally 5 and 6. Monitor to see how much they took in, where they need help, and their general level of enthusiasm for the text. This will make for a much more interactive class.

Sts read the review and find the relevant paragraphs for 1–4. Have them underline the specific parts in each paragraph which give them the answer.

Check answers. Ask sts what they thought of the text, story, and review. Do they know any similar rags to riches stories or stories of people who have married for money?

Answers

1 para 3   2 para 1   3 para 6   4 para 2

B Read through **Write it right!** with the class. Sts match the points with the underlined parts of the review (1–4). Peercheck. Classcheck.

Answers

1 contrasting the book with others like it
2 offering plot details
3 praising the author
4 using descriptive adjectives

C Sts read through the sentences and try and fill in the blanks, then read the review to check. Classcheck.

As follow-up, ask sts in groups to try and relate the plot of *Brooklyn* based on what they have learned from the review. Ask: *Have you read any similar books? Does the review make you want to read the book? Why? / Why not?*

Answers

1 unfolds   2 impression   3 spoil   4 down, turner
5 highly

D Your turn! Go through the instructions with the class and check sts understand what they have to do. Tell them to use the phrases in C and some of the techniques in B.

Board other useful phrases to help, e.g.

The plot centers around …

The story depicts …

The book contains / covers / explains …

The book is written for / aimed at …

They can also use the phrases in **How to say it**.

When sts have finished writing their reviews, tell them to exchange them with a partner, and check each other's work for spelling and grammar mistakes. When they are happy with them, have them post them online or they can stick them on the classroom wall.

Optional activity

When sts have written their book reviews, put them in groups to read them out to other sts without saying the name. Other sts in the group listen and guess which book they're describing.

To end the task, ask: *Have any of your reviews persuaded any of you to read a book (or at least see the movie of it)?*

» Workbook p.32.

> ♪ In my dreams I have a plan. If I got me a wealthy man, I wouldn't have to work at all

6.5

11 Writing: A book review

A Read the review about a work of fiction and find the paragraph(s) where …

1 the character's personality and a conflict are introduced.
2 something unusual about the book is first mentioned.
3 a recommendation is given.
4 the plot and main character are first introduced.

B Read *Write it right!* Then match each point to the underlined examples in the review (1–4).

> **Write it right!**
>
> A good book review maintains interest throughout the review. Some common techniques are:
> - praising the author.
> - using descriptive adjectives.
> - contrasting the book with others like it.
> - offering plot details.

C Book reviews also contain many other specific expressions that capture the reader's attention. Test your memory. What are the missing words? Then check in the review.

1 As the story _____ , we learn (what a complicated decision that is).
2 We're left with the _____ that she doesn't really wish to leave.
3 I wouldn't want to _____ the pleasure of reading this (absorbing narrative).
4 I couldn't put this book _____ . It was a real page-_____ .
5 I _____ recommend *Brooklyn*.

D Your turn! Choose a book you discussed in **10B** and write a book review in about 280 words.

Before
Note down the setting, plot, and characters if your book is fiction, and the organization and main themes if it is non-fiction. Then decide your recommendation.

While
Organize your book review in five to six paragraphs, following the model. Use *Write it right!* techniques from **B** and expressions from **C**.

After
Post your review online and read your classmates' work. Which book would you most like to read?

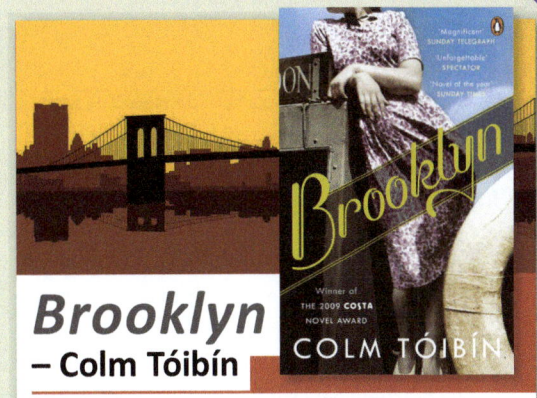

Brooklyn – Colm Tóibín

1 ¹So many books have been written about the immigrant experience in the United States that it would be hard to imagine that anything new could possibly be said. Yet Colm Tóibín's novel *Brooklyn* delivers something very special and unique – a calm, measured depiction of two ways of life, along with the feelings and motivations of the characters that inhabit both.

2 ²The plot centers around Eilis Lacey, a young woman unable to find work in her native Ireland in the early 1950s. Her well-meaning older sister, Rose, arranges a visit for her with a local priest, who's just returned from a trip to New York City. Dazzled by his description of the employment and social opportunities that await her, she decides to emigrate from her home in Enniscorthy, the same Irish town the author is from. As the story unfolds, we learn what a complicated decision that is.

3 Before Eilis's departure, we're left with the impression that she doesn't really wish to leave her hometown and has no reason but the practical for doing so. Nevertheless, she is eager to please her mother and sister. The protagonist, like the members of her family, is somehow unable to express her emotions openly, but ³Tóibín is a master at capturing his character's underlying feelings. Yet perhaps because she is young, or simply passive by nature, Eilis boards the ship as planned, without ever expressing regret, on her way to a new destiny.

4 ⁴The book contains vivid, unforgettable images of Eilis's passage. As readers, we absorb her mood and feelings as she is seasick on the ship and first takes in the sparse Brooklyn boardinghouse where she will live. We are drawn into her loneliness and homesickness as she goes to her job in the upscale department store that has hired her, and then returns alone in the evening. And we follow her avidly as she meets a young Italian-American man and slowly falls in love.

5 Eilis is called back to Ireland as the result of unforeseen family events. I wouldn't want to spoil the pleasure of reading this absorbing narrative by saying more. What I can add is that I couldn't put this book down as I read about her changing perceptions and took in her new maturity. It was a real page-turner, and more than a few surprises await you.

6 I highly recommend *Brooklyn* to anyone looking to understand not only a quintessential American experience, but also the individuality of those who undertook the journey. You won't be disappointed.

Review 3
Units 5–6

1 Listening

A ▶R3.1 Listen to a museum guide discussing the graffiti artists Os Gêmeos. Complete 1–5.

1. Os Gêmeos are known not only in Brazil, but also _____ .
2. Their work includes family, social, and political _____ , and is influenced by Brazilian _____ .
3. Their early influences came from _____ culture, and they started out as _____ .
4. The Brazilian government has commissioned them to paint large _____ and also some _____ .
5. They've become so popular because of their success in appealing to our _____ .

B Make it personal In pairs, share opinions about these Os Gêmeos paintings. Use falling intonation tag questions and some words from the box.

> amazing bizarre bring out colorful creative dull (un)imaginative
> (un)inspiring (un)original point out thought-provoking vibrant

> This one's really bizarre, isn't it!

> Actually, I think it's … . As the guide said, Os Gêmeos …

2 Grammar

A Read the paragraph. Circle the correct answers.

> I'm really sick and tired of ¹[**my neighbors not taking out / that my neighbors don't take out**] their garbage. ²[**With the aim of / In an effort to**] improve the situation, I decided to talk to them. ³[**Given the fact that / Thanks to**] they are elderly, I tried to be understanding. The man wasn't very nice, though, and I really didn't like ⁴[**that he yells / his yelling**] at me. ⁵[**With a view to / In view of**] finding a solution, I explained that I could smell rotting food in my apartment, and that I was very uncomfortable about ⁶[**that they don't take / their not taking**] the situation seriously. ⁷[**With a view to / So as to**] lower the tension, I said I'd give them one more week before I speak to the building management.

70

Review 3 (Units 5–6) R3

Warm-up

See p.61 and 105 of the Teacher's Book for warm-up ideas.

As there is no reading in this Review, you could

- have them re-read a text they enjoyed or struggled with from the last two Units, or
- use one of the texts from the Test Generator
- ask them to choose a song (e.g. the full text of one of the song lines) and use that as a reading, as well as a chance to sing
- have sts choose an authentic text they think the rest of the class would enjoy reading.

1 Listening

A ▶ R3.1 Refer sts to the photo of the graffiti art by Os Gêmeos on p.66. Ask: *What do you remember about the artists? Where are they from? Has their work grown on you at all? Have you seen any other good graffiti since the lesson?*

Have them turn to p.70, and read sentences 1–5. Ask if they can guess any of the missing words. Play the audio for them to check and complete the others.

Classcheck and ask: *What four types of art have Os Gêmeos done?* (paintings, portraits, murals, and graffiti).

Answers
1 abroad   2 art, folklore   3 hip hop, breakdancers
4 murals, subway trains   5 emotions

» See Teacher's Book p.325 for Audio script R3.1.

B Make it personal   Before sts do this, quickly review tag questions. Board the following, and ask sts to complete them with the correct tags:

1 *She really has talent, _____ ?*
2 *The murals look South American, _____ ?*
3 *You didn't like his paintings, _____ ?*
4 *He's really awful, _____ ?*

Remind them that intonation goes down when the tag question is giving an opinion. Ask sts which of the four questions above are giving opinions (1 and 4). Have them practice saying them with the correct intonation.

Go through the adjectives in the box and check the meanings and pronunciation. Ask: *Which of the adjectives would you use to describe the Os Gêmeos paintings?* Put sts in pairs to share their opinions about them, using the adjectives and falling intonation tag questions. Have pairs join with another pair, and exchange opinions.

Monitor, and help sts if they are struggling with the intonation.

Classcheck by asking volunteers to share their opinions with the class.

Optional activity

For further practice of tag questions, ask sts to write five statements about five other sts in the class (one for each). They can be about anything, and they don't have to be sure whether they're true or not. Make sure they don't show their statements to anyone else. Go around and help where necessary. When they are ready, ask sts to go and find the sts they wrote about and check if their statements are true by using tag questions – with rising intonation if they're not sure, and falling intonation if they are sure. In feedback, ask a few sts to tell you how many of their statements were correct.

2 Grammar

A Ask: *Do you ever have problems with your neighbors? What about?*

Ask sts to read the text quickly for gist and find out what this person's problem is with their neighbors. Peercheck. Tell them to re-read the text and choose the correct options. Peercheck. Classcheck.

Answers
1 my neighbors not taking out
2 In an effort to
3 Given the fact that
4 his yelling
5 With a view to
6 their not taking
7 So as to

R3

B Make it personal Go through the instructions, and focus on the example. Check meanings of the expressions in the box, and refer sts back to the grammar table in 9A on p.57 to remind them of formal structures they can use.

Elicit a couple more examples to check sts understand the task, e.g. *I can't accept my boyfriend yelling at me. Thanks to the advice of my sister, I'm going to break up with him. / My teacher isn't very supportive of my doing badly on the exams. I'm going to find a tutor to help me.*

Put sts in pairs to share their information. Have them mingle to see if anybody has something very similar or very surprising. Classcheck by asking a few sts to read out their blog entries.

Tip

Make sure sts avoid writing about each other, so as not to cause offence.

3 Writing

Brainstorm areas sts could write about, e.g. not getting a job, not studying enough, not getting along with someone, failing to stick to a diet, not saving money.

Weaker classes: Start a paragraph together on the board, as an example, e.g.

I haven't been very happy about my math teacher's assigning so much homework this semester. I really haven't enjoyed working on assignments on weekends. I'm also very tired of getting up so early to finish my work. In an effort to find a solution, I've decided to speak to him etc.

As sts finish, ask them to swap and read each other's paragraphs to give other sts more time.

Sts swap paragraphs with a (new) partner and proofread each other's writing. Display the texts on the wall or post them on the class website.

4 Self-test

Remind sts of the aim of this section: to help them consolidate vocabulary and grammar, and practice proofreading.

Sts do the test individually, then paircheck. Encourage them to look back through the grammar and vocab sections in Units 5 and 6 if they're unsure about any of the sentences. If sts score less than 15 out of 20, suggest they re-do the exercise in a few days' time, to see if they get a better score. If they do really well, they could also repeat the exercise later, but without referring to Units 5 and 6 this time. Fast finishers can produce more sentences of their own with recent class errors that you have focused on, for the rest of the class to correct.

Stronger classes: Ask sts to identify six phrasal verbs in the sentences, and write new sentences for each of them (*fall through, spell out, work out, bring out, call off, put together*).

Answers

1. Because of the terrible weather, our plans fell **through** and, as a result, our hike was called **off**.
2. I fell flat on my **face**, and I came close to **having** a nervous breakdown!
3. In view of **the fact that** I didn't get a bonus, I started staying home on weekends **so as** to save money / to save money.
4. I heard that Bob and Sue broke up last month, but I still hoped they could work things **out**.
5. I'm going to put **together** a proposal to improve our classroom and try to spell **out** all the steps clearly.
6. Three **out of** five people say you can get used to subtitles as long as you **are** open to them.
7. Even **if** it rains this weekend, I plan to go camping whether **or not** anyone else goes.
8. Jim says he really **does** like the movie because it **goes** into so many interesting themes.
9. **In case** you haven't noticed, our Internet connection is dead, **even if** the power is on elsewhere.
10. A good dubbing brings **out** the personality of the original actors, even if the voices and lips are **out** of sync.

Optional activity

Do this as an "auction." Put sts into small groups and tell them you're giving each group $100. Board the name of each group, writing $100 next to each name. Tell them that you'll go through each sentence in turn, and first ask them to "bid" up to a maximum of half of their money, depending on how confident they are they can correct it. Board the bids, then give each group one minute to correct the sentences. Go around and check their answers. If they've corrected it successfully, the group wins back double the amount of their bid. If it's incorrect, they lose their bid. The winning group is the one with most "money" at the end.

5 Point of view

Go through topics a–c with the class, and brainstorm a few ideas for each one. Individually, sts choose one and make some preparatory notes.

Review expressions for giving opinions, and supporting them (see p.62).

Weaker classes: Sts can write out their argument in full, but get them to rehearse it before they record it, so they don't have to read directly from their notes.

Encourage sts to listen to each other's recordings and give each other feedback. Brainstorm what "convincing" might mean: more accurate, more fluent, better pronunciation/ intonation, quicker, funnier, etc. The main aim is for them to encourage each other, and grow in confidence by doing things which perhaps they thought they wouldn't be able to do very well.

Stronger classes: Hold a class debate on one of the topics. (See teaching procedures on p.106.)

Review 3 5–6

B Make it personal Complete the online blog about two disappointing people, using more formal structures where possible. Then add a sentence with an expression from the box to explain what you've done to improve the situation. Share your information with a partner.

| Given | In view of | So as to | With a view to | In an effort to | Thanks to | With the aim of |

1 I can't accept _____ . _____ , I _____ .
2 _____ isn't very supportive of _____ , I _____ .

OK, listen to what I wrote: "I can't accept my manager's making me work overtime. Given that I have so little free time, I've decided to find a new job."

That does seem like a good solution!

3 Writing

Write a paragraph about something that hasn't gone well or that you feel you haven't been successful at.

1 Start with an expression in the box and use possessive adjectives + -ing forms.

| I haven't been happy about … | I haven't been comfortable with … |
| I really haven't enjoyed … | I'm very tired of … |

2 Use formal conjunctions and prepositions from 2B to suggest a solution.

4 Self-test

Correct the two mistakes in each sentence. Check your answers in Units 5 and 6. What's your score, 1–20?

1 Because of the terrible weather, our plans fell and as a result, our hike was called.
2 I fell flat on my head, and I came close to have a nervous breakdown!
3 In view of I didn't get a bonus, I started staying home on weekends so to save money.
4 I heard about that Bob and Sue broke up last month, but I still hoped they could work things over.
5 I'm going to put a proposal to improve our classroom and try to spell all the steps clearly.
6 Three of five people say you can get used to subtitles as long as you will be open to them.
7 Even though it rains this weekend, I plan to go camping whether anyone else goes.
8 Jim says he really do like the movie because it comes into so many interesting themes.
9 Unless you haven't noticed, our Internet connection is dead, as long as the power is on elsewhere.
10 A good dubbing brings through the personality of the original actors, even if the voices and lips are off of sync.

5 Point of view

Choose a topic. Then support your opinion in 100–150 words, and record your answer. Ask a partner for feedback. How can you be more convincing?

a It's essential to fail in order to succeed. OR
   Failure is a devastating experience and should be avoided at all cost.
b Dubbed movies really spoil the experience of going to a movie theater. OR
   Some movies can be dubbed very successfully and have advantages.
c Graffiti isn't real art even if it's creative. OR
   Graffiti is a serious art form and should be given even more attention.

7 » What are our most important years?

1 Listening

A ▶ 7.1 In pairs, look at the photos and answer the lesson title. Then listen to the start of an interview. Did you agree with Dr. Castro?

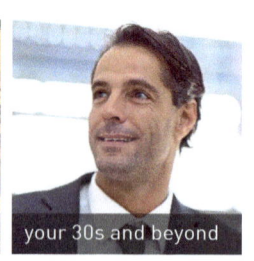

childhood   adolescence   your 20s   your 30s and beyond

B ▶ 7.2 Note down two reasons Dr. Castro might give to support her opinion. Listen to check. Were any of your ideas mentioned?

C ▶ 7.2 Listen again. Check (✔) the statements she agrees with.)
1. ☐ Society is more forgiving of mistakes you make in your teens.
2. ☐ Your 20s should be a sort of rehearsal for adult life.
3. ☐ It's harder to reinvent yourself in your 30s and 40s.
4. ☐ These days it's relatively easy to succeed in your 20s.

D ▶ 7.3 Read *Animal idioms*. Then look at the pictures on the right and guess the missing words. Listen to check.

> **Animal idioms**
>
> There are dozens of common English expressions based on animals:
>
> Who **let the cat out of the bag** (= accidentally revealed a secret) about the surprise party?
>
> I know this is true! I heard it **straight from the horse's mouth** (= from a reliable source).
>
> I was planning to go skydiving, but I **chickened out** (= decided not to do it out of fear) at the last minute.

1 _____ a can of worms (= do something that will lead to problems)

2 take the bull by the _____ (= deal with a difficult situation)

3 You can't teach an old dog new _____ (= It's hard to abandon old habits.)

4 get out of the rat _____ (= abandon a competitive lifestyle)

E Make it personal In groups, discuss 1–3.
1. Look at the lesson title again. Did you change your mind after the interview? Why (not)?
2. Which of the idioms from D do you associate with people your age? Your parents' or children's ages? Why?
3. Choose a statement from C you (dis)agree with. Support your opinion with a story about yourself.

> I agree with number 3. You can't teach an old dog new tricks, as they say!

> I totally disagree. My mom went back to school and started a whole new career.

What are our most important years? 7.1

Lesson Aims: Sts discuss age and learn vocabulary to talk about important milestones in our life.

Skills	Language	Vocabulary
Listening to a radio interview about the importance of your 20s Discussing the right age to do certain life events	Talking about age and milestones, e.g. *When you are in your twenties, there's more at stake. Our lives take off in our twenties.*	Milestones: *come to terms with, come of age, get off track, make it through, the stakes are higher, take charge* Animal idioms: *let the cat out of the bag, hear it straight from the horse's mouth, chicken out, open a can of worms, take the bull by the horns, not be able to teach a dog new tricks, get out of the rat race*

Warm-up

Ask: *What have been the most important milestones in your life so far, e.g. starting school, graduating from high school, passing your driving test, having your first boyfriend? How old were you at the time?*

Draw a time line with six years / dates representing milestones of your own for the class to guess what happened on each, and ask for more details, e.g. *You left home on January 1st, 2000?* Ask sts to play the same guessing game in pairs. Any coincidences / surprises?

1 Listening

A ▶ 7.1 Focus on the photos. Ask sts to describe the people. Ask: *How old do you think they are?* Ask the lesson title question: *What are our most important years?*

Tell sts they are going to listen to a radio interview. Play the audio and ask: *What does Dr. Castro think are the most important years of our life? Do you agree with her?*

Board: *Can we talk about the elephant in the room?*, and ask sts what they think the interviewer means by this. Elicit that the elephant is a metaphor for an "obvious truth which no one wants to discuss."

Answer

Dr. Castro thinks our 20s are the most important.

▶ See Teacher's Book p.325 for Audio script 7.1.

B ▶ 7.2 Ask sts why they think Dr. Castro says the 20s are the most important age. Encourage sts to guess. Play the audio for them to check their guesses. Ask sts if any of their ideas were mentioned.

Ask: *Do you agree / disagree with her reasons? Why?*

Answers

She mentions the following reasons:
Most of the choices we make in our 20s have life-long consequences.
If there's something you want to change about yourself or about the way you live your life, in your 20s is the time to do it (because your brain is still changing) ... it's harder to reinvent yourself after that age.

▶ See Teacher's Book p.325 for Audio script 7.2.

C ▶ 7.2 Have sts read the statements. Elicit the meaning of *rehearsal* (practice). Re-play the audio and ask them to check the ones Dr. Castro agrees with. Classcheck.

To check sts' understanding, board: *You went against conventional wisdom.* Ask: *What's the conventional wisdom?* (Most people believe / argue that our childhood years – or maybe adolescence – are the most influential.)

Answers

Checked: 1 and 3

D ▶ 7.3 Read **Animal idioms** with the class. Ask: *Are you familiar with any of the idioms? Are there similar idioms in your language?* Sts look at the pictures and try to guess the missing words. Play the audio for them to check.

Class feedback. Ask sts: *Do you know anyone who has gotten out of the rat race? Have you been in a situation where someone you know has taken the bull by the horns? Have you ever felt like you have opened up a can of worms? Do you know anyone who has disproved the theory that you can't teach an old dog new tricks?*

Answers

1 open   2 horns   3 tricks   4 race

▶ See Teacher's Book p.326 for Audio script 7.3.

Optional activity

In pairs, sts prepare a short situation for each idiom in D. Monitor and help as necessary. When finished, have each pair act out their situation, saying *Bleep!* instead of the idiom, for the class to guess it.

Weaker classes: Sts in pairs write out the situations first.

E Make it personal Have sts discuss 1–3 in groups.

1 Ask: *How did you answer the title question at the beginning of the lesson? Have you changed your mind after hearing Dr. Castro?* Ask sts to raise their hands if they have. Did most sts change their minds? If they didn't, ask them to explain why not.

2 Elicit a few answers from sts, e.g. *I associate no. 3 with my parents. They are definitely too old to change their habits!*

3 Refer sts to the model in the speech bubbles. Encourage them to use the animal idioms where appropriate to support their opinion. Invite sts to share their stories with the class.

7.1

2 Vocabulary: Milestones

A ▶ 7.4 Tell sts 1–6 are quotes made by Dr. Castro in the audio in 7A. Have them complete them with the expressions in the box. Remind them to put the verbs in the correct form. Play the audio for them to check. Elicit which of the expressions always has a negative meaning (*get off track*). Elicit or teach the opposite *stay on track*.

Classcheck. Ask: *Which of the five phrasal verbs have you heard / do you already use?*

> **Answers**
> 1 come of age   2 get off track   3 the stakes are higher
> 4 made it through   5 come to terms with   6 take charge
> Negative meaning: get off track

Tip

Monitor for any pronunciation problems. Play the audio for them to check, pausing after each one to elicit correct pronunciation where you heard errors.

B Go through the quotes 1-4. Ask: *Where and when have you felt this way about situations in your lives?* Put sts in pairs to share stories and brainstorm ideas. Have them chose one, preferably from their own experience, prepare a short dialog, then act out the situation for the class, who has to guess who is talking to who.

Weaker classes: Have sts write out their conversation first, e.g.

A: *How are you feeling about your break-up?*

B: *Well, it's been a year now, but I still haven't come to terms with the idea that she's left me.*

C Focus on the title of the text. Ask sts to say what they think the right age is. Have them discuss in pairs. Encourage them to give their reasons.

Refer sts to the cartoon, and ask them to explain the joke (the reader is assuming that all the events happened over several years at least, until the punchline when they find out that it all took place in one weekend.)

Sts read and complete the text with the expressions in A. Class feedback. Ask sts which of the opinions 1–3 they agree / disagree with and why. For homework, ask sts to write their own paragraph for the blog, saying what they think the right age is.

> **Answers**
> 1 the stakes are higher   2 gets off track   3 make it through
> 4 come of age   5 take charge   6 coming to terms with

» Song lyric: See Teacher's Book p.348 for notes about the song and an accompanying activity to do with the class.

Optional activity

Board: *What's the right age to leave home?* Sts, in pairs, then write three sentences using the expressions about the topic, similar to the sentences in C. Monitor and help where necessary, correcting any errors. When they have finished, put pairs together into groups of four to share their ideas and see if other sts agree.

D Make it personal Go through the list of events, and ask sts: *What age did you or your children do these things? In retrospect, do you think this was too early / too late?* If you have an older class, you might want to add *retire* to the list.

Put sts in groups to discuss the best age for each event. Focus on the models in the speech bubbles. Highlight the use of *at least*, and teach the opposite *no older than*, e.g. *You should be no older than 30 when you …*

Encourage sts to refer to their own experiences to justify their opinions, e.g. *That's not true. My dad started his own business servicing friends' cars before he'd even come of age, and was able to retire at 50.*

Focus on **Common mistakes**. Point out that we can use the phrase *at my age* as an adverbial phrase, e.g. *It's very difficult to change jobs at my age*, *It's amazing that she's traveling alone at her age*.

Class feedback. Ask sts if they mainly agree or disagree. Ask: *Do any of your classmates have controversial opinions?*

» Workbook p.33.

♪ And isn't it ironic ... don't you think? It's like rain on your wedding day. It's a free ride when you've already paid

2 Vocabulary: Milestones

A ▶ 7.4 Using context, complete 1–6 with a form of the expressions in the box. Listen to check. Which expression always has a negative meaning?

> come to terms with   come of age   make it through   the stakes are higher
> get off track   take charge

1 Yes, but I would argue that when we _____ (= reach adulthood), we make the decisions that have the greatest impact on our future.
2 Because that's when our lives either take off or _____ (= start to go in the wrong direction).
3 But when you're in your 20s, _____ (= there's more at risk).
4 I _____ (= survived) my 20s, and even the rough times, but I wish I'd been more focused.
5 We need to _____ (= accept) the fact that most of the choices we make in our 20s have life-long consequences.
6 So it's really in your 20s that you need to _____ (= assume control) and determine your destiny.

B In pairs, choose a situation for sentences 1–4. Then role-play a short conversation.
1 "It started well, but it *got off track* halfway through. I nearly fell asleep towards the end."
2 "It's been a year, but I still haven't *come to terms with* the idea that she's left me."
3 "I don't know how I *made it through* the first week. But then I got used to it."
4 "I think he really needs to *take charge* of the situation and try to fix it."

> So, how was the lecture? Did I miss anything important?

> Well, it started well, but it got off track halfway through. I nearly ...

> We met, fell madly in love, got engaged, had a lovely wedding and honeymoon. Then things turned sour, we grew bitter, separated, and divorced. It was quite a busy weekend!

C Complete 1–6 with the expressions in **A**. Which opinion(s) do you agree with?

WHAT'S THE RIGHT AGE TO GET MARRIED?

→ Not until you're in your 30s. If things don't work out, ¹_____, especially if there are children involved.

→ When a relationship ²_____, couples need to stick together so they can ³_____ the bad times, and that takes a lot of maturity. So I'd say wait until you're in your mid-20s at least.

→ There's no such thing as "the right age." Once you've ⁴_____ and feel you're mature enough to ⁵_____ of your own life without depending on other people, I'd say go for it!

→ I got divorced last year, and I'm still ⁶_____ being on my own again. So, right now, I'm the last person you should ask!

D Make it personal In groups, decide on the best ages for these activities. Use expressions from **A**.

> get your child a cell phone   let your child start dating   start learning a foreign language
> travel on your own for the first time   have a baby   become a boss   start your own business

> You should be at least 40 before you start your own business.

> Yes, the stakes are much higher when the company is yours!

Common mistakes

(who are)
People at / in / of my age aren't mature enough to have a baby!

are
Couples who ~~have~~ the same age get along best.

» 7.2 Would you like to live to be 100?

3 Language in use

A ▶ 7.5 Listen to a sociology professor discuss changing attitudes toward older people. In pairs, answer 1–2.

1 How does he define "ageism"?   2 Is he optimistic or pessimistic about the future?

B ▶ 7.5 Listen again without looking at the statements below. Then check (✔) the ones you remember Dr. Suárez making to support his prediction of a changing workplace.

1 ☐ By 2050, most of you will have been working for several decades, and you will have developed many valuable skills by that time. You won't be ready to stop.
2 ☐ Nevertheless, some of you will have decided you'd like to spend more time with family.
3 ☐ Many more people will have discovered they can reinvent themselves. The majority of the population will have accepted 60 is the new 40.
4 ☐ The proportion of older workers will have changed because the number of new workers will have slowed considerably.
5 ☐ Society will have been gradually accepting this demographic change, and older workers won't have been fired prematurely.
6 ☐ Older workers also won't have developed the physical limitations they have today.

C In pairs, which statements from B do you agree with? Why (not)? Can you add one more of your own?

> I agree with number 6. Look how far medicine has advanced in the last 50 years.

> Yes, but isn't that wishful thinking? There are limits to how much the aging process can be delayed.

D **Make it personal** What age-related behaviors might be more / less common by 2050?

1 Look at the photos. Do any of today's age-related behaviors surprise you? Make notes.

2 Read *Clarifying opinions*. Then in groups, share your reactions to the photos. Be sure to clarify any ideas your classmates don't seem to understand.

> **Clarifying opinions**
>
> You may use expressions such as *What I mean(t) is that …*, *What I was trying to say is that …*, and *Let me put it another way* to clarify opinions you realize were too broad or weren't clear:
>
> Sexism will have disappeared. [very broad]
>
> What I mean is that people will have more open attitudes. [more specific]

> I think many older women will be dating younger men. For one thing, sexism will have disappeared.

> You've got to be kidding! But I do think people won't be aging as quickly, and of course, women will still live longer on average.

> Well, what I mean is that people will have more open attitudes and abandon the old stereotype that the man must be older.

Would you like to live to be 100? 7.2

Lesson Aims: Sts listen to a lecture about ageism and discuss how things might have changed by 2050.

Skills	Language	Vocabulary	Grammar
Listening to a lecture about attitudes towards older people	Clarifying opinions, e.g. *What I was trying to say is that …, Let me put it another way …*	life expectancy, ageism, demographic, age (v), advance (v), retire, health care	Future perfect and future perfect continuous

Warm-up

Books closed. Dictate this question. *The first person who's going to live to be 150 has probably already been born. Could it be you?* Sts check spelling in pairs, then answer it. Classcheck.

Focus on the lesson title question: *Would you like to be 100?* Initially ask for a show of hands, then ask sts to discuss the question in pairs and note down a list of advantages / disadvantages of living to be that age. Class feedback.

3 Language in use

A ▶ 7.5 Tell sts they are going to hear a sociology professor giving a lecture about ageism. Ask: *How would you define ageism? Can you give some concrete examples?* Sts discuss in pairs. Have the class share some examples, and allow them to disagree if they wish to.

Play the audio and have sts answer 1 and 2. Ask sts whether their definition of ageism was similar to the professor's. Classcheck. Ask sts if they have thought of any other examples of ageism in their society.

Answers
1 negative, discriminatory attitudes towards older people
2 optimistic

▶ See Teacher's Book p.326 for Audio script 7.5.

B ▶ 7.5 Have sts cover the statements. Re-play the audio. Then ask sts to check the statements they remember Dr. Suarez making. Peercheck. Classcheck. Ask: *What is the retirement age in your country nowadays? At what age would you like to retire?*

Weaker classes: Ask sts to read the statements first before they listen. You could also ask sts to make notes while they listen and use these to help them complete the exercise.

Answers
Check 1, 3, 4, and 5

Tip

Always set a clear listening task, ideally a different one for each repeat listening, so it's never exactly the same. This helps sts avoid the feeling of having failed the first / previous time. Checking in pairs after each listening can help with this, too. The exception is when sts are trying to make sense of a short, tricky extract, which they need to hear several times. So, here, ask sts to *Listen and try to remember as much as you can of what the professor says*. Or *Listen and calculate how much more you understood this second time*. Then paircheck before uncovering the statements.

C Put sts in pairs to discuss the predictions in B. Ask them to discuss which they agree with. Refer them to the models in the speech bubbles as examples. Discuss the meaning of *wishful thinking* (the formation of beliefs according to what might be pleasing to imagine rather than being based on evidence or reality).

Ask sts to make one prediction of their own.

D Make it personal

1 Ask sts to look at the photos. Ask: *What can you see?* Elicit the following:

Picture a – an older woman marrying a younger man;
Picture b – a very young girl working on the cash register (in what is presumably the family business);
Picture c – older people taking an exercise class;
Picture d – young people working in a fast-food restaurant. Ask: *Are these things common in your society today? Which are frowned upon?*

2 Go through **Clarifying opinions** with the class. Drill pronunciation of the phrases and ensure that sts stress the correct words: *What I **meant** is that …, What I was trying to say is that …, **Let** me **put** it a**no**ther way …*

Have sts share their reactions to the photos. Refer sts to the examples in the speech bubbles. Encourage sts to ask their classmates for clarification if necessary, e.g.
A: *I'm not sure what you mean.*
B: *Let me put it another way …*

Optional activity

Before sts discuss their reactions in D2, choose one st from each group to leave the class with you. Explain they must secretly question everything people say, or "act dumb." This will encourage other sts to clarify their opinions and use the expressions in the box.

7.2

>> Song lyric: See Teacher's Book p.349 for notes about the song and an accompanying activity to do with the class.

4 Grammar: Future perfect and future perfect continuous

Tip

It's useful to look for parallels across the tenses, so board *Present / Past perfect* and *Perfect continuous* forms and rules. Put sts in pairs to remember all they can. Monitor and check their perceptions. Classcheck anything they think the forms and uses have in common. Go back to this once you've been through the grammar box, to look for further similarities and links.

A Have sts read through the grammar box. Check they understand the example sentences. Point out that we often use the contracted form in spoken English, e.g. *We'll have worked since our twenties.*

Ask sts to translate the sentences into their language. Ask: *Is there a future perfect continuous form in your language?* Sts check the correct words in the rules. Classcheck.

Refer sts to the **Common mistake**. Elicit why we use the future perfect and not the future perfect continuous in this case (because the sentence refers to a future event which is over or complete – the person will be 90). Refer them to rule 2.

Answers

1 sometimes   2 future   3 only the future perfect

Tip

Despite their names, the future perfect and future continuous don't always refer to the future, e.g. *I sent her the letter two weeks ago, so she'll have received it by last Friday.* The most important part of this construction is the use of *will* as a prediction. Since the future is less certain than the present or the past, we naturally make more predictions about the future.

>> Refer sts to the **Grammar expansion** on p.150.

B Refer sts to the statements in 3B and have them underline the examples of the future perfect and the future perfect continuous.

Have them write the correct rule numbers next to each one. Peercheck. Classcheck.

Answers

Rule 1: most of you will have been working, Society will have been gradually accepting
Rule 2: you will have developed, some of you will have decided, people will have discovered, population will have accepted, older workers will have changed, the number of new workers will have slowed, older workers also won't have developed
Rule 3: older workers won't have been fired

C Sts read the text and choose the correct options 1–7. Classcheck. Have them underline time phrases in the text, e.g. *By 2050, for some time, for over 50 years.* Tell sts that the present perfect simple and continuous are often used with time phrases. Elicit which ones (*by + time / date / then / that time / the time*, etc.).

Ask sts: *Which of the statements do you agree with?* Teach *I'm inclined to agree with ..., I can't say I agree with ...,* as ways of politely agreeing / disagreeing.

Answers

1 will have reached   2 will have exceeded   3 will have been living   4 won't have stopped   5 will have been improved   6 will have been using   7 will have become
Both choices are correct in 3 and 6

5 Pronunciation: Reduction of future forms in informal speech

A ▶ 7.6 and 7.7 Sts read and listen to the rules. Have them listen to 1–3 and mark the stress, then listen again and repeat. Have sts practice saying the sentences in pairs.

Optional activity

Demonstrate how the future forms are reduced by first drilling only the stressed syllables in the first sentence with the class:

will – work – fif – years – won't – bored – all

As you do this, establish a clear rhythm by clapping your hands or clicking your fingers. Once you've drilled it a few times, maintain the same rhythm and "slot in" the other syllables, in their reduced form. Explain to sts that English is a stress-timed language, which means we time what we say by the number of stressed syllables, not by the number of words, and this is why many sounds become reduced in natural speech.

B **Make it personal** Brainstorm ideas together with the class, e.g. *By 2050 our cities will have grown so much it will be impossible to get around. While health care will have improved a lot there will be a lot more pressure on the health services. Social problems will have worsened and a shortage of housing will have become a real problem.* Have sts discuss in pairs. Class feedback. Ask: *Are you optimistic or pessimistic about the future?*

>> Workbook p.34.

♪ Wherever you go, whatever you do, I will be right here waiting for you

7.2

4 Grammar: Future perfect and future perfect continuous

A Read the grammar box and check (✔) the correct rules (1–3).

Future perfect and future perfect continuous: active and passive

We			**worked**	since our twenties.
			been working	for 50 years by the time we retire.
I	will	have	**seen**	many social changes by then.
People	won't			
These changes			**been accepted**	by the vast majority of people.
Older people			**been forced**	out of the workplace prematurely.

1 The future perfect and continuous ☐ sometimes ☐ never have the same meaning.
2 When a future event will have ended by the time referred to, use the ☐ **future perfect** ☐ future perfect continuous.
3 In passive sentences, use ☐ either form ☐ only the future perfect.

» Grammar expansion p.150

B Underline examples of the future perfect and future perfect continuous in 3B. Next to each one, write rule numbers 1, 2, or 3.

Common mistake
Even when I'm 90, I won't have ~~been forgetting~~ *forgotten* my English.

C Circle the correct options (1–7). In which two are both choices correct? Which do you agree with?

→ By 2050, every two out of nine people ¹[**will have reached** / **will have been reaching**] the age of 60, and life expectancy ²[**will have exceeded** / **will have been exceeding**] 76 years.
→ The majority of people ³[**will have lived** / **will have been living**] in urban areas for some time.
→ While we ⁴[**won't have stopped** / **won't have been stopping**] aging, health care ⁵[**will have been improving** / **will have been improved**] significantly by then and will be linked to happiness.
→ And, of course, by then, we ⁶[**will have been using** / **will have used**] technology for over 50 years, and our proficiency ⁷[**will have become** / **will have been becoming**] impressive.

5 Pronunciation: Reduction of future forms in informal speech

A ▶ 7.6 and 7.7 Read and listen to the rules. Then listen to and repeat 1–3.

In rapid, informal speech, future perfect forms are often reduced:
will have been = *will /ə/ been*   won't have been = *won't /ə/ been*
In more formal speech, and when a vowel follows, say *will've* and *won('t)'ve*:
will have exceeded = *will /əv/ exceeded*   won't have exceeded = *won't /əv/ exceeded*

1 I will have been working for 50 years and won't have been bored at all.
2 We will have been exposed to many new things.
3 Employers won't have expected people to retire early.

B Make it personal The sentences in 4C are all positive changes. What negative changes can you imagine might take place in the same areas? Use reduced future forms where possible.

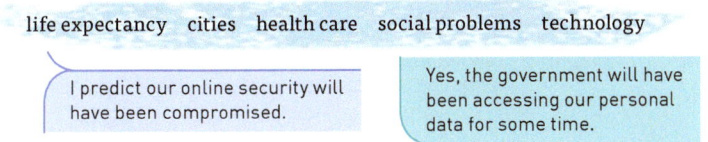

life expectancy   cities   health care   social problems   technology

> I predict our online security will have been compromised.

> Yes, the government will have been accessing our personal data for some time.

75

7.3 Do babies ever surprise you?

6 Reading

A Read the first two paragraphs and cover the rest. In pairs, guess the things babies might be capable of.

Five Things You Didn't Know Babies Could Do

Himanshu Sharma

There's simply no better way to put it: babies are essentially vegetables. Sure, they're cute and everything, but at the end of the day, ¹we all know that they're primitive organisms who are yet to develop the basic functions to qualify as cognitive human beings. As the babies grow, they will slowly develop various functions necessary to survive in the world.

But as research is gradually finding out, ²babies are capable of much more than we usually give them credit for.

5 Distinguishing faces, even of other species

If you've ever spent time with a baby, you'll know that they're not so great at recognizing people by their faces. They don't seem to behave in a particularly different way when they see someone they have met earlier, unless it's their mother or someone they spend a lot of time with. The ability to tell faces apart from each other is something they acquire much later in their lives. ³Or that's what the babies would rather have you believe, anyway.

Babies are actually pretty good at identifying faces, even when it comes to creatures of different species. In an experiment conducted by researchers at the University of Sheffield and University of London, six-month-old babies were found to be as good as adults at recognizing human faces that they had seen earlier. But, shockingly, they were actually better at recognizing monkey faces than the adults. How many of us can tell monkeys apart by their faces? We bet it's not a lot. Yet, apparently, six-month-old babies can do just that. We lose the ability to recognize the faces of different species and races as we grow older, because an adult's facial recognition is based more on familiarity than absolute facial indicators, but babies still carry this vestigial ability up to a certain age.

4 Judging character

⁴The ability to judge how likely someone is to help you comes built in as an evolutionary trait. It's a social skill that's essential to operating in a society as well as to survival. This was especially true during the hunter-gatherer times, when knowing if someone was likely to kill you and steal your belongings was pretty helpful. It's a crucial ability, and—surprisingly enough—one that comes with the package at birth instead of being developed over years of social communication, as we're generally inclined to assume.

Researchers set up an experiment and made some babies watch a puppet show. One puppet was shown to be climbing a mountain, while the second and third puppet would either help the climber up or throw him back down, respectively. When the babies were offered the last two puppets, 14 out of 16 10-month-olds and all 12 six-month-olds preferred the helper over the hinderer. While researchers still don't know whether it's an informed decision, ⁵drooling infants seemingly staring blankly at things sure register far more information than we knew.

3 Learning language in the womb

Learning a whole new language is a process that takes a long time to perfect, especially when it comes to conversing in a social environment. The verbal cues, gestures, subtle winks, and other aspects of communicating take years to master. While it is something that we get better at as we grow older, this development starts much earlier than you'd think: before you're even born.

Babies apparently learn their native language from their mothers in the womb and can identify their mother tongue when they're barely hours old. Researchers recorded the vowel sounds in the native tongues of some 30-hour-old babies and studied their reactions to see if they recognized the sounds. The researchers plugged a pacifier into a computer and made the babies suck on it. Sucking for a shorter period of time meant that the sound was familiar, and vice versa. As it turned out, the babies appeared to recognize the sounds played in their mother tongue, indicating that we're born with at least a rudimentary sense of what our native language sounds like.

Do babies ever surprise you? 7.3

Lesson Aims: Sts learn about babies and the skills they have.

Skills
Reading an article about research that has been carried out on babies' abilities

Language
Adjective-noun collocations, e.g. *social skill, social communication*

Warm-up

Ask sts the lesson title question: *Do babies ever surprise you?* Ask: *How much experience have you had with babies? Have you ever babysat? Do you have any babies in your family?* Ask sts to discuss in pairs, then feedback as a class.

6 Reading

Tip

It's a good idea not to pre-teach too many words before reading a text, because this deprives sts of practice in guessing unknown words from context, which is a useful skill to have outside the classroom. Sometimes, however, the meaning of the word might be too difficult to guess, especially if it's an authentic text. When planning your lesson, look through the text for words which you think your sts won't know. Cover up the word and see if you can still understand the phrase or sentence without if. If you can, then you don't need to pre-teach it. If it's too difficult, then it's worth pre-teaching.

A Refer sts to the photo and ask: *Are any of you twins? Do you have twins in your family?* If not, ask: *Would you like to be a twin? Looking at the photo, what adjectives spring to mind?* Try to elicit: *cute, sweet, delightful, gorgeous* or *boring, dull, uninteresting, exhausting*! Ask: *Do you agree with your classmates?*

Sts cover up the text apart from the first two paragraphs in the tinted box. Ask them to read the title and guess what two of the things babies can do might be. Give a funny example yourself, e.g. *Stop their parents from sleeping, Annoy fellow passengers, Cost you all your savings in diapers!*, and elicit others. Rather than call them out, have sts note down their ideas to compare with those in the text after reading it all (before they do 6D).

Tell sts to read the first two paragraphs and ask them if they agree with this assessment of babies. Elicit or teach the meaning of *vegetables* in this context (informal use meaning a person who is incapable of conscious responses or activity).

Refer sts back to the second paragraph and have them discuss in pairs what they think babies might be capable of. Class feedback. Have sts share their ideas.

Tip

Before doing exercise 6B, have sts uncover the text and read only the headings in red. Ask them to work in pairs and quickly guess what skills will be mentioned in each section. Monitor but don't check, as they will get their own feedback when they do 6B.

7.3

B ▶ 7.8 Have sts read and listen and underline the explanation of the skills babies have in each paragraph.

Weaker classes: Pause the audio after each section.

Ask: *Do any of these skills surprise you?* Ask sts if they remember the pronunciation of the pink-stressed words. Drill them and check. Ask: *Which are cognates in your language?* Ask sts to find ten other cognates in the text.

As further reading practice, put sts into groups of five and allocate one section of the text (1–5) to each member of the group. Tell them to make notes about the experiment described in their section. In turns sts tell the rest of the group about the experiment in their own words. Class feedback. Ask: *Which is the most convincing experiment?*

Answers

5 We lose the ability to recognize the faces of different species and races as we grow older, because an adult's facial recognition is based more on familiarity than absolute facial indicators, but babies still carry this vestigial ability up to a certain age.
4 The ability to judge how likely someone is to help you comes built in as an evolutionary trait. This was especially true during the hunger-gatherer times, when knowing if someone was likely to kill you and steal your belongings was pretty helpful.
3 Babies apparently learn their native language from their mothers in the womb and can identify their mother tongue when they're barely hours old… we're born with at least a rudimentary sense of what our native language sounds like.
2 this section of the brain lit up in response to a real social interaction – facial expressions, social gestures, and so on – but did not respond to, say, an arm manipulating a random object. This suggests that babies are wired to recognize social clues from birth.
1 it's an evolved mechanism that lets us function in a social environment … what is a surprise is how early we develop this crucial ability.

Optional activity

If any of your sts have children of their own, or baby siblings or nephews / nieces, ask them if they agree with the facts in the article from their own experience, and to share any funny stories they have about their own babies.

▶ Song lyric: See Teacher's Book p.349 for notes about the song and an accompanying activity to do with the class.

C Ask sts to re-read the article, and in pairs, explain the authors' opinions (1–7) in their own words. Refer sts to the example in the speech bubble.

Weaker classes: Go through the blue highlighted expressions first and discuss the meanings.

Classcheck by inviting individual sts to explain the opinions to the class.

Ask sts: *What did you think of the article? Did you learn anything new?*

Elicit and drill pronunciation of the words highlighted in pink. Tell them they can ask you the meaning and pronunciation of three more words maximum (not those in yellow, which are dealt with in 7B). Any others they should look up at home, because you are not a walking dictionary! They may argue which ones, so let them vote!

Answers

1 yet to = who until now have not developed
2 capable of = able to do
3 would rather = would prefer to
4 comes built in = already exists
5 seemingly staring blankly = giving the impression of looking at nothing in particular
6 wired to = have an instinctive / innate ability to
7 isn't much use for = isn't very helpful to

D Make it personal Ask sts: *What other skills do you think babies have?* Compare with their original guesses from 6A. Ask: *Were any right? Did you learn much from the text?*

Refer sts to the example in the speech bubble. Ask sts to search on the Internet for more information. They can do this for homework. Have them report back any interesting facts to the class.

7 Vocabulary: Adjective-noun collocations in writing and speech

A Refer sts to **Finding common adjective-noun collocations**. Ask sts to look through the text and find the underlined words. Ask: *Which of these are cognates in your language?* Go through the meanings and drill pronunciation.

Ask sts to write a sentence of their own with each of the collocations, e.g. *Having great social skills helps you meet interesting people.* Refer them to the penultimate paragraph and ask them find one more collocation with social (social environment).

Answers

social skill, social communication, social environment, social interaction, social gestures, social clues

B Make it personal Go through the yellow-highlighted words in the text and check meanings. You could ask sts to choose one each, and look it up in a dictionary, then invite volunteers to explain the meaning to the rest of the class.

Ask the question in the Student's book: *Have you ever felt you weren't treated appropriately for your age?* Refer sts to the example in the speech bubble, and elicit a few more examples, e.g. *In the early stages of my teenage years, my parents still treated me like a baby. They were always checking where I was going and what time I was coming in.*

▶ Workbook p.35.

♪ I hear babies crying. I watch them grow. They'll learn much more than I'll ever know. And I think to myself, What a wonderful world

2 Understanding social interactions

In our daily lives, we often need to know the context of a social interaction to respond accordingly. The mind can collate data on what's going on around you and suggest the best course of action based on that information. Of course, babies can't do that, but they do know the basics of social communication.

Researchers studied babies between 24 and 120 hours of age. They employed a technique known as near-infrared spectroscopy to monitor the part of the brain responsible for social interactions. What they found was that this section of the brain lit up in response to a real social interaction—facial expressions, social gestures, and so on—but did not respond to, say, an arm manipulating a random object. ⁶This suggests that babies are wired to recognize social clues from birth.

There had been similar studies on older babies before, but this was the first time social interactions were studied in babies as young as 24 hours. Interestingly, the older babies were better at successfully differentiating the various types of communication, suggesting that this ability rapidly develops in the early stages of life.

1 Fairness

Our sense of fairness is something that probably helps us save a ton of money by not getting ripped off all the time. It's no surprise that we have it; it's an evolved mechanism that lets us function in a social environment. But what is a surprise is how early we develop this crucial ability. According to science, babies as young as 15 months are able to distinguish a fair deal from an unfair one.

Babies were made to sit on their parents' laps and look at a video of someone distributing food to two people. This was done twice. The first time, the food was distributed equally. The second time, one recipient got more food than the other. The babies were more surprised and hence stared longer at the unfair transaction compared to when the food was divided equally. ⁷Even if a baby's basic sense of fairness isn't much use for either the baby or anyone else, it's surprising that this ability starts developing way before it's actually needed in life.

B ▶ 7.8 Read and listen to the article. In pairs, recall explanation for each skill babies have. Were you surprised?

> It seems logical babies would be better at recognizing faces.

C Re-read and, in pairs, explain the author's opinions in the numbered sentences 1–7. Replace the blue highlighted expressions with a similar meaning.

> In sentence 1, he's saying that everyone thinks babies still haven't developed cognitive functions.

D 🌐 **Make it personal** Search on "Things babies can do." What other surprising things did you discover?

> Did you know babies can yell at birth, but not cry? Tears can't be formed until they're about three weeks old.

7 Vocabulary: Adjective-noun collocations in writing and speech

A Read *Finding common adjective-noun collocations*. Find the underlined collocations with *social* in context. Which are you familiar with?

> **Finding common adjective-noun collocations**
>
> News sources often use adjective-noun collocations that are common in conversation. For example:
>
> It's a *social skill* that's essential.

B Make it personal Have you ever felt you weren't treated appropriately for your age? Look at the highlighted adjective-noun collocations in the article. Then use them and the collocations from A to share stories in groups.

> My parents didn't even have a rudimentary sense of how teenagers think. For example, when it came to social interactions, they didn't seem to remember peer pressure.

7.4 Do you seem younger or older than you are?

8 Language in use

A ▶ 7.9 Listen to the start of a community lecture. Complete the notes.

- Nature vs. nurture: the influence of [1]_____ vs. [2]_____.
- Stage theorists vs. others: development is [3]_____ vs. it's affected by [4]_____.

B ▶ 7.10 Read the quotes from the street interviews. Then listen to the rest of the lecture. Match the people in the order you hear them (1–6) to their photos.

WHAT IS "AGE-APPROPRIATE" BEHAVIOR?

A ☐☐ It's my grandmother who walks two miles a day. And she's pushing 90!

B ☐☐ It's my younger brother who's more mature. He's wise beyond his years.

C ☐☐ We're not the ones who will reform society. We seem to have run out of ideas and just conform to expectations.

D ☐☐ Act my age? No way! It's a crazy situation I find myself in now. I'm the one who puts food on the table.

E [1]☐ My teacher is in her early 70s, and she's really young at heart. It's my classmates who seem old-fashioned.

F ☐☐ It's not old people who are boring. They have so much insight and first-hand experience. It's us!

C ▶ 7.10 Listen again. Match opinions a–d to the six people in B. Did anyone surprise you?
   a Nature is more important than nurture.
   b Nurture is more important than nature.
   c Stage theory is usually accurate.
   d People simply don't fit into neat stages.

D In pairs, explain the meaning of the highlighted expressions in context.

> I think to be pushing 90 means "she's almost 90." If you think about the meaning of *push*, it makes sense!

E Make it personal What are your views on human development?
   1 In groups, choose opinions from B. Note down examples from your life or the lives of others.
   2 Share a story about yourself or someone you know to illustrate your views. Use expressions from A.

> I'd say life stages are unpredictable, and I have first-hand experience, too! People my age might be in college, but I dropped out to become a singer.

> What convinced you to do it?

78

Do you seem younger or older than you are? 7.4

Lesson Aims: Sts learn vocabulary to talk about human development and the influence of nature vs. nurture.

Skills	Language	Vocabulary	Grammar
Listening to a lecture on nature vs. nurture	Using emphasis, e.g. *It's a tough situation that we have to face. It's their parents that don't set expectations.*	to be pushing 50 / 60 etc., be wise beyond your years, conform to, act your age, be young at heart, first-hand experience	Cleft sentences, e.g. *It's your attitude that has to change.*

Warm-up

Ask sts the lesson title question: *Do you seem younger or older than you are? Do you feel younger or older than you are?* Board the following quotes: 1) *Act your age.* 2) *Age is just a number, maturity is a choice.* 3) *Live your life and forget your age.* 4) *I see no good reason to act my age.* 5) *My age is very inappropriate for my behavior.* Ask sts to discuss what they mean, and choose their favorite.

7 Listening

A ▶ 7.9 Ask sts to look at the notes. Check the meaning of *vs.* (abbreviation of versus) = against. Ask: *What do you think nature vs. nurture mean?*

Tell sts that they are going to listen to a lecture on the current theories of life-span development. Have them listen and complete the notes. Classcheck.

Highlight the pronunciation of *nature* /ˈneɪ·tʃər/ and *nurture* /ˈnɜr·tʃər/. Elicit other words with similar pronunciation, e.g. *lecture, adventure, creature, mixture*. Tell sts that in words where the last syllabus is stressed, e.g. *mature*, the pronunciation changes to /məˈtʃʊr/.

Answers

1 heredity   2 physical and social world and our experiences
3 predictable   4 environment

» See Teacher's Book p.326 for Audio script 7.9.

Tip

When the sounds /t/ and /j/ combine in natural speech, it often produces the sound /tʃ/ as in /ˈneɪ·tʃər/. The same sometimes happens with the voiced sound /d/ and /j/, which produces /dʒ/ as in *residual* /rɪˈzɪdjʊəl/.

B ▶ 7.10 Explain that sts are going to listen to interviews which took place as part of college research into Nature vs. Nurture. Have them look at the photos of the people interviewed and the comments they made. Ask: *How old do you think the people are?* Ask sts to listen and say what order they hear the interviews. Check answers.

Answers

1 E   2 C   3 B   4 D   5 A   6 F

» See Teacher's Book p.326 for Audio script 7.10.

C ▶ 7.10 Play the audio again for sts to match the opinions with the people in B. Peercheck. Classcheck. Ask: *Did anyone surprise you? Whose views are most similar to yours?*

Answers

A d   B d   C a   D c   E b   F c

D Sts discuss the meaning of the highlighted expressions in pairs. Refer sts to the example in the speech bubble. Classcheck. Ask sts to think of someone they know who: *is pushing 90, wise beyond their years, conforms to expectations, acts their age, is young at heart*. In pairs, ask sts to tell each other who the person is and how old they are, e.g. *My sister doesn't act her age. She's 26, but still lives at home, and has my mom cooking for her and washing her clothes!!*

Answers

she's pushing 90 = she's almost 90
wise beyond his years = with more knowledge and experience than most people have at his age
conform to = comply with
act my age = behave in a way which is appropriate to your age rather than someone younger
first-hand experience = experience obtained personally

Optional activity

Ask sts to choose three of the expressions and write a description of a situation or person corresponding to each. Monitor and help where necessary. When they are ready, put sts into small groups to read out their descriptions for other sts to guess the expression.

E Make it personal

1 Put sts in groups. Ask them to choose opinions from B which they can relate to or have experience of in some way. Tell them to make notes. Refer sts to the speech bubble as an example.

2 If you like, you can put sts in pairs, and have them role play an interview like in B, with one st being the researcher and the other being the member of the public being interviewed. Encourage them to use the highlighted expressions from B.

Class feedback. Ask: *Did you find out anything interesting or surprising about your classmates?*

165

7.4

>> Song lyric: See Teacher's Book p.349 for notes about the song and an accompanying activity to do with the class.

9 Grammar: Cleft sentences

Tip

It can often help sts if grammar terminology has a wider association, so elicit the meaning of *cleft*, as in *cleft lip*, meaning split or divided into two, a defect some people have the misfortune to be born with. Once sts have studied the grammar box, ask them why they think these are called "cleft sentences."

A Go through the examples in the grammar box. Ask sts why you might want to use cleft sentences (to emphasize what you want to say about the subject or object in a sentence by building up to it in the first part of the sentence). Ask sts if there is a similar structure in their language.

Ask sts to write S or O next to each sentence, then find five sentences in 8B.

To practice, have sts in pairs cover the right-hand side of the box and remember the rest of each sentence. Then cover the left-hand side and remember the beginnings.

> **Answers**
>
> 1 S 2 S 3 S 4 S 5 O 6 O 7 O
> It's my grandmother who walks two miles a day!
> It's a crazy situation I find myself in now.
> It's my younger brother who's more mature.
> It's my classmates who seem old-fashioned.
> It's not old people who are boring.
> It's not their behavior, as such, that bothers me.

>> Refer sts to the **Grammar expansion** on p.150.

B Ask sts to quickly read the text about Leo. Ask: *How would Leo feel if he saw an 80 year old on a skateboard?* (envy). Ask sts to rewrite the underlined parts of the text as cleft sentences, and go through the example. Peercheck. Classcheck. Then ask: *What does the text tell you about Leo? How do you feel about Leo and his point of view?*

Ask: *Do you own a skateboard? How would you feel if you saw an 80 year old on a skateboard?*

> **Answers**
>
> 1 It's not their behavior, as such, that bothers me. – S
> 2 It's my expectations that aren't being met. – S
> 3 It's the complete surprise that leaves me speechless. – S
> 4 It's a sight (like that) I just haven't expected. – O
> 5 It's envy that I feel. – O
> 6 It's my own fears that are getting in the way of positive thoughts. – S

C Go through **Alternatives to cleft sentences** with the class. Sts find two examples in 8B. Peercheck. Classcheck.

> **Answers**
>
> 1 I'm the one who puts food on the table.
> 2 We're not the ones who will reform society.

D Sts read the whole conversation and check understanding. Ask: *Why are the parents not acting their age?* (because they are borrowing money from their son / daughter). *Why is the son / daughter not acting his / her age?* (because he / she is too young to buy a car).

Have them rewrite the underlined responses using alternatives to cleft sentences. Tell sts that when the main action is in the past (e.g. *borrowed money*), the first part of the sentence is also in the past (*It **wasn't** me who ...*). Peercheck. Classcheck.

> **Answers**
>
> 1 I wasn't the one who borrowed the money.
> 2 They were the ones who borrowed $200 from me.
> 3 I'm the one who needs the money.
> 4 You're the one who's not acting your age.

Optional activity

Ask sts to rewrite the answer to exercise D as cleft sentences. Peercheck, then classcheck. Ask sts if they think they sound natural.

E **Make it personal** Put sts in pairs. Have them discuss questions 1–3.
1 Ask sts if they agree with their partner.
2 Ask them to think about members of their family or teachers!
3 Ask sts if they know any children who don't act their age. Ask if they think it is the fault of their parents. Focus on the example in the speech bubble.

Class feedback.

Tip

Monitor hard and try to head off as many errors as you can, e.g. with a gesture, prompt, ask the listener if the speaker is right. If time, have sts then repeat the activity with a different partner, this time congratulating them on errors they have self-corrected from the first time.

>> Workbook p.36.

♪ If you ever get close to a human, And human behavior. Be ready, be ready to get confused

7.4

9 Grammar: Cleft sentences

A Read the grammar box. Write S (subject) or O (object) next to each sentence. What clue gave you the answer? Then find five cleft sentences in 8B. Write S or O next to each.

Cleft sentences: subject and object focus

It's	older people	who / that	have a perspective on life. ¹
	your attitude	that	has to change. ²
	not how long you live		always determines your savings. ³
	saving now		will pay off later. ⁴
	an unusual phase of life	(that)	we find ourselves in. ⁵
	a tough situation		we have to face. ⁶
	a way of dealing with the future		he's looking for. ⁷

A cleft sentence can focus on a subject or object:
Subject: *Your attitude* has to change. → It's your attitude that has to change.
Object: We have to face *a tough situation*. → It's a tough situation (that) we have to face.

» Grammar expansion p.150

B Rewrite the underlined parts of Leo's responses (1–6) as cleft sentences.

Does anything tend to bother you, Leo?
Yes, when I see people not acting their age, it really bothers me. ¹I'm not bothered by their behavior, as such. But ²my expectations aren't being met. For example, if I see an 80-year-old on a skateboard, ³the complete surprise leaves me speechless. I guess you could say, ⁴I just haven't expected a sight [like that]. As for what bothers me, ⁵I think I feel envy. If I can't skateboard now, how will I skateboard at 80? ⁶My own fears are getting in the way of positive thoughts!

1 *It's not their behavior, as such, that bothers me.*

C Read *Alternatives to cleft sentences*. Find two alternatives in 8B.

Alternatives to cleft sentences

Cleft sentences with pronouns may sound unnatural and, at times, even ungrammatical when the pronoun is a subject. Instead, use *the one(s)*:

~~It's not him~~ who wants to change jobs. → He's not the one who wants to change jobs.

D Change the underlined responses (1–4) using alternatives to cleft sentences.
A: Why did you borrow money from your parents?
B: ¹I didn't borrow money.
A: What do you mean?
B: ²They borrowed $200 from me. They're really not acting their age!
A: What's it got to do with age? And besides, aren't they out of work?
B: ³I need the money. I want to buy a car.
A: ⁴Maybe you're not acting your age. You're only 17!

E Make it personal In pairs, discuss 1–3. Use cleft sentences (and alternatives) where possible.
1 Do you agree with the opinions in 8C?
2 Do you know any adults who don't act their age?
3 Do you think parents are at fault when children don't act their age?

> Are parents at fault when children don't act their age?

> Yes, because it's their parents that don't set expectations.

79

» 7.5 What would your ideal job be?

10 Listening

A ▶ 7.11 Listen to Mia talking to her friend Jack about having a younger boss. Complete the missing words (1–5) in Bill's suggestions.

1. Maybe it's time for some new _____.
2. It's your age you have to take out of the _____.
3. Just relax, be yourself, but still show _____.
4. He also might appreciate your _____ information with him.
5. You're the one who has the most to _____ if you help him solve his problems.

B In pairs, what do these expressions from A mean?

1. "take [something] out of the _____"
2. "[you] have the most to _____"

C ▶ 7.12 Listen to the next part of the conversation. Complete the chart.

	Mia	Her boss, Tim
Character traits	1	4
Qualifications	2	5
Experience	3	6

▶ 7.13 Listen to Mia and her boss. Check (✔) 1, 2, or 3. Do you think Jack's advice made a difference?

Tim becomes interested in what Mia is saying because …
1. ☐ she asks his advice.   2. ☐ she presents a solution.   3. ☐ both 1 and 2.

11 Keep talking

A In pairs, brainstorm jobs you feel you're ideally suited for, but where you might be seen as too young (or old).

1. Plan two reasons for each category: character traits, qualifications, and experience.
2. Counter the argument about your age with reasons from 1.

B ▶ 7.14 **How to say it** Complete the chart. Listen to check.

Formal requests	
What they said	What they meant
1 I hope I'm not _____.	You might be busy.
2 I had an idea for the report I wanted to _____ by you.	I want to know what you think.
3 _____ it be OK if I went ahead?	Can I go ahead?
4 I wonder if I could _____ work at home tomorrow.	I'd like to work at home tomorrow.
5 Would you be so _____ as to close the door?	Please close the door.

C Imagine you got the job in A. Role-play a conversation with your boss and ask to work on an important project. Use *How to say it* expressions.

> May I come in for a minute? I hope I'm not …

> Yes, by all means.

> I had an idea I wanted to … by you. I wonder if I could … work on the … project? You know I'm very … so I thought I'd be perfect for it.

What would your ideal job be? 7.5

Lesson Aims: Sts listen to a discussion about the problems of having a younger boss, and learn language to write a job-application letter.

Skills	Language	Vocabulary
Listening to an employee discussing problems she has with her boss Writing a job-application letter using formulaic expressions	Communicating in the office, e.g. *I hope I'm not interrupting. Would you be so kind as to …, Would it be OK if I went ahead?*	Jobs: *experience, qualifications, opportunity, opening, entry-level, position, skills, full-time, on-the-job, run by, interrupt*

Warm-up

Put sts in pairs to answer the lesson title question. Board extra questions for them to add in, e.g. *Would you be good at it? Why? What (job) experience / qualifications do you have? What character traits make you suitable?* Ask sts to discuss the questions in pairs. Classcheck. Do sts have similar dreams?

10 Listening

A ▶ 7.11 Focus only on the photo. Give sts two minutes to say all they can about it and guess what the listening will be about. Classcheck. Ask: *Have you ever worked for a boss who is younger than you? Have you ever had colleagues reporting to you who are older than you?*

Have sts read Jack's suggestions 1–5. Play the audio for sts to complete them. Peercheck. Classcheck. Ask: *How old is Mia?* (50) *How old is her boss?* (half her age – 25)

Answers
1 strategies   2 equation   3 him respect   4 sharing
5 gain

» See Teacher's Book p.327 for Audio script 7.11.

B Sts complete the expressions. Put them in pairs, and have them discuss the meanings. Ask: *Are there similar expressions in your language?* Classcheck.

Answers
1 remove something from the situation, don't let something be a factor, disregard something
2 you will benefit most, you will be the one who is better off

C ▶ 7.12 Focus on the chart, then sts listen to Mia and Jack and complete it. Peercheck. Classcheck. Ask: *Do you notice a difference in Mia's attitude?* (She's beginning to see her boss in a more positive light).

Answers
1 very open and receptive to customers' needs
2 master's in business management
3 three decades of experience working in marketing
4 communicates well, quite creative
5 MA in business management
6 worked in sales for five years

» See Teacher's Book p.327 for Audio script 7.12.

Weaker classes: Board the answers in random order. Sts listen and match the answers to each person in the recording.

D ▶ 7.13 Tell sts Mia's now in her boss' office. *Can they guess what will happen?* Sts listen and check 1, 2, or 3. Highlight the phrase *Could I see the numbers?* (financial forecasts) We can also ask *Could I see the figures?* Ask: *How do Tim and Mia treat each other?* Elicit *politely* and *with respect.* Ask: *Do you think Jack's advice has worked?*

Answers
Check 3 (both 1 and 2)

» See Teacher's Book p.327 for Audio script 7.13.

11 Keep talking

A Ask sts to choose two or three jobs each which they would be ideal for (but may be too old or too young).

1 Have them think of reasons why they would be good at the job from the categories: character traits, qualifications, and experience.

2 Elicit and board examples to start them off, e.g.
   A: *I'd make a really good head teacher, but I'm too young.*
   B: *That doesn't matter. You have good qualifications and lots of experience.*
   A: *I think I'd be a good tennis coach, but I'm too old now.*
   B: *No way! You've played tennis for years, and have a great understanding of the game. Age isn't important.*

In pairs, ask sts to write out similar mini exchanges, and act them out. Invite a few sts to act them out for the class.

B ▶ 7.14 **How to say it** Have sts complete the sentences, then play the audio for them to check. Elicit the meaning of *go ahead* (start doing it / begin).

Answers
1 interrupting   2 run   3 Would   4 possibly   5 kind

C Put sts in pairs. Have sts write out their conversations together. Make sure they take turns playing each role.

Weaker classes: Give sts a copy of audio script 7.13 to help them.

7.5

12 Writing: A job-application letter

A Ask: *How many jobs have you applied for? How many did you get? Have you ever applied for a job in writing? When was the last time? Did you get it?*

Focus on the letter. Ask the class: *Who's it from? Who's it to?*

Tip
To create a more communicative class, and prevent stronger sts dominating, first set a gist reading task, e.g. *What job is she applying for? Where is it? Do you think she'll get it?* Give sts two minutes to read and answer, then check in pairs. This allows weaker sts extra time to digest more of the letter before going into the detailed tasks.

Ask the class: *What character traits do you think would make a good hotel receptionist?* Brainstorm answers.

Take sts through the rubric and tasks. Sts re-read the letter and find 1–4. Peercheck. Classcheck. Having read her letter, do they think she'll get the job? Why (not)?

> **Answers**
> 1. excellent communication skills, attentive to detail, enjoys interacting with customers and serving their needs, dynamic, pro-active
> 2. BA in Hotel Management, speaks four languages fluently
> 3. several summer jobs working as an assistant in reception
> 4. problem-solving room assignments, checking in customers, and answering routine questions

Stronger classes: Ask sts to cover up the letter and work in pairs to remember as many of the things in A as they can. Elicit sts' ideas, then ask them to find them in the letter and check.

B Read through **Formulaic expressions (2)** with the class. Ask sts what the equivalent expressions are in their language. Sts complete blanks 1–6 in the letter with the correct expressions. Classcheck.

Stronger classes: Have sts try to complete the letter before reading *Formulaic expressions*. Then read the letter to check.

> **Answers**
> 1. I am writing in response to
> 2. I believe I am highly suited to
> 3. As you will see in
> 4. would be a perfect fit for
> 5. In this capacity
> 6. I hope you will give my (resume) careful consideration

C Read through **Write it right!** Point out that the introduction and the conclusions of job applications are especially short. Is this similar in their language?

Sts find other noun phrases and *-ing* forms in the letter. Classcheck. Refer sts to the **Common mistake**, and remind them that *work* is uncountable and therefore never used with an indefinite article.

> **Answers**
> On-the-job experience would allow me to translate the theoretical to the practical.
> My academic background has familiarized me with many aspects of the hotel industry.
> Helping customers has strengthened my desire to have a future career in hotel management.

D Sts rewrite sentences 1–4 using an *-ing* form. Do the first one together on the board, as an example. Have sts continue with 2–4. Peercheck. Classcheck.

> **Answers**
> 1. Using my writing skills would be fulfilling. (copy writer)
> 2. Responding to emergencies taught me to make rapid decisions. (emergency services)
> 3. Studying linguistics helped me develop an interest in computing language. (programmer)
> 4. Working at such a world-famous hospital would be the dream of a lifetime (nurse / doctor)

E Your turn!

Go through the instructions with the class, and check sts understand what they have to do. Remind them to include the address and date on their letter. They should begin the letter with *Dear Sir or Madam*, and end it with *Sincerely*, as in the example.

Have sts post their finished letters online or stick them on the classroom wall. Tell them to read at least five of their classmates' letters. Ask: *Would you give the applicants a job? Why / why not?*

Optional activity
Put sts in pairs and ask them to swap their letters with another pair. Ask sts to read the letters they were given and think of questions they'd like to ask to find out more information. When they are ready, put the pairs together to role-play interviews for the job. In feedback, ask sts if they would give the jobs to the sts who applied for them, and why / why not.

» Song lyric: See Teacher's Book p.349 for notes about the song and an accompanying activity to do with the class.

» Workbook p.37.

♪ Workin' 9 to 5. What a way to make a livin'. Barely gettin' by. It's all takin' and no givin'

12 Writing: A job-application letter

A Read the letter. Then identify ...
1. five positive character traits the writer mentions.
2. two qualifications for the job.
3. one example of her past experience.
4. three specific responsibilities she's had.

General Director, Meliá Hotels
April 12, 2017

Dear Sir or Madam:

1. ¹_____ your online ad of March 31, where you posted an opening for an entry-level receptionist in your hotel chain. ²_____ the position, and am attaching my résumé.

2. Having graduated from Anhembi Morumbi University in São Paulo with a BA in Hotel Management, I am eager to put my skills to use. ³_____ my résumé, I speak four languages fluently: English (my native language), Portuguese, Spanish, and German. Therefore, I believe my profile ⁴_____ in one of the São Paulo branches of the Meliá Hotels group. However, I'm open to opportunities in Rio de Janeiro, as well.

3. Working in your prestigious hotel chain would be rewarding work for me. I have excellent communication skills and am attentive to detail. In addition, I enjoy interacting with customers and serving their needs. In several summer jobs where I've worked as an assistant in reception, I have been praised as dynamic and pro-active. My past responsibilities have included problem-solving room assignments, checking in customers, and answering routine questions. ⁵_____, I have learned to interact with a wide variety of people from many backgrounds and nationalities. Helping customers has strengthened my desire to have a future career in hotel management.

4. While I am aware this would be my first full-time hotel assignment, I consider myself a quick learner. My academic background has familiarized me with many aspects of the hotel industry. On-the-job experience would allow me to translate the theoretical to the practical.

5. ⁶_____. Thank you very much in advance.

Sincerely,
Linda Baker

Common mistake

Working there would be a ~~rewarding~~ work for me.
rewarding

B Read *Formulaic expressions (2)*. Then complete 1–6 in the letter with the expressions given.

Formulaic expressions (2)

Formulaic expressions like these are commonly used in job-application letters.
I believe I am highly suited to (this sort of assignment).
As you will see on (p.2) / in (the attached sample) ...
In this capacity, (I answered phones).
I am writing in response to (your job opening).
I hope you will give my (résumé) careful consideration.
(I) would be a perfect fit for (this job).

C Read *Write it right!* In paragraphs 3 and 4, underline two more examples of sentences beginning with noun phrases and one of a sentence beginning with an *-ing* form.

Write it right!

Job-application letters are fairly short and often include sentences beginning with ...
1. noun phrases as subjects:
   My past responsibilities have included problem-solving ...
2. *-ing* forms used as nouns, as opposed to sentences beginning with *it*, which take longer to get to the point:
   Working in your prestigious hotel would be rewarding work for me.

D Change 1–4 into sentences beginning with an *-ing* form. What kind of job might each person be applying for?
1. It would be fulfilling to use my writing skills.
2. It was responding to emergencies that taught me to make rapid decisions.
3. It was studying linguistics that helped me develop an interest in computing language.
4. It would be the dream of a lifetime to work at such a world-famous hospital.

E **Your turn!** Choose a job you brainstormed in 11A and write a job-application letter in about 280 words.

Before
List the character traits, qualifications, and experience that make you an excellent candidate.

While
Write four to five paragraphs, following the model in A. Use formulaic expressions and begin sentences with noun phrases (including *-ing* forms).

After
Post your letter online and read your classmates' work. Whose letter is most convincing?

8

What makes a restaurant special?

1 Listening

A ▶ 8.1 Listen to the start of a lecture on business practices. Which picture (1–2) does the speaker imply the dinner will be like?

B ▶ 8.2 In pairs, guess what happened next. Listen to check. Then answer 1–3.
1 Who came to the dinner?
2 What were they given at the end?
3 What was the true reason for the dinner?

C ▶ 8.2 Listen again. What do 1–4 mean in context? Choose a or b.
1 bland   a ☐ smooth, not irritating   b ☐ tasteless
2 shrug off   a ☐ not care   b ☐ brush off, remove
3 baffled   a ☐ puzzled   b ☐ frustrated
4 oblivious to a ☐ unaffected by   b ☐ unaware of

D ▶ 8.3 Listen to the last part. Why didn't the companies sue the site? Check (✔) the correct answer.
1 ☐ They probably wouldn't succeed.
2 ☐ It probably wasn't in their interest.
3 ☐ both 1 and 2

E Make it personal Does advertising work? In groups, discuss 1–3.
1 How effective do you think campaigns like the one described in **A** really are?

> Very effective! These days any video offering the unexpected goes viral almost immediately.

2 Which quotes (a–f) do you like most / least? Why? Take a class vote.

> a "The only people who care about advertising are the people who work in advertising." (George Parker)
>
> b "Don't find customers for your product. Find products for your customers." (Seth Godin)
>
> c "Advertisers constantly invent cures to which there is no disease." (Author unknown)
>
> d "Ads sell a great deal more than products. They sell values, images, and concepts of success and worth." (Brené Brown)
>
> e "Advertising teaches people not to trust their judgment. Advertising teaches people to be stupid." (Carl Sagan)
>
> f "Let's gear our advertising to sell our goods, but let's recognize also that advertising has a broad social responsibility." (Leo Burnett)

3 Guess why the quotes were all written by men. Similar opinions?

What makes a restaurant special? 8.1

Lesson Aims: Sts hear about a smart marketing prank and learn expressions with *take*.

Skills	Language	Vocabulary
Listening to a lecture on business practices Sharing stories of bad service	Describing negative experiences, e.g. *On top of that ..., To make matters worse ..., As if that were not enough ..., To add insult to injury ...*	Expressions with *take*: *take legal action, take a stand, take matters in your own hands, take offense, take the blame, take the internet by storm* *bland, shrug off, baffled, oblivious, advertising, tasty, tasteless*

Warm-up

Board: *What's the best restaurant experience you've had?* for sts to answer in small groups as they come into class. Classcheck.

Focus on the lesson title question. Brainstorm factors onto the board with the class. Have them vote for their top three to make it "special."

1 Listening

A ▶ 8.1 Focus on the pictures. Ask: *What do you think is happening in each of the pictures? Why do you think the people in picture 2 look unhappy?*

Explain that sts are going to hear the start of a lecture on business practices. The speaker talks about a dinner that a Brazilian website called *Reclame aqui* set up. It invited a lot of heads of business to the dinner. Ask sts to listen and find out whether the dinner will be like picture 1 or picture 2.

Play the audio. Elicit that the dinner will be the worst dinner of their lives.

Answer

Picture 2

» See Teacher's Book p.327 for Audio script 8.1.

B ▶ 8.2 Ask: *What do you think happened next?* Encourage sts to make a few guesses, e.g. *the waiter was rude, the food was cold.* Teach the word *portion*, e.g. *the portions were tiny.* Play the audio for sts to check. Then have them answer 1–3. Re-play the audio if necessary.

Classcheck. Ask: *What was the reaction of the executives?* (they didn't understand what was going on).

Answers

1 nine executives from companies which had received the greatest number of complaints on the reclame aqui website
2 a piece of paper saying, "Did you feel disrespected? Well, so do thousands and thousands of your customers, according to the data on our site."
3 to reproduce the level of service that customers usually get when they do business with the companies, and to highlight how frustrating / annoying it is to receive such bad service

» See Teacher's Book p.327 for Audio script 8.2.

C ▶ 8.2 Ask sts if they know the meanings of words 1–4. If not, play the audio again for them to figure out the meaning from the context (or give them a copy of the audio script). Drill pronunciation of the words.

Ask them to choose meanings a or b. Classcheck. Ask: *Which foods would you describe as bland?*

Answers

1 b   2 b   3 a   4 b

D ▶ 8.3 Ask sts to guess why the companies didn't sue the site. Play the audio for them to check. Classcheck. Ask: *What did you think of the prank? Do you think it was a good idea? Do you think it will change the way the executives run their companies?*

Answer

3

» See Teacher's Book p.328 for Audio script 8.3.

Optional activity

Ask sts to think of other events they could organize for different companies, e.g. a garage which only offered superficial repairs. Sts then share their ideas in groups and present the most interesting to the class.

E Make it personal

1 Put sts in small groups to discuss question 1. Refer them to the model in the speech bubble, and check the meaning of *go viral* (sharing of something by email or social media). Discuss the fact that many companies now use social media as a big part of their marketing campaigns, rather than more traditional newspaper, TV, or magazine ads.

2 Go through the quotes with the class, and discuss the meaning. Back in their groups, have sts say which they like most / least and why. Have a class vote.

3 Have sts discuss question 3 in their groups. Class feedback by inviting sts to share their opinions with the class. Say: *Think of an ad which stuck in your mind. Why did it stick? Did you buy the product?* If you can, ask sts to show the ads to the class when they discuss this.

» Song lyric: See Teacher's Book p.350 for notes about the song and an accompanying activity to do with the class.

8.1

2 Vocabulary: Expressions with *take* for discussing events

Tip

Elicit the differences between *bring* and *take* and collocates for both, including any phrasal verbs, e.g. *take after, take back, take in, take off, take out, take up; bring up, bring back*. You could refer sts to the Phrasal Verb bank on SB p.164.

A ▶ 8.4 Ask sts to study the expressions in the box. Ask: *Which do you know already?* Ask them if they remember what these expressions referred to in the context of the *reclame aqui* lecture.

Tell sts they are going to hear excerpts from the lecture in 1, with the relevant expressions missing. They have to say the correct expression when they hear a beep. Remind them to use the correct form of *take*.

Weaker classes: Give sts a copy of the audio script with the *take* expressions blanked out. Have them fill in the blanks.

Answers

1 took matters into its own hands   2 took the internet by storm   3 taking a stand   4 took offense   5 take legal action   6 take the blame

» See Teacher's Book p.328 for Audio script 8.4.

B Have sts read the sentences and guess the correct prepositions. They can search in dictionaries or on the internet to check. Peercheck. Classcheck. Sts then make the sentences true for them, e.g. *I don't really take offense at jokes aimed at minority groups, but I don't like them.*

Answers

1 against   2 against   3 at   4 for

Optional activity

Once sts have guessed the correct prepositions, check answers with the class but don't discuss the meanings yet. Call out the phrases at random and have sts race to find the meaning on their mobile device, before sharing it with the class.

C ▶ 8.5 Elicit the meaning of *nightmare* and *purchase* then have sts guess what it means as a phrase (a disastrous buy). Play the audio and ask sts to listen for gist. Ask: *What nightmare purchase did Ruth make?* (A washing machine). Have them read the questions, then listen again and make a note of the answers. Sts write full answers to the questions using the expressions in A. Peercheck. Classcheck.

Ask: *Have you ever had a similar experience to Gary?*

Answers

1 Very. It would take everyone by storm.
2 He took offense.
3 The store's, but they didn't take the blame.
4 Very. She promised she would take matters into her own hands.
5 He might take legal action.

» See Teacher's Book p.328 for Audio script 8.5.

D Make it personal

1 ▶ 8.6 **How to say it** Go through examples 1–4 in the chart with the class. Have sts try to fill in the blanks, then play the audio for them to check. Check sts understand the meanings. Ask: *Do you have similar expressions in your language?*

Drill stress and pronunciation. Then have sts practice saying the expressions in pairs. Encourage them to use the contracted form *As if that **weren't** enough …*

Answers

1 top   2 matters   3 enough   4 add

2 Sts work individually making notes about the worst restaurant experience they have had, using the prompts in the Student's book.

Ask: *Did you complain? Did you get your money back?*

3 Put sts in groups to share their stories. Refer sts to the models in the speech bubbles. Class feedback. Ask sts to relate the story of someone in their group.

Refer sts to **Common mistakes**. Elicit the meaning of *tasteful* (showing good taste). Ask: *What is the opposite of tasty?* (bland). *What synonyms for delicious do you know?* (mouthwatering, succulent, moreish, yummy). *And for bland?* (unseasoned, watered down, flavorless).

Optional activity

Sts could act out their experience for the class. Other sts then vote on the worst experience.

» Workbook p.38.

♪ No one learned from your mistakes. We let our profits go to waste. All that's left in any case. Is advertising space

2 Vocabulary: Expressions with *take* for discussing events

A ▶ 8.4 Listen to excerpts 1–6. When you hear the "beep", say one of the expressions below. Use the correct form of *take*. Continue listening to check.

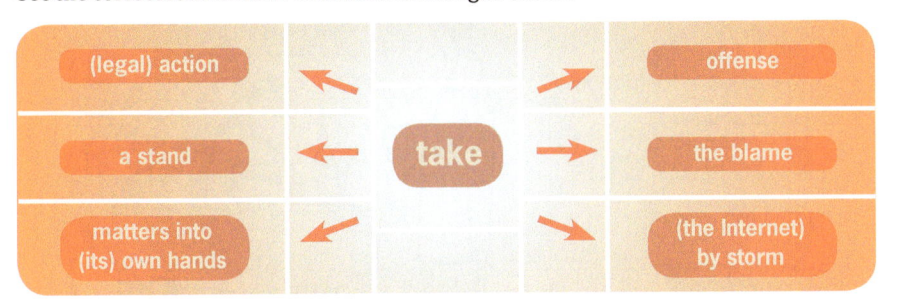

- (legal) action
- a stand
- matters into (its) own hands
- take
- offense
- the blame
- (the Internet) by storm

B 🌐 In groups, use your instincts to guess the correct preposition (1–4). Search on the expression to check. Then change the sentences so they're true for you.

1 I wish more people would take a stand [**about** / **against**] GM foods.
2 In my country, it's easy to take legal action [**over** / **against**] cyber stalkers.
3 I take offense [**at** / **with**] jokes aimed at minority groups.
4 I sometimes get into trouble at work because I take the blame [**for** / **of**] my colleagues' mistakes.

C ▶ 8.5 Listen to two friends, Gary and Ruth, talking about a nightmare purchase. Take notes on 1–5. Then answer using expressions from **A**.

1 How popular does Ruth think a campaign like that would be in the U.S.?
2 How did Gary react when Ruth mentioned the old washing machine?
3 Whose fault was the wrong delivery?
4 How apologetic was the manager?
5 What does Gary say he might do in the end?

D Make it personal Talk about bad service!

1 ▶ 8.6 **How to say it** Complete the chart. Listen to check.

Describing negative experiences	
What they said	What they meant
1 On _____ of that, (it took them three days to get back to me).	To make a bad situation worse or more painful ...
2 To make _____ worse, (she said it was the delivery company's fault).	
3 As if that were not _____, (they charged my credit card again).	
4 To _____ insult to injury, (they didn't even apologize).	

2 What was the worst experience you've ever had at a restaurant? Think through a–b and make notes.
  a the most relevant details (What / Where / When / Who / Why / How long)
  b the outcome and what you learned from the experience

3 In groups, share your stories. Use *How to say it* expressions and ones with *take*. Who had the worst experience?

> I once had to wait an hour before my order was taken, so I took matters into my own hands.

> What did you do? Grab food from the kitchen?

> I stood up and yelled "Fire." So to add insult to injury, they accused me of creating a disturbance!

Common mistakes
tasty
The food was ~~tasteful~~ / tasteless.
tasteful
The decoration was ~~tasty~~ / tasteless.

» 8.2 Are you a demanding customer?

3 Language in use

A Read the cartoon. Do you agree? What advice would you give the waitress?

B ▶ 8.7 Listen to Raúl and his private English tutor, Julia. Check (✔) the problems with his text.
- ☐ There are a few grammar mistakes.
- ☐ It's too wordy.
- ☐ It's too formal.
- ☐ The vocabulary is too simple.

Cartoon speech bubbles:
- "The customer is always right, the customer is ALWAYS right."
- "Could I have the cheese omelette, but without the cheese and eggs?"
- "I'd like a glass of naturally distilled spring water with a slice of organic lemon."

FRAN.

C ▶ 8.8 Listen to the next part of their conversation. Underline the sentences in sections 1–4 of Raúl's draft handout that Julia suggests changing. Which reason in **B** does she give?

> **Guidelines for dealing with complaints – draft**
> Once you realize that a customer is dissatisfied, try to imagine yourself in his or her position, even if you're not to blame. Then follow these four easy guidelines:
> 1. It is critically important that your customers communicate how they feel. They need time and space to express their dissatisfaction. Then, apologize – even if you feel their criticism is unfair.
> 2. Listen actively. It is essential that you not draw any conclusions until you know all the facts. Then repeat your customer's concerns to make sure you have correctly identified the key issues.
> 3. If you can respond to the issue at hand immediately, do it. It is crucial that problems be resolved quickly.
> 4. A customer may insist that he or she speak to the manager. If that happens, try to find someone in a position of authority to support you.

D ▶ 8.8 Try to remember Julia's suggested changes. Cross out the words and write the new ones in Raúl's handout. Then listen again to check. Did you get them all?

E **Make it personal** In pairs, discuss 1–3. Similar opinions?
1. Which of Raúl's guidelines in **C** should companies follow more often? Would you add any others?
2. Should businesses refund or exchange damaged products with "no questions asked"?
3. Do you notice the writing style of letters businesses send? How informal should it be?

> I'd add that a salesperson shouldn't answer the phone when the customer is talking!

84

Are you a demanding customer? 8.2

Lesson Aims: Sts learn to use the subjunctive and formal vs. informal language.

Skills	Language	Grammar
Listening to a st talking with his tutor in an English lesson Making a short formal speech	Using formal language, e.g. *It's essential not to be late. I suggest that he seek help immediately.*	The subjunctive

Warm-up

Focus on the lesson title question. Ask: *Which adjectives could replace "demanding"?* (e.g. difficult, pleasant, agreeable). Brainstorm ideas onto the board. Ask: *Which adjective is you?* for sts to confess to each other! Then ask: *Do you complain if you aren't happy with the service you get in a store or restaurant?*

3 Language in use

A Tell sts to read the cartoon then react to it in pairs. Classcheck. Who found it funny? Ask: *Are the customers being difficult? Does the waitress really believe that "the customer is always right"? What advice would you give the waitress?* Elicit *to be patient*. Ask: *Have any of you worked in a restaurant or had an experience like this?* In groups, sts discuss any experiences they have had with annoying or demanding customers. Have sts share their stories with the class

B ▶8.7 Focus on the photo of Raúl and his English teacher, Julia. Explain that Raúl has brought a draft handout about customer service that he wants Julia to help him correct. Go through the list of problems, and elicit the meaning of *wordy* (too many words). Have sts listen and check the problems the tutor mentions. Classcheck. Ask sts: *What does the tutor think of Raúl's written English?* (very good)

Answers

It's too wordy. It's too formal.

≫ See Teacher's Book p.328 for Audio script 8.7.

C ▶8.8 Tell sts they are going to hear Raúl and Julia going through his handout. The tutor is suggesting ways of improving it. Have them read it first and elicit their opinions / suggestions, then listen and underline the sentences she suggests changing. Classcheck.

Answers

1 It is critically important that your customers communicate how they feel.
2 It is essential that you do not draw any conclusions until you know all the facts.
3 It is crucial that problems be resolved quickly.
4 A customer may insist that he or she speak to the manager.
They're too formal.

≫ See Teacher's Book p.328 for Audio script 8.8.

Tip

In English, we often make what we say more formal by adding distance. We can do this by using longer words with a Latin origin e.g. *request* instead of *ask*. We also do this simply by adding more words to a sentence, as in Raúl's handout.

D ▶8.8 Sts try to remember the changes the tutor suggests. You could do the first one together on the board. Write the original sentences out, then cross out the words that are not needed. Sts continue correcting 2–4. Play the audio for them to check.

Answers

1 It's important for your customers to say how they feel.
2 Don't jump to conclusions until you know all the facts.
3 Problems must be resolved quickly.
4 A customer may want to speak to the manager.

Optional activity

To provide a change of pace, print each of the points in Raúl's handout onto a large piece of paper and display them around the classroom. Sts walk around and cross out the extra sentences in pencil.

E Make it personal Ask: *How important do you think customer service is?*

Go through questions 1–3 with the class. Put sts in pairs to discuss them. Refer them to the example in the speech bubble. Ask: *Which question does this refer to?* (1). Class feedback. Invite sts to share their views with the rest of the class.

Ask: *Do you receive much junk mail? Do you read it or throw it away? Is it normally written in a formal or informal way? Any suggestion for ways to reduce junk mail?*

Optional activity

Ask sts to describe norms in their country/ies, i.e. how far companies follow Raúl's guidelines and how easy it is to get refunds / exchanges.

177

8.2

> Song lyric: See Teacher's Book p.350 for notes about the song and an accompanying activity to do with the class.

4 Grammar: The subjunctive

Tip

First, board *The subjunctive*, and ask: *What do you know about the subjunctive in English? Is it easier or harder than the equivalent form in your language?* See how much of what's in the grammar box you can elicit first. Note: If only one or two stronger sts do all the talking, or it simply gets too complicated to explain easily, move on as fast as you can to avoid the rest of the class feeling uncomfortable!

A Read through the examples in the grammar box and check the meanings.

Weaker classes: Ask sts to underline the verbs in each part of the sentences. Ask: *Which verbs are in the ... present / past / base form?*

Tip

Ask sts to mentally translate the sentences into their own language. This doesn't mean they have to start speaking a lot of L1, but mental translation is an inevitable process whenever there is doubt, so it's often better to give them a minute just to note the similarities and differences. They can always quickly compare with a neighbor, figure out any uncertainties they have, then come back to plenary, without you having to get involved in any L1 discussion at all.

Have sts check the correct rules a–c, then rewrite sentences 1–4 using the subjunctive.

> **Answers**
> a were   b base   c doesn't change
> 1 It's important that customers say how they feel.
> 2 It's essential you don't jump to any conclusions until you know all the facts.
> 3 It's crucial that problems are resolved quickly.
> 4 A customer may insist that he speak to the manager.

> Refer sts to the **Grammar expansion** on p.152.

B ▶ 1.5 Read **Using the subjunctive** together. Have sts read the article **Plain English**. Elicit the meaning of *plain* (simple / not complicated).

Sts rewrite sentences 1–6 using the subjunctive to make them more formal.

Ask sts to imagine where they might hear these things said. Refer them to the speech bubble as an example. Classcheck. Focus on the **Common mistake** and point out that we cannot use an object pronoun (*him*) as the subject of the verb (*take*).

> **Answers**
> 1 It's important that you meet the deadline. (architects discussing submitting their plans for a project)
> 2 It's essential that you not be late. (friend talking to a person going for a job interview)
> 3 I suggest that you seek help immediately. (someone talking to a friend who is struggling with a subject at school)
> 4 I wish dad were here to witness this day. (daughter talking to mother on graduation day)
> 5 It's critical that all the requirements be met. (two managers assessing job applications)
> 6 She demanded that the contract be revised. (lawyers talking about a client)

C Make it personal

1 Have sts choose one or two sentences from the right column of the Plain English article in B, and plan a short speech around it. Weaker sts can do this in pairs.

Refer them to the speech bubble as an example of an introduction. Brainstorm points that the school director could make in his or her speech and board them, e.g. *It's essential not to be late for lessons. If you are falling behind, then I suggest you seek help immediately from your subject teacher. It's critical that you work hard leading up to your exams.*

They can use the same context or think of their own.

2 Put sts in groups to deliver their speeches. If sts are working in pairs, have them each deliver half the speech. Monitor around the class and make a note of good uses of the subjunctive. Invite one or two sts to deliver their speeches to the whole class.

Tip

When giving feedback on sts' language after a speaking activity, pick out any good examples of language use (as well as errors), and drill them around the class.

> Workbook p.39.

♪ Oh cherie amour, pretty little one that I adore. You're the only girl my heart beats for. How I wish that you were mine

8.2

4 Grammar: The subjunctive

A Read the grammar box and check (✔) the correct rules (a–c). Then, without looking back at 3B, rephrase the underlined parts of 1–4 using the subjunctive. Use the word in parentheses.

The subjunctive: verbs and expressions with *it's*

I wish		the shirt were	on sale.
I demanded		he give	me a refund.
I insist	(that)	the manager see	me right now.
I suggest		we look into	this matter.
It was important		you not be	rude.
It's essential		she research	her purchase.

a After *wish*, the subjunctive form for *he* and *she* is ☐ was ☐ were.
b After other verbs, and expressions with *it's*, the subjunctive is the ☐ base ☐ past tense form.
c When the first verb is in the past, the subjunctive form ☐ changes ☐ doesn't change.

» Grammar expansion p.152

1 <u>It's important for your customers to say</u> how they feel. (important)
2 <u>Don't jump to any conclusions</u> until you know all the facts. (essential)
3 <u>Problems must be resolved</u> quickly. (crucial)
4 A customer <u>may want to speak</u> to the manager. (insist)

B Read *Using the subjunctive*. Then complete 1–6 below. Imagine a context for each.

Using the subjunctive

The subjunctive is relatively uncommon in English, and is used in formal speech and writing. In conversation, other structures are frequently used:
It's important **for you not to be** rude. / **Please don't be** rude.
They suggested **speaking** to you. / They **said to speak** to you.

Plain English: All it's cracked up to be?

Writers often recommend a communication style that's short, clear, and to the point. But are we going too far in that direction? In this course, you'll learn how to make your language more emphatic – useful skills for writing and formal speeches.

Instead of:	It might be better to say:
1 Do your best to meet the deadline.	It's important … the deadline.
2 Don't be late.	It's essential … late.
3 He should seek help immediately.	I suggest … help immediately.
4 I'm sorry Dad isn't here to witness this day.	I wish … here to witness this day.
5 All the requirements must be met.	It's crucial …
6 She said the contract had to be revised.	She demanded …

I think in number 6, some lawyers might be talking about a client.

Common mistake

She suggested ~~him to take~~ legal action.
(that) he take

C **Make it personal** Be convincing!
1 Choose at least one sentence from the right column of B, decide a context, and plan a short speech.
Note down at most five key points.
2 In groups, deliver your speeches. Whose points were clearest? Who sounded the most formal?

Thank you very much for joining me here today. As I think most of you know, I'm the new school director. I'd like to begin by …

85

8.3 What are the worst aspects of air travel?

5 Reading

A Read the title. Does Barbara Apple Sullivan expect to be treated well? What clue is there? Read the first four paragraphs to check.

B In pairs, guess why Barbara had a "reinvigorated customer experience." Then read the rest to check. Make certain you understand the highlighted words, and search online for images, if necessary.

> I think she might have been given a free flight ...

The True Story Of Amazing Customer Service From – Gasp! – An Airline

1. When Barbara Apple Sullivan accidentally dropped her passport in a Charles de Gaulle airport mailbox just before boarding a flight, she was certain she'd be stuck for days. But thanks to a Delta employee, she made it on board and had her future travel plans transformed forever.

2. "Keep Climbing."

    That is the slogan for Delta Airlines' latest advertising campaign, which highlights its promise for a "reinvigorated customer experience." So often I have seen this television commercial and others like it, paying little attention to the message and the value proposition. My only takeaway was reassurance that the planes were pointed upward and not downward.

3. In such a saturated industry, it is difficult for any airline to differentiate the customer experience. The planes themselves are virtually identical. The food, if it exists, is universally awful. Airport security is conducted by an entity over which the airlines have virtually no control. And virtually everyone who flies has a personal horror story. Is it really possible to redefine the customer experience?

4. It was my personal experience with a single employee that emblazoned Delta's value proposition in my mind forever. Their promise came to life in a real, tangible way. More than any advertising, more than an impactful website, more than those tasty biscotti cookies served on the plane, this really was a reinvigorated customer experience.

5. Allow me to set the scene. To my horror, I inadvertently dropped my passport in a mailbox at Charles de Gaulle airport last Sunday morning (it was bundled with all my VAT refund envelopes). The instant the mail left my hand and dropped to the bottom of the mailbox, I realized my error. Two airport employees told me it was impossible to open the mailbox on a Sunday since postal workers, who do not work on Sundays, have sole authority to open the box. I was told I must wait until Monday, go to the U.S. Embassy in Paris, and request an emergency passport before I would be able to fly. In desperation, I approached the Delta ticket counter and told them I had a BIG problem.

6. One gentleman behind the counter, Mr. Karim Sayoud, took my problem as though it were his own. He calmed me in my increasing panic, explained what he could do and immediately called the U.S. Homeland Security Customs and Border Control representative station at the airport.

7. Mr. James Wilkinson from U.S. Homeland Security came to interrogate me. All I had was my passport number. I had nothing else. No copy of my passport, no social security card, and the address on my driver's license did not match my passport. After providing enough correct answers to convince him that I was in fact who I said I was, he agreed to let me travel, subject to the French authorities that retain final approval.

8. Karim Sayoud left his position at the Delta ticket counter, escorted me to Delta check-in, and he convinced his colleagues to accept my baggage (without the certainty that I would be on the flight) and issue a boarding pass. He then escorted me through French passport control and security, encouraging the authorities to let me through, and ultimately to the Delta gate agents. It was there that I was finally able to breathe a sigh of relief.

9. Sayoud didn't stop there. After I was successfully on the flight, he took it upon himself to make certain that my passport was retrieved from the mailbox the following day and returned to me in New York. He actually taped a handwritten note on the mailbox so the postal worker would see it and return the passport to Delta once it was retrieved. He phoned and emailed me multiple times each day updating me on the status. Lo and behold, my passport arrived at my address by FedEx – a true customer-service miracle made entirely possible by one dedicated employee.

—Barbara Apple Sullivan, is CEO and a managing partner of Sullivan, a multidisciplinary brand-engagement firm based in New York City. Follow them on Twitter at @sullivannyc

What are the worst aspects of air travel? 8.3

Lesson Aims: Sts read a story about a member of staff who goes the extra mile, and talk about strangers' acts of kindness.

Skills	Language	Vocabulary
Reading a text about a passenger's experience at the airport Telling stories about sts' own experiences of help from strangers	Talking about helpful people: *He took it upon himself to …, She went to great lengths to …, He moved mountains to …*	Expressions of *help*: *take it upon oneself, go to great lengths, go out of your way, go the extra mile, move mountains, take it from there, see to it that* Airport travel: *passport, ticket counter, check-in, boarding pass, passport control, gate agents, baggage*

Warm-up

Board: *Air travel*. Ask sts to think of as many words as they can related to air travel, e.g. *check-in desk, departures, security gate, board the plane, gate, baggage, passport control, boarding pass, take off, land, baggage reclaim*.

Ask the lesson title question: *What are the worst aspects of air travel? Do you fly a lot? When did you last fly? How was the flight? What is the worst experience you have had of air travel?* Students discuss the questions in pairs, then feedback.

5 Reading

A Ask: *Have you ever lost your passport? Were you about to travel? What did you do? How easy was it to get a new one?*

Tip

Set the parameters for success in the lesson. Tell sts that today will involve practicing reading a difficult authentic text. If they can get the gist the first time, and most of the main ideas the second time, they will have done well.

Have sts read the title. Elicit that Barbara does not expect to be treated well. The clue is in the word *Gasp*, which is what we do when we are surprised or astonished! Ask sts to mime the word *gasp*. Establish that she is clearly being sarcastic.

Ask: *Why might she feel so negative about airlines?* Elicit answers (previous experiences, negativity about them making large profits out of routes where they are the only option, etc).

Then ask sts to read the first four paragraphs to check.

Tip

Set a clear feasible first reading task, e.g. *How many negatives can you find in the four paragraphs?* (broken advertising promises, poor value, the only guarantee is that they take off and land, planes are all the same, terrible food or none at all, unhelpful airport security, other passengers' negative experiences) Give them enough time because this is complex, unfiltered authentic language and they will almost certainly struggle the first time they read it.

Paircheck then classcheck. Ask: *Did you find any positives?* (the fancy cookies and one nice employee) Tell them not to worry too much about the complicated language, but that you're not going to translate every word because it's natural to struggle with authentic text. Indeed that's the whole point, getting them used to reality, and celebrating comprehension of the difficult, rather than spoon-feeding with highly edited text as may have happened to them at lower levels.

B Put sts in pairs to make guesses about what Barbara's positive experience might be. Refer them to the speech bubble. Elicit other expressions for speculating, e.g. *Maybe / Perhaps she …, It's possible that …, She probably …* Invite sts to share their guesses. They read the rest of the text to check.

Class feedback. Ask: *How close were your guesses? Have you ever had a similar experience? Have you ever dropped something in a mailbox by mistake?*

If you've done the warm-up and elicited all the highlighted words, there shouldn't be any problem with comprehension. If not, double check.

8.3

C ▶ 8.9 Have sts read the statements carefully. Play the audio and ask them to follow the text in their books.

Tip

Pause a couple of times for sts to breathe, look up, and tell a partner how they are feeling. When sts look at each other, you tend to get more honest feedback than when they look at you! This makes the whole experience in a mixed ability class more human, and more real, allowing them to express difficulty, discomfort, etc. Then they take a deep breath and continue! You can also clarify quickly if they desperately want to understand a word / idea, so they are "unblocked" and able to concentrate again.

Sts mark the statements T or F, and correct the false ones. Classcheck. Drill pronunciation of the words highlighted in pink.

> **Answers**
> 1 F (She was mailing VAT refund envelopes) 2 F (postal workers have sole authority to open the box) 3 T 4 F (the French authorities had final approval) 5 T

Optional activity

Ask sts if there were any new words in the article that they'd like to check the meaning of, but don't answer any questions at this stage. Instead, sts make a note of which words they want to find out about. Put sts into pairs to share their words and find out if their partner knows the meanings. After this, put sts into small groups to share and ask again. Ask each group to choose two words they would like to ask you about. Explain the meanings and check understanding.

D **Make it personal** Have sts discuss the questions in pairs.

Class feedback. Further the discussion by asking: *Do you think this level of customer service is normal or was it an exceptional case? What impression does Barbara now have of the company Delta? What value would you place on customer service from the company's point of view?*

» Song lyric: See Teacher's Book p.350 for notes about the song and an accompanying activity to do with the class.

6 Vocabulary: Expressions of help

A Read **Describing helpful behavior** with the class. Drill pronunciation of the bold expressions, and check the meanings. Ask: *Which of the expressions did you already know? Are there similar expressions in your language?*

Tell them to cover the chart, and write full sentences about Karim's story using the cues in 1–6. Sts re-tell the story in pairs.

Stronger classes: In pairs, sts roleplay telling Karim's story in the following roles: 1) Barbara to a friend and 2) Karim to his wife. Sts change roles and re-tell the story with a new partner.

> **Suggested answers**
> 1 When Karim learned about the problem, he took it upon himself to …make sure Barbara got her passport / calm her down / call U.S. Homeland Security Customs and Border Control.
> 2 He then went the extra mile, left the counter, and escorted her to the Delta check-in counter.
> 3 He moved mountains to make sure the authorities allowed her through and let her board the plane.
> 4 On Monday, he took it from there and saw to it that Barbara's passport was retrieved from the mailbox and returned to her in New York.
> 5 He went out of his way and even taped a note on the mailbox for a postal worker.
> 6 He then went to great lengths to keep Barbara updated and posted her passport by Fed-Ex to arrive the next day.

B **Make it personal**

1 Focus on the pictures. Ask: *What do you think happened?* Have sts guess in pairs.

> **Suggested answers**
> 1 The little boy got lost, and the police officer helped him find his parents.
> 2 The boy was having difficulty putting on his backpack because of his crutches. The girl helped him.
> 3 The girl was late for the bus, and was running to try and get it. The bus driver waited for her.

2 Put sts in groups. Have them share their stories about helping strangers or strangers helping them. Class feedback. Ask: *Which is the most remarkable story you have heard?* Ask some sts to share their stories with the class.

Ask: *What do you think of the idea of karma?* Board the following quotes, and discuss them together: *What goes around comes around. As you shall sow, so shall you reap.*

For homework, you could ask sts to look up *Acts of Kindness* on the Internet, and read about people who carry out random acts of kindness. Ask them to report back to the class any they are particularly impressed by.

Optional activity

After sts have discussed the situations in 1, they choose one and describe what happened to the class, without saying which photo it is. Sts listen and guess the situation.

» Workbook p.40.

♪ *You've got a friend in me. When the road looks rough ahead, And you're miles and miles, From your nice warm bed*

C ▶ 8.9 Listen to and re-read the article. T (true) or F (false)? Correct the false statements.
1. Barbara accidentally dropped her passport in a mailbox when she was mailing letters.
2. Airport employees in Paris are allowed to open mailboxes if they have the keys.
3. Karim Sayoud first tried to reassure Barbara and then had a security and border-control representative interview her.
4. Whether Barbara was allowed to fly was ultimately up to U.S. Homeland Security.
5. Karim Sayoud took multiple steps to make sure Barbara got her passport back.

D Make it personal In pairs, how unusual do you think Barbara's story is? If you'd had the same experience at an airport, train, or bus station, would you have gotten the same level of help? Why (not)?

> If this had happened to me, it wouldn't have occurred to me to ask Delta for help.

6 Vocabulary: Expressions of help

A Read *Describing helpful behaviour*. Then cover the chart and use the cues 1–6 to retell Karim's story.

Describing helpful behaviour

Common expressions of help, like the one underlined in the text, often have similar meanings.

Karim Sayoud	took it upon himself went to great lengths went out of his way went the extra mile moved mountains	to make	sure Barbara got her passport.
	took it from there	and made	
	saw to it that	she was fully satisfied.	

1. When Karim learned about the problem, he [take / upon / himself] to …
2. He then [go / extra / mile], left the counter, and …
3. He [move / mountains] to make sure the authorities …
4. On Monday, he [take / from / there] and saw to it that Barbara's passport …
5. He [go / out / way] and even … for a postal worker.
6. He then [go / great / lengths] to keep Barbara updated and …

B Make it personal Share stories about Good Samaritans.

1. The unlucky people in the pictures were all helped by thoughtful people. In pairs, share what you think happened, using expressions from A.

2. Has a stranger ever gone out of his / her way for you? Or vice versa? In groups, share your stories. Whose is the most remarkable?

> A guy I'd never met before really went to great lengths for me once and …

» 8.4 Have you ever borrowed money?

7 Language in use

A ▶ 8.10 Listen to two friends, Alba and Paul, discussing bureaucracy. In pairs, answer 1–2.

1 What was the problem?
2 Guess what Alba decided to do.

B ▶ 8.11 Listen to the complete conversation. Match the comments with the topics (a–f). There's one extra.

1 As much as you might try to plan your life, there are always unpleasant surprises.
2 However generous he may have been, for us it was a nightmare.
3 Whatever compromises you feel are reasonable, none will be convincing.
4 For all the good arguments you come up with, they just won't budge.
5 As exciting as it sounds, some things just aren't worth it.

a ☐ paying taxes
b ☐ getting an inheritance
c ☐ having a lot of money
d ☐ Spanish bureaucracy
e ☐ government bureaucrats
f ☐ Alba's uncle's restaurant

8 Vocabulary: Words for discussing money

A Read *Money terms*. Then complete 1–6 below with a form of the words in the box.

> **Money terms**
>
> Terms involving money can vary quite a bit across languages. For example, the Spanish verb *cobrar* can mean "to charge (an amount)," "to get paid (a salary)," "to cash (a check)," or "to collect (a debt)." In English, these are all separate verbs. Always learn money terms in context. A noun and a verb may be identical or have different forms.
>
> "I'm afraid they're going to *tax* (v.) me a lot this year." "The *tax* (n.) is very high, too."
> Tom might *inherit* (v.) a lot of money. He's going to have a big *inheritance* (n.)

| borrow   charge (n. / v.)   inherit   loan (n. / v.)   profit (n. / v.)   tax (n. / v.) |

1 *Stand by Us* Electronics has terrible customer service, but they sure make a nice _____ .
2 If I _____ a lot of money, I'd quit my job the next day.
3 Never go to that store on Fourth Street. They _____ me double for a purchase last week. I think they did it on purpose.
4 Ever since the recession, it's really hard to get a _____ . I don't think I'll be able to buy a house — there's so much red tape!
5 I never let people _____ my computer, even if they beg me to!
6 A great state to shop in is Delaware. There's no state _____ .

B Make it personal In groups, discuss 1–2. Any memorable stories?

1 Have you ever had a very (un)pleasant experience with red tape or bureaucracy? What was the situation?
2 Do you know of anyone whose life changed after inheriting money? Any interesting stories?

> Yes, I had an uncle who became a well-known painter. When he no longer had to work, he started to spend his whole day taking art courses.

> I sure wish I could do that!

88

Have you ever borrowed money? 8.4

Lesson Aims: Sts learn vocabulary to talk about money and listen to someone talking about her experience of inheriting a restaurant.

Skills	Language	Vocabulary	Grammar
Listening to a friend discussing the problem she had with a restaurant she inherited Discussing customer service in your city	Talking about frustrating situations, e.g. *As much as you try to please customers, you're not succeeding. For all the help you give me, I won't shop here again.*	Money vocabulary: *borrow, charge, inherit / inheritance, loan, profit, tax, generous, bureaucracy, red tape, recession*	Adverb clauses to emphasize conditions or contrasts, e.g. *However reasonable the price may seem, the watch still doesn't work.*

Warm-up

Ask sts the lesson title question: *Have you ever borrowed money? Do you have a mortgage? Did you borrow money from a friend or a bank? If you borrowed from a bank, was it difficult? Was there a lot of paperwork involved? Have you ever lent anyone any money? Did you get it back? Have you ever inherited any money?* Classcheck anything interesting sts learned about their partner.

7 Language in use

A ▶ 8.10 Put sts in pairs to say all they can about the photo, and guess how it might somehow be linked to borrowing money. Monitor and re-elicit their funniest ideas.

Ask sts to define *bureaucracy* (overly complicated and rigid administrative procedures which make it difficult to get things done). Ask: *Do you think there is too much bureaucracy in your country?*

Tell sts the people from the photo, Alba and Paul, are talking about a problem she had related to bureaucracy. They have to listen and find out what it was. Check answers.

Ask: *What do you think Alba decided to do?*

Optional activity

Before sts listen, board the following: *buying a house, getting married, having a child, buying a car, paying taxes*. Put sts in groups and ask them to rank them according to how much bureaucracy each one involves. When they have finished, nominate one st from each group to share their ideas with the class.

Answer

Alba and her sister inherited a restaurant from her uncle but then had to pay inheritance tax on the property before they could even accept it.

>> See Teacher's Book p.328 for Audio script 8.10.

B ▶ 8.11 Have sts listen to the rest of Alba and Paul's conversation and find out if their guesses were correct (she decided not to accept the restaurant). Have sts listen again and match the comments with the topics.

Weaker classes: Pause the audio after the relevant bits so sts can note down the answers as they go along.

Answers

1 d 2 f 3 a 4 e 5 b

>> See Teacher's Book p.329 for Audio script 8.11.

8 Vocabulary: Words for discussing money

A Books closed. Brainstorm vocabulary related to money with the class, e.g. *pay, spend, price, cost, charge, cash, check, payment, borrow, loan*.

Books open. Read through **Money terms** with the class. Ask: *Which of these expressions are you familiar with?*

Drill pronunciation of the words in the box, then ask sts to complete the sentences.

Tip

To make this more communicative, do it as a dictogloss. Have sts cover the text. Dictate the first five sentences, then have sts write down all they can remember and compare in pairs. Repeat this procedure twice more. Then uncover the text for them to check, correct their versions, and read the two examples.

Peercheck. Classcheck. Check meaning of *recession* (period of significant economic decline which has an impact on wages and employment). Elicit the opposite *inflation*.

Answers

1 profit 2 inherited 3 charged 4 loan 5 borrow
6 tax

B Make it personal Elicit the meaning of *red tape* (an idiom for excessive bureaucracy or adherence to official rules and formalities, which comes from the traditional practice of binding legal documents in red tape). Brainstorm situations which involve a lot of red tape, e.g. opening a bank account, buying a house, applying for a visa or passport.

Put sts into small groups to discuss questions 1 and 2. Set this up with a personal anecdote if you have one.

Class feedback. Ask: *What interesting stories did you hear?* Have a few sts report back to the class anything surprising they learned from their classmates.

>> Song lyric: See Teacher's Book p.350 for notes about the song and an accompanying activity to do with the class.

8.4

9 Grammar: Adverb clauses to emphasize conditions or contrasts

Tip
Cover the grammar box and begin with the **Common mistake**. If possible, add in any others you've heard sts make recently, or invent any that you know they would make as a result of direct mother tongue translation. Get sts to explain why they are wrong and elicit the correct forms.

A Go through the examples in the grammar box with the class. Check they understand them. Elicit the meaning of *discount* (reduction in price).

Sts complete the rules. Peercheck, then classcheck. Focus on the **Common mistake**. *Which rule is that breaking?*

Elicit another example of each structure to ensure they have the patterns clear, e.g. *However generous the offer may seem, it is still too expensive. Whatever advice you might give me, I will do what I think best.*

For further practice, in pairs, sts can cover different columns from the box and try to remember the rest of the sentences and test each other.

> **Answers**
> a may or might b present c nouns, adjectives

» Refer sts to the Grammar expansion on p.152.

B Tell sts that *No matter …* is an alternative way of expressing the adverb clauses in A. Like the adverb clauses in A, it suggests that the action it refers to will not make any difference. We use *No matter what* with nouns and *no matter how* with adjectives or adverbs.

Have sts write 1–5 next to the sentences in 7B, and then, after going through the example with them, ask sts to rephrase the sentences using *No matter what* or *No matter how …* Peercheck. Classcheck.

> **Answers**
> 4 No matter how much you might try to plan your life, there are always unpleasant surprises.
> 1 No matter how generous he may have been, for us it was a nightmare.
> 2 No matter what compromises you feel are reasonable, none will be convincing.
> 5 No matter what good arguments you come up with, they just won't budge.
> 3 No matter how exciting it sounds, some things just aren't worth it.

Stronger classes: Ask them to write their own sentences using the expressions in bold, in order to give advice on dealing with difficult customers. Monitor and help where necessary. When they have finished, put sts in groups to share their ideas.

C Ask sts: *What countries have you visited? Was customer service better or worse than in your country? What would you guess customer service is like in Japan?* Ask sts to read the text quickly and find out if they were right. Have sts re-read the text and choose the correct options. Classcheck.

> **Answers**
> 1 As important as 2 However 3 Whatever
> 4 As much as 5 Whatever

Optional activity
Ask sts to write a similar paragraph about customer service in their own country/ies, using the phrases from A. This could either be done here or after the discussion in D.

D Make it personal Focus on the survey. Go through the businesses in the left hand column. Ask: *What experience have you had of dealing with these businesses recently? What did you buy? What was the customer-service like?* Ask them to check one of the columns (poor, average, good, excellent) for each business depending on their experience.

Ask sts to discuss their answers in groups. Refer them to the models in the speech bubbles, as an example. Encourage them to say why they have scored the businesses high or low, and tell their classmates about any customer-service experiences they have had, e.g. *I bought a skirt from a clothing store recently, and the zip was broken. I took it back to the store, and they gave me a refund immediately. The assistant was very sympathetic and helped me choose another skirt.*

In their groups, have sts collate their survey answers and rank the businesses in order (1 = best customer service; 5 = worst customer service). Class feedback. Ask one member of the group to report back their groups' results to the rest of the group. Ask: *What conclusions can you draw from the class' results? Is customer service generally good or bad in your city?*

» Workbook p.41.

It's a bittersweet symphony, this life. Try to make ends meet. You're a slave to the money, then you die

9 Grammar: Adverb clauses to emphasize conditions or contrasts

A Read the grammar box and complete the rules (a–c).

Adverb clauses to emphasize conditions or contrasts		
1 **However** reasonable the price	**may** seem,	the watch still doesn't work.
2 **Whatever** discount you	**might** give me,	it won't be sufficient.
3 **As useful as** the manual	**may** be,	it isn't helping.
4 **(As) much as** you	**try** to please customers,	you're not succeeding.
5 **For all the** help you	**give** me,	I won't shop here again.

a Sentences 1–3 use the modal verbs _____ or _____ to express a condition.
b A condition can also be expressed using the _____ tense.
c Conditions or contrasts with *whatever* are followed by _____, whereas ones with *however* are often followed by _____ or adverbs.

» Grammar expansion p.152

B Write the numbers from the grammar box (1–5) next to the sentences in 7B. Then rephrase each one so it begins with *No matter* …

No matter how much you might try to plan your life …

Common mistake

However ~~the price seems low~~ *low the price seems*, it's too high!

C Choose the correct answer (1–5) to emphasize a condition or contrast.

¹[**As important as / as much as**] it may be to be polite to customers, sometimes sales people are downright rude. However, anyone who has ever been to Japan knows that employees there have a few things to teach us. ²[**However / Whatever**] annoyed they may feel privately, you would never know it as the customer. ³[**Whatever / For all the**] questions you may have, they will always be answered with a smile. The reason is simple. ⁴[**For all the / As much as**] you may think it is unnatural or even super-human to be so polite, it is actually good for business. How do we know this? By asking customers, of course! ⁵[**However / Whatever**] surveys we've done on customer-service quality, Japan always comes out on top!

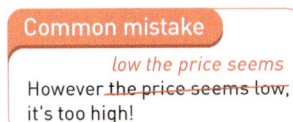

D Make it personal Discuss customer service where you live.

1 Check (✔) the customer-service quality for your city for each kind of business. In groups, defend your choice. Use adverb clauses to emphasize conditions or contrasts, where possible.

Customer-service quality	Poor	Average	Good	Excellent
car dealers				
banks				
cell-phone carriers				
clothing stores				
electric companies				

2 Reach a consensus and share it with the class. How many groups agree?

> Cell-phone carriers are the worst. Whatever problem you might have, they try to convince you it's your own fault.

> Oh, but I've actually had a good experience with [name of company].

8.5 What was the last complaint you made?

10 Listening

A ▶ 8.12 Listen to the start of Amber's call to a phone company. What's the problem? Guess what she says next.

B ▶ 8.13 Listen to part two. When you hear "beep," choose Amber's response and write the number. Continue listening to check. There's one extra choice.

a ☐ You mean you save these conversations? I must have made a mistake. But could you please try to accommodate me?
b ☐ Could you please check if there's an earlier opening? It's essential that it be taken care of today.
c ☐ I have an important deadline. I'm not going to be home on May 12.
d ☐ I'd like to wait if at all possible. I'm really quite worried about this.
e ☐ However limited the number may be, it's really important that you find a solution.

C ▶ 8.14 Guess the polite responses 1–5. Then listen to part three and circle the ones you actually hear. Which words make them rude in this context? Why did the speakers use this tone?

1 Mr. Bell [**says** / **claims**] you recorded me.
2 I need my phone connected [**immediately** / **as soon as possible**].
3 [**I've already provided** / **I believe you have**] this information.
4 [**I'd really appreciate your accommodating** / **I insist that you accommodate**] me.
5 [**Could you possibly speak more softly?** / **I suggest you lower your voice**].

> In the first one, Amber had made a mistake with the date, but she doesn't really believe it. So the word ...

D **Make it personal** In pairs, discuss 1–2.

1 Who do you sympathize with more, Amber or Ms. McGuire?
2 Were you surprised by the outcome? Why (not)? Would it be different where you live?

> I sympathize with Amber. It's natural to be upset after so many calls!

11 Keep talking

A Choose a type of business where you would like to have a real problem resolved. Note down the details. Be sure to include ...

1 the problem.
2 the steps you've already taken.
3 what exactly you'd like the company to do.
4 what action you'll take if they don't.

store   bank   company   car dealer

B Plan your phone call. Individually, review expressions from 10B and C, and try to imagine the conversation.

C In groups of three, role-play the conversation. Which of you should work for a phone company?

1 **A:** Place the call.
   B: Respond as an employee.
   C: Evaluate whether **A** and **B** are convincing and give suggestions for improvement.
2 Change roles until all the phone calls have been made. Choose one to share with the class.

> [name of business] May I help you?

> Yes, I'm calling concerning a problem I've had with (a purchase) ...

What was the last complaint you made? 8.5

Lesson Aims: Sts learn formal language to make complaints by telephone and by letter.

Skills	Language	Vocabulary
Listening to a conversation between a phone company and a customer Writing a complaint letter	Making formal complaints: *I believe you have this information. I insist that you accommodate me. I need my phone connected immediately.* Talking on the telephone: *I'll put you through …, Please don't hang up …, Please hold the line …, I'll put you on hold*	Formal expressions: *be convinced that, be given to understand, be led to believe*

>> Song lyric: See Teacher's Book p.350 for notes about the song and an accompanying activity to do with the class.

Warm-up

Ask sts the lesson title question: *What was the last complaint you made? Was it by phone, in writing or in person?* Ask: *When did you last call a company to complain about something? How long did it take you to get through to someone? Was the person who answered the phone polite? Did they figure out the problem? Were you satisfied with their response?*

10 Listening

A ▶ 8.12 Focus on the photo. Ask: *How do you think Amber is feeling?* (annoyed) *What type of conversation is she having?* (frustrating) Pre-teach *landline* (telephone). Play the audio. Ask sts to listen and find out what the problem is. Ask: *Do you have a landline telephone?* Have sts guess what she says next.

Answer

She expected her phone number to be transferred to her new address the day before but in fact it's not scheduled to be done for another week.

>> See Teacher's Book p.329 for Audio script 8.12.

B ▶ 8.13 Tell sts Amber's conversation continues but they will hear it with blanks indicated by a beep.

Pre-teach: *put (you) on hold, hang up* and *put (you) through*. Have sts listen and choose the correct responses from a–e when they hear the beeps. Peercheck. Classcheck by re-playing the audio.

Answers

1 b   2 e   3 a   4 d

>> See Teacher's Book p.329 for Audio script 8.13.

C ▶ 8.14 Focus on the responses 1–5. Ask sts to consider the options in parentheses and guess the one they think is the most polite. Play the audio for sts to circle the one they hear. Ask: *Did the speakers use the polite responses?* (No)

Ask sts which words in particular make the responses sound rude. Have them make a note of them. Check answers. Ask: *Why did the speakers use this tone?* (because they were annoyed)

Class feedback. Ask: *Have you had similar conversations? Do you find it difficult to be polite when you are annoyed?*

Answers

1 claims   2 immediately   3 I've already provided
4 I insist that you accommodate
5 I suggest you lower your voice

1 claims make it sound as if she thinks he was lying
2 immediately is too strong
3 already sounds accusatory
4 insist is peremptory and sounds like an order
5 suggest sounds sarcastic and like an order

>> See Teacher's Book p.329 for Audio script 8.14.

D **Make it personal** Put sts in pairs to discuss questions 1 and 2. Class feedback.

Stronger classes: Have sts rewrite the dialog so that there is a satisfactory outcome, i.e. the company resolves Amber's problem.

11 Keep talking

A Ask sts: *Have you had a similar problem to Amber? How was it resolved?* Ask sts to think of other situations they have been in, where they have needed to complain to a company. Ask: *Do you have a real problem right now that needs resolving with a company?* If so, sts can use this to base the activity on. If not, ask them to choose a problem they have had in the past or invent one.

Ask sts to make notes about the problem using the prompts in the Student's Book.

B Tell sts to imagine they are going to call the company and try to resolve the problem. Have them plan their phone call, and note down language they can use from 10B and 10C. Encourage them to use polite expressions.

C 1 Put sts in groups of three. One person is the caller, one person represents the company, and one person listens to the call for training purposes. Review some of the phone language the employee in 10B and 10C used and board it, e.g. *Who am I speaking to? How may I help you today? I'm sorry to hear that, Please hold while I put you through, Don't hang up, I'm going to put you on hold, Sorry to keep you waiting.*

2 Have sts change roles and roleplay their own conversations.

Class feedback. Ask: *Who was the most successful at getting the company to help them?*

8.5

12 Writing: A complaint letter

A Ask the class: *How many times have you studied "letters or emails of complaint" in English?* (it's common to the point of being an ELT cliché, but important for exams, and is a rich way to practice very useful functional language) *What did you learn?* (to see how much they can remember and how much of the lesson they think they already know). Then tell them: *Well this one is special and particularly useful, as it involves saving you money!* to motivate them to want to read on!

Have sts read the letter quickly to find out what Jacob Banks is complaining about. Ask: *Have you had problems with a credit card in the past? Have you ever had to complain to the company? What happened?*

Read the list of topics with the class. Ask sts: *Which order would you put them in if you were writing a letter of complaint?* Have them read the letter and match paragraphs 1–5 with the functions. Classcheck. Ask: *When did you last write a letter of complaint in your language? Would you normally send it by post or by email?*

> **Answers**
> 1 introduce the topic and create sympathy
> 2 fully describe a problem
> 3 document evidence of previous steps
> 4 give an opinion on the company's practices
> 5 make a strong request

Optional activity

If you've recently written a letter of complaint and are happy to share it, show it to the class before looking at the example in **A** and ask sts if they think it's effective. Tell them what action resulted from it.

B Ask sts to find the underlined expressions in the letter (numbered 1–10). Ask them which they are familiar with. Sts match them with the informal expressions listed. Peercheck. Classcheck.

Highlight the use of the present perfect in the letter *I have tried repeatedly...*, *Your company has refused to reinstate my card*. Remind sts that we use the present perfect when we are talking about an action that we carried out in the past at a non-specific time.

> **Answers**
> 1 without success   2 fix things   3 you can help me
> 4 fixed things   5 even though   6 I could easily have given   7 If I'm not happy   8 take you to court   9 I don't have to do that   10 please write back

C Read **Write it right!** with the class. Sts find two more passive expressions in paragraph 3 with a similar meaning to *I was told …* Peercheck. Classcheck.

Elicit other ways to say this, e.g. *I was informed that …*, *I was advised that …*

> **Answers**
> I was led to believe that …
> I was given to understand that …

D Sts find examples of 1 and 2. Check answers. Ask them to also find an example of an adverb clause (refer them to the grammar box on page 89), e.g. *however reasonable your policies may seem, I believe that good customer service takes into account the specific situation …*

> **Answers**
> 1 In the event that I do not receive satisfaction, I will have no choice but to …
> 2 I insist that my account be reactivated immediately
>   In fact, it is imperative that this issue be resolved …

Tip

If time, as with any functional exchange like this, there is potential for roleplay here. Sts could act out the exchange between them for fun, obviously making it much less formal. You could tell them the situation and do this before reading the letter, or do it after they have read it, as a lively finish to the lesson.

E Your turn! Read through the instructions with the class, and check sts know what to do. Point out that in his letter, Jacob Banks is very specific about what happened and when, and he also quotes the names of the people he spoke to. Encourage sts to do this in their letters. Also remind them to use the correct salutation, and to sign off with *Sincerely, …*

When sts have written their letters, have them swap them with a classmate, and check each other's work, before they post them online.

Tip

To correct this quickly and in an original way, using a fluorescent highlighter, color all the phrases which are correct and give it back to sts to try to improve it. Focusing on the positive like this can be motivating, and trying to get more of it "in color," i.e. correct, can get some sts more into the idea of process writing.

» Workbook p.42.

♪ I'm in the phone booth, it's the one across the hall. If you don't answer, I'll just ring it off the wall

8.5

12 Writing: A complaint letter

A Read Jacob Banks's complaint letter and match paragraphs 1–5 to their main function.

- [ ] give an opinion on the company's practices
- [ ] introduce the topic and create sympathy
- [ ] document evidence of previous steps
- [ ] make a strong request
- [ ] fully describe a problem

B Match the formal expressions 1–10 in the letter with these more informal ones with a similar meaning.

- [ ] you can help me
- [ ] even though
- [ ] I could easily have given
- [ ] I don't have to do that
- [ ] fix(ed) things (two expressions)
- [ ] If I'm not happy
- [ ] please write back
- [ ] take you to court
- [ ] without success

C Read *Write it right!* Then find two more passive expressions in paragraph 3 that both have the same meaning.

> **Write it right!**
>
> Complaint letters use formal expressions in the passive that mean "I was told," but which avoid mentioning the person who gave the information:
>
> I **was convinced (that)** the problem would be resolved promptly.

D In paragraphs 4 and 5, find …
1. an example of a formal way to express a condition.
2. two examples of the subjunctive.

E Your turn! Choose a consumer problem you brainstormed in 11A and write a formal complaint in about 280 words.

Before
Plan the main function of each paragraph. Note down very specific details on the problem and what steps you've already taken.

While
Write five to six paragraphs to support your complaint, following the model in **A**. Use passive expressions from *Write it right!*, some formal expressions from **B**, and formal structures from **D**.

After
Post your complaint online and read your classmates' work. Whose letter got the most sympathy?

Ms. Eleanor Fernández
Director of Customer Service

Dear Ms. Fernández:

1. I am writing concerning the cancellation of my credit card on September 5, 2016. I have tried repeatedly, but ¹to no avail, to ²resolve the matter with your staff. I am a college student, and as this is my first and only credit card, I am hopeful ³you will be able to assist me.

2. On September 1, I attempted to pay my monthly bill of $355.66, but mistakenly authorized a payment of $3355.66. Within a day, my checking account was frozen because of an overdraft, and my credit card was suspended. While my bank immediately ⁴rectified the problem, canceling payment and authorizing a new payment in the correct amount, your company has refused to reinstate my card. In fact, the suspended card has now been canceled because of "possible fraudulent activity."

3. On September 2, I spoke to Mr. Ethan Adams, and I was led to believe that the problem would be resolved promptly. On September 4, when I still could not use the card, I spoke to Ms. Kira Russo. I was given to understand that I would have access to the card that very evening. However, when the card was not active on September 5, I called a third time and spoke to Mr. Sean McGee. ⁵Notwithstanding the fact that I had been offered previous reassurances on two occasions, Mr. McGee informed me that the card had been canceled. When I asked to speak to a manager, I was connected to Ms. Hannah Cook, who insisted that company policy had been followed, and I would need to apply for a new card.

4. I understand that fraud is a legitimate concern, and I appreciate the need for online security. Nevertheless, however reasonable your policies may seem, I believe that good customer service takes into account the specific situation, in my case a simple human error. ⁶I would have been happy to provide whatever form of identification was required.

5. I insist that my account be reactivated immediately. In fact, it is imperative that this issue be resolved by September 15 so that I can pay my college tuition. ⁷In the event that I do not receive satisfaction, I will have no choice but to post the incident on Twitter and YouTube, as well as ⁸consider legal action. I sincerely hope ⁹these steps will not be necessary.

Thank you very much in advance for your assistance, and ¹⁰I look forward to a response.

Sincerely yours,
Jacob Banks

Review 4
Units 7–8

1 Speaking

A Look at the photos on p.72.

1 Note down milestones for each phase of life using some of these expressions.

> act your age   come of age   come to terms with   conform to expectations   first-hand experience
> get off track   make it through   the stakes are higher   take charge   young at heart   wise beyond your years

2 In groups, share insights about what (you think) it's like to be each of the ages in the photos.

> By the time you're in your 30s, the stakes are a lot higher if you feel you've chosen the wrong profession. I've decided to find a new job."

> I'm not sure I agree. Even if you get off track, you're still young and can start over.

B Make it personal Do you believe in nature or nurture? Give examples of people you know about.

> I believe in nature. Haven't you read those studies of identical twins separated at birth who turn out to be exactly alike?

2 Grammar

A Rewrite the opinions (1–6) using cleft sentences.

1 Your age doesn't determine how creative you are. *It's not your age that determines how creative you are.*
2 The recession prevents many young people from getting jobs even if they've tried many times.
3 Having friends makes a difference when life gets tough even if your family is supportive.
4 Your parents made you the person you are now even if school is an influence.
5 Getting old doesn't cause depression; you can enjoy life at any age.
6 We have to face the challenge, though, even if we don't want to.

B Make it personal In pairs, share two true opinions from A.

> Given   In view of   So as to   With a view to   In an effort to   Thanks to   With the aim of

> It's your age that determines how creative you are. Young people have more ideas.

> I don't agree at all. My grandmother writes beautiful poetry.

C Complete the conversation with the verbs in parentheses in the future perfect (simple or continuous) form, or the subjunctive. (Some have more than one answer.)

Teacher: I suggest your son ¹_____ (try) to study harder before exams.
Parent: Yes, I wish he ²_____ (be) a better student. The problem is, he's on the soccer team and by the end of the year, he ³_____ (play) 50 games. He's never home.
Teacher: It's essential that he ⁴_____ (improve) his grades. If not, he won't get into college. He's already failed math twice.
Parent: I know. I'm really quite worried. Next year, he ⁵_____ (take) the same course for three years in a row.
Teacher: It was important that he ⁶_____ (study) for the exam last week, but I don't think he did.
Parent: I promise I'll talk to him when I get home.

Review 4 (Units 7–8) R4

Warm-up
See p.61, 105, and 149 of the Teacher's Book for warm-up ideas.

Board the following questions to feed into their discussion: *Do you know any identical twins? Are they similar in personality? What do you think the challenges of being an identical twin are? Do you think it's possible to change your personality?*

1 Speaking

A 1 Review the expressions in the box. Refer sts to 2A on p.73 and 8B on p.78, if they need reminding. Highlight and drill the stressed words within the phrases with reduction of *your, of, to, are, at*. Focus on the photos on p.72 and ask sts to note down the four different life phases they represent: childhood, adolescence, your 20s, your 30s, and beyond. Ask: *What age would you say adolescence covers?* Elicit between 13 and 19; it describes the transition between childhood and adulthood.

Give sts a few minutes to note down milestones for each of the ages using the expressions in the box. Peercheck. Classcheck.

Possible answers
Childhood: starting school, learning a second language
Adolescence: going to college, learning to drive
Your 20s: getting married, getting your first job
Your 30s and beyond: starting your own business, retiring

Optional activity
To review the expressions, ask sts to choose two of them and write a definition for each. Monitor and help where necessary. When they have finished, put sts into small groups. Sts read out their definitions for other sts to guess the expressions.

2 Give sts a few minutes to think about what they think it is like to be each of the ages in the photos; the advantages and disadvantages. Put them in groups to share their ideas. Focus on the speech bubbles as an example. Encourage them to use the expressions in the box in 1 if appropriate.

Class feedback. Ask: *What do you wish you'd known 10 or 20 years ago?* As follow-up, ask sts to think of advice you would give to people at different ages, using the expressions in the box, e.g. *When you get to your 30s and beyond, it's important to stay young at heart. Do what you feel like, and don't conform to expectations. / In your twenties, be careful to stay on track, and focus on your career while you don't have any responsibilities.*

B Make it personal Brainstorm what sts learned about nature vs. nurture from 8A–D on p.78. Focus on the speech bubble. Ask sts to move and work with sts who they haven't talked to recently, in order to freshen the topic up and avoid repetition. In new groups, ask sts to discuss the question: *Do you believe in nature or nurture?* Encourage them to give reasons for their views, and give examples where they can of people they know.

2 Grammar

A Focus on the example and explain what sts have to do. Review what sts remember about the word *cleft* and cleft sentences. Refer them to the grammar section on p.79 if necessary. Sts individually work through 2–6, rewriting them to include cleft sentences. Peercheck. Classcheck. Fast finishers can produce a locally relevant example for others to rewrite.

Answers
1 It's not your age that determines how creative you are.
2 It's the recession that prevents many young people from getting jobs, even if they've tried many times.
3 It's having friends that makes a difference when life gets tough even if your family is supportive.
4 It's your parents who made you the person you are now even if school is an influence.
5 It's not getting old that causes depression; you can enjoy life at any age.
6 It's a challenge we have to face, though, even if we don't want to.

B Make it personal Ask sts to choose two statements they agree with from A. Include any that fast finishers may have produced. Put them in pairs to share their opinions. Encourage them to agree / disagree, and to give their reasons.

Classcheck by asking a few sts to share their ideas with the class. Ask: *Which of the statements do you and your partner agree on?*

C Ask sts to quickly read through the conversation and, in pairs, summarize what it's about. Sts complete the conversation as instructed.

Weaker classes: Have sts quickly review the rules for the subjunctive in the grammar section on p.85 first.

Peercheck. Classcheck by asking a pair of sts to read out the conversation for the rest of the class. Ask other sts to correct any mistakes they hear.

Answers
1 try
2 were
3 will have played
4 improve
5 will have taken / will have been taking
6 study

R4

D Refer sts back to the grammar section on p.89 before they do this activity.

Go through the example then ask sts to rephrase 2–6. Peercheck. Classcheck.

For more practice, ask sts to write their own true sentences using each of the adverb clauses of condition, e.g. *However hard I try, I can't get the hang of whistling.*

Answers

1 However old you may be, it's not your age that determines how creative you are.
2 For all the times they've tried, it's the recession that prevents many young people from getting jobs.
3 As much as your family may be supportive, it's having friends that makes a difference when life gets tough.
4 As useful as school is, it's your parents who made you the person you are now.
5 Whatever age you may be, you can enjoy life. It's not getting old that causes depression.
6 It's a challenge we have to face though, as much as we don't want to.

Optional activity

When sts have written their sentences in D, nominate sts to pick a sentence at random and read it out to the class, omitting the adverb clause of condition. Other sts listen and guess which adverb clause of condition is missing.

3 Reading

A Books closed. Ask: *Do you shop online? What problems have you had?* Invite sts to share their ideas with the class. Ask sts to turn to p.93. Tell them to read the text and check whether any of the problems were mentioned.

Ask them to re-read it and note down five consumer problems and three actions you can take.

Classcheck, and ask: *Have you ever taken any of the actions suggested in the text?* Allow them to look up a maximum of three words in a dictionary, the rest they can check at home.

Answers

Consumer problems: unexpected fees (e.g. having to pay shipping charges to return a purchase); damaged merchandise; deliveries arriving late / not at all; deliveries being left outside their homes without permission; poor quality; being the victim of fraud

Actions you can take:

Contact the Consumer Protection Office to mediate complaints and conduct investigations

Contact the Federal Trade Commission to investigate fraud and get useful tips for getting your money back – and use the e-consumer government website to help you file complaints against international businesses

Contact the Better Business Bureau to help you locate reputable businesses (then you won't need the other services).

B Make it personal Read the directions to the class. With a show of hands see how many have an e-purchase story to share (of their own or somebody else's). For those that don't, have them sit together and make one up, or just act as group secretary and note down problems, etc. during the speaking phase.

In groups, sts share their stories, asking questions and helping each other to tell their story as well and in as much detail as they can. Monitor and gather the most useful feedback you can give them.

Optional activity

After they have shared their stories in pairs, ask sts to choose one and roleplay a conversation about what happened.

4 Self-test

Sts do the test individually, then paircheck. Use the procedure on Teacher's Book p.62.

Answers

1 When I had children my career **went** off track, something that was very hard to come to terms **with**.
2 They say couples who **are** the same age get along best, but it's hard to meet people **(who are)** my age.
3 When I'm old, I won't **have saved** enough for retirement, but I will **have been** working since my 20s.
4 My sister isn't the one who **has / will** have problems because she's not the one who will **have been taking** care of our parents.
5 Would it be OK if I **apply** for the job? I'm sure it will **be fascinating** work.
6 We need to all take a stand **against** climate change and take legal action **against** companies that don't protect the environment.
7 It was important that you **not be** rude, but, unfortunately, you insisted that our manager not **speak** at all.
8 I'm going to suggest **that she** go out of **her** way for our customers.
9 **Notwithstanding** the fact that I've written to the manager three times, it's been **to** no avail.
10 By the time you open your new store, I will **have been** coming here for 10 years and would really appreciate **whatever** discount you may be able to offer me.

5 Point of view

Go through topics a and b with the class, and brainstorm a few ideas for each one. Follow the procedure on Teacher's Book p.62.

Stronger classes: Hold a class debate on one of the topics. (See teaching procedures on p.106.)

D Rephrase the sentences in A. Use the adverb clauses of condition (1–6) at the beginning or end of the sentence.

1. *However + adjective / adverb ...*
2. *For all the ...*
3. *As much as ...*
4. *As useful as ...*
5. *Whatever + noun ...*
6. *As much as ...*

> However old you may be, it's not your age that determines how creative you are.

3 Reading

A Read the article on e-shopping. Note down five consumer problems and three actions you can take.

> **THE TRUTH ABOUT ONLINE SHOPPING**
>
> Nearly half of all online consumers have problems with online purchases, with issues ranging from unexpected fees to damaged merchandise. While there are more online customers than ever before, most never think about deliveries arriving late, not at all, or being left outside their homes without permission. Quality is hard to judge online, and some items may be better in a real store. Returning a purchase may require that you pay shipping charges. And finally, some consumers are victims of outright fraud. Many of them have no idea of their rights.
>
> In the U.S., you have various options. Your state may have a Consumer Protection Office that can mediate complaints and conduct investigations. The Federal Trade Commission investigates fraud and offers useful tips for getting your money back. There's even an e-consumer government website to help you file complaints against international businesses. But most important, the Better Business Bureau helps you locate reputable businesses so you will not need these other services.

B Make it personal Using your notes in A, share a story about an e-purchase. Include the problem, what you've done until now, and what you plan to do to resolve it.

> For all the promises [name of business] may make, they never tell you about [type of problem]. When I bought ...

4 Self-test

Correct the two mistakes in each sentence. Check your answers in Units 7 and 8. What's your score, 1–20?

1. When I had children, my career came off track, something that was very hard to come to terms.
2. They say couples who have the same age get along best, but it's hard to meet people are my age.
3. When I'm old, I won't have been saving enough for retirement, but I will be working since my 20s.
4. My sister isn't the one who have problems because she's not the one who will have been taken care of our parents.
5. Would it be OK if I will apply for the job? I'm sure it will be a fascinating work.
6. We need to all take a stand about climate change and take legal action over companies that don't protect the environment.
7. It was important that you were not rude, but, unfortunately, you insisted that our manager not spoke at all.
8. I'm going to suggest her to go out of the way for our customers.
9. Notstanding the fact that I've written to the manager three times, it's been no avail.
10. By the time you open your new store, I will be coming here for 10 years and would really appreciate however discount you may be able to offer me.

5 Point of view

Choose a topic. Then support your opinion in 100–150 words, and record your answer. Ask a partner for feedback. How can you be more convincing?

a The 20s are the most important decade. OR
   Childhood is far more critical than your 20s.
b In 50 years, many social changes will have occurred. OR
   Change takes place slowly, and life won't have changed as much as people imagine.

9

Would you like to be a teacher?

1 Listening

A ▶ 9.1 Read the photo caption and guess the answer. Listen to the start of a radio show to check.

> Homeschooling is becoming [**more** / **less**] popular in the United States.

B ▶ 9.2 In groups, complete the chart. Then listen to the second part. How many of your ideas were mentioned?

Homeschooling	
What I (think I) know	What I'd like to know
It's popular in some European countries.	*Do parents prepare all the lessons?*

C ▶ 9.2 Listen again. Check (✔) the advantages mentioned. How many of your questions from B were answered?
Homeschooling ...
1. ☐ enables students to do well academically later in life.
2. ☐ brings families closer together.
3. ☐ enables parents to cater to individual needs.
4. ☐ helps to avoid unnecessary interpersonal conflicts.
5. ☐ gives students more free time to pursue their own interests.

D ▶ 9.3 Listen to the third part. Circle the correct inferences.
Carlos feels that ...
1. parents [**worry** / **don't worry enough**] about protecting their kids from outside influences.
2. [**not all** / **most**] parents have the natural aptitude to be good teachers.
3. both parents [**generally** / **don't always**] agree on whether to homeschool.
4. kids need to interact with [**only a few** / **all kinds of**] people to develop emotional intelligence.
5. homeschooling might make kids [**self-centered** / **lonely**].

E Make it personal Share your thoughts on homeschooling. Any big differences?
1. 🌐 Search on "homeschooling" to answer any remaining questions you have from B.
2. Which of the advantages / disadvantages in C and D are the most important? Can you add others?
3. Would you like to have been homeschooled? Would you ever homeschool your own children? Why (not)?

> On balance, I'm opposed to homeschooling, and it's not an option I'd choose for my kids.

> Really? But how can you be so sure?

Would you like to be a teacher? 9.1

Lesson Aims: Sts listen to interviews with people who have experience of home-schooling and discuss current trends in education.

Skills	Language	Vocabulary
Listening to a radio program about homeschooling Asking and answering questions about education	Making tentative comments, e.g. *It looks as if ..., It would appear that ..., This might have to do with the fact that ..., There might be some truth in that ...*	Verbs beginning with *out*: *outperform, outgrow, outweigh, outlast, outperform, outnumber, outsmart*

Warm-up

Board: *Who's the best / worst teacher you've had? What subject did he / she teach?* for sts to think about and answer in pairs as they come into class. Monitor then, after a few minutes, add: *What makes a good / bad teacher?* After they've answered in pairs, brainstorm positive and negative qualities onto the board in two columns.

Ask the lesson title question. Sts say why (not) and if so, which subject they'd teach. Which subject is most popular?

1 Listening

A ▶ 9.1 Focus on the photo. Ask: *Who do you think the people are? What are they doing? Where? Is it easier to teach one st or a class of sts?*

Focus on the caption and ask sts to guess the answer. Ask: *Do you know anyone who is homeschooled? Did / do you mainly enjoy school? Would you like to be homeschooled? Why / Why not?*

Play the audio and have them check the answer.

Ask: *How many sts were homeschooled in the U.S. in 2016?* (2.3 million)

Answer

more

▶▶ See Teacher's Book p.330 for Audio script 9.1.

B ▶ 9.2 Focus on the chart. Brainstorm a few ideas for each column with the class. Questions for the second column might include: *Do you need any qualifications / experience to teach your own children? Do the parents get any help? Who decides what sts study?* Have sts continue individually, noting down more ideas in each column.

Tell sts they are going to hear an interview with Susan Crane who homeschooled her son. Play the audio for sts to check if their ideas were mentioned. Class feedback. Ask: *Why did she decide to homeschool her son? Was her experience of homeschooling positive or negative?*

Tip

Before class, familiarize yourself with the audio script. When brainstorming ideas for questions for the second column, try to feed in one or two questions which you know will be answered in the recording.

▶▶ See Teacher's Book p.330 for Audio script 9.2.

C ▶ 9.2 Have sts read the list of advantages 1–5. Ask: *Which do you think are true?* Play the audio again and have sts check the advantages Susan mentions.

Classcheck, then ask sts: *Which questions did you write down that were not answered in the audio?* Board these, and discuss them with the class.

Answers

Check: 1, 3, and 4

D ▶ 9.3 Explain that sts are going to hear an interview with a second guest, Carlos Diaz, who was homeschooled himself.

Have them read through 1–5 before they listen. Play the audio. Sts circle the correct options. Classcheck. Ask: *How did Carlos decide to educate his own children?* (in a public school)

Highlight the form of the noun *homeschooling*, (not *homeschool*). Board the common mistake: *I think homeschool is a good idea.* Ask sts to correct it (*I think homeschooling is a good idea.*).

Answers

1 worry 2 not all 3 don't always 4 all kinds of
5 self-centered

▶▶ See Teacher's Book p.330 for Audio script 9.3.

E Make it personal

1 Give sts some time to carry out research on the Internet if they still have questions unanswered from B.

2 Put sts in pairs to discuss the advantages and disadvantages. Have them agree together on which are most / least important, and then add any others they can think of. Class feedback. Ask sts to share their views. Ask: *Do you mostly agree / disagree?*

3 Put sts in groups to discuss whether they would like to have been (or like to be) homeschooled, and whether they would choose to homeschool their own children. Refer sts to the models in the speech bubbles. Elicit other phrases sts could use in their discussions and board them: *On the whole ..., In general ..., I'm in favor of ..., I'm for ..., I'm totally against ..., I (don't) like the idea of ...*

Finish the discussion with a vote on who, in an ideal world where money was not an issue, would / wouldn't prefer homeschooling.

9.1

2 Vocabulary: Verbs beginning with *out*

A ▶ 9.4 Ask: *How many words do you know beginning with out-? Brainstorm ideas. Any verbs?*

Read **Out-verbs** with the class. Go through the examples and check understanding. Ask sts how they would translate these in their language.

Elicit other example sentences with *outsmart*, *outnumber*, and *outsold*, e.g. *Men outnumber women in our class.*

Model pronunciation. Tell sts that out is never stressed in *out*-verbs.

Focus on the mind map and ask sts to guess the meaning of the verbs (*outperform* = perform better than; *outlast* = last longer than; *outgrow* = grow too old / big for; *outweigh* = be more significant than). Have sts practice saying the verbs (outperFORM, outLAST, outGROW, outWEIGH.).

Sts complete sentences 1–4. Remind sts to put the verbs in the correct forms. Peercheck. Classcheck.

Stronger classes: Ask sts to find more verbs with the prefix out, e.g. *outlive, outplay, outdrink* and write definitions for them.

Tip

Nouns beginning with out do stress the first syllable, so OUTput, OUTcome and OUTback.

Answers

1 outlasted   2 outweigh   3 outperform   4 outgrow

Tip

Draw sts' attention to the general meaning of *out* here i.e. "more than."

▶ Song lyric: See Teacher's Book p.351 for notes about the song and an accompanying activity to do with the class.

B Read the questions with the class. Sts rephrase them using *out*-verbs.

Put sts in pairs to ask and answer the questions. Make sure they take turns asking the questions. Elicit an answer to 1 as an example, e.g. *Maybe because women have more patience with children?* Class feedback. Ask: *Did you agree on the answers?*

Answers

1 Why do female teachers outnumber male teachers?
2 Is it a myth or fact that students who read widely tend to outperform those who don't?
3 When it comes to single-sex schools, do the pros outweigh the cons?
4 On college campuses, why do PCs tend to outsell tablets?

Stronger classes: Ask sts to write further questions for the verbs in A and any other verbs they found, on a topic of their choice. Monitor and help where necessary. When they are ready, sts walk around the class and ask their questions to other sts. Even if they only have one question, they can do it as a *Survey the class activity*, asking everybody and then feed back a summary of their answers.

C Make it personal

1 ▶ 9.5 **How to say it** Ask sts to look at the comments in the *What they said* column, and ask if they remember who said them (1 = presenter, 2 = presenter, 3 = Susan, 4 = Susan). Sts complete the chart, then listen to check. Have them practice saying the sentences in pairs, covering one column and remembering the other, testing each other, etc.

Stronger classes: Ask sts to draw their own conclusions about homeschooling using each of the expressions in the box, e.g. *It looks as if homeschooling is becoming very popular.* Say: *Imagine 100 years from now. How might things be similar / different?*

Answers

1 if   2 appear   3 do   4 truth

2 Discuss the meaning of the headlines with the class. Discuss the meaning of the headlines with the class. Focus on the difference between *bull* and *bully*, and elicit the meaning of *ramp up, enhance,* and *packing into classrooms*. Ask: *Are these trends familiar in your country? Are there any other trends becoming popular in your country?* Have sts work individually noting down possible reasons for the trends.

Tip

If sts are tiring of educational trends, ask them to suggest a topic they'd prefer to talk about, e.g. healthcare, transportation, fashion, etc.

3 Have sts discuss their ideas in pairs. Refer them to the examples in the speech bubbles. Encourage them to use the **How to say it** expressions and *out*-verbs where appropriate. Class feedback. Invite some sts to share their ideas with the rest of the class and open up to a class discussion.

▶ Workbook p.43.

♪ I can move to another town, Where nobody'd ask where you are now. LA or Mexico, No matter where I go, I can't outrun you

9.1

2 Vocabulary: Verbs beginning with *out*

A ▶ 9.4 Read *Out-* verbs. Then complete 1–4 with forms of the verbs in the mind map. Listen to check.

> **Out- verbs**
>
> The prefix *out-* in verbs usually means "better," "greater," "further," "longer," etc.
> He's a savvy politician who always manages to **outsmart** his rivals. (= be smarter than)
> In my neighborhood, houses **outnumber** apartments. (= There are more houses.)
> Adele **outsold** every female singer on the planet in the mid 2010s. (= sold more than)

1 Schools have stood the test of time and _____ countless societal changes and paradigm shifts.
2 Do the advantages of homeschooling _____ the potential drawbacks?
3 Apparently, homeschooled kids tend to _____ their public school peers on standardized tests to get into college.
4 We need to expose children to different people and environments to help them _____ their immaturity.

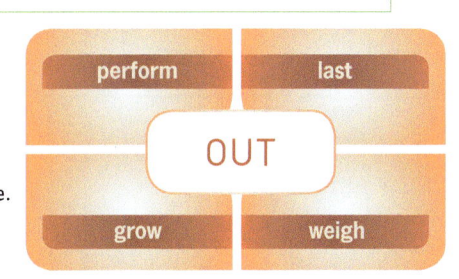

Mind map: perform | last | OUT | grow | weigh

B Rephrase 1–4 using *out-* verbs. There may be more than one possible answer. Then ask and answer in pairs. Any disagreements?

1 Why are there more female than male teachers?
2 Is it a myth or fact that students who read widely tend to do better than those who don't?
3 When it comes to single-sex schools, are the pros greater than the cons?
4 On college campuses, why do PCs tend to sell more than tablets?

C Make it personal "Into" or "out of" the mainstream?

1 ▶ 9.5 **How to say it** Complete the chart. Listen to check.

Drawing tentative conclusions	
What they said	What they meant
1 It looks as _____ (it's crossing over into the mainstream).	It seems that …
2 It would _____ that (the homeschool population is continuing to grow).	It seems that …
3 This might have to _____ with the fact that (homeschooling offers both parents and children a great deal of flexibility).	Maybe this is related to …
4 There might be some _____ to this.	Maybe this is true.

2 Read the headlines showing different educational trends in the United States. Which ones seem to be gaining popularity in your country, too? Note down some possible reasons.

1 Career-focused learning is back: High schools, community colleges, and companies push for a renewed emphasis on technical skills.

2 Not just for fun: Increasing evidence that music classes enhance performance in other subjects.

3 TAKING THE BULL BY THE HORNS: SCHOOLS RAMP UP ANTI-BULLYING EFFORTS

4 Size matters: Schools are packing more and more students into classrooms – and this is not a good

3 In pairs, compare your ideas. Use *out-* verbs and *How to say it* expressions. Similar opinions?

> Career-focused learning might have to do with the fact that these days, everyone needs to be an entrepreneur.

> Yes, new tech start-ups are beginning to outnumber traditional companies!

» 9.2 What is alternative medicine?

3 Language in use

A Read the excerpt from an article on acupuncture and answer 1–2.

1 The writer most likely thinks acupuncture …
☐ definitely works. ☐ might work. ☐ is ineffective.

2 In pairs, looking only at the cartoon …
a summarize what acupuncture is.
b list three conditions it might be used for.

ACUPUNCTURE

Acupuncture, the stimulation of points along the skin using thin needles, is thought to be effective for a variety of medical conditions. But it is really? Patients are reported to have been cured of pain, but some scientists say research is inconclusive, and it's unclear if this is a placebo effect. The technique is believed to relieve neck pain, migraines as well as less severe headaches, and lower back pain, and while many patients are thought to be helped, these scientists say more studies are needed. Of course, this is a Western point of view. In quite a few Asian countries, acupuncture is mainstream medicine, and in Mainland China, Japan, Hong Kong, and Taiwan, nearly everyone will tell you that acupuncture is known to have reduced patient suffering.

B Which view of acupuncture do you agree with? Is acupuncture popular where you live?

> I don't know if acupuncture is effective. I'd like to see more scientific evidence.

4 Pronunciation: Stress on three-word phrasal verbs

A ▶9.6 Complete the text with forms of the verbs in the box. Listen to a conversation between Emma and Luke to check. How many verbs did you know?

| come down with | give up on | go through with | grow out of | watch out for |

When Emma was a senior in high school, she ¹_____ (= began to suffer from) migraines at least once a week. Her mom thought she would ²_____ (= stop having) them, but she often missed school. The doctors couldn't help and Emma almost ³_____ (= stopped hoping for) a cure. Fortunately, though, her mom ⁴_____ (= was looking for) new treatments, and she discovered aromatherapy. Even though it didn't help right away, Emma decided to ⁵_____ the treatment (= finish it to the end).

B ▶9.7 Listen to the verbs in A and check (✔) the correct rule. Then repeat each one.

Three-word phrasal verbs are always stressed on the ☐ first ☐ second ☐ third word.

C Make it personal In pairs, discuss 1–3. Include three-word phrasal verbs, where possible.

1 Have you ever tried acupuncture or aromatherapy? Would you like to?
2 Why might some people be opposed to alternative medicine?
3 Do you know anyone who's had a medical problem that wouldn't go away? Would either treatment have helped?

> My grandmother came down with the flu and developed asthma, but I don't think acupuncture would have helped …

What is alternative medicine? 9.2

Lesson Aims: Sts learn how to form passive expressions with infinitives and talk about health using three-word phrasal verbs.

Skills	Language	Vocabulary	Grammar review
Listening to a conversation between friends about aromatherapy. Reading a blog about alternative medicine	Talking about medical problems, e.g. *My grandmother came down with the flu. I developed asthma when I was young.*	Three-word phrasal verbs: *come down with, give up on, go through with, grow out of, watch out for*	Passive expressions with infinitives, e.g. *Patients are believed to have been cured.*

Warm-up

Ask the lesson title question: *What is alternative medicine?* In pairs or groups ask sts to try and come up with a definition, e.g. *remedies or therapies which are used instead of standard medical treatments.*

Brainstorm what sts know about alternative medicine. Ask: *Have you tried any of them? Which? Was it successful? Do you prefer alternative or traditional medicine?*

3 Language in use

A Focus on the word *Acupuncture*. Model pronunciation /ˈakjʊˌpʌŋktʃer/, with the stress on the first syllable. Ask: *Have you ever had acupuncture? Did it work?*

Focus on the cartoon. Ask: *Do you find it funny? What are synonyms for "odd"?* (strange, weird) *Have you ever had a feeling like this?* Sts read the excerpt and answer questions 1 and 2. Discuss the meaning of *placebo effect.* (The phenomenon where an ineffective or fake treatment actually works simply because the patient believes that it will.)

Check answers to 1 and 2, and ask: *In which countries is acupuncture mainstream medicine? Is it mainstream in your country? Do you think it should be?*

> **Answers**
> 1 might work   2 a) stimulation of points along the skin using thin needles   b) neck pain, migraines, and other headaches, lower-back pain

B Ask: *Which view of acupuncture do you agree with? Do you imagine acupuncture will be mainstream in 100 years? If not, why not?*

Weaker classes: Clarify the views in the article in **A** by asking: *Who has doubts about acupuncture, based on the article in* **A**? (scientists, who say there is not enough scientific evidence). *Who believes it works?* (Many people in Asian countries because they have seen evidence of it reducing pain.)

Discuss how popular acupuncture is where sts live.

>> Song lyric: See Teacher's Book p.351 for notes about the song and an accompanying activity to do with the class.

4 Pronunciation: Stress on three-word phrasal verbs

A ▶ 9.6 Focus on the phrasal verbs in the box. Ask: *Which do you know?* Ask sts to read the text quickly ignoring the blanks. Ask: *What was Susan's problem? What alternative medicine did she try to cure it? Do you think it worked?*

Have sts complete the text with the correct form of the verbs in the box. Then play the audio for them to check.

Stronger classes: In pairs, ask sts to tell their partner about ailments they have had using the phrasal verbs, e.g. *I used to get asthma a lot, but I grew out of it.*

> **Answers**
> 1 came down with   2 grow out of   3 gave up on
> 4 was watching out for   5 go through with

>> See Teacher's Book p.330 for Audio script 9.6.

B ▶ 9.7 Have sts say the phrasal verbs in **A**, and mark the stress. Play the audio for them to check. Then have them listen and repeat.

Elicit other three-word phrasal verbs sts might know, e.g. *look up to (s.o.), get on with (s.o.), get around to (doing sth), miss out on (sth).* Have sts practice saying them with the correct stress.

> **Answers**
> second

C **Make it personal** Go through the three questions with the class.

When sts have discussed the questions in pairs, open up to a class discussion and invite pairs to share anything interesting they learned from their classmates.

Ask: *Which of your classmates is the biggest fan of alternative medicine? Who's the biggest critic?*

Optional activity

Put sts in pairs and give each one an alternative medicine, e.g. *homeopathy, aromatherapy, acupressure, reflexology.* Make sure you don't include any of the therapies mentioned in **5D**. Ask sts to research their therapy online and find out a) what it is and b) any evidence that it works. When they are ready, put sts in groups to share what they found out and discuss whether they think it's useful or not.

9.2

5 Grammar: Passive expressions with infinitives

Tip

A great technique to invigorate grammar charts like this is to have sts read the grammar box for a minute, then cover it and, in pairs, remember all they can of the contents, patterns, and rules.

A Go through the grammar box with the class and check understanding of the example sentences by asking them to make them active. Can they think of any other verbs which could be included here? (e.g. *said, supposed, alleged*) Sts check the correct rules, then classcheck.

Ask them to think of other infinitives you could add to the passive expressions, e.g. *The treatment is reported to be very tiring for the patient. Patients are known to improve very quickly.*

> **Answers**
>
> 1 passive, present   2 active, present   3 active, passive
> 4 happened in the past

Weaker classes: Introduce the structure by boarding the following sentence: *People report the treatment works well. The treatment ...* and elicit the rest of the sentence (*is reported to work well*). Elicit that it's the passive (with an infinitive), then look at exercise **A** with the whole class.

>> Refer sts to the **Grammar expansion** on p.154.

B Sts find four more examples in **3A**. Focus on the answer to the first one in the speech bubble, as an example. Classcheck. Tell sts that these impersonal expressions (e.g. *It's known to, It's believed to*) are very common in English. Elicit others that sts might know, e.g. *It's understood to ..., It's claimed to ..., It's supposed to ..., It's considered to ..., It's deemed to ...*

> **Answers**
>
> 1 Acupuncture ... is thought to be effective ... (red because it is active and in the present)
> 2 The technique is believed to relieve neck pain ... (red because it is active and in the present)
> 3 ...many patients are thought to be helped ... (blue because it is passive and refers to the present)
> 4 acupuncture is known to have reduced patient suffering (green because it is active and refers to the past)

C Focus on the blog about alternative medicine. Ask sts to quickly scan the text and find all the alternative medicine therapies mentioned (homeotherapy, biofeedback, Bach flower remedies, Feng Shui, hypnotherapy). Ask: *Which of these have you heard of?*

Sts rewrite the underlined sentences 1–6 as instructed.

Peercheck. Classcheck. Ask: *Which of the therapies sounds most convincing?*

> **Answers**
>
> 1 Homeotherapy is thought to be helpful.
> 2 Patients are believed to be assisted by biofeedback.
> 3 They're reported to provide relief (for personality problems and emotional issues).
> 4 Many people are known to have been cured.
> 5 Feng Shui is known to have helped some people.
> 6 It's reported to be a miracle treatment.
> Sentences 2 and 4 contain passive infinitives (*to be assisted* and *to have been cured*)

Optional activity

Ask sts to add their own comments to the "forum" using a passive expression. When they are ready, invite sts to board their comments, and ask other sts if they agree.

D **Make it personal** Read out the types of alternative medicine, modeling pronunciation. Ask: *Which of these have you heard of / tried?* If there are sts in the class who have tried the therapies, ask them to explain what they are to the rest of the class.

Ask sts to choose one of the therapies or one from **C**, and note down reasons why they would be effective. They can do some research on the Internet if they like to find out more information. Put sts in groups, and have them tell their classmates about the therapy they chose and why they think it would be effective. Encourage them to use passive expressions where possible.

When they have finished, ask: *Which of the therapies do you think sounds most effective? Which would you try? Why?* Try to get the class to agree on the best alternative treatment.

Optional activity

Sts could write a paragraph summarizing their arguments, either in class or for homework.

>> Workbook p.44.

♪ Say something, I'm giving up on you. I'm sorry that I couldn't get to you. Anywhere I would've followed you

5 Grammar: Passive expressions with infinitives

A Read the grammar box and check (✔) the correct rules (1–4).

Passive expressions in sentences with active and passive infinitives

The treatment	is	reported / thought	to	work well. / have helped.
Patients	are	known / believed		be easily influenced. / have been cured.

1. The blue phrases are ☐ active ☐ passive. They refer to the ☐ present ☐ past.
2. The red phrase is ☐ active ☐ passive. It refers to the ☐ present ☐ past.
3. The green phrase is ☐ active ☐ passive, and the purple phrase is ☐ active ☐ passive.
4. The green and purple phrases describe events that ☐ happened in the past ☐ are happening right now.

» Grammar expansion p.154

B Find four more examples in 3A of passive expressions in sentences with infinitives. In pairs, say why each infinitive is like the red, green, blue, or purple example.

> The first one is "Acupuncture is thought to be effective": I think it's red. The infinitive is "to be" and it refers to the present. It's active because the subject is "acupuncture."

C Rewrite underlined sentences 1–6 from the forum to contain passive expressions and infinitives. Begin with the words in italics. How many infinitives are passive, too?

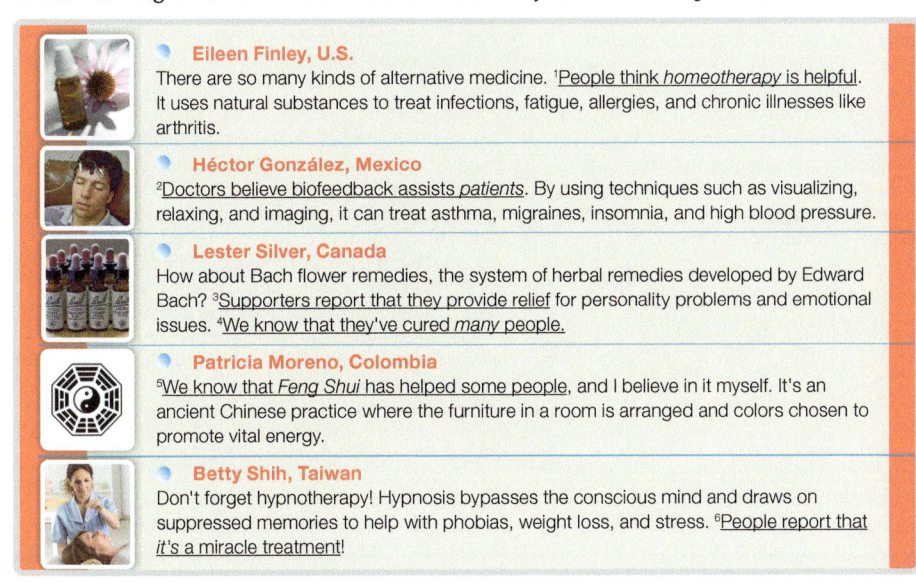

Eileen Finley, U.S.
There are so many kinds of alternative medicine. ¹People think *homeotherapy* is helpful. It uses natural substances to treat infections, fatigue, allergies, and chronic illnesses like arthritis.

Héctor González, Mexico
²Doctors believe biofeedback assists *patients*. By using techniques such as visualizing, relaxing, and imaging, it can treat asthma, migraines, insomnia, and high blood pressure.

Lester Silver, Canada
How about Bach flower remedies, the system of herbal remedies developed by Edward Bach? ³Supporters report that they provide *relief* for personality problems and emotional issues. ⁴We know that they've cured *many* people.

Patricia Moreno, Colombia
⁵We know that *Feng Shui* has helped some people, and I believe in it myself. It's an ancient Chinese practice where the furniture in a room is arranged and colors chosen to promote vital energy.

Betty Shih, Taiwan
Don't forget hypnotherapy! Hypnosis bypasses the conscious mind and draws on suppressed memories to help with phobias, weight loss, and stress. ⁶People report that *it's* a miracle treatment!

D 🌐 **Make it personal** What are the best alternative treatments?

1. Choose two treatments from **C** or search on "types of alternative medicine" to find information about one of those below.

    dance therapy   fasting   massage therapy   Reiki   vitamin therapy   yoga therapy

2. Note down at least two reasons why they would be effective. For which ailments?
3. In groups, state your case. Use passive expressions with infinitives where possible.

> Dance therapy is reported to be helpful for physical disabilities and eating disorders.

> That may be, but it's also just fun and a great way to lose weight.

97

9.3 What unconventional families do you know?

6 Reading

A Read the first three paragraphs of the article. In pairs, list three possible advantages and three disadvantages of single parenting. Then read the rest. Were any of your ideas mentioned?

Four Reasons It's Better To Be A Single Parent
By Kerri Zane

Although the gold standard in child rearing has traditionally been a dual family unit, being a single parent has myriad benefits. Rather than navigating the treacherous territory of constant parental compromise, you can independently make choices for your children that you feel are best. Eleven years ago, when my former husband and I split, I saw my divorce as a glorious opportunity to parent solo. No more discussing the finer points of gymnastics vs. volleyball. I didn't have to debate dessert after dinner vs. never ever letting sugar touch lips. And there was no longer a lengthy discussion over the reason my daughters needed braces.

While the state of rock-steady marital bliss in the United States continues to falter, more and more adults are joining the ranks of contented uncoupled family units. In fact, based on the latest Census Bureau statistics, there are over 14 million single-parent households with children under the age of 18. That is a lot of people and a good reason to celebrate. Which is why March 21 has been designated as National Single Parents' Day. It is a time to honor all those tenacious individuals who do what they do, day in and day out, to support, nurture and care for their kids.

As the single mom expert and author of the Amazon best-selling book, *It Takes All 5: A Single Mom's Guide to Finding The REAL One*, I would like to honor the day and offer you four solid reasons why it's better to be a single mom or dad than half of a parenting pair.

1. No Negotiations Necessary
While your married counterparts continue to disagree on the state of their children's welfare, you get to make unilateral choices. In the long run this is better for your offspring's well-being. A child's behavior can be negatively affected by adult arguing. It will either leave them crying their eyes out or running for cover. With no one else in the house to challenge your choices, you may continue to be the cozy constant security blanket your children need. Granted, there is a financial price to pay when you are the sole provider, but children need to learn that sometimes we can't give them everything they want. And often times what they thought was a "must-have," really isn't. Ultimately, if it is that important, you will find a way. Payment plans are designed for the single parent!

2. Stellar Independent Role Model
One of the best gifts I was able to give my two daughters was the knowledge that they can make it on their own. Change a light bulb without a dad in the house — snap Mom. Swoop a stylish up-do for your teen with no mom in sight — yeah Dad. You embody the idea that it's better to "want" to be in a relationship because there is a loving bond, rather than you "need" to be in a relationship because there is stuff to be done or procured. When your child sees you as a completely whole and independent adult, they will learn to emulate your healthy behaviors.

3. Relationship Options May Vary
Our society is shifting away from the bonds of matrimony. A recent Pew study revealed that just over half of adult Americans are married, the lowest rate in decades. Children will be enlightened and possibly relieved that they are no longer tied to that traditional lifestyle. Marriage is optional and sometimes not applicable. Long-term relationships without wedding bands can be stronger. My idols in this arena are Kurt Russell and Goldie Hawn; they've been together for nearly 30 years. These lessons are particularly important for girls, who've been raised on the fictitious belief that Prince Charming would sweep them off their feet to live happily ever after. There is a real possibility that they can become enormously disappointed when their fairytale ending turns into a hardcore courtroom reality.

What unconventional families do you know? 9.3

Lesson Aims: Sts read an article about being a single parent and learn common collocations and compounds.

Skills	Vocabulary
Reading an article about the advantages of being a single parent	Common collocations and compounds: *fictitious belief, overriding desire, prospective mate, lengthy discussion, unilateral choices*

Warm-up

Ask: *What is your idea of the conventional family?* Ask the lesson title question: *What unconventional families do you know?* Brainstorm different family units, e.g. *single-parent families, families with gay parents, families whose parents are unmarried, foster families, extended families.*

Ask: *How many people do you know who live with one parent? How many people do you know who are separated / divorced from their husband or wife? Do you know any siblings who live apart? Do you know anyone who has adopted or fostered a child? What is the biggest / smallest family you know?*

6 Reading

A Ask sts to cover the text apart from the first three paragraphs. Focus attention on the title of the magazine article and the photo. Ask: *Who is in the photo? What are they doing?* Encourage sts to guess, e.g. *I think it is a father and daughter. The man looks like he's been working ...* Get sts to guess what the article will be about and what ideas might be mentioned.

In pairs, have them note down possible advantages and disadvantages of being a single parent. Sts then read the rest of the article, and check which of their ideas were mentioned.

Possible answers

Advantages: parent makes all the parenting decisions, parent has more time for their child(ren), child benefits from not witnessing poor adult relationships, children learn to be independent faster, two birthday celebrations

Disadvantages: financial stresses, loneliness, being overloaded with work (both profession and housework), sometimes difficult to discipline child

Tip

As this is a complex, authentic text, with some hard cultural references, set a task to help sts focus and feel more success, e.g. *Find out as much as you can about the writer of the article Kerri Zane in the first three paragraphs, and why she decided to write the article.*

Sts share what they have found out. (She's divorced, has daughters, has been a single parent for 11 years, has written a book, wants to celebrate National Single Parents' Day.) Ask: *Did you know this day existed? Does it seem like a good idea? Are there too many "special" days nowadays? Any you'd get rid of?*

Optional activity

Board the following, in random order: *Making your own decisions; Changing times; Who I am.* Ask sts to read the first three paragraphs and match the titles to each one. Peercheck then classcheck.

9.3

B Have sts read through statements 1–6. Check understanding. Have sts find and underline the evidence in the text. Classcheck.

Tip

You could produce a more interactive class by putting sts into trios here, and assigning each of them two different statements, then have them share their answers. They have yet to hear the full text, so all sts will get the chance to re-read the whole thing.

As follow-up, ask: *Overall, do you agree that it's better to be a single parent? What do you think a child of a single-parent family would say? Do you think they would say it is better to have one parent?*

Answers

1 … you get to make unilateral choices. In the long run this is better for your offspring's well-being.
2 Granted, there is a financial price to pay when you are the sole provider …
3 …it's better to "want" to be in a relationship because there is a loving bond, rather than a "need" to be in a relationship because there is stuff to be done or procured
4 These lessons are particularly important for girls, who've been raised on the fictitious belief that Prince Charming would sweep them off their feet to live happily ever after.
5 Marriages are like your freshman year in college. You have the tendency to pack on the pounds.
6 The best way to handle the inevitable life shifts is to stay positive, reach out for support from your friends and family …

Weaker classes: Show sts the answers, but in random order, and ask them to match them to statements 1–6.

» Song lyric: See Teacher's Book p.351 for notes about the song and an accompanying activity to do with the class.

C » 9.8 Read **Common collocations and compounds**. Play the audio, pausing after each highlighted phrase to give sts time to figure out the meaning. Tell sts also to keep an eye out for the words highlighted in pink and try to remember the pronunciation. Classcheck.

Ask sts to look through the article again and find the expressions in the Writer's style column. Tell sts these are underlined in the text. Point out that these collocations and compound nouns are less common, and have been "put together" by the writer. Ask sts to try and explain what they mean.

Stronger classes: Ask sts to write their own sentences with the words highlighted in yellow, e.g. *After a lengthy discussion, we agreed to accept the new proposal.* Have them omit the yellow words, then swap sentences with a partner, and try to guess the missing words.

Answers

fictitious belief – something that is accepted out of convention even though it isn't true
overriding desire – a wish to have something more than anything else
prospective mate – a person likely to become your spouse
lengthy discussion – a conversation that takes place over a long period of time
unilateral choices – decisions made by only one person
child rearing – the process of bringing up a child or children
fairytale ending – an extremely happy or fortunate ending
security blanket – a familiar blanket held by a young child as a source of comfort (when used metaphorically, something that gives a person a sense of protection)

Optional activity

Sts test each other in pairs. One st says the first word, then the second st, with his / her book closed, says the collocation or compound.

D Make it personal

Tip

Perhaps the best reading comprehension activity, is to ask sts for their emotional reaction to a text. So, ask the class, e.g. *Did you enjoy that text and the ideas in it? Do you like her style? How did you feel reading that the first second and third time? How do you feel now, knowing that you've understood a long, hard authentic text?* Try to extract all the positives you can.

Go through questions 1–3 together.

1 Elicit the opposite of *balanced* (one-sided / biased). Ask: *Did Kerri point out any disadvantages of single – parenting?*
2 In their pairs, have sts review the advantages and disadvantages they listed in A. *Did they have similar points?* Ask sts: *Which of your points were not mentioned in the article?* They will probably say the disadvantages, reinforcing the view that Kerri's article is one-sided. Have sts agree on the most important advantages / disadvantages and decide if the advantages outweigh the disadvantages or vice versa.
3 Focus on the models in the speech bubbles as an example exchange, and encourage sts to replicate similar exchanges.

When they have finished discussing question 3, widen out to a class discussion. Tell sts to imagine being a child in a single parent family, and think about the advantages / disadvantages from their point of view.

» Workbook p.45.

♪ I'm a survivor. I'm not gonna give up. I'm not gonna stop. I'm gonna work harder

4. Building a Better Body

Marriages are like your freshman year in college. You have the tendency to pack on the pounds. One study found that women could gain five to eight pounds in the first few years of their wedded bliss and a whopping 54 pounds by the ten-year anniversary mark. Their single counterparts stay slim. Most of us have an **overriding desire** to want to be attractive to **prospective mates** of the opposite sex. The result of a divorce? A slimmer, trimmer you — aka the Divorce Diet. Take a look at Tom Cruise who reportedly lost 15 pounds after splitting with Katie. Jennie Garth lost 20 and Demi Moore has been stick thin since the departure of her sweetheart, Ashton Kutcher.

Many reports will tell you that being a single parent is stressful. It is. But no more stressful than being a married parent. Ultimately, we all want to step into our own with confidence and take every curveball life throws us with our independent spirit intact. The best way to handle the inevitable life shifts is to stay positive, reach out for support from your friends and family, relish the time you spend with your children and most importantly, create a daily space for some much deserved me-time.

Happy National Single Parents' Day to you!

B Statements 1–6 are true, according to the author. Underline the evidence in the article.

1. Children benefit when only one parent makes all decisions.
2. Single-parenting can be financially challenging.
3. Relationships should be based on love rather than mutual dependence.
4. Women grow up believing that they're destined to find the perfect partner.
5. People tend to put on weight in marriage, just like when they start college.
6. Optimism and meaningful relationships can help you cope with life's changes.

C ▶ 9.8 Read *Common collocations and compounds*. Then listen to and re-read the article focusing on the highlighted phrases. In pairs, use context to work out what they mean.

Common collocations and compounds

Adjective–noun collocations and compound nouns are common, but distinguishing common expressions from an author's personal style can be hard. Memorize expressions you see frequently.

	Common	Writer's style
collocations	fictitious belief, overriding desire, prospective mate, lengthy discussion, unilateral choices	parental compromise, tenacious individuals
compound nouns	child rearing, fairytale ending, security blanket	parenting pair, divorce diet, life shifts

> A "fictitious belief" is obviously a belief that is false. I don't believe in Prince Charming!

D **Make it personal** In pairs, react to the author's article. Discuss 1–3. Use common collocations and compounds. Do you both agree?

1. How balanced is her presentation of single parenting?
2. How many of your points in A were mentioned? Which are most important?
3. Which statements in B do you agree with? Why (not)?

> I don't agree with number 1. A good partner helps in decision-making and provides you with a security blanket, too.

> But what about Kerri Zane's arguments? Don't you agree that ...?

9.4 How often do you work out?

7 Language in use

A ▶9.9 Match a–e to the photos. Then listen to conversations 1–5 and match them to the photos.

| a a treadmill   b stretching   c weightlifting   d sit-ups   e abs |

A   B   C   D   E

B ▶9.10 In pairs, take the quiz. Listen to a personal trainer to check. Any surprises?

Test your fitness IQ!	A fact	Hmm … Not so simple!
1 Running on a treadmill will protect your knees.		
2 Calorie counters in fitness machines are usually accurate.		
3 You don't need to sweat to burn calories.		
4 Stretching before weightlifting prevents injury.		
5 If you do lots of sit-ups, you'll get toned abs.		

C ▶9.11 Read *Verbs ending in -en*. Then complete 1–5 with verbs formed from words in the box. Listen to check.

> **Verbs ending in -en**
>
> The *-en* suffix can be used to make verbs from adjectives or nouns.
> 1 Light and color: *I'm going to have my teeth **whitened** (adj: white) tomorrow.*
> 2 Size, density, and movement: *Don't **lengthen** (n: length) your workout beyond your level of endurance and **lessen** (adj: less) your expectations for quick progress.*
> 3 Others: *Things have **worsened** (adj: worse) and his neighbor has **threatened** (n: threat) him.*

| bright   fresh   soft   strength   weak |

1 Most treadmills include padding that can <u>stop</u> your knees from hurting because, just like a cushion, it _____ any impact you may feel, unlike a hard surface outdoors.
2 Some machines can overestimate calorie count by over 40%! These numbers might put a smile on your face and _____ your day, but don't <u>let</u> them fool you! You can't <u>count on</u> them being right!
3 Sweating <u>keeps</u> you from overheating – and having to stop to _____ up every five minutes! But rest assured that you can burn hundreds of calories without necessarily dripping in sweat.
4 Some studies show that stretching before weightlifting won't necessarily <u>enable</u> you to perform better and might actually _____ your muscles!
5 Toning exercises will <u>help</u> you _____ your abs, but may not give you a really flat tummy.

D 🌐 **Make it personal** Search on "fitness myths" and find at least one more to share in groups. Whose was the most surprising?

> Here's one to brighten your day! Working out actually lessens your craving for food!

100

How often do you work out? 9.4

Lesson Aims: Sts learn vocabulary to talk about working out, and bust some of the myths relating to fitness.

Skills	Vocabulary	Grammar
Listening to a personal trainer on a radio podcast, answering listeners' questions about working out	Fitness vocabulary: *treadmill, stretching, weightlifting, sit-up, abs* Verbs ending in *-en*: *brighten, freshen, soften, strengthen, weaken*	Overview of verb patterns, e.g. *make* + object + base form, *cause* + object + *to* infinitive

Warm-up

Ask: *Why do people work out?* Elicit as many reasons as possible, e.g. *to lose weight, to get in shape, to meet people, prevent injury, to relieve anxiety / depression.*

Ask the lesson title question: *How often do you work out?* Follow this up by asking: *Do you go to a gym or do you work out at home? Do you have a fitness app? Do you get advice from a personal trainer or do you do your own thing?*

7 Language in use

A ▶ 9.9 Focus on the photos. Ask: *What are the people doing?*

Say the words in the box, and have sts repeat. Ask: *What are abs an abbreviation of?* (abdominal muscles) Sts match the words with the photos. Tell sts they are going to listen to conversations at the gym. Ask them to match each conversation with a photo.

Classcheck. Tell sts we often call a treadmill a running machine.

Ask: *Which of these activities do you do regularly? Which have you done in the past? What else can you do to work-out?* (jogging, push-ups, leg lifts, step exercises, squats, crunches)

Optional activity

Books closed. Before doing exercise **A**, elicit the words by demonstrating / showing yourself and drilling the words around the class. Then sts open their books and do the exercise.

> **Answers**
> A c 4 B d 5 C a 1 D e 3 E b 2

> See Teacher's Book p.331 for Audio script 9.9.

B ▶ 9.10 If necessary, explain the word *calories*. Ask: *Have you ever used a calorie counter?* Sts take the quiz in pairs. Tell them they are going to listen to a personal trainer talking on a radio fitness pod. Play the audio for them to check their quiz answers.

Classcheck. Ask: *How many questions did you get right? Which are the most surprising?* Go through the statements, and have sts explain why 1, 2, 4, and 5 are "not so simple," according to the fitness trainer, e.g. 1 *Although a treadmill softens the impact on the knees, people tend to take shorter strides which actually increases risk of injuries.*

> **Answers**
> 1 Hmm... not so simple 2 Hmm... not so simple
> 3 A fact 4 Hmm... not so simple 5 Hmm... not so simple

> See Teacher's Book p.331 for Audio script 9.10.

C ▶ 9.11 Read **Verbs ending in -en** with the class. Ask sts what these verbs are in their language. Elicit the opposites of the verbs (*whiten – blacken; lengthen – shorten; lessen – increase; worsen – improve; weaken – strengthen*).

Weaker classes: Focus on the adjectives in the box, and ask sts what the verb forms are. Ask them to say the verbs ensuring that they stress the first syllable in each case, e.g. BRIGHTen, FRESHen.

Sts complete 1–5 with the correct verbs. Remind them to put the verbs in the correct form. Play the audio for them to check. Classcheck. Check understanding of the underlined verbs. These will be referred to in **8A**.

Ask sts if they know any other verbs ending in *-en*, e.g. *lighten, sadden, broaden, widen, deepen, flatten, quicken, sharpen, thicken.* Ask them which of the categories 1, 2, or 3 they fit into.

> **Answers**
> 1 softens 2 brighten 3 freshen 4 weaken
> 5 strengthen

Optional activity

Ask sts to write example sentences for three of the other verbs ending in *-en* that you elicited. Monitor and help where necessary. When they have finished, ask them to blank out the verbs and read them to a partner to guess what they are.

D Make it personal

Brainstorm a few ideas to get sts started, e.g. *Swimming is the best form of exercise. Squats are bad for your knees. Eat less to lose weight. Running will make you fit.* Ask sts to research why these statements are not accurate. Sts can do the research at home if you don't have time in the lesson. In the following class, sts share what they learned in groups. Invite a few volunteers to present their "fitness myth" to the rest of the class.

Class feedback. Ask: *Which myth is the most surprising?* Have sts complete the following sentence then find out if anyone has written something similar: *For me personally, the best way to keep fit is …*

9.4

8 Grammar: Overview of verb patterns

Tip
To help with upcoming pronunciation, and encourage sts to explore lexical sets, board the word *courage* and elicit pronunciation, a definition (the ability to do something frightening, strength in the face of pain or grief), the synonym (*bravery*), the adjective (*courageous*) and verbs (*encourage* and opposite *discourage*). Ask them for some examples of courageous people.

A Go through the grammar box, and check sts understand the examples. To immediately personalize, ask sts in pairs to go through them and say which ones they can imagine saying themselves or agreeing with. Feedback any interesting discoveries.

Tell sts that sadly, there are no rules to follow, they just have to learn the verb patterns. It will help them to list verbs with similar patterns together in their vocabulary books, e.g. *help s.o. do stg., make s.o. do stg., let s.o. do stg.*

Sts complete the rules with a–d. Refer them back to the underlined verbs in **7C**. Sts add them to the appropriate rules as an example.

Answers
1 b (enable)   2 a (let / help)   3 d (count on)
4 c (stop / keep)

» Refer sts to the **Grammar expansion** on p.154.

» Song lyric: See Teacher's Book p.351 for notes about the song and an accompanying activity to do with the class.

B ▶ 9.12 Have sts read through the sentences and check they understand the underlined verbs. Explain or elicit the meaning of *give stg. a shot* (to try something out).

Sts circle the correct answers, then write a–d next to the underlined verbs.

Peercheck. Classcheck. As you correct number 3, focus on the **Common mistake**. To consolidate it, ask: *Is this what you would say if you translated directly from your language?*

Answers
1 from giving (c)   2 you to see (b)   3 help (a)
4 to cool (b)   5 to stretch (b)   6 listening (d)

C Ask sts to read through **Fact or myth?** Explain or elicit the meaning of *dose* (quantity – usually of a medicine or drug – recommended to be taken at any one time). Ask: *Which of these facts or myths have you heard before?*

Ask sts to re-phrase the sentences beginning with the underlined words and using the verbs in parentheses. Do the first one together as an example. Peercheck. Classcheck.

Focus on the photos. Ask: *Do the people there remind you of anybody? How many hours a day do you now spend in this position? How much fact-checking do you do on your cell phone?*

Answers
1 Cold showers can help you lose weight faster.
2 Large doses of vitamin C stop you from getting the flu.
3 Cell phones prevent teens from developing social skills.
4 Bike lanes don't dissuade people from using their cars.
5 Taking notes by hand enables students to remember information better.
6 Violent video games encourage children to behave aggressively.
7 A GPS lets you find your location more easily than maps.

D Make it personal

1 Sts re-read the statements in **C**, and choose three. It will be easier if they choose ones they have personal experience of.

2 Put sts in groups of three or four. Have them take turns telling their classmates which statements they have chosen and whether they think they are fact or myth. Encourage them to react to each other, agreeing or disagreeing, and backing up their opinions with any personal experiences. Focus them on the speech bubbles as an example.

Class feedback. Ask: *Did you all agree?* Read out the statements one by one, and ask sts to vote on whether they think they are facts or myths. Ask: *Which are the most controversial?* As follow-up, ask sts to write one fact and one myth. In groups, they read them out. Their classmates decide which is the fact and which is the myth.

Optional activity

Ask sts to research some of the statements online to see what other people think, then report back to the class.

» Workbook p.46.

♪ Something in the way you move, Makes me feel like I can't live without you. It takes me all the way. I want you to stay

9.4

8 Grammar: Overview of verb patterns

A Read the grammar box and write a–d in the white boxes for patterns 1–4. Then choose an underlined verb from **7C** for each example.

	Verb patterns with adjectives, gerunds, base forms, and infinitives			
a	My coach	**makes**	me	**stay** focused.
b	Exercise	**encourages**	people	**to socialize**.
		will **cause**	your blood pressure	**to drop**.
c	Parents	should **discourage**	young kids	**from overexercising**.
d	I	really **appreciate**	your	**helping** me.

verb + object + ...
1 ☐ infinitive (e.g., _____)   3 ☐ -ing form (e.g., _____)
2 ☐ base form (e.g., _____)   4 ☐ preposition + -ing form (e.g., _____)

» Grammar expansion p.154

B ▶ 9.12 Circle the correct answer. Listen, check, and write a–d next to each underlined verb.
1 Maybe you won't <u>dissuade</u> ☐ me [**from giving** / **to give**] it a shot then.
2 I <u>urge</u> ☐ [**that you see** / **you to see**] your doctor before you begin exercising.
3 <u>Have</u> ☐ your doctor [**help** / **helping**] you choose the best exercise program for you.
4 Sweat is a sign that your body is <u>reminding</u> ☐ itself [**to cool** / **of cooling**] down.
5 My doctor <u>warned</u> ☐ me not [**to stretch** / **stretch**] before weightlifting.
6 I won't <u>insist on</u> ☐ your [**listen** / **listening**] to me instead.

Common mistake
Can you help me ~~choosing~~ *choose* a good gym?

C Rephrase 1–7. Use the correct form of the verbs in parentheses and begin with the underlined words.

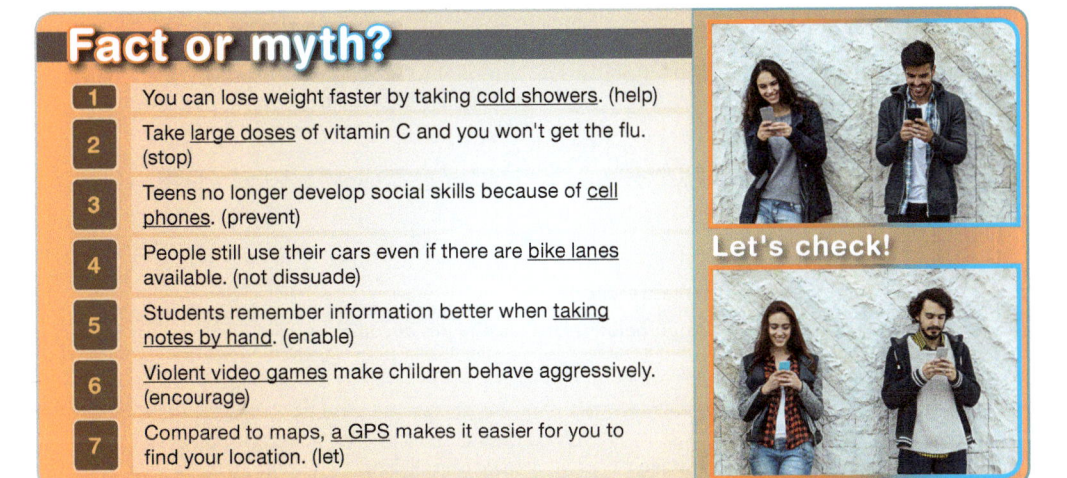

Fact or myth?

1 You can lose weight faster by taking <u>cold showers</u>. (help)
2 Take <u>large doses</u> of vitamin C and you won't get the flu. (stop)
3 Teens no longer develop social skills because of <u>cell phones</u>. (prevent)
4 People still use their cars even if there are <u>bike lanes</u> available. (not dissuade)
5 Students remember information better when <u>taking notes by hand</u>. (enable)
6 <u>Violent video games</u> make children behave aggressively. (encourage)
7 Compared to maps, <u>a GPS</u> makes it easier for you to find your location. (let)

Let's check!

D **Make it personal** Fact or myth? In groups, do 1–2.
1 Individually, choose three statements from **C**. Write M (myth) or F (fact) next to each one.
2 In groups, support your opinion. Use verb patterns from **A**. Who's most convincing?

Cold showers really help people lose weight! They make your metabolism work faster.

I've heard that, too. I went on a "cold-shower diet" once, but I gave up after a month!

101

» 9.5 What are the pros and cons of dieting?

9 Listening

A ▶ 9.13 Use the photo to guess what a raw vegan diet includes. Listen to Terri and Hugo and cross out the foods that don't belong.

B ▶ 9.13 Listen again. Terri most likely …
☐ thinks Hugo has made a good decision.
☐ considers the diet a bit weird.
☐ is firmly opposed to Hugo's choice.

C ▶ 9.14 Listen to the rest. T (true), F (false), or NI (no information)? Correct the false statements.
1 A raw vegan diet contains no carbohydrates.
2 Carbohydrates aren't found in fruit.
3 A salad is a better protein source than fruit.
4 Adults usually find the diet easy to get used to.
5 Lack of vitamin D can have dangerous consequences in children.

D **Make it personal** In pairs, would you like to try a raw vegan diet? Support your opinion with at least three reasons.

> I think it would be very hard to find places to eat.

> Not any longer. There are lots of "raw" restaurants these days.

10 Keep talking

A ▶ 9.15 **How to say it** Complete the chart. Listen to Terri's responses to check.

Reacting to new information	
What they said	What they meant
1 I should _____ judgment.	I should be more open minded.
2 Did I hear you _____ ?	You must be joking.
3 Who in their _____ mind (would eat so many bananas)?	You'd have to be crazy (to eat so many bananas).
4 _____ , but no thanks!	No way!

B In groups, report on out-of-the-mainstream choices!

1 🌐 Search for an article online on a topic below. Is it basically pro or con? Note down the main arguments.

FOUR WAYS TO GET OUT OF THE MAINSTREAM!

| 1 Quit your high-stress, high-paying job now! Be a "taxi" tour guide or dog walker, instead. | 2 Repelled by an image-conscious society? Support a ban on plastic surgery ads. | 3 Let your children be "free to roam." Reject structured after-school activities. | 4 Become "technology free." Throw out your cell phone and delete your Facebook profile. |

2 Would you personally consider this choice? Support your "decision" with information you've found. Use *How to say it* expressions where possible.

> An article called [name] says being a "taxi" tour guide pays well.

> I should reserve judgment, but is that safe?

What are the pros and cons of dieting? 9.5

Lesson Aims: Sts listen to someone explaining what a raw vegan diet is, discuss the pros and cons of opting out of the mainstream, and write a report on pros and cons.

Skills	Language	Vocabulary
Writing a report on pros and cons, using bullet points	Reacting to new information, e.g. *Did I hear you correctly? Who in their right mind would ...?*	Food vocabulary: *raw, carbohydrates, fat, protein, diet, vegan, vitamin supplement, malnutrition, low-fat, dairy products*

Warm-up

Ask the lesson title question: *What are the pros and cons of dieting?* Ask: *Have you ever tried a special diet? Do you know anyone who is vegetarian / vegan? How difficult is it to limit what you eat to specific foods?*

» Song lyric: See Teacher's Book p.351 for notes about the song and an accompanying activity to do with the class.

9 Listening

A ▶9.13 Focus on the photo. Board the following food groups: 1) *bread / pasta*, 2) *dairy*, 3) *sugar*, 4) *eggs and meat*, 5) *fruit*, 6) *vegetables*. Have sts match them with the food on the plate. In pairs, give them two minutes to name all the foods in each category. Classcheck.

Ask: *Do you know anyone who is vegan? Which of the foods on the plate do you think vegans can't eat? Why do you think it is a good idea to eat raw food?* (to preserve the vitamins)

Tell sts they are going to hear two work colleagues discussing going out to lunch. Play the audio for them to check what food vegans can't eat. Classcheck.

Answers
Cross out: bread, pasta, dairy, meat, fish, egg

» See Teacher's Book p.331 for Audio script 9.13.

B ▶9.13 Re-play the audio. Sts check the correct option. Classcheck. Ask: *Do you know any restaurants in your town which would be suitable for people on a raw vegan diet? Would you like to have Hugo come over for dinner?! What would you give him to eat?*

Answers
Terri most likely considers the diet a bit weird.

C ▶9.14 Ask sts to read the statements and check any unknown words. Ask: *Which do you think are true?* Play the rest of Terri and Hugo's conversation, and ask sts to mark the sentences T, F, or NI.

Answers
1 F (It contains 80% carbohydrates)   2 F (Carbohydrates are found in bananas and dates)   3 NI   4 F (Adults often feel nauseous at first).   5 T

» See Teacher's Book p.331 for Audio script 9.13.

D Make it personal Sts discuss whether they would like to try a raw vegan diet, giving their reasons. Focus on the speech bubbles as examples.

If sts need prompting, ask: *Which foods would you most miss if you were vegan? Do you think you would be able to get enough nutrients? Do you think it would be hard to find places to eat in your town / city?*

Class feedback by inviting some sts to tell the class what their partner thinks about a raw vegan diet.

Optional activity

Put sts in pairs to research online and find a recipe which is part of a raw vegan diet. Ask them to share it with the class and have sts vote for their favorite one.

10 Keep talking

A ▶9.15 **How to say it** Have sts complete the sentences, then play the audio for them to check. Ask sts how they would say these expressions in their language. Re-play the audio, pausing after each expression for sts to repeat. Ask sts to practice the sentences in pairs. Monitor and check pronunciation and stress.

Answers
1 reserve   2 correctly   3 right   4 Thanks

B 1 Go through the four topics together, eliciting explanations of any trickier vocabulary. Ask: *Which is the biggest issue for people your age? Which do you feel the most strongly about?* Have sts choose one and do some Internet research. Ask them to note down the main arguments in support of the topics.

Weaker classes: Brainstorm a few ideas together for the first topic as an example: *High-stress, high-paying jobs put you under a lot of pressure to work long hours. There is little time to do non-related work activities or pursue hobbies. Taking time off and working in a less-pressurized job for a while gives you time to take a breather and have some fun. Money isn't the key to happiness.*

2 In groups, ask sts to tell their classmates what they found out and whether they would consider the choice themselves. Class feedback. Ask: *Have you ever made any decisions which go against mainstream thinking? How easy is it to make decisions which take you out of the mainstream? Which of the courses of action in 1 would you be most likely to take?*

9.5

11 Writing: A report on pros and cons

A Lead into the topic. Ask: *Did / Do people write reports about you? When was the last time you read a report? Have you ever had to write one? If so, what makes a "bad" report?* (lack of clarity, inaccuracy, overlong, boring, no conclusion, etc.) Elicit answers to see how important reports are for them. And then ask: *What do you remember from the lesson about homeschooling?* (9.1)

Have sts read the report, and check a, b, or c. Classcheck. Ask them which of the paragraphs 1, 2, or 3 list the pros and which list the cons (pros: 1 and 2; cons: 3). Ask: *How useful is the report for someone trying to make a decision about homeschooling? As a report, whether or not you are into the topic, do you think it is "good"? Yes, no, why?*

Tip

Asking these questions (above) will give sts a chance to express their disinterest, should they have any! It's much better to let it out, than keep it bottled and de-motivate by over-insisting on or faking interest in something that might not excite them.

Don't prompt them but see if they pick up on the two personal sentences (11B). Congratulate them if they do.

> **Answer**
> c wants parents to make their own decisions

B Read through **Guidelines for good reports** with the class. Ask sts to identify the thesis and conclusion in the report in **A**. Ask: *Is the report short and succinct? Does it avoid repetition?*

Have them cross out the two personal statements. Classcheck.

> **Answers**
> My neighbors struggled with this decision.
> I was homeschooled and it wasn't for me.

Tip

As you go through the guidelines in **B**, elicit examples of each tip from the report.

C Go through **Write it right!** together. Sts match the sections in the report (1, 2, or 3) with a, b, and c. Peercheck. Classcheck. Highlight the use of the ellipses in sections 1 and 2, which indicate that there is missing text (completed by the bullets which follow).

> **Answers**
> a 3   b 2   c 3

D Ask sts to read the list. Ask: *What does each of the bullet points begin with?* (subject pronoun, verb, -ing form, subject pronoun). Sts rewrite them so they all begin in a similar style. Peercheck. Classcheck.

> **Possible answers**
> take into account the time involved
> set aside money for materials
> find possible friends for your children
> always be patient in your "home classroom"

E Your turn! Read through the instructions with the class and check sts understand what they have to do. When they have finished their reports, encourage sts to proofread them carefully, and then ask a classmate to double check for mistakes.

Tip

Be sure to give them as much freedom as they like about the topic, as there is little point in asking sts to produce a report on something they aren't really interested in.

Sts post their reports online. Alternatively, they could pin them on the classroom wall, allowing sts to mingle and read each other's reports.

If sts do the report for homework, assign each st a partner to email their report to for peer correction. Ask sts to give their classmates' reports a score out of 5 for consistency, clarity, and balance.

Class feedback. Ask sts: *Which of the reports did you find most interesting? Did any of them persuade you to consider this choice in the future?*

Weaker classes: To set up the activity, plan a report for topic 1 together on the board, with sentence starters for each paragraph:

Para 1 (intro). *Extensive research has been done on the problems of being in a high-stress, high-paying job …*

Para 2 (pros) *Among the many benefits of quitting a high-pressure job are …* (e.g. more free time to pursue hobbies, time to spend with family and friends, less pressure).

Para 3 (benefits) *It is claimed that people who have less stressful, low paid jobs are …* (e.g. healthier, more relaxed, not so anxious)

Para 4 (cons) *Nevertheless, potential arguments for keeping a well-paid job are persuasive.* (e.g. less money to spend, less job satisfaction, reaction of friends / family.)

Para 5 (conclusion)

» Workbook p.47.

♪ I am beautiful no matter what they say. Words can't bring me down. I am beautiful in every single way

9.5

11 Writing: A report on pros and cons

A Read the report on the pros and cons of homeschooling. It can be inferred that the writer …

a ☐ is for homeschooling.
b ☐ is against homeschooling.
c ☐ wants parents to make their own decisions.

Extensive research has been done on homeschooling, a growing trend in the United States and many other countries. Nevertheless, it is unclear whether observed benefits are actually caused by homeschooling, as opposed to other factors. For that reason, the decision to homeschool continues to be a very personal one. My neighbors struggled with this decision.

---

1 Among the many reasons given for homeschooling are the ability to …
  - customize the curriculum and offer more individual attention.
  - experiment with pedagogical methods different from those used in schools.
  - enhance family relationships.
  - provide a safe environment for learners.
  - impart a particular set of values and beliefs.

2 It is claimed that students who are homeschooled …
  - outperform their peers on achievement tests, regardless of parents' income or level of formal education.
  - do above average on measures of social and psychological development.
  - succeed at college at a higher rate than the general population, are more tolerant, and are more involved in community service.

3 Nevertheless, potential arguments against homeschooling are just as numerous.
  - Time: Organizing lessons, teaching, giving tests, and planning field trips are labor-intensive activities.
  - Cost: Buying the newest teaching tools, computer equipment, and books can eat into the family budget.
  - Effort: Ensuring adequate opportunities for socialization with other children, including those from other countries and backgrounds, calls for careful planning.
  - Patience: Separating the roles of parent and teacher requires a calm attitude.

I was homeschooled and it wasn't for me. Every child is a unique individual, as is every parent who homeschools. A child's needs and how optimum learning can be achieved remain the overriding concerns.

B Read the *Guidelines for good reports*. Then cross out two personal sentences in the report in **A** that don't belong.

> **Guidelines for good reports**
>
> A good report on a topic …
> - has a clear thesis and conclusion.
> - is short and succinct.
> - keeps the reader interested by avoiding repetition: different verbs or nouns start each point.
> - does not include irrelevant personal information or opinions.

C Read *Write it right!* Then find the section that …

a ☐ has items beginning with nouns.
b ☐ has ones with verbs.
c ☐ contains nouns with *-ing* forms.

> **Write it right!**
>
> For lists in reports, begin each item in a section with a similar style. For example, in section 1, all points begin with infinitives.
> Homeschooling offers the ability **to** …
> - customize the curriculum.
> - experiment with different methods.
>
> Sections don't all need to be identical, just consistent. They may also begin with nouns or verbs.

D Rewrite the list with a consistent style. There may be more than one solution.

If you are considering homeschooling …
- it's important to take into account the time involved.
- set aside money for materials.
- finding possible friends for your children is important, too.
- you should always be patient in your "home classroom."

E **Your turn!** Choose a topic that you discussed in **10B** and write a report in about 280 words that includes two to three lists.

Before
Plan the main function of each list. Note down specific information for three to five bullet points. Search online for more details if necessary.

While
Write three to four sections, following the model in **A**. Include a clear thesis and conclusion, and refer to *Write it right!* for style.

After
Post your report online and read your classmates' work. Give suggestions for clarity and consistency.

10 Why do friends drift apart?

1 Listening

A ▶ 10.1 Listen to Henry reminiscing about his college years. How close is he to his old friends? Why?

B ▶ 10.2 Listen to the second part. Label Mike (M) and Bruce (B) in the pictures. There's one extra.

And the guy kind of looked like Shrek. *He did!*

I'm so worried about Thursday. *Oh yeah?*

It's just a phase. It will pass. *Thanks. I hope you're right.*

C ▶ 10.2 Match 1–4 with the topics a–d. Listen to check. Do you understand the expressions in context?

1 "The writing was on the wall."
2 "What a riot he was!"
3 "Whatever became of him?"
4 "Go figure."

a ☐ Henry's sister wonders what Bruce is doing.
b ☐ Henry was surprised by Bruce.
c ☐ Bruce was different from Mike.
d ☐ Henry and Mike didn't have much in common.

D ▶ 10.3 Listen to the last part. In pairs, explain 1–2. Will Henry follow the advice? Why (not)?

1 what Henry meant by "abducted by aliens"
2 Henry's sister's advice, "Don't judge a book by its cover."

> He might mean / be suggesting …

E Make it personal Do opposites attract?

1 ▶ 10.4 **How to say it** Complete the chart with a form of *say* or *tell*. Listen to check.

Clarifying: Expressions with *say* and *tell*	
What they said	What they meant
1 I guess it goes without _____ (that) …	It must be obvious that …
2 Truth be _____ , …	Honestly, …
3 There's no _____ why, but …	It's hard to explain why, but …
4 _____ what you will …	You might have your reservations …
5 Easier _____ than done!	That's easy to suggest, but hard to put into practice!

2 Note down answers to a–c. In pairs, tell each other about someone you see often, but who's very different from you. Use *How to say it* expressions.

a Who's the person? Are you in close touch with him / her out of choice or obligation?
b Do your differences bother you, or have they strengthened your relationship. In what way?
c Have you ever fallen out temporarily? What happened?

> My friend María is my polar opposite. There's no telling why we're friends!

> So are you saying you don't enjoy her company?

104

Why do friends drift apart? 10.1

Lesson Aims: Sts learn vocabulary to talk about friendships, and listen to a conversation about old friends drifting apart.

Skills	Language	Vocabulary
Listening to a brother and sister talking about old friends	Clarifying (expressions with *say* and *tell*), e.g. *I guess it goes without saying that we didn't really care if we saw each other. Truth be told I thought he was boring.*	Friendship idioms: *the life of the party, go beneath the surface, go back a long way, see eye to eye, breath of fresh air, What a riot he was, birds of a feather* Idiomatic expressions: *The writing was on the wall, Go figure, Whatever became of him?*

Warm-up

Board these questions for sts to answer in pairs: *Who is / are your oldest friends? How long have you known them? Why do you think you've remained friends? What makes a good friend?* Classcheck.

Then ask the lesson title question and brainstorm answers.

1 Listening

A ▶ 10.1 Explain that Henry is looking at some college photos and talking to his sister about his college years. Focus on the question: *How close is he to his old friends? Why?* Play the audio and elicit the answer.

> **Answer**
> Henry is not close to his old friends. Since they left college they have grown apart. They got along better as a group than one-to-one.

» See Teacher's Book p.332 for Audio script 10.1.

B ▶ 10.2 Before sts listen, focus on the pictures of Henry and his friends. Point out that Henry is in each of the pictures with three different friends. Get them to identify Henry (on the right in picture 1).

Tell sts they are going to hear Henry talking about two of the friends in the pictures, Bruce and Mike. Have sts listen and guess which is Bruce and which is Mike. Classcheck. If sts labeled 3 as Bruce, explain that although Henry mentions playing squash with Bruce, he also says that Bruce is always laughing and joking, so it can't be no. 3.

> **Answers**
> 1 Bruce 2 Mike

» See Teacher's Book p.332 for Audio script 10.2.

C ▶ 10.2 Read the expressions 1–4. Ask: *Do you remember who said them, Henry or his sister?* Ask sts if they remember what the comments referred to. Play the audio for them to listen and match.

Weaker classes: Pause the audio after each expression to make it easier.

Classcheck. Discuss the meaning of the expressions. (1 = It was inevitable, 2 = What fun he was, 3 = What happened to him?, 4 = That's surprising. / Who would've thought that?)

> **Answers**
> 1 d 2 c 3 a 4 b

Optional activity

Ask sts to choose one of the phrases and write a short conversation of two-three lines leading up to it. Sts read out their conversation to a partner who then guesses which phrase comes next.

D ▶ 10.3 Play the end of the conversation. Ask: *Why doesn't Henry see Leona anymore?* (Because she's changed, and Henry no longer has anything in common with her.)

Put sts in pairs to discuss the meaning of 1 and 2. Classcheck.

Ask: *What advice does Henry's sister give?* (to give Leona a chance; even though she has changed) *Will he take the advice?* (probably).

> **Answers**
> 1 abducted by aliens – many people genuinely believe that they have been taken against their will by aliens and subjected to psychological testing – and this is a take on that belief and essentially means that he thinks she's had an extreme change of personality
> 2 don't judge a book by its cover – metaphorical phrase which means you shouldn't base your opinion of something or someone on its or their outward appearance alone

» See Teacher's Book p.332 for Audio script 10.3.

E Make it personal

1 ▶ 10.4 **How to say it** Ask sts to read through the expressions in the *What they said* column. Ask: *Who said these?* (Henry - 1, 2, 3, and 5. Henry's sister - 4)

Sts complete the expressions, then listen to check.

> **Answers**
> 1 saying 2 told 3 telling 4 say 5 said

2 Give sts time to think about the questions and make notes. In pairs, sts share their stories. Focus on the speech bubbles as models, and have them guess the meaning of *polar opposite* (completely different).

Classcheck by inviting volunteer pairs to share what they found out.

10.1

» Song lyric: See Teacher's Book p.352 for notes about the song and an accompanying activity to do with the class.

2 Vocabulary: Friendship idioms

A ▶ 10.5 Focus on the word *friendship*.

Tip

It's useful to look for links to similar sounding / looking words, so ask: *What other words do you know ending in -ship?* There aren't many but most have to do with people, e.g. *partnership, relationship, ownership, leadership, censorship, championship*. The suffix *-ship* means *position held*, i.e. having the rank, position, skill or relationship of (the stated type).

Read through the comments. Ask sts if they remember who said them. Have them try to match from memory. Tell sts they will hear Helene the cyber teacher giving the answers, then explaining the meanings of the comments. Have them listen, check their answers, and listen to the definitions. Ask: *Were Helene's explanations clear? Any you'd like to hear again?*

Classcheck by asking sts to give the definitions in their own words.

> **Answers**
> 1 f   2 d   3 a   4 c   5 b   6 e

» See Teacher's Book p.332 for Audio script 10.5.

Optional activity

Ask sts to think of people they know (or have known in the past) who the idioms can describe. Give them a few minutes to think of a person for each idiom, and make notes if they want to. When they are ready, sts discuss the different people in pairs.

B Ask sts: *How many really close friends do you have? Are they like you or are they very different?*

Tip

If sts respond animatedly to any of your introductory plenary questions, it's often a good idea to break them into impromptu pairs, so they can all talk at once. It may not have been part of your plan, but these spontaneous, student-lead sessions are often the most successful part of lessons.

Get sts to cover the text and brainstorm different types of friends from their own experience. What might the text say? Have sts read the text and rephrase the underlined sentences. Paircheck. Ask them to think of someone they know who fits each of the descriptions. In pairs, sts tell each other about that person. Focus sts on the speech bubble as an example. Classcheck, by asking a few sts to tell the class about the person.

Class feedback. Ask: *Which of the categories would you say your close friends fit into?*

> **Answers**
> 1 He's a breath of fresh air.
> 2 Lorna and I are birds of a feather.
> 3 she can go beneath the surface
> 4 we don't see eye to eye
> 5 we go back a long way
> 6 He's a riot.
> 7 He's the life of the party.

C Make it personal

1 Ask sts what they know about the famous people who wrote the quotes (in parentheses). Put sts in groups to discuss what they think the quotes mean. Have them agree on a good explanation for each. Focus them on the speech bubble as a model. Classcheck by asking a spokesperson for each group to share their explanations with the class. Agree as a class on the best one.

Background information

George Herbert (1593–1633) was a Welsh-born poet, orator, and Anglican priest.
Aristotle (322 BCE–384 BCE) was a Greek philosopher and scientist. Together with Socrates and Plato, he laid much of the groundwork for western philosophy.
Emily Giffin (1972–) is an American author of several novels commonly categorized as "chick lit" (literature which appeals to young women).
Helen Keller (1880–1968) was an American author, political activist, and lecturer. She was the first deaf-blind person to earn a bachelor of arts degree.
John Churton Collins (1848–1908) was a British literary critic.
Mandy Hale is a blogger turned New York Times best-selling author and speaker.

2 Ask sts: *Which of the quotes do you agree / disagree with? Which is your favorite?* Hold a class vote.

Optional activity

Stronger classes: Sts search online or even try to write their own quotes about friendship, then walk around the class and share them with other sts. In feedback, ask sts to tell you which they liked best. If your institution permits, it's nice to display these quotes for other classes to read.

» Workbook p.48.

> If you wanna be my lover, You gotta get with my friends. Make it last forever, Friendship never ends

2 Vocabulary: Friendship idioms

A ▶ 10.5 Match each question or comment (1–6) to its reply (a–f). Listen to check.

1. The three of you were inseparable!
2. Bruce was the exact opposite, always the life of the party.
3. Our conversations never went beneath the surface.
4. You guys go back a long way, right?
5. Do you still see her?
6. OK, so you don't see eye to eye on everything. So what?

a ☐ Yeah, all you could talk about was soccer and video games.
b ☐ No, she was a breath of fresh air, though.
c ☐ We do! We went to high school together.
d ☐ Yes, what a riot he was!
e ☐ But it's important to agree on things, isn't it?
f ☐ Yes, we were birds of a feather.

B Rephrase underlined sentences 1–6 using highlighted expressions from **A**. Use the correct tense. Then choose two expressions to describe someone you know.

Five types of friends you need to have in your life. Who are yours?

> INTERESTING CATEGORIES. HERE'S MY LIST. — Louise762

1. **THE HONEST CONFIDANT:** GUY
   [1]He's a welcome change. He's still the one I turn to when I need to hear the truth, and nothing but the truth.

2. **THE SOUL MATE:** LORNA
   [2]Lorna and I are very similar in character. She's a terrific listener, and when we're having a serious conversation, [3]she can see beyond the obvious and have insights that none of my other friends can.

3. **THE POLAR OPPOSITE:** JULIA
   It's funny how Julia and I have become friends even though [4]we don't seem to agree on anything. But, honestly, why would I want to surround myself with people just like me?

4. **A FRIENDLY NEIGHBOR:** RON
   Ron moved to the neighborhood in 2005, so [5]we've known each other for ages! He's really helpful and dependable, and above all, a good listener.

5. **A WORK PAL:** HUGO
   In an office full of boring people, Hugo is a breath of fresh air. [6]He makes me laugh! [7]He's a lot of fun! He's always telling jokes, even when we're stressed out.

> My next-door neighbor is a breath of fresh air. He's always in a good mood!

C Make it personal What's the nature of friendship?

1. In groups, explain what the quotes below mean to you.

   1. "The best mirror is an old friend." (George Herbert)
   2. "A friend to all is a friend to none." (Aristotle)
   3. "And like a favorite old movie, sometimes the sameness in a friend is what you like the most about her." (Emily Giffin)
   4. "I would rather walk with a friend in the dark than alone in the light." (Helen Keller)
   5. "In prosperity our friends know us; in adversity we know our friends." (John Churton Collins)
   6. "You will evolve past certain people. Let yourself." (Mandy Hale)

   > The first one must mean, "An old friend sees you as you really are and reflects that back."

   > But do you agree? Don't friends sometimes see someone like themselves?

2. Vote on your three favorites. Why do they resonate?

10.2 Who's the oldest person you know?

3 Language in use

A ▶ 10.6 Listen to the start of a lecture. Which factor may be most important for longevity, according to the speaker? Which two photos (1–3) are her Aunt Agatha?

B ▶ 10.7 Listen to the rest of the lecture and complete the slide. Any surprises?

THE KEY TO LONGEVITY
- Regular ¹_____ _____ is just as important as diet and ² _____.
- ³_____ _____ can be much more harmful than ⁴_____.
- The size of our ⁵_____ _____ is slightly more important than the ⁶_____ of our ⁷_____ – but only during ⁸_____ and old age.
- In other words: The more ⁹_____ your ¹⁰_____ are, the ¹¹_____ and ¹²_____ your life may be.

C ▶ 10.8 Read *To as a preposition*. Then correct the mistakes, if any, in 1–5. Listen to check.

> **To as a preposition**
>
> If *to* is followed by the base form of a verb, it's part of an infinitive:
> I wouldn't **want to live** to a hundred if that means having a boring, overly healthy lifestyle.
>
> If it's followed by the *-ing* form, it's a preposition:
> I can understand why people **look forward to retiring**. There's more to life than just working.
>
> It's easy to know which is which. Try putting a noun after *to*. If you can, it's a preposition:
> I know I should **limit myself to (having) two cups** of coffee a day, but I can't!

1 What's the secret to living a long and healthy life?
2 Let me try to answer this question by way of a personal anecdote.
3 She came close to win a marathon.
4 Aunt Agatha managed to track down some of her school friends.
5 Social connections might be the key to have good overall health.

D **Make it personal** In groups, discuss 1–2. Similar opinions?
1 Re-read the sentences in the box in **C**. Modify them so they're true for you.
2 Which potential risks would you give up?

delicious, but fatty food   fun, but potentially dangerous sports
travel by plane, car, or motorcycle   weekend parties, but not enough sleep
a well-paid, but totally sedentary job

> The key to living longer is having a good time, so I'm never giving up parties.

Who's the oldest person you know? 10.2

Lesson Aims: Sts learn to use degrees of comparison and vocabulary to talk about old age and the key to longevity.

Skills	Vocabulary	Grammar
Listening to a lecture on the effect social contact has on quality of life and life expectancy Reading about marriage in old age	Phrases and verbs with *to*: *look forward to, limit yourself to, want to, the secret to, come close to, the key to, try to, manage to*	Degrees of comparison, e.g. *The more friends you have, the happier you'll feel.*

Warm-up

Have sts ask you the lesson title question for a change, plus follow-up questions of their own. Then you ask them, plus *What's his or her secret?* and board prompts for sts to talk around in pairs, e.g. *Are they happy? Do they have a lot of friends? Is loneliness a problem for old people where you live? Are there social clubs and organizations for old people? How can we reduce social isolation for old people? What are you looking forward to when you get old?*

3 Language in use

A ▶10.6 Ask: *What factors do you think are important for a long life, e.g. diet, exercise, good genes, lack of stress, luck?* Focus on the photos.

Tip

Do this books closed and gamelike to make it more communicative. Sts will have seen the photos when they looked at the question title, so see how much detail they can remember in pairs. When they run out of things to say, have them open books for only 10 seconds then close again, then tell each other any detail they missed. Books open. Ask sts: *Any questions? How good are your (visual) memories?*

Ask: *What are the women doing?* (puzzle / celebrating a birthday with friends / exercise class). Ask: *How do you think these activities might affect longevity?*

Tell sts they are going to hear a lecture on the subject. The speaker mentions her aunt who is in two of the photos. Ask sts to listen and say which is her aunt. Classcheck.

Tip

Play it again if the majority seem to want you to, but set a further detail task, e.g. *note two items you understood this time you missed the first.* Paircheck to share them.

Answers

According to the speaker, the most important factor for longevity may be having a wide circle of friends and acquaintances.
Photos 2 and 3

▶▶ See Teacher's Book p.332 for Audio script 10.6.

B ▶10.7 Focus on the text. Ask sts to read it quickly for gist ignoring the blanks. Have them guess some of the missing words. Play the audio for them to check and complete the text. Drill pronunciation of *adolescence*.

Ask: *Do you know any elderly people? Do they have good friends? Do you think that's the key to their long lives?*

Answers

1 social contact   2 exercise   3 social isolation   4 obesity
5 social networks   6 quality   7 relationships
8 adolescence   9 meaningful   10 relationships
11 longer   12 healthier

▶▶ See Teacher's Book p.333 for Audio script 10.7.

▶▶ Song lyric: See Teacher's Book p.352 for notes about the song and an accompanying activity to do with the class.

C ▶10.8 Go through the box with the class. Have sts write their own example sentences using the phrases in bold (*want to ..., look forward to ..., limit yourself to ...*).

Sts correct the mistakes in 1–5. Play the audio for sts to check. Elicit other verbs sts know which take *to* infinitive or *-ing* form, e.g. *agree to* + inf., *pretend to* + inf., *arrange to* + inf., *be the answer to* + *-ing* form, *admit to* + *-ing* form.

Optional activity

Books closed. Do the exercise as a race, showing one sentence at a time. Ask sts to call out if the sentence is correct, or what the mistake is.

Answers

3 winning   5 having

D Make it personal   Put sts in groups to discuss 1 and 2.

1 If necessary, elicit some examples to get sts started, e.g. *I'd want to live to a hundred, especially if I had grandchildren. I'm not looking forward to retiring.*

2 Have sts say which of the risks they currently take, then ask and answer: *Do you eat delicious, but fatty food? Do you participate in fun, but potentially dangerous sports? Do you go to weekend parties, and not get enough sleep?*

Then get them to discuss which they would / wouldn't give up and why.

Class feedback. Ask: *Did you have similar opinions? Who is the biggest risk-taker in your group?*

10.2

4 Grammar: Degrees of comparison

Tip

Begin by having sts cover the last two columns of the box and guess some ways in which each sentence might end. Monitor and collect their best / funniest ideas for feedback with the class. Then uncover and reveal the "right" ideas. Ask sts to self-correct any of their own ideas before moving on.

A Take sts through the grammar box a sentence at a time, asking them each time if they agree if appropriate or to modify those with pronouns to make them true for themselves.

If necessary, you could ask them to translate the sentences into their language to bring out any major differences in form.

Remind sts that with adjectives ending in *y*, the final *y* changes to *i* in the comparative form, e.g. *happy* > *happier*.

Sts put the sentences 1–7 in the correct categories. Peercheck. Classcheck.

Answers

Parallel or equal meaning: 1, 2, 5
Big differences of degree: 3, 6
Small differences of degree: 4, 7

Optional activity

Have sts write their own grammar box in pairs, St A re-writing sentences 1, 3, and 5, St B 2, 4, and 6. Have them compare their grammar box with another pair. Are any sentences exactly the same?

» Refer sts to the **Grammar expansion** on p.156.

B Sts read the sentences, and compare them with sentences 1–4 in the text in 3B.

Have them check the ones which mean the same. Do the first one with the class as an example. Peercheck. Classcheck.

Answers

Check 1 and 4

C Sts read the text and rephrase sentences 1–6. Do the first one together as an example. Peercheck. Classcheck. Ask: *Do you have elderly relatives who are happily married? Would you agree with the article?*

Focus on the **Common mistake**. Board the following phrases, and ask sts to complete them: *The harder you work ..., The richer you are ...*

Answers

1 The older you are, the more dependent you are on other people ...
2 Married people take nowhere near as many risks as single people.
3 ... the health differences between married and single people aren't quite as significant as they used to be.
4 Research also shows that people who are single, especially men, are living a whole lot longer than ever before.
5 Widows and widowers are slightly less healthy than people who are married.
6 ... social isolation can be every bit as bad for your health as lack of exercise.

Optional activity

Stronger classes: Have sts cover the words in the box and rephrase the underlined sentences. When they have finished, sts uncover the box and amend any of their sentences that they want to.

D Make it personal Have sts read through questions 1–3. Focus on the speech bubbles as models. Review phrases for expressing views, e.g. *Well, it depends on ..., That may be ..., but don't you think ...?, I couldn't agree more, I totally disagree, Hang on a minute, let me finish.*

Put them in groups of three to discuss, and encourage them to come up with some fun ideas for question 3! Class feedback. Invite sts to share their views, and open out into a class discussion. Ask: *Do you know any old people who live on their own and are happy? If you had to choose one factor as the ultimate key to happiness in old age, what would it be?*

» Workbook p.49.

♪ It's my life. It's now or never. I ain't gonna live forever. I just want to live while I'm alive

10.2

4 Grammar: Degrees of comparison

A Read the grammar box. Then put sentences 1–7 in the categories below.

Degrees of comparison with *the ... the*, *more / ... er*, and *as ... as*			
1 **The more friends**	you have,	**the happier**	you'll feel.
2 **The healthier**	your diet (is),	**the longer**	you'll live.
3 I'm	much / far / a (whole) lot	**clos**er to my sister **than** (to)	my mom.
4 She's	a little / a bit / slightly	**more** traditional **than**	we are. / us.
5 Friends are	every bit / just	**as** important **as**	family.
6 Family is	nowhere near		friends.
7 Friends are**n't**	quite	**as** close **as**	family.

» Grammar expansion p.156

Parallel or equal meaning	Big difference of degree	Small difference of degree

B Check (✔) the sentence(s) that mean(s) the same as the four points in 3B.
1. ☐ Regular social contact is every bit as important as diet and exercise.
2. ☐ Social isolation is nowhere near as harmful as obesity.
3. ☐ For a small part of our lives, the size of our social network isn't quite as important as the quality of our friendships.
4. ☐ Meaningful relationships have a big impact on your health and lifespan.

C Rephrase the underlined sentences using the words in the box. Keep the same meaning.

1 The older   2 nowhere near   3 not quite   4 a whole lot   5 slightly   6 every bit

Marriage in later life

- ¹When you're older, you're more dependent on other people, and for many, this means one's husband or wife. So to what extent does marriage improve life expectancy?
- Marriage has traditionally been a non-biological factor that correlates positively with life expectancy. For one thing, ²married people take risks far less often than single people. Marriage also gives you more social and economic support.
- However, ³the health differences between married and single people are slightly less significant than they used to be. This may be because people are committing to each other in different ways.
- ⁴Research also shows that people who are single, especially men, are living much longer lives than ever before. It would appear that they are taking more responsibility for their own health and well-being.
- ⁵Widows and widowers aren't quite as healthy as people who are married. No one really knows exactly why. Maybe married people can count on an extended family to help them out. Besides, the widowed are more likely to be isolated, and ⁶social isolation can be very bad for your health.

D Make it personal In groups, discuss 1–3. Any interesting ideas?
1. Were you aware of the research in 3B? Is it convincing? Why (not)?
2. Does being married help with social integration where you live?
3. In what ways might being married actually shorten some people's lives?

Common mistake
the sooner you'll finish
The sooner you start, ~~you will finish sooner~~.

> Well, the less fulfilling your relationship is, the shorter your life might be! Doesn't stress shorten life?

> That could be, but you don't have to stay in an unhappy marriage.

10.3 How easy is it to make friends where you live?

5 Reading

A In pairs, guess the author's answer to the article question. To what extent can nationality predict human behavior?

B ▶ 10.9 Read and listen to the article. Check (✔) all that apply. Does the author seem to agree with your answers in **A**?

The author compares Germans and Americans in _____ terms.
1. ☐ social   2. ☐ economic   3. ☐ historical   4. ☐ gender-related

Are American Friendships Superficial?

Why do many immigrants consider American friendships superficial?

1 I was speaking to a German woman who has lived in the United States for a decade and has made it her permanent home. She was describing her likes and dislikes about the U.S. in comparison to Germany. For example, on the positive side, she was enthusiastic about the opportunities for work and advancement she had found here based on her skills and accomplishments – as opposed to Germany, where an insistence on the right credentials is often insurmountable. On the negative side, however, she complained that American friendships are superficial.

2 I have heard this criticism before, with variations – "no deep friendships," "people form and dissolve relationships too easily," "you don't know if you can really trust people," and so forth.

3 She also described a misunderstanding with a co-worker, who referred to her as a friend. "You're not my friend," she said. "You're an acquaintance. We go out for coffee together and chat about things. That's not friendship." The woman was offended – not surprisingly. Telling someone in the U.S. "You're not my friend," is tantamount to saying "You're my enemy." It took quite a while for her to overcome this misstep.

What is going on here?

4 To begin with, in a conversation Germans tend to be quite direct. (An American might joke that their words are so long that there is no time left to beat around the bush.) Where an American might say "From my point of view, I see it this way," a German might simply say, "I think X." Direct speech can seem inconsiderate to Americans. In this regard, Brazilians are to Americans as Americans are to Germans. Americans who are new to Brazil complain that "You never know what Brazilians think." or even "People are always lying to me." From the Brazilian point of view, they're being considerate, modulating what they say according to the non-verbal reactions of the other person, so as to have an agreeable conversation.

5 Germany is also part of the Old World. A family may live in the same town, or even the same house, for several centuries; everyone knows everyone, and personal relationships develop gradually over extended periods of time. The United States has only been around for two centuries. We are a nation of immigrants, and time begins for many families with their arrival here. Our history of wagon trains and the conquest of the West involved a similar internal migration experience – breaking the ties of family and friendship, and then forming new ones.

6 American individualism means that we give more emphasis to our own needs in forming and dissolving relationships than do cultures organized around traditional forms and relationships. This means that people who don't know one another can form groups to satisfy common needs. In criticizing what she viewed as the superficiality of our friendships, the German woman also praised the existence of numerous informal groups – around hobbies, interests, work, self-improvement, religion, and so forth – that make it possible to meet new people.

7 For generations, America has been the world center of capitalism; and capitalism prizes a mobile labor force. Thus, it is not surprising that many Americans have developed the ability to form and dissolve relationships, as they are periodically uprooted to earn a living or advance a career in another city, state, or region.

8 I should also mention that, during her childhood, the place where the woman grew up was in East Germany. Before reunification, the Stasi (secret police) were an omnipresent danger. People never knew, if they told someone their true thoughts and feelings, whether the information could be passed on to be used against them. Trusting someone as a friend could mean putting your life in their hands – a much greater commitment than friendship here. Even though that time has passed, the more intense commitment involved in friendship lingers on.

9 German-English dictionaries define friend as *Freund* and vice versa. But clearly, despite many features in common, the two words are not equivalent. Friendship in the United States and Germany is similar but not the same. As I told the woman about her co-worker, "She was your friend, but not your *Freundin*."

How easy is it to make friends where you live? 10.3

Lesson Aims: Sts learn vocabulary to talk about friendships, and discuss different nationalities' views of friendship.

Skills
Reading an article about American friendships vs. German friendships
Discussing stereotypes

Vocabulary
Words with both prefixes and suffixes, e.g. *discouraging, interdependence, counterproductive, impolitely*

Warm-up

Explore the lesson title question: *How easy is it to make friends where you live?* and the difference between meeting friendly people and making real friends. Ask: *Are there social clubs, sports clubs, associations where you can go and meet new people? How do you normally make new friends? What nationality are your friends? How many real friends do you have of another nationality? How did you meet them? Is your friendship with them different in any way from your other friends?*

Board the following words: *acquaintance, pal, chum, buddy, bosom buddy, companion, contact, colleague*. Ask sts to think of five or six people they come into contact with each day, and say which of the words they would use to describe them. Have them rank the people in order of how good a friend they are from 1–5, (1 = close friend, 5 = superficial). Ask: *How important is it to have a good friend you can confide in?*

5 Reading

A Ask: *Do you know any American people? Do you have any good friends who are American?* Refer sts to the title of the text: *Are American friendships superficial?* Ask: *What do you think?* Have sts guess the author's view on this. (Note: They have no real way of knowing unless they have read the text in advance of the lesson, it's just a guess for fun, to make them commit and then want to read on.)

Focus on the second question: *To what extent can nationality predict human behavior?* Elicit sts' views. Ask: *Do you have any friends of different nationalities? How different is your friendship with them than with friends of your own nationality?*

B ▶ 10.9 Tell sts they're going to listen and read the article to check their guesses and to do the second task here. Elicit and drill pronunciation of *social, economic, historical,* and *gender-related*. As they read have them check 1–4.

Tip

For a change here, we suggest you go straight into listening and reading together. This is relaxing, and many sts really enjoy it, but the problems come when sts find it too difficult, too long, or the text uninteresting. Why not give them a choice? Ask: *Would you prefer to listen and read it all or read it silently then listen and re-read, or read it all then listen to it all (which will be too hard)?* If they aren't sure, try a different technique on paragraphs 1–3: paragraph 1 they listen and read only; paragraph 2 they read it silently, then listen and read; paragraph 3 they read it silently then listen with the text covered. Then ask them to express their opinions and how they would like to go on. Remind them if necessary that the aim of a Reading lesson should be to practice the skill itself, not just to input vocabulary or grammar. So they need to try to read faster, slower, and so on and talk about their feelings about Reading.

Ask sts to *Show me with your fingers approximately how much you understood* (1 finger = 10%, 5 = 50%, 10 = 100%) so you get some immediate, visible feedback, and give them a chance to express their feelings. If they are at all negative, tell them not to worry, the rest of the lesson will clarify and help them a lot.

Peercheck the words they have checked 1–4. Classcheck. Ask sts to compare the author's views with their answers to **A**. Ask sts: *How long had the German woman been living in the U.S.? What two advantages of living in the U.S. did she give?* (more opportunities for work, easy to meet new people through informal groups based on hobbies or interests, for example).

Answers
Check 1 and 3

10.3

C Have sts re-read the article and find the relevant words and phrases. Peercheck.

> **Answers**
>
> German friendships: "You're an acquaintance. We go out for coffee together and chat about things. That's not friendship." / Germans tend to be direct. / Old World / everyone knows everyone / personal relationships develop gradually / Trusting someone as a friend … a much greater commitment than friendship here / more intense commitment involved in friendship lingers on
>
> American friendships: superficial / "no deep friendships," "people form and dissolve relationships too easily," "you don't know if you can really trust people" / Direct speech can seem inconsiderate to Americans / Our history … breaking the ties of family and friendship, and then forming new ones / American individualism … more emphasis to our own needs in forming and dissolving relationships / people who don't know one another can form groups to satisfy common needs / numerous informal groups – around hobbies, interests, work, self-improvement, religion, and so forth – that make it possible to meet new people

D Sts do the activity individually, then check answers with a partner. Classcheck.

Stronger classes: Ask sts to find five other words which are new to them in the article. Ask them to look up the words in a dictionary, and write definitions or synonyms for the words, as in 1–4, along with the number of the paragraph where the word can be found. Ask them to exchange their definitions with a classmate, then try to guess their classmates' words.

> **Answers**
>
> 1 tantamount to   2 beat around the bush   3 agreeable
> 4 lingers

Optional activity

Ask sts to write an example sentence for each of the phrases 1–4. Monitor and help where necessary.

E Make it personal Put sts in groups of three to discuss the questions.

Before sts begin, quickly review the differences between Germany and the United States.

When sts have exhausted their ideas, invite them to report back to the rest of the class on their discussion. Open out to a class discussion.

Optional activity

Put sts in pairs and ask them to come up with a list of tips for making friends in their country. When they have finished, put pairs together in small groups to share their ideas.

6 Vocabulary: Words with both prefixes and suffixes

A Go through **Double affixation** together with the class and check everyone understands. Ask sts to do the activity, then check answers in pairs.

> **Answers**
>
> 1 dis / courage / ing (the *e* is dropped)   2 in / effect / ive
> 3 inter / depend / ence   4 un / rely / able (*y* changes to *i*)
> 5 counter / product / ive   6 mis / understand / ing
> 7 im / polite / ly

B ▶ 10.10 Tell sts to look at the three columns. Check meanings of the root words. Have them add prefixes and suffixes to the root words to form new words.

Tell them they are going to listen to two conversations, in which these new words are mentioned. Pre-teach or elicit meaning of *an only child* (child with no siblings). Ask them to listen and check.

> **Answers**
>
> 1 immaturity   2 distasteful   3 unacceptable
> 4 irresistible   5 illogical   6 inexpensive

» See Teacher's Book p.333 for Audio script 10.10.

C ▶ 10.10 Elicit the stereotypes referred to in the conversations ("Only children are often spoiled" and "Old people don't keep up with technology").

Ask: *What do you hear in the conversations which disproves the stereotypes?* (In conversation 1, one of the speakers is an "only child" as well as her husband, and neither of them is spoiled (according to the speaker). In conversation 2, one of the speakers is 80, and streams albums, uses Netflix, and has an iPhone.)

» Song lyric: See Teacher's Book p.352 for notes about the song and an accompanying activity to do with the class.

> **Answers**
>
> "Only children" are often spoiled.
> Old people don't keep up with technology.

D Make it personal Ask: *Do you have any experience of your age group or the place where you live being stereotyped? Why can this be a problem? Which groups of people do we tend to stereotype?* (e.g. teenagers, women drivers).

Have sts complete 1–5 with their own ideas. Then put them in groups to compare.

Class feedback. Ask: *Which are the most common stereotypes?* Encourage sts to disprove them with their own experiences. Focus on the speech bubble as an example.

» Workbook p.50.

♪ You won't ever find him being unfaithful. You will find him, You'll find him next to me

10.3

C Re-read the article. Circle words or phrases that show the woman's views on friendship in Germany. Underline those for the United States.

D Scan the article and find …
1. an expression that means "equivalent to": _____ (paragraph 3)
2. an idiom that means the *opposite* of "get straight to the point": _____ (paragraph 4)
3. an adjective that means "pleasant": _____ (paragraph 4)
4. a verb that means "remains, but is gradually disappearing": _____ (paragraph 8)

E Make it personal Friendships across cultures. In groups, discuss 1–2.
1. When it comes to making friends, is your country more like Germany or the United States?
2. Do you have any friends from other cultures? To what extent have they challenged your views on …?

- the relative importance of family
- socializing and dating
- gender roles
- money

> Here in [name of country], we would never tell anyone "You're not my friend." I think we're more like the U.S.

6 Vocabulary: Words with both prefixes and suffixes

A Read *Double affixation*. Then write the root words (1–7) as they are spelled in isolation. Were any letters dropped or changed?

> **Double affixation**
>
> Many adjectives, nouns, and adverbs are made up of a prefix, a root word, and a suffix:
> In Germany, an insistence on the right credentials is often **insurmountable**.
> Here, *in-* means "not," *surmount* means "overcome," and *-able* means "that can be."
> " So, *insurmountable* means "that can't be overcome." Remember: spelling sometimes changes, too.
> I was shocked by their **unfriendliness**. (un + friendly + ness)

1. discouraging 3. interdependence 5. counterproductive 7. impolitely
2. ineffective   4. unreliable   6. misunderstanding

B ▶ 10.10 Match the three columns to find six words. Then write the full words with the correct spelling. Listen to two conversations about stereotypes to check.

Prefix		Root word		Suffix	
dis	in	1 mature	4 resist	able	ible
il	ir	2 taste	5 logic	al	ive
im	un	3 accept	6 expense	ful	ity

C ▶ 10.10 Listen again. Summarize each stereotype in one sentence. Any truth to them?

D Make it personal Complete 1–5 with popular stereotypes where you live. In groups, compare your ideas. Which ones are most common?

1. _____ are bad drivers.
2. _____ can be a bit rude.
3. _____ tend to be lazy.
4. _____ is a dangerous place.
5. _____ (You choose!)

> Here in [name of city], [neighborhood] is really dangerous.

> That's just a stereotype! I live there, and I've never had any problems.

10.4 Have you ever met someone new by chance?

7 Language in use

A ▶ 10.11 Listen to the start of a radio show. Choose the correct answer.

> "Six Degrees of Separation" means we're [further away / closer] to people than we think.

B ▶ 10.12 Look at the pictures on the right and read the conversation excerpts. Listen to the next part. Check (✔) the callers that believe the "Six Degrees of Separation" theory.

C ▶ 10.12 Listen again and note down key details. In pairs, summarize each story.

> So in the first one, this guy was in a bad mood and went out to eat …

D ▶ 10.13 Read *Expressions with odds*. Then listen and match excerpts 1–5 with the correct pattern (a–e). Continue listening to check.

> **Expressions with *odds***
>
> The word *odds*, meaning "chances" is very common in English and takes various patterns.
> The odds **of** see**ing** him were **50 to 1**.
> What are **the odds that** I could get that job?

a ☐ the odds of [object] [verb]-*ing* …
b ☐ the odds of [verb]-ing …
c ☐ The odds are against you …
d ☐ the odds that …
e ☐ the odds are [number] to [number] that …

E **Make it personal** In groups, use only the pictures from **B** and your notes from **C**, to decide which story is most surprising. Do you know of any similar experiences? Use expressions with *odds*.

> Number 5 is the most surprising. What are the odds of falling in love with a place that quickly?

> I think it's possible if you were looking to make a change in your life.

1 Had Sarah not come by with Tom, I wouldn't be married to her now! ☐

2 Should you need anything at all while Beth is away, just come by. You know I don't mind. ☐

3 Were I to have dialed a different phone number, my whole life would have been different! ☐

4 Had I called even a minute later, I might not have arrived in time. Eric saved my life! ☐

5 Were we to spend even one more day here, I'd never be able to leave. This is the most beautiful view I've ever seen. ☐

Have you ever met someone new by chance? 10.4

Lesson Aims: Sts learn to make inverted conditional sentences and learn expressions with *odds* to discuss chance meetings.

Skills	Language	Vocabulary	Grammar
Listening to a radio show about the theory Six Degrees of Separation Discussing sts' own experiences of "missed connections"	Talking about missed opportunities, e.g. *Had I seen her a second sooner, I could have spoken to her. Had I apologized, we would still be friends now.*	Expressions with *odds*, e.g. *What are the odds of …?, The odds are against you, The odds are very low, The odds are 100 to 1 that you will …*	Inverted conditional sentences, e.g. *Were I to have gone home, we never would have met.*

Warm-up

Books closed. Scramble and board the lesson title question: *chance met ever someone you new have by?* for sts to order. When they tell you the correct order, answer the question and tell them, e.g. how you met your partner. Then tell them to answer it in pairs. Board *How did you meet your partner / best friend / roommate?* Have sts share any interesting stories. Ask: *Do you believe in fate?*

7 Language in use

A ▶ 10.11 Board the following saying: *It's a small world.* Ask sts if they know what it means. (We say this when a coincidence happens resulting from people knowing each other or meeting each other unexpectedly.)

Ask: *Have you heard of Six Degrees of Separation?* Focus on the meaning in the box. Ask sts which they think is correct. Tell sts they are going to hear a radio show guest talking about the theory. Have them listen and choose the correct answer.

Classcheck. Ask: *When did the theory develop?* (1929) *What does the radio presenter think might have made the theory even truer today?* (the Internet). Ask sts to try and explain the theory in their own words.

> **Answers**
> closer

▶▶ See Teacher's Book p.333 for Audio script 10.11.

B ▶ 10.12 Focus on the pictures, and read the excerpts with the class. Ask sts if they can guess what the anecdotes are about.

Tell sts they will hear the people in the pictures calling in to the radio to tell anecdotes about meeting people or things happening by chance. Have them listen and check which of the callers believes in the Six Degrees of Separation theory.

Check answers. Ask: *Which of the stories did you enjoy the most? Who was easiest / hardest to understand? Have you ever called in to a radio show?*

> **Answers**
> Check 1, 4, and 5

▶▶ See Teacher's Book p.333 for Audio script 10.12.

C ▶ 10.12 Tell sts to listen again and note down the key details. Have them think about: when, where, and why it happened; what actually happened; and who was involved.

Sts retell the stories in pairs. They can jointly tell each story or take turns telling one, while their partner listens and prompts them when they need help. Invite one or two sts to re-tell one of the stories to the class. Ask: *Which ones do you think support the theory of separation? Which do you think were bound to happen anyway?*

Optional activity

Ask sts to think of a time they met someone they already knew in an unexpected place (e.g. a neighbor on vacation). Give them a few minutes to think of the details, then put them in groups to share their experiences.

D ▶ 10.13 Go through **Expressions with** odds together with the class. Have sts look through expressions a–e. Ask them if they remember how these were used in the audio in **C**. Play the audio for them to listen and match.

Classcheck. Elicit the actual sentences with *odds* used in each excerpt and board them, e.g. *The odds are 100 to 1 that you'll meet your wife when you're in such a foul mood.* Tell sts that we often use the word "slim" with expressions with odds, e.g. *The odds of … ing were very slim.*

You could also teach the expression *Against (all) the odds …*, e.g. *Against (all) the odds, our team won the championship last week.*

> **Answers**
> a 5   b 3   c 4   d 2   e 1

▶▶ See Teacher's Book p.334 for Audio script 10.13.

E Make it personal Ask sts to think about each story and say what aspect of it is most surprising, e.g. *in story 1, the odds of you wanting to chat to anyone when you are in a bad mood are very low.*

Have them agree on which is the most surprising story overall, and share any similar experiences they might have had. Class feedback. Ask: *Do you believe in the theory of Six Degrees of Separation?*

10.4

> Song lyric: See Teacher's Book p.352 for notes about the song and an accompanying activity to do with the class.

8 Grammar: Inverted conditional sentences

A Cover the grammar box, look only at the title and see if sts can either remember any examples, and / or produce new ones of their own, as in the song line above.

Go through the examples in the grammar box with the class. Check sts understand the meanings. Ask them how they would say them in their language.

Uncover the grammar box and talk sts through the examples. Say them formally so they get the idea that this is educated, relatively formal English. Check sts understand both the meanings and nuances. Ask them if they invert for emphasis / to be more formal in a similar way in their language. Refer sts to the **Common mistake** to exemplify the rule about *Had not* being contracted and elicit another negative example, e.g. something fun like *Had I not done my homework, you would have shouted at me!*

Draw sts' attention to the use of the comma after the first clause. Ask them to choose the correct meanings a or b. Peercheck. Classcheck.

> **Answers**
> 1 a 2 b 3 a 4 a 5 b

Stronger classes: Ask sts to turn the examples in the grammar box into questions, e.g. *Were you to apologize, could you resume your friendship with Richard?* This will be useful practice for D, where they might need to use the question form.

Refer sts to the **Common mistake**.

>> Refer sts to the Grammar expansion on p.156.

Optional activity

For further practice, ask sts to cover the right-hand column in the table and complete the sentences in a different way. Monitor and help where necessary. When they are ready, sts read out their endings in random order in pairs, and their partner listens and guesses the correct beginning.

B Focus on the pictures and excerpts in 7B again. Have sts underline the inverted conditional clauses. Class check.

Weaker classes: To check sts have really grasped the grammar point, ask them to rephrase the sentences using an *If* clause, e.g. *If Sarah hadn't come by with Tom, I wouldn't be married to her now!*

> **Answers**
> 1 Had Sarah not come by with Tom …
> 2 Should you need anything at all while Beth is away …
> 3 Were I to have dialed a different phone number (Had I dialed …)
> 4 Had I called even a minute later …
> 5 Were we to spend even one more day here …

C Cover the page and board the forum title, *remember-dot-me-dot-com*. Ask sts to say it correctly and guess what it might be. Then give a clue that it's a forum based on the exact opposite of Six Degrees of Separation to see if they can express it.

Uncover the forum and have sts read the entries in pairs and, for fun, imagine the context, people, their age, and what happens next. Enjoy their ideas!

Ask: *Do these remind you of any similar situations you or any friends of yours have been in?*

Peercheck. Classcheck. Tell sts to take care to use *Were* with I, e.g. *Were I ever to see you again*, not ~~Was I ever to see you again~~ …

> **Answers**
> 1 Had we talked just a moment longer,
> 2 Should you want to get in touch at any time,
> 3 Had you not gotten a phone call,
> 4 Were I ever to see you again,
> 5 Had she tried, I said to myself,
> 6 Were you to take the same train again at 3:30 pm,

D Make it personal Brainstorm a few examples of "missed connections," e.g. arriving at a party just after someone had left, losing someone's contact details. If sts have not had any experiences of their own, they can research stories on the Internet by googling "missed connections" for ideas.

Put sts in groups. First have them share their stories giving details of when / where / why / what and who. Focus on the speech bubble as an example.

Then have sts ask and answer questions 2–4. Class feedback. Ask: *Which story did you most enjoy listening to?*

>> Workbook p.51.

🎵 I lost a friend, Somewhere along in the bitterness. And I would have stayed up with you all night, Had I known how to save a life

8 Grammar: Inverted conditional sentences

A Read the grammar box and choose the correct meaning below (a or b) for 1–5.

Inverted conditional sentences for present, past, or future time		
Were	we to apologize[1],	we could resume our friendship with Richard.
	I to have gone[2] home,	we never would have met.
Should	you wish to come[3] today,	just give us a call.
Had	he contacted[4] me on Facebook,	we could have seen each other.
	she not gone[5] to the party,	we wouldn't be married today.
Inverted conditional clauses can be used instead of *if*-clauses and sometimes add emphasis. They tend to be slightly more formal. *Had* is not contracted, and past sentences like *Were I to have gone …* mean the same as *Had I gone …*		

» Grammar expansion p.156

1 a ☐ If we apologized b ☐ If we had apologized
2 a ☐ If I went home b ☐ If I'd gone home
3 a ☐ If you want to come today b ☐ If you came today
4 a ☐ If he'd contacted me on Facebook b ☐ If he contacted me on Facebook
5 a ☐ If she'd gone to the party b ☐ If she hadn't gone to the party

Common mistake
Had you not
~~Hadn't you~~ called, I would have worried.

B Underline the five inverted conditional sentences in **7B**. Which sentence(s) with a form of *be* can be reworded with a form of *have*?

C Rephrase the underlined clauses 1–6 in the forum entries. Use inverted conditional sentences and a form of the verbs in parentheses.

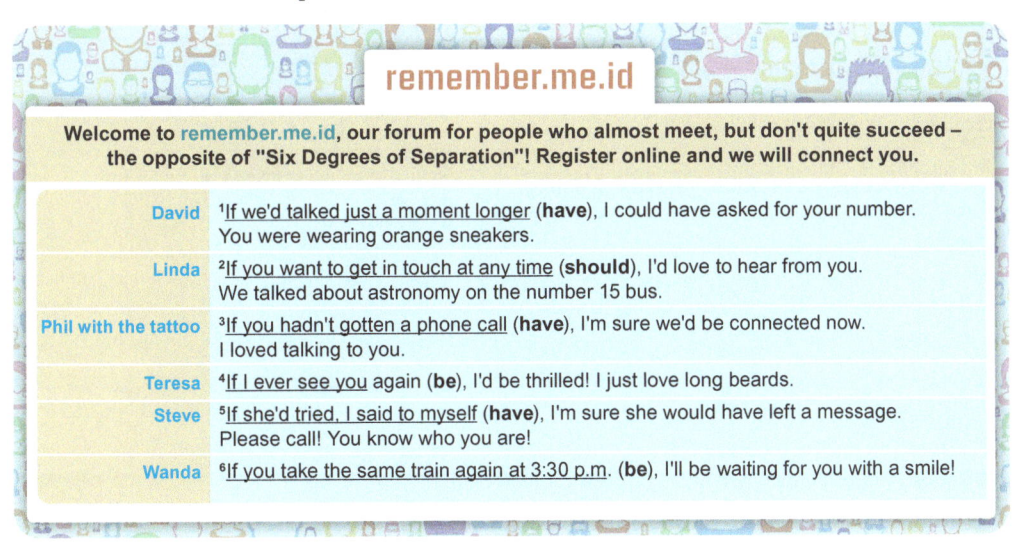

remember.me.id

Welcome to **remember.me.id**, our forum for people who almost meet, but don't quite succeed – the opposite of "Six Degrees of Separation"! Register online and we will connect you.

David [1]<u>If we'd talked just a moment longer</u> (**have**), I could have asked for your number. You were wearing orange sneakers.

Linda [2]<u>If you want to get in touch at any time</u> (**should**), I'd love to hear from you. We talked about astronomy on the number 15 bus.

Phil with the tattoo [3]<u>If you hadn't gotten a phone call</u> (**have**), I'm sure we'd be connected now. I loved talking to you.

Teresa [4]<u>If I ever see you</u> again (**be**), I'd be thrilled! I just love long beards.

Steve [5]<u>If she'd tried, I said to myself</u> (**have**), I'm sure she would have left a message. Please call! You know who you are!

Wanda [6]<u>If you take the same train again at 3:30 p.m.</u> (**be**), I'll be waiting for you with a smile!

D **Make it personal** Have you ever had an important "missed connection"? In groups, share a true or invented story. Whose is most surprising?

1 When / Where / Why / What / Who? Note down a few details.
2 What would have happened had you been able to connect?
3 If you could go back in time, what would you have done differently?
4 Were you to meet this person again, what would you do?

> When I was on the train last week, I saw an old girlfriend out of the corner of my eye. Had I reacted even one second sooner, I could have spoken to her!

111

>> 10.5 How persuasive are you?

9 Listening

A In pairs, imagine you want to persuade a slightly antisocial friend to come to a party you're giving. What strategies would you use?

> I might say, "I've only invited people you know."

B 🔊 ▶ 10.14 Listen to / watch the first part of a video on persuasion (0:00–3:05). What do the party invitation and restaurant tipping have in common?

C 🔊 ▶ 10.14 Listen / Watch the first part again. Which statements do the speakers believe? Write Y (yes) or N (no). Correct the wrong ones.

1 Integrity is important when trying to persuade others.
2 Social plans don't involve obligation.
3 It's not only the size of a gift that counts, but also how the recipient feels.
4 Pleasant surprises make a strong impression.
5 It's usually not noticed when gifts are personalized.

D **Make it personal** In pairs, which statements in C do you agree with? Support your opinion with a personal story.

> I definitely agree with number 1. I'll never forget the time that ...

E 🔊 ▶ 10.15 Listen to / watch the "persuasion of liking" from 7:40 to 9:05. How did liking potato chips help the business students persuade others?

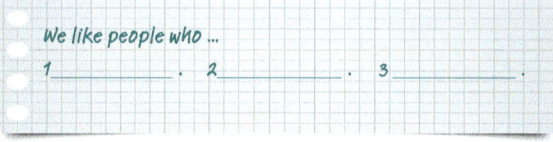

F 🔊 ▶ 10.15 In pairs, can you recall why we like people? Complete the notes. Then listen to / watch the second part again to check.

> We like people who ...
> 1_____ . 2_____ . 3_____ .

10 Keep talking

A Choose two questions and note down at least three points for each.

1 How can we persuade our parents, teachers, or boss to give us more independence?
2 Why is it difficult, but important, to sometimes say "no," even to those we like?
3 How have you been influenced by friends / family? Did they use strategies from 9E?

B Share opinions in groups, using these expressions. Any interesting stories or ideas?

> They're far more likely to ... if ...   They persuaded me to ...
> I'm nowhere near as ... by ... as ...   The more they ... , the more I ...

> I got to know my friend Victoria when she cooperated with me on a project. The closer I got to her, the more she influenced me ...

How persuasive are you? 10.5

Lesson Aims: Sts watch a video about the art of persuasion, and write a persuasive essay.

Skills	Language	Vocabulary
Watching a video about the art of persuasion Writing a persuasive essay	Sharing opinions: *They're far more likely to ... if ...*, *They persuaded me to ...*, *I'm nowhere near as ... by ... as*, *The more they ..., the more I ...*	Phrases for structuring an essay: *after all, therefore, however, at this point, as we all know, nevertheless, finally, by now, moreover*

Warm-up

Ask the lesson title question: *How persuasive are you? Are you easily persuadable? Which of your family members / friends are easy / difficult to persuade? Do / Did you have strategies for persuading your parents to agree to things? Has anyone ever persuaded you to do something really silly?*

9 Listening

A Read them through rubric and put sts in pairs to brainstorm answers. Use the speech bubble as an example. Classcheck. You could have them act out a role play, with St A acting out the part of the party host, trying to persuade St B, the reluctant guest, to come to the party.

B 🔊 ▶10.14 Focus on the pictures. Ask: *How could these be related to a talk on persuasion?* Play the first section of the video. Classcheck. Ask: *Do you tend to tip more if you are offered a gift in a restaurant?*

> **Answers**
> They both have an obligation to give when you receive, e.g. a return invite, or a tip to the waiter in exchange for a mint.

» See Teacher's Book p.335 for Video script 10.14.

C 🔊 ▶10.14 Ask sts to read the statements, and say whether they think they are true or false. Play the audio for them to check. Peercheck. Classcheck.

To recap on what they have heard and check comprehension, ask: *Do people generally consider all the information available to them when making decisions?* (No). *Why is this?* (because we are overloaded with information and we need shortcuts) Ask: *What six shortcuts have the researchers identified which help guide our decision making?* (reciprocity, scarcity, authority, consistency, liking, and consensus).

> **Answers**
> 1 Y 2 N (Social plans do involve obligation) 3 Y 4 Y
> 5 N (It is noticed when gifts are personalized)

D **Make it personal** Give sts preparation time to think of ideas and personal experiences before the discussion. Put sts in pairs to discuss the statements in C.

E 🔊 ▶10.15 Say: *Remember the six shortcuts that guide human behavior and help us to persuade people to do things are: reciprocity, scarcity, authority, consistency, liking, and consensus.* Tell sts that they are going to watch part of the video in which they talk about liking. Read the question in the Student's Book, *How did liking potato chips help the business students persuade others?* Ask sts to guess the answer, then have them watch the video to check. Classcheck.

> **Answer**
> It helped them to find a similarity between them before they started negotiating, and it helped to secure a much higher percentage of agreements.

» See Teacher's Book p.335 for Video script 10.15.

F ▶10.15 Put sts in pairs, and have them complete the notes. Then re-play the video for them to check. Classcheck.

Class feedback. Ask sts if they think they are persuaded by the six shortcuts. Ask: *Which do you think has the biggest effect on our decisions?*

> **Answers**
> 1 are similar to us 2 pay us compliments
> 3 cooperate with us

10 Keep talking

A Go through the questions with the class. Ask sts to make notes for two of the questions.

B Before you put sts in groups, elicit example sentences using the expressions in the box, e.g. *They're far more likely to agree to give me more time off if I work hard and help my colleagues.*

Stronger classes: Ask sts to act out a role play. St A is the boss, and St B the employee. St B needs to take a day off work to go to a wedding. St B needs to persuade his / her boss to let them have the day off.

Class feedback. Ask sts to share any interesting stories with the rest of the class. Ask: *Do you think the strategies you heard about in the video are helpful?*

233

10.5

11 Writing: A persuasive essay

A Ask: *When was the last time you read (a book / article / blog / piece) or watched (a movie / show / video) that persuaded you to change your lifestyle / beliefs? Why did it work?* (convincing, well-written / produced / realistic / hadn't really thought about it before, etc.)

Tip

For fun, focus on the word "essay." Ask: *What's the first thing that comes into your head? How do / did your teachers at school persuade you to write them?* (threats of punishment or failure) *Does/Did it work?* (Well, yes, …) *So, what do you think I, your teacher, am going to do if you don't do this assignment!?*

Read them through the rubric. Sts read the first paragraph and underline the topic sentence. Focus on the question at the end of the paragraph, and have sts try to answer it before they read on. Classcheck.

> **Answers**
> Research on the science of persuasion shows that we like people who are similar to us, pay us compliments, and cooperate with us.

B Sts read the rest of the essay and find the sentences which state the subtopics.

Tip

Have them read in pairs and pause at the end of each paragraph and do a different task. After paragraph ….

2: they can answer the question,
3: they can try to summarize together what they understood from what they just read,
4: they can say and compare how similar they are to their own parents,
5: they can share what they admire about their own parents, and
6: they can tell each other how they feel after reading it all!

Send them back again to look for the sentences, as they will have forgotten the task by now, but no matter!

Classcheck.

> **Answers**
> Para 4: Nothing pleases parents more than to think that they and their children are alike.
> Para 5: Next come praise and admiration.
> Para 6: _____, people who lend a helping hand seem reasonable and thoughtful.

C Read through **Write it right!** with the class. Check meanings of the phrases in the box, then ask sts to write the strategy number 1, 2, or 3 next to them. Elicit other similar words sts may know in each category, e.g. *consequently, even so, in the end, ultimately, furthermore, besides*. Have sts re-read the essay and complete the blanks 1–9 with an appropriate phrase. Peercheck. Classcheck.

> **Answers**
> Strategy 1: After all, As we all know
> Strategy 2: Therefore, However, Nevertheless, Moreover
> Strategy 3: At this point, Finally, By now
> Possible answers: 1 However / Nevertheless   2 As we all know   3 After all   5 Moreover   5 Therefore   6 Nevertheless / However   7 Finally   8 At this point   9 By now

Optional activity

Ask sts to write the numbers 1, 2, and 3 on separate sheets of paper. Go through the information in the box with sts, then ask them to close their books. Call out the expressions in the box randomly, one at a time. Ask sts to hold up the piece of paper with the number of the correct strategy. When you have finished, sts do **C** as in the book.

D Have sts read the pairs of sentences. Ask them to rewrite them, using the words in parentheses. Tell them that 1, 2, and 4 can be rewritten as a single sentence.

Peercheck. Classcheck.

> **Answers**
> 1 As we all know, people love personal attention, so tips may be bigger if you give it.
> 2 I find it hard to say no, which undoubtedly is not such a good quality.
> 3 Undoubtedly, friends understand us better than family. Moreover, they tend to be more objective.
> 4 Since my friends have persuaded me to be a little calmer, at this point you'd never know I was once a nervous wreck.

E Your turn! Read through the instructions with the class and check that sts understand what they have to do. Be sure they are all happy with a topic, and let them choose another appropriate one of their own if they wish to. Make sure they follow the *Before, While,* and *After* steps. Monitor and help, as necessary.

Sts could do this for homework, but have them plan the essay in class first so you can give them feedback. Assign each st a partner to email their essay to for peer correction.

Weaker classes: You could put sts in pairs and have them choose one of the topics in **10B** together. Then they can brainstorm ideas together and plan their paragraphs together before writing them up individually.

» Song lyric: See Teacher's Book p.353 for notes about the song and an accompanying activity to do with the class.

» Workbook p.52.

♪ Just say yes, just say there's nothing holding you back. It's not a test, nor a trick of the mind, Only love

11 Writing: A persuasive essay

A A persuasive opinion essay has a clear topic sentence, which may state subtopics to be developed in separate paragraphs. Read paragraph 1. What is the topic sentence?

B Read the rest. Then find three sentences in paragraphs 4, 5, and 6 that state each subtopic.

C Read *Write it right!* and write the strategy number (1, 2, or 3) next to the words in the box. Then complete 1–9 in the essay with an appropriate item.

Write it right!
A good persuasive essay appeals to the reader's feelings, and logically builds a persuasive argument. To do so, the writer uses several strategies.
1. Words and expressions that appeal to the reader's common sense, e.g. *undoubtedly*.
2. Conjunctions to link ideas, e.g. *as a result*.
3. Time markers to build the argument toward a conclusion, e.g. *next*.

- [ ] After all
- [ ] At this point
- [ ] Finally
- [ ] Therefore
- [ ] As we all know
- [ ] By now
- [ ] However
- [ ] Nevertheless
- [ ] Moreover

D Connect the pairs of sentences logically, using the words or expressions in parentheses.
1. People love personal attention. Tips may be bigger if you give it. (as we all know, so)
2. I find it hard to say no. That's not such a good quality. (which, undoubtedly)
3. Friends understand us better than family. They tend to be more objective. (undoubtedly, and moreover)
4. My friends have persuaded me to be a little calmer. You'd never know I was once a nervous wreck. (since, at this point)

E Your turn! Choose a topic that you discussed in **10B** and write a persuasive essay in 280 words.

Before
Using your notes from **10A**, plan four to five paragraphs.

While
Write your essay, following the model in **A**. Include a clear thesis statement, and start a new paragraph for each sub-theme. Use strategies from *Write it right!* to build your argument.

After
Post your essay online and read your classmates' work. Whose is most convincing?

The psychology of persuasion

1 Persuasion involves just a little basic psychology, and this is true whether your target is a parent, a teacher, or even your boss. Research on the science of persuasion shows that we like people who are similar to us, pay us compliments, and cooperate with us. As a result, we are more likely to do what they request. How then can we apply this science in our everyday lives?

2 Let's look at an example, one we've all identified with at some point: How can we persuade our parents to give us more independence? Does this challenge have anything to do with being liked?

3 Undoubtedly, your first reaction will be "no." You may point out that your parents don't "like" you, they "love" you, and, not only that, their "love" is permanent. ¹_____, to agree to your request, they do need to "like" you at the moment you make it. ²_____, it is possible to "love" someone and not "like" the person at every given moment. So let's look at the research step by step.

4 Nothing pleases parents more than to think that they and their children are alike. ³_____, not only have they invested a lot of time and energy in your upbringing, but you are likely to be here when they're gone – their legacy on earth, so to speak. In the case of children, if they are just like their parents, this also implies shared values, and shared values imply trust. ⁴_____, if you think like your parents, you are less likely to make decisions they would be against. Let's take a case in point: You'd like to borrow the family car for a long weekend. What similarities between you and your parents come to mind? Most people will think being cautious is a character trait to emphasize. ⁵_____, you might start by saying, "You know how careful I am, Mom (or Dad). I'm just like you."

5 Next come praise and admiration. You may be opposed in principle to excessive praise and feel pouring it on is "false" or "manipulative." ⁶_____, is that necessarily so? What if the feeling is real? You might say, "I've always admired you, Dad (or Mom) for thinking things over so carefully. It shows you're open to considering all sides of an argument." Don't be surprised if your parent then announces that he or she admires this about you, too! Good feeling is being created all around, and you're well on your way to dissuading your Dad (or Mom) from saying "no."

6 ⁷_____, people who lend a helping hand seem reasonable and thoughtful. Your parents are more likely to be persuaded if you appear to have these traits. Here you might start by saying, "I know you get up really early on Mondays and don't want to spend Sunday evening worrying. So I promise I'll have the car back no later than 6:00 p.m." ⁸_____, all three principles of persuasion are in place, and the odds are clearly in your favor. ⁹_____, you're nearly guaranteed a "yes" answer!

Review 5
Units 9–10

1 Listening

A ▶ R5.1 Listen to a professor discussing traditional and innovative learning. Check (✔) the statements that can be inferred. The professor probably feels …

1. ☐ traditional techniques can be made to be innovative.
2. ☐ good lectures require very knowledgeable speakers.
3. ☐ it's easier to take notes than to participate in class.
4. ☐ a lecture is more innovative if it incorporates video.
5. ☐ the virtues of lectures need to be promoted more.

B **Make it personal** In pairs, discuss which statements in A you agree with.

> There might be some truth to number 3.

> Yes, note-taking discourages us from participating actively.

2 Reading

A Read the article. Underline at least one sentence in each section where the writer could have been talking about children.

▶ HOW TO SET GOOD LIMITS WITH FRIENDS

Setting limits with friends may be difficult, but just as you would with your children, the sooner you establish them, the better. A number of years back, we befriended a new couple in the neighborhood, who made it a habit to pay us a surprise visit every Saturday night. Had they not arrived with a delicious cake each time, we might have caught on sooner that they had an issue with boundaries. Here are a few pieces of advice based on this experience. They may not be innovative, but are known to work!

1 Be direct. If you're not clear, the other person may have trouble grasping what it is you're trying to communicate. Once you've planned what to say, go through with it, even if your message is that you find someone's behavior unacceptable.

2 Avoid guilt and self-doubt. Don't let a fictitious belief that "others come first" sabotage your legitimate need to act. Trust your instincts, which will outweigh any second thoughts you may have.

3 Do not backpedal. Despite the fact that you may have an overriding desire to please, don't allow yourself to be persuaded by your friends' point of view. In the end, they will appreciate your having held your ground. Consistency is every bit as important to friends as to children.

B **Make it personal** In pairs, discuss setting boundaries with friends. Is the advice in the article helpful? Use degrees of comparison where possible.

> I've followed point 1. The more honest you are, the closer you and your friends will be.

Review 5 (Units 9–10) R5

Warm-up
See p.61, 105, and 149 of the Teacher's Book for warm-up ideas.

1 Listening

A ▶ R5.1 Books closed. Ask sts: *What comes to mind when we say traditional learning?* Elicit: lectures, teacher at the front of the class, note-taking. *What comes to mind when we say innovative learning?* In pairs, sts brainstorm. Classcheck. Be sure they include: online learning, homeschooling, interactive learning, videos, flipped teaching.

Ask sts to read statements 1–5. Play the audio and ask sts to check the statements which can be inferred. Peercheck and monitor hard to see how many sts managed to get most of it the first time. Play the audio a second time if necessary. Classcheck.

Answers
Check 1, 2, 4, and 5.

» See Teacher's Book p.334 for Audio script R5.1.

B Make it personal Put sts in pairs to discuss the statements in A.

Focus on the example in the speech bubble, and board other language they can use, e.g. *There's no truth in …, I totally agree with …, I'm not sure about …*

Encourage sts to give reasons for their views. Classcheck by asking some sts to share their views with the class. Ask: *Would you prefer to go to lectures or learn by other more innovative methods?*

2 Reading

A Focus on the title of the blog. Ask sts to explain what it means and to think of an example. Ask what "boundaries" they think friends should have. Ask: *Which of the following do you think is crossing "friendship boundaries": gossiping behind your friend's back, being dishonest, stopping in to visit without arranging it beforehand, making daily phone calls?* Ask them to think of others. Ask: *Do you have friends who cross boundaries?*

Ask sts to read the first sentence of the blog. Ask sts what kind of boundaries you would normally set with children. Ask sts to quickly read the blog and underline one sentence in each section which could equally apply to children. Peercheck. Classcheck.

Answers
If you're not clear, the other person may have trouble grasping what it is you're trying to communicate.
Trust your instincts, which will outweigh any second thoughts you may have.
In the end, they will appreciate your having held your ground.

B Make it personal In pairs, sts discuss setting boundaries with friends. Focus on the model in the speech bubble as an example.

Ask: *Do you think it is necessary to set boundaries with friends? Is it more necessary with some friends than others? Do you find it easy? Do you think the advice in the blog is useful? Can you think of any more guidelines?*

Tip

Ask sts to try to think of and add in personal examples from their parents' and even their grandparent's own lives to support their opinions here. How important have close friendships been in their lives? Were there any obvious boundaries, stated or implicit?

R5

3 Grammar

A Ask: *Have you ever tried to lose or gain weight? Were you successful? How did you do it?*

Have sts read the text quickly and find out what three tips the article suggests (adding food like fruit and vegetables to your diet, fast-paced stroll, drinking water). Peercheck, then classcheck.

Refer sts back to the grammar sections on p.97 and p.101, and quickly review the rules, or alternatively have sts try and complete the blanks first, only referring back to the grammar sections if they get stuck.

Sts re-read the article and complete blanks 1–8 with the correct form of the verbs in parentheses.

Peercheck. Classcheck. Ask: *Do you think the tips are useful?*

> **Answers**
> 1 is known, have helped   2 help, appreciate   3 cause, to avoid   4 encourages, to dislike   5 appreciate, giving   6 is believed, be   7 are thought to have lost   8 makes, feel

B Make it personal Put sts in pairs. Have them choose two sentences they find interesting. In pairs, say whether they agree or disagree with them. Invite sts to share their answers with the class. Ask: *Do you mostly agree / disagree with your partner? What other tips do you know for losing weight? Does anybody know any amazing success stories?*

Optional activity

Ask sts to prepare a short presentation on how to lose weight. Give them plenty of time to prepare their advice, and encourage them to use the grammar patterns from Lessons 9.2 and 9.4. When they are ready, sts give the presentations to the class. Other sts listen and choose the best one.

4 Writing

Ask sts to make notes for topics a, b, and c. Tell them to refer them to 2A for ideas for topic a. Brainstorm a few ideas for topics b and c, e.g. Giving honest feedback: give positive as well as negative feedback, when giving negative feedback don't use harsh or hurtful words, speak kindly and quietly, don't give difficult feedback when you are angry or upset with someone.

Asking a parent to respect your privacy: be prepared to compromise, e.g. keep your door open when you are using the computer, so they can walk by and see what you are looking at, but ask them not to log on to your computer without asking you, ask them not to go into your room when you are not there, be honest and open about unimportant stuff that you don't mind them knowing about.

Give sts time to write their advice. When finished, they can exchange with a classmate, and give each other "honest feedback"! If their classmates have good suggestions, give them time to review their writing incorporating their comments. Sts post their final versions online, and read each other's advice. Class feedback. Ask: *Did you read any useful advice? Which of it will you take on board?*

Optional activity

Do this as a speed writing activity. Sts work in pairs, with one st writing and the other feeding in ideas / what to write. Explain that you will give them a very strict time limit of five minutes to write their paragraph and no more. When they start, count down the minutes so it's very clear when their time is up. After the five minutes, explain you will give sts an extra minute to change / correct anything in their paragraphs, but they cannot add anything more. Sts then write a second draft individually with more time to do so.

5 Self-test

Follow the procedure on Teacher's Book p.62.

> **Answers**
> 1 Adele **strengthened** her fan base and **outsold** every other performer.
> 2 In the past, these types of treatments are thought **to have helped** people even if it seems **illogical**.
> 3 My angry reaction to what you said might have to **do** with you **refusing** to listen!
> 4 **Immaturity** often makes **children think only** about themselves.
> 5 I love my work so there's really **no telling why** I'm looking forward to **retiring**.
> 6 **The** more friends you have, **the happier** you'll be.
> 7 Jim **isn't** quite as close to us **as** he used to be.
> 8 My uncle was the **life** of the party – a true breath of **fresh** air!
> 9 **Should you** wish to come, accommodating you isn't **insurmountable**.
> 10 I'm far **more** qualified than my résumé shows, and were you **to** hire me, you wouldn't regret it.

6 Point of view

Follow the procedur en Teacher's Book p.62.

Stronger classes: Hold a class debate on one of the topics. (See teaching procedures on p.106.)

3 Grammar

A Read the advice on how to lose weight. Complete 1–8 with the verbs in parentheses and grammar patterns from Lessons 9.2 and 9.4. Some have more than one answer.

Top three ways to lose weight

1. You might not believe this, but adding foods to your diet ¹*is known* to *have helped* (help, know) people lose weight! Healthy fruits and vegetables make great snacks and ² _____ us _____ (appreciate, help) food even more.

2. Joining a gym may actually ³ _____ us _____ (avoid, cause) exercise, contrary to popular opinion. That's because "working out" sounds like work, so it ⁴ _____ us _____ (dislike, encourage) it. You may ⁵ _____ my _____ (appreciate, give) you the advice to just walk more. A fast-paced stroll ⁶ _____ to _____ (be, believe) boring, but that's rarely true!

3. Many people ⁷ _____ _____ (lose, think) weight just by drinking water. If that sounds odd, it's simply because it ⁸ _____ us _____ (feel, make) less hungry.

B Make it personal Choose two sentences and, in pairs, explain why you agree or disagree.

> I disagree with number 1. Adding foods may be known to have helped people lose weight, but it's so easy to add the wrong foods.

4 Writing

Write your opinion on one of these topics. Follow the model in 2A, and include three pieces of advice.
a Setting limits in relationships b Giving honest feedback c Asking a parent to respect your privacy

5 Self-test

Correct the two mistakes in each sentence. Check your answers in Units 9 and 10. What's your score, 1–20?

1. Adele strengthened her fan base and sold out every other performer.
2. In the past, these types of treatments are thought to help people even if it seems unlogical.
3. My angry reaction to what you said might have to see with you refuse to listen!
4. Unmatureness often makes children to think only about themselves.
5. I love my work so there's really no telling to why I'm looking forward to retire.
6. More friends you have, more happy you'll be.
7. Jim is quite as close to us than he used to be.
8. My uncle was the laughter of the party – a true breath of cool air!
9. You should wish to come, accommodating you isn't unsurmountable.
10. I'm far qualified than my résumé shows, and were you hire me, you wouldn't regret it.

6 Point of view

Choose a topic. Then support your opinion in 100–150 words, and record your answer. Ask a partner for feedback. How can you be more convincing?

a Society should discourage women from raising children alone. OR Society should make single parenting easier.
b Friends naturally drift apart after college. OR With a little effort, college friendships can be lifelong.
c We're never more than six steps away from the perfect person. OR Meeting the perfect person depends largely on effort.

11 What was the last risk you took?

1 Vocabulary: Risk-taking expressions

A ▶11.1 Read the quiz and, using your intuition, complete the highlighted expressions with *safe*, *safety* or *caution*. Listen to two colleagues, Phil and Lisa, to check.

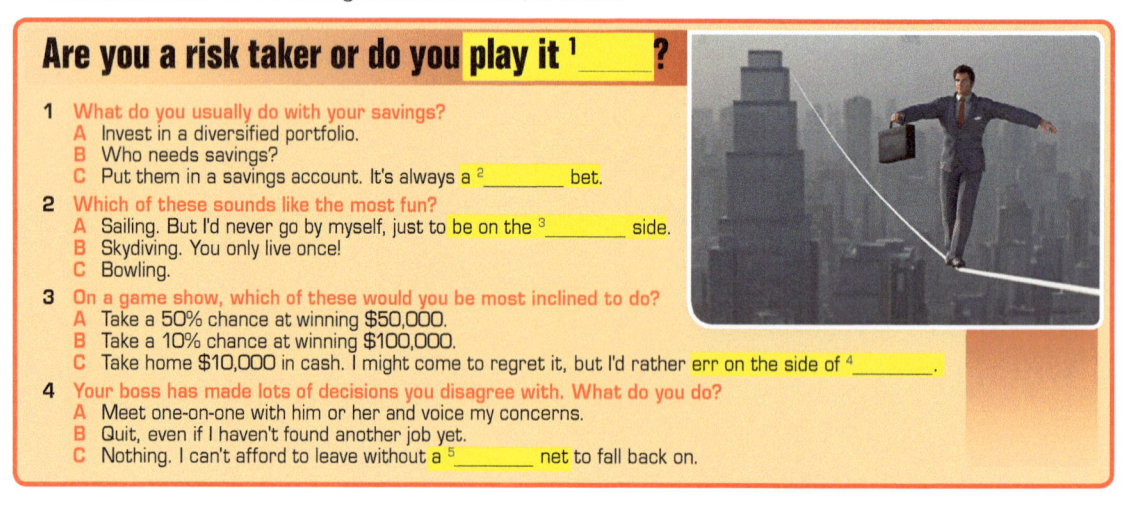

Are you a risk taker or do you play it ¹____?

1 What do you usually do with your savings?
   A Invest in a diversified portfolio.
   B Who needs savings?
   C Put them in a savings account. It's always a ²____ bet.

2 Which of these sounds like the most fun?
   A Sailing. But I'd never go by myself, just to be on the ³____ side.
   B Skydiving. You only live once!
   C Bowling.

3 On a game show, which of these would you be most inclined to do?
   A Take a 50% chance at winning $50,000.
   B Take a 10% chance at winning $100,000.
   C Take home $10,000 in cash. I might come to regret it, but I'd rather err on the side of ⁴____.

4 Your boss has made lots of decisions you disagree with. What do you do?
   A Meet one-on-one with him or her and voice my concerns.
   B Quit, even if I haven't found another job yet.
   C Nothing. I can't afford to leave without a ⁵____ net to fall back on.

B ▶11.2 Take the quiz in pairs. Do you have more A, B, or C answers? Listen to the results. How accurately do they describe you?

> I chose B three times. Well, while it's true I'm sometimes impulsive, I don't make risky decisions!

C ▶11.2 Listen again. Note down four more expressions with *safe*, *safety*, and *caution*. Which expression(s) in A can you replace with them in context?

D Rephrase 1–5 using expressions from A and C. There may be more than one answer. Then make each sentence true for you.

1 When I invite people over, I always end up cooking too much. Well, <u>it's better to do too much than too little</u>.
2 If you want to have good Italian food, try Massimo's. <u>You can't go wrong</u> if you eat there.
3 My friends say I should <u>stop being so careful</u>, quit my job, and have my own business.
4 I always put away 10% of my paycheck every month. That way I'll have <u>some savings for a rainy day</u>.
5 I love going to the gym. But I never work out more than an hour and always <u>take special care</u> to avoid injuring myself.

E Make it personal What makes people more / less prone to risk-taking?

1 Individually, check the two most important factors. Note down a possible reason for each.
2 In groups, share your thoughts. Any major disagreements?

☐ gender ☐ age ☐ upbringing ☐ job ☐ marital status ☐ zodiac sign ☐ ____

> For me, upbringing is most important. If you're taught to err on the side of caution, you'll be that way for life.

> I don't agree. You can learn not to play it safe.

116

What was the last risk you took? 11.1

Lesson Aims: Sts listen to someone trying to persuade a colleague to take a risk and accept a new opportunity abroad.

Skills	Language	Vocabulary
Listening to someone trying to decide whether to take a job abroad Acting out a role-play	Expressing hesitation: *There's just too much at stake, I need to sleep on it.* Expressing encouragement: *What do you have to lose? What's the worst that could happen?*	*a safe bet, be on the safe side, err on the side of caution, a safety net*

Warm-up

Ask sts: *Do you consider yourself to be a risk-taker or are you quite cautious?* Ask the lesson title question: *What was the last risk you took? Did it work out well or badly? Are you glad you took the risk?* Board the following adjectives: *cautious, prudent, adventurous, daring, careful, wary, bold, reckless*. Ask sts to list them in two groups: risk-taker / non risk-taker. Ask them which of the adjectives they would use to describe themselves.

1 Vocabulary: Risk-taking expressions

A ▶ 11.1 Focus on the photo and the title of the quiz. Sts read the quiz and fill in the blanks, as instructed. Tell them they are going to hear two friends, Phil and Lisa taking the quiz. Play the audio and have sts listen out to see if they have completed the blanks correctly.

Peercheck. Classcheck. Elicit the adjective and adverb forms of *caution* (cautious / cautiously).

> **Answers**
> 1 safe 2 safe 3 safe 4 caution 5 safety

▶▶ See Teacher's Book p.335 for Audio script 11.1.

B ▶ 11.2 Have sts read the quiz questions, and check any unknown words. They do the quiz in pairs. Ask: *Which answer did you choose most A, B, or C? Which was the most popular answer in the class?*

Play the audio for them to find out the results. Ask: *How accurately do they describe you?*

Weaker classes: Give sts a copy of the audio script for them to check the results.

Optional activity

Ask sts to work in pairs and write two more questions for the quiz, with corresponding A, B, and C options. Monitor and help, correcting any errors and feeding in language where necessary. When they have finished, combine pairs into small groups and have them ask each other their questions.

▶▶ See Teacher's Book p.335 for Audio script 11.2.

C ▶ 11.2 Re-play the audio and have sts listen out for four expressions with *safe, safety,* and *caution*. Then discuss which expressions in A they can be replaced with. Classcheck.

> **Answers**
> 1 For safety's sake (can replace *to be on the safe side*) 2 throw caution to the wind (can replace *play it safe* – but note that it changes the question to the opposite meaning) 3 exercise caution (can replace *play it safe / err on the side of caution*) 4 better to be safe than sorry (can replace *I'd rather err on the side of caution*)

Weaker classes: Board the expressions from the recording, but jumble up the words in each one. Sts listen and put the words in the correct order before matching them to the expressions in A.

D Ask sts to rephrase 1–5. Do the first one together as an example. When sts have finished, check answers by asking sts to read out their sentences.

Have sts make the sentences true for them. Elicit an example, e.g. *When I invite people over, I never cook enough food.* Put sts in pairs, and have them read out their sentences to each other.

> **Answers**
> 1 it's better to be safe than sorry / it's better to err on the side of caution
> 2 It's (always) a safe bet.
> 3 throw caution to the wind
> 4 a safety net
> 5 exercise caution / err on the side of caution / play it safe

E Make it personal Go through the list of factors, and ask sts to think about which of them are most important in affecting whether you are prone to taking risks.

1 Individually, sts check the two factors they think are most important, and a possible reason for each.
2 Put sts in groups to share their ideas. Invite one or two sts to share their ideas with the class.

Optional activity

Ask sts to also come up with additional factors which might make people prone to caution, including those in their own lives.

▶▶ Song lyric: See Teacher's Book p.353 for notes about the song and an accompanying activity to do with the class.

11.1

2 Listening

A ▶ 11.3 Begin with the photo, asking: *Where / Who are they? What time of day is it? How are they feeling? What's going on?*, etc. Take them through the rubric. Ask: *Has anybody here had a promotion recently?*

Have sts read through the list of concerns Phil has. Ask: *Do you think he is a risk taker?* Play the audio and have sts number the concerns in the order they hear them. Check answers. Ask: *Which is the extra one?* (miss his family). *Why might that not be an issue?* (no kids, etc.) Ask: *Do you think Lisa is more of a risk-taker than Phil? What would you do in Phil's shoes? What would you be most concerned about?*

Weaker classes: Ask sts to listen initially for general comprehension. Board the following questions:
1 What job has Phil been offered? (sales manager)
2 Where is the new job? (Mexico City)
3 Does Phil have a girlfriend? (No)
4 Were his parents risk-takers? (No)

Ask sts to listen to the audio and answer the questions.

> **Answers**
> 1 lack leadership skills
> 2 not be able to overcome the language barrier
> 3 have trouble getting settled in a foreign country
> 4 not be good at the job

» See Teacher's Book p.335 for Audio script 11.3.

B ▶ 11.4 and 11.5 Play audio 11.4 and have sts follow in their books. Ask one or two sts to say the expression *What do you mean?* using one of the intonation patterns. Other sts try and guess which of the two intentions they are trying to convey.

Tell sts they are now going to hear excerpts from audio 11.3 which include the expressions 1–4. Have sts write 1 or 2, depending on the meaning the speaker is trying to convey in each case. After each of the pairs of excerpts, they will hear the correct answers. Classcheck. Then get sts to do the same in pairs, taking turns trying to elicit the different responses from their partner, either as Lisa, or better, as themselves.

> **Answers**
> 1 a1 b2   2 a2 b1   3 a2 b1   4 a1 b2

» See Teacher's Book p.336 for Audio script 11.5.

Tip

Exact rules about intonation can be difficult to pin down, and specific patterns can sometimes be difficult to hear. It's a good idea therefore to give sts lots of opportunities to listen, notice, and try out different ways of saying things for themselves.

C Make it personal

1 ▶ 11.6 **How to say it** Ask sts to read the expressions in the chart. Ask: *Who says 1, 2, and 3?* (Phil) and *Who says 4, 5, and 6?* (Lisa).

Have them try to complete 1–6 from memory. Play the audio for sts to listen and check. Re-play the audio and ask sts to pay attention to the stress and pronunciation. Have them practice in pairs. Ask sts if there are similar expressions in their language, and which of those here they like the best.

> **Answers**
> 1 stake   2 takes   3 sleep   4 lose   5 happen   6 go

Tip

Asking sts which of a set of phrases, or new words in any text they like best, adds an extra level of processing and personalization that usually helps them to remember that little bit better.

Optional activity

After checking answers, test / recycle the language with sts by asking them to close their books. Call out one of the missing words at random and ask sts to tell you the whole expression. Sts can then practice in the same way in pairs.

2 Go through the list of situations. Ask: *Have you ever been in any of these situations?* Put sts in pairs. Have them role play one of the situations, then swap roles. Ensure they use the expressions in 1. Monitor and make a note of common errors for feedback session.

Class feedback. Board any common errors, and ask sts to correct them.

Ask: *Have you ever turned down a good opportunity because you were scared to take a risk?*

» Workbook p.53.

♪ Don't listen to a word I say. Hey! The screams all sound the same. Hey! Though the truth may vary. This ship will carry our bodies safe to shore

2 Listening

A ▶ 11.3 Listen to Phil tell Lisa about the promotion he's been offered. Order his concerns 1–4. There's one extra.

Phil fears he might …
- ☐ not be able to overcome the language barrier.
- ☐ lack leadership skills.
- ☐ not be good at the job.
- ☐ miss his family and friends.
- ☐ have trouble getting settled in a foreign country.

B ▶ 11.4 and 11.5 Read and listen to *Intonation and intentions*. Then listen to four pairs of excerpts. When you hear the beep, choose Lisa's response (a or b). Continue listening to check.

> **Intonation and intentions**
>
> Changes in intonation may convey completely different intentions and / or emotions:
>
> Phil: Blame it on my upbringing.
> Lisa: What do you mean? (= "Tell me more.")
>
> Phil: I'm not sure I have what it takes …
> you know, to be a sales manager.
> Lisa: What do you mean? (= "I disagree.")

1 "So …"   a ☐ Anyway …   b ☐ What's the problem?
2 "Oh, come on!" a ☐ Just say yes, please. b ☐ Don't be silly!
3 "Of course."   a ☐ Without a doubt!   b ☐ Don't worry! You can trust me.
4 "What?"   a ☐ You've got to be kidding! b ☐ Please explain.

C Make it personal Get out of your comfort zone!

1 ▶ 11.6 **How to say it** Complete the chart. Listen to check.

Expressing hesitation and encouragement	
What they said	What they meant
Hesitation	
1 There's just too much at _____.	The risks are too high.
2 I'm not sure I have what it _____.	I might not have the necessary qualities.
3 I need to _____ on it.	I can't make a decision right now.
Encouragement	
4 What do you have to _____?	What could go wrong?
5 What's the worst that could _____?	What's the worst case scenario?
6 Why not just _____ with the flow?	Why not just take things as they come?

2 In pairs, role-play one of the situations below.

A: Choose a situation and note down three things that might go wrong.
B: Offer reassurance and try to get **A** out of his / her comfort zone.

What might you have to lose if you …?

spent all your savings on a great vacation   created your own YouTube channel
told an old friend you had feelings for him/her   started posting political views on Facebook
applied to sing in a reality show   adopted two puppies from a rescue organization

> I'd love to spend a month traveling across Europe, but things are kind of up in the air at work. There's too much at stake.

> Hmm … If you did go, what's the worst that could happen?

117

11.2 Do you enjoy riding a bike?

3 Language in use

A ▶ 11.7 Listen to a program on bike safety. It can be inferred that [**only the instructor has** / **both the instructor and participants have**] thought about safety before.

B ▶ 11.7 Use the pictures to guess the missing words in the safety tips. Then listen again to check.

BICYCLE SAFETY TIPS FROM OUR STAFF AND PARTICIPANTS

1. "You <u>might want to take</u> some basic precautions even when you're buying a new bike. Make sure the _____ of your _____ can support your _____."

2. "I <u>won't ride</u> my first day in a new city. I explore the area on _____ to be sure I won't have any _____ when I'm riding."

3. _____ "The driver <u>could have looked</u> before opening his _____. It was a close call! If drivers are looking at all, it's only for _____. So be careful!"

4. "They all <u>should have mastered</u> the basics in a few days, but one _____ had poor _____. So don't be too hard on yourself."

5. "You <u>might try riding</u> only during the day at first. Then make sure to buy a _____. Your _____ is reduced at _____."

6. "It <u>shouldn't be hard to remember</u> one important rule, though. Always ride _____, and not _____ traffic."

C ▶ 11.8 Listen to an eyewitness account from two points of view. What safety rule did each person violate? Whose behavior is more dangerous?

D ▶ 11.9 Listen to excerpts 1–6 from the conversation. Choose the missing phrase or sentence below for each "beep". Continue listening to check.

- [ ] froze in her tracks
- [ ] My hair stood on end.
- [ ] screeched to a halt
- [ ] I could feel the color draining from my face.
- [ ] screamed at the top of my lungs
- [ ] swerved to avoid hitting me

E **Make it personal** Choose a situation. In pairs, role-play a real or imagined "eyewitness account." Use at least four expressions from D.

speeding bike or motorcycle   distracted pedestrian   child in the road   reckless bus or car driver

> You look shaken. What exactly happened?

> I sure am! You see, I was minding my own business and suddenly, I just froze in my tracks. This motorcycle was coming right at me!

Do you enjoy riding a bike? 11.2

Lesson Aims: Sts listen to eyewitness accounts of a road incident, and role-play giving eyewitness accounts themselves.

Skills	Language	Vocabulary	Grammar
Listening to a cycling instructor giving tips on bike safety, and listening to two eyewitness accounts of a traffic incident Role-playing an eyewitness account of a road incident	Expressing fear, e.g. *I froze in my tracks. I could feel the color draining from my face. I screamed at the top of my lungs.*	speeding, distracted, reckless, pedestrian, swerve, screech to a halt	Special uses of modals: expectation, suggestion, refusal, and annoyance

Warm-up

Begin with an image of a bike and ask sts to label all they can: *frame, handlebars, gears, brakes, chain, saddle, pedals, bell, wheel, puncture, suspension, lock, helmet*, etc. Feedback the words onto the board.

Ask: *Do you have a bicycle? Do you enjoy riding a bike? Where do you ride it? Do you ride it to school / work? Do you wear a helmet? Are there bike lanes in your town? Have you ever had an accident on your bike? Have you ever knocked anyone over on your bike? How do you think they could make cycling safer in your town?*

3 Language in use

A ▶ 11.7 Ask: *Have you ever taken a bicycle safety course? What did you learn?* Tell sts they are going to hear an instructor talking about bicycle safety on a training course. Play the audio. Tell them to listen for gist, and choose the correct option. Classcheck.

> **Answer**
> Both the instructor and participants have thought about safety before

» See Teacher's Book p.336 for Audio script 11.7.

B ▶ 11.7 Cover the texts for sts in pairs to say whatever they can / want to about the pictures. Then get them to try to remember the safety tips. Consider playing the audio once more to help them, but don't let them uncover the texts until they have guessed.

Sts read the texts and try to remember / figure out the missing words. As they do so, they should begin to notice some of the errors they made in pairwork, without you having to tell them. Play the audio for them to check. Peercheck. Classcheck. Show them which part of the foot is the *ball*.

> **Answers**
> 1 Make sure the **ball** of your **foot** can support your **weight**.
> 2 I explore the area on **foot** to be sure I don't have any **distractions** when I'm riding.
> 3 The driver could have looked before opening his **door**. But if drivers are looking at all, it's only for **cars**.
> 4 They should have mastered the basics in a few days, but one **student** had poor **balance**.
> 5 Then make sure to buy a **headlight**. Your **visibility** is reduced at **night**.
> 6 Always ride **with**, and not **against** traffic.

C ▶ 11.8 Explain that sts are going to hear accounts by a pedestrian and a cyclist involved in a road incident. Ask them to listen and find out which safety rule each of them violated. Discuss whose behavior was the most dangerous.

Ask: *Have you ever been knocked over by a cyclist?*

> **Answers**
> The cyclist was cycling against the flow of traffic.
> The woman crossed the road without looking properly / waiting for the lights to change.

» See Teacher's Book p.336 for Audio script 11.8.

D ▶ 11.9 Go through the excerpts with the class and discuss the meanings. Get sts to mime them to demonstrate understanding, and perhaps then test each other in pairs. Ask sts if they remember who said these expressions. Play the audio and have sts choose the missing phrases for each beep. Classcheck.

> **Answers**
> 1 screamed at the top of my lungs (pedestrian)
> 2 swerved to avoid hitting me (pedestrian)
> 3 screeched to a halt (pedestrian)
> 4 froze in her tracks (cyclist)
> 5 I could feel the color draining from my face. (cyclist)
> 6 My hair stood on end. (cyclist)

» See Teacher's Book p.336 for Audio script 11.9.

E Make it personal Ask: *Have you ever had to give an eyewitness account to the police?* If possible, sts use real experiences to base their roleplays on. If not, have them imagine a situation from those listed.

Brainstorm expressions they can use to respond with when playing the role of the listener, e.g. *What exactly happened? Very dangerous, I agree. And then? Can you tell us what happened next? That's not good.*

Monitor around the class while sts are doing their roleplays, and offer help where needed. Choose a couple of pairs to act out their roleplay for the whole class.

Tip

Have sts draw a basic plan of the place where the accident happened and use this to describe it during their roleplay. You could also ask sts to perform their roleplay for the class and ask other sts to listen and draw a plan of what happened.

11.2

4 Grammar: Special uses of modals

A Read through the grammar box together.

Tip

Check comprehension by having sts work in pairs, imagine the context and who's saying them to whom, and then say them to each other with appropriate intonation to express the function in that context, (e.g. optimistically and slightly worried for the two examples of expectation in a). Give a couple of different intonation examples yourself to set this up.

Have them complete the rule. Refer sts back to 3B, and ask them to find the underlined examples, then match them to the uses a–d. Peercheck. Classcheck.

Ask sts to write their own personalized sentences using each of the modals, e.g. I **should** wear a helmet when I'm cycling, but I find them very uncomfortable. It **shouldn't** be difficult to pass my English exams. I just need to work hard.

Answers

1 obligation   2 possibility   3 future
Examples in 3D
1 b   2 c   3 d   4 a   5 b   6 a

Tip

Although they all have special uses, modals also have one thing in common, that they express the speaker's attitude or opinion at the time of speaking. You can demonstrate this to sts by boarding:
1 She's happy.
2 She might be happy.

We can rephrase the second sentence as *I think it's possible she's happy*. In the examples in the box, *should* = I think it's a good idea; *might* = I think it's possible; *won't* = I think it's inevitable; *could* = I think it was possible.

Encourage sts to ask any question they want to about modals. They're one of the most difficult areas of English grammar at any level, and sts only really use them fluently and accurately at very high levels. Allay fears and encourage them to try to use them whenever they can. Through trial and error, practice, and feedback, they will get better.

» Refer sts to the **Grammar expansion** on p.158.

B Focus on the title of the blog, and have sts read the blog entries. They match the modal verbs highlighted in bold (1–8) with functions mentioned in the grammar box.

Sts then make four sentences true for them. Elicit an example from a stronger st, and board it, e.g. *My brother won't wear a helmet, even though he knows it's dangerous.*

In pairs, sts compare their sentences. Classcheck by asking some sts to read them out to the class.

Answers

1 obligation   2 expectation   3 suggestion   4 possibility
5 possibility   6 annoyance   7 future event   8 refusal

» Song lyric: See Teacher's Book p.353 for notes about the song and an accompanying activity to do with the class.

C Focus on the pictures and get sts to cover the captions below. Ask: *What's happening*? Elicit answers.

Ask: *What are they saying?* In pairs have them invent speech bubbles and exchanges / mini dialogues, or even do a quick impromptu roleplay between the people illustrated. Have them share the best ones.

Ask: *Which of the situations in the blog in B do the pictures relate to?* Have sts complete the blanks with modal verbs. Classcheck.

Answers

1 might, won't (item 6)
2 could, shouldn't (item 1)
3 might, won't (item 8)

Optional activity

Sts in pairs choose another one of the situations from B and write a short extract, as in C. Monitor and help where necessary. When they are ready, combine pairs into small groups to read out their extract for other sts to guess which item in B it refers to.

D Make it personal Put sts in new pairs to re-enact the roleplays from 3E. Encourage them to use modals where appropriate. Focus on the speech bubbles as a model. Monitor and celebrate good use of modals. Choose the best ones you hear to re-enact for the whole class at the end.

» Workbook p.54.

♪ Oh, I would do anything for love. I would do anything for love, but I won't do that. No, I won't do that

11.2

4 Grammar: Special uses of modals

A Read the grammar box and complete the rule. Then write a–d in the boxes next to the underlined examples in 3B.

Special uses of modals: expectation, suggestion, refusal, and annoyance	
a expectation	It **shouldn't be** dangerous. I think it's safe.
	She **should have landed** by now. I'll check the flight online.
b suggestion	We **might as well forget** it then. We wouldn't be happy with a car that doesn't have the latest safety features.
	You **might want to take** some precautions. I've heard travel there is dangerous.
c refusal	He **won't listen** to me. I've told him to wear a bike helmet!
d annoyance	She **could have called** at least. I was really worried something had happened to her!

Modal verbs have more than one meaning. *Should* also expresses ¹o_____, *might* and *could* also express ²p_____, and *will* also describes a ³f_____ event.

» Grammar expansion p.158

B Using your completed grammar box in A, say the function expressed by each word in bold (1–8). Then make four sentences true for you.

OUR CITY, THE TRANSPORTATION BLOG

◆ You ¹**should** watch out for pedestrians at all times. These days, people are on their cell phones when they cross the street!

◆ It ²**shouldn't** be hard to learn to ride a motorcycle. It just involves good balance, like a bike.

◆ You ³**might** as well put your energy into bike, not car, safety. Pretty soon there's going to be nowhere to park around here.

◆ I'm afraid something ⁴**might** have happened to the plans for more traffic lights. The city is doing nothing!

◆ If I hadn't looked up, I ⁵**could** have been killed. The corner of 8th and Warren is the most dangerous intersection in the city.

◆ The cops ⁶**could** have been a little more understanding. It's hard to move your car after a snowstorm.

◆ Starting next year, there ⁷**won't** be any cars on Broom Street. They're turning it into a pedestrian walkway.

◆ I'm not letting my son drive until he's 21! He ⁸**won't** wear his seat belt, even though he knows it's illegal.

C What are the people saying? Complete 1–3 with appropriate modal verbs. Which items in B are they talking about?

1 A ticket! You _____ want to be a little more understanding. I _____ move my car until you plow this street!

2 Hey, watch out! You _____ have looked where you were going! It _____ be too hard to put that phone away for a second.

3 You _____ as well forget getting a license! And I _____ let you in the car with me in the future either!

D Make it personal In new pairs, role-play your situations from 3E again. This time, comment with special uses of modals in A.

> You won't believe what just happened. This motorcycle was coming right at me, and I had to jump out of the way.

> That's awful. He could have been a little more careful. They're always speeding through here.

» 11.3 Are you in favor of online dating?

5 Reading

A Read the article on online dating up to the heading "Big Mistake." In pairs, brainstorm possible reasons for the author's mistake. Then read the next paragraph to check. Are you surprised?

> I think she might have stolen something from his house.

B Make sure you understand the section titles below. Then read the rest. Put the titles back into the article (1–7).

> Ask the right questions   Be safe at home   Call for backup, Part 1   Call for backup, Part 2
> Gentlemen first   Know when to bail   Pick a safe spot for your first date

How to Stay Safe While Dating
by Ken Solin

Follow these tips to stay safe during your first few encounters with someone new

I was walking on California's Stinson Beach in August 2009 when I struck up a conversation with a woman who seemed utterly delightful. Captivated, I invited her to dinner at my house that evening.

Big mistake!

After dinner, she refused to leave. And, according to her, why should she? My acquaintance of 12 hours bizarrely insisted that we were living together. The situation felt menacing — would I find a rabbit stew boiling on the stove? — so I summoned my next-door neighbor, a woman, for help. The two of us spent 45 minutes coaxing my surprise head case to leave, but it took a threat to call the police to finally get her out the door.

Does it jar you to find a man writing about dating safety? Don't let it. Scary situations can pop up for anyone in the dating world — female or male, online or not. That's why everyone who is part of that world must take some basic steps to ensure his or her physical safety. At the very least, consider adopting the approaches below; all of them draw on my 12 years of recent online dating experience.

1 _____ When you've exchanged emails with a prospect and you feel it's time to furnish phone numbers, the man should offer his first. If he doesn't, the woman should ask him to do so. I can't think of any good reason why a legitimately eligible man would withhold his digits; if he does, that's ample cause to feel unsafe. Give the dude a pass.

2 _____ A busy daytime cafe is ideal. There isn't much privacy, but you'll be grateful for the presence of others if an unpleasant situation develops. If your date refuses to meet at a cafe or insists on a less public place, simply move on.

3 _____ I once had a coffee date with a woman who grew increasingly angry – and vocal – over her mistreatment by an ex-boyfriend. When she turned her attack on me, I got up and left – and was thankful for an audience to witness my exit.

4 _____ If a coffee date shows up with a bad attitude, a bad temper or a foul mouth, head for the door. Do likewise if he or she attempts to corral you into a relationship. If you feel truly threatened, explain the situation to the cafe manager and ask him or her to walk you to your car.

5 _____ I was enjoying a second date at a restaurant when my companion took a call during dinner. I was pretty sure I knew what was going on.

"I'm just fine," she told the caller, then stowed the phone with an apologetic smile.

"What would your friend have done if you hadn't picked up?" I asked her.

"She had instructions to call the police," she replied.

Good tip. Smart woman.

6 _____ Certain queries can reveal a lot of info in a short amount of time about a person you've just met. You might ask, for example, if your date has close friends: a "yes" indicates he or she is capable of connecting with others; a "no" suggests a lack of intimacy skills.

7 _____ As I learned the hard way with my would-be Glenn Close, it's unwise to welcome anyone into your abode unless you know them well. If you're unsure, consider asking another couple to join you.

120

Are you in favor of online dating? 11.3

Lesson Aims: Sts read about the dangers of online dating, and discuss safety tips.

Skills	Vocabulary
Reading an article about how to stay safe while dating	Whether to look up words: deciding when you need to look up new words *coax, pop up, draw on, eligible, screen*

Warm-up

Ask: *Are you in favor of online dating? Have you ever used an online dating website or do you know anyone who has? Do you think it is a good way of meeting people? Why do you think more people are using them these days? What are the dangers?* Tell sts that since 2013 use of online dating websites has tripled in the 18–24 age group, and doubled in the 55–64 age group.

Ask the lesson question title: *Are you in favor of online dating?* Divide the class in half, down the middle, and tell those on the left to call out arguments in favor, those on the right arguments against, e.g. because of all the dangers. Take turns, as if it were a game of tennis, an argument from the left, then one from the right, until they run out of ideas.

5 Reading

A Ask: *Have you seen the film "Fatal Attraction"?* Elicit the main actors (Glenn Close and Michael Douglas.) Ask them to quickly describe the plot (see Background information). Ask: *Have you ever had a girlfriend or boyfriend who has become obsessive?*

Focus on the photo, and elicit what's going on, what they might be saying, and how the date is going.

Tip

With the right class, for fun, you could have them enact an impromptu spontaneous roleplay.

Tell sts to cover the text and then unveil it line by line as they hear it. Read out the title of the article and then read them the first paragraph as far as *Big mistake!* Put sts in pairs to speculate about what the mistake was. Sts uncover and read the next paragraph to check.

Answer

His date would not leave the house.

Background information

Fatal Attraction is a 1987 movie starring Michael Douglas and Glenn Close. It is about a married man who has a brief affair with a woman he meets through business. After the brief affair, she becomes more and more psychotic, attempting suicide and at one point breaking into the man's family home and cooking their child's pet rabbit in a stew. This scene gave rise to the term "bunny boiler" commonly used to describe a rejected lover who goes to great lengths to win someone back.

B Focus on the section titles. Teach the meaning of to *bail on someone* (to stand someone up / break a date with someone). Ask sts how the seven titles might be related to "staying safe while dating," and what the dangers might be. Give sts about four minutes to skim and match the section titles with the correct paragraphs 1–7 alone, then move into pairs to finish and check. Peercheck. Classcheck.

Tip

Changing from individual to pair work during any longer reading activity adds new energy to it, and helps level out some of the more obvious differences in a mixed ability class.

Answers

1 Gentlemen first
2 Pick a safe spot for your first date
3 Know when to bail
4 Call for backup, Part 1
5 Call for backup, Part 2
6 Ask the right questions
7 Be safe at home

Optional activity

Ask sts to cover up the titles and read the article, thinking of their own titles for each one, then compare answers in pairs. Sts then read the title in the box and match them to the paragraphs. Peercheck, then classcheck. Ask if anyone's guesses were the same as the titles given.

» 11.3

C ▶ 11.10 Sts listen and re-read the article.

Tip
Since this will be the first time they hear at least the first part, try having them shadow read, i.e. listening, mouthing the text, and saying it under their breath as they hear it. For fun, you can pause occasionally when they do this, and tell them to keep going for a line or two, them play the audio for them to hear and compare their pronunciation with the audio. Then ask if they noticed anything very different from what they said.

Ask: *Which tip do you think is most important?* Discuss with the class.

Finally, have sts go back and practice pronunciation of the pink words in pairs. Elicit peer explanations of as many as you can.

D Make it personal Have sts discuss the questions in pairs. You could ask the following questions to prompt ideas: *Are women more vulnerable than men when online dating? What information do you think it is safe / not safe to give people on your first date?*

Give sts a few minutes to discuss these questions and those in the Student's Book. Classcheck by asking volunteers to share their ideas with the rest of the class.

Class feedback. Link back to the lesson title. Ask: *Would you use online dating? Why / why not? What excuses could you make to get out of a date that wasn't going well?*

> **Possible answers**
>
> Gather some basic information, e.g. email address / phone number before you agree to meet. Check them out online – are they who they say they are, check they aren't married, etc. Don't rely on your date for transportation after the date – drive or take public transportation.

Optional activity
Ask sts to research tips for online dating online, then compare the advice they found in small groups. In feedback, ask each group to share their best three tips with the class.

» Song lyric: See Teacher's Book p.353 for notes about the song and an accompanying activity to do with the class.

6 Vocabulary: Whether to look up words

A Focus on the heading, cover the text below and have sts brainstorm their own "policy" on this first. Since we all have permanent, instant access to a bi-lingual dictionary on our cell phones, perhaps they find looking things up easier than in the past? Does that perhaps mean it's more practical to do so more often than live with uncertainty? Discuss.

Go through **Deciding when to look up words** together with the class and check everyone understands. Explain that the reading task is also a factor. If they only need to get the gist of a text, then they probably don't need to look up so many words. If they are reading a text to get specific information, they will probably need to look up more words.

In pairs, sts go through the yellow highlighted words and say whether they will look them up or not. Classcheck by going through each of the words, and asking sts to put up their hand if they chose to look them up. Did they mostly agree?

B ▶ 11.11 Tell sts they are going to hear two teachers discussing the text in 5B. They are deciding which of the blue highlighted words they are going to ask their sts to look up. Have them listen and note down the words that are not chosen.

Ask sts if they agree and whether they can guess the meanings without using a dictionary. Ask sts to go through the other blue highlighted words. Ask: *Which do you know? Are any of them cognates?* Have them look up the ones they don't know and can't guess.

> **Answers**
>
> to bail, strike up, utterly, stew, head case, jar

» See Teacher's Book p.337 for Audio script 11.11.

C Make it personal Focus on the topics. Ask sts if they have any experience of these. If so, suggest they choose these topics. If not, allow them to suggest more, e.g. training for a sports event, or getting ready for an important party.

Brainstorm language they can use from the article in 5B, e.g. *It's unwise to ..., If you ..., Try (+ ing form), I strongly urge you ..., keep in mind that ...*

Ask sts to work in groups and write tips. Classcheck by asking them to share their tips with the rest of the class. Ask: Which tip is the most important / useful?

Optional activity
Have each group make a poster with their best tips and some illustrations / cut-outs from magazines / online. They then present these to the class and display them on the walls.

» Workbook p.55.

♪ Heartbreaks and promises, I've had more than my share. I'm tired of giving my love, And getting nowhere

« 11.3

My current girlfriend (whom I met online, by the way) invited me into her home after only our second date. I accepted, thanking her for her trust, but later mentioned that she could have been putting herself at risk.

We all want to believe the best about people, but a date you don't really know deserves only a ==modicum== of trust. So rather than ==rolling the dice== when it comes to your personal safety, try following the steps above. Who knows? They might even be a ==short==cut to finding the right person out there.

Note: Dating services' official rules for dating online are located under their websites' terms of use. They suggest a==ppro==priate behavior, but ==screening== is minimal – so I strongly urge you to use the tips above to create your own safety zone. Keep in mind that you can block any other member if you ever start to feel that safety is an issue.

C ▶ 11.10 Listen and re-read to check. Which tip do you think is most important?

D Make it personal What are the best safety rules? In groups, answer 1–3.
1 Should women and men follow the same safety advice? Why (not)?
2 Is any advice missing? Can you add at least one more piece?
3 What online dating safety stories have you heard or read about? Give advice. What new tips have you picked up?

> OK, let's see. Men need to be careful with their phone numbers, too.

6 Vocabulary: Whether to look up words

A Read *Deciding when to look up words*. Then re-read the sentences in the article where the yellow ==highlighted== words appear. In pairs, explain whether you will look them up and why (not).

> **Deciding when to look up words**
>
> Stopping to look up lots of words decreases reading pleasure. Before looking up words, ask yourself these questions:
> 1 Have you seen the word before?
> **Yes** Go to question 2. **No** It may be infrequent. Keep reading.
> 2 Is it necessary to understand the word?
> **Yes** Go to question 3.
> **No** The sentence makes sense. Keep reading.
> 3 Do you want to learn this word right now for active use?
> **Yes** Look it up. Find the meaning that matches the text.
> **No** Try to figure out the meaning from context and keep reading.

> *Coaxing* must come from the verb *coax*. I've never seen or heard it before, have you?

> No. But, following rule 3, let's not look it up. I wonder what it means, though.

> I think it might mean "to convince." It's pretty clear he's trying to get her to leave.

B ▶ 11.11 Listen to a conversation between two teachers and note down the words not chosen. Then find them among the blue ==highlighted== words. Do you agree? If not, follow rule 3 in **A**.

C Make it personal Create your own safety tips! In groups, choose two topics and create five tips for each one. Use highlighted blue and yellow words where useful.

How to safely …

be a celebrity   go on a crash diet   become a political activist   be a police officer   hire employees

> First: If you want to be a celebrity, you might need to hire a bodyguard.

> Yes, strange situations can pop up!

11.4 What does the sea make you think of?

7 Listening

A In pairs, if you and saw this sign at the beach, would you go in the water? Why (not)?

B ▶ 11.12 Listen to a couple talking at the beach. Note down one convincing argument each person gives. Are you more like Bob or Andrea?

C ▶ 11.13 Which of these are more likely to kill you than a shark attack? Listen to check. Were you surprised?

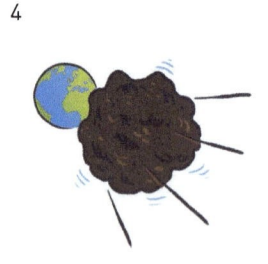

1 2 3 4

D ▶ 11.14 Listen to the end of the conversation. Which reason 1–3 does Andrea give for saying that the numbers "can't be taken at face value"?

1 ☐ They don't take people's location into account.
2 ☐ Not all oceans have sharks.
3 ☐ The figures haven't been updated in a while.

8 Pronunciation: Stressing function words for emphasis

A ▶ 11.15 Read and listen to to the rules. Then read exchanges 1–4 and guess the stressed words in the responses.

> As we saw on page 67, auxiliaries may be stressed for emphasis. Other normally unstressed function words like conjunctions, articles, and pronouns, are sometimes stressed, too.
> BOB: You worry too much. Come on! Have some fun!
> ANDREA: I **am** having fun. But I want to have fun **and** be safe. And I want **you** to be safe, too.

1 ANDREA: Do you want to get eaten by a shark? ☐
  BOB: Do I want what?
2 ANDREA: There are an estimated 64 attacks each year, but few are fatal. ☐
  BOB: Few. Not none, so the odds might not be in our favor!
3 ANDREA: That doesn't make any sense! Sharks are color blind! ☐
  BOB: Color blind? They are?
4 ANDREA: It's written right here! The evidence is clear! ☐
  BOB: I think it's anything but clear.

B ▶ 11.16 Listen to check. In pairs, first repeat and then extend each exchange.

C **Make it personal** In pairs, choose a picture from 7C and role-play a conversation where you don't agree on risk. Pay close attention to word stress.
  A: You're extremely risk-averse.
  B: You don't mind taking risks.

> Get away from that tree! You could be hit by lightning.

> I could be, but I won't be! What are the chances of that?

What does the sea make you think of? 11.4

Lesson Aims: Sts listen to a couple discussing the chances of being attacked by a shark, and go on to assess the risk in other situations.

Skills	Language	Vocabulary	Grammar
Listening to a couple on the beach talking about the risks of being attacked by a shark	Stressing function words for emphasis: *Do I want* what? *I think it's anything* but *clear.*	research, statistics, facts, evidence, studies	Definite and indefinite articles: general and specific uses

Warm-up

Board the lesson title question: *What does the sea make you think of?* If possible, play an evocative seaside recording and give them a minute to listen and dream before they answer. Put sts in groups, and have them write as many words as they can associated with the sea. Possible words include: *waves, currents, jelly fish, fish, shells, stones, seaweed, sand, wading, swimming, surfing.*

Ask: *Do you enjoy swimming in the sea? Why / Why not?*

7 Listening

A Focus on the sign. Ask: *Where might you see a sign like this? Have you ever been to a beach resort where there are known to be sharks in the water? Would you go in the water?*

B ▶ 11.12 Explain that sts are going to listen to a couple on the beach discussing the risks of being attacked by a shark. They listen and note down one convincing argument from each person. Ask the question in the Student's Book: *Are you more like Bob or Andrea?*

Follow up by asking: *What do you think are the odds of being attacked by a shark?* and use this as an opportunity to review expressions with *odds.* (see 7D on p.110)

Answers

Ann: There was a warning sign, Roy is wearing red shorts
Roy: The chances of being killed by a shark are statistically slim, sharks are color blind

▶ See Teacher's Book p.337 for Audio script 11.12.

C ▶ 11.13 Focus on the pictures. Ask: *What is happening?* (boy is being struck by lightning, girl is being bitten by a dog, plane is going to crash, earth is being hit by an asteroid). Ask sts to rank them in order of likelihood (1 = most likely to happen, 4 = least likely). Ask: *Which are more likely to kill you than a shark attack?*

Play the audio for sts to check. Class feedback. Ask: *Are you surprised? Does that change your mind about whether you would swim or not?*

Answer

All of them

▶ See Teacher's Book p.337 for Audio script 11.13.

D ▶ 11.14 Focus on the question in the Student's Book: *Which reason does Andrea give for saying that the numbers "can't be taken at face value"?* Check sts understand the expression *take at face value* (to accept something as it appears). You could get them to cover reasons 1-3 and guess what they might be first, and which she will choose. Play the audio. Sts choose reason 1, 2, or 3.

Classcheck by asking: *Is the couple's risk of being attacked higher or lower than average?* (higher) *Why?* (they're in an area where sharks have been sighted).

Answer

Reason 1

▶ See Teacher's Book p.337 for Audio script 11.14.

8 Pronunciation: Stressing function words for emphasis

A ▶ 11.15 Go through the information in the box together. Ask two sts to read out the exchange between Bob and Andrea, stressing the words marked.

Focus on exchanges 1–4, and ask sts to guess which are the stressed words.

Answers

1 what 2 so 3 are 4 but

B ▶ 11.16 Play the audio for sts to check. Put sts in pairs, and have them act out the exchanges. Monitor and be sure they are stressing the correct words. Encourage sts to extend the conversations if they can.

Optional activity

Board the following: 1 *I AM listening!* 2 *Who is?* 3 *She said what?* 4 *They ARE?* Explain that these are responses to things people have said. In pairs, ask them to think of what the first person said. Go around and check what they're writing makes sense, then ask sts to practice saying the mini-conversations.

C Make it personal Refer sts to the example in the speech bubble. You might want to review the risk-taking expressions sts learned in 11.1 at this stage. Put sts in pairs and allocate them roles A or B. Have sts role play a situation from 7C. Then tell them to swap roles and choose another situation to act out in their new roles.

Invite a few pairs to act out their roleplay for the class.

11.4

9 Grammar: Definite and indefinite articles

Tip

Divide up the board into three sections, and at the top write *no article, the, a / an*. Put sts into small groups to discuss what rules they can remember about when we use each one. After a few minutes, give out board pens and have them come and write their ideas in the right section. Classcheck. Sts then read the rules in the box and compare with the rules they thought of. Ask them if anything in the box is new.

A Go through the examples in the grammar box with the class. Ask sts if they would use a definite / indefinite article in their language in each case. If sts complain about the complexity of article rules in English, remind them that at least there are only three forms, a / an / the, as compared to most other languages, which have far more!

Refer sts to the mini dialogues in 8A and underline the indefinite and definite articles in each one. They write a–f next to them.

Classcheck. Books closed. Board the incorrect sentence from the **Common mistakes** box. Ask sts to correct it. If possible, board some more recent examples of errors that you've heard them making, or that you know they would make if they translated from their language, for them to correct too.

Answers

1 c (a shark) 2 d (an estimated 64) 3 a (Sharks)
4 e (The evidence)

» Refer sts to the **Grammar expansion** on p.158.

» Song lyric: See Teacher's Book p.354 for notes about the song and an accompanying activity to do with the class.

B Ask sts to read the text quickly for gist. Ask: *Which of the things mentioned do you worry about?* Have sts re-read the text and correct the mistakes in the underlined phrases. Classcheck and ask sts to match the underlined phrases with the rules a–f in A.
(1 b, 2 a, 3 e, 4 c, 5 a, 6 a, 7 d, 8 c).

Answers

2 Flu outbreaks? 3 The human brain 6 plane crashes
8 a sedentary lifestyle

C Read **Quantifiers and pronouns** with the class. Elicit other quantifiers sts know.

Tip

Board the following sentences to show examples of other quantifiers. Tell sts we only use certain quantifiers with uncountable nouns, e.g. *less of, little of, much of, part of, a bit of, a good / great deal of, a little of, the whole of*.

*I'm worried about the risks of being hit by lightning and being bitten by a dog, even though I know **neither of them** is a huge risk.*

*There have been a lot of incidents involving sharks on this beach but **none of them** have been serious.*

*There is a lot of research on cell-phone use but **little of it** is reliable.*

*I've done a lot of work over summer break, but **a good deal of it** was very badly paid.*

Have sts rephrase the underlined sentences using the words in parentheses. Do the first one together as an example. Explain that they will need to change the relevant pronouns and the form of the verbs. Have sts refer back to subject–verb agreements taught in Unit 1 on page 9, if necessary. Peercheck. Classcheck.

Answers

1 There is a lot of research on cell-phone use, but how reliable is it?
2 And let's not forget the WiFi equipment we're surrounded by and the radiation it emits.
3 Well-paid jobs aren't easy to come by these days.
4 There seems to be competing evidence about whether eggs are good for you.
5 Digital music is more affordable than it's ever been.

D Make it personal Have two sts read the model dialog in the speech bubbles. Divide the class into groups of three. Ask sts to go through the concerns in C, and say how much they worry about these things.

Have them discuss other concerns they have. Ask them to decide on the most common concern sts have within their group. Open up to a class discussion and find out what the class' most common concerns are.

» Workbook p.56.

♪ Baby, this is what you came for. Lightning strikes every time she moves. And everybody's watching her, But she's looking at you

11.4

9 Grammar: Definite and indefinite articles

A Read the grammar box. Then write a–f next to mini-dialogues 1–4 in **8A**.

Definite and indefinite articles: general and specific uses

general	a countable nouns	**Precautions** need to be taken.
	b non-count nouns	**Research** tells us that the risks are real.
specific	c first mention	Is this **a risk** you're willing to take?
	d adjective + number	**A record ten** attacks were recorded in 2016.
	e shared knowledge	**The study** was conducted in Japan.
	f adjective = group of people	**The rich** tend to live longer.

» Grammar expansion p.158

B Correct the mistakes in article use in some of the underlined phrases (1–8).

Common mistakes
some / a piece of   *advice is / suggestions are*
Mark gave me ~~an~~ advice. His ~~advices are~~ always good.

Are you worrying about the right things?

These days, it's hard to choose what to worry about. ¹Climate change? Resistant bacteria? ²The flu outbreaks? Whichever the answer, remember: Your brain is wired to conspire against you! Although ³human brain can respond well to risk, it's not good at deciding which modern threats are actually worth worrying about. This is because our survival instincts are activated by the choices that kept our ancestors safe, in ⁴a world where dangers took the form of ⁵predators, not terrorists. As a result, we tend overestimate the odds of rare events, such as ⁶the plane crashes, while downplaying the real risks, such as lack of exercise. According to a recent study, for example, ⁷an astounding 83 million Americans are living ⁸sedentary lifestyle.

C Read *Quantifiers and pronouns*. Then rephrase the underlined sentences in 1–5. Replace the bold words with those in parentheses.

Quantifiers and pronouns

Notice the pronoun differences between countable and non-count nouns.

Non-count	Countable
The article offers lots of **advice**.	The article offers lots of **suggestions**.
Most of **it** is useful, some of **it** is not.	Most of **them** are useful, some of **them** are not.
	One of **them** in particular is terrible.

1 There are a lot of **studies** on cell-phone use, but how reliable are they? (research) I keep worrying about the risks posed by the radiation.
2 Exactly! And let's not forget the WiFi **devices** we're surrounded by and the radiation they emit. (equipment)
3 The recent unemployment statistics are pretty scary, and I worry about losing my job. Well-paid work isn't easy to come by these days. (jobs)
4 There seem to be competing **facts** about whether eggs are good for you. (evidence) Why can't scientists decide?
5 Digital songs are more affordable than they've ever been. (music) How will artists make money?

D Make it personal In groups, which concerns do you share from **C**? What other concerns are important to you? Be careful with articles.

Teen obesity is a major problem. I read that an astonishing 17 percent of teens are obese.

Yes, schools need to pay more attention to teaching good nutrition.

123

11.5 Have you ever had an allergic reaction?

10 Listening

A ▶ 11.17 Listen to the beginning of a lecture on allergies. Complete the notes.

> Percent suffering in U.S. ¹_____ (Adults ²_____ Children ³_____)
> Three main causes of fatalities: 1) ⁴_____, 2) ⁵_____, 3) ⁶_____
> Anaphylactic ⁷_____ : Name comes from ⁸_____

B ▶ 11.18 Listen to the second part and take notes. In pairs, share two important facts that you've learned. Were they similar?

> Anaphylactic shock can come on quickly. It's important to seek help immediately!

C ▶ 11.19 These symptoms are mentioned in the second part. In pairs, brainstorm other possible causes for them. Then listen to check. Were your ideas mentioned?

cramps   hives   sense of impending doom

swelling   itching   wheezing

> Wheezing, for example, might occur if you had asthma.

11 Keep talking

A In groups, choose a topic where you'd like to know more about safety. Choose from those below or think of your own.

home safety   sailing / operating a boat   horseback riding
side effects to everyday medications   hotel and vacation safety

B Brainstorm three specific questions about your topic you don't know the answer to. Search online by entering each question in a search engine.

C Share your information with the class. Be sure to explain any new words. Which topic did you learn the most about?

> You shouldn't have any problems at a hotel if you make sure the entrance is in a well-lit area. Always err on the side of caution!

> Also check that your door has a dead-bolt lock. That means one that has a heavy sliding bar that moves when you turn it.

Have you ever had an allergic reaction? 11.5

Lesson Aims: Sts listen to a lecture on allergies and write a statistical report.

Skills	Language	Vocabulary
Listening to a lecture about allergies Writing a statistical report	Using number phrases to present statistics, e.g. *Only eight foods account for 90 percent of these allergic reactions. One in every 13 children is affected.*	Numbers: *Two thirds, Seventy percent, One out of three, The number of ..., half, some, most of*

Warm-up

Board and drill the word *allergies*. Ask: *What are the most common allergies? Do you / Does anyone you know have any (unusual ones)? What precautions do you / they have to take? Can any allergies kill you?* Discuss as a class.

Focus on the lesson title question: *Have you ever had an allergic reaction?* Invite any students who have to tell the class what happened. Prepare an anecdote yourself in case none of them have a story to tell.

10 Listening

A ▶11.17 Focus on the notes. Ask sts to guess what kind of words are missing, e.g. *numbers, nouns, adjectives*. Play the audio and have sts complete the notes. Classcheck. Ask: *Did you know any of this information before?*

Answers

1 16 %   2 30%   3 40%   4 medicines   5 food allergies
6 insect stings   7 shock   8 Ancient Greek

» See Teacher's Book p.338 for Audio script 11.17.

B ▶11.18 Pre-teach *epinephrine*, which is a medication used to treat anaphylactic shocks. Sufferers from severe allergies carry with them epiPens which are used to inject a dose of epinephrine in the case of emergencies.

Play the audio with the second part of the lecture, and have sts note down the key points. Peercheck and listen again as necessary.

In pairs, sts tell their partner two facts they have learned. Ask if these were the same.

Weaker classes: Before sts listen, pre-teach vocabulary in C (*cramps, itching, hives, swelling, sense of impending doom, wheezing*), using the pictures.

Possible answers

rapid onset; epinephrine shot used as an antidote to reaction; affects skin, respiratory system, gastrointestinal system, heart and central nervous system; symptoms include swelling, hives, itching, flushed face, abdominal pain, cramps, wheezing, breathing difficulties, headaches, anxiety, sense of impending doom

» See Teacher's Book p.338 for Audio script 11.18.

C ▶11.19 Focus on the pictures and drill the symptoms from audio 11.18. Ask: *Have you ever suffered from these symptoms? What was the cause? What other possible causes of these symptoms can you think of?*

Focus on the example in the speech bubble. Play the final part of the lecture for sts to check.

Classcheck. Ask sts if their ideas were mentioned. Did they have any other ideas that weren't mentioned?

Answers

cramps: eaten too much
hives (also itching and swelling): insect bite
sense of impending doom: seizure, panic attack
wheezing: asthma

» See Teacher's Book p.338 for Audio script 11.19.

Optional activity

Books closed. Elicit the words through mimes / simple descriptions. Sts then look at the pictures / words in the book.

» Song lyric: See Teacher's Book p.354 for notes about the song and an accompanying activity to do with the class.

11 Keep talking

A Go through the topics and elicit what sts already know about them regarding safety, e.g. always leave a light on at home when you go out, always wear a helmet when you go horseback riding. Allow sts to get into groups with classmates who are interested in the same topic.

B In their groups, sts brainstorm three questions they would like to research.

Elicit a few example questions for one of the topics to get sts started, e.g. *How do you do an emergency stop on a horse? What is the quickest way to dismount? Do you need to wear protective clothing? What type of boots should you wear?*

Sts research the answers online in class or for homework.

C Elect a spokesperson for each group to present the safety information they have found out. Focus on the examples in the speech bubbles as models.

Class feedback. Ask: *What topic did you learn most about? What was the most interesting thing you learned?*

257

» 11.5

12 Writing: A statistical report

A Board two quotes: "98% of all statistics are made up" and "Statistics mean never having to say you're certain." Ask: *Do you agree? What does the word "statistics" make you think of? Is it positive or negative one?*

Have sts read the report quickly. Ask: *Who is the report intended for?* (teachers) *What's your first reaction to it?* Focus on the charts and ask sts to explain the figures. Ask: *What other types of charts / graphs could you include in a statistical report?* (pie charts, line graphs, Venn diagrams)

Have sts read it again more carefully and underline the numbers. Check they can say the numbers. Class feedback. Ask: *Which is the most surprising fact?*

Optional activity

While sts are underlining the numbers, board them. When they have finished, ask sts to close their books. Point to the numbers on the board and ask sts if they can remember what each one refers to.

B Read through **Write it right!** with the class. Sts complete sentences 1–5 from the report. Peercheck, then classcheck, by asking sts to find the sentences in the report.

> **Answers**
> 1 have   2 indicate, is   3 is   4 come   5 report

Optional activity

Board the following sentences:

1 *Hotel crime is increasing! One state, Florida, …756 crimes in just two years.*
2 *Half of these crimes … thefts, and 38% … crimes committed in hotel rooms.*
3 *A number of studies … evidence that home accidents in the UK … 6,000 deaths a year.*
4 *The number of people poisoned … a problem, too.*
5 *Leisure … always safe, either! Almost 1,000 people in the U.S. … boating collisions each year.*

Ask sts to think about what they think each answer is, but not write anything yet. Elicit their ideas, but don't give any answers. Sts then write their answers. Peercheck, then classcheck.

(Possible answers: 1 reports 2 are, are 3 provide/offer/give, cause 4 is 5 isn't, have/are involved in)

C Go through the instructions, and make sure sts are clear about what they have to do. Tell them they should aim to write about 250–300 words. They can present their statistics in any type of chart or graph, e.g. a pie chart, bar graph or line graph, but they should try to include at least two.

Highlight a few expressions from the report that they might find useful, e.g. *(the numbers) break down as follows, on average, only, many of, more than, is steadily rising / falling, one in every, close to*. Go through the Before and While stages and get sts to highlight the key things to remember. Sts can start their report in class, and finish it for homework. Assign each st a partner to exchange reports with to proofread before they post them online.

Tip

Ensure they feel free to choose another topic of their own if they'd prefer to research something else, and help them come up with ideas. What are they really into, e.g. music, fashion, food, their soccer team's performances? What trend or aspect would they be interested in finding out more about?

» Workbook p.57.

♪ I've been through the desert on a horse with no name. It felt good to be out of the rain

11.5

12 Writing: A statistical report

A Read the report, underlining the numbers. Which is the most surprising fact?

B Read *Write it right!* Then complete 1–5 with a singular or plural form of the verb in parentheses. Read the report again to check.

> **Write it right!**
>
> When you use numbers, subject–verb agreement can be tricky. Here are three rules to help you:
> 1. When you use fractions, percentages, or words like *half*, *some*, *most*, and *all*, the **object** of the preposition determines the verb:
>   Two thirds / 70% of the **voters are** undecided.
>   Half / Most of the **information** I got **is** useless.
> 2. After *one*, the verb is always singular:
>   **One** out of every three homes **has** Netflix.
> 3. *The number* takes a singular verb. *A number*, which means *many*, takes a plural verb:
>   **The number** of people with allergies **is** high.
>   And **a number** of them **have** severe reactions.

1. Seven percent of children _____ allergies. (have)
2. A number of studies _____ that the number of children _____ rising. (be)
3. One in every 13 children under 18 _____ affected by allergies. (indicate, be)
4. In the U.S., many of the most common allergic reactions _____ from fish allergies. (come)
5. Three out of every 15 people with allergies _____ peanut and tree nut allergies. (report)

C Imagine you've been asked to write a statistical report on one of the topics in 11A to a specific audience responsible for safety, such as insurance companies, vacation resorts, or doctors. Your report will need to highlight possible dangers and give recommendations.

Before
🌐 Choose your audience and plan two charts to support your message. Search on questions designed to produce statistics, such as "How many people …?"

While
Write three to four paragraphs to summarize your charts, following the model in **A**. Address your audience in paragraph 1 and give recommendations in the conclusion. Use expressions with numbers from *Write it right!*, paying careful attention to subject-verb agreement.

After
Post your report online and read your classmates' work. Whose statistics best supported the report?

FOOD ALLERGIES:
please read carefully

Five out of every 100 Americans have food allergies – that's an astonishing 15 million people, or close to 4%. What's more, the rate is even higher in children. One in every 13 children under the age of 18 is affected. In other words, on average, over 7% of children have food allergies. In addition, a number of studies indicate that the number of children is steadily rising. Teachers: please review this information carefully.

Only eight foods account for 90 percent of these allergic reactions: milk, eggs, peanuts, tree nuts (walnuts, almonds, hazelnuts, cashews, etc.), soy, wheat, fish, and shellfish. Yet these foods can be very dangerous. Food allergies may cause anaphylactic shock, a sudden reaction that, if not treated quickly, may be fatal.

By age, allergies in children and teenagers break down as follows:

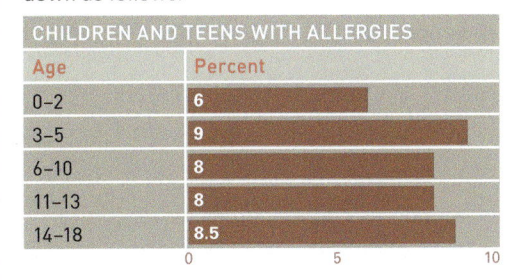

CHILDREN AND TEENS WITH ALLERGIES	
Age	Percent
0–2	6
3–5	9
6–10	8
11–13	8
14–18	8.5

Among those diagnosed, the scope of the problem can be seen in this chart:

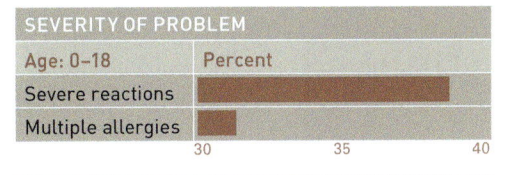

SEVERITY OF PROBLEM	
Age: 0–18	Percent
Severe reactions	(≈39)
Multiple allergies	(≈31)

Some allergies can be outgrown, but fish and shellfish allergies are usually lifelong. In the U.S., many of the most common allergic reactions come from fish allergies – more than 6.5 million adults have them. Peanut and tree nut allergies tend to be lifelong also. More than three million adults report such allergies. Alarmingly, food allergies overall are so common that, in the U.S., someone ends up in the emergency room every three minutes, for a total of 200,000 visits a year.

Epinephrine auto-injectors can save lives! Should you be faced with an emergency, do not attempt to treat a student yourself. Take him or her immediately to the nurse's office and call 911. Every minute counts.

12 What brands are the wave of the future?

1 Listening

A ▶ 12.1 Look at the cartoon. What do you think the professor's lecture will be about? Listen to check.

> Maybe he / she will talk about how bad the economy is right now.

"What if we don't change at all ... and something magical just happens?"

B ▶ 12.1 Listen again. Check (✔) the points the professor makes.
1. ☐ Innovation involves risk-taking.
2. ☐ It's hard to change well-established practices.
3. ☐ Companies spend many years planning changes.

C ▶ 12.2 Listen to part two. Correct the mistake in each line of the student's notes.

Microsoft
1. 80s & 90s: high profits due to ~~PC~~ *software* sales
2. Mid 2000s – present: huge drop in computer sales, esp. laptops
3. *Surface* tablet: impressive sales at first
4. Future of PCs: 3D gaming won't increase sales

D ▶ 12.3 Listen to part three and complete the notes. Were your surprised?

National Geographic
1. Early days: American _____
2. Challenge in the 90s: number of _____ went down
3. John Fahey's role: change _____ of company
4. Digital presence: top non-celebrity account on _____

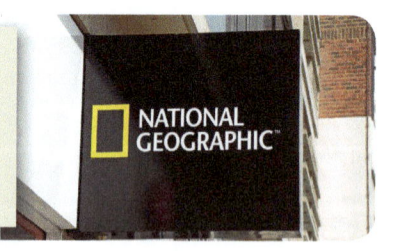

E 🌐 **Make it personal** Brands that have come and gone! In groups, do 1–3.
1. Individually, search on "brands that disappeared" to find an interesting story.
2. Read the case study and quickly note down the key points.
3. Share your stories. What should each company have done differently?

> Here's one ... the amazing story of Blockbuster, the video rental company. They turned down a partnership with Netflix. Can you believe it?

What brands are the wave of the future? 12.1

Lesson Aims: Sts listen to a lecture on innovation and learn language to talk about figures and trends.

Skills	Language	Vocabulary
Listening to a lecture on the importance of innovating and hearing case studies on successful businesses, Microsoft and National Geographic	Describing trends: *The number of traffic deaths has plunged since 2006. PC shipments have plummeted. The decline in sales might level off.* Expressing cause and reason: *Many bankruptcies stem from fear. It paved the way for other innovations.*	Verbs describing trends: *level off, soar, skyrocket, plummet, plunge, fall* Expressions to describe cause and reason: *pave the way for, give rise to, be closely related to, stem from*

Warm-up

Board the sentences for sts to choose the right option:
What brand / make of car do you drive?
What brand / make of cigarette did you used to smoke?

Elicit that *make* is the manufacturer, (used almost exclusively for cars) and *brand* the name of the product; the one we know it by. Elicit examples of both.

Ask: *Which are the most popular brands in your age group?* Have the class come to an agreement on the three most successful brands of their time. Ask: *What determines whether a brand continues to be successful? Do you think these brands will survive the test of time?* Focus on the lesson title question. *What are their predictions?*

1 Listening

A ▶ 12.1 Focus on the cartoon and the caption. Ask: *What's happening?* (business meeting) *What do you think they are discussing?* (how to change the fortunes of the business around) *How competent do you think they are?* From the caption, try to elicit that the company is not used to "change" or innovation.

Tell sts they are going to hear a professor giving a business lecture. From the cartoon and lesson title, have them guess what it will be about. Then play the audio for them to check.

Weaker classes: Give sts a copy of the audio to check.

Classcheck. Ask: *Which companies are mentioned as being innovative?* (Apple, Starbucks, Honda) Ask: *What is your impression of them? Which other companies would you say are innovative?*

> **Answer**
> How companies stay ahead in the market and avoid bankruptcy by constantly reinventing themselves

» See Teacher's Book p.338 for Audio script 12.1.

B ▶ 12.1 Have sts read statements 1–3. Ask: *Do you agree with these?* Re-play the audio and have sts check the points the professor makes. Classcheck.

> **Answers**
> Check 1 and 2

C ▶ 12.2 Ask sts: *What do you know about Microsoft? Who has used Windows (the Microsoft operating system)? Who has a desktop computer / laptop / tablet? Have you heard of the Surface tablet? What's your dream computer / mobile?*

Have them read the notes and make guesses about the content of the lecture. Play the audio and ask sts to correct the mistakes in the notes. Peercheck. Classcheck. Re-play the audio if necessary.

> **Answers**
> 2 laptop > desktop   3 impressive > slow   4 won't > might

» See Teacher's Book p.338 for Audio script 12.2.

D ▶ 12.3 Ask: *What do you know about National Geographic? Have you ever read their magazine? Or watched their TV channel?* Ask sts to read the notes and guess what the next part of the lecture will be about. Play the audio and ask sts to complete the notes.

Peercheck. Classcheck. Ask: *What did you learn from the lecture? What was the most surprising?*

> **Answers**
> 1 treasure   2 subscribers   3 image   4 Instagram

» See Teacher's Book p.338 for Audio script 12.3.

E Make it personal Ask sts if they know of any brands which have disappeared. Board the following if they can't recall any: *Woolworth, Blockbuster* (videos), *Avon* (cosmetics). Ask them what they know about these companies.

1 Sts research other companies which have disappeared, in class if you have online access or for homework. Have each group choose a different company if possible.
2 Sts share their information in groups, and note down the key points of the company's case study. Tell them they are going to present their case study to the rest of the class. Elect a spokesperson. Have them rehearse in front of their own group first.
3 Sts take turns presenting their case studies to the class, then discuss together what the company could have done differently. Finally, ask them to predict which famous names will be next to disappear, and why.

12.1

2 Vocabulary: Verbs describing trends

Tip

Divide the class in half, then in pairs. Tell the left-hand pairs to cover the second column and guess the endings, tell the right-hand pairs to cover the beginnings and try to guess them by looking at the endings. Listen and enjoy their guesses. Ask them which was harder and why. Then have them swap roles, covering the opposite side to see if they can remember the beginnings / endings they saw before, and match them to the correct ending / beginning they can now see. Don't let this go on too long, but it should be fun, and motivate them to want to get the exercise right!

A ▶ 12.4 Have sts match the two halves of the sentences, then play the audio for them to check. Go through the yellow highlighted words, and ask sts to guess the meanings using the context. Drill pronunciation of these words.

Sts then write the highlighted words under each graph. Classcheck.

> **Answers**
>
> 1 d 2 c 3 a 4 e 5 b
> Graph 1: soar, skyrocket
> Graph 2: level off
> Graph 3: plummet, plunge

Tip

A lot of verbs for describing graphs come from the world of flying, such as the verbs here. Another area they come from is that of describing mountains, e.g. *climb, reach a peak, descend*. Point this out and see if sts can think of any others. Ask if it's similar in their language.

B Focus on the blog title. Ask: *What good news have you had or heard recently?*

Ask sts to form sentences using the cues. Tell them to think carefully about which form of the verb to use (*simple past* or *present perfect*), and focus on the **Common mistake**. Remind sts that we use the simple past with a specific time in the past and the present perfect with non-specific times in the past or a period of time leading up until the present.

Board the following and ask sts to compare:

Unemployment has soared since 2015.

Unemployment soared in 2015.

Peercheck. Classcheck. Elicit other verbs sts might know to describe trends, e.g. *escalate, rocket, plunge, drop*. Have sts write four of their own sentences using these verbs or the verbs in **A**. Monitor and correct as many errors as you can while sts write. If time, have them share their sentences. Any identical ones?

> **Answers**
>
> 1 In Canada the number of traffic deaths has plunged since 2006.
> 2 In Spain unemployment fell from 2013 to 2016.
> 3 In India the generation of solar electricity has soared over the past few years.
> 4 In the UK life expectancy has risen since 1990.
> 5 In the U.S. obesity rates in men leveled off in 2016.
> 6 Globally poverty has plummeted in the last two decades.

Optional activity

Ask sts to research other good news stories from the news now. Ask them to write two facts, then delete the verb. Put sts in pairs to read out their facts for other sts to guess the missing verb.

C Make it personal

1 ▶ 12.5 **How to say it** Focus on the professor's statements 1–4 in the chart, and ask sts to guess the missing words from memory. Play the audio for them to listen and check. Classcheck.

Re-play the audio, asking them to repeat. Have them practice saying the expressions simultaneously in pairs, synchronizing together and imitating the model as closely as they can.

> **Answers**
>
> 1 stem 2 closely 3 given 4 way

2 Go through the instructions and the model in the speech bubble. If you have online access, give sts time to research the figures in class. Alternatively, they can do the research for homework.

In their groups, sts change 1–6 in **B** to make the sentences true for their region, using the expressions in **C** to explain them.

Classcheck by asking each group to read out one of their sentences. Board them and ask other members of the class to correct them, if necessary.

Elicit more sentences about trends sts are aware of using the expressions in **B**.

» Song lyric: See Teacher's Book p.354 for notes about the song and an accompanying activity to do with the class.

» Workbook p.58.

♪ The world I love. The trains I hop, To be part of, The wave can't stop. Come and tell me when it's time to

2 Vocabulary: Verbs describing trends

A ▶ 12.4 Match the two halves. Listen to check. Then write the highlighted verbs under each graph.

1 Since the mid 2000s, sales of cell phones and tablets have increased worldwide,
2 The *Surface* line had a bumpy start,
3 If 3D gaming remains popular,
4 It seems the magazine had lost of some its edge,
5 National Geographic is the top non-celebrity account on Instagram,

a ☐ the decline in PC sales might **level off**.
b ☐ and the number of followers continues to **soar** month after month!
c ☐ but its sales eventually **skyrocketed**.
d ☐ while PC shipments have **plummeted**.
e ☐ and the number of subscribers began to **plunge**.

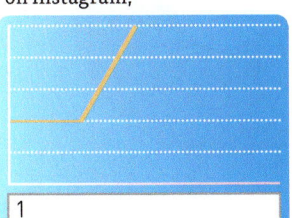

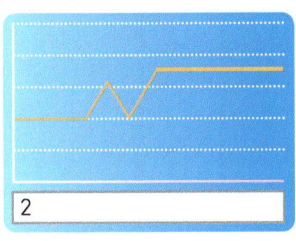

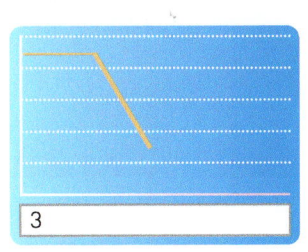

1	2	3

B Form sentences using cues 1–6. Notice the *Common mistake*.

Good news from around the globe:

1 Canada: number / traffic deaths / plunge / since 2006
2 Spain: unemployment / fall / from 2013 to 2016
3 India: generation of solar electricity / soar / over the past few years
4 UK life expectancy / rise / since 1990
5 U.S. obesity rates / men / level off / in 2016
6 Globally: poverty / plummet / in the last two decades

Common mistake

have
Sales ∧ plunged in / over the last three years.

C Make it personal Discuss trends in your region.

1 ▶ 12.5 **How to say it** Complete the chart. Listen to check.

Expressing cause and reason	
What they said	What they meant
1 (Many bankruptcies) _____ from (fear).	Negative outcome A is caused by B.
2 (Innovation) is _____ related to (risk and uncertainty).	A has a lot to do with B.
3 (Mobile computing) has _____ rise to (new challenges).	A has caused B.
4 (The TV channel) paved the _____ for (other innovations).	A made B possible.

2 In groups, change 1–6 in **B** to give true information for your region. Use expressions from **C** to explain the possible reasons. Can you think of any other trends?

> The number of traffic deaths around here has soared. It probably stems from raising the speed limit.

12.2 What songs have changed the world?

3 Language in use

A ▶ 12.6 Listen to a podcast about music and society. Note down one reason why each song below was influential.

Believe, Cher, 1998

Do They Know It's Christmas, Band Aid, 1984

B ▶ 12.6 Listen again. Check (✔) the points the music critic makes.
1. ☐ Most singers use Auto-Tune these days, which is objectionable.
2. ☐ Auto-Tune has made singers less unique.
3. ☐ Fundraising songs should be as catchy as possible.
4. ☐ Music may have lost some of its impetus for social change.

C ▶ 12.7 Complete 1–5 with a form of the highlighted phrasal verbs. Listen to check.

> **bring about:** make something happen
> **catch on:** become popular
> **fall back on:** use as a last resort
> **get across:** make an idea clear or convincing
> **grow on:** become more appealing over time
> **warm up to:** begin to like something or someone

1. Cher didn't refuse to be "auto-tuned," and the song instantly _____.
2. Today, most people – regardless of talent – can take a shot at singing if they can _____ Auto-Tune. It makes you wonder if singers are just one step away from being completely replaced by robots.
3. *Do they know …?* wasn't a tune I instantly _____, and I remember being underwhelmed when I first heard it.
4. But the song eventually _____ me, maybe because of the message it was trying to _____.
5. What's remarkable about *Do they know …?* is that it showed artists their influence could be used to _____ real change.

D Read *Transitive and intransitive phrasal verbs*. Then write 1–3 next to the phrasal verbs in C.

> **Transitive and intransitive phrasal verbs**
>
> Phrasal verbs can be transitive or intransitive:
> 1. Intransitive phrasal verbs don't take an object: Why did Abba **break up**?
> 2. Transitive ones need an object. Many are separable: They **called** the concert **off** / **called off** the concert.
> 3. Others are inseparable, including most three-word phrasal verbs: Can we **go over** the contract once more? (NOT ~~go the contract over~~); I'm **looking forward to** their next release.

What songs have changed the world? 12.2

Lesson Aims: Sts talk about songs which have changed society, and discuss important books which have had an impact on them.

Skills	Language	Grammar
Listening to a podcast about music and society	Phrasal verbs: *bring about, catch on, fall back on, get across, grow on, warm up to*	Passive forms with gerunds and infinitives

Warm-up

Ask: *How important is music in your life? What are your favorite songs? Why?* In pairs have sts list their five favorite songs of all time, then compare lists. Ask: *Do you have any in common?* Ask the lesson title question: *What songs have changed the world?*

3 Language in use

A ▶ 12.6 Focus on the photos. Ask: *Do you know these songs? Do you like them? What do you know about the artists / songs? Why do you think each song was influential?* If possible, play the songs before sts hear the audio.

Play the audio for sts to check and note down one reason for each song.

> **Answers**
>
> *Believe* led to the use of Auto-Tune throughout the music industry.
> *Do they know …?* showed artists could bring about change through music. (The song led to other fundraising anthems.)

» See Teacher's Book p.339 for Audio script 12.6.

Background information

Believe was the lead single from Cher's 22nd studio album of the same name. It was different from her previous music style and was seen as an attempt to appeal to a younger audience. It was the first commercial single to use auto-tune.

Do They Know It's Christmas? BandAid was written in 1984 by Bob Geldof and Midge Ure in order to raise money for the 1983–1985 famine in Ethiopia. Sung by a galaxy of stars, it became the fastest-selling single in UK history, selling a million copies in its first week.

B ▶ 12.6 Ask sts to read the statements. Ask: *Which of these points did you hear the music critic make?* Re-play the audio for them to check.

Ask *When were the biggest charity rock songs made, according to the music critic?* (in the 80s and 90s) *Which other fund-raising songs were mentioned?* (*We Are the World* and *That's What Friends are For*). *Do you know any others?*

Class feedback. Ask: *What do you think of the technique of auto-tuning? Which other songs do you know which strongly feature it?*

> **Answers**
>
> Check 2 and 4

C ▶ 12.7 Focus on the phrasal verbs. Ask: *Which of these do you know?* Have sts read the five extracts from the audio, and complete them with the correct phrasal verb. Remind them to use the appropriate form. Play the audio for them to check. Re-play the audio pausing after each phrasal verb for sts to repeat.

Have sts write their own sentences with each of the phrasal verbs, e.g. *I didn't like Rihanna's latest song at first, but it's beginning to grow on me.*

Peercheck. Classcheck.

> **Answers**
>
> 1 caught on   2 fall back on   3 warmed up to
> 4 grew on, get across   5 bring about

D Read **Transitive and intransitive phrasal verbs** with the class. Have sts copy the verbs from **C** into three lists, 1 (intransitive), 2 (transitive), and 3 (separable). Have them add any other phrasal verbs they know to the lists. Peercheck. Classcheck.

Tip

Remind sts of the list on SB p.164. Ask how they are doing remembering them all.

> **Answers**
>
> 1 catch on   2 get across   3 bring about, fall back on, grow on, warm up to

Optional activity

Books closed. Board:

1 *The single never really caught on sales.*
2 *It was a good idea, I just couldn't seem to get across it to the producer.*
3 *If I don't make it as a singer I can always fall my job back on.*

Explain that there is one mistake in each sentence, and ask sts to correct them in pairs. Elicit their ideas, but don't give any answers yet. Sts open their books and read the information in the box, then check their answers from before. Peercheck, then classcheck. Elicit why each of the sentences on the board is wrong.

265

E **Make it personal** Focus on the names of the writers of the quotes (in parentheses), and ask sts if they have heard of any of these people. Put sts in groups to discuss the quotes. Ask them to discuss what they mean and agree on their favorite.

Classcheck by having a st from each group report back to the class.

As follow-up, ask: *Do you know any other famous music-related quotes?* For homework, you could ask sts to research two or three quotes, and share them with the class in the next lesson.

Stronger classes: Ask sts to make up their own music-related quotes.

> **Answers**
> 1 catch on
> 2 get across
> 3 bring about, fall back on, grow on, warm up to

Background information

Erykah Badu (1971–) American singer-songwriter, record producer, disc jockey, activist, and actress.

Albert Schweitzer (1875–1965) French-German theologian, organist, philosopher, and physician.

Mart Twain (1835–1910) American writer, entrepreneur, publisher, and lecturer.

Shawn Fanning (1980–) American computer programmer, entrepreneur, and angel investor. He developed Napster.

4 Grammar: Passive forms with gerunds and infinitives

» Song lyric: See Teacher's Book p.354 for notes about the song and an accompanying activity to do with the class.

A Board a mistake with "not" in the wrong position for sts to correct, e.g. the last example in the grammar box. *The singer was disappointed to not be invited to join the group.*

Have sts read through both columns of the grammar box. Highlight the gerund and infinitive forms, and check they understand the example sentences. Ask: *Is this similar to your language?* Re-highlight the position of *not* in the negative sentence, compared to where it would be in their language. Get them to find the passive sentences in 3C and match them with the rules 1–6. Peercheck. Classcheck.

Have sts say out loud the example sentences in the grammar box and underline the stressed syllables. Elicit or point out that the auxiliary *be / being* is usually not stressed.

> **Answers**
> Cher didn't refuse to be "auto-tuned." (4)
> It ... one step away from being completely replaced by robots. (2)
> I remember being underwhelmed. (1)
> their influence could be used (6)

» Refer sts to the **Grammar expansion** on p.160.

B Ask sts to skim the text and find the titles of four books. Ask: *Have you read any of these books? Did you like them?* Have sts read the text and rewrite the underlined parts (numbered 1–6) using the passive with *be*, *to be*, or *being*. Do the first one together as an example.

Classcheck, and ask: *Which of the books would you like to read? Have you read any books which have changed the way you approach these things, (i.e. set priorities, cope with stress, read poetry, feel about reading).* Expand this to any other books they would recommend as being "life-changing" in any way.

Stronger classes: Ask sts to choose one of the categories and write about a book they have read which changed their approach to this.

> **Answers**
> 1 why priorities should be set
> 2 how this important task can be accomplished
> 3 I was so upset not to be considered for my dream job
> 4 I'd prefer to be forced to read ...
> 5 being told what to read
> 6 I still recall being surprised by the author because I hadn't known that...

C **Make it personal** Give sts time to think about books, movies, plays, and articles which have had a big impact on their lives. According to the age and interests of the class, you could add songs, poetry, and even people to the list too to broaden this out further.

Go through the events listed and ask sts how the book / movie / play or article has affected the way they approach these things. Put them in pairs to discuss.

Focus on the speech bubbles as a model.

Class feedback. Ask sts to report back what they found out about their partner.

Optional activity

Ask sts to think of books / movies / etc. for two of the categories, and make notes on each on their own. Monitor and help where necessary. When they are ready, sts describe their things for their partner to listen and guess which category.

» Workbook p.59.

♪ I want to thank you for giving me the best day of my life. Oh just to be with you is having the best day of my life

E Make it personal In groups, agree on your two favorite quotes. Explain what they mean and why you like them.
1 "Music and the music business are two different things." (Erykah Badu)
2 "There are two means of refuge from the miseries of life: music and cats." (Albert Schweitzer)
3 "The trade of critic, in literature, music, and ... drama, is the most degraded of all trades." (Mark Twain)
4 "Independent artists and labels have always been the trend setters in music and the music business." (Shawn Fanning)

> In the first one, I think she means that the music business is motivated by profit.

4 Grammar: Passive forms with gerunds and infinitives

A Read the grammar box. Underline the four passive sentences in **3C** and write 1–6 next to each one.

Passive forms with gerunds and infinitives: after parts of speech and as subjects	
Use gerunds ...	Use infinitives and base forms ...
1 after certain verbs: Cher **enjoyed being played** on the radio again.	4 after certain verbs: Band Aid **hoped to be remembered** for the song.
2 after prepositions: She didn't object **to being** "**auto-tuned**."	5 after adjectives, nouns, and indefinite pronouns: The song is **unlikely to be forgotten**.
3 as subjects: **Being considered** cool again was her goal.	6 after modals: Its lyrics **should** not **be taken** at face value.
In negative sentences, the preferred form for *not* is before the infinitive: The singer was **disappointed not to be** invited to join the group.	

B Rewrite 1–6 in the passive, using *be*, *to be*, or *being*. Which books, if any, would you like to read?

» Grammar expansion p.160

BOOKS THAT CHANGED THE WAY I ...

● **SET PRIORITIES:** *THE ONE THING*, BY GARY KELLER.
Do yourself a favor and read *The One Thing*. In it, the author shows us ¹why people should set priorities in the first place, and ²how we can accomplish this important task.

● **COPE WITH STRESS:** *HOW TO STOP WORRYING AND START LIVING*, BY DALE CARNEGIE.
I read this book at a very stressful moment in my life. ³I was so upset they didn't consider me for my dream job. Thanks to this book, I was able to pull myself together.

● **READ POETRY:** *TRANSFORMATIONS*, BY ANNE SEXTON.
Up until recently, if someone asked me whether I enjoyed reading poetry, I'd usually reply: ⁴"I'd prefer someone forced me to read the small print on a cereal box". But *Transformations*, which turns well-known fairy tales into poems, taught me how to appreciate it!

● **FEEL ABOUT READING:** *20,000 LEAGUES UNDER THE SEA*, BY JULES VERNE.
Over the years I've learned that ⁵having people tell you what to read is a surefire way to make you hate books! *20,000 Leagues ...* was the very first book I chose to read, and this made all the difference! ⁶I still recall that the author surprised me because I hadn't known that science fiction could be so engaging.

C Make it personal In pairs, has a book / movie / play / article ever had an impact on the way you ...?

approach friendships / romance   cope with stress   deal with money   have fun   see the world

> I don't remember ever being that influenced by a single book or movie. How about you?

> Actually, *Eat, Pray, Love* made me rethink my work schedule!

12.3 What futuristic programs have you seen?

5 Reading

A Imaginative drawings of the future were once common. Look at two postcards of "future" transportation. In pairs, answer 1–2.

1. Where could the people be going?
2. What else might artists have imagined 100 years ago?

> Well, the first one looks like a flying train. Aren't they on top of a building?

B ▶ 12.8 Read and listen to the article. Underline details describing how the future will be. Which (if any) do you see in A? Are you surprised by anything in the article?

Here's how people 100 years ago thought we'd be living today

In 100 years, there will be flying taxis and people will travel to the moon routinely. Knowledge will be instilled into students through wires attached to their heads. These may sound like the predictions of modern-day futurists, but they're how people a century ago saw the future – otherwise known to you and me as the present.

These vintage European postcards illustrate a view of the 21st century that is remarkably prescient in some ways and hilariously wrong in others, says Ed Fries, who selected them from his private collection.

In the 10 years since he left Microsoft, where he was co-founder of the Xbox project, Fries has worked on what he calls "a random collection of futuristic projects." He's advised or served on the board of companies working on 3-D printing, depth-sensing cameras (like those used in Kinect), and headsets for reading brain waves. Earlier this month, he presented some of his favorite postcards at a neurogaming conference in San Francisco, using them to illustrate pitfalls in predicting the future that remain relevant today.

One thing you see in the cards is a tendency to assume some things won't change, even though they undoubtedly will. In one image, a couple flags down an aerotaxi. That's futuristic enough, but the man is wearing spats and carrying a cane, while she has a parasol and an enormous hat with a feather. Did they really think transportation would undergo a revolution while fashion stayed frozen in time? "In every one of these you see a mix of a futuristic concept with stuff that looks to us to be very old fashioned," Fries said.

At the same time, there's virtually no hint in the postcards of the truly transformative technologies of the last century – namely personal computers and the Internet. Sure, there are video phones, but the image is projected on a screen or a wall. Moving pictures were just coming into existence, Fries says, so that wasn't a huge leap. But the idea of a screen illuminated from within seems to have been beyond their imagination.

All in all, people at the turn of the 20th century did a pretty good job of extrapolating the technology of their time, Fries says. But their imagination was limited by the world they lived in. The same is true today – at least for those of us who aren't the visionaries of tomorrow.

Fries thinks what sets those farsighted people apart has something to do with ignoring conventional wisdom. "The future is changed by people who have a crazy idea and follow it wherever it may lead," he said. "That's why I like hanging out with wacky people like at that neurogaming conference. One of them is probably going to change the world."

What futuristic programs have you seen? 12.3

Lesson Aims: Sts read about future predictions made 100 years ago, and make their own predictions for 100 years from now.

Skills	Vocabulary
Reading an article about what people 100 years ago thought life would be like today Using a dictionary	*prescient, random, pitfall, spat, undergo, namely, leap, farsighted, wacky*

Warm-up

Ask: *What do you remember about "The War of the Worlds" from lesson 4.2? How many "Star Wars" movies have you seen? Or "Back to the Future"? Which other movies about the future did you enjoy? Do you like science fiction? Do you read any science magazines?*

Focus on the lesson title question. Programs here refers to TV, but expand to video games, futuristic apps, astrology, anything "futuristic." Ask: *Are you optimistic or a pessimist about our future?* Have sts brainstorm in groups how they think we will be traveling around and communicating 30 years from now, e.g. *Will we teleporting?* Classcheck their best ideas.

5 Reading

Optional activity

Picture dictation. For fun, pairs have St A close their book and St B look at one of the pictures and dictate it, for St A (who can't see it) to draw, e.g. *In the middle of the picture, draw a primitive helicopter with a pilot at the front and two passengers sitting in the back.* It doesn't need to be a complex picture, just a simple line drawing, unless of course they're good artists. Monitor, help with prepositions of place, and enjoy their pictures. Once done, let them open their books, compare with the original, and show the rest of the class their work!

A Focus on the postcards. Ask: *What can you see?* (Elicit: type of air taxi, underwater boat / submarine, propeller, woman carrying shopping bags, people having a meal, waiter, porter). *When do you think the postcards were drawn? What type of publication might they have appeared in?*

Sts discuss questions 1 and 2 in pairs. Classcheck by asking sts to share their ideas. Finally, ask: *What did the artists get right / wrong about future transportation?*

B ▶ 12.8 Sts read and listen to the article, and underline any details describing how the future will be.

Tip

Once the audio stops, ask sts in pairs to cover the text and remember as much of it as they can together. Have them also say which parts they a) liked the best and b) found the hardest.

Peercheck. Elicit that you can see a flying taxi in **A**. Discuss any surprising facts from the article.

Tip

Tell them to hold back on looking up the words in yellow just yet, and don't explain them yourself, as they will do that in **6B**.

Classcheck, and ask: *When predicting the future, what two aspects, according to Fries, were largely ignored by people at the turn of the 20th century?* (fashion and technology).

Re-play the audio and pause after each paragraph for sts to practice saying the pink-stressed words together. Again resist explaining *prescient* and *undergo* until **6B** if you can.

Finally, ask: *Did you enjoy that topic / reading experience? How hard was it? Does it make you want to see more postcards? What do you think transportation will be like 100 years from now?*

Answers

Paragraph 1: ... there will be flying taxis and people will travel to the moon routinely. Knowledge will be instilled into students through wires attached to their heads.
Paragraph 4: a couple flags down an airtaxi.
The first postcard looks as if it's an airtaxi.

12.3

C Make it personal Give sts time to research vintage postcards in class if you have online access or ask them to do it for homework. If possible, ask them to bring in copies to show the class. They could also search on "future travel" and look for images to see if the technology / fashion portrayed, is radically different from now.

Class feedback. Ask: *What are the most common topics shown on vintage postcards?* (e.g. space travel, sea travel, communication, clothes, air travel) *Were predictions about the future generally accurate?*

Optional activity

Ask sts to research actual predictions for the future, 50 years from now, then share their ideas in groups. When they have shared what they found, ask them to reconsider the predictions in light of what they read in the article, i.e. how many of these predictions do they think are limited by the world we live in now, and how many do they think are truly farsighted?

» Song lyric: See Teacher's Book p.355 for notes about the song and an accompanying activity to do with the class.

6 Vocabulary: Using a dictionary

A Books closed. Board *leap*. Ask: *Is it a noun, verb, or adjective? What does it mean?* Don't confirm answers at this stage, as sts will find out later in the activity.

Books open. Get sts to read **Looking up words**, and answer questions 1 and 2. Classcheck. Elicit a few more sentences using the word *leap* either as a noun or a verb. Tell sts that *leapt* is used in British English

Remind sts that when looking up words in a dictionary, they should also check the pronunciation.

For further practice, give them three more words (e.g. *smack, flirt, plunge*), ask them to look them up in a dictionary, and answer the questions in **Looking up words**.

> **Answers**
> 1 Questions 1a, c and 3 can be answered.
> 2 Countable. We took a chance. = We took a leap in the dark.

Tip

Remind sts that just as important as looking a word up in a dictionary is recording it well for future use. If they can recall the word / expression they looked up before quickly and easily, they're more likely to use and remember it. Ask sts to share the different ways they like to record lexis.

B Go through the yellow-highlighted words and ask for a show of hands if sts know the words. Don't let them call out translations or even definitions or they will spoil it for others. Ask which ones they think they can guess from the context. Of those they can't guess, ask them to choose five to look up, using a monolingual dictionary, even if they prefer bi-lingual ones. You could take this opportunity to discuss the pros and cons of each (both are useful at this level). In pairs, sts compare what they learned. Ask: *Did you choose to look up the same words or different ones?*

Classcheck by asking individual sts to tell the class which words they looked up and what they learned.

C Make it personal Explain what sts have to do. Put them in groups and have them plan their postcards. Refer them to questions 1, 2, and 3 to help them plan. Encourage them to use the yellow highlighted words in their discussion.

Sts can draw futuristic forms of transportation for their postcard, or they can choose another area, such as food, fashion, housing, or communication.

When they have agreed on what to put on their postcard, get them to all draw one individually. Sts who really don't want to draw can work in a pair with someone who does. They can choose the best one to present to the rest of the class.

» Workbook p.60.

♪ Good friends we've lost along the way. In this great future, you can't forget your past. So dry your tears I say ...

12.3

C **Make it personal** In groups, search on "vintage postcards of the future." Share your favorite one.

> Here's one that's cool: a ship that turns into a train with wheels once it hits land. I wonder why those were never invented.

6 Vocabulary: Using a dictionary

A Read *Looking up words* and study the definition of *leap*. Answer 1–2.
1 Which questions from the box can be answered from the definition below?
2 🌐 Look up *leap* in a monolingual dictionary and find the noun. Is it countable or uncountable? How do you say, "We took a chance"?

> **Looking up words**
>
> When looking up words, follow these helpful guidelines:
> 1 Study the examples, and consider these questions: and consider these questions:
>   (a) Which prepositions are possible? (b) Does the word seem formal or informal?
>   (c) Does it have a figurative meaning, too?
> 2 Pay attention to collocations. What other words does the new word go with?
> 3 Decide the part of speech. Is the word a noun? If yes, is it countable or uncountable?

> **leap** /liːp/ **verb** Other forms: **leaped** /liːpt/ or **leapt** /lɛpt/; also **leaping**
>
> **1** to jump from a surface **2** to jump over something **3** to move quickly
>
> **Examples:**
> **1** He leaped from the bridge.
> **2** He leaped over the wall.
> **3** The cat leaped into the air. / We leaped at the chance. (fig)

B Choose five highlighted words from 5B to look up. In pairs, explain what you learned.

> I chose *farsighted* and learned it has both a medical and figurative meaning ...

C **Make it personal** In groups, plan and draw your own futuristic postcard! Consider 1–3. Use highlighted words from 5B.
1 Study the postcards in 5A again. How might these areas be different?
2 Can you imagine fashion 100 years from now? Or would you prefer to draw current fashions like the postcard artists did?
3 Will there be anything truly transformative by 2050?

Jobs
Energy
Fashion
Transportation

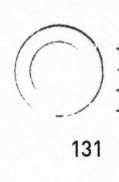

> I know it might sound a little wacky, but I think we should draw a ...

12.4 How unpredictable has your life been?

7 Language in use

A ▶ 12.9 What do you know about these people? Read the website and guess the missing words. Listen to check.

THESE 19TH CENTURY AUTHORS FOUND THE UNEXPECTED!

① Charles Dickens never would have imagined his ¹_____. Since his father couldn't pay his debts, he **got arrested** in 1824 and **got thrown in** debtor's prison. His whole family, including Charles, **had** their home **taken away** and had to join the father in ²_____. Then, as a young man, the future ³_____ **was exposed** to terrible ⁴_____ conditions in a factory. As a result, he soon had a wealth of ⁵_____ for his 15 novels, among them *Great Expectations* and *A Tale of Two Cities*. It turned out the hardships of his youth were worth it.

Dickens

② George Sand did not find what she was ⁶_____ when she traveled to the island of Mallorca, in the winter of 1838, with Polish ⁷_____ Frédéric Chopin. Sick with tuberculosis, Chopin **was being treated** in France, but **was getting pressured** by his doctor to find a milder ⁸_____. He thought a stay in Mallorca would be well worth the effort. They **had** their wishes **fulfilled** when they found a beautiful house in the town of Valldemossa. But, ⁹_____ for Chopin, he couldn't **get** his ¹⁰_____ **cured** because the humidity actually worsened it, and the couple had to return to France. Sand, though, now had material for a book: *A Winter in Mallorca*.

Chopin

Sand

B Answer 1–6. Which story did you find more surprising?
Who …

1 wasn't able to pay his or her debts?
2 lost their home and went to prison?
3 experienced bad working conditions?
4 encouraged Chopin to find a new climate?
5 was happy to find a beautiful house?
6 was still sick upon returning to France?

> I found the Dickens story shocking. I had no idea that he'd spent time in prison.

C ▶ 12.10 Read *Expressions with worth*. Then listen to two conversations about *Great Expectations*. Answer 1–2, using the expressions in the box.

Expressions with *worth*

Worth expressions usually imply there's value in the effort involved. The expressions are often interchangeable. However, if you're not expressing effort, *worth* can sound unnatural. Compare:

Is it **worth it** to read this long book? It's 600 pages!

Let's go to Henry's for dinner. The food is really ~~worthwhile~~ **good**.

be worth it   be worth the effort / trouble   be worth + verb + *-ing*
be worth someone's time   be worthwhile

Common mistake

It's
~~It~~ worth being frugal.

1 In conversation 1, why might the book a good choice for Mike?
2 In conversation 2, why might it not be a good choice?

D **Make it personal** In groups, have you ever done something you never thought would be worthwhile that led to an unpredictable result? Use expressions from **C**. Whose story is most surprising?

> I never thought it would be worth the effort to join a theater group. But I ended up getting the lead in a play!

132

How unpredictable has your life been? — 12.4

Lesson Aims: Sts read about 19th century authors, and discuss the unpredictable turns in their lives.

Skills	Language	Grammar
Reading a text about two 19th century authors whose hard lives provided materials for the books they wrote. Discussing unpredictable outcomes	Using causative and passive expressions with *get* to convey different registers, e.g. *Do you want to get us killed? I got accepted to Harvard.*	The passive with *get* and *be*, and the causative with *get* and *have*, e.g. *Tom was getting hassled. She got / had her photo taken.*

Warm-up
Ask the lesson title question: *How unpredictable has your life been? Have you been surprised by the way a life event turned out, e.g. a job you ended up getting, someone you ended up marrying, an award or prize you won? Do you believe that everything happens for a reason?*

7 Language in use

A ▶ 12.9 With the text covered, ask sts to focus on the pictures and the title of the text. Ask: *What do you know about these people?* Have them guess when they were born (Dickens 1812, Chopin 1810, and Sand 1804). Ask: *What do you know about life in the 19th century?*

Sts read the text and guess the missing words. Then play the audio for them to check. Classcheck.

Stronger classes: For listening practice, you could ask sts to keep the text covered while you play the audio. Pause after each sentence, and ask sts to transcribe it. When they have finished, they uncover the text and compare it with their version.

> **Answers**
> 1 future 2 prison 3 writer 4 working 5 material
> 6 expecting 7 composer 8 climate 9 unfortunately
> 10 illness

Background information
Charles Dickens was an English writer and social critic in the 19th Century. He created some of the world's most well-known fictional characters such as Oliver Twist and Scrooge, and his fiction often highlighted the terrible conditions that the poor of the time used to live in.

George Sand was a French writer in the 19th Century. She was well-known for her romantic affairs with well-known creative people, such as Frédéric Chopin.

Frédéric Chopin was a Polish composer and pianist in the 19th Century. He was a childhood prodigy and composed many of his earlier works before the age of 20. He was ill throughout most of his life, and died in Paris at the age of 39.

B Ask sts to read the questions and explain any unknown words. Ask them if they remember the answers. Have them re-read the text to check. Peercheck. Classcheck.

> **Answers**
> 1 Charles Dickens' father 2 Charles Dickens' family
> 3 Charles Dickens 4 Chopin's doctor 5 Chopin and Sand
> 6 Chopin

C ▶ 12.10 Go through **Expressions with worth**. Focus on the expressions in the box below, and explain or elicit what they mean. Have sts think of examples using each of them, e.g. *I don't think it's worth the effort to run / running for the train. We'll miss it anyway.*

Tell sts that the meaning is the same for all the expressions. They should take note that *be worth it* is always followed by *to* + infinitive. However, *be worth* is followed by an *-ing* form. Board the following examples for them to compare:

*Is it worth it **to read** this long book?*

*Is it worth **reading** this long book?*

They should also note that be worth the *effort* can be followed by **either** *to* +infinitive or *-ing* form, but the other expressions are only used with the *-ing* form.

Focus on questions 1 and 2. Tell sts they are going to hear Mike talking to two different people about the book Great Expectations by Charles Dickens. Play the audio and have sts answer the questions.

Classcheck, and ask: *Have you read the book? Did you like it? Do you think it's worthwhile for Mike to read it?*

> **Answers**
> 1 It's worth reading (or worthwhile) because it's a good historical novel – and his girlfriend is from London.
> 2 It's not worth it (worth reading, worth the effort) because Mike wants to understand modern England (and it's long and depressing).

» See Teacher's Book p.339 for Audio script 12.10.

D Make it personal Ask: *Have you ever done something you never thought would be worthwhile that led to an unpredictable result?* Focus on the example in the speech bubble, and maybe give sts a further example of your own, e.g. *I often wondered whether spending hours learning English words at school was really worth the effort, but in the end I became an English teacher!!*

Put sts in groups to discuss the question. Monitor, helping with vocabulary. Invite sts to share their stories with the class. Discuss which story was most surprising.

12.4

» Song lyric: See Teacher's Book p.355 for notes about the song and an accompanying activity to do with the class.

8 Grammar: The passive and causative with *get*

Tip

As a lead-in, board the verb *get* and ask sts to come up with as many meanings as they can, with a useful personal example (e.g. *receive, become, understand, go to / arrive at somewhere, achieve, be, have*) plus all the phrasal options.

A Board a sentence with a mistake to correct, e.g. *We got washed our car.* Highlight the word order in the causative sentences (the past participle always comes after the object). Have they ever made this mistake?

Go through the example sentences in the grammar box, and elicit what tense the verbs are in. Check the meaning of the verbs *hassle* (annoy) and *assign* (delegate / give out). Ask sts how they would formulate the example sentences in their language.

Highlight the word order in the causative sentences (the past participle always comes after the object).

Focus on the bold words in **7A**, and ask sts to rephrase them as instructed. Do the first one together as an example. Peercheck. Classcheck.

> **Answers**
>
> Dickens was arrested. He was thrown in debtor's prison. He got their home taken away. He got exposed.
> Chopin was getting treated. He was being pressured. They got their wishes fulfilled. He couldn't have his illness cured.

» Refer sts to the **Grammar expansion** on p.160.

B Go through **Spoken grammar** together. Model stress and intonation of the example sentences. Have sts repeat after you, encouraging them to express the appropriate emotion.

Sts read sentences 1–5. Help with any unknown words. Ask them to rephrase the underlined parts with a *get* passive or causative.

Optional activity

Fast finishers can come up with another example of their own to add to the activity.

Peercheck. Classcheck.

Put sts in pairs, and have them take turns reading out their rephrased sentences. Their partner responds appropriately. Focus on the speech bubble, as a model, and have two sts read it out.

Weaker classes: Brainstorm a few replies they can use: *How annoying! Is it very painful? Don't worry, she won't find out! Great job! I'm so happy for you! You're right! Let's go somewhere else.*

> **Answers**
>
> 1 Do you want us to get killed?
> 2 I just got my foot stepped on.
> 3 You could get fired. / She could get you fired
> 4 I got awarded
> 5 Do you want me to get taken to court (by the neighbors)?

C ▶ 12.11 Focus on the pictures, and encourage sts to guess what happened, prompting them if necessary by asking: *Where are they? What is the relationship between the two people? How are they feeling?*

Tell sts they will hear a short conversation for each picture. When they hear a beep, they need to rephrase the last phrase they heard with *get*. Rather than call out their answer, have them turn and say it to a partner, so everyone gets the same chance.

Weaker classes: Play the audio right through once so sts can get the gist before they do the task. Classcheck.

> **Answers**
>
> 1 I got promoted to manager.
> 2 You could get hurt!
> 3 I got it twisted in the subway!
> 4 You want to get us evicted?

» See Teacher's Book p.339 for Audio script 12.11.

D Make it personal Put sts in pairs. Have them use the pictures to create new roleplays and practice patterns a–d from B. Point out that the pictures are just there to spark ideas and that they are free to change the situation to anything that appeals to them. Tell them to take turns playing each role. Monitor and make sure they are using *get* expressions correctly, and encourage them to respond with emotion.

Ask sts to act out their best situation to the class.

> **Possible answers**
>
> 1 See example speech bubbles
> 2 A: I want to get my ball out of the pool. I'm going to dive in.
>   B: You could get hurt / killed.
> 3 A: My arm's killing me. I was running for the train and I got it caught in the doors.
>   B: Poor you!
> 4 A: I'm looking to give away Dana's dog.
>   B: Our roommate's dog? Do you want to get us arrested? You can't give away someone else's pet.

Optional activity

When sts perform their best roleplays to the class, don't let them say which picture it refers to. Other sts in the class watch / listen and guess the picture.

» Workbook p.61.

♪ And I'm in so deep. You know I'm such a fool for you. You've got me wrapped around your finger. Do you have to let it linger?

8 Grammar: The passive and causative with *get*

A Read the grammar box. Then rephrase the verbs with *get* in 7A with a form of *have* or *be*, and the ones with *have* or *be* with a form of *get*.

The passive with *get* and *be*; the causative with *get* and *have*

Passive: *get = be*	Tom	**was getting** / **is being**	**hassled** / **pressured**	a lot by his boss. / to resign.
	I	**got** / **was**	**fired** / **left**	on Tuesday. / without a job.
Causative passive: *get = have*	She	**got** / **had**	her short story **accepted** / her photo **taken**	by the magazine. / as a result.
	We	**'ll be getting** / **might have**	more work **assigned** / our vacations **taken**	soon! / away.

>> Grammar expansion p.160

B Read *Spoken grammar: Using the get passive*. Then rephrase the underlined parts of 1–5 with a *get* passive or causative. In pairs, A: Read a sentence with emotion; B: Respond with feeling! Change roles.

Spoken grammar: Using the *get* passive

The *get* passive and causative, in spoken English, often convey nuances of meaning and register. For example:

a informality: Guess what! I **got accepted** into Harvard!
b emphasis: You **could get hurt** if you keep that up!
c negative intent: I **got** my wallet **stolen** as I was walking home.
d unintended consequence: Do you want to **get** me **arrested**?

1 Hey, you're going 90 miles an hour! Slow down. <u>Do you want us to die</u>?
2 Ouch! <u>Some creep just stepped on my foot</u>! I think he did it on purpose!
3 What! You're reading your boss's email? <u>She could fire you</u> and with good reason!
4 Fantastic news! <u>They awarded me</u> first prize for my painting!
5 Firecrackers are illegal! Do you want <u>the neighbors to take me to court</u>?

> Hey, you're going 90 miles an hour! Slow down. Do you want us to get killed?

> I'm sorry! I'm just worried we might miss our flight.

C ▶ 12.11 Guess what happened in pictures 1–4. Then listen to four conversations. After the "beep," rephrase the sentence with *get*. Continue listening to check.

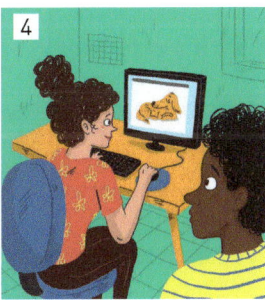

D Make it personal In pairs, using only the pictures, role-play new situations. Use the passive or causative with *get*.

> Big news! I got my picture taken for the newspaper!

> You did? That's awesome.

12.5 What will make a better society?

9 Listening

A ▶ 12.12 Listen to the start of a lecture on building a utopian society. In pairs, answer Professor Orwell's question.

B ▶ 12.13 Listen to part two. Complete Jennifer's reasons. In pairs, are any convincing?

There will be no …
1 housing shortage because buildings will be _____.
2 food shortage because people will have _____.
3 pollution because everyone will have a _____ for transportation.

> I think … sounds ridiculous!

C ▶ 12.14 Listen to part three and take notes. Give one argument to show how …
1 the housing crisis may diminish.
2 hunger will remain a problem.

D ▶ 12.15 Read *Whatsoever*. Then add *whatsoever* to 1–6, only if possible. Listen to check.

> **Whatsoever**
>
> Like *at all*, *whatsoever* can be used to emphasize negative ideas. Notice its position in these sentences:
> I have **no** idea **whatsoever** what a utopian society is.
> There's **nothing whatsoever** we can do to change the current situation.
> It can also be used in questions with *any*:
> Is there **any** doubt **whatsoever** that climate change is getting worse?

1 But rest assured, there's no connection to the famous novel, *1984*.
2 To me, a true utopia makes life just enjoyable and worth living.
3 I have no doubt that those things will come, too.
4 For one thing, the housing shortage will disappear.
5 There won't be any emissions where we live.
6 Is there any evidence that any of these changes might actually come about?

10 Keep talking

A In your view, is the world getting better or worse? Choose three areas.

access to quality education   animal rights   international relations
environmental issues   hunger   public health / homelessness

B Note down reasons. Can you find any evidence to support your opinion?

C In groups, share your ideas. Any disagreements?

> I think the world is getting worse. For example, homelessness is on the rise.

> Hmm … What's your evidence?

134

What will make a better society? 12.5

Lesson Aims: Sts listen to a lecture on building a better society and write an opinion essay.

Skills	Language
Writing an opinion essay, using a variety of verb and noun phrases	Emphasizing negative ideas using *whatsoever*, e.g. *I have no idea whatsoever! There's nothing whatsoever we can do to change the current situation.*

Warm-up

Ask: *Have you heard of George Orwell? What do you know about him? Who has read his novel 1984?* If sts have read it, ask them to explain what it is about. Board the words *totalitarian* and *dystopian*, and discuss what they mean.

Ask the lesson title question: *What will make a better society? Do any modern cities or communities come close to your ideal?* Have sts discuss in groups. Open up to a class discussion.

Background information

George Orwell was an early 20th Century British writer, whose real name was Eric Arthur Blair. Most of his work was about social injustice and opposition to totalitarianism. One of his most famous books was *1984* which describes a totalitarian state of the future where everyone is watched by the leader "Big Brother" and monitored by the thought police. It tells the story of how one man tries to escape this life and the terrible consequences he faces because of it.

9 Listening

A ▶ 12.10 Tell sts they are going to hear the start of a lecture on utopian society. Play the audio, elicit the question the lecturer asks, and board it. Ask: *What's the very first word that comes to mind when I say "utopia"?*

Put sts in pairs to discuss the question. Classcheck by inviting them to share ideas with the class.

Ask: *What is funny about the speaker's name?*

» See Teacher's Book p.339 for Audio script 12.12.

B ▶ 12.13 Tell sts they are going to hear the speaker interacting with three sts, Jennifer, Michael, and Oscar. Sts listen to the second part of the lecture and complete Jennifer's reasons. Classcheck. In pairs, sts discuss Jennifer's points, and if they are convincing or not. Try to elicit that her ideas are a bit far-fetched and idealistic.

Ask: *Do you think the other sts are convinced by Jennifer's arguments?* (not really) *What are their main concerns?* (environment and basic needs such as food, education, housing, and medical care)

Answers
1. built underground 2. 3D printers 3. drone

» See Teacher's Book p.339 for Audio script 12.13.

C ▶ 12.14 Sts listen to the final part of the lecture and take notes. Elicit an argument for 1 and 2. Classcheck.

Answers
1. Cities have already shown they can fit more people.
2. World hunger has declined in the last 25 years, but not fast enough.

» See Teacher's Book p.340 for Audio script 12.14.

D ▶ 12.15 Read **Whatsoever** with the class. Drill pronunciation /wɒtsəʊˈɛvər/. Explain that *whatsoever* and *at all* are interchangeable.

Ask sts what a comparable phrase would be in their language. Sts rewrite sentences 1–6, adding *whatsoever* if they can. Play the audio for them to check.

Answers
1. But rest assured, there's no connection whatsoever to the famous novel, *1984*.
3. I have no doubt whatsoever that those things will come, too.
5. There won't be any emissions whatsoever where we live.
6. Is there any evidence whatsoever that any of these changes might actually come about?

10 Keep talking

A Go through the areas listed. Ask sts: *Do you feel optimistic / pessimistic about the future of these things?* Give sts time to think about them, and choose three they feel most passionate about.

B Ask sts to research the areas they chose and find facts and statistics to back up their views. Do this in class, if you have online access, otherwise have them do the research for homework.

C Put sts into groups to share their ideas. Monitor around the class and help with vocabulary. Classcheck by asking one or two sts to present their ideas to the class.

Ask: *Did your groups feel generally optimistic or pessimistic about the future? Which were the biggest areas for concern?*

12.5

11 Writing: An opinion essay

A Focus on the essay title and have sts raise a hand if they think the world is generally getting better, or if they think it's worsening.

Tip

Make it clear that you will give sts literally just one minute to scan through the essay, to see the author's point of view. Classcheck. Ask: *How did you do it? Who, for example, read the first and last line of each paragraph? Who only read the last paragraph? Any other tactics? How useful / easy is a quick read like this?*

Have sts read the essay carefully and check one of the boxes. When deciding, ask sts to consider if Oscar a) backs up the points he makes with facts, and b) whether he presents a balanced argument. Collate their answers, by asking sts to raise their hand if they checked boxes 1, 2, or 3. Did sts agree?

B Sts re-read the essay and complete it with topics from 10A.

Classcheck. Ask them to skim the text and underline the positive points he makes (advances in medicine are bringing us closer to curing diseases, fall in homelessness, increase in life expectancy, decrease in international conflicts), and the negative points (steep rise in the planet's temperature, destruction of the Earth's biosphere, extinction of increasing number of species).

Ask: *Is Oscar optimistic or pessimistic overall? What does "apocalypse" mean?* (end of the world, catastrophe) *What might the opposite of "apocalypse" be?* (something like good fortune, happiness, a miracle)

> **Answers**
> 1 public health 2 international relations
> 3 environmental issues

C Read **Write it right!** together. Focus on sentences 1–5, and ask sts to note the tense of the verbs (present perfect). Tell sts to take care to retain the same form when they rephrase the sentences. Focus on the example *has increased steadily > there has been*. Sts rephrase 2–4 individually, then peercheck. Fast finishers can try to add a locally relevant one of their own for the class to rephrase.

Classcheck by asking sts to read out their rephrased sentences.

> **Answers**
> 1 There's been a steady increase in life expectancy.
> 2 There's been a slow but steady improvement in international relations.
> 3 The number of international conflicts has decreased significantly.
> 4 There's been a steep rise in the planet's temperature.
> 5 There's been a sharp fall in homelessness in some places.

» Song lyric: See Teacher's Book p.355 for notes about the song and an accompanying activity to do with the class.

D Your turn! Read through the instructions together, and clarify the aim (to write an essay entitled *Is the world getting better or worse?*).

Before they begin, ask sts to quickly scan the essay once more for phrases they can use a) to present a balanced argument, b) to give their opinions, and c) to link ideas.

Board them for sts to refer to when writing their essays:

a) *However, although, there's also been, while I don't quite agree ...in the long run ..., despite*

b) *in my view, I feel, it doesn't seem as if, it would seem to me*

c) *as opposed to, as well as, all of this might help to explain why, in the long run, in fact*

Make sure sts follow the *Before*, *While*, and *After* stages. Sts can plan their essays in class, and write up their finished essays for homework. Monitor and give feedback on their plans.

Before sts post their essays online, make sure they proof-read them carefully, or exchange them with a partner and proof-read each other's. Class feedback. When sts have had a chance to read some of their classmates' essays, get their feedback, and ask: *What does the class think are the most pressing issues? Are most sts pessimistic or optimistic?*

» Workbook p.62.

♪ If you wanna make the world a better place, Take a look at yourself, and then make a change

12.5

11 Writing: An opinion essay

A Read Oscar's essay in response to Professor Orwell's question. In your opinion, is he …
1. ☐ convincing?
2. ☐ somewhat convincing?
3. ☐ not convincing?

B Complete the essay with words from **10A**.

C Read *Write it right!* Then rephrase 1–5 using verb or noun phrases. Scan the essay to check.

> **Write it right!**
>
> Good writers know how to use words and structures flexibly to avoid repetition. Verb phrases can be written as noun phrases without a change in meaning:
>
> | Verb phrase (verb + adverb) | Noun phrase (adjective + noun) |
> |---|---|
> | CO_2 levels have **risen steadily**. | There has been **a steady rise** in CO_2 levels. |
> | Average earnings **dropped slightly**. | There was **a slight drop** in average earnings. |

1. Life expectancy has increased steadily.
   There's been a steady increase in life expectancy.
2. International relations have improved slowly but steadily.
3. There's been a significant decrease in the number of international conflicts.
4. The planet's temperature has risen steeply.
5. Homelessness has fallen sharply in some places.

D Your turn! Write an opinion essay in response to Professor Orwell's question in about 280 words.

Before
Decide how optimistic you feel about the future of the world. Then choose two to three issues from **10A** and, using your notes, plan the content of each paragraph.

While
Write a four to five paragraph essay, following the model in **A**. Refer to *Write it right!* to vary your use of noun and verb phrases.

After
Post your essay online and read your classmates' work. What were the most pressing issues?

Is the world getting better or worse?

Let's face it. This year hasn't been the most positive of years. Last year was tough, too. But is the world really getting worse? When our social media feeds are filled with bad news after bad news, reasons for optimism can seem few and far between. However, if we look at the world as a whole, as opposed to individual countries, in my view things are actually getting better.

Take ¹_____ for example. Although access to health care is still an issue in many countries, recent advances in stem-cell research, gene therapy, and nanotechnology mean we're inching closer to a cure for diseases such Alzheimer's, Parkinson's, and multiple sclerosis, as well as some forms of cancer. There's also been a sharp fall in homelessness in some places. All of this might help to explain why there has been a steady increase in life expectancy.

Second, there has been a slow but steady improvement in ²_____. Since World War II, the world has seen no "Great Wars," and the number of international conflicts has decreased significantly. Some historians refer to the period we are living in as the "Long Peace." While I don't quite agree since the world is still a dangerous place, in the long run, I feel globalization will make it safer.

We're still faced with serious ³_____. In the past two decades, there's been a steep rise in the planet's temperature, which has caused glaciers to melt and seas to rise at unprecedented rates. The continued destruction of the Earth's biosphere and the extinction of an ever-increasing number of species are just some of the daunting challenges we're up against. Will we be able to meet them? Only time will tell, but at least awareness has increased.

Yet, despite all the problems in the world today, it doesn't seem as if we're on the edge of the apocalypse – at least not yet. In fact, looking back through the lens of history, it would seem to me that the opposite might be closer to the truth.

Review 6
Units 11–12

1 Listening

A ▶ R6.1 Listen to a conversation between two friends, Phil and Melinda. Her primary tone is …
 a angry and sarcastic.   b angry, but resigned.   b sarcastic, but hopeful.

B ▶ R6.1 Listen again and fill in the modal verbs. Then match them with their functions (a–e).
1 He _____ have just asked.
2 You _____ want to file a report.
3 This _____ be a bad corner.
4 They _____ come here.
5 It _____ be that hard to locate it.
6 He _____ have at least dropped the bag.

a ☐ possibility
b ☐ suggestion
c ☐ expectation
d ☐ annoyance
e ☐ refusal

C In pairs, role-play Phil and Melinda's conversation from memory.

> Stop, thief! Can you believe it? I just got my purse snatched!

2 Speaking

A Look at the cartoon on p.126.

1 In two minutes, note down as many possible trends that you can imagine over the next ten years, using these words and expressions:

> a steady increase   a steep rise   be closely related to   bring about   drop slightly   give rise to   level off   plummet   plunge   rise significantly   skyrocket   soar   stem from

2 In groups, share ideas. Similar opinions?

> Homelessness is going to skyrocket. There's not enough housing.

> Actually, I think it's likely to level off. Doesn't at least some of it stem from the recession?

B **Make it personal** Choose three question titles from Units 11 and 12 to ask a partner. Ask at least three follow-up questions for each. What did you learn about each other?

> What does the sea make you think of?

> Jellyfish! I'm always getting stung by them when I go swimming.

3 Writing

Write a persuasive paragraph summarizing three trends you predict from 2A.

1 Note down evidence. 🔍 Search online for one key fact about each trend, as necessary.
2 Express your arguments using verbs from the box. Change some to nouns to vary the wording.

> decrease   drop   fall   improve   increase   level off   rise

"There will be a dramatic increase in salaries."

Review 6 (Units 11–12) R6

Warm-up

See p.61, 105, and 149 of the Teacher's Book for warm-up ideas.

1 Listening

A ▶ R6.1 Ask sts to listen to the conversation between Phil and Melinda, and choose the correct option. Peercheck and ask additional comprehension questions for them to answer in pairs, so more of them talk. Ask: *What's Melinda angry about?* (She had her bag stolen). *Why's she critical of the police?* (Because they are not patrolling an unsafe area). *What else did you manage to pick up?*

> **Answer**
> a

▶ See Teacher's Book p.340 for Audio script R6.1.

B ▶ R6.1 Ask sts to read the extracts from Phil and Melinda's conversation. Ask them if they remember who said these things, Phil or Melinda. Have them try and fill in the modal verbs from memory before playing the audio a second time for them to check. Peercheck.

Classcheck by re-playing the audio, pausing after each comment for sts to repeat. Encourage them to imitate the same tone of voice, rhythm, and reductions. Ask sts to practice saying them in pairs.

Put sts in pairs to try and role-play Phil and Melinda's conversation. Brainstorm the nature of their relationship, e.g. get sts to imagine their jobs, age, the chemistry, and possible problems between them, etc. to help them come up with the imaginative roleplays.

Weaker classes: Have sts sketch out the roleplay in noteform first.

Monitor and help as needed. Ask one or two pairs who seem to be having the most fun to act out their roleplays to the class. If time, and sts are into this, have them swap roles and act out the roleplays in new pairs.

> **Answers**
> 1 could, d   2 might, b   3 might, a   4 won't, e
> 5 shouldn't, c   6 could, d

Weaker classes: Board the modals before they listen, in random order. Sts complete the sentences, then listen and check.

C Put sts in pairs to try and role-play Phil and Melinda's conversation.

Weaker classes: Have sts write out the roleplay first.

Monitor and give help where needed. Ask one or two pairs to act out their roleplays to the class. When sts have finished, have them swap roles and act out the roleplays in new pairs.

2 Speaking

A Focus on the cartoon on p.126. Ask sts what they think the people could be talking about (falling sales / profits). Elicit suggestions using the boxed expressions, e.g. *Sales / profits have plummeted. There has been a steady decrease in sales / profits. Sales have dropped sharply. Sales / profits have plunged.*

1 Brainstorm some of the trends sts talked about in lesson 12.1, e.g. traffic deaths, unemployment, generation of solar electricity, life expectancy, obesity rates, poverty, use of cell phones / tablets. Give sts two minutes to note down any other current, local, or international trends they can think of using the expressions in the box.

2 Put sts in groups to share their ideas. Focus on the speech bubble as an example. Elicit a couple more examples, e.g. *Use of cell phones is going to level off.* Encourage sts to comment on their partner's ideas, and challenge them if they disagree.

Class feedback. Invite sts to share their ideas with the class.

Optional activity

Review the expressions first by drawing simple graphs on the board and eliciting which phrase(s) could be used to describe them. Sts then test each other in pairs by drawing similar diagrams.

B Make it personal Sts look back at the lesson title questions in Units 11 and 12 and choose three to ask a partner, plus at least follow-up questions. Focus on the example and elicit a few other answers to this question.

Put sts in pairs to ask and answer their questions. When they have finished, they can swap partners and ask the questions again or ask a different series of questions from another lesson title.

Class feedback. Ask: *What was the most surprising thing you learned about your partner?*

3 Writing

Focus on the cartoon. Ask: *Who do you imagine is talking to whom? Have you ever heard anyone say this? Do you believe him?*

Go through the instructions with the class. Ask sts to quickly review **Write it right!** on p.135 before they begin. Sts might also find it helpful to refer to the report and **Write it right!** on p.125, too.

Review the pronunciation and meanings of the boxed verbs, e.g. by asking which are opposites.

Sts write their paragraphs individually. If they do this in class, ask the fast finishers to swap and read each other's paragraphs to give the rest more time. When everyone has finished, sts swap paragraphs with a (new) partner, read, and proofread each other's writing. Display the texts on the wall or post them on the class website.

4 Grammar

A Before sts do the activity, give them a minute to read the text quickly for gist, and say whether the number of homeless are a) rising b) falling c) doesn't say. (The answer is "doesn't say"). Ask: *How do you say that long number?*

Ask them to read the text again and add or delete an article in 1–9.

Weaker classes: Ask sts to refer to the Grammar section on p.123 of the Student's Book for help.

Peercheck. Classcheck.

Answers

1 a homeless problem 2 ✓ 3 ✓ 4 relatives
5 homeless people 6 a number of efforts
7 the last survey 8 ✓ 9 shelter

B Go through the example together. Put sts in pairs. Ask them to take turns going through 2–9 in **A** and explain why the items are correct or incorrect.

Monitor and give help where needed. Class feedback. Ask: *Are you more confident now about article use?*

Suggested answers

4 There is no article as the writer is referring to "relatives" in general.
5 As above.
6 We need the indefinite article because it's the first time it's been mentioned.
7 We need the definite article here because it is shared knowledge.
9 No article needed, as this refers to shelter in general.

Optional activity

Board the following questions:

How bad is homelessness / unemployment in your country?

Is it getting better or worse? Why?

What can be done to help the homeless / unemployed?

Sts discuss the questions in pairs / small groups, before sharing their ideas with the class.

5 Self-test

Follow the procedure on Teacher's Book p.62.

Answers

1 When trying out a new recipe, I always play it **safe** since there's no safety net to fall back on.
2 We can't just go with the flow because there's **too / so** much at stake.
3 Susan gave me some well-intended advice, but actually, most of **it wasn't** too useful.
4 Apparently one out of every three people **has itching** when stung by a bee.
5 I really warmed up **to** Auto-Tuning and didn't even realize they'd fallen **back on it**.
6 I enjoy **being** recorded when I sing and **hope not to** make any errors.
7 My brother was being **hassled** by his boss, and then he got **fired** on Thursday.
8 The new restaurant is expensive but worth it, and the food is really **good**.
9 There's nothing **whatsoever** we can do about the steady rise in pollution here.
10 We're **being** (getting) pressured by **the** new boss more than ever.

6 Point of view

Follow the procedure on Teacher's Book p.62.

Stronger classes: Hold a class debate on one of the topics. (See teaching procedures on p.106.)

4 Grammar

A Add or delete articles (1–9) where needed. Check (✔) those that are correct.

> Is there any doubt whatsoever that we have ¹homeless problem in the U.S.? ²A random study even showed that people walk by ³the homeless without even looking. Participants who saw ⁴the relatives on the street didn't even recognize them when they were disguised as ⁵the homeless people! Nevertheless, every two years, ⁶number of efforts is made in the U.S. to count the number of homeless in major cities. ⁷Last survey shows ⁸a staggering 578,424 people were without ⁹the shelter.

B In pairs, explain why the items are correct or incorrect.

> Number 1 is incorrect. It has to be a homeless problem. It's the first time it's been mentioned.

5 Self-test

Correct the two mistakes in each sentence. Check your answers in Units 11 and 12. What's your score, 1–20?

1. When trying out a new recipe, I always play it safety since there's no safe net to fall back on.
2. We can't just do with the flow because there's much at stake.
3. Susan gave me some well-intended advice, but actually, most of them aren't too useful.
4. Apparently, one out of every three people have the itching when stung by a bee.
5. I really warmed up Auto-Tuning and didn't even realize they'd fallen it back on.
6. I enjoy to be recorded when I sing and don't hope to make any errors.
7. My brother was being hassle by his boss, and then he got fire on Thursday.
8. The new restaurant is expensive but worth, and the food is really worth the trouble.
9. There's nothing whatever we can do about the steady rising in pollution here.
10. We're having pressured more by new boss more than ever.

6 Point of view

Choose a topic. Then support your opinion in 100–150 words, and record your answer. Ask a partner for feedback. How can you be more convincing?

a. You think upbringing determines whether you're open to risk-taking. OR
   You think age is the most important factor in risk-taking.
b. You think online dating is generally safe and you should go with the flow. OR
   You think online dating calls for detailed safety precautions.
c. You think books are more influential than music in changing the world. OR
   You think the power of music in promoting social change shouldn't be underestimated.
d. You think limited access to quality education is a major social problem. OR
   You think access to quality education has been steadily improving.

Unit 1 — Grammar expansion

1 Subject-verb agreement with possessives (do after 1.2)

In American English, it is ungrammatical to use a plural possessive adjective or pronoun to refer back to a singular subject. Indefinite pronouns are singular:

Everyone should take	**his or her**	seat.
People should take	**their**	seat**s**.

In informal conversation, you may hear sentences where a singular subject has the plural possessive *their* or *theirs*, but such sentences should be avoided in formal speech and writing.

Common mistakes

Anyone who wants to open ~~their~~ *his or her* own business can.

Someone dropped ~~their~~ *a* wallet.

In other possessive constructions, the verb agrees with the subject of the sentence:

One of my parents' friends	**has**	a great new idea.
Each of our team's members	**is**	sending in a proposal.

2 More on expressing continuity (do after 1.4)

Use the past continuous to give background information, but use *used to* or *would* for repeated actions, and *used to* or the simple past to express a state:

I **was going**	to school at the time.
I **belonged**	to a gym.
I **used to / would**	go there every week.
I **used to**	have a personal trainer.
Eventually I **decided**	to become a trainer, too.

Use modal verbs in continuous tenses to express ideas that are or will be in progress:

Probability	You **must be moving**	soon. I can see you're packing.
Possibility	We **might be starting**	our own business, but things are a little up in the air.
Advice	You **should be looking**	for a job. You're already 25!

Sometimes the continuous verb is close in meaning to a non-continuous form:

Possibility	We **might start**	our own business if we find a good location.

But sometimes the meaning is very different:

Obligation / Necessity	You **must move**	within three months. The landlord needs the apartment.

How long ... ?, for, and since

The present perfect and present perfect continuous have the same meaning when used with *How long ...?*, *for*, or *since*:

How long **have you done** this kind of work?	I've **done** it **for two years**.
How long **have you been working** here?	I've **been working** here **since 2015**.

But use only the present perfect with stative verbs:

How long **have you had** this car?	I've **had** it **for three years**.

Unit 1

1A Correct the two mistakes in each sentence. There may be more than one solution. (You may wish to review the rules on p. 9, too.)

1. One of my friends' classmate have an idea for a new start-up.
2. Everyone need to be cautious with their major decisions.
3. Many people worries about investing his or her money.
4. Two hundred dollars are a lot for someone to pay for their English course.
5. Having business strategies are important for anyone who wants their own start-up.
6. My teacher, as well as all my friends, think one of us have a great idea.
7. Keeping your fears in check are important if you're someone who are planning a lifestyle change.
8. Some of my parents' best advice were in his or her letter.
9. Everyone should take their umbrella because something tell me it's going to rain.
10. One of my sister's friends have told me that two years aren't long enough to learn English.

1B In pairs, explain the reasons each sentence is ungrammatical.

> Number 1 is kind of hard. I wasn't sure about "friends'."

> You have many friends so that's correct, but "classmate" needs an "s" because there are many students in the class. And then the verb ...

2A Circle the correct options to complete the texts about each first time experience.

1. Speaking of "firsts," I'll never forget the first time I ¹[**acted** / **was acting**] in a play. I ²[**was living** / **would live**] in Spain, so the play ³[**used to be** / **was**] in Spanish. I ⁴['**d been practicing** / '**d practiced**] my part one last time before we ⁵[**went** / **were going**] on stage, but I ⁶[**was still** / **was still being**] nervous. I ⁷[**would worry** / **worried**] that ⁸[**I might be forgetting** / **I might forget**] my part. However, when we finally ⁹[**performed** / **were performing**] the play, it ¹⁰[**was** / **was being**] a fabulous success.

2. It may not seem like a big deal, but the first time I ¹[**was** / **had been**] on an airplane was so exciting. I only ²[**used to fly** / **flew**] from Washington, D.C. to Chicago, less than two hours away, but in those days, it ³[**wouldn't be** / **wasn't**] so common to fly, and it ⁴[**used to be** / **would be**] much more expensive. When I ⁵[**got** / **was getting**] there, I then ⁶[**was having to** / **had to**] take a bus through the corn fields of Illinois up to Wisconsin, where I ⁷[**was visiting** / **used to visit**] a friend. The fields ⁸[**went** / **were going**] on for miles. But what I remember most of all is that a girl ⁹[**had lost** / **was losing**] her knapsack, and the whole bus ¹⁰[**must spend** / **must have spent**] a half hour looking for it.

2B Make it personal In pairs, share an experience about yourself beginning with "Speaking of 'firsts' ..." or "It may not seem like a big deal, but ..."

> Speaking of "firsts," I'll ever forget the time I spent the night on a sailboat. The wind was picking up, and it had just started to rain when ...

Bonus! Language in song

♪ **Some people** want diamond rings. **Some** just want everything. But **everything** means nothing.

Rewrite the song line changing the bold words in order to *only one of us*, *each of us*, and *most things*. Add any other necessary changes.

Unit 2 — Grammar expansion

1 Sentences with complements and conjunctions (do after 2.2)

In conversation, repetition can be avoided both when you agree and don't agree.	
I actually like small apartments.	I **do**, too. / So **do** I.
My mom doesn't throw anything out.	Mine **doesn't** either. / Neither **does** mine.
I don't like this neighborhood.	But I **do**. Let's at least give it a chance.
I'm not happy in this apartment.	But I **am**. And we just moved in last year.

You can also avoid repetition with possessives and with indefinite pronouns. When there is a compound noun, only the second noun is possessive.		
Possessives	My house is a lot smaller than my **sister's**. My yard is smaller than **hers**, also.	
	But my house is bigger than **Jim and Amy's**. And my kitchen is bigger than **theirs**, as well.	
Indefinite pronouns	We don't have a garden, but my brother has **one**.	
	Last year, we planted vegetables, but this year, we don't have **any**.	

Finally, you can avoid repetition when referring to an entire idea or sentence.	
Do you feel like going out to dinner tonight?	I don't think **so**.
Would you consider renting one of these apartments?	I guess / suppose **so**.
We have a lot of junk here!	I told you **so**.
However, you cannot use *so* to refer to a specific noun.	
What was your reaction to *this neighborhood*?	I like **it**.

Common mistakes

Our garden is nicer than my ~~sister~~ garden. → *sister's*
I really like my new home, and my friends ~~like~~, too. → *do*
Do you like the apartment? I think ~~that yes~~. → *so*

2 More on comparatives with *so* and *such* (do after 2.4)

Use *so much* before comparative forms of adjectives, to compare non-count nouns, and to refer to a whole idea.
Use *so many* when comparing count nouns.

Adjectives	It's	so much	harder	living in a small apartment.
			less expensive	here than in New York.
			more crowded	on the subway than the bus.
Non-count nouns	There's		more information	than there used to be.
			less time	than when we were kids.
Ideas	We like it here		more	than we thought we would.
	We miss home		less	than we expected.
Count nouns	There are	so many	more people	that I can never get a seat.
	We have		fewer services	than we once had.

Common mistakes

It's so much ~~more noisy~~ than what we were used to. → *noisier*
There are so many ~~less~~ people than there once ~~was~~. → *fewer* ... *were*

Unit 2

1A Rewrite the sentences, shortening them to avoid repetition.
1. My whole family has trouble throwing things out, and I have trouble throwing things out.
2. There aren't that many good English coursebooks, but I have a good English coursebook.
3. Many of my friends want to get married, but I don't want to get married.
4. A lot of people I know want to live alone, and I want to live alone.
5. I've looked at a lot of apartments, and I hoped to find an apartment, but I haven't found an apartment. (two changes)
6. My friends say their ideas about the future have changed recently, and my ideas about the future have changed. (two changes)

1B Make it personal Change two sentences in A so they're true for you. In pairs, compare opinions.

> My whole family has trouble throwing things out, and so do I!

> I don't! My apartment is so small I hardly fit in it myself.

1C Correct the mistakes in these shortened sentences.
1. Maybe you don't like small apartments, but I like.
2. They haven't saved money for unforeseen events, but I've saved.
3. My view is nicer than Ted and Mary's, and my kitchen is bigger than them.
4. My neighborhood is a lot more interesting than Sally and Bill.
5. We don't have a pool in our back yard, but my sister has.
6. My parents asked me if I wanted to move, and I said I thought yes.
7. We can't find a good moving company, but maybe you can recommend one good.
8. Our old apartment had big closets, but this one doesn't have some.
9. My boyfriend asked me if I wanted my independence, but I said I didn't think it.
10. I don't know for sure if we're buying this place. My husband wants, so I guess that yes. (two mistakes)

2A Complete the paragraph with comparatives containing *so many* or *so much* and the words in parentheses.

Most major cities have changed substantially in the last 50 years, and Washington, D.C. is no exception. There are ¹<u>so many more people</u> (people) than there used to be, and it's ² _____ (busy) all the time. It's true that the Metro, which opened in 1976, was a welcome addition to the nation's capital, one that makes it ³ _____ (easy) to get to work. But the trains are ⁴ _____ (crowded) than the old buses used to be. Since I still have to drive to a *Park and Ride* station to get the train, I'm aware that there's ⁵ _____ (traffic) everywhere, too. And forget about driving to work! There are ⁶ _____ (parking spaces) than there once were. In fact, there are hardly any! Everywhere, especially in neighboring Maryland and Virginia, there are ⁷ _____ (buildings) and just ⁸ _____ (congestion) everywhere. I have to say I like the "new" Washington, D.C. ⁹ _____ than the city I remember from my childhood.

2B Make it personal Rewrite the paragraph about a city you know, changing the details as necessary. In pairs, share your stories.

Most major cities have changed substantially in the last 10 years, and ...

> **Bonus! Language in song**
>
> ♪ So many tears I've cried. So much pain inside. But baby it ain't over 'til it's over.
>
> Explain why the first sentence in the song line uses *so many*, but the second line *so much*.

287

Unit 3 — Grammar expansion

1 More on subject and object questions (do after 3.2)

Clauses with question words can be embedded in both *yes-no* and information questions.		
Does	**whether I have good pronunciation**	matter?
How does	**where I study**	affect my test results?
Why is	**how my accent sounds**	important?
When does	**what we say**	offend people?

Common mistakes

Does ~~how do I pronounce~~ *how I pronounce* my "r" really make any difference?

Why is what she ~~do~~ *does* your business?

2 More on participle clauses (do after 3.4)

Both active and passive participle clauses, including perfect participles, can also be negative.		
Active clause	**Not** living near a university,	Jack wasn't able to go to college.
	Not having driven in years,	I didn't feel comfortable starting again.
	After **not** being able to pay her bills,	Amy had to find a job.
Passive clause	**Not** respected by his boss,	Elmer decided to quit.
	Not having been seen in a while,	Marie suddenly showed up.

"Dangling" participles, common in informal conversation where the subject is understood, may sound very natural. However, they are ungrammatical.		
Conversational, but ungrammatical	Not being outgoing,	it's hard to meet new people.
Written		I find it hard to meet new people.

For clarity, the closer the participle clause is to the subject, the clearer the sentence. For this reason, participle clauses often go at the beginning, and not the end, of a sentence:
Having loved the violin as a child, **I** decided to study music and go to a conservatory.

Unit 3

1A Rephrase the questions without the word *it*.
1. Does it really matter what you study in college?
   Does what you study in college really matter?
2. Why should it be important how much you practice in public speaking?
3. When is it relevant whether you cram for a test?
4. How does it make you lose weight what you have for breakfast?
5. Why is it my parents' business what I do on weekends?

1B Correct one mistake in each question.
1. Do whether I can become bilingual really important?
2. How does what school do I choose affect my career?
3. Why does whether women has children keep them from finding jobs?
4. Does whether do I feel confident as a public speaker improve my performance?
5. How does what our teacher tell us about grammar help us speak more accurately?
6. Does how much TV we watch in English improves our vocabulary?

1C Make it personal Choose three questions from **A** and **B** to ask a partner.

> Does what you study in college really matter?

> I don't think it matters too much. Often you end up working in another area anyway.

2A Rewrite the paragraph, making the underlined participle clauses negative when the meaning requires it. Leave participle clauses that make sense as is.

> My husband and I are both bilingual in Spanish and English, so naturally we wanted our children to be, too. ¹Having been raised bilingual ourselves, we weren't sure where to begin. So ²knowing how to go about it and ³having been given useful advice by anyone, we looked for books in the library. We decided we would both speak both languages. ⁴After giving that a try, though, we didn't think it was working. ⁵Knowing which language to speak, my children were confused, so we decided I would always speak English, and my husband Spanish. ⁶Having tried that now for several weeks, we're all a lot happier.

2B Correct the dangling participles, changing any necessary words so each sentence has a clear subject.
1. Not being confident about my accent, it could seem to people that I'm shy.
   Not being confident about my accent, I could seem shy to people.
2. Not having been elected president, Tom's attitude wasn't very good.
3. After not graduating last year, it was hard for me to find a job.
4. Not enjoying practicing at all, my violin just sat in a closet.
5. Not feeling loved by his girlfriend, Greg's weekends were kind of depressing.

2C Make it personal Share something you didn't do or that didn't happen, and the result, with a partner. Begin with a negative participle clause.

> Not having started my assignment until a day before it was due, I missed the deadline.

> So what happened?

> **Bonus! Language in song**
>
> ♪ And promise you kid that I'll give so much more than I get. I just haven't met you yet.
>
> Rewrite the song line beginning with the participle clause, *Having not even met you yet …* Make any other changes needed.

289

> Unit 4

Grammar expansion

1 More on emphatic inversion (do after 4.2)

When there is a subject and a verb in both clauses, adverbs and adverbial expressions sometimes invert them in the first clause and sometimes in the second. There is no rule. The expressions must be memorized.		
First clause	**No sooner** had I walked in the door	than the police rang the bell.
Second clause	**Not until** I saw the strange objects	**did I believe** the news.
Other **first clause** adverbials are: hardly (ever), never, seldom, rarely, only then, not only, scarcely, only later, nowhere, little, only in this way, in no way, on no account		
Other **second clause** adverbials are: not since, only after, only when, only by + -ing		

Emphatic inversion and register
Emphatic inversion is used in conversation for dramatic effect: **Never** in my life **had I met** anyone like him!
However, it is especially common in writing: **On no account** can we claim that these events are real. (written, formal) **There's no way** we can claim (that) these events are real. (conversational, neutral / informal)

> **Common mistake**
>
>   *college have*
> Not since I was in ~~college, have~~ I had so little money.
> Do not put a comma between the clauses when you use emphatic inversion.

2 More on formal relative clauses (do after 4.4)

Formal relative clauses often begin with prepositions. When the sentences are rephrased informally, the preposition goes at the end.	
Formal	Jane met someone **with whom** she had a lot in common.
	It's an interesting dilemma **to which** I imagine there are no answers.
	That's the researcher **in whose office** we had the meeting.
Informal	Jane met someone (**who**) she had a lot in common **with**.
	It's an interesting dilemma (**that**) I imagine there are no answers **to**.
	That's the researcher **whose office** we had the meeting **in**.

However, sometimes formal relative clauses begin with indefinite pronouns or nouns.	
Indefinite pronoun	The researchers, **some of whom** had different ideas, had trouble reaching a consensus.
	I looked at a lot of tests, **a few of which** seemed quite valid.
Noun	The test identifies **the frequency with which** we experience these emotions.
	We had a meeting this morning **the outcome of which** is still unclear.
These relative clauses have no informal equivalent, and the only way to express the same ideas more informally is to rephrase them: The researchers had trouble reaching a consensus **since / because** some of them had different ideas. The test identifies **how frequently** we experience these emotions.	

> **Common mistakes**
>
>   *the results of which*
> We've finished analyzing the study, ~~which results~~ were very surprising.
>   *whom*
> The students, most of ~~them~~ are under 30, are very open to new experiences.

Unit 4

1A Rephrase the sentences so they're more emphatic, beginning with the words in parentheses.
1. I haven't had a dream like this since I was a child. (not since)
2. I didn't realize the incident was serious until I saw it on TV. (only when)
3. I only came to understand the events later. (only later)
4. I absolutely didn't imagine our proposal would be accepted. (in no way)
5. Everyone started laughing, so we realized that Ron had made an April Fools' joke. (only after)
6. We almost never consider the consequences of our actions. (seldom)

1B In pairs, check the inverted subjects and verbs. Write 1 when the adverbial requires inversion in the first clause, and 2 for the second clause.

1C Rewrite the paragraph so it's more formal, using the adverbials in parentheses.

> I just couldn't have imagined some of the truly mean April Fools' jokes I've seen ¹(never), but the perpetrators hardly ever suffered any consequences ²(rarely). Take the case of the friendly and genial office colleague at my former job. As soon as his coworkers had arrived at work, he would invite them to come to his cubicle for a piece of gum ³(no sooner … than). Of course, they never suspected they might be chewing, and maybe even swallowing, something else ⁴(in no way)! But right when they put it in their mouths, we would hear a piercing scream ⁵(only when)! They almost never knew why it tasted so bad ⁶(seldom). You see, the gum was actually Play Doh, a sticky substance used by children for art projects. My colleagues never found out that it began as a wallpaper cleaner in the 1930s ⁷(hardly ever)!

1D Make it personal Using at least three adverbials, share a story about a prank or joke you've experienced.

> Nowhere had I heard about the joke that my friend Hilary played on me!

2A Correct the sentences so that each one has a formal relative clause with *whom*, *which*, or *whose*.
1. There are many amateur personality tests, some of them aren't very rigorous.
2. That's the convention center in it we stayed for the conference.
3. I studied the five domains into them our personalities can be classified.
4. Reliability is a trait which importance many people underestimate.
5. The scientist I work with him has just published an article.
6. The roommates, I lived with them as a freshman, were easy to get to know.
7. The woman I lived in her apartment just got elected to public office.
8. Which speed the train was traveling when it crashed was very high.

2B Make it personal Make three formal statements about your class or classmates. Your partner will say which he or she agrees with.

> Most of the people with whom we're studying English seem very motivated.

> I totally agree. If you get to this level, you have to be!

Bonus! Language in song

♪ Never in my wildest dreams, did I think someone could care about me.

Which word or phrase in the song can be replaced by the word *little* without changing the meaning?

Unit 5 — Grammar expansion

1 More on formal conjunctions and prepositions (do after 5.2)

		Most conjunctions and prepositions are neutral in register because often the content of the full sentence determines the level of formality. However, some distinctions can be made.
To express purpose:		
Formal	With a view to With the aim of In the interest of	reducing costs, the post office has eliminated Saturday delivery.
Neutral	(In order) to	reduce costs, the post office has stopped delivering mail on Saturday.
Other formal ways to express purpose: *so as to*, *in an effort to*		
To express reason:		
Formal	In light of On account of Owing to	increasing life expectancy / the fact that life expectancy is increasing, people need to save more money.
Neutral	Because of As a result of	
Other formal ways to express reason: *given*, *in view of*, *thanks to*		
To refer to something:		
Formal	With regard to Regarding	our communication of last week, we are still expecting a response.
Neutral	As far as	prices go, they couldn't possibly be higher.
	When it comes to	prices, they couldn't possibly be higher.
In formal speech and writing, shorter noun phrases, as opposed to longer clauses, are often used: In view of exhorbitant prices, we need to take emergency measures. (formal) Because prices are through the roof, we need to act now! (informal)		

> **Common mistake**
>
>   *the fact (that)*
> In light of / On account of / Owing to ∧ you didn't pay your rent on time, we're going to have to evict you.
>
> You may also say, "In light of / On account of / Owing **to not having paid** your rent on time, you're going to have to move." Remember: If you use a participle clause, it must have a subject!

2 More on objects + *-ing* forms after prepositions and verbs (do after 5.4)

When changing a noun to a possessive form in a more formal sentence, make certain the apostrophe is in the correct position.			
Neutral to formal	They accepted	**our team's**	submitting a project.
	I read about	**the protester's**	disrupting the event.
	We're supportive of	**the employees'**	taking a longer vacation.
Informal	They accepted	**our team**	submitting a project.
	I read about	**the protester**	disrupting the event.
	We're supportive of	**the employees**	taking a longer vacation.
Sense verbs are not followed by possessive forms: I saw **the man** climbing in the window. The cat is in our bed! I felt **it** tickling me.			

Unit 5

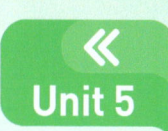

1A Rephrase the sentences so they're more formal, using the words in parentheses. Make any other changes necessary.

1. Because we need better security, we will be installing alarms throughout the building. (in the interest of)
2. Since you failed the final exam twice, I'm afraid you're going to have to repeat this course. (in light of)
3. In order to attract more customers, we're going to start doing more promotion. (with the aim of)
4. As far as the complaint you made recently about cockroaches, we'll send the exterminator this weekend. (with regard to)
5. Because we've had so many problems, we may have to postpone our vacation. (on account of)
6. As a result of having had very low sales, we can't offer raises this year. (owing to)
7. When it comes to the interpretation of dreams, I have some good books to recommend. (regarding)

1B Make it personal Rephrase the sentences so they are *less* formal. Then choose one topic to discuss with a partner. Any major disagreements?

1. Owing to the many world problems that face us, I don't think I'm going to have children.
2. In the interest of getting a good job, I'm going to delete my Facebook page so a potential employer can't see it.
3. Regarding understanding politics, I'm really not the slightest bit interested.
4. In light of the fact that we live a long life, I think it's silly to watch your diet too much.
5. So as to start over from scratch, I'm going to change schools.

> For the last one, you can say, "To start over from scratch, I'm going to change schools." That could be a very good idea.

> I'm not sure I agree. Even if things aren't going well, it's good to give things a chance.

2A Complete the sentences with an object and *-ing* form of the verb, adding any words needed. Then rephrase the sentences informally.

1. Jim witnessed <u>his daughter's getting arrested</u>. (daughter / get arrested) And now he's very upset with her.
   Jim witnessed his daughter getting arrested.
2. All parents have an investment in _____. (child / succeed) That's why they spend so much money.
3. I'm not happy about _____ so often. (husband / travel) He's never around!
4. We're worried about both new _____ so nervous. (managers / become) Maybe we're about to be fired!
5. The other team has an interest in _____ the award. (our school / win) If we win, they won't have as much competition next year.
6. George resented _____ with his old girlfriend. (Phil / go out) He was hoping to get back together with her.
7. Marcy was aware of _____ about her behind her back. (classmates / talk) They would start whispering as soon as they saw her.

2C Make it personal Complete the sentences with the *-ing* form of a verb so they are true for you. Then share two with a partner.

1. I don't mind my teacher …
2. I really appreciate my mother …
3. I'm definitely going to insist on my children …
4. I'm interested in our school …
5. I'm uncomfortable with my neighborhood …
6. I'm grateful for my country …

> I'm grateful for my country('s) taking pollution seriously.

Bonus! Language in song

♪ All is quiet on New Year's Day. A world in white gets underway.

Create a new song line beginning with *In view of*, *thanks to*, or *given*. Do you like the way it sounds? Why (not)?

Unit 6 — Grammar expansion

1 More adverb clauses of condition (do after 6.2)

Adverb clauses of condition also can be expressed more formally.		
As long as …	**Assuming** (that) the movie has subtitles,	viewers who don't speak the language can still enjoy it.
	Provided (that) your novel is accepted,	you'll be on your way to beginning a career as a writer.
	On the condition (that) the concepts are explained,	all students can understand and enjoy art.
(Even) if …	**Supposing** (that) 50 percent have a talent for music,	it's still true that the other 50 percent don't.
Even though …	**Despite the fact that** many young people don't like to read,	schools should still promote a love of literature.
	Irrespective of the fact that we have few museums,	our mayor realizes the importance of art.
	Notwithstanding the fact that books are expensive,	public libraries are free.

Common mistakes

Supposing ~~the fact~~ (that) your class hates to read, they may still like comics.
　　　　　the fact
Despite ∧ that many movie theaters have disappeared, some still remain.

2 More on emphasis (do after 6.4)

To emphasize a noun, you may begin the sentence with a *what*-clause.	
What a great **book**	it was.
What bad **English**	that actor spoke.
What bad **reviews**	the play got.
And to emphasize an adjective, you may begin with a *how*-clause.	
How bad the information was	that they gave us.
How right we were	about Jamie's novel.
Unlike auxiliaries to express emotion or emphasis (see p. 67), *what* and *how* clauses may begin a conversation. Compare: A: *What a boring movie that was*! I'm sorry we came to see it. B: Yes, it *did seem* kind of slow, didn't it?	

Common mistakes

　　　　　　great
What ~~a great~~ art this museum has.
　　　　　　　the play we saw was!
How enjoyable ~~was the play we saw~~!

Unit 6

1A Complete the paragraph to create formal adverb clauses of condition that mean the same as the words in parentheses. Do not use the same words twice.

> ¹_____ (even though) increasing numbers of people move from country to country as they seek employment, newspapers and publishers have not kept up with the need to truly internationalize their offerings. ²_____ (as long as) they speak the local language, English speakers living abroad may wish to read books in their original version, but at least one prominent e-reader based in the United States has been known to offer only an English translation for certain titles! ³_____ (as long as) there is a potential e-reader audience for the original text, publishers should be obliged to provide it. ⁴_____ (even if) some people wish to read translations, it is still true that others don't, just as not everyone wishes to see dubbed movies. ⁵_____ (as long as) publishers can break even on production costs, they need to remember that we live in a globalized age. ⁶_____ (even though) they undoubtedly have a large audience for the translation, they would do well to increase their marketing efforts to reach readers who can enjoy their texts in the languages in which they were originally written.

1B Make it personal Complete the sentences with true opinions. Use formal adverb clauses of condition. Then try to convince a partner.

1. _____, all students should be promoted to the next grade.
2. _____, movie theaters should remain open.
3. _____, at least 50% of people my age don't enjoy doing crossword puzzles.
4. _____, many people still never go to museums.
5. _____, I could imagine reading a book a week.

2A Rewrite the first sentences in 1–6 for emphasis, beginning with the words in parentheses.

1. That was a really great play! (what) I hadn't heard of the actors before.
2. The writer was awful in the way he expressed himself! (how) I'm not reading anything else by him.
3. There were scary actors that came on stage in the second act! (how) I didn't expect that.
4. She did a really bad job! (what) I'm hiring a different photographer next time.
5. You have an active imagination! (what) A movie like that could never happen in real life.
6. The paintings in this exhibit were intriguing! (how) I loved the artist.

2B Complete the conversations. Use auxiliaries to express emotion or emphasis.

1. A: What a boring movie that was. It didn't even have a plot.
   B: But *it did have a plot*! I agree it was a little slow, though.
2. A: How incompetent that actor was in how he delivered his lines. He couldn't even remember them.
   B: But _____. I read the play and they were correct.
3. A: What bad news I got today from the museum director. I can't even tell you.
   B: But _____. I'm always here to listen.
4. A: How stimulating our class was today. I love Shakespeare.
   B: Are you sure? I thought you hated him.
   A: But _____. I just didn't know enough English to understand him.

2C Make it personal Using the models in B and C, make three true sentences with *what* or *how* clauses. Then share them with a partner.

> What a boring class we had last week on American literature! I didn't learn anything.

> But you did learn something! You told me yourself you'd never heard of Raymond Carver previously.

Bonus! Language in song

♪ Near, far, wherever you are, I believe that the heart does go on.

Identify the auxiliary used for emphasis in this song line. What is being emphasized?

Unit 7 — Grammar expansion

1 Summary of future tenses (do after 7.2)

The future perfect emphasizes the completion of an action and is often used with *by the time*. The future perfect continuous always implies the action is ongoing.

- By the time I retire, I **will have had** at least three careers.
- Unlike my parents, when I'm 90, I **will have been using** Facebook my whole life.

Going to and *will* are both used to make predictions. Use *going to* when you're more certain about your prediction or have present evidence. Always use a perfect tense with *for* and *since*.

- A few years from now, our government **is going to run out** of money.
- By 2050, people **will** still **be working** when they're 80.
- By the time I'm 80, I **will have lived** here *for* 50 years because I have no intention of ever moving.
- In the future, people **will have been telecommuting** *since* their very first job.

Common mistake

By the end of the century, 90-year-olds ~~will use / will be using~~ social media for many years.
(*will have used / will have been using*)

2 More formal uses (do after 7.2)

The future perfect or future perfect continuous is sometimes used to speculate about past events and is usually more formal than the present perfect or present perfect continuous.

Neutral	No doubt you **'ve seen** that movie already and **have been telling** everyone else to do the same.
More formal	No doubt you **will have been** impressed by the performance and **will have been listening** to the orchestra's recordings.

When predicting the future, you may omit the word *going* for a more formal sentence. A contracted sentence is not as formal.

Neutral	If we**'re going to be** happy in our old age, we need to focus on our relationships. (active) If we think we**'re going to be rewarded** for living to 100, think again! (passive)
More formal	If I**'m** ever **to graduate**, I'd better start studying. (active) If we **are to live** longer, we need to change our eating habits. (active) Benefits **are to be paid** beginning at 65. (passive)

3 Cleft vs. pseudo-cleft sentences (do after 7.4)

English has many ways to move information to the front of a sentence for emphasis. Sentences beginning with words like *what*, *when*, and *where* are called "pseudo-cleft" sentences.

Cleft sentences	**It's** younger people	**who / that** have a few things to learn. (subject)
	It's the unimaginable	**(that)** no one can predict. (object)
Pseudo-cleft sentences	**When** I'm really tired	is on the weekends.
	What I thought I once wanted	has all changed now.

Unit 7

1A Circle the correct forms.

Since I come from a family with lots of longevity, I ¹[**'ll live** / **'m going to live**] to be 100. When I ²[**will start** / **start**] my second century, I hope I ³[**will still be able** / **will have still been able**] to ride a bike. By that point, I ⁴[**will have earned** / **will have been earning**] the distinction of having been an avid cyclist for over 90 years, and I ⁵[**will have been participating** / **will have participated**] in at least 2,000 bike races! I ⁶[**won't be racing** / **won't have been racing**] any longer in my second century, and I ⁷[**won't have been giving** / **won't have been given**] any medals, but I ⁸[**will have been passing** / **will have passed**] the longevity test. I hope my friends ⁹[**will have been exercising** / **will be exercising**] for as many years as I have because I definitely don't want to do this alone!

1B Make it personal Rewrite the paragraph in A beginning with sentence 2, changing "century" to "decade." In pairs, share your hopes for the next ten years.

> When I start my next decade, I hope I …

2A Rewrite the sentences to make them more formal.

1. No doubt your daughter has discovered a solution to peer pressure by now.
2. If we're going to be comfortable economically, we need to save money.
3. I'm sure older people have considered all the options before choosing a nursing home.
4. The government has planned for the fact that pensions are going to be cut back even further by the 2030s.
5. No doubt our planet has been suffering for generations, and we're just paying attention now.

2B Make it personal Choose three sentences from A and make them true. In groups, share opinions.

> No doubt my friend [name] …

3 Change the underlined parts of the responses to cleft or pseudo-cleft sentences. Begin with the word in parentheses.

1. A: I just can't believe Bob didn't throw out the garbage.
   B: <u>The small things always get to you</u>. (it)
2. A: We're not ready to work until we're 75.
   B: That's not a problem. <u>We're not ready for global warming</u>. (it)
3. A: Are you planning to go to grad school?
   B: I'd love to, but <u>I have no idea where I'll get the money</u>. (where)
4. A: Do you ever think about the future?
   B: Sometimes, but <u>I really can't tell you what I'll be doing in 10 years</u>. (what)

> **Bonus! Language in song**
>
> ♪ Wherever you go, whatever you do, I will be right here waiting for you.
>
> Rewrite the song line ending with the words *for fifty years*. What tense did you use?

Unit 8 — Grammar expansion

1 More on using the subjunctive (do after 8.2)

In formal speech, the subjunctive can be used with these verbs and expressions.	
Verbs	advise, ask, command, demand, desire, insist, prefer, propose, would rather, recommend, request, suggest, urge
Expressions with *it* ... (that)	It is best, critical, crucial, desirable, essential, imperative, important, preferable, recommended, urgent, vital, a good idea, a bad idea

The subjunctive can also be used in negative, passive, and continuous sentences. Remember that the subjunctive verb is not conjugated and remains in the base form.		
Negative	I suggest	(that) he **not speak** to me in that tone!
Passive	It's critical	(that) he **be fired** immediately.
Continuous	I absolutely insist	(that) you **be waiting** for me when I arrive.

Nevertheless, the subjunctive is limited in English. Do not use it to express the following.		
The future	I'm not leaving	until the manager sees me.
want, *would like*	I want	you **to refund** my money!
	I'd like (for)	
Emotion	I'm really happy	I **can exchange** this product.
	Sally was angry	the manager **didn't speak** to her yesterday.

In neutral or informal speech, the subjunctive is often avoided.		
Expressions with *it*	It's important	**for** stores **to respect** their customers.
	It's essential	she **expresses** her frustration. (primarily British)
Some verbs	I'd prefer	**for** your staff **to be** a little more polite.
	I recommended	he **should see** the manager. (primarily British)
would rather	I'd rather	you **gave** me the money today!

Common mistakes

I'd like ~~that your manager~~ *(for) your manager to* speak to me now!
I want ~~that she~~ *her to* pay attention.

2 More on adverb clauses with *-ever* words to emphasize conditions (do after 8.4)

Nouns, adjectives, and adverbs may follow *however*. Be careful with count and non-count nouns.			
Non-count noun	However	**much** (money) you spent,	I won't be responsible.
Count noun		**many** times you try to persuade me,	we can't give you a refund.
Adjective		**calm** he may seem,	he's furious inside.
Adverb		**long** you might wait,	we can't see you today.

All of the *-ever* words may express conditions in the past, as well as the present or future. The meaning is sometimes clearest with *may* or *might*.			
Past Continuous	Whichever	one you'**ve chosen** / **may have chosen**,	the purchase is non-refundable.
	Whatever	excuse he'**s given** / **might have given**,	I'm not really interested.

Unit 8

1A Correct the mistakes.
1. On top of that, when I wanted that the waiter apologize, he refused.
2. I suggest your staff to treat me appropriately!
3. I insisted the clerk didn't do that again.
4. The customer took offense when I requested for him to show me the receipt.
5. I demanded my sister gets a refund.
6. I suggest you no use that tone of voice with me ever again!
7. My boss insisted the customer was removed from the store.
8. We were pleased the waiter be understanding when he talked to us.
9. I'll hold on until the owner agree to talk to me.
10. I'd like that this product be replaced right away.

1B Create sentences using the prompts. Which opinions can be expressed using more than one structure?
1. [important / an airline / go / extra mile / customers]
   It's important (that) an airline go the extra mile for customers.
   It's important for an airline to go the extra mile for customers.
2. [I / want / electric company / improve / where I live]
3. [I / rather / stores / not charge / so much / for high-quality merchandise]
4. [add / insult / injury / our government / would like / us / pay / higher / taxes]
5. [everyone / need / take / stand / and demand / restaurant service / improve]
6. [We / demanded / cell-phone service / improve / never / did]

1C Make it personal Make three sentences in B true for you. In pairs, share your opinions.

> Lines at [name of airport] are longer than ever. It's imperative airlines take a stand against inefficiency!

2A Respond to these situations. Begin with an adverb clause, using the words in parentheses.
1. A man calls a store 10 times demanding to speak to the manager.
   Manager to receptionist: _____ (however, times)
2. A woman only wants to buy products she can return, but the store has a "no-returns" policy.
   Sales clerk to woman: _____ (whichever, one)
3. A young man is worried about buying a bed for his overweight father. She reassures him.
   Sales clerk to man: _____ (however, weigh)
4. A polite car salesperson tries to sell a young woman an overpriced car. In the end, she decides against it.
   Woman to salesperson: _____ (however, helpful)

2B Make it personal In pairs, exchange opinions on stores or restaurants near you. Use adverb clauses containing *-ever* words.

> Do you ever go to [name of restaurant]? Service there is pretty good.

> Yeah, well, however polite the waiters may be, the food leaves a lot to be desired.

Bonus! Language in song

♪ It's a bittersweet symphony, this life. Try to make ends meet. You're a slave to the money, then you die.

Which two expressions can be used to combine the last two sentences: *(as) much as*, *however*, or *for all the*? Create two new possible song lines.

Unit 9 — Grammar expansion

1 More on passive expressions in sentences with infinitives (do after 9.2)

Acupuncture / The treatment / It	is	reported	to	be	effective. I think I'll try it.
	was			have been	helpful in the past and still is.
	has been	shown		help	patients, including me.
	still hasn't been			have helped	people as much as some people claim.
	might be	thought		be	helpful, but I'm not so sure.
	may have been			have been	out of the mainstream, but it no longer is.

1. If you are unsure what a sentence means, try changing it to an active one.
   Acupuncture **has been reported** to help patients, including me. (passive)
   People **have reported** that acupuncture helps patients. (active)
2. Choose the tense based on the part of the sentence you wish to emphasize. Without additional context, the meaning may be clearer with only one verb in the past. Compare:
   a. Acupuncture **was reported** to help patients. (The reporting is in the past. Nothing is said about whether patients are still being helped.)
   b. Acupuncture is reported to **have helped** patients. (Patients have been helped in the past up to and including the present. Nothing is said about exactly when the reporting took place.)

Common mistakes
Acupuncture was known to ~~had~~ *have* helped people many years ago.
It was reported to ^ *have* cured many diseases.

2 More on verb patterns (do after 9.4)

All verb patterns form questions in familiar ways. Only the first verb changes in the formation of the question.		
Does your coach	**make** you	**practice** a lot?
What will	**encourage** people	**to lose** weight?
Should teachers	**force** students	**to do** homework?
Has your brother	**appreciated** you	**teaching** him karate?

Passive questions are also very common.		
Have you	**been discouraged**	**from going** on a diet?
Will we	**be encouraged**	**to exercise** more?
Should students	**be forced**	**to take** so many exams?
Were you	**made**	**to wear** those ugly shoes as a kid, too?

Common mistakes
Have you been discouraged ~~to try~~ *from trying* hypnotherapy?
Did your teacher make you ~~stayed / to stay~~ *stay* late?

Unit 9

1A Choose the correct meaning below for sentences 1–8.

1. Feng Shui <u>was reported</u> long ago to have existed before the invention of the compass.
2. It <u>has been known</u> to be effective for thousands of years.
3. The 1901 Boxer Rebellion in China <u>was believed</u> to <u>have been caused</u> by Westerners violating principles of Fung Shui during the construction of railroads.
4. Feng Shui <u>may have been thought</u> to be a factor, but today the rebellion <u>is known</u> to have had broader causes.
5. Feng Shui <u>may be seen</u> to be an Asian custom, but Westerners practice it, too.
6. It still <u>hasn't been shown</u> to help people definitively, but it continues to be very popular.
7. Many other kinds of alternative medicine <u>have been thought</u> to have developed a long time ago, too.
8. They<u>'ve been reported</u> to <u>have been tried</u> in many countries.

1. Historians [**now report** / **reported earlier**] that the compass was invented before Feng Shui.
2. People [**once knew** / **still know**] that it is effective.
3. People [**originally believed** / **believe now**] that Feng Shui caused the Boxer Rebellion.
4. Historians [**no longer think** / **still think**] Feng Shui caused the rebellion.
5. People [**used to think** / **still think**] Feng Shui is an Asian custom.
6. Proponents [**once showed** / **are still trying to show**] that Feng Shui definitely helps people.
7. Historians [**used to think** / **may still think**] other kinds of alternative medicine are old, too.
8. Doctors [**report** / **used to report**] they've been tried in many countries.

2A Complete questions 1–5 using the verb patterns on p. 154 and forms of the words in parentheses.

1. A: _____ them recently? (anyone / really / appreciate / you / help)
   B: Yes, my sister has. I helped her move just last week.
2. A: _____ alternative medicine? (people / encourage – passive / try)
   B: I think they should. It's been known to help many!
3. A: _____ anything you didn't want to as a kid? (you / ever / make – passive / do)
   B: I sure was! My mom made me clean up my room every Saturday.
4. A: _____ something new? (you / ever / discourage – passive / try)
   B: Yes, unfortunately. I really wanted to be homeschooled, but my parents were opposed to the idea.
5. A: _____ their wallet to a thief? (anyone you know / ever / force – passive / hand over)
   B: Yes, my mom was held up just a few weeks ago.

2B Make it personal Choose two questions from **A** to ask a partner. Answer with true information.

... something new?

Yes, I wanted to try rock climbing, but everyone said it was dangerous.

> **Bonus! Language in song**
>
> ♪ Something in the way you move makes me feel like I can't live without you. It takes me all the way. I want you to stay.
>
> Change the first sentence to a question so you are asking someone about yourself. Be sure to change all the pronouns, too.

Unit 10 — Grammar expansion

1 More comparative patterns (do after 10.2)

More comparative patterns					
My friends are	half	as	important	as	my family (is).
My parents aren't	twice		sympathetic		my friends (are).
I have	three times		**many** friends		Bob (does)
They pay me			**much** attention		Ann (does).
I have	four times	more	money	than	my sister (does).
We have	slightly / far	fewer	friends		we used to (have).
I'm under	much / far / a lot	less	pressure		my friends (are).

> **Common mistakes**
>
> She criticizes me half / twice ~~more than~~ *as much as* my mother.
> He has ~~less~~ *fewer* friends than anyone else.
>
> You may say *three times more*, but not *twice more*. *Less* is ungrammatical before a countable noun, even if you may, at times, hear native speakers say it in informal speech.

2 Summary of conditional sentences (do after 10.4)

Inverted conditional sentences are often distinguished from other types of conditional sentences only by register. The sentences below show a sequence from least to most formal.			
Present or future meaning	**If you change**	your mind,	everyone **will be** happy.
	If you changed If you were to change Were you to change Should you change		we **would/could give** you a discount.
Past meaning	**If I had left** Had I left Were I to have left	a message,	I'm sure he **would/could have** come.
Present inversions with *had* and past inversions with *should* are restricted to highly formal or poetic usage: Had he more money (present), I would marry him. Should you have had second thoughts (past), I wouldn't have proceeded with the plan.			

Unit 10

1A Write sentences with comparative patterns in blue from p. 156 and the information given. There may be more than one answer.

1. My class: 30 students – the other classes: 10 students
   My class has three times as many students as the other classes (do).
   My class has three times more students than the other classes (do).
2. High school grades: important – college grades: double the importance
3. My friends: very understanding – my parents: not very understanding
4. Our cities ten years ago: high unemployment – now: double the unemployment
5. Me: three good friends; my best friend – 15 good friends
6. Your English: very fluent; my English – not as fluent

1B Correct five mistakes in comparative patterns.

A: People have far less friends and less support than they used to because everyone moves around so much.
B: But the good thing about the U.S. is you can make new friends just by joining informal clubs.
A: Yes, but that's hard to do. I had twice more friends before I moved from Washington, D.C. to Los Angeles. And on top of that, now I have to drive such long distances everywhere.
B: It's true. I drive less miles when I want to see friends. But I have half of many as you! I don't know how you do it. Even though you just moved a year ago, you still have twice as much friends as I do!

1C Make it personal Choose two sentences from A. In pairs, share true information.

> Our class has slightly fewer students than the other classes.

> Do you really think so? It seems big to me!

2A Express present or future suggestions or requests informally or formally, according to the cues. Then underline the language in each sentence that shows the register.

1. Mother to child: [clean room / take out for ice cream]
2. Sales clerk to elderly customer: [need help / ask]
3. Employee to boss: [try new approach / double sales]
4. Teenager to younger sister: [not stop that right now / get really mad]
5. Passenger to flight attendant: [have peanuts left over / give me some?]
6. Police officer to driver: [continue to argue / arrest you]

2B Make it personal In pairs, review your sentences in A. Do you agree the register is appropriate?

> OK, number 6: Should you continue to argue, I'll arrest you.

> Police officers are never that formal and polite! I have, "If you continue to argue, I'll arrest you ..."

> Maybe you're right. But it's good for them to be polite in my opinion!

Bonus! Language in song

♪ Where did I go wrong? I lost a friend, Somewhere along in the bitterness. And I would have stayed up with you all night, had I known how to save a life.

Rewrite the inverted conditional sentence using an *if*-conditional clause. Does it refer to present, past, or future time?

2C Change your sentences in A to the past. Which now express a criticism instead of a suggestion or request?

Unit 11 — Grammar expansion

1 More on using modals (do after 11.2)

Modal verbs are very common and fulfill many functions. Below is a summary of common uses. Those with a star haven't been presented earlier in *Identities*.

Possibility	Jim **may / might / could have gone** home early.
Probability	Laura isn't here yet, so she **must be working** late tonight.
Certainty	Laura **couldn't have taken** that train. I saw her on the earlier one.
Obligation	You really **must call** your mother! It's been more than a month!
Advice / Criticism	You **shouldn't have let** so much time go by without talking to her.
Expectation	Fix your flat tire? That **shouldn't be** too hard to do.
Ability	I **could speak** French when I was young, but I **can't speak** it any longer.
Implied *if*-clause	You just found out the airport is closed? I **could have told** you that! (if you'd asked me)
Request	**Could / Can** you **open** the window? It's boiling in here.
*Request / command with annoyance or anger	**Can't** you **sit** still for even for second! **Won't** you just **be** quiet and listen! You can ask questions later. **Would** you **watch** where you're going! You almost ran me over!
Future decision	I**'ll pick** you **up** after school. Call me when your class ends.
Refusal	I **won't give** you any more money, no matter how many times you ask.
*Rhetorical question	**Must** I **listen** to that music blaring? I'm trying to concentrate! **Couldn't** you **have** at least **tried** not to spill your coffee? What a mess!
Habitual past action	I used to love to swim, and I **would go swimming** every afternoon.
Permission	Rows 15–30 **may / can** (less formal) now **begin** boarding.
Suggestion	You **might try** doing yoga to help you relax.
Invitation	**Would** you **like** to come to dinner Saturday? We'd love to have you. We're thinking of going to the beach Sunday. **Will** you **join** us?

2 Articles and subject-verb agreement (do after 11.4)

Use of the definite article and whether the verb that follows is singular or plural may differ in some cases from your language. Here are some tips to help you.

Countries: Memorize which countries have articles. All take a singular verb, even if they end in *s*.	The United States has fifty states. The Philippines is a country with numerous islands. Indonesia consists of many islands, too. Peru is famous for Machu Picchu.
Collective nouns such as organizations, companies, and stores take a singular verb in American English, and may or may not have an article. Nouns that refer to a category, however, are plural.	The federal government is located in Washington, D.C. Richmond has published *Identities*. Macy's sometimes offers discounts. The fish in that restaurant is very good. (= cooked fish) The young take too many risks. Fish are sometimes caught in this bay. (= living fish)
Shared knowledge: Use *the* when you refer to something a second time or the listener knows what you're referring to.	Where are the kids? I don't see them anywhere. I didn't eat the dessert. It didn't look very appetizing.
Fractions may take a singular or plural verb. Expressions involving **time**, **money**, or **distance** generally require a singular verb.	According to a recent survey, two thirds of adults don't have satisfying jobs, but one third of adults does. 30 miles is a very long way to travel to school! Five dollars is a lot to pay for a soda!

Unit 11

1A Rephrase the underlined sentences with modal verbs. There may be more than one answer.

1. A: Did you hear there was a motorcycle accident this afternoon? I hope it wasn't Ethan.
   B: <u>I'm positive it wasn't</u>. He's always so careful.
   It couldn't have been.
2. A: <u>Stop pointing that umbrella at me</u>! Do you want me to lose an eye?
   B: You don't have to be so nasty about it.
3. A: <u>I expect that Tom is here by now</u>. His plane was due in at 4:00.
   B: Yes, I was just thinking the same thing.
4. A: <u>Aren't you able to talk more quietly</u>? I'm trying to sleep.
   B: Oh, sorry. I didn't realize we were talking loudly.
5. A: Excuse me, is it OK if I turn on my tablet?
   B: Yes. <u>Passengers are now allowed to use portable devices</u>.
6. A: I still haven't run five kilometers in under 30 minutes.
   B: <u>Maybe a good idea is to run more on weekends</u>.
7. A: I'm having Chloe and Alex over for dinner Sunday. <u>I'd like you to come, too</u>.
   B: Oh, I'd love to. Just let me know what to bring.

1B **Make it personal** Role-play the conversations with a partner. Use modal verbs in the cue sentences.

1. A: (Make a request)
   B: Sure! That shouldn't be too hard to do.
2. A: (Express a possibility)
   B: I could have told you that! I knew all along.
3. A: (Ask a rhetorical question)
   B: You don't have to be so sarcastic. How would I know it was bothering you?
4. A: (Ask permission)
   B: Sure! Go right ahead.
5. A: (Make an angry command)
   B: But we're not! I swear we aren't!
   A: I saw you doing it. Stop it immediately!
6. A: (Make a suggestion)
   B: That's a good idea. I think I'll try it.

2A Correct the mistakes.

1. Steak are a good source of iron.
2. The old is traveling much more now than in the past.
3. They say 25 percent of the young people is unemployed, but everyone I know have a job.
4. The bicycles are usually safe, and bike I have has extra safety features.
5. Japan is the country that have to worry about earthquakes.
6. Ten dollars an hour aren't very much to earn in my opinion!
7. Half of all teenagers has nothing to do after the school.
8. The fruit are important for a balanced diet, but the fruit sold here are never fresh.

2B **Make it personal** Choose three sentences and start a conversation with a partner. Change them as needed so they are true.

> Fish is a good source of protein, but the frozen fish sold here is tasteless.

> That's a shame. You might want to try cooking fresh fish. It's easy!

> **Bonus!** Language in song
>
> ♪ Oh, I would do anything for love. I would do anything for love, but I won't do that. No, I won't do that.
>
> Which function is expressed in this song line: expectation, a suggestion, refusal, or annoyance? Underline the verb.

Unit 12 — Grammar expansion

1 More on passive forms with gerunds and infinitives (do after 12.2)

Passive forms with gerunds and infinitives are also common in questions:	
Gerunds ...	**Infinitives and base forms ...**
1 After certain verbs: **Did** you **like being videoed** by a total stranger?	4 After certain verbs: How **do** you **hope to be remembered**?
2 After prepositions: **Were** you **counting on being** promoted?	5 After adjectives, nouns, and indefinite pronouns: **Is** she the politician most **likely to be elected**?
3 As subjects: Why is **being chosen** important to you?	6 After modals: Why **might** he **be fired**?

After verbs and adjectives, be certain to use the correct prepositions:	
Are you **terrified** of **being caught**?	Was she **worried** about **being fired**?
How did you **succeed** in **being considered**?	Why do your kids **object** to **being left alone**?
Is she very **discouraged** at (by) **not being chosen**?	Were you **congratulated** on **being elected**?

When the question is negative, the meaning may change based on the position of the negative:	
	Meaning
Weren't you **relieved about being fired**? Our boss was a nightmare anyway.	The person *was* fired.
Were you **relieved about** not **being fired**? It's so hard to find a job these days.	The person *wasn't* fired.
Weren't you **hoping to be promoted**? I know you've been here a long time.	The person *wasn't* promoted.
Were you **hoping** not **to be promoted**? You didn't sound happy when they announced it!	The person *was* promoted.

2 More on the *be* and *get* passive (do after 12.4)

The *be* and *get* passives can both be used when talking about actions or something that has changed. But the two passives are not identical and are not always interchangeable.
The *get* passive shows greater informality, emphasis, and negative intent as explained on p. 133: Get down from there! You could **get hurt**!
Only the *be* passive can be used with stative verbs, such as *say, tell, like,* etc.: He **was liked** by everyone in the class. Those criminals **are known**, but the police does nothing about them!
Only the *be* passive is usually used for longer, planned events: The new museum **was opened** in the summer of 2017. The bridge **was built** to ease the flow of traffic.
The *get* passive is common with verbs like *killed, injured, wounded, paid, hired, fired, laid off,* and *accepted*, which have a clear beneficial or adverse effect on the subject. Neutral verbs, however, generally use the *be* passive: Andy **got / was paid** $1,000 for just two hours of work. BUT Her shoes **were purchased** at the expensive store down the street.

Unit 12

1A Complete the passive questions using the verbs in parentheses.
1. What school would you like _____ to? (accept)
2. Do you mind _____ to work late? (ask)
3. Do you object more to _____ by your teachers or by your parents? (criticize)
4. How do you want _____ of by people? (think)
5. Are you excited about _____ for the soccer team? (choose)
6. Have you succeeded in _____ for a job you really wanted? (hire)

1B Make it personal Choose two questions to ask a partner. Answer with true information.

> What school would you like to be admitted to?

> Well, I'd really like to go to ... , but tuition has skyrocketed, so I might have to fall back on ...

1C Choose the most logical response in italics (a or b) for conversations 1–4.
1. A: I'm waiting for an acceptance letter to UCLA.
   B: a *Are you scared of not getting in?*
      b *Aren't you scared of getting in?*
   A: No, why would I be?
   B: It's just that I've heard it's a hard school.
2. A: I've been working here for four years now.
   B: a *Are you worried about not being promoted?*
      b *Aren't you worried about being promoted?*
   A: Not really. It would just mean more work if I were.
3. A: I ran into Andrea yesterday.
   B: a *Oh, was she upset at not being invited to the wedding?*
      b *Oh, wasn't she upset at being invited to the wedding?*
   A: I think she was OK with it. This way she doesn't have to buy a gift.
4. A: I'm going to the conference tomorrow.
   B: a *Didn't you mind being asked to give a presentation?*
      b *Did you mind not being asked to give a presentation?*
   A: I was relieved! I don't like speaking in front of lots of people.

2A Change the *get* passive to *be* when it is ungrammatical or unnatural. Check (✔) if it is both correct and natural.
1. My house got broken into last week. They took all my jewelry.
2. I got told that flying cars will have been invented by 2050.
3. I think this shopping center got opened around 10 years ago.
4. The tickets got sold so quickly, we weren't able to buy any.
5. My dad got laid off last month, but luckily he's already found a new job.
6. It's gotten said that global warming is the most serious threat to our planet.

2B In pairs, explain your choices in A.

> The first one sounds fine with *get*. It shows emphasis, and it's used to talk about an adverse effect.

2C Make it personal Write three questions to ask a classmate about the future? How long can you continue the conversation?

> **Bonus! Language in song**
>
> ♪ I want to thank you for giving me the best day of my life. Oh just to be with you is having the best day of my life.
>
> Make the song lines negative. In which position does the negative make the most sense?

Grammar expansion answer key

Unit 1

1A
1. One of my friends' classmate**s has** an idea for a new start-up.
2. Everyone need**s** to be cautious with **his or her** major decisions.
3. Many people **worry** about investing **their** money.
4. Two hundred dollars **is** a lot for someone to pay for **his or her** English course.
5. Having business strategies **is** important for anyone who wants **his or her** own start-up.
6. My teacher, as well as all my friends, think**s** one of us **has** a great idea.
7. Keeping your fears in check **is** important if you're someone who **is** planning a lifestyle change.
8. Some of my parents' best advice **was** in **their** letter.
9. Everyone should take **his or her** umbrella because something tells me it's going to rain.
10. One of my sister's friends **has** told me that two years **isn't** long enough to learn English.

2A
1
1. acted
2. was living
3. was
4. 'd practiced
5. went
6. was still
7. worried
8. I might forget
9. performed
10. was

2
1. was
2. flew
3. wasn't
4. used to be
5. got
6. had to
7. was visiting
8. went
9. had lost
10. must have spent

Bonus!
Only one of us wants diamond rings. Each of us just wants everything. But most things mean nothing.

Unit 2

1A
1. My whole family has trouble throwing things out, and I do, too. / so do I.
2. There aren't that many good English coursebooks, but I have one.
3. Many of my friends want to get married, but I don't.
4. A lot of people I know want to live alone, and I do, too. / so do I.
5. I've looked at a lot of apartments, and I hoped to find one, but I haven't.
6. My friends say their ideas about the future have changed recently, and mine have, too. / so have mine.

1C
1. Maybe you don't like small apartments, but I do.
2. They haven't saved money for unforeseen events, but I have.
3. My view is nicer than Ted and Mary's, and my kitchen is bigger than theirs.
4. My neighborhood is a lot more interesting than Sally and Bill's.
5. We don't have a pool in our back yard, but my sister does.
6. My parents asked me if I wanted to move, and I said I thought so.
7. We can't find a good moving company, but maybe you can recommend one / a good one.
8. Our old apartment had big closets, but this one doesn't (have any).
9. My boyfriend asked me if I wanted my independence, but I said I didn't think so.
10. I don't know for sure if we're buying this place. My husband wants to, so I guess we are.

2A
1. so many more people
2. so much busier
3. so much easier
4. so much more crowded
5. so much more traffic
6. so many fewer parking spaces
7. so many more buildings
8. so much more congestion
9. so much less

Bonus!
"tears" are countable, "pain" is uncountable.

Unit 3

1A
1. Does what you study in college really matter?
2. Why should how much you practice in public speaking be important?
3. When is whether you cram for a test relevant?
4. How does what you have for breakfast make you lose weight?
5. Why is what I do on weekends my parents' business?

1B
1. **Is** whether I can become bilingual really important?
2. How does what school ~~do~~ I choose affect my career?
3. Why does whether women **have** children keep them from finding jobs?
4. Does whether ~~do~~ I feel confident as a public speaker improve my performance?
5. How does what our teacher tells us about grammar help us speak more accurately?
6. Does how much TV we watch in English improve~~s~~ our vocabulary?

2A
1. correct
2. not knowing how to go about it
3. not having been given useful advice by anyone
4. correct
5. Not knowing which language to speak
6. correct

2B
2. Not having been elected president, Tom didn't have a very good attitude.
3. After not graduating last year, I found it hard to find a job.
4. Not enjoying practicing at all, I just left my violin in a closet.
5. Not feeling loved by his girlfriend, Greg felt his weekends were kind of depressing.

Bonus!
Having not met you yet, I promise you kid that I'll give so much more than I get.

Unit 4

1A
1. Not since I was a child have I had a dream like this.
2. Only when I saw it on TV did I realize the incident was serious.
3. Only later did I come to understand the events.
4. In no way did I imagine our proposal would be accepted.
5. Only after everyone (had) started laughing did we realize that Ron had made an April Fools' joke.
6. Seldom do we consider the consequences of our actions.

1B
1. 2 (have I had)
2. 2 (did I realize)
3. 1 (Only later did I)
4. 1 (In no way did I imagine)
5. 2 (did we realize)
6. 1 (Seldom do we)

1C
Never could I have imagined some of the truly mean April Fools' jokes I've seen, but **rarely** did the perpetrators suffer any consequences. Take the case of the friendly and genial office colleague at my former job. **No sooner** had his coworkers arrived at work **than** he would invite them to come to his cubicle for a piece of gum. Of course, **in no way** did they ever suspect they might be chewing, and maybe even swallowing, something else! **Only when** they put it in their mouth would we hear a piercing scream! **Seldom** did they know why it tasted so bad. You see, the gum was actually Play Doh, a sticky substance used by children for art projects. **Hardly ever** did my colleagues

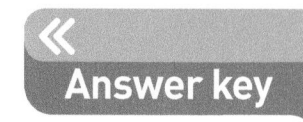

find out that it began as a wallpaper cleaner in the 1930S!

2A
1. There are many amateur personality tests, some of which aren't very rigorous.
2. That's the convention center in which we stayed for the conference.
3. I studied the five domains into which our personalities can be classified.
4. Reliability is a trait the importance of which many people underestimate.
5. The scientist with whom I work has just published an article.
6. The roommates with whom I lived as a freshman were easy to get to know.
7. The woman in whose apartment I lived just got elected to public office.
8. The speed at which the train was traveling when it crashed was very high.

Bonus!
Little did I think anyone could care about me.

Unit 5

1A
1. In the interest of improving security, we will be installing alarms throughout the building.
2. In light of the fact that you failed the final exam twice, I'm afraid you're going to have to repeat this course.
3. With the aim of attracting more customers, we're going to start doing more promotion.
4. With regard to the complaint you made recently about cockroaches, we'll send the exterminator this weekend.
5. On account of the fact that we've had so many problems, we may have to postpone our vacation.
6. Owing to very low sales, we can't offer raises this year.
7. Regarding the interpretation of dreams, I have some good books to recommend.

1B
1. Because of / As a result of the many world problems that face us, I don't think I'm going to have children.
2. (In order) to get a good job, I'm going to delete my Facebook page so a potential employer can't see it.
3. When it comes to understanding politics / As far as politics goes, I'm really not the slightest bit interested.
4. Because (of the fact that) we live a long life, I think it's silly to watch your diet too much.
5. (In order) to start over from scratch, I'm going to change schools.

2A
2. All parents have an investment in their child's succeeding.
   All parents have an investment in their child succeeding.
3. I'm not happy about my husband's traveling so often.
   I'm not happy about my husband traveling so often.
4. We're worried about both new managers' becoming so nervous.
   We're worried about both new managers becoming so nervous.
5. The other team has an interest in our school's winning the award.
   The other team has an interest in our school winning the award.
6. George resented Phil's going out with his old girlfriend.
   George resented Phil going out with his old girlfriend.
7. Marcy was aware of classmates' talking about her behind her back.
   Marcy was aware of classmates talking about her behind her back.

Bonus!
In view of (thanks to, given) the fact that all is quiet on New Year's Day, a world in white gets underway.

Unit 6

1A
1. Despite the fact that / Irrespective of the fact that / Notwithstanding the fact that
2. Assuming (that) / Provided (that)
3. Assuming (that) / Provided (that)
4. Supposing (that)
5. Provided (that) / On the condition (that)
6. Despite the fact that / Irrespective of the fact that / Notwithstanding the fact that

2A
1. What a great play!
2. How awful the way the writer expressed himself was! / How awful the writer was in the way that he expressed himself.
3. How scary the actors that came on stage in the second half were!
4. What a bad job she did!
5. What an active imagination you have!
6. How intriguing the paintings in this exhibit were.

2B
1. it did have a plot
2. he did / could remember them
3. you can tell me
4. I didn't hate him

Bonus!
Does, the heart is being emphasized

Unit 7

1A
1. 'm going to live
2. start
3. will still be able
4. will have earned
5. will have participated
6. won't be racing
7. won't have been given
8. will have passed
9. will have been exercising

2A
1. No doubt your daughter will have discovered a solution to peer pressure by now.
2. If we are to be comfortable economically, we need to save money.
3. I'm sure older people will have considered all the options before choosing a nursing home.
4. The government will have planned for the fact that pensions are going to be cut back even further by the 2030s.
5. No doubt our planet will have been suffering for generations, and we're just paying attention now.

3
1. It's the small things that always get to you.
2. It's global warming (that) we're not ready for.
3. where I'll get the money I have no idea
4. what I'll be doing in 10 years, I really can't tell you

Bonus!
Wherever you go, whatever you do, I'll have been right here waiting for you for fifty years. (future perfect continuous)

Unit 8

1A
1. On top of that, when I wanted ~~that~~ the waiter **to** apologize, he refused.
2. I suggest your staff ~~to~~ treat me appropriately!
3. I insisted the clerk **not** do that again.
4. The customer took offense when I requested ~~for him to~~ **he** show me the receipt.
5. I demanded my sister gets a refund.
6. I suggest you no**t** use that tone of voice with me ever again!
7. My boss insisted the customer **be** removed from the store.
8. We were pleased the waiter **was** understanding when he talked to us.
9. I'll hold on until the owner agree**s** to talk to me.
10. I'd like ~~that~~ this product **to** be replaced right away.

1B
2. I want the electric company to improve service where I live.
3. I'd rather stores not charge so much for high quality merchandise.
4. To add insult to injury, our government would like us to pay higher taxes.
5. Everyone needs to take a stand and demand restaurant service improve.
6. We demanded that cell-phone service improve, but it never did.

2A
Possible answers:
1. However many times they call, we can't see them today.
2. Whichever one you buy, the product is non-returnable.
3. However much he weights, the bed will be comfortable for him.

Answer key

4 However helpful you (may) have been, I think the car is too expensive for me.

Bonus!

As much as you try to make ends meet, you're a slave to the money, then you die.
However much you try to make ends meet, you're a slave to the money, then you die.

Unit 9

1A

1 reported earlier
2 still know
3 originally believed
4 no longer think
5 still think
6 are still trying to show
7 may still think
8 report

2A

1 Has anyone really appreciated you helping them recently?
2 Should people be encouraged to try alternative medicine?
3 Were you ever made to do anything you didn't want to as a kid?
4 Were you ever discouraged from trying something new?
5 Has anyone you know ever been forced to hand over their wallet to a thief?

Bonus!

Is there something in the way I move that makes you feel like you can't live without me?

Unit 10

1A

Possible answers

2 College grades are twice as important as high school grades.
High school grades are half as important as college grades.
3 My parents are (much) less understanding than my friends.
4 Our cities have twice as much unemployment now as they did 10 years ago.
5 I have (far) fewer good friends than my best friend (does).
6 My English is (a lot) less fluent than yours (is).

1B

A People have far **fewer** friends and less support than they used to because everyone moves around so much.
B But the good thing about the U.S. is you can make new friends just by joining informal clubs.
A Yes, but that's hard to do. I had twice **as many** friends before I moved from Washington, D.C. to Los Angeles. And on top of that, now I have to drive such long distances everywhere.

B It's true. I drive **fewer** miles when I want to see friends. But I have half as many as you! I don't know how you do it. Even though you just moved a year ago, you still have twice as **many** friends as I do!

2A

Possible answers

1 <u>If you clean</u> your room, I'll take you out for ice cream.
2 <u>Should you need</u> any help, just ask.
3 <u>Were you to try</u> a new approach, you could double sales.
4 <u>If you don't stop</u> that right now, I'll get really mad.
5 <u>If you were to have</u> any peanuts left over, would/could you give me some?
6 <u>If you continue</u> to argue, I'll arrest you.

2C

1 If you had cleaned your room, I would have taken you out for ice cream. (criticism)
2 Were you to have needed help, you could have asked. (criticism)
3 Had you tried a new approach, you could have doubled sales. (criticism)
4 Had you had any peanuts left over, would you have given me some?
5 Were you to have continued to argue, I would have arrested you.

Bonus!

And I would have stayed up with you all night if I had known how to save a life – past time

Unit 11

1A

Possible answers

2 Would you stop pointing that umbrella at me!
3 Tom must be here by now.
4 Could you talk more quietly?
5 Passengers may now use portable devices.
6 You might try running more on weekends.
7 Will you come, too?

1B

Students' own answers.

2A

1 Steak **is** a good source of iron.
2 The old **are** traveling much more now than in the past.
3 They say 25 percent of young people **are** unemployed, but everyone I know **has** a job.
4 **Bicycles** are usually safe, and **the** bike I have has extra safety features.
5 Japan is **a** country that **has** to worry about earthquakes.
6 Ten dollars an hour **isn't** very much to earn in my opinion!
7 Half of all teenagers **have** nothing to do after **school**.
8 **Fruit is** important for a balanced diet, but **the** fruit sold here **is** never fresh.

2B

Students' own answers

Bonus!

Refusal – won't do

Unit 12

1A

1 to be accepted
2 being asked
3 being criticized
4 to be thought
5 being chosen
6 being hired

1C

1 b
2 a
3 a
4 b

2A

1 ✓
2 was told
3 was opened
4 ✓
5 ✓
6 been said

Bonus!

I don't want to thank you for giving me the best day of my life. Oh just not to be with you is having the best day of my life. / I want to thank you for not giving me the best day of my life. Oh just to be with you is not having the best day of my life.

Audio scripts

Unit 1

1.1 page 6 exercise 1A

L = Lucy, B = Ben

L: Well, I imagine it's a real handful, I know. But overall, it seems you're happy being a psychologist?
B: Most days I guess ...You know I used to dream of being a teacher.
L: You did?
B: Yeah, when I was a young boy. I even tried it for a year after I graduated from college ... But the initial enthusiasm wore off after a while and I ... Well, what's done is done.
L: Good thing you realized it early.
B: Yeah, I guess I don't regret that my teaching career never really took off. But let me tell you about my first interview! It was pretty surreal.
L: What happened?
B: I kind of blew it ... well, totally blew it – not the interview itself, but the sample lesson. It wasn't my fault, to be fair.
L: What do you mean? They asked you to observe a lesson?
B: No, they actually had me teach a group of real students. I guess they were still unsure about me.
L: Wow! That must have been stressful.
B: Tell me about it. I'd never spoken to a crowd – big or small – before ... I mean, not in a position of authority, anyway.
L: But what happened exactly? How did the observation go?

1.2 page 6 exercise 1B

L: How did the observation go? Did they tie you to a tree or something?
B: Well, actually, as far as I can recall, the kids were pretty harmless. Most of them, anyway.
L: So ...
B: I can still see it as if it were yesterday. I had to teach a group of sixth graders a number of spelling rules, which, as you can imagine, wasn't exactly a topic that set the class on fire.
L: I'm sure it didn't.
B: Even the principal was yawning and looking as if he was about to doze off.
L: Oh, no ...
B: I don't remember exactly what I'd planned for the lesson. It's completely slipped my mind. Anyway, it doesn't really matter because I never even had the chance to pull it off.
L: What do you mean?
B: All of a sudden, a piercing scream – you know, like the ones you hear in a Stephen King movie – wakes everybody up.
L: You've got to be kidding!
B: I'm serious! And are you ready for this? What had happened was that just as I was getting started, a big black vulture flew into the room through an open window!
L: No way!
B: Yep. It swooped down toward the students in the front row, then up again, 'til it eventually landed on an empty desk.
L: A vulture in the classroom? What a way to kick off your teaching career! No wonder it didn't last!
B: Yeah, maybe that's why! Anyway, the vulture sent everyone into a frenzy. Some kids ran out of the room, others burst into tears ...
L: What did *you* do?
B: I ducked under the table.
L: You what?!
B: Yep. I was so scared I couldn't think straight.
L: What about the principal?
B: I have no idea! I have a vague recollection of hearing him call my name, but who knows.
L: Oh, boy.
B: But I was so terrified, like, frozen under the table, I couldn't move. The vulture must have felt sorry for me, because after a minute or two it flew away.
L: And then what?
B: You should have seen the room. Tables overturned, papers everywhere ... It was like a bomb had gone off.
L: What a nightmare! And the kids?
B: Well, by then they'd all rushed off and left me and the principal in an empty classroom. But you're not going to believe this ... I got the job anyway!
L: You did?
B: Yeah, he decided I didn't have to do a sample lesson after all. "Saved by the bell" so to speak! Well, I guess he couldn't afford not to take me on – two teachers were on maternity leave and another one had just been fired. But come to think of it, it could have been a lot worse.
L: How?
B: What if it had been a snake?!

1.5 page 7 exercise 2C

Hello! You may remember me from last year. I'm your cyber teacher, Helene.

1 Our first phrasal verb is *wear off*. When something "wears off," it gradually disappears or stops, like Ben's enthusiasm. Remember he says, "I even tried it for a year, but the initial enthusiasm wore off after a while." So, what other words go with *wear off*? A <u>novelty</u>, something new and different, can wear off, too. For example, the cell-phone game *Angry Birds* used to be popular, but soon the novelty wore off. An <u>effect</u> can also *wear off*, for example, when you take medicine. You may need to take some more after a while as the effect has worn off.

2 Next we have the phrasal verb *take off*. Today we will look only at examples of "take off" that mean to succeed or get started, like Ben's career. He says, "Yeah, I guess I don't regret that my teaching career never really took off." A <u>plane</u> also *takes off* as I'm sure you already know. In this case, "get started" means to "become airborne." And finally, a <u>business</u> can *take off*, too, as in "Our new business took off right away. We made a profit the very first year." Notice that this meaning of *take off* is intransitive, and is different from the familiar meaning of *take off* meaning "remove" as in "Take off your shoes," which is transitive – it needs a direct object.

3 Let's move on to our next phrasal verb, *pull off*, which means "to accomplish something or make it happen, sometimes despite difficulties." Remember that Ben says, "I never even had the chance to pull off the lesson." You can *pull off* a trick, as in "I had hoped to play a trick on him, but I couldn't pull it off." Or you can *pull off* a crime, as in "The gang pulled off a spectacular robbery and managed to steal three million dollars."

4 Finally, we've got one more phrasal verb, *go off*, which means "to be activated," or in some cases, "to explode." Ben says, "Tables overturned, papers everywhere ... It was like a bomb had gone off." An alarm clock can also *go off*, as in "The alarm on my phone went off at six and I'm exhausted!" And, in fact, any kind of alarm can *go off*, as in "The fire alarm went off and we smelled smoke." Remember, though, that bells and telephones do not *go off*. They "ring." And it looks like our bell just did! So I'll be back again soon.

1.6 page 8 exercise 3A

S = Show host

S: Here's something that might shock you: The average American buys 64 pieces of clothing per year – yes, 64 – most of which are trendy outfits meant to be worn a couple of times and then quickly disposed of. Tired of hearing her friends complain about having nothing to wear – despite their closets full of clothes – IT manager Elena Fernández left her job and created *Lists* and *Twists*, a company that has shipped more than 100,000 dollars in products since 2015.

1.7 page 8 exercise 3B

E = Elena, S = Show host, K = Keith

E: *Lists* and *Twists* is, in a nutshell, a clothes subscription service. Think Netflix for fashion and you get the idea. When you sign up, you fill out a quick survey and tell us the sort of stuff you're into. Then, based on your preferences, one of our stylists selects seven articles of clothing, puts them in a bag, and has them shipped to you – and this is more than our competitors offer. You can keep your clothes as long as you want and when you're done, simply put them in a box and send them back. Then the process starts again: Our team suggests new clothes based on your comments and purchase

311

history, and you get a brand new bag. You can become a member for about 60 dollars a month. If 60 dollars sounds like a lot of money, that's nothing compared to what most of the designer clothing available usually costs.

S: Here's another case of need meets vision, vision meets opportunity. Musician Keith Smith grew up in London and later moved to L.A., so he knows just how hard it is to park your car when you live in a big city. Last year, he saw a window of opportunity. Keith refinanced his apartment, sold his car, and started Personal Attendant, which is making headlines everywhere.

K: Finding parking in a big city can be nothing short of a nightmare: Meters all over the place, expensive lots, and signs that no one understands. This is where Personal Attendant comes in. We connect you to hundreds of Personal Attendants in your city. All you need to do is access our company's app before you leave home. Basically, this is how it works: the app asks where you're going and tracks you as you make your way to your destination – just like your parents used to do on the weekends! Five minutes before you arrive, it matches you with a Personal Attendant, who'll be waiting for you, hop into your car, and take it to the nearest Personal Attendant-affiliated lot. Then when you're ready to pick up your car, your Personal Attendant will return it to you. All of this for eight dollars a day, whether you use our service for one hour or ten – and that's something that sets us apart from our competitors. The feedback we've been getting from our clients, as well as the number of positive press reviews, reflects our commitment to excellence. Meeting your needs is our number 1 priority!

▶ **1.11** page 12 exercises 8A and B

DJ = Radio presenter, R = Roy

DJ: The first 10 years of this century will probably go down as a pretty depressing decade: natural disasters, terrorist attacks, financial meltdowns. But there's also a lot to be thankful for. Can you imagine a world without Facebook? Or Wikipedia? Or even YouTube? Here in the studio with me is Roy Martínez, author of *The 2000s*. We asked him what he thought the three defining moments of the 2000s were and he sent us a list. Hi, Roy. Welcome to our show.

R: Pleasure to be here.

DJ: We were all scratching our heads when we saw *Slumdog Millionaire* on your list. Erm ... Why did you pick a movie? By the way, for those of you who haven't seen it, *Slumdog Millionaire* tells the story of a young man who made millions on a TV show, but, you know, was far more interested in finding his missing girlfriend.

R: Yeah, the movie took the world by storm when it was released in 2008, grossing nearly, what, $400 million, I think. It went on to win eight Academy Awards and ...

DJ: Eight?

R: Yeah, including best picture. *Slumdog Millionaire* set a new world record: It was the first time an international production had won so many Oscars, and this set in motion a number of important changes.

DJ: You mean the fact that it was an international movie?

R: Yes. When the movie came out, some people called it the world's first globalized masterpiece. Even though it was a British script, it was set and filmed in India with local actors.

DJ: And you think this will open the door to new international talent?

R: Without a doubt.

DJ: Would you agree with that assessment, though? I mean, that the movie is a masterpiece?

R: Definitely. Twenty minutes into the movie and I understood what all the hype was about.

DJ: Yep, same here. The invention of new technology words is number two on your list, correct?

R: Yeah. Until the year 2000, the word "dot. com," as in the "dot.com crisis" didn't even exist, and "blog" wasn't invented until 2002. You may feel some of these new words didn't exactly set the world on fire initially, but by 2010, everyone had been using words like "texting" and "to Google" for years. But keep in mind that before 2004, we didn't even have a verb that meant "to text." I think that's remarkable.

DJ: Yes, and a memory has come back to me. Texting was popular in Japan several years before the technology reached the U.S. and on a visit to Tokyo, I actually watched as a subway car full of people moved their thumbs over their phones. I had no idea what they were doing! And I sure didn't have a word for it, either!

R: But think of it this way ... maybe some of these early words set the stage for more new ones. "To Google" and "cloud computing" were invented in 2007 and "Twitter" in 2008. But believe it or not, the verb "to tweet" didn't make it into the language until 2013. Maybe you're still not sure how to use that one yet, are you?

DJ: Hmm ... I see what you mean. It takes a few years until we feel comfortable with these new words.

R: Yes, and here's an important thing to keep in mind. Our view of language has changed. Now we *expect* to learn new words that we didn't know even a few years ago! And *that* I think is really groundbreaking.

DJ: Yes, if you put it that way ... So, why did you single out Wikipedia as the game changer of the 2000s?

R: Hmm ... I think the Internet took a major leap forward with the launch of this mammoth, ever-expanding online database, because it was built and edited by people like you and me ...

DJ: Uh huh.

R: Since it was introduced in 2001, Wikipedia has set new rules for how we build and share knowledge. It, erm, it kind of changed the hierarchy of information on the web, and gave average users a voice – a voice they'd never had before. This paved the way for the Twitters and the Facebooks and the Snapchats.

DJ: Why do you think Wikipedia has come in for so much criticism?

R: Good question. Well, does it have its flaws? Yes. Is the information always reliable? No, of course not. But what's really at stake is the fact that we no longer know who or what the "official" sources of information are. And that can be pretty disturbing.

DJ: Yeah. Who does knowledge belong to?

R: Exactly.

DJ: So, erm, Roy, what've you been up to these days?

R: I've been working on a new book, and it's different from anything I've ever written. It's set for a December release, so, stay tuned! It'll be my first ...

▶ **1.12** page 14 exercise 10A

T = Todd, A = Amy

T: I just read this really sobering article.

A: What's it about?

T: A cross-cultural relationship and the things that can happen. This poor guy moved to Japan, met a woman, and ...

A: That sounds pretty positive to me!

T: But wait. He gives at least twelve rules for how to avoid conflict in cross-cultural marriages.

A: What do you mean? All relationships involve potential conflict.

T: It's not the same. For example, he says your interest in the other person's culture might be the very thing that's the problem. You arrive in a new country fascinated. However, the interest may wear off. And even if it doesn't, it's only when you're into the relationship that it hits you how much your whole approach to life is actually determined by the culture you grew up in.

A: So, what happened between this couple?

▶ **1.13** page 14 exercise 10B

T: Well, the real problem started when they were planning the wedding. They chose the date and everything seemed great. But they had never talked about whether the guests could actually attend. It turned out his fiancée's brother had to work because, it seems, in Japan, especially if you work for a big company, work obligations might come first.

A: You've got to be kidding! Her own brother didn't attend the wedding?

T: That's what I'm telling you. The expectations weren't the same. The article says to never assume anything! Every single aspect of your life with your partner has to be discussed.

A: That's for sure. But how do you really know if you've uncovered a difference?

T: Well, that can be hard, but, for example, if your partner says something "isn't important," it might mean that it's actually very important.

A: Why is that?

T: Because saying something isn't important implies you already have an idea of how it will turn out. However, that idea is based on your past, which you and your partner haven't shared.

A: I'm a little lost, I think. Can you give me an example?

T: Yeah, how about this? Let's say we're going to be very late for dinner at someone's house, and you say it's not important. That might mean that you think arriving late is fine. But maybe I think the opposite because in my culture, it's rude.

A: Oh, I see.

T: And this couple, listen to this: She had a job that she hated, but instead of looking for a new one, she just seemed to express a sort of stoicism.

A: What do you mean? Is there something culturally specific about that? My grandparents are very stoic!

T: Well, I'm not really sure. She just felt you had to try to adjust. It drove her American husband nuts.

A: I'll bet. But why was she like that?

T: You're asking me? How would I know? Maybe she thought things might change if she was just patient.

A: Sometimes they do, you know, especially on a job.

T: Yes, but the article implies this might be a cultural trait. Another problem this couple had was that for her, security was very important. She wanted her husband to give up his dream of being an entrepreneur and work in the family business.

A: What's so cross-cultural about that? It could happen here, too.

T: Well, apparently for her, it was "common sense" that he would choose security first. You know, just logical. I think it's a profound cultural difference.

A: I'm not sure I agree. To me it sounds just personal. Let's face it. Some people find security very important.

T: My impression is that she expected him to change once they married, but, you know, you can never change anyone.

A: Hmm ... it could be that's cultural, but then again, maybe not. So what happened in the end?

▶ **1.14** *page 14 exercise 10C*

T: Well, this couple had a few things going for them. He spoke very good Japanese, and she spoke very good English, and they were able to express their thoughts with great subtlety. So once they started to bring things out into the open, he realized how important family was to her.

A: How could family be important if her brother didn't even go to their wedding?

T: It was important in another way. Family acceptance was important. Once he understood that, he decided to join her family's business.

A: Wasn't he just giving up a part of himself, his identity?

T: Well, you could say they both tried to merge a little. For example, realizing how important communication was to him and how different their cultures were, she stopped taking things for granted. And she stopped assuming things were just common sense.

A: So they're still married?

T: Yes! They've been married for 20 years. Anything is possible if you just give it a try!

Unit 2

▶ **2.1** *page 16 exercise 1A*

L = Luke, J = Julia

L: Nice poster.

J: It's a vision board, actually. Pretty cool, uh?

L: What's a vision board?

J: It's, erm ... It's, erm, it's kind of a collage representing some of the things you want to achieve in life ...

L: Uh huh.

J: Or maybe a change in your lifestyle.

L: So you pick the photos yourself?

J: Yeah. Not only photos, though. Look! You can include quotes, sayings, pictures of places you want to go to, images that bring back memories you'd like to make part of your life again. The possibilities are endless.

L: Right, OK ...

J: But it's got to be stuff that will motivate and inspire you. You know, things you'll want to look at throughout the day.

L: So you're saying the images will help to keep you focused on whatever you want to achieve?

J: Yeah, but there's more to it than that. I've always believed that we attract ...

▶ **2.2** *page 16 exercise 1B*

J: I've always believed that we attract whatever we think about, good or bad.

L: Uh huh.

J: So, when you can visualize your thoughts, you make them more concrete ...

L: In other words, you're saying that a vision board really can help you meet your goals?

J: Exactly.

L: The whole idea seems so far-fetched! You can stare at a picture of a new car 'til you're blue in the face, but it won't just fall into your lap. It's not enough just to put your mind to something. You've got to do your part and go the extra mile – you know, save money for a long time, if necessary.

J: Yes, of course, you've got to work toward your goals, even if they seem unattainable. But our minds help us do that. If you're clear about what you really want and stay focused, it really makes a difference. I've read lots of books about it.

L: Oh, come on! Surely you don't believe any of this stuff is based on actual research? If we got everything we thought about, we'd have no social problems, no poverty ... These people only want to sell books and get rich!

J: You're such a skeptic! Speaking of books, though. Remember that book I told you about?

▶ **2.3** *page 16 exercise 1C*

J: Remember that book I told you about? The one I'd been meaning to write forever?

L: Yeah?

J: Well, guess what, no more excuses. This time I'm determined to get it published.

L: Wow! Good for you!

J: Yeah, I don't know why I put it on hold for so long, but now my mind's made up. I'd love to be able to work from home, as a writer, so whenever I look at this photo of a home office, I remind myself that I must keep writing, no matter what.

L: That's the spirit! And how about this one right here? Don't tell me you're planning to go back to college?

J: Actually, I might take an online course.

L: You mean like a degree?

J: Yeah. I'm torn between an MA in literature and an MBA.

L: Wow!

J: But there's a lot at stake.

L: Like what?

J: I'm not sure I'm going to be able to juggle all the assignments and a full-time job – oh, and the book! I guess I need to give it some more thought, especially if I have to look for another place to live.

L: What do you mean look for another place to live?

J: Well, I've been toying with the idea of selling this house...

L: You what?

J: ... yeah ... and moving into a much smaller place.

L: So that explains the photo. But you love this house!

J: I know, but I'm trying to convince myself that I don't need so much space and so much stuff to be happy. Just look at my closet!

L: Yeah, it's pretty packed.

▶ **2.5** *page 17 exercise 2C*

Hello! This is Helene, your cyber teacher. And I'm back with a few more collocations.

OK, Number 1: Earlier you learned that an idea can be far-fetched or unlikely. You can also talk about a *far-fetched story*, a *far-fetched explanation*, and a *far-fetched example*, as in "Did you really believe that story? It sounds pretty far-fetched to me!"

Number 2: We learned that a goal can be unattainable, meaning it cannot be reached or achieved. What other things do you think might be unattainable? Unfortunately, too many things! Some common words that go with "unattainable" are *an unattainable objective* – objective, as you know, means a "goal" – *an unattainable wish*, and *an unattainable target*, such as a sales target. Of course, the antonym, as you can probably guess, is *attainable*, and fortunately, some of our wishes, such as learning English, are definitely attainable ones!

Number 3: Speaking of goals again, we learned that you can meet your goals. What else can you hope to meet besides, of course, a soulmate? You can *meet a deadline*, usually

313

a tight one, *meet the requirements* for a school program or job, or *meet someone's expectations*. Meet is a very versatile verb, with lots of uses.

Number 4: Finally, one more collocation for today. Earlier, we learned that you can work toward a goal. You can also *work toward a degree*, like a law degree, *work toward a solution* like to a problem, and work toward a career in something, like journalism. *Work toward* means to move gradually in the direction of something, and in all these cases, you move gradually toward your goal. By the way, you can also say *work towards*, in case you were wondering. Both *toward* and *towards* are correct.

▶ 2.6 *page 18 exercises 3A and B*

C = Crystal, B = Barry

C: … we could have a housewarming party or something? Well, looks like we've made it. It took us a week, but we're finally unpacked!
B: Hey, where's the Kandinsky?
C: The one we kept near the stairs? I threw it out.
B: You what?! I loved that painting. You did, too!
C: Yeah, but it didn't go with the new curtains. We'll get ourselves brand new things!
B: You're unbelievable!
C: I know! Hey, just look out of the window! What a view, huh?
B: Yeah, I have to admit I like the surroundings, especially these tree-lined streets.
C: I knew you would! … in fact, that's what I thought the first time I saw this place – on Day 1, when I called you to tell you about it. So, why so grumpy?
B: Listen, Crystal, it's a nice place, but it feels kind of claustrophobic, don't you think?
C: Well, compared to our old house, yes, but it's still larger than Julie and Bob's apartment. If they could settle for a little less space, I don't see why we can't.
B: Well, I suppose we can downsize. Especially now that we're living off our pension and savings.
C: It's a new phase of life. It's going to be great … Hey, did you check out the neighbors? They're all in their mid 20s.
B: Yeah, young enough to be our kids.
C: What's wrong with that? I'd love to hang out with a younger crowd for a change!

▶ 2.7 *page 18 exercise 3C*

C: You'll come to love our new home. I'm convinced! Besides, who needs all that space anyway? Think of all the time and energy we spent on the upkeep of the house. The blocked drains, the broken pipes, the …
B: All kinds of creatures living in the ceiling …
C: Exactly! And think of the money we're going to save on insurance, taxes, and bills. We won't have to pay any of those now.
B: That's true. We won't have to. We might even be able to afford a few extras.
C: See?
B: By the way, you do realize there are still five or six boxes at our old place?

C: So?
B: What do you mean, "so"? You haven't even asked what's in them. Some of our possessions won't fit in this apartment.
C: I'm sure most of them will. Barry, listen, I know we may have to get rid of a few things, but look on the bright side. We'll finally be able to declutter our lives!
B: Hmm …
C: You see, I've been reading this book about living in small spaces, and I'm totally convinced that less is more.
B: Nope. Less is less, Crystal.
C: Come on, Barry. Cheer up! We'll find a solution. We always have.

▶ 2.11 *page 21 exercise 6A*

Hello, this is Helene, your cyber teacher, and I'm back with some more collocations! Collocations help you sound natural, so try to memorize as many of these as you can.

Number 1, *convey*: The word *convey* means "to make something known or communicate it." People, places, or things can all be the subject of *convey*. We can "convey a message" or "convey an idea" using words, pictures, or even body language. A place can "convey a sense of freedom" – in other words, it makes you feel free. And, of course, other words can follow "sense," too: "convey a sense of joy and a sense of happiness."

Number 2, *crave*: *Crave* means "to long for or want something greatly." And there are many things we all crave! You can "crave excitement," "crave attention" – like some celebrities do – and "crave peace and quiet" if you've been busy or stressed out. You can also crave things like "candy" or "your grandmother's delicious cooking."

Number 3, *ubiquitous*: *Ubiquitous* means "widespread," and many things are ubiquitous and all around us. We can talk about a "ubiquitous influence or presence," as in "David Bowie's ubiquitous influence on pop culture" or "a politician's ubiquitous presence in the media." Or even a "ubiquitous fashion." And, as the article says, nothing could be more ubiquitous than our many electronic devices!

Number 4, *cater to*: To *cater to* someone or something is a common verb, and, as you probably know, it means "to supply what a specific audience desires or requires." So, for example, a TV show can "cater to a young, male, or female audience," and a teacher can "cater to students' needs." A business might "cater to the different interests" or "different tastes" of specific groups.

Number 5, *upscale*, our last collocation for today: *Upscale* means "appealing to those with money." So you can say "an upscale neighborhood," "an upscale restaurant," or "an upscale market." Many things can be "upscale," for example, a five-star hotel is an "upscale hotel." And we'd all love to stay in one of those! Well, that's it for today. Hope you've enjoyed your cyber lesson, and I'll be back again soon.

▶ 2.12 *page 22 exercise 7A*

E = Sleep expert, S = Student

E: Thank you so much for coming today. As you know, you've all been invited to participate in a study here at the Sleep Center. Now I know you were probably expecting older people and are wondering why on earth you were chosen.
S: Yes, I was wondering, in fact.
E: Good. That's what we're going to find out today as we explore the sleep habits of people in their 20s.
S: Can I go get some coffee? I'm really tired!
E: I'd like to ask you to wait until we take a break. But, I have a question … are you a morning or an evening person?
S: I'm not sure anymore. I've changed a bit. Now I get up earlier, but I'm still working on it … as you can see! My first two years of college, I was such a night owl that I wrote most of my assignments between 1:00 and 4:00 a.m. Sometimes, I didn't sleep a wink before exams! I looked like a zombie, but it was so much easier to study at night.
E: Thanks. Let's explore this a bit. Now, I've been told you're all science majors. Over here …

▶ 2.13 *page 22 exercises 7B and C*

E = Sleep expert, S = Student (1–5)

E: So, let's get started. What are your sleep habits like? You, in the red T-shirt.
S2: In my case, I've always gotten up early, but until recently, you know, some days I just spent the day yawning, staring at the clock, wishing I could go back to bed …
E: I know the feeling!
S2: Eventually I figured out that a lot depended on what I did as soon as I woke up.
E: Really? How's that?
S2: I know, it sounds weird, but I just observed myself. I looked for studies on sleep habits, but there were so few that it was hard to figure out how morning habits could ruin your day – you know, when time drags and you can't think straight. But finally I succeeded.
S3: This is fascinating. How?
S2: Well, I stopped starting my day with coffee.
S3: I could never do that!
S2: Try it. Helping yourself to a cup of freshly made coffee is more a matter of tradition than anything else. There are physiological reasons why your body may, in fact, need a little more time before it can make the most of caffeine.
E: Very interesting. Why's that?
S2: I read that when you wake up, your body begins to produce hormones to help you stay alert.
E: Like cortisol?
S2: Yes, exactly … if you drink coffee first thing in the morning, it's like adding fuel to the fire – you burn out faster.
S3: So, in other words, you're saying that if you drink coffee as soon as you wake up, you end up with so much energy that you run out of stamina faster, and you're tired by noon. But if you drink it later in the day, you get an extra energy boost?

Audio scripts

S2: Yes, that's a really good way to summarize it.
S3: That's such useful advice, thanks a lot.
E: I think you people know more about sleep than I do. Let's get a few more opinions. Are you a morning or evening person? Um, you, on the end in the white shirt.
S4: Hi. I used to be an evening person, but not anymore. I would spend the day dozing on and off, which made me very unproductive.
E: I can imagine.
S4: So a few years ago I tried to change my biorhythm. I forced myself to wake up at around seven, get down to work right after breakfast, and call it a day before dinner, no matter what.
E: Not easy for an evening person, I'm sure.
S4: No, but the key to my change was my first activity of the day.
E: How's that?
S4: I would make my bed.
E: Making your bed first thing in the morning. That sounds like a no-brainer.
S4: Yes, but it's the most important thing you'll do all day.
E: Why is it such a big deal?
S4: It sets the tone. Knowing that you were able to accomplish the very first task of the day puts you in a positive frame of mind. Just like some people do 30 push-ups or sit-ups, it's the same kind of "I did it" type of thing.
E: Makes sense.
S4: You see, my mornings are so hectic I have to skip breakfast sometimes. There's just no time. In fact, there's so little I have to run for the bus.
E: That's not very healthy ...
S4: Well, no, but making the bed is like a sacred ritual for me ... come rain or shine. It's the only calm thing I do!
E: Thanks. Just one more. Our first participant is patiently waiting for his coffee. And you? Coffee: friend or foe?
S5: Neither! I turn on my cell phone when I get up. It's such useful advice to do something productive.
E: And then?
S5: Well, all too often I have so little time and so many urgent messages, it's hard to put them on hold, even though I know it's not a good idea to handle email when I'm still drowsy. I've lost count of the number of times I had to hit "unsend" as soon as I'd sent a message.
E: So, why do you keep doing it?
S5: I'm in control of my day! There's no such thing as waking up on the wrong side of the bed.
E: That's an interesting way to look at it. This has been a very interesting discussion. Let's take a 15-minute break and then we'll ...

⏵ 2.14 *page 24 exercises 9A–D*

G = Shawn Groff, I = Mona Iskander,
W = Sarah Watson, M = Mayor Michael
Bloomberg, J = John Infranca, S = Speaker

G: ... a micro loft here in Vancouver. It's about 260 square feet ... and everything is really compact. It's got to be multi-functional ...
I: Shawn Groff is a 26-year-old employee at Whole Foods, who lives in a building that consists solely of what are known as micro-apartments.
G: We're standing in every room. We're standing in my kitchen and my dining room and my living room and my bedroom and my bathroom is just around the corner. The table comes up ...
I: His dining room table is also ... his bed.
G: The whole thing folds down which is classic Murphy bed style.
I: For about $950 a month he learns to make do with his 260 square foot space.
G: Voila! If I have company and I need another chair, I can use my coffee table again and they can enjoy as well. This a solution for people like myself, in the stage of my life, where I don't have that many things and I don't feel like I need that much space, I'm not really home that often. You ask yourself what you really need, um, and if you're honest about that a lot of things become unnecessary.
I: He happens to live in Vancouver, Canada, one of the first North American cities to embrace the tiny living concept. But the idea is catching on in a number of cities in the United States as well, like Seattle, San Francisco, New York, Boston, Washington D.C., Providence and Cleveland. They've all been pursuing projects to develop this new model. Sarah Watson is the deputy director of a non-profit research group in New York, the Citizen's Housing and Planning Council. For the last five years, the organization has been studying new concepts in housing. Watson says the number of people living by themselves in the United States has increased dramatically. In the 40s and 50s, it was less than 10 percent. Today that population is closer to 30 percent. People are getting married later, getting divorced at higher rates than they once did and are living longer. And Watson says the supply of housing for single people hasn't kept up with this changing demographic.
G: If the population changes but there's not housing supply to follow what happens is people start going underground and living informally, and that's why you see this huge growth in this craigslist market, people trying to make room in housing stock that's not designed for it.
I: And the problem is only going to get worse. For instance, New York's population is expected to rise by approximately 600,000 people by the year 2030. That's about an 8 percent increase.
W: We can't just keep building taller buildings, so there has to be some new ways to accommodate these people within it. So this whole space is 325 square foot.
I: So her organization lobby to convince Mayor Michael Bloomberg's administration to consider new types of housing in New York, including micro apartments, like this one on display at a recent exhibit at the Museum of the City of New York.
W: ... The shelf stays horizontal, you don't even have to clear your books.
I: So, it's basically an experiment?
W: Right. It's an experiment and the city's using it to properly test what happens if you just relieve a few elements, a few controls, erm, really to see what the options could be.
M: This, for many cities, is a selling point.
I: John Infranca is a Law professor at Suffolk University in Boston who studies affordable housing and land use policy.
J: I think it's good for cities in terms of being able to retain, um, young professionals, recent college graduates who might otherwise be priced out of the city in that that'll add a certain, you know, dynamism to the city. Um, Boston for instance, is really pushing that front that they want to retain their recent graduates who are ... otherwise can't afford to live there. And those graduates are going to be important for the city's broader economy to grow.
I: But there has been backlash. In Seattle, community groups have voiced concerns that these units crowd too many people together and that they make neighborhoods less stable as young people come and go. In Vancouver, critics worry that micro apartments will replace housing for the poor. For example, the apartment building where Shawn Groff lives used to be a single room occupancy building. Locals complained its residents were being forced onto the street.
S: ... Critics say that these are really geared towards young, high-income people who are moving to the city for the first time. It's not really addressing the needs of, um, lower middle-income workers who also need the housing.
W: A lot of these pilots that are happening in cities are definitely on the higher end because they're happening in high value areas, but we believe if you could really think through the design concepts of these small spaces and situate them in other locations, you know, you can, you're really changing the price point for that, um, and you can target different populations.
W: We have a small one drawer dishwasher ...
I: And Watson believes micro units make sense for the way many people live today.
W: There's a reason why this is catching on in the country because, you know, you can live quite comfortably now with your music collection and your, you know, your books all on a very tiny laptop. I mean it's actually transformed our need for space in the last five years, technology. So, you couple that with new transformable furniture and you can really maximize a small space in a positive way.

Review 1 (Units 1–2)

⏵ R1.1 *page 26 exercise 2A*

T = Teacher, S = Student 1

T: We may not think about it consciously, but how we dress defines our lifestyle and social standing. No area encompasses the areas of psychology, sociology, and economics more than fashion. In choosing a personal style, we meet our need for individuality. When we attempt to imitate the clothing style of a

Audio scripts

pop icon, we meet our need to belong to, and identify with, a group. And when we buy brand-name products, we convey that we have reached a certain level of prosperity. Today we are going to see how clothing reflects our lifestyle in another context, that of China. Yes, Amanda?

S1: Does that include Hong Kong?

T: Yes, it does. We'll get to that in a minute. However, we will be focusing on Mainland China and the cities along the coast, especially Shanghai and Beijing. You may wonder why I'm speaking about China today in a class on lifestyles. It's because China represents a merger between East and West and choosing to embrace that merger means choosing a way of life. Famous designers, including Christian Dior and Yves St. Laurent, have created fantastic, exotic designs drawing on Chinese motifs and cinema.

▶ R1.2 page 26 exercise 2B

T = Teacher, S = Student (1–3)

T: We may not think about it consciously, but how we dress defines our lifestyle and social standing. No area encompasses the areas of psychology, sociology, and economics more than fashion. In choosing a personal style, we meet our need for individuality. When we attempt to imitate the clothing style of a pop icon, we meet our need to belong to, and identify with, a group. And when we buy brand-name products, we convey that we have reached a certain level of prosperity. Today we are going to see how clothing reflects our lifestyle in another context, that of China. Yes, Amanda?

S1: Does that include Hong Kong?

T: Yes, it does. We'll get to that in a minute. However, we will be focusing on Mainland China and the cities along the coast, especially Shanghai and Beijing. You may wonder why I'm speaking about China today in a class on lifestyles. It's because China represents a merger between East and West and choosing to embrace that merger means choosing a way of life. Famous designers, including Christian Dior and Yves St. Laurent, have created fantastic, exotic designs drawing on Chinese motifs and cinema.

S2: Really? I didn't know that.

T: Yes, and the reverse is true, as well. E-commerce and social media have revolutionized China. Customers are increasingly used to buying online. China is such a sophisticated fashion market that 45 percent of people in Beijing and Shanghai claim to have their own personal style. Hong Kong, which you mentioned Amanda, is a fashion setter, so many middle class people follow trends there. Consumers have an international outlook, which means many travel abroad on vacations.

S3: I recently saw Chinese tourists right here in San Diego.

T: Yes, that's true, Todd. However, you may think they're copying your fashions when they buy at Macy's or Nordstrom's, but they're not. If international designers are lucky, they can team up with Chinese designers to create unique Chinese brands. The Chinese want innovation, personalization, and value for money. They're working toward their own vision, not meeting your expectations.

S1: I'm still not sure I see the connection to lifestyle, though.

T: Very good point, Amanda. Those who choose to embrace both the East and West may make lifestyle decisions beyond fashion. For example, the travel Todd mentioned. Or they may eat a broader range of foods, or spend time seeking out international exhibits and films. A lifestyle is a way of life, and openness can be considered a lifestyle.

Unit 3

▶ 3.1 page 28 exercise 1B

T = Teacher, H = Hugo, M = María

T: Really? Who would have thought it! How about you, Hugo? Do you speak any other languages?

H: Well, I've been to Brazil a few times, and I've taken some Portuguese courses. So I can carry on a simple conversation. And I speak French and a little English.

T: What do you mean a little English? Don't be so modest! You're an advanced student! And an excellent one at that!

H: Well, yeah, but I've never lived in the States, for example. I think you need to spend some time in an English-speaking country to have a really good command of the language.

M: What makes you say that?

T: Good question, María.

H: Well, you see, when I finished high school, I spent a year in Paris working as an au pair. I only spoke a little French when I arrived. I mean, I knew how to order food, ask for directions ... but nothing beyond that.

T: You mean you could get by?

H: Yeah, but after a few months, my French improved a lot – and really fast.

M: Did you take a course or something?

H: No way! I couldn't afford to. I learned from the kids, the host family, and all the friends I made when I was there.

T: You mean you picked it up naturally by talking to native speakers?

H: Uh huh. Plus, I'm not shy, which might have helped. I suspect you learn a language more easily when you're an extrovert.

T: Hmm ...That's debatable, I think.

▶ 3.2 page 28 exercise 1C

H: Anyway, when I came back to Mexico, I was practically bilingual. Well, maybe not bilingual. My French – at least my spoken French – was much better than my English. But I've forgotten lots of words, and I'm not as fluent as I used to be.

T: So your French is a bit rusty ...

H: Yeah, that's the word. And I need to catch up on my reading. It's been a while!

M: You're right. Reading for pleasure is the only way to increase your vocabulary.

T: Well, definitely one good way. But do you agree with Hugo? Do you need to live in another country to master the language?

M: Well, I've never set foot in a foreign country. I've learned all the English I know in this school. And I ... I think my English is better than before.

T: Yes, it's improved by leaps and bounds! I mean, you need to be really advanced to use the expression "set foot in"!

M: Well, if you say so ... I'm not a gifted learner, though. In the beginning I used to struggle a lot. I was always lost in class.

T: Well, it's natural to feel out of your depth sometimes.

M: I guess. Anyway, I've lost count of the number of grammar and vocabulary exercises I've done. Not to mention all the apps I've downloaded ...

T: Yes, I know you have! You've put a lot of effort into your work! And it's paid off! If you're willing to go the extra mile, you can make a lot of progress, whether or not you're naturally good at languages ...

M: Yes, and I don't think living abroad is automatically going to make you fluent. Take my dad, for example.

H: What about him?

M: He spent six months in the UK when he was in his twenties, but he keeps saying my spoken English is better than his.

T: Hmm ... interesting.

H: Did he use to hang out with a lot of Spanish speakers?

M: Yeah. I think most of his friends were from Mexico and Spain ...

H: So that might explain it.

M: But, honestly, why do you need to live abroad when you can access the Internet and immerse yourself in a foreign language without leaving your home? And YouTube is fantastic! When I watch videos, I feel as if I'm there.

H: Well, I'm not sure I agree. Even if you're exposed to a lot of English, it's not the same as actually living abroad. When you live in another country, you absorb the culture ... You, erm, you become "one of them," and that's really important.

▶ 3.5 page 29 exercise 3A

H = Hugo, M = María

1

H: I spent a year in Paris working as an au pair. I only spoke a little French when I arrived. I mean, I knew how to order food, ask for directions ... but nothing beyond that.

T: You mean you could get by?
Number 1. *To get by*, in this context, means "to just barely manage or survive." So when Hugo says he knew how to order food and ask for directions, he is saying he could just barely *get by*.

2

M: Did you take a course or something?

H: No way, I couldn't afford to. I learned from the kids, the host family, and all the friends I made when I was there.

T: You mean you picked it up naturally by talking to native speakers?
Number 2. *To pick something up* in this context means "to acquire by experience." Hugo *picked up* French by talking to his host family and friends.

3
H: My French – at least my spoken French – was much better than my English. But I've forgotten lots of words, and I'm not as fluent as I used to be.
T: So your French is a bit rusty …
Number 3. *Rusty means oxidized, like metal after the rain*. But here it is figurative, not literal, meaning here: "to be slow through lack of practice." When Hugo says he's forgotten words and isn't as fluent as he used to be, he's saying he's out of practice.

4
M: I've learned all the English I know in this school. And I … I think my English is better than before.
T: Yes, it's improved by leaps and bounds!
Number 4. To *improve by leaps and bounds*, as I'm sure you've guessed, means to improve "extremely rapidly." María's teacher is trying to tell her that her English isn't only better than before, it's much better. This expression can also be used with verbs that mean "to expand" as in "The town grew by leaps and bounds."

5
M: I'm not a gifted learner, though. In the beginning I used to struggle a lot. I was always lost in class.
T: Well, it's natural to feel out of your depth sometimes.
Number 5. To be or feel *out of your depth* means "to feel beyond the limits of your capabilities." When María says she was always lost, she's saying she felt *out of her depth*.

6
M: I've lost count of the number of grammar and vocabulary exercises I've done. Not to mention all the apps I've downloaded …
T: Yes, I know you have! You've put a lot of effort into your work!
Number 6. *To put a lot of effort into something* means "to devote a lot of time and energy to it." And María has certainly *put a lot of effort* into doing exercises and downloading apps. But wait, we're not quite done. Maybe you thought the answer was *that's debatable*, which means that something can be questioned and is open to debate. If María's teacher had said "that's debatable," it's not an ungrammatical answer. But he would be saying that María was lying about doing so many exercises!

▶ 3.6 *page 30 exercise 4A*

… so please feel free to interrupt me at any time, OK? The first question I'd like to examine is: To hash or not to hash? Hashtags are probably the most popular way to categorize content on social media and you'd be hard pressed to find someone who's never heard of them. So, just in case you've been living in a cave for the past ten years hashtags let you search by topic, which, to a certain extent, filters out some of the less relevant results. So, for example, if you type the hashtag #learn English# in Twitter, you'll see lessons, newspaper articles, and more. Hashtags are an integral part of online communication – and, in some respects, of our culture at large.

▶ 3.7 *page 30 exercise 4B*

… of our culture at large. But there's more to tagging your messages than simply making them easier to find. As your social media profiles become integrated with your personal and professional identity, your choices of hashtags are often seen as part of your character. In other words, your personal and professional identity are both reflected more clearly when your messages are stronger. A well-chosen, creative hashtag is a bit like a witty afterthought. What it can do is give your text more color and depth – a humorous twist, like a clever punchline, if you will. It can also help you convey certain non-verbal emotions, too, that would only come across in face-to-face communication, like a smirk, a sigh, a smile, or even rolling your eyes. Think of an emoticon without the silly faces, and you get the idea. Beyond that, certain hashtags have political and social significance and the power to unite people who happen to support specific causes, and this, in turn, helps them realize they're part of a larger community of like-minded individuals. A few years ago, for example, …

▶ 3.8 *page 30 exercise 4C*

L = Lecturer, S = Student (1 and 2)
L: More and more people, however, are starting to wonder what the point of using hashtags is when regular words can get the job done just as well. In other words, why not say, "Hey, I'm having a lot of fun" instead of #havingfun? True, but the problem is not the hashtag itself. It's the fact that most people still haven't learned how to use hashtags well. Let me show you three examples. Take a look at the first tweet on the slide: "Having lunch at Au Bon Pain. Love this place! #lunch. What's wrong with this hashtag?
S1: Hmm … It states the obvious, I think.
L: Exactly! We're fully aware that she's not building a spaceship or running a marathon, right? Hashtags like these don't add much to the original message. They're just noise, so to speak and, honestly, why people use them is beyond me. How about the second tweet, the one with the link to the article? What's wrong with it?
S2: I can't make it out!
S3: Neither can I!
L: Exactly. This hashtag is confusing to say the least and how it can help the reader isn't clear. When I first read it, it took me about ten seconds to figure out there were actually eight, no, nine words lumped together! If you absolutely have to write a long hashtag, make sure the word boundaries are as clear as possible. Now, take a look at the last one, the one about Pinocchio and Rihanna. It looks harmless on the surface, I know, but is "funny" an effective hashtag?
S1: I didn't find it funny!
S2: I did!
L: You see? Just because something cracked you up doesn't mean other people are going to find it funny, too. Personally, I find that tweet a bit lame – to put it mildly, but that's beside the point. Some people will like it, some won't, so your hashtag can't make that sort of assumption. Now, whether hashtags are here to stay remains to be seen, but, at any rate…

▶ 3.11 *page 34 exercises 8B and C*

V = Veronica, C = Caroline
V: There are more reasons for raising a child bilingually than you may think. Hi, I'm Veronica with watchmojo.com and today we're speaking with Caroline Erdos, a speech language pathologist from the Montreal Children's Hospital on the dos and don'ts of raising a child learning two languages from birth. What are the benefits of raising a child who knows more than one language?
C: Well, there are several cognitive advantages, so for example, bilingual children have been found to have better abilities at problem solving in that ignoring irrelevant information when they're problem solving. There are also advantages later in life, for example, adults with Alzheimer, the adults who are bilingual will tend to, um, only begin showing signs of Alzheimer later than the monolingual individuals.
V: Do you always have to have one parent speak one language, the other parent speak another language and their teacher stick to one language?
C: One can choose the formula one wants, so it could be one parent one language at home, two different languages in the home, or it could be one language in the home one language at daycare, there are various formulas. What that does is ensure that there is a sufficient amount of input in each language, so for example, a child with whom we only read in a language would not necessarily be exposed to vocabulary concerning academics or sports, but if we're holding many conversations with that child in that language, then we're covering a wide range of vocabulary.
V: Will learning more than one language ever confuse your child?
C: No, generally children are quite able to learn two languages and, in fact, worldwide there are more individuals who are bilingual than individuals who are monolingual.
V: Now, should parents worry if the child uses two languages in one sentence?
C: No, actually it's quite natural phenomena for individuals who are bilingual to use words from the other language and, in fact, children tend to do that more if they're around adults who they know speak both languages and if they do that in a context where the adults do not speak both languages, they're usually doing it because they don't have the word in one language

and they'll borrow from another language. It's not something to worry about.
V: Will a child who's learning more than one language speak later on in life than someone who's just learning one language?
C: In fact, studies have looked at comparing language milestones, um, between bilingual children and monolingual children and the milestones appear to be very similar, so the babbling occurs around the same age whether a child is monolingual or bilingual. First words, uh, first word combinations, sentences.
V: Are there any situations where maybe it's not ideal to teach your child two languages?
C: Not that I know of. Even in the extreme case of children who have language disorders or, what we call language impairment, um, those children, whether they're bilingual or monolingual, they're language skills will look the same, so bilingualism does not further exacerbate even a child with language difficulties. Of course, the child will have difficulty learning the second language because that child had difficulty learning a first language, but to the extent that that child can learn one language, she can learn a second language.
V: So is it ever too late to introduce a new language for your child?
C: It probably is never too late, but the later a child is introduced to a language, um, the less likely that child is to lose the accent. There is some critical age that is yet unidentified but beyond that age, that's what we're seeing, is that one can learn a language very well but will not necessarily master the language in terms of pronunciation.
V: As a parent what can you do to make sure that your child will learn both languages to the best of his or her ability?
C: Well, they can make sure the child is getting a sufficient amount of input, so at least 30 per cent of what the child hears should be in a given language if that child is expected to be productive in that language. They should also make sure that the person who is speaking to the child masters the language so the child is getting an adequate language model and the exposure should be sustained. It should not be just sporadically throughout the year, it should be as often as possible and in a sustained, continuous manner.
V: Well thank you, it was really great having you.
C: It's my pleasure.

3.13 page 36 exercise 11A

P = Paula, D = David

P: Well, I'm off to the gym. Have to practice my backhand.
D: Again? You seem to practice your tennis a lot.
P: You're right. I do. "Practice makes perfect," remember.
D: Yeah, I wish! That doesn't seem to apply to everything.
P: You mean, practice? Yeah, you could be right. That's what I thought the other night.
D: Why? What happened?
P: Well, I went to a concert, and I don't know. The soloist just didn't have any spark. A violinist.
D: You mean he was just going through the motions?
P: It sure seemed that way. And you're not going to believe what happened after the intermission.
D: I'm dying of suspense.
P: Just as he's about to begin, he decides he doesn't want to continue! And he escapes out a side door. Then he has a friend call to say he's suddenly become "indisposed" and is in the hospital.
D: No!
P: It's true! My cousin who knows him told me the whole thing! When the conductor – who doesn't quite believe the excuse, you know – confronts him, Arthur – that's his name – admits he doesn't want to do anything any longer that requires perfection. Really. Well, the conductor tries to convince Arthur perfection isn't fixed, and that the interpretation is in the performance. But Arthur now sees the violin as his enemy, as an instrument that demands a perfection he can't possibly deliver.
D: Wow! That's just incredible. Had he ever performed before?
P: No, I think this was his very first time in front of such a large audience …

3.14 page 36 exercise 11B

P: Poor Arthur – as soon as he came on stage, he just seemed totally out of it.
D: In what way?
P: Well, even though he had a great technique, and he seemed to own a very expensive violin, there was no emotion. He was just kind of mechanical. As if someone had once told him he had talent, but he didn't really believe it.
D: I've been thinking … this is so interesting! That's how I feel about the piano. I've been playing for six years, and I just don't seem to be making much progress. In fact, I really have my doubts about my playing! And what's more. I'm terrified of performing, so I can't even begin to imagine giving a concert. Maybe you can give me some advice, based on … well, maybe you picked up some pointers at this concert.
P: Well, OK. I can try. But why do you feel so insecure?
D: I don't know. It's like … everything has to be perfect. I feel paralyzed. No matter how long I practice, it just never seems good enough. Not when I think about Beethoven!
P: That's the problem. You're setting yourself impossibly high standards. You just have to enjoy yourself. What difference does it make if it's perfect anyway?
D: People might laugh at me.
P: Oh, come on, David! What are the odds of that happening? Adults don't laugh at people who make an effort. Only children do. And not all kids, either! Try not to think too much about the audience.
D: Maybe you're right. Or I could even just decide I don't have to play the notes correctly.
P: Well, don't go to the other extreme! You need to hit a middle ground. Do your very best, but don't worry about being perfect. Kind of like speaking another language, you know.
D: You mean to say that learning a language is like learning an instrument?
P: All learning is the same if you ask me. You have to put a lot of effort into it and go the extra mile. It's part motivation, a lot of hard work … and being gifted doesn't hurt, of course, but it's not the main thing.
D: So do you think I could learn to ski if I really put my mind to it?
P: Yeah, I do. Why not give it a shot? You might not be in the Olympics, but you can still have a great time on the ski slopes!

Unit 4

4.1 page 38 exercise 1A

I = Interviewer, W = Dr. Wallace

I: … our interview with Dr. Emilia Wallace, author of Dream on: *What we learn about ourselves at night*. …By the way, I love Dream on. The book is thoroughly-researched and very reader-friendly at the same time. Congratulations.
W: Thank you very much.
I: No wonder it's been getting such rave reviews. It is a masterpiece.
W: Well, I wouldn't go so far as to call it a masterpiece, but it's, erm, it's a solid effort.
I: Your review of the current literature on dreams is especially praiseworthy.
W: Well, what I set out to do was evaluate the existing research in the light of my own experience as a therapist.
I: I see. So, here's the first – and inevitable – question: Do dreams actually mean something? In other words, if I dream about a snake, are we simply talking about random neural signals? Or does the fact that it's a snake, rather than, say, a kitten, matter in any significant way?
W: Well, dreams have a number of functions, one of which is simply to "de-clutter" your brain while you sleep. And some dreams are simply your body reacting to outside stimuli, such as noises and smells.
I: Like when you hear the phone ring and dream about a fire-engine siren?
W: Exactly. But there might be more to it than that. The general consensus seems to be that some recurring dreams have an emotional basis and can help us understand who we really are beneath the surface.
I: So you're saying the snake could represent my feelings toward my mother-in-law? Or my boss?
W: It could, well, yes.

4.2 page 38 exercises 1B and C

I = Interviewer, W = Dr. Wallace, C = Caller (1–3)

I: ... and we have our first caller, from Vermont. Hi, you're on the air.
C1: Hi, Dr. Wallace. Erm ... I have this recurring dream in which I'm in a car, and it's totally out of control. The brakes fail, and I end up losing control of the steering wheel, and ... Well, I always wake up before the worst happens.
W: Well, this is a common type of dream and, trust me, I've had my share. More often than not, dreaming about car crashes means that maybe you're pushing yourself too hard.
C1: Hmm ...
W: Sound familiar?
C1: Disturbingly so, yeah.
W: ... and maybe setting yourself impossibly high standards.
C: Yep, that's me.
W: Highly competitive, results-oriented individuals often have this sort of dream ...
C: So the car heading for a crash is a kind of metaphor? Or could it be that I might have an accident one of these days?
W: No, no. It really sounds as if your nightmare is stress-related. Nothing to worry about.
I: So you're saying there's no such thing as prophetic dreams?
W: Hmm ... We should be cautious about these claims. You see, the jury is still out on whether that's true, so I'd rather not give you an unequivocal "yes" or "no" at this point.
I: And our next caller is from Dallas. Hi. What's your question?
C: Erm ... I have a recurring dream of being chased through the woods by a tall, ghost-like figure.
W: And you can't make out who or what it is?
C: No!
W: Does it look more like a man or a woman?
C: I'm not even sure it's human.
W: I see. And how fast does it run?
C: Slowly at first, and then it starts to catch up.
W: Well, dreams of being chased usually mean that certain circumstances might be closing in on you, and that you're feeling vulnerable and trying to run away.
C: Uh huh.
W: But there's another possible meaning. It could also represent something you blame yourself for that maybe you haven't come to terms with yet. You know, as if you're afraid of being caught as a result of something you've done.
C: Makes perfect sense.
W: So what you should do is try to identify what it is that you're running away from and confront your fear head on. Only then will you get to the bottom of the problem.
C: And then these dreams will go away?
W: Yes, just relax. There's no doubt in my mind that they will.
I: And here's our third caller, from South Carolina.
C: Hi, Dr. Wallace. I, erm ... I keep dreaming about my teeth ... that they're falling out ...
W: Uh huh.
C: One by one, with just a light tap.
W: Dreams about our teeth usually reflect our anxieties about how other people perceive us. So this sort of dream may have its origins in our fear of rejection. The more image-conscious we are, the worse it gets.
C: Hmm ...
W: Remember that you also use your teeth to bite, to tear, to chew, so they do symbolize power as well. So maybe it's that you're having trouble getting your ideas across, making your points forcefully ... Just struggling to find your voice, so to speak. Does that ring true? That is, more than being image-conscious? I'd say this explanation is more likely.
C: No, not really, doctor. But thanks anyway.

4.3 page 38 exercise 1D

I: It's been a pleasure to have you in the studio tonight. Any final thoughts?
W: Yeah. Erm ... Even if we assume, for the sake of argument, that dreams are emotionally-charged phenomena, rather than random neurochemical reactions, they can't be interpreted out of context, since symbols may not always have universal significance.
I: Oh, yes, without a shadow of a doubt.
W: For example, a dream about your mother might have a very different meaning if you're from a culture where your mother plays a dominant role in your decision-making throughout your life, as opposed to a more subservient role.
I: So, in other words, we should take these claims with a grain of salt. Any interpretation might be valid!

4.6 page 40 exercises 3A and B

Welcome to "Today in history," where we review spectacular events you may not be aware of.

October 30, 1938, a day that will live in infamy! Orson Welles was only 23 when his theater company decided to create a radio play based on a famous science-fiction novel. The show aired on a Sunday, at 8:00 p.m, and millions of Americans had their radios on as a voice announced: "The Columbia Broadcasting System and its affiliated stations present Orson Welles and the Mercury Theater on the air in *The War of the Worlds* by H.G. Wells."

Orson Welles, no relation to the writer H.G. Wells, introduced the play, which was followed by a weather report and a music number. At one point, someone broke in to report that a certain observatory had detected a sequence of explosions on Mars, which, not surprisingly, took listeners by surprise. Then the music came back on, but it was followed by another interruption. Apparently, a huge meteor had crashed into a farm in New Jersey – except that it wasn't a meteor, but an army of Martians, which the radio announcer described as "large as bears," with "V-shaped salivating mouths" and "eyes that gleamed like serpents." Not only did the creatures look hideous, they were evil, too, annihilating whoever came their way and releasing poisonous gases into the air, which threw listeners nationwide into a frenzy.

As it turns out, the reports – which had chilling sound effects and incredibly convincing performances – were part of the radio play! The whole thing was so realistic that millions of listeners were under the impression that the U.S. was, in fact, under attack. Panic broke out as thousands of people clogged the highways, desperately trying to flee the attack – where they were headed is anyone's guess, of course! Never before had a radio show inadvertently caused so much panic.

News that the show had wreaked havoc in the country eventually reached the studio, and only when Welles realized the seriousness of the situation, did he interrupt the show to explain what was going on. The nation breathed a sigh of relief to learn that it was all fiction, of course, but the general public had a hard time believing that the show was never intended as a hoax. The radio station came in for a lot of criticism for unleashing terror across the country, and Orson Welles reportedly said that *The War of the Worlds* would be the end of his career. But the opposite happened. Welles eventually signed a movie deal which led to *Citizen Kane*, arguably the greatest American film of all time.

4.7 page 40 exercise 3C

Hello, This is Helene, your cyber teacher again, back to look at some new expressions all related to chaos and our reactions to it.

Number 1: *throw someone into a frenzy*: The radio program describes how *The War of the Worlds* "threw listeners nationwide into a frenzy", and, as you've probably guessed, this expression means to "cause someone to have an intense emotional reaction." It's a fixed expression, but, of course, you can change who was thrown into a frenzy. So, for example, you can say, "When I learned the exam was tomorrow, it threw me into a frenzy."

Number 2: *clog the highways*: "Panic broke out as thousands of people clogged the highways." Think about it. "To clog" means to "block" or "stop up," like a toilet or a drain, so to "clog the highways" means that they were "filled up" – in other words, there was a tremendous traffic jam. This is a figurative use of the verb "clog."

Number 3: *flee the attack*: Flee means "to run away from" so "desperately trying to flee the attack" means "to run away from" or "to escape" the attack. You may know that "flee" also collocates with other events you may want to escape, so you can "flee a fire," "flee an accident," or the more general "flee the scene."

Number 4: *breathe a sigh of relief*: a sigh is a long, audible breath, like this Aaaaaah and since we obviously breathe air, this is another figurative use. *The nation breathed a sigh of relief* means "The nation felt tremendously relieved and maybe even let out a long audible breath." like this, Phew!!!

Number 5: *wreak havoc*: The verb *wreak* means to "cause great damage or harm" and havoc is a situation with great damage or confusion, so *wreak havoc* is a fixed expression essentially meaning to "cause great damage or confusion," which is exactly what Orson Welles did when he *wreaked havoc* in the country.

Audio scripts

Well, I hope you never find yourselves in a dangerous or chaotic situation, but just in case, you'll now be armed with some great new expressions! See you soon.

4.9 page 44 exercise 7B

R = Reporter, P = Psychologist

R: ... which brings me to the key question: Just how accurate is personality testing? Today we have psychologist Will Morganstern with us to answer that question.
P: It depends on the type of research on which the test was based and on the subsequent data analysis. There are a number of respectable tests out there, based on years of research, such as Myers Briggs, which identifies and describes as many as 16 distinctive personality types.
R: 16? Wow!
P: Yes, impressive. But Myers Briggs is one of the few exceptions. The web is full of amateur tests, all of which have come in for a lot of criticism in recent years – and quite deservedly so.
R: Are you talking about things like "Pick the eye that you're immediately drawn to" or those psychoacoustic studies on sounds that bother people?
P: Exactly. These tests provide vague personality descriptions, with which it's hard to disagree. If you ask me, they're in the same league as fortune-telling, horoscopes, telepathy and that sort of thing.

4.10 page 44 exercise 7C

P: ... they're in the same league as fortune-telling, horoscopes, telepathy and that sort of thing. But well-researched or not, every personality test has a number of failings, most notably the fact that they build their scales around polar opposites.
R: What do you mean by polar opposites?
P: For example, shy people can be really outgoing in some situations, while, say, a driven, focused individual may procrastinate on certain occasions, so you can't classify people as strictly A or B. The human psyche is far, far more complicated.
R: I see.
P: Besides, no single test is capable of capturing the complexities of people's personalities because they change in response to different external factors, such as positive events like falling in love or negative ones like a traumatic experience or accident. And this is not even to mention the people with whom we interact daily: our family, close friends, classmates, and coworkers.
R: Why do so many companies still use personality profiling tests to screen their employees?
P: As a rule, personality tests – even the most rigorous ones – have low predictive validity; that is, they don't do a very good job of anticipating actual on-the-job behavior, which raises the question ...
R: What's the point of using them?

P: Exactly! And you can imagine how dangerous these tests can be in the wrong hands. For my latest book, I interviewed over a hundred recruiting managers, some of whom admitted to using test results as an excuse not to hire or promote someone.
R: What do you think the future holds for ...?

4.12 page 46 exercise 9A

J = Julie, S = Seth

J: Hey Seth, look at this. One of those surveys that wants our opinion.
S: Again? What's the question this time?
J: Whether an employer has a right to know if an applicant has a criminal record. I'm going to answer ... after what happened to Bob. I just can't stop thinking about him.
S: You mean how he was fired when they found out he had a prior conviction?
J: Uh-huh, he–
S: He should have been up front – I mean, about the prior conviction. An employer has a right to decide whether a criminal should be hired. I'd –
J: You mean an *ex*-criminal! Once you've served your time, you're not a criminal any longer. Why is it the employer's business?
S: Maybe, but don't you think it says a lot about you, I mean, just the fact that you committed the crime to begin with?
J: No, actually, I don't. That's my whole point. This is so interesting ... just like the podcast I listened to last week.
S: What do you mean?
J: I mean that the prejudice stays with us. We secretly feel criminals can't be rehabilitated. And so if a potential employer knows you have a criminal record, your chances of getting a job are extremely slim.
S: But we can't just hide our pasts. That would be like a ... like a conspiracy, almost.
J: What?!
S: Transparency is what allows us to trust people. Otherwise, life would just be like an April Fool's joke. And the truth always comes out, for example, when your boss starts to wonder why you're so secretive and refuse to talk about six years of your life.
J: I'm not sure I agree. Rarely do we find out everything about anyone anyway.
S: True enough.
J: And imagine if it was a crime in which no one was injured and no damage was really done. Wouldn't you just want to forget it? In fact, in some states, if the conviction was expunged – that means basically deleted because you were pardoned – it's illegal to use it against a job applicant, even if you find out about it.
S: Hmm. That may be, but I guess I've always been opposed to censorship in any shape or form. It just doesn't feel right. The employer has a right to know about your past. The company has to hire you with all the information on the table.

4.13 page 46 exercise 9B

J: You know, it's not just criminal records. I think censorship has its uses. In fact, I think it's essential in a civilized society.
S: You do? How? I think it's just a cover-up.
J: Well, for one thing, there's such a thing as too much information, most of which you have no need for whatsoever. We have no need to see sensitive government documents, for example.
S: I want to know what my government is up to! I'm not in favor of Big Brother!
J: That may be, but would you know what to do with the information you were given? You might get nervous. Overplay its importance. And you might exaggerate threats. Look at the famous radio play *The War of the Worlds* by Orson Welles. Not only were there no Martians, but there was no attack, either.
S: That's not the same as a *real* invader.
J: Well, maybe not, but let's take another example: parental censorship. I think it's a good thing.
S: What kind of parental censorship?
J: Like software that blocks access to certain sites. Kids don't have the maturity to know what they're looking at.
S: Don't you think it would be better, though, to talk to them? Why so much control? Seldom do kids not respond well when their parents trust them.
J: Hmm ... well, maybe. But how about reading? Shouldn't some novels be banned from school? And kids shouldn't be reading them at home, either, until they're 18. Books can be depressing. They might cause nightmares. And at the very least, they can have a negative influence on young people.
S: I just don't believe in any of this. Life isn't a bed of roses. Kids will be more resilient if they know what the real world is like! It's just not fair otherwise.
J: OK, one more example. What about history? Should textbooks be honest? This could be really scary. If teachers and textbooks were totally honest, kids might end up not trusting anybody. There's a lot of evil in the world, most of which we don't really need to know about.
S: I think it's the opposite. If we conceal information, kids will be suspicious as soon as they find out.

Unit 5

5.1 page 50 exercises 1A and B

DJ1: ... those huge promotional campaigns that can make or break a product.
DJ2: You know what they say – there's no such thing as bad press, but some companies try too hard! So instead of making a splash, they make the headlines – and attract people's attention for all the wrong reasons – like Snapple, the New York-based beverage company did a few years ago.
DJ1: Yes, in 2005, Snapple sought to break a world record, so it came up with a creative if crazy idea: erect the world's largest popsicle ... in downtown Manhattan.

The idea was to generate lots of publicity, of course. They were on the verge of something big, but the campaign never materialized.
DJ2: What happened?
DJ1: Their plans fell through, and the whole thing ended in a sticky mess.
DJ2: Why is that?
DJ1: The company, which had been trying to create excitement for a brand new line of frozen treats, built a 25-foot-tall, 17.5-ton popsicle, or you could say "snapsicle," took it to Union Square in a freezer truck and tried to raise it using a huge crane.
DJ2: They needed a *crane*?
DJ1: Yes! But the company's officials quickly realized there was something wrong when the pink, sugary liquid started to pour all the way down onto East 17th Street.
DJ2: You mean the gigantic popsicle started to melt?
DJ1: It did, before everyone's eyes, really fast, flooding Union Square with a sticky, strawberry-kiwi flavored liquid. It was like a scene straight out of a disaster movie.
DJ2: Oh my goodness!
DJ1: Authorities feared that the giant frozen treat would crumble – I mean, it was roughly 80 degrees outside – so, the company decided to call the whole thing off and stopped raising the popsicle with the crane. They called the fire department to close off the surrounding streets …
DJ2: And prevent the liquid from spreading even further!
DJ1: Exactly.
DJ2: Sounds as chaotic as a snowstorm with unploughed side streets!

▶ 5.2 page 50 exercise 1C

DJ2: But was it an oversight? I mean, didn't they see it coming?
DJ1: You mean that the giant popsicle wouldn't be able to withstand the heat?
DJ2: Yeah. It's hard to know, though, because there wasn't much in the news about a possible cause.
DJ1: I doubt it was the heat. The temperature was normal for the beginning of summer. Also, they're usually very though when planning big campaigns, and it was a high-stakes operation, meaning that if it failed, it would be a disaster. It might have been a glitch or something – maybe software-related.
DJ2: You mean in the production process?
DJ1: Yeah. For example, the software might have indicated the popsicle was colder than it was.
DJ2: Or maybe the popsicle got mushy on its way to New York, you know, because of vibrations from inside the truck.
DJ1: Hmm … You don't think a rival company would have …
DJ2: What?
DJ1: You know, done something to ruin their campaign.
DJ2: Well, we can't rule it out, can we? Or maybe it was just Murphy's Law!

DJ1: Yeah. "When something can go wrong, it will." Well, folks, it looks like we're out of time. We'll be right back after the break. Stay tuned.
DJ2: Speaking of Murphy's law, I still remember the day I defended my PhD thesis as it if were today.

▶ 5.6 page 51 exercise 3D

DJ2: Nice to have a short break before we go on the air again. But anyway, speaking of Murphy's law, I still remember the day I defended my Ph.D. thesis as if it were today.
DJ1: Wow! Lots at stake, uh?
DJ2: You bet.
DJ1: What happened?
DJ2: I'd been getting ready for months and, really, I knew my stuff inside out. Nothing could go wrong – except that it did, and I fell flat on my face. Well, not exactly, but close.
DJ1: What happened?
DJ2: At one point the data show stopped working and, in a strange twist of fate, my computer started acting funny too, and then…
DJ1: But hadn't you tested it beforehand?
DJ2: Of course! I'd even updated PowerPoint to the latest version. Who knows what happened!
DJ1: Sounds awful!
DJ2: A nightmare! Then things got out of hand. I started sweating and stammering, but everybody told me to calm down … It took me a while to pull myself together, but I did … and restarted the computer. It was back to square one! I had to start the presentation all over.
DJ1: I don't know what I would have done in your shoes!
DJ2: Guess what, the data show worked, but my computer froze. Again!
DJ1: Oh, no!
DJ2: I came this close to having a nervous breakdown!
DJ1: What happened then? Did they cancel the whole thing?
DJ2: No, luckily, someone lent me a laptop and I was able to continue.
DJ1: Did you pass?
DJ2: I did! Don't ask me how. I have to say, I really sympathize with Snapple!

▶ 5.8 page 52 exercises 4A and B

The beginning of every new year is often the perfect time to make a fresh start and get around to doing the things we'd been putting off forever, whether it's getting serious about shedding a few pounds, cutting corners here and there so you can learn how to live within your means, or perhaps making amends with people you might have fallen out with. The list goes on and on. This raises two questions. One, why do so many people wait for the new year to start anew? Do they expect that this will somehow strengthen their resolve? The second – and more important question – is, why do so many resolutions fall through? Why is it difficult to turn the page, get your act together, and follow through with your plans? Why is it so hard to stick to your resolutions?
To answer these and other questions, we have with us today, Doctor Alexander Wolinsky, along with several guests who have graciously agreed to share their experiences.

▶ 5.9 page 52 exercise 4C

W = Dr. Wolinsky, G = Guest (1 and 2), P = Presenter
W: Changing our behavior can be exceedingly difficult, and given what we know about the nature of the human psyche, this shouldn't come as a surprise. Breaking a lifelong habit means letting go of things that may be rooted in a number of unresolved issues – issues we might have struggled with for years and years.
G1: It took me 10 years to quit biting my nails. Looking back, I realize that I was a bit obsessive in general. Maybe I still am!
P: Yes, and with a view to better understanding the problem – that is, the problem of breaking old habits – a number of researchers have looked at the success rates of people's New Year's Resolutions. They found out that in the first few weeks, most people tend to follow through with their resolutions, though with varying degrees of enthusiasm. Around February, they begin to lose steam, and toward the end of the year, they're often back to square one. There are individual variations, of course, but the failure rate – if we can put it that way – is consistently high across a wide range of age groups and personality types.
W: One reason might be the fact that we sometimes set unrealistic, almost unattainable goals that we know we're not going to stick to.
P: So you're saying some people sabotage themselves so as not to succeed?
W: Yes. Deep down they know they're bound to fail, and the more they fail, the less likely they are to try again.
G2: Yes, for example, three years in a row, I resolved to spend more time with my family. But my boss was totally unreasonable. So I just stopped trying, I was so discouraged.
P: I know how you feel. And here's another problem. Nearly every conversation about New Year's resolutions tends to revolve around outcomes. How much weight do you want to lose? How much money do you want to make? In other words, when making New Year's resolutions, we tend to see the end goal of whatever we're planning to start. But in view of what we know about recent motivational theories, this rarely works.
W: The problem is that resolutions don't deliver new results – new lifestyles do. So instead of focusing on the outcome, you should focus on the process, on the new habits you want to acquire. They should be their own reward.

Audio scripts

▶ **5.11** *page 56 exercise 8A*

1
A: So our project is due on Tuesday, right, Barbara?
B: Yes, why?
A: Well, I'm going to be away this weekend, actually. Do you think you could finish up the last part?
B: I'm not happy about you asking me at the last minute, Roger. You're not pulling your weight, you know. I thought you were more responsible.

2
A: It's over, John. I really can't take this any longer. What you did last night was the last straw.
B: Take what, Anne? I didn't do anything.
A: That's what I mean. Never apologizing. Never wrong. I thought you were a little more mature. I guess I was wrong!

3
A: Susan, I'm afraid I need to have a few words with you. The Robinson account is very important to us. I'm concerned about your not being in touch with the company.
B: I just got out of the hospital, Bill! Why didn't you explain I'd had emergency surgery?
A: I know I don't sound sympathetic, but that's really no excuse. Business comes first.
B: You know what? I hadn't imagined that you were so cruel. My resignation is effective at 5:00 p.m. today.

4
A: Simon, we have some concerns about your plagiarizing. This essay doesn't appear to be your own work.
B: Of course it is, Ms. Lombardi! I'm offended.
A: This is a serious matter, Simon. I thought you were capable of an honest response. The essay you submitted has already been published. Here it is. Look.
B: It must be a mistake.
A: Mistake or not, I'm going to have to pursue this with your parents.

5
A: Do you know what happened? When I asked Amy if she wanted to come Saturday, there was a long pause, as if she was thinking about how to say no.
B: Oh, I don't think it was that. She's just very shy.
A: Amy, shy? I had absolutely no idea!

6
A: Ma'am, tail light's broken. May I see your license?
B: Yes, certainly.
A: Hmm ... I'm not sure how to tell you this, but I'm afraid we have a warrant out for your arrest, from 1986.
B: 1986, officer? That was over 30 years ago. What did I do?
A: You failed to return a library book. Stolen property.
B: Stolen property! This is ridiculous!
A: I understand that you're upset, ma'am, but I need to ask you both to follow me to the station.
B: The station! You had a kind face. I really thought you were more understanding.

▶ **5.12** *page 56 exercise 8B*

1
A: Roger seemed so studious. He was always taking notes and asking questions.
B: Is that why you're so surprised now?
A: It sure is! I never expected to be stuck with all the work. I resent him expecting me to do everything! I thought I could count on his help, but I can't. It looks as if I'll have to team up with someone else.

2
A: I was talking to Marjorie yesterday.
B: Oh, did she tell you about John?
A: Yes, I heard about you breaking up and that you couldn't work things out. I can see why you didn't want to stay with him!
B: When I first met him, he was so considerate. He would always ask how my day was. He used to cook me a wonderful dinner if I was feeling down. But then he started to show his true colors! Now he only thinks about himself!

3
A: So tell me, Susan. Why have you decided to resign?
B: I can't work with Bill.
A: Bill and I have some legitimate concerns about your not sticking to the deadline. I know that might strike you as heartless.
B: I would have been happy to discuss legitimate concerns. But Bill actually told me that business came before my health. When I first met him, I had no idea he was so cold and unfeeling. He came by my office often to see how my work was going.

4
A: Is Simon your student?
B: Unfortunately, yes.
A: The principal is appalled at the boy's cheating and plans to take the matter up with his parents.
B: Yes, I know. It seems he lied when confronted with the evidence.
A: Did you have any idea he was capable of cheating on a major exam?
B: None, whatsoever. Whenever social issues came up in class, he would talk about values and ethics. Shows how easy it is to be fooled.

5
A: I heard when Georgina invited Amy to the party, she just stood there. At least 10 seconds passed before she said stiffly that she'd like to come.
B: She appreciated us inviting her, even though it didn't come off that way. You know how shy she is. But still, we might wind up being good friends.
A: Yes, but it was a complete surprise to Georgina. She said Amy was always raising her hand in class and offering to give presentations.
B: Could be, but those aren't social situations.

6
A: Did you hear I was arrested?
B: You, arrested! They don't arrest people your age, Laura!
A: That's what you think. The officer seemed so understanding. You know, good manners. Soft southern accent. But he was hard as nails. All this because I lost a library book 30 years ago.
B: Oh, is "lost" a euphemism for "stole"?
A: Knock it off, Dennis. I have no idea what happened to the book. But the police officer insisted on our coming to the station. At first, I thought he'd let us off.

▶ **5.13** *page 58 exercise 10A*

E = Ed, M = Monica

E: Whoa! You could get yourself killed in this city!
M: That's for sure! I'm so sick of that sound.
E: Did you just see him as he went into that turn? He was racing down this street at 40 miles an hour. Maybe even 50!
M: They say distracted drivers are the main cause of pedestrian fatalities. They speed. They have no idea where they're going. You know, "Uh, oh" ... here's my turn! Just like this guy.
E: I know ... but wait, I have an idea!
M: You do? What is it?
E: Well, in my new job at City Hall, maybe I could send a proposal to the Motor Vehicle Bureau. I have an idea for a new driving test, modeled after the London taxi exam.
M: But you've only been on the job three days, Ed! Isn't all of this a little premature? And isn't the Motor Vehicle Bureau a separate agency?
E: Well, yes, but I'm going to put together a proposal anyway. And maybe I can submit it next week. Someone has to do something!

▶ **5.14** *page 58 exercise 10B*

E: They turned down my proposal. Guess it's back to square one. If we live that long, that is!
M: Not again! So what did your proposal entail? What was the general idea?
E: Well, I got the idea from the London taxi exam. It's called "The Knowledge Test." Future taxi drivers have to memorize the shortest route from point A to B anywhere in the city. It takes two to four years to learn all the streets in London.
M: What?! Are you saying you wanted new drivers to spend four years preparing for a driver's license? That's insane! And how does learning the city make you slow down? Besides, an exam has to work for the whole state.
E: Calm down, Monica. A simplified version. The rationale was that since most pedestrian accidents take place right here in the city, there would be a special exam for city drivers. I really thought they'd go for it. Remember, the goal was to eliminate distractions. And that can be done by knowing your city backwards and forwards.
M: But ... but ... people have to get to work. They can't spend years studying to pass a driver's exam. And one designed for taxis. Suppose you only had to know one part of the city?

Why would you need to pass an exam like that?

E: Hmm ... that's what the email they sent said, so I guess you've got a point. Well, what would you do about these drivers?

M: I'd put speed bumps ... everywhere! On every single street, say every three blocks. That way, even if you did speed up, you'd soon have to slow down. And maybe we could scare people. I saw highway signs in Mexico that did that. It must have been a bad strip because you know what they said?

E: No, what?

M: "After an accident, nothing is the same."

E: That's creepy, Monica!

M: So let's go back to the speed bumps, then.

E: But do you have any idea what that would cost? A fortune! And it would turn driving into a roller-coaster ride.

M: Listen, if the secret is learning to be a good driver, why not focus on a person's reflexes? If you have slow reflexes, you're disqualified! If you talk in the car, sightsee while you drive, forget it. It's the whole person we need to measure!

E: What? How would you do that?

M: Through several road tests, not just one. And several different examiners. When it comes to driving, you just can't be too careful.

E: I think you're on to something. Will you help me put together a revised proposal? It's got to be airtight this time! It has to spell out all the different steps ... and show how to get from point A to point B.

M: What do you mean? Back to directions?

E: What I mean is they have to see exactly how our proposal will lead to a reduction in pedestrian fatalities. It has to be more logical than my last one. *And* it has to be cost effective.

M: But you know none of this is really your job, Ed. Are you really sure you should be doing another proposal? It's one thing to talk to me, but another to keep pestering an agency you don't even work for. In fact, your boss might not like this initiative.

E: I don't care! Let them fire me. At least deep down I'll know I tried to make our city safer!

▶ **5.15** *page 58 exercise 10C*

M: Well ... OK, let's get started. How many driving exams exactly?

E: How about three? And each will have a different focus. So for example, the first would be a standard exam. Can you parallel park? Do you understand and obey traffic signs? You know, the typical stuff.

M: Yes, in the second, the examiner could begin to focus on driver psychology, and a sensor could measure the level of driver awareness. Are the driver's eyes always on the road? Does he or she scan the whole road and check the rear-view mirror frequently to anticipate problems? Or does he or she only look at a point directly in front of the car?

E: Great. Of course a team of psychologists would be needed to write the test. And the cars would have to be equipped with the sensors.

M: That doesn't seem too hard to accomplish. What happens in the third test?

E: In the final test, the examiner evaluates the driver's future ability to handle distraction because obviously in a driving test, no one will be sending text messages.

M: I see. So in the final test, perhaps the focus would be on the driver's conversation. Does the driver change topics frequently? The goal would be to measure the driver's attention span.

E: You know what? I think we need to consult a psychologist before submitting our proposal.

M: Great idea. But now I think we should go over our key points and list the three tests as bullet points. You know, proposals need to be short and sweet.

Unit 6

▶ **6.1** *page 60 exercise 1A*

Not too long ago, the publishing world was in hysterics over the future of paper books. As readers switched to their brand new digital devices, e-book sales went through the roof, print sales plunged, and a number of bookstores went out of business. Many publishers and authors feared that the industry would never recover. But, as fate would have it, the digital apocalypse never came. Although some analysts once predicted that e-books would overtake print by the mid-2010s, digital sales appear to have leveled off, and now it seems that some early e-book adopters are either going back to print or juggling both. And, shockingly, some surveys show that even some so-called digital natives actually prefer reading on paper. To explain the surprising resilience of paper books, joining me in the studio tonight is Dr. Robert Soars, author of *Print is Far From Dead*.

▶ **6.2** *page 60 exercises 1B and C*

H = Host, S = Sr. Soars

H: Dr. Soars, thank you for joining us.

S: Thanks for having me.

H: So it looks as if paper books aren't going anywhere?

S: Not in the foreseeable future, I don't think.

H: But how can that be? I mean, it's so much easier to browse an online store, pick out your favorite titles, and download them! And then you can take your e-reader wherever you go.

S: I know!

H: And if you're keen to read a foreign book in its original version but don't understand a word, you just click the word and a translation entry pops up. I mean, how cool is that?

S: Uh huh.

H: Oh, and as an added bonus, you can't wear out or accidentally tear e-books. You should have seen the number of paper books I had to recycle last year!

S: Yeah, sounds familiar.

H: So how come paper books are still popular?

S: Well, here's the thing, we tend to think of reading as an essentially abstract activity involving thoughts, ideas, and metaphors.

H: Which it is, right?

S: Well, yes and no. You see, reading involves a certain degree of physicality.

H: You've lost me here.

S: To our brains, text is a concrete part of the physical world we live in, which means that the whole reading experience is inherently tactile.

H: So you're saying that e-books fail to recreate this sort of, erm ... this sort of hands-on experience?

S: To some extent, yes. Some people expect books to look, feel, and even smell a certain way. So much so that when they really like an e-book, they even go out and buy a paper version ...

H: So they can physically turn the pages?

S: That's right. A paper book has an easily identifiable size, shape, and weight, which brings out its more concrete nature. Some people find it easier to take notes, highlight, or even cross out sentences in a paper book ... I mean, using a pen or pencil.

H: Well, guilty as charged!

S: You see? Another reason why paper books remain popular has to do with the fact that with a paper book, it's easier to flick back and forth across pages, you know, if you want to re-read an earlier section, for example. Sure, an e-reader allows you to do that, but it's slightly more complicated.

H: So you're saying paper books really have the reader in mind?

S: Yes, and that's why they're here to stay.

▶ **6.3** *page 60 exercises 1D and E*

H: What about phones? That's where my kids do most of their reading. Is it true that when people read stuff on their phones, they don't put the same amount of mental effort into the process?

S: Well, some studies point out that people reading on their phones take lots of shortcuts.

H: Like, for example?

S: They tend to skip over whole sentences and even paragraphs ... If a text doesn't grab their attention right away, they rarely make it past the first paragraph. They're also more likely to ignore unknown words rather than work out their meaning in context or look them up.

H: But some of these can be important reading strategies, too, right?

S: Yes, as long as you can use them flexibly. Sure, you need to be able to run your eyes over a text quickly ... you need to be able to get the gist of a text. But equally important is the ability to pore over a challenging text, read between the lines, and understand what was not directly stated. And this sort of careful reading you're more likely to do with either an e-book or, of course, a paper book.

▶ **6.5** *page 62 exercise 3A*

G = Grace, N = Noah

G: ... and, really, it blew me away. I just love Edith Piaf. So glad they decided to show *La Vie en Rose* again. It's just timeless!

N: My eyes hurt!

Audio scripts

G: What?
N: All that text!
G: You mean the subtitles?
N: I can't stand them!
G: Really? But –
N: Yeah. In Germany, where I used to live, most films are dubbed, and nearly every foreign TV show, too. I mean, like 8 out of 10, unless it's pay per view or something. Or cult shows from smaller networks.
G: No way! How could you possibly dub a film like this?! It's such a classic.
N: Well, in a few cities, like Berlin, you can find the occasional theater where movies can be seen in their original versions ... And they take dubbing really seriously, too. Each foreign actor is matched up with a German voice – like a signature voice – so the whole thing feels more authentic. There's even an award ceremony specifically for voice actors!
G: I would have thought the subtitled versions would be more popular.
N: Yeah, go figure. I read a study once that besides Germany, the European countries with the highest rejection rates are ...
G: You mean for subtitles?
N: Yeah ... Austria, Italy, and Spain, where it can be very difficult to find the original version of a movie in a theater.

6.6 page 62 exercise 3B

G: Why do you think that happens – that is, that they don't show the original?
N: Well, I can only speak for myself, but when I watch a movie with subtitles, I feel like I'm missing out on all sorts of nuances in the actors' expressions because I'm paying attention to the text ...
G: Uh huh.
N: And I end up reading the subtitles whether or not I understand what's being said. I guess I do it out of sheer habit – just in case I might have missed something. I mean, I speak French and I was able to understand a lot of what they said, but I still found myself looking at the text over and over.
G: Hmm ... I'm not big on dubbed movies, to be honest. The new voices, the translation ... It's like the whole thing prevents me from really immersing myself in the movie. And it annoys me how the actors' lips and their voices are always a little out of sync, even if the dubbing is done well. Sometimes I just feel like getting up and walking out of the theater.
N: I know, but it's just so much easier to watch a film that's been dubbed! Besides, don't you think that movies and TV shows are meant to be watched – not read? I mean, that's how the director intended them!
G: But when you're an actor, your native language is part of your identity and it helps you convey emotion. You just can't do without the original voice! And do you really want to hear an actress playing Edith Piaf speaking English or Spanish?
N: Hmm ... Well, I don't mind the occasional subtitle as long as there's not too much text to process. Otherwise, I find I'm out of patience pretty quickly!

6.7 page 62 exercise 3C

1 In Germany, nearly every foreign TV show is dubbed. I mean, like 8 out of 10, unless it's pay per view or something.
  The answer is number 4, "selection from a group." 8 out of 10 means "from a group of 10, something is true for eight."
2 I end up reading the subtitles whether or not I understand what's being said. I guess I do it out of sheer habit – just in case I might have missed something.
  The answer is number 2, "caused or motivated by." Out of sheer habit means something was "caused or motivated by" sheer habit.
3 It annoys me how the actors' lips and their voices are always a little out of sync, even if the dubbing is done well.
  The answer is number 3, "not having." Out of sync means "not having" rhythm or being in sync.
4 Sometimes I just feel like getting up and walking out of the theater.
  The answer is number 1, "movement from within outwards." To walk out of the theater means to walk "from within the theater to the outside."
5 I don't mind the occasional subtitle as long as there's not too much text to process. Otherwise, I find I'm out of patience pretty quickly.
  The answer is number 3, "not having." Out of patience means "not having" patience.

6.9 page 66 exercises 7A and B

D = Donna, J = Jason

D: Hey, this is cool! An article on street art.
J: Street art?
D: Yeah, graffiti artists. Look. Bet you can't guess where they're from.
J: Well, their names are right there.
D: True, but what's in a name? Pick one. Let's see how you do.
J: OK. "El Bocho." He sounds Mexican. In the tradition of Diego Rivera. Didn't he do people like that, too?
D: You mean, short and squat? Well, I wouldn't say exactly like that! But anyway, El Bocho isn't Mexican. He lives in Berlin. And he's really well known in the Berlin graffiti scene.
J: You mean he's German?
D: Not exactly. He's from Spain originally. But his name does sound Mexican. Let me look it up. Wow, according to my dictionary, in Argentina and Uruguay, it means a person's head!
J: OK, let's keep going. Os Gêmeos. This artist must be Brazilian. I like him.
D: How do you know it's a him?
J: Well, aren't most graffiti artists men? Personally, I've never seen graffiti done by a woman. Anyway, I wonder what the name means.
D: I have seen some women graffiti artists. And, in fact, next I'll ask you to guess which of the remaining artists happen to be women. But to answer your question, the name means "the twins" in Portuguese. Their names are Otávio and Gustavo Pandolfo, and they're from São Paulo. They've both been painting graffiti for almost 20 years.
J: Let's see. Maya Hayuk. She's obviously a woman.
D: You get a point! What did you think of her art?
J: Hmm ... I'm not sure.
D: Sounds as if you didn't really like it. Didn't the vibrant colors appeal to you?
J: I did like it. It's just that I really like graffiti with a message. And I'm having trouble figuring out what hers is.
D: Any idea where she's from?
J: Hayuk? Is the name native American?
D: I honestly have no idea. But she was born in the city of Baltimore and lives and works in Brooklyn, New York.
J: I think we've done enough guessing. Just tell me quickly about the others.
D: OK, There's Inti, from Valparaíso, Chile. His name comes from the Incan sun god and the Quechua word for "sun."
J: Interesting. The mural does seem very South American, doesn't it?
D: Yes, he also likes to draw political themes and represent South America around the world. And finally, we have two more women. Firstly, there's Olek, originally from Poland although she now lives in New York. I read she used to be essentially homeless until her art was discovered.
J: You're kidding! I love the bicycle.
D: It does look original, doesn't it? I wish I could buy one!
J: And the last artist?
D: Kashink from Paris. And get this? She's been drawing a thin mustache on her upper lip for a few years and "wears" it every day.
J: Cool. I guess you could call that a kind of graffiti!
D: Yes. I bet you hadn't realized how creative graffiti could be.
J: Well, I had realized. But still, I always thought graffiti was mainly done on buildings.

6.13 page 68 exercise 9B

K = Kenna, S = Stan

K: What are you reading?
S: Just this book about musicals. Doesn't sound too exciting, does it?
K: Oh, but I love musicals! I think my favorite of all time was *Mamma Mia*.
S: Well, you might enjoy it then. *The secret life of the American musical: How Broadway shows are built*. By Jack Viertel. This book is a really good read.
K: I didn't know musicals had a secret life! It does sound interesting!
S: Yeah, he explains what they all have in common – you know, why people keep going to them. And in case you haven't seen many,

it's easy to follow. It's written with a broad audience in mind.

K: In what way?

S: Well, if you're really into musicals, you'll smile at the connections he makes between them. But if you've never really given them much thought – that is, for millenials like us, it's just a fabulous introduction.

K: So what kind of stuff do you learn specifically?

6.14 page 68 exercise 9C

S: First the book covers the entire history of the American musical. Even if you've never heard of Rodgers and Hammerstein and have never seen *Oklahoma!*, this book will fill you in on lots of interesting facts.

K: I'd like to learn more about the history of musicals.

S: They're all there: *My Fair Lady, Hair, West Side Story* ... and you can learn about recent musicals, too, like *Hamilton*.

K: What's that one about?

S: Alexander Hamilton, you know, one of the Founding Fathers of the United States – the one who died in a duel with Aaron Burr.

K: Oh, that Hamilton! So what else does this book go into? I mean, after all, I can read Wikipedia to learn about individual musicals, and I can even listen to the songs on YouTube.

S: Yes, that's a good point. What's really unique about the book is that it captures what musicals have in common. Take the first act. There's always an opening number to define what the musical is about, then a song where a character professes to want something, a love song that introduces a bit of doubt, and a catchy musical number to keep the audience awake.

K: And every musical is the same?

S: Yes, pretty much. The second act, then offers more plot twists, an obligatory song early on by the star, and, of course, a show-stopping number late in the act that gives the audience something to hum when leaving the theater. It was originally called an "eleven o'clock number" to match the time it traditionally occurred.

K: Wow. Now I understand something I never really understood before.

S: What's that?

K: Well, often people who know very little English, when they visit New York, they try to see a Broadway musical. And I used to think, "How can they enjoy the show if they can't understand the lyrics or what's being said?" But now I see that as long as they know how musicals are structured, they're all set. They don't actually need to understand.

S: Exactly!

6.15 page 68 exercise 9D

K: So does this book talk about the future of the musical? I mean, things have changed a lot in the past 75 years. What about the role of technology?

S: Hmm ... I don't really know. Do you mean technology might make the musical obsolete?

K: Anything's possible, isn't it? And the U.S. now has immigrants from virtually every country, something that wasn't true when the musical was invented. Will the modern musical evolve to reflect their cultural traditions?

S: You've stumped me there. I wish I had a crystal ball. The book does talk a little about the social and political evolution of the musical, though.

Review 3 (Units 5–6)

R3.1 G = Guide, V = Visitor (1 and 2)

G: Thank you for joining us today. We are lucky enough to have on loan to us a special exhibit by the graffiti artists Os Gêmeos. First, I'd like to tell you a little bit about their background.

V1: Doesn't their name mean "the twins"?

G: Yes, it does, in fact. Otávio and Gustavo Pandolfo are identical twin brothers. Their work is quite diverse and has made a distinct impact both at home and abroad. They've done family portraits, social and political art, and paintings that draw on Brazilian folklore. It's fascinating, really.

V2: Just out of curiosity, can I ask a question? How did they get into graffiti to begin with?

G: Believe it or not, via hip hop culture, which reached Brazil in the 1980s. They were teenagers then, and they started out as breakdancers. When they turned to graffiti, initially, they just tried to imitate New York artists, having met a couple of them who were in Brazil for various reasons. Nowadays, however, they have a distinctly Brazilian presence, abroad as well as at home. There's the famous mural they've done in ...

V1: Oh, so they paint murals?

G: Yes, and most interestingly, their work has also been commissioned by the government. If you're ever in São Paulo, you can see one of their murals on Paulista Avenue. Not only that, but the Brazilian government has even invited them to paint some subway trains!

V2: That is impressive! I've always associated subway graffiti with vandalism.

V1: Why do you think they're so popular? I mean, it sounds as if they appeal to art historians and street kids alike.

G: I think it's because they paint with a view to appealing to our emotions, rather than reason. They don't just stick to the predictable. If you allow yourself to just feel as you look at their art, and don't focus too much on working out the meaning, you'll enter a world of subtlety and magic. Over here, for example ...

Unit 7

7.1 page 72 exercise 1A

H = Host, C = Dr. Castro

H: And we're very lucky tonight to have Dr. Julia Castro with us, author of *The critical years of our lives*. Thanks for joining us, Dr. Castro.

C: Thanks for having me.

H: So, first, can we talk about the elephant in the room?

C: Oh, the article! I had no idea it would be so controversial!

H: Basically, you went against conventional wisdom and argued that it's not early childhood that sets us up for life – or adolescence – but the 10 years from 20 to 30 ...

C: Yeah, most people still seem to believe that the first few years are the most important, but the critical decade is really your 20s. So I guess I opened a can of worms! You have no idea how many angry tweets I got!

H: But what about milestones like graduating from high school or getting a driver's license? These are things we usually do before our 20s.

C: Yes, but I would argue that when we come of age, we make the decisions that have the greatest impact on our future.

H: Why's that?

C: Because that's when our lives either take off or get off track.

7.2 page 72 exercises 1B and C

C: You see, when you're a teenager, you make lots of mistakes, but you also get lots of second chances. But when you're in your 20s, the stakes are higher.

H: In what ways?

C: When I was 22, maybe 23, I'd already graduated from college, and I had a steady job to help me make ends meet, but, you know, looking back, I don't think I took life seriously enough. I just breezed through my 20s, assuming that adulthood wouldn't begin until I turned 30. Well, guess what, I was wrong. So in my 30s, I had to take the bull by the horns and work twice as hard to make up for all the lost time and wasted opportunities.

H: Uh huh.

C: I made it through my 20s, and even the rough times, but I wish I'd been more focused. We need to come to terms with the fact that most of the choices we make in our 20s have life-long consequences. If you drop out of college, pick the wrong career, choose the wrong partner ... you can't just turn back the clock and say, "Well, maybe I rushed into marriage too early, so let me start over" or "Hmm ... maybe I'm not cut out to be a lawyer after all."

H: So it's really in your 20s that you need to take charge and determine your destiny.

C: Yes, absolutely. And if there's something you want to change about yourself or about the way you live your life, that's the time to do it.

H: Why's that?

C: Because our brains keep changing throughout our 20s – especially the frontal lobe, which is responsible for decision-making. This means that once you're in your 30s or 40s, it's not as easy to reinvent yourself.

H: So you can't teach an old dog new tricks?

C: Well, it's not as black and white as that. I've interviewed a few 40-somethings who decided to quit their high-paying jobs,

Audio scripts

get out of the rat race, and turn their lives around, but most of them wish they hadn't waited so long.
H: You have a teenage son, correct?
C: A daughter. She's turning 20 next year.
H: Do you think she'll have it easier than you? I mean, than your generation?
C: Hmm ... I think in many ways the odds are against her – especially with this economy.

▶ 7.3 page 72 exercise 1D

1
C: So I guess I opened a can of worms! You have no idea how many angry tweets I got! Number 1: *open a can of worms*. Opening a can with worms inside would be unpleasant, to say the least. So this idiom means, "We're about to do something that will lead to problems."

2
C: So in my 30s, I had to take the bull by the horns and work twice as hard to make up for all the lost time and wasted opportunities. Number 2: *take the bull by the horns*. As you can imagine, grabbing a bull by its horns would be difficult, not to mention dangerous. So this expression means, "deal with a difficult situation."

3
H: So you can't teach an old dog new tricks?
C: Well, it's not as black and white as that. Number 3: *You can't teach an old dog new tricks*. The meaning of this expression is fairly clear. It means, "It's hard to abandon old habits."

4
C: I've interviewed a few 40-somethings who decided to quit their high paying jobs, get out of the rat race, and turn their lives around. Number 4: *get out of the rat race*. A race is competitive, and when we "get out of the rat race," we abandon a competitive lifestyle or situation.

▶ 7.5 page 74 exercises 3A and B

D = Dr Suárez, S = Students (1–3)

D: OK, if everyone could quickly try to find a seat, we'll get started. Thank you. Today we're going to explore a topic that may not concern you just yet, but that all of us will have to face one day – if we're lucky, that is – attitudes toward the elderly. You've probably heard the word "ageism," negative, discriminatory attitudes towards older people, and it's a positive sign that English has such a word. Not all languages do. In the English-speaking world, government and private organizations are devoting considerable energy to combating this form of discrimination, so today I'd like to look at the future. How will attitudes have changed by the year 2050?
S1: That's when I turn 60!
D: Yes, I think it's a good benchmark for most of you! So to start, by 2050, most of you will have been working for at least 30 years. And you will have developed many valuable skills by that time. You won't be ready to retire, either professionally or personally.
S2: I'm sure I'll want more free time, though.
D: That may be. However, there are other options, and many more people will have discovered them. For example, you may choose to work part time. Or you could reinvent yourself and begin to do more creative work.
S3: Really? Start something new at 60? Isn't that a little late?
D: What I meant is that even if the change is only partial, it's never too late to learn new skills and have new experiences. My feeling is that the majority of the population will have accepted that 60 is the new 40. The reason is that the proportion of older workers will have changed.
S1 Safety in numbers!
D: I'll buy that! Just to give you an idea, the number of new employees in the workforce will have slowed to four or five times fewer workers than what we saw between 1950 and 2000. You'll be needed!
S2: Wow!
D: And personally, I feel employees your age won't have been given early retirement or even worse, simply fired. Society will have been coming to terms with this demographic change for decades.
S3: Ageism will be a thing of the past!
D: Well, we still need to be realistic, Josh, so we're not disappointed.
S3: I guess I got carried away with enthusiasm. What I was trying to say is that compared to now, we will be a more progressive society.
D: Yes, there is good evidence that we have reason to be positive about the future.

▶ 7.9 page 78 exercise 8A

Age is certainly a relative concept, and all of you who have come to this lecture tonight have some interest in understanding current theories of life-span development. So, what do we mean by this term? Our life span, of course, is the period of time that we actually live. There are many theories, but among the questions they consider, two are very important:
1 Is nature or nurture more important? By *nature*, I mean, the influence of heredity. Are we basically just born a certain way? Or to what degree does nurture, the physical and social world, and our experiences, influence us?
2 Does everyone follow a similar course of development? Or are there many possible ones?
Let's look at the second question a bit more. There are two possibilities. Those who believe everyone follows a similar course of development, sometimes called "stage theorists," believe the life span is predictable: we're born, we move from childhood to adulthood, we train for a profession, we marry and have children, and when they leave home, we enjoy retirement. Sound familiar? Many popular books have been written about what are believed to be predictable stages. Other theorists, however, believe these stages aren't predictable at all and that a person can be greatly affected by his or her environment. So to illustrate this point ...

▶ 7.10 page 78 exercises 8B and C

P = Presenter, S = Speaker (1–6)

P: To illustrate this point, let's look at several short interviews we conducted. First, I need to get this video working.

1
P: Hello, we're from a university psychology research program. Can we ask you both a few questions?
S1: Hmm ... sure, I can't say no to research.
P: Do you believe nature is more important in our development – that is, the influence of heredity? Or do you believe that nurture takes precedence – or in other words, that our physical and social world has enormous influence on us?
S1: Take a real case, the class I just came from. We're not born cool or old-fashioned. My teacher is in her 70s, and she's really young at heart. It's my classmates who seem old-fashioned. This must be nurture!

2
P: And you?
S2: I believe in nature. Every generation has equal potential. Without fail, young people are brimming with new ideas. Young minds are vibrant! But I've lived long enough to see what happens. People my age ... we're not the ones who will reform society. We seem to have run out of ideas and just conform to expectations. And the next generation will, too. It's human nature. No pun intended!
P: Thank you very much. An interesting take on things. ... OK, let's move on to the second question: Do we all follow a similar course of development, or, in other words, is stage theory accurate? We have two more interviews.

3
P: Hello, we're from a university psychology research program. Can we ask you both a few questions?
S3: Sure! Why not?
P: Do you believe we all move through predictable stages in life? That is, we all have a similar course of development? Or do you believe the stages of life are not predictable and there are many possible ones?
S3: Nope. Not predictable. People just can't be characterized that easily. You'd think I'd be very mature, right? A working man? But actually, it's my younger brother who's more mature. He's wise beyond his years. He's only 17, but it's as if he totally skipped the adolescent part of the life span.

4
P: How about you? Do you "act your age," so to speak?
S4: Act my age? No way! It's a crazy situation I find myself in now. For example, in my family, I'm the one who puts food on the table. My parents have both lost their jobs. But if it weren't for that, they'd be taking care of me, and I'd be in college. So I think the stages of life usually are predictable unless something happens.
P: Oh, I'm sorry to hear that. Thank you for your time.

5

P: Hello, we're from a university psychology research program. Can we ask you both a few questions?
S5: If it's fast ...
P: Yes, I promise. Do you believe we all move through predictable stages in life? That is, we all have a similar course of development? Or do you believe the stages of life are not predictable and there are many possible ones?
S5: Definitely the second. Compare my mom and grandmother, for example. It's my grandmother who walks two miles a day. And she's pushing 90! My mom doesn't move from the couch! It's true Grandma had a heart attack a few years ago, but everything changed after that. You know, a whole new outlook on life. I think that proves life doesn't have predictable stages.
P: Thank you. And you?
6
S6: Actually, I believe the opposite. What I see is that pretty much people do follow the same course. For example, if you talk to older people, their life stories always seem to build on previous ones, and there's a lot of similarity from person to person. But it's not old people who are boring. They have so much insight and first-hand experience. It's us! And don't you think, or at least, isn't it possible that your grandmother just started expressing her philosophy more? But maybe it was slowly developing all along?
S5: Oh, I don't know ...
P: Thank you. You may both wish to pursue this topic and see where it leads you. ... And I'd like all of you to think about these interviews while we take a ten-minute break. I'll see you back here at 8:00.

7.11 page 80 exercise 10A

J = Jack, M = Mia

J: How's your new job?
M: Well, to be honest, it could be better. My boss is half my age! He could definitely be my son. I feel a little ... well ... superfluous. Maybe they don't need my expertise.
J: You could think of it this way, though. Someone chose him to be your boss. So he must have managerial talent.
M: That's what you say! All I know is I've only been on the job for a week, and we've already had two arguments.
J: Hmm ... that's not good. Maybe it's time for some new strategies.
M: What kind of strategies? I can't hide the fact that I'm 50! He can see how many years I've been working from my résumé. And besides, I have twice his level of experience. He's even new to the industry.
J: The problem is you're dwelling on it, and it's your age you have to take out of the equation.
M: So what can I do exactly?
J: First, don't say anything to call attention to it. No comments like, "When I started in this business 25 years ago ... " You'll just make him feel uncomfortable. Or worse, you could seem like a dinosaur.
M: OK, and what else?

J: Don't stereotype him. You've only known him a week. You may be jumping to conclusions. Just relax, be yourself, but still show respect. Remember, think "boss," not "toddler." He also might appreciate your sharing information with him.
M: What! So he can steal my ideas? What if he's just after his own recognition?
J: There you go again ... stereotypes. You're the one who has the most to gain if you help him solve his problems.
M: Thanks, Jack. Maybe I'll try being extra polite, too. You could be right. He might just feel insecure.

7.12 page 80 exercise 10C

J: Before your next conversation with your boss, it might be good to think about your qualifications and his – you know, just to keep things in perspective.
M: What do you mean? Why he hired me?
J: Yes. What were the character traits, qualifications, and experience that convinced him?
M: Well, during the interview, he told me I seemed very open and would be receptive to customers' needs. And of course, I was qualified because of my master's in business management. And then, as you know, I've had three decades of experience working in marketing ...
J: See! You need to begin by assuming he respects you and not that he's challenging you. And how about him? Why do you think he was chosen to lead the department?
M: Tim? He communicates very well, and actually, he's quite creative, too. He always seems to be looking for innovation.
J: And what are his qualifications and experience? You've only told me what he's lacking.
M: Well, actually, he has an M.A. in business management, too. And he did work in sales for five years.
J: So that's what you need to think about when you see him next!
M: Yes, I think you're right. I'll try my best!

7.13 page 80 exercise 10D

M = Mia, T = Tim

T: Yes?
M: May I come in for a minute?
T: Yes, sure. What can I help you with?
M: I'm sorry to disturb you. I hope I'm not interrupting. But I had an idea for the report I wanted to run by you to see what you thought. If you think it's worth pursuing, perhaps I could develop it.
T: Yes, by all means.
M: Well, I've calculated we could save $100,000 over three years by changing distributors.
T: That's very interesting, Mia. Could I see the numbers?
M: Would you mind if I provided them on Thursday? I'm still working on the details. But would it be OK if I went ahead in this direction?
T: Certainly.

M: And if I could ask a small favor ... I wonder if I could possibly work at home tomorrow. It's freedom from distraction that I need – just for a day.
T: Yes, that would be fine. As long as it's a one-time event, of course.
M: Thank you, Tim. I'll get back to work then.
T: I'm looking forward to your report. Would you be so kind as to close the door behind you?

Unit 8

8.1 page 82 exercise 1A

... the Internet is full of sites where customers complain about faulty products, sloppy services, misleading ads, and so on. In 2016, a Brazilian site called "reclame aqui" – or "complain here" – had an interesting idea. Instead of simply providing a forum where angry customers could speak their minds, the site went a step further and took matters into its own hands in an effort to improve business practices. To celebrate its 15th anniversary, "Reclame aqui" produced a two-minute video that went viral in a matter of days and took the Internet by storm – at least in Brazil. Here's what the campaign did: The site invited as many as 100 executives from different companies – retailers, banks, automakers, cell phone carriers, you name it – to a free dinner at a restaurant guests were told had just opened its doors to very positive reviews. As expected, most people politely declined, or simply ignored the invitation, but some said yes, blissfully unaware of the fact that the place was filled with hidden cameras and that they were about to have one of the worst – if not the worst – dinner of their lives.

8.2 page 82 exercises 1B and C

... they were about to have one of the worst – if not the worst – dinner of their lives. Everything that could go wrong did: the orders got mixed up more than once, the food took forever to arrive, and when it did, it was either too spicy or too bland. The nine executives from different companies who showed up complained loudly, of course, but the waiters couldn't have cared less. When asked to call the manager, they simply shrugged it off, claiming no one was available – just the sort of thing we keep hearing over and over, right? The executives, who were expecting top-notch service, were all baffled. What on earth was going on? Was this some sort of strike against bad working conditions, with the waiters all taking a stand? Well, little did they know that it was all a prank: the site was trying to reproduce the level of service that customers usually get when they do business with the companies in question. You see, as it turns out, the 100 invitations had been sent to the companies with the greatest number of complaints on the site: "The bottom 100," so to speak. So, at the end of the meal, still scratching their heads and oblivious to what was going on, the nine men and women didn't get the check, but a piece of paper saying, "Did you feel disrespected? Well, so do thousands

Audio scripts

and thousands of your customers, according to the data on our site."

▶ 8.3 page 82 exercise 1D

How did those people react, you must be wondering. Well, not surprisingly, they took offense when they found out a video of the dinner had been posted on the website. But their faces were digitally blurred on the video, and at no time were the companies' names mentioned, which would have tarnished their reputations. So my guess is that there wouldn't have been any grounds for a lawsuit, even if they'd wanted to take legal action. But, honestly, why would the companies want to expose their own weaknesses and draw even more attention to themselves? Besides, it's not the site's fault that these businesses don't value their customers. Why should it take the blame? Now whether and how this campaign will improve business practices remains to be seen. What do you think? I'd like to hear your views.

▶ 8.4 page 83 exercise 2A

1 Instead of simply providing a forum where angry customers could speak their minds, the site went a step further and (pause) took matters into its own hands.
2 "Reclame aqui" produced a two-minute video that went viral in a matter of days and (pause) took the internet by storm.
3 Was this some sort of strike against bad working conditions, with the waiters all (pause) taking a stand?
4 How did those people react, you must be wondering. Well, not surprisingly, they (pause) took offense.
5 So my guess is that there wouldn't have been any grounds for a lawsuit, even if they'd wanted to (pause) take legal action.
6 Besides, it's not the site's fault that these businesses don't value their customers. Why should it (pause) take the blame?

▶ 8.5 page 83 exercise 2C

G = Garry, R = Ruth

G: Wow! That was a brilliant campaign, don't you think?
R: Absolutely. I wish an American site would do something like that. It would be really popular.
G: You bet. You know, if I had my way, I'd invite the guys at Magnet to a dinner like that!
R: Why? What happened?
G: Well, you know I bought a new washing machine, right?
R: At long last! I don't understand how you kept that old piece of junk for so long!
G: Oh, come on! It worked until last week, didn't it? I don't believe in planned obsolescence.
R: Yeah, I'm sorry. Anyway, is the new one any good?
G: I don't know.
R: What do you mean?
G: Oh, it's a long story. First, they shipped it to the wrong address.
R: Oh, no!
G: Yeah. I sent a complaint through the site, which, by the way, is really difficult to navigate. And on top of that, it took them three days to get back to me.
R: Three days?
G: Yeah. To make matters worse, she said it was the delivery company's fault, even though it was clear that the store had misspelled the name of the street.
R: Typical!
G: Anyway, she promised to send me another one in a day or two. Guess what, a week went by and ... no sign of the washing machine. And as if that were not enough, they charged my credit card again.
R: Oh, no!
G: So I called them and spoke to a man named Joe and, again, they promised a quick delivery.
R: And they sent it to the wrong address again?
G: No, but as they were unloading the truck, they dropped the box, and it hit my car! The bumper fell off!
R: You've got to be kidding me!
G: I'm not! And to add insult to injury, they didn't even apologize! Can you believe it? So, I call them again and speak to the manager, who says she's sorry – well, duh! – and promises she will personally take care of my problem.
R: You mean pay for the damage?
G: Yes. Well, I hope they do. I threatened to take them to court otherwise.

▶ 8.7 page 84 exercise 3B

R = Raúl, J = Julia

R: Hi, Julia, sorry to keep you waiting.
J: Please, don't apologize. I just got here myself.
R: Great. Um, before we start the lesson, could I ask you to help me with something today? I brought this handout I'd like to give out at the office.
J: Sure. What's it about?
R: I have to give a talk about customer service to the summer interns ... But then, I'd like to give them a summary to refer to. The problem is, I think what I've written sounds kind of formal.
J: OK. Let's take a look.
R: Thanks. Here it is.
J: Once you realize that a customer is dissatisfied, try to imagine yourself in his or her position, even if ... Uh huh ... OK ... Wow! Your written English is very good, Raúl.
R: Thank you!
J: The text sounds great, but, you know, for a young person, I'd say things a little differently.
R: But which sentences are too formal?
J: We'll get to that, but for starters, in English, it's always best to be short and to the point. For example, that whole first sentence could be shortened to "Always put yourself in the customer's position."
R: You're kidding! So the problem isn't formal language?
J: Only partly. I'd make it all simpler.
R: OK.

▶ 8.8 page 84 exercises 3C and D

J: But for formal language, let's look at number 1: "It's critically important that your customers communicate how they feel." Well, if you feel really, really strongly, it's OK to say that, but you don't want to scare away your interns! Why not just say, "It's important for your customers to say how they feel"?
R: Good idea. So, number 2, "It is essential that you not draw any conclusions until you know all the facts" – guess I should change that, too, right?
J: Uh huh.
R: I could say, "It's essential for you not to jump to conclusions."
J: But then you'd have two sentences in a row that were almost alike. And some of these words: "essential," "critically important" ... they really make it sound like a serious issue.
R: So how about, "Don't jump to conclusions until you know all the facts."
J: Yes, that sounds perfect. And, in fact, "jump to conclusions" is a great expression. Now I bet you can do the others without me!
R: OK, look at number 3, instead of "It is crucial that problems be resolved quickly," how about simply, "Problems must be resolved quickly"?
J: Perfect. One more. Can you find it?
R: Yes, number 4, "a customer may insist that he or she speak to the manager"... how about just, "a customer may want to speak to the manager"?
J: Great job, Raúl. See how much friendlier it sounds now?
R: I do. But I'm just so used to using the subjunctive from Spanish. Does it sound ... um, you know, pompous?
J: Not at all. You can use it in English, especially in writing and when you want to speak more formally. It can be especially useful if you're trying to emphasize things. But you know, you're trying to make your audience feel comfortable, just like customers.
R: Great advice, Julia. I've learned so much from you!

▶ 8.10 page 88 exercise 7A

P = Paul, A = Alba

P: So much red tape and paperwork ... I'm so sick of bureaucracy.
A: If you think you have problems here in the U.S., you should try living in Spain!
P: Why? What's it like there?
A: Terrible – the bureaucracy, that is! As much as you might try to plan your life, there are always unpleasant surprises. And just hope you never inherit anything from a long-lost, rich relative!
P: You're kidding! I'd love to come into some money. What could be better?!

A: Think twice. Let me tell you what happened to my sister and me.
P: I'm all ears.
A: We had an uncle we hadn't seen in years, who lived alone in the country. He had no children and no immediate descendants. And guess what? He left us the restaurant he had bought 50 years before!
P: That sounds great!
A: Oh, that's what you think. However generous he may have been, for us it was a nightmare.
P: But you've always dreamed of having a place in the country. Couldn't you just turn it into a vacation home?
A: I bet you didn't know that in Spain, you have to pay taxes on the property before you can even accept the inheritance. The amount varies by region, but where he lived, it was 20 percent of the profit.
P: You've got to be kidding! How much was the profit?
A: The restaurant was worth 200,000 euros. So we suddenly owed 40,000 – that's about 45,000 U.S. dollars – money we obviously didn't have.
P: What on earth did you do?

8.11 page 88 exercise 7B

P: So much red tape and paperwork ... I'm so sick of bureaucracy.
A: If you think you have problems here in the U.S., you should try living in Spain!
P: Why? What's it like there?
A: Terrible – the bureaucracy, that is! As much as you might try to plan your life, there are always unpleasant surprises. And just hope you never inherit anything from a long-lost, rich relative!
P: You're kidding! I'd love to come into some money. What could be better?!
A: Think twice. Let me tell you what happened to my sister and me.
P: I'm all ears.
A: We had an uncle we hadn't seen in years, who lived alone in the country. He had no children and no immediate descendants. And guess what? He left us the restaurant he had bought 50 years before!
P: That sounds great!
A: Oh, that's what you think. However generous he may have been, for us it was a nightmare.
P: But you've always dreamed of having a place in the country. Couldn't you just turn it into a vacation home?
A: I bet you didn't know that in Spain, you have to pay taxes on the property before you can even accept the inheritance. The amount varies by region, but where he lived, it was 20 percent of the profit.
P: You've got to be kidding! How much was the profit?
A: The restaurant was worth 200,000 euros. So we suddenly owed 40,000 – that's about 45,000 U.S. dollars – money we obviously didn't have.
P: What on earth did you do?

A: First we went to see a lawyer, but he wasn't very helpful. He basically told us, "Whatever compromises you feel are reasonable, none will be convincing." The system is rigid. There's just no room to maneuver on these sorts of taxes.
P: Gee, this is starting to sound unpleasant.
A: It sure was. In the end, we couldn't get a loan from the bank, either, because neither of us had full-time jobs, so we had no choice but to turn down the inheritance.
P: What do you mean? How do you "turn down" an inheritance?
A: Basically, you just say you don't want it, and if there are no other heirs, the government takes it. Because, you know, these bureaucrats, for all the good arguments you come up with, they just won't budge.
P: But that's so unfair!
A: I know, but there's nothing you can do. It's how the system works. Sometimes you hear these awful family stories. For example, say a family has two homes and the parents wanted to leave one to each child. If one child can't accept his or her inheritance, it would pass by law to the other. So the son or daughter with the most money might end up getting everything.
P: What an awful system!
A: It's not great, I'll tell you. In some parts of the country, an inheritance is turned down by a full 15% of those who receive one. And obviously, with the economy the way it's been, it's gotten worse.
P: So you're saying that as exciting as it sounds, some things just aren't worth it.
A: That's right. You start to wish no one had left you anything. You just can't imagine how stressful ...

8.12 page 90 exercise 10A

R = Recorded message, B = Mr. Bell, A = Amber

R: Please hold the line. We will be with you momentarily. This conversation may be recorded for quality assurance.
B: Good morning. Alexander Bell speaking. How may I help you today?
A: I wasn't expecting that name!
B: That's what everyone says. What might I assist you with?
A: Well, I just moved, and my number was supposed to be transferred yesterday, but it hasn't happened. My landline is still dead.
B: Who am I speaking with today?
A: Amber Wilkins.
B: I'm sorry to hear that, Ms. Wilkins. And is this the number you're calling about?
A: No, it isn't. The phone is dead. I'm calling about 212-555-7654.
B: Let me check the records. Let's see ... I'm afraid the transfer isn't scheduled until a week from now, Tuesday, May 19.

8.13 page 90 exercise 10B

B: I'm afraid the transfer isn't scheduled until a week from now, Tuesday, May 19.
A: But I'm positive I requested Tuesday, the 12th. (beep)

1
A: Could you please check if there's an earlier opening? It's essential that it be taken care of today.
B: I'm sorry about that, Ms. Wilkins. Let me put you on hold for just a moment.
B: Sorry to keep you waiting. Unfortunately, we won't be able to reschedule for an earlier date. We have a limited number of technicians.

2
A: However limited the number may be, it's really important that you find a solution. I depend on this line for my work, Mr. Bell.
B: We have a recording of your having requested May 19. Unfortunately, it's a bit late to reschedule. (beep)

3
A: You mean you save these conversations? I must have made a mistake. But could you please try to accommodate me? It's crucial that I have access to this phone.
B: I'm afraid no one's available at the moment. But I'll make a note in your file for a manager to call you. (beep)

4
A: I'd like to wait if at all possible. I'm really quite worried about this.
B: Please hold, Ms. Wilkins. I'll put you through now.
RM: Please hang up and try your party again. "Please hang up and try ..."
A: I can't believe it. I've been disconnected!

8.14 page 90 exercise 10C

H = Mr. Holmes, A = Amber, G = Ms. McGuire

H: Good morning. David Holmes speaking. How may I help you today?
A: Yes, I was being transferred to a manager and was disconnected. My phone was supposed to be connected yesterday.
H: Your name and phone number, please?
A: Amber Wilkins. The number is 212-555-7654.
H: One moment please.
G: Ms. McGuire speaking.
A: I've got a serious problem, Ms. McGuire. I just spoke with Alexander Bell who claims you recorded me asking for a May 19 connection date. But the date I wanted was yesterday. And I need my phone connected immediately!
G: Please start from the beginning. Your name and phone number, please?
A: Amber Wilkins. 212-555-7654. I've already provided this information.
G: Yes, we have your connection scheduled for next week. I'm afraid we're fully booked this week.
A: Listen, I've been a loyal customer for over 10 years. I insist that you accommodate me.

Audio scripts

G: I suggest you lower your voice, Ms. Wilkins.
A: How dare you tell me to lower my voice. I'm changing phone providers!
G: You're certainly within your right to do so, Ms. Wilkins. Now I will transfer you back to Mr. Bell so he can disconnect your service.

Unit 9

9.1 page 94 exercise 1A

P = Present, S = Susan, C = Carlos

P: Generally considered the world's most resilient institutions, schools have stood the test of time and outlasted countless societal changes and paradigm shifts. But parents sometimes choose to take a different route and teach their own children at home – or, in other words, homeschool them. Up until recently, homeschooling was considered a cutting-edge and "alternative" form of education, but it looks as if it's crossing over into the mainstream. As of 2016, it is estimated that there are about 2.3 million home-educated students in the United States, and it would appear that the homeschool population is continuing to grow at a steady rate. But what are the pros and cons of not sending your kids to school? Do the advantages of homeschooling outweigh the potential drawbacks? Here in the studio tonight are two parents, people with very different takes on homeschooling. Susan, Carlos, thanks for joining us.
S: Hi, thanks for having me
C: Pleasure to be here.

9.2 page 94 exercises 1B and C

P: Susan Crane, a small business owner from Tulsa, resorted to homeschooling when her now 19-year-old son Jonathan was diagnosed with severe allergies that made school attendance nearly impossible.
S: Yes, there were days when he just couldn't leave the house!
P: So, homeschooling was never your number one choice?
S: No, not really. Peter – that's my husband – and I weren't sure we'd be up to the challenge. I mean, neither one of us had a teaching qualification, and we'd never done any teaching before.
P: Uh huh.
S: But we did all right, I guess. When Jonathan turned 15 and the allergies began to subside, we enrolled him in a local public school, and, to our surprise, he had no trouble whatsoever keeping up – or getting along – with the other students. Now he's just been accepted to both Harvard and Columbia, and we couldn't be prouder.
C: Congratulations!
S: Thanks. Which goes to show that, well, we probably made the right decision.
P: It would seem that stories like yours are becoming more and more common. I read this really interesting article to prep for this interview and, apparently, homeschooled kids tend to outperform their public school peers on standardized tests to get into college. Why do you think that's been happening?
S: Hmm … Good question. I think this might have to do with the fact that homeschooling offers both parents and children a great deal of flexibility.
P: Uh huh.
S: When homeschooling Jonathan, we were able to choose what got taught, when, and how. For example, math was never his forte, so we decided to wait until he was a little older to tackle things like linear algebra or …
C: Just out of curiosity … How well did you know all of that stuff yourself?
S: Some of it slowly came back to us as we studied and prepared lessons, but, oh yeah, sometimes we had to hire outside tutors to help us out.
P: I see.
S: Another advantage of homeschooling is that there's no peer pressure, no competition, no bullying … When you homeschool your kids, they can dress and act and think the way they want, without fear of ridicule or the need to fit in, which means they can focus a 100 percent on their studies, which is what Jonathan did.
P: Is it possible to juggle homeschooling and a full-time job, do you think?
S: Personally, I would say no, or, at least, it's certainly not advisable. Even though when you teach one to one, you don't have as many disruptions as in a traditional classroom – you know, classroom management, discipline, and so on – and you might be able to cover the curriculum in fewer hours, all children need lunch breaks and recess. Not to mention the fact, that even if you telecommute or have flexible hours, your new job as a homeschool teacher includes a lot more than actual teaching time. There are lessons to prepare, tests to write … it shocked us to realize how much time was involved!
P: In other words, your advice to parents is quit your job first.
S: Well, there may be a few super moms and dads who can pull off both, but for most of us, yes, this is very much a full-time job. I would say one parent needs to be totally dedicated to it – or if parents team teach like we did, outside work needs to be part time only.
P: Thank you, Susan. To sum up then, overall, despite the learning curve, yours was a very positive experience?
S: Yes, absolutely.

9.3 page 94 exercise 1D

P: Welcome back, and now we'll hear from our second guest, Carlos Díaz. Carlos, you were homeschooled, correct?
C: Yeah, from kindergarten through fifth grade.
P: But your children go to a public school?
C: Uh huh. I can't fathom the idea of homeschooling my children – even if my wife and I didn't work full time.
P: Why's that?
C: Well, my brother and sister and I were homeschooled because, well, I guess Mom and Dad wanted to – perhaps subconsciously – shelter us from the outside world – from bullying, from peer pressure, you know, all the things Susan mentioned. But, though not exactly a nightmare, the whole experience was a complete waste of some of the best years of our lives.
P: That sounds pretty harsh!
C: I know, but it's kind of sad to think that our worldview until the age of 11 was shaped by so few people – just family and a couple of close friends.
P: Yeah, I see where you're coming from.
C: Also, Dad – who ended up doing most of the teaching – wasn't cut out to be a teacher, so most of our lessons just dragged on and on. You know, left to his own devices, I think he might have sent us to a regular school, but Mom didn't realize Dad wasn't the ideal teacher. It took them a few years to come to the conclusion that we'd be better off going to a public school and studying with people from different backgrounds, and with a range of values and personalities.
P: So you don't recommend homeschooling?
C: Look, I don't mean to generalize beyond my own experience – look at how great Susan's son did – but I think kids need opportunities to develop their emotional intelligence from a young age. They need to learn how to read social cues, overcome interpersonal challenges and, you know, just grapple with the ins and outs of face-to-face interaction.
P: Well, proponents of homeschooling say it's a myth that children don't develop social skills. There are a number of studies that …
S: Yeah, Jonathan had no trouble making friends in high school!
C: I'm sure he didn't, and, again, I don't mean to make any sweeping generalizations. But, you see, children are born thinking the world revolves around them, and the problem with homeschooling is that it might reinforce this tendency. We need to expose children to different people and environments to help them outgrow their immaturity.
S: Yes, there might be some truth to this. I mean …

9.6 page 96 exercise 4A

E = Emma, L = Luke

E: I used to have terrible migraines. My mom thought I might grow out of them, but it went on for years.
L: That sounds awful.
E: It was. By the time I was a senior in high school, I was coming down with a migraine at least once a week. I often had to miss school.
L: That sounds really hard.
E: And there really wasn't any way to make up the lost time, so I had to repeat senior year.
L: I'm sorry to hear that.
E: Thanks. I almost gave up on ever being cured. But my mom was always watching out for new treatments, so we heard about aromatherapy.

L: Aromatherapy?
E: Yes, it uses essential oils from plants to treat stress and anxiety. Even though my doctor said there wasn't really any clear evidence that it would help me, I started seeing an aromatherapist and decided to go through with the treatments. And in the past three years, I haven't had a single migraine!
L: That's wonderful. How does it work?
E: Well, there are various types of oils. Some can be inhaled and some can be diluted and applied to the skin. It's important to be very careful, though, and work with a specialist. The oils are potent and can interact negatively with some medicines. And some can be toxic when applied directly.
L: Really interesting. I had no idea there was that much to know about it!

▶ 9.9 *page 99 exercise 7A*

1
A: Looks like someone wants to lose weight!
B: Yeah. I've been running on this thing for 40 minutes.

2
OK, now keep your legs straight and feet together … Yeah, just like that. Stand, and without bending your knees, reach down as far as possible … A little more … Good. Remember to put your weight through your heels, not your toes.

3
A: Wow! I wish my stomach looked like that! So flat. You look like a fashion model!
B: Thanks. I've been working out a lot.

4
A: Wow, way to go! Now let's try something a little more challenging.
B: 100 pounds? You've got to be kidding!

5
OK, breathe out and pull your stomach in when you go up. Breathe in when you go back down. Ready, steady, go. 1 and 2 and 3… Let's do 25 of these.

▶ 9.10 *page 100 exercise 7B*

T = Trainer, C = Colleague

T: Welcome back to *Fitness on the go*, the weekly fitness podcast for people on the run – just like you and me! Thanks for tweeting us your questions. We'll try to answer as many as we can today. So, let's get right down to it. Here's a tweet from @lazyrunner. Hi Lazyrunner. Hope you're with us today. Lazyrunner writes: "Is it true that running on a treadmill – as opposed to, say, running on the street – is gentler on your knees?" Well, the thing about running is that it's a high-impact exercise, so it creates a lot of stress on your knees no matter where you run …
C: You just talked thousands of listeners out of even trying!
T: But here's the good news: Most treadmills include padding that can stop your knees from hurting because, just like a cushion, it softens any impact you may feel, unlike a hard surface outdoors. That's why many people consider them to be safer than jogging outside.
C: Oh, well, maybe you won't dissuade me from giving it a shot then.
T: But that's only half the story. You see, a few studies have shown that people tend to take shorter steps, shorter strides, when they're on a treadmill, and this can actually increase the risk of injury. So, in a nutshell, the answer is, it depends. Either way, I urge you to see your doctor before you begin exercising.
C: Yes, that's critical! Have your doctor help you choose the best exercise program for you. Here's another tweet. "Speaking of treadmills, can we trust those calorie counters?"
T: Treadmills and stationary bikes know nothing about your biorhythm, general health, and fitness level, all of which determine how many calories you're burning when you work out.
C: Yeah, that's what I thought.
T: Some machines can overestimate calorie count by over 40%! These numbers might put a smile on your face and brighten your day, but don't let them fool you! You can't count on them being right!
C: So, you're saying 100 calories might actually be 60?
T: That's right. But, you know, sometimes they guess right, so they're better than nothing.
C: Wow, I had no idea! Anyway, while we're on the subject of cardio, let's talk about sweating. Our next tweet: "Is it true that you absolutely have to sweat to burn calories?"
T: You see, sweat is a sign that your body is reminding itself to cool down.
C: Like a biological response?
T: Yes. Sweating keeps you from overheating – and having to stop to freshen up every five minutes! But rest assured that you can burn hundreds of calories without necessarily dripping in sweat.
C: Oh, this is good news! Let me read another tweet. This one's from @robertbrown. "My doctor warned me not to stretch before weightlifting. Has he lost his mind?"
T: Well, this is a tricky question, but your doctor might be on to something, Robert. You see, the jury's still out on how helpful stretching really is. Some studies show that stretching before weightlifting won't necessarily enable you to perform better and might actually weaken your muscles! This doesn't mean that there's no need to warm up, of course, but static stretching might–
C: What's that?
T: Stretching your muscles with your body at rest … that might not be the best way to do it. But not all experts agree, your doctor for one, so, I won't insist on your listening to me instead!
C: OK, we have time for one more tweet before our commercial break. @Gwen_Chicago asks: "I do 100 sit-ups every day. Will I get the abs of my dreams?"
T: Gwen, I hope you don't mind me saying this, but, no. Toning exercises will help you strengthen your abs, but may not give you a really flat tummy. If you want that, you'll have to incorporate cardio into your exercise routine … and watch your diet, of course.
C: That's the hardest part. At least for me, it is!
T: Thank you everyone. We'll take a quick break and …

▶ 9.13 *page 102 exercises 9A and B*

T = Terri, H = Hugo

T: Free for lunch?
H: Sure, but I might have to choose the restaurant.
T: Because you're treating me?
H: No, it's that I'm a raw vegan.
T: Sorry, Hugo, I didn't catch what you said.
H: A raw vegan.
T: I'm embarrassed to admit I don't really have any idea what that is.
H: It's pretty much what it sounds like. I only eat food that's raw, and I don't eat food of animal origin, so that rules out not only meat and fish, but eggs and dairy products.
T: Is it … totally raw, like in cold?
H: Well, it doesn't need to be cold, no, but it can't be cooked at a temperature above 48 degrees centigrade or 118 degrees Fahrenheit.
T: So … is it possible to achieve a balanced diet?
H: Sure! Don't I look healthy?

▶ 9.14 *page 102 exercise 9C*

H: Don't I look healthy?
T: Of course! I never would have thought you were on a raw vegan diet.
H: But … uh … it sounds as if you don't think it's healthy.
T: You're right. I should reserve judgment. So, what do you eat exactly?
H: First, the balance of carbohydrates to protein to fat is 80–10–10. I follow that rigorously.
T: You mean, carbohydrates aren't bad for you?
H: It depends what kind. I get mine from fruit, like bananas and dates. You could say I'm an LFRV.
T: A what? It sounds like a religion or something.
H: Low-fat-raw-vegan! It's a lot faster to say LFRV.
T: So what exactly do you eat in a typical day?
H: Let's see … 24 bananas or 48 dates or 5.3 liters of orange juice. Sometimes I mix it all in a blender. I get my protein and fat from the juice. And then most days I eat a low-fat salad to get protein, minerals, and vitamins.
T: Did I hear you correctly? You eat 24 bananas a day? Don't you feel kind of …
H: Nauseous? Yeah, that's what everyone says. Well, to tell you the truth, I did at first. I felt awful!
T: Are you sure this is healthy, Hugo? I'm a little worried.
H: You do have to be careful. For example, I take a vitamin supplement for vitamin D and vitamin B12. And here's something very important. People may tell you otherwise, but this diet is for adults, not kids.
T: I can imagine! Who in their right mind would eat so many bananas?

331

Audio scripts

H: It's no joke. There have been scary stories of kids failing to grow properly, who suffer from malnutrition and rickets, and I even read one about a girl with holes in her teeth. Vitamin D is critical for normal development.
T: You're rapidly causing me to lose my appetite, Hugo! Would it be OK if we just went to a salad place for lunch?
H: You mean, you don't want to try Raw foods on State Street?
T: Thanks, but no thanks! But I have to say, I admire people like you who are out of the mainstream. Look at me. Nine-to-five job, traditional family, even more traditional diet …

Unit 10

10.1 page 104 exercise 1A

S = Sister, H = Henry

S: Wow! Look at you! That's a great picture!
H: Oh, those were the days. Such memories …
S: I remember. The three of you were inseparable.
H: Yes, we were birds of a feather – same tastes, same interests, same idols …
S: And you haven't seen each other in what …?
H: I'd say at least five years.
S: Oh, what a shame.
H: I know! After we graduated, we kept in touch for a while, but, then you know, we just went our separate ways. We tried to get together last year, but we couldn't find a time that worked for everyone, and, well, it just never happened.
S: Oh, that's too bad.
H: Well, I guess that's the way it goes.
S: But before last year, I mean, had you guys ever fallen out or anything?
H: No, never. But I guess it goes without saying that we didn't really care if we saw each other.
S: So why do you think you drifted apart like that?
H: Hmm … maybe what we had was essentially a group relationship.
S: What do you mean?
H: Well, our one-on-one interactions were usually a bit awkward.

10.2 page 104 exercise 1C

S: Awkward? Why?
H: Well, take Mike, for example. We had an interesting dynamic, the two of us. We liked each other, we did, but, for some reason, we felt a bit uncomfortable when we were alone together.
S: Like where?
H: Like when, you know, we'd arranged to meet somewhere, and Mike and I were the first to arrive and we had to wait for the others …We didn't seem to have that much to talk about.
S: Oh, I see what you mean.
H: We found it really hard to connect. Mike was OK as part of a group, but, truth be told, I thought he was a bit boring, you know, always going on and on about homework and tests and …
S: Hmm… So, the writing was on the wall, wasn't it? I mean, you both knew you'd lose touch eventually.
H: Yeah, I guess. Bruce, though … Bruce was the exact opposite – always the life of the party.
S: Yes, what a riot he was! You used to play squash together, right?
H: Uh huh. Twice a week. It was fun. We were constantly laughing and making sarcastic remarks. Sometimes our conversations sounded as if they could have been taken from a sitcom! But when Bruce and I were alone together, we couldn't get out of the "this is hilarious!" mode.
S: So it felt a bit forced?
H: Exactly! We were always trying to outwit each other. I mean, I don't remember ever talking about something meaningful with him. There's no telling why, but our conversations never went beneath the surface.
S: Yeah, all you could talk about was soccer and video games. But, say what you will about Bruce, he was still fun to be around.
H: Oh, definitely.
S: Whatever became of him? Do you have any idea?
H: None whatsoever. I looked for him on Facebook one day, out of curiosity, and it seems he'd deleted his account. Both Facebook and Instagram! And he was such a computer geek! Well, go figure.

10.3 page 104 exercise 1D

S: So, … what about Leona? Why isn't she in any of the pictures?
H: I think she was the one who took the photos.
S: You guys go back a long way, right?
H: We do! We went to high school together … and then we both ended up at the same college!
S: Do you still see her?
H: No. She was a breath of fresh air, though. Always so positive and idealistic. Of all my friends, Leona is the one I wish I'd kept in touch with.
S: Didn't you hang out once or twice a couple of years ago?
H: Yeah, but she'd changed a lot.
S: Really? How?
H: She'd always been a bit of a rebel, you know … always fighting for justice and trying to make the world a better place. She couldn't have cared less about status and material possessions and, you know … I liked that about her. I really did.
S: Uh huh.
H: Turns out that when we met, it was as if the old Leona had been abducted by aliens or something.
S: Aliens?
H: I could barely recognize her. She kept going on and on about her job at the law firm, and her brand new car and … I kept thinking to myself, "Whatever happened to the Leona I used to know?"
S: Well, don't judge a book by its cover. Just because she talks about her career and loves her new car doesn't necessarily mean she's given up on her ideals. You can still be friends.
H: Yeah, well, easier said than done. We have so little in common!
S: OK, so you don't see eye to eye on everything. So what? You know what they say, opposites attract!
H: Hmm … But it's important to agree on things, isn't it? I think our values are just … different. But you could be right. I mean, maybe I should …

10.5 page 105 exercise 2A

Hello. This is Helene, your cyber teacher. You haven't seen me in a while! Today we have some very good, new expressions, all related to friendship.
1
S: The three of you were inseparable!
H: Yes, we were birds of a feather.
To be birds of a feather means you're very much alike. If you think about it, birds that have the same feathers are all from the same species.
2
H: Bruce was the exact opposite, always the life of the party.
S: Yes, what a riot he was!
To be *the life of the party* means "to be a lot of fun." Someone who's the life of the party is often the center of attention, in a positive way. And when someone is *a riot*, it means that he or she really makes people laugh.
3
H: Our conversations never went beneath the surface.
S: Yeah, all you could talk about was soccer and video games.
When a conversation doesn't *go beneath the surface*, as I'm sure you can guess, it means it's shallow, just like water.
4
S: You guys go back a long way, right?
H: We do! We went to high school together.
When two people *go back a long way*, it means they've known each other for a long time. For example, Henry might have said, "Leona and I go back a long way."
5
S: Do you still see her?
H: No, she was *a breath of fresh air*, though.
Helene: If you say someone is a breath of fresh air, it means the person is "a welcome and refreshing change." Henry goes on to say that Leona was positive and idealistic.
6
S: OK, so you don't *see eye to eye* on everything. So what?
H: But it's important to agree on things, isn't it?
As Henry's answer implies, if you don't see eye to eye, it means "you don't agree." But I don't agree with Henry personally. I love a good argument! Well, folks, I think that's all for today. See you again soon.

Audio scripts

10.6 page 106 exercise 3A

... related to a very wide range of factors. So, here's the million-dollar question: What's the secret to living a long and healthy life? Let me try to answer this question by way of a personal anecdote. This is my late aunt Agatha on her 88th birthday. What a remarkable woman! One of seven children, she never married, but had a huge social network – and I'm talking about a real life, face-to-face social network. She knew practically everyone on her street! Luckily, all the neighbors got along well and were always there for each other. Through Facebook – yes, she was on Facebook – Aunt Agatha managed to track down some of her school friends and kept in touch with them. She also met lots of new people at the book club and at the gym – she was big on yoga and, are you ready for this? When she was in her 70s, she came close to winning a marathon! Unfortunately, three years after this photo was taken, because of circumstances beyond her control, she had to move to a nursing home, where she lost touch with nearly all of her friends and neighbors. It so happens that Aunt Agatha – who'd always been in perfect health – died within six months. I think this story illustrates how important it is to have a wide circle of friends and acquaintances, not only for the sake of your mind, but for the sake of your body. Recent research suggests that social connections might be the key to having good overall health, from adolescence well into your senior years. Let me show you a summary of three studies conducted from 2010 to 2016 …

10.7 page 106 exercise 3B

… a summary of three studies conducted from 2010 to 2016, two of which were in the U.S. and one in Australia. First of all, it appears that regular social contact – and, by the way, I'm using the terms social contact, ties, and connections interchangeably – is just as important as diet and exercise. Some of these studies – and they're all described in your handouts – actually suggest social contact might be even more important than diet and exercise, which is good news for a sociable couch potato like me. The second one is a bit of a shocker. Yes, social isolation can be much more harmful than obesity. Not slightly more harmful – much more harmful! Remember, though, that we're talking about one study, so, clearly, more research is needed. Here's another interesting finding: The size of our social networks is slightly more important than the quality of our relationships – but only during adolescence and old age. This might have to do with the fact that our relationships tend to change more frequently during that time. So, long story short: The more meaningful your relationships are, the longer and healthier your life may be. It would seem that human beings are wired for connectedness, just as our planet thrives on biodiversity.

10.8 page 106 exercise 3C

1 What's the secret to living a long and healthy life?
Number 1 is correct. *To* is a preposition and a noun can follow. For example, you can also say, "What's the secret to life?"
2 Let me try to answer this question by way of a personal anecdote.
Number 2 is correct. *To* is part of an infinitive, and a noun cannot follow. In this particular case, you may also say, "Let me try answering this question," and there is no change in meaning.
3 She came close to win a marathon.
Number 3 is incorrect. The correct sentence is "She came close to winning a marathon." It is possible to put a noun after *to*, for example, "She came close to stardom." Therefore, to is a preposition and must be followed by the -ing form.
4 Aunt Agatha managed to track down some of her school friends.
Sentence 4 is correct. *To* is part of an infinitive, and a noun cannot follow. In this case, the infinitive is the phrasal verb *to track down*.
5 Social connections might be the key to have good overall health.
Sentence 5 is incorrect. The correct sentence is "Social connections might be the key to having good overall health." It is possible to put a noun after to, for example, "Social connections might be the key to longevity." Therefore, *to* is a preposition and must be followed by the *-ing* form.

10.10 page 109 exercises 6B and C

Conversation 1
A: Poor mother.
B: Yeah. I sympathize!
A: Bet he's an only child.
B: What makes you say that?
A: Well, my sister has a twelve-year-old, and he's spoiled rotten. He can be really nasty and disrespectful at times.
B: Really?
A: Uh huh. Some of it has to do with immaturity, of course, but I think his mother is the one to blame. I mean, she puts up with just about anything. The other day he told her to mind her own business! Can you believe it?! Oh, and don't get me started on all the distasteful jokes! That would have been unimaginable when we were growing up. I think it's totally unacceptable.
B: Absolutely.
A: If he was my son, things would be different. For one thing, I …
B: Well, I'm an only child myself, and I wasn't spoiled. Well, at least I don't think I was.
A: Maybe you're an exception to the rule.
B: Rule? What are you talking about? My husband is an only child, too, and …

Conversation 2
A: Nice headphones. What are you listening to?
B: Drake's latest.
A: Oh, I like him.
B: You've heard of Drake?
A: Yeah, I streamed one of his albums … He has a nice voice, that kid, and the melodies are irresistible.
B: What do you mean you *streamed* his album? Uncle Brian, you use Spotify?
A: What? You think I still listen to CDs?
B: Erm … Yeah …
A: Oh, no, they take up too much space. Your Aunt Brenda convinced me to get rid of most of them – and the DVDs, for that matter, too. I mean, who needs DVDs when there's Netflix? Keeping them would just be illogical!
B: I didn't think you even knew what Netflix was!
A: I love Netflix! It has tons of shows, it's user-friendly, and relatively inexpensive. And they have a great iPhone app.
B: Wow!
A: Oh, come on! Give me some credit. Just because I'm in my 80s doesn't mean I live in the past!
Did you match the columns correctly and catch the six words? They are: 1 immaturity, 2 distasteful, 3 unacceptable, 4 irresistible, 5 illogical, 6 inexpensive

10.11 page 110 exercise 7A

The Six Degrees of Separation theory, developed in 1929 and popularized in a 1990 play, claims that we're never more than six steps away from everyone and everything on earth. And now, in the Internet age, that seems to be truer than ever. But maybe it was always true. After all, the theory was developed nearly a century ago. Now let's see what our callers have to say.

10.12 page 110 exercises 7B and C

H = Host, C = Caller (1–5)
H: Now let's see what our callers have to say. Hello, you're on the air. Do you believe in Six Degrees of Separation?
C1: Thank you. One day, I was in a really bad mood after work, so I figured I'd have a quick bite at an outdoor restaurant. And just as I was getting ready to pay, my neighbor Tom walked by with his sister. I thought she was the most beautiful woman I'd ever seen. So I asked Tom to introduce us. The rest is history. We got married two years ago. So it just goes to show: Had Sarah not come by with Tom, I wouldn't be married to her now! I'd say the odds are 100 to 1 that you'll meet your wife when you're in such a foul mood! But it happened to me! So I'd say definitely. I mean, I ended up marrying my neighbor's sister! Can you believe it?
H: A great story. Caller 2, you're on the air.
C2: Well, I really hate to impose on people, you know, but a couple of years ago, right before my wife Beth was due to go on a long business trip, I was visiting my friend Gary – my oldest friend. He knows I hate asking for help, so he kept repeating, "Really, should you need anything at all while Beth is away, just come by. You know I don't mind." So one day I did. Anyway, while I was there, he got a call from a friend who was selling his house. It was in a neighborhood we were dying to live in, and

Audio scripts

so we bought it! But the odds that I probably would have seen an ad online are pretty high, I guess. I think it's overblown – the theory, that is.

H: I'm not so sure. It sounds like serendipity to me! Caller 3.

C3: So here's a good one. I had just started teaching English in Bogotá and wanted to find a partner for a Spanish-English language exchange. All the requests on the bulletin board were in Spanish, except for one, which was in English. So I thought, "That might be useful in case I have questions." Of course I never imagined Pedro would become my boyfriend, much less my husband. I thought I'd leave Colombia in a year. But here we are, twenty years later. Were I to have dialed a different phone number, my whole life would have been different! Still, I'm not so sure about the theory. The odds of finding an English speaker were maybe low, but then this was a language school, after all. So I'd say there was a logical explanation.

H: Another happy ending. Caller 4.

C4: This one has a happy ending, too, of the best kind! Everyone's worst nightmare. I started to have chest pains. But I thought, "This couldn't possibly be a heart attack. I'm only 45 years old." And I waited, hoping the pain would go away. I had all the classic symptoms: sweating, pain down one arm. After an hour, I was scared, and so even though it was 3:00 a.m., I decided to call my best friend, Eric. I mean, the odds are really against you if you wait too long. But fortunately, he came over immediately and in 10 minutes, we were at the hospital. A good thing, too! Had I called even a minute later, I might not have arrived in time. Eric saved my life! But ... and this is the best part of all. I'm now married to my doctor, who's originally from Lithuania! What could be a better example?

H: A close call! Never ignore those symptoms. But what a great ending. Caller 5.

C5: Twenty years ago, I became good friends with an American named Ruth, who was living here in London. Well, just last year, we decided to take a trip together to visit a friend of hers in Greece. What a place! After three days, I said, "Were we to spend even one more day here, I'd never be able to leave. This is the most beautiful view I've ever seen." Anyway, one thing led to another, and Ruth's friend said I could come live with her. What are the odds of a stranger offering you a home?! So, absolutely! In fact, I just read a book about "Six Degrees of separation".

H: Thank you all. As for me, I believe in it, without a doubt! Why else would I have hosted this show? If you're not convinced, just be patient and ...

▶ 10.13 *page 110 exercise 7D*

1 I'd say the odds are 100 to 1 that you'll meet your wife when you're in such a foul mood!
The correct pattern is e, "the odds are number to number that ... ," in this case, "100 to 1."

2 But the odds that I probably would have seen an ad online are pretty high, I guess.
The correct pattern is d, "the odds that ... ," followed by a sentence.

3 The odds of finding an English speaker were maybe low, but then this was a language school, after all.
The correct pattern is b, "the odds of verb + *ing*," in this case, "finding."

4 I mean, the odds are really against you if you wait too long.
The correct pattern is c, "the odds are against you ... ." In this case, the expression is followed by an *if*-clause.

5 What are the odds of a stranger offering you a home?!
The correct pattern is a, "the odds of object", in this case, "a stranger" + verb + *ing*," in this case, "offering."

▶ 10.14 *page 112 exercises 9B and C*

R = Dr. Robert Cialdini, S = Steve Martin

R: Researchers have been studying the factors that influence us to say yes to the requests of others for over sixty years and there can be no doubt that there is a science to how we are persuaded and a lot of this science is surprising. When making a decision it would be nice to think that people consider all the available information in order to guide their thinking, but the reality is very often different. In the increasingly overloaded lives we lead, more than ever, we need shortcuts or rules of thumb to guide our decision-making. My own research has identified just six of these shortcuts as universals that guide human behavior. They are; reciprocity, scarcity, authority, consistency, liking and consensus. Understanding these shortcuts and employing them in an ethical manner can significantly increase the chances that someone will be persuaded by your request. Let's take a closer look at each in turn.

S: So the first universal principle of influence is reciprocity. Simply put, people are obliged to give back to others the form of behavior, gift or service that they have received first. If a friend invites you to their party, there's an obligation for you to invite them to a future party you are hosting. If a colleague does you a favor, then you owe that colleague a favor. And in the context of a social obligation people are more likely to say yes to those that they owe.

One of the best demonstrations of the principle of reciprocation comes from a series of studies conducted in restaurants. So the last time you visit a restaurant there's a good chance that the waiter or waitress will have given you a gift, probably at about the same time that they bring your bill, a liqueur perhaps or a fortune cookie, or perhaps a simple mint. So here's the question; does the giving of a mint have any influence over how much tip you're going to leave them? Most people will say no, but that mint can make a surprising difference. In the study, giving diners a single mint at the end of their meal typically increased tips by around 3 percent. Interestingly, if the gift is doubled and two mints are provided tips don't double ... they quadruple, a 14 percent increase in tips. But, perhaps most interestingly of all is the fact that if the waiter provides one mint, starts to walk away from the table, but pauses, turns back and says "For you nice people, here's an extra mint", tips go through the roof, a 23 percent increase influenced, not by what was given but how it was given. So the key to using the principle of reciprocation is to be the first to give and to ensure that what you give is personalized and unexpected.

▶ 10.15 *page 112 exercises 9E and F*

S: The fifth principle is the principle of liking, people prefer to say yes to those that they like. But what causes one person to like another? Persuasion science tells us that there are three important factors; we like people who are similar to us, we like people who pay us compliments and we like people who cooperate with us towards mutual goals. As more and more of the interactions that we are having take place online it might be worth asking whether these factors can be employed effectively in, let's say, online negotiations. In a series of negotiations studies carried out between MBA students at two well-known business schools, some groups were told, "Time is money, get straight down to business". In this group around 55 percent were able to come to an agreement. A second group, however, were told "Before you begin negotiating, exchange some personal information with each other, identify a similarity you share in common, then begin negotiating". In this group 90 percent of them were able to come to successful and agreeable outcomes that were typically worth 18 percent more to both parties. So to harness this powerful principle of liking be sure to look for areas of similarity that you share with others and genuine compliments you could give before you get down to business.

Review 5 (Units 9–10)

▶ R5.1 *page 114 exercise 1A*

P = Professor, S = Student (1–3)

P: Today I'd like to consider a new aspect of the innovative learning debate. So what comes to mind when I say the words "innovative learning"?

S1: I tend to think of approaches like home-schooling that do away with the traditional classroom altogether.

S2: I think of distance learning, which has added so much flexibility to our options, especially for students who also have to work while going to college.

S3: What I think of is just recognizing a wide range of learning styles.

P: Good. Now I'm going to go into a topic you may not find innovative since it's been around for some time – but still worth looking at: how to mix traditional learning and technology. Today we're going to talk about the ideal lecture.

S1: Can a lecture be ideal?
P: We're going to find out. I hope I haven't dissuaded you from listening.
S2: I've given up on choosing lecture courses, but maybe that will change after today!
P: Yes, that's a common reaction. You may feel the traditional lecture is didactic, rather than interactive, and encourages a passive stance on the part of the student. But what might some of the advantages be?
S3: I'm not really sure, to be honest.
P: Have you ever thought that it lets you get away from the fast-paced, interactive world of technology? Lectures are known to be appreciated when delivered by a knowledgeable speaker with breadth and depth. The benefits might, in fact, outweigh the disadvantages.
S1: Just because we don't have to talk?
P: Not exactly. Good lectures clarify complex issues, drawing on the speaker's tremendous experience. They can strengthen and enhance your understanding of a topic. What might encourage students to get the most enjoyment from them?
S2: I'd say incorporating video. The more dynamic they are, the more likely it is that we'll pay attention.
P: Yes, at times, the delivery is every bit as important as the content. Good visuals are often irresistible. Were lecturers to pay attention to presentation, they'd have fewer yawns in class. So far I haven't seen any here today, so I guess that's a good sign!
S3: I totally agree. I'm nowhere near as likely to become distracted if there's a good video.
S1: So it may be a fictitious belief that lectures have gone out of style?
P: In a sense. Innovation could mean playing up the virtues of this supposedly old-fashioned medium. Combined with supportive visuals at the optimum moments, a good lecture can widen our understanding of virtually any topic.

Unit 11

11.1 *page 116 exercise 1A*

L = Lisa, P = Phil

L: Too much time on your hands?
P: What? Oh, you mean this!
L: "Are you a risk taker or do you play it safe?" Hmm ... Interesting.
P: Let me try it on you.
L: OK.
P: "What do you usually do with your savings?"
L: Oh boy!
P: "A: Invest in a diversified portfolio; B: Who needs savings?; C: Put them in a savings account. It's always a safe bet."
L: Hmm ... Probably A. What's the next one?
P: "Which of these sounds like the most fun? A: Sailing, but I'd never go by myself, just to be on the safe side; B: Skydiving. You only live once!; C: Bowling."
L: Well, I'm not really into bowling. And I'm scared of heights, so definitely not skydiving. I think I'd go with A – sailing, but not alone.
P: OK. Number 3: "On a game show, which of these would you be most inclined to do? A: Take a 50% chance at winning $50,000; B: Take a 10% chance at winning $100,000; or C: Take home $10,000 in cash. I might come to regret it, but I'd rather err on the side of caution."
L: Gee, I don't know! A 10% chance seems so unlikely. But I don't think I'd settle for 10,000 either. So A. I think I'd go for the $50,000 prize.
P: Right, next one. "Your boss has made lots of decisions you disagree with. What do you do?"
L: She sure has!
P: "A: Meet one-on-one with him or her and voice my concerns; B: Quit, even if I haven't found another job yet; C: Nothing. I can't afford to leave without a safety net to fall back on."
L: Oh, definitely C.
P: Yeah, me too. Here's the next one ...
L: Erm ... Phil, listen, I've got to get back to work. How many questions are there?
P: Ten, but they're all pretty similar. You chose mostly As, right?
L: Uh huh. Let me see what it says ...

11.2 *page 116 exercises 1B and C*

L: Uh huh. Let me see what it says. "Mostly A answers: You're a thinker. For safety's sake, you always weigh the pros and cons of each and every decision you make." Hmm ... that's true. "Sometimes, however, you throw caution to the wind because deep down you know that the bigger the risk, the bigger the potential payoff." Yeah, that sounds a lot like me. Or am I the next one? Let's see. "Mostly B answers. You're a gambler. You think rules are meant to be broken. You thrive on action, uncertainty, and challenge, so you tend to seek out highly stimulating experiences. You're impulsive and you often make hasty – sometimes reckless – decisions. It wouldn't hurt to exercise caution once in a while." Hmm ... Not, definitely not me. How about you, Phil?
P: Oh, I haven't finished it yet, but I chose lots of Cs.
L: What does C say? "You're a worrier. Your favorite saying is, 'Better to be safe than sorry.' You tend to avoid taking risks and, on the rare occasions when you do, you usually have a plan B to fall back on. You're always ready for the worst-case scenario, even though it rarely materializes! Loosen up and live a little!" Hmm ... Is this accurate?
P: Yeah, I think so. I find it really hard to get out of my comfort zone, and, because of that, I might be about to let a once-in-a-lifetime opportunity go to waste.

11.3 *page 117 exercise 2A*

L: What are you talking about?
P: Are you sure we're here alone?
L: Yes. Everyone's left. It's already 7:00.
P: There's an opening for ... Listen, this is between you and me, OK?
L: Of course.
P: Melinda wants to promote me to sales manager ...
L: That's fantastic! Congratulations! I could totally see you doing that job.
P: In Mexico City!
L: No way!
P: Yep. It seems like a good opportunity, I know, but I don't think I'm going to accept it.
L: What? Have you lost your mind? Why not? You don't have a girlfriend at the moment, you don't have kids, your parents are healthy ... What do you have to lose?
P: Blame it on my upbringing.
L: What do you mean?
P: Well, my parents were pretty strict, so I didn't take many risks. I guess I'm scared.
L: Of what?
P: I don't know. There's just too much at stake. What if things don't work out?
L: Oh, come on! What are the odds? You're really good at your job.
P: Thanks, but I'm not sure I have what it takes ... you know, to be a sales manager.
L: What do you mean?
P: Maybe I'm just not cut out for ...
L: What?
P: Leadership.
L: Oh, I'm sure you'll have some kind of mentor in your new office, someone to set you on the right path. And you know what they say, leaders are not born, they're made.
P: But what about my Spanish? How am I supposed to manage a team of ten people – and highly experienced people at that – if I don't speak their language fluently? They won't take me seriously!
L: Listen, maybe the first few weeks will be tough ...
P: You think?
L: But you're going to keep studying Spanish when you're there, right?
P: Yes, I'm sure I will.
L: And don't forget you'll be exposed to the language 24–7, too, which means you're going to get really fluent faster. Besides, I would assume that most of them speak at least some English, right?
P: Yes, I've been told they do.
L: So ...?
P: Still, I don't know what it would be like to start over in another country. You know, get used to the weather, find a place to live ...
L: Oh, I'm sure your colleagues will help you find an apartment! Assuming, of course, that the company won't take care of that, which they might. Don't worry! Listen, Phil, what's the worst that could happen?
P: Quite simply, I might fall short, and then I could be out of work, too.
L: Worst comes to worst, I'm sure Melinda will give you your current job back. She thinks the world of you. Why not just go with the flow?
P: So you really think I should say yes?
L: Of course!
P: I wouldn't be throwing caution to the wind?
L: Well, in a sense, yes, but it's a chance to get out of your comfort zone. You might never forgive yourself if you didn't.
P: I know, I know.

Audio scripts

L: So you're going to do it?
P: I need to sleep on it.
L: Oh, come on! Just say yes, please!
P: You'll end up wearing me down!

11.5 page 117 exercise 2B

Number 1. Excerpt 1
L: So you're going to do it?
P: I need to sleep on it.
Number 1. Excerpt 2
L: Besides, I would assume that most of them speak at least some English, right?
P: Yes, I've been told they do.
L: So … ?
In the first excerpt, *so* means (beep) and in the second, it means (beep). In the first excerpt, the answer is a. *So* means "anyway." And in the second, the answer is b. It means, "What's the problem?"

Number 2. Excerpt 1
P: What if things don't work out?
L: Oh, come on!
Number 2. Excerpt 2
P: I need to sleep on it.
L: Oh, come on!
In the first excerpt, *Oh, come on!* means (beep) and in the second, it means (beep). In the first excerpt, *Oh, come on!* means "Don't be silly!" and in the second, it means "Just say yes, please!"

Number 3. Excerpt 1
P: Listen, this is between you and me, OK?
L: Of course.
Number 3. Excerpt 2
P: So you really think I should say yes?
L: Of course!
In the first excerpt, *Of course!* means (beep) and in the second, it means (beep). In the first excerpt, *Of course!* means "Don't worry! You can trust me" and in the second, it means "Without a doubt."

Number 4. Excerpt 1
P: Yep. It seems like a good opportunity, I know, but I don't think I'm going to accept it.
L: What?
Number 4. Excerpt 2
P: Maybe I'm just not cut out for…
L: What?
P: Leadership.
In the first excerpt, *What?* means (beep) and in the second, it means (beep). In the first excerpt, *What?* means "You've got to be kidding!" and in the second, it means "Please explain."

11.7 page 118 exercises 3A and B

I = Instructor

I: Welcome to City Awareness, our training course on responsible bicycle safety for those over 25. I'm very pleased that you've shown up today, and our goal, of course, is to teach you not only to enjoy a great sport, but to enjoy it safely. Let me start with a common myth. "It's like riding a bicycle," we often say when talking about skills we'll never lose. But how good were those skills to begin with? While it's true we may have learned to ride a bike when we were young – five, six, seven years old – none of us ever learned how to defend ourselves in twenty-first century traffic. Before I show you a video on the 10 most important safety features, let's just spend a minute brainstorming. Why are you here today?
A: I'm here because I'm nervous. I used to ride on the sidewalk when I was growing up. But now that's illegal where I live. It fills me with dread to have to ride where cars are moving!
I: It shouldn't be hard to remember one important rule, though: always ride with and not against, traffic. That means with the flow of traffic, and naturally stay as far to the right as possible if there's no bike lane. In fact, did you know that riding against traffic can be up to three times as dangerous as riding with it?
A: No, I had no idea.
I: Yes … so, what else comes to mind?
B: Bike riding can really reduce stress, but only if you start out feeling relaxed.
A: That's easier said than done!
B: I'd say it helps if you learn your surroundings first. If I'm traveling and I rent a bike, for example, I won't ride my first day in a new city. First, I make sure I know my way around. I always buy a map and explore the area on foot to be sure I won't have any distractions when I'm riding.
I: That's a good point. Distracted riding can be every bit as dangerous as distracted driving. In fact, you might try riding only during the day at first. Then make sure to buy a headlight. Your visibility is reduced at night. But you need to keep an eye on traffic conditions as far ahead of you as possible, just like in a car.
A: Speaking of conditions up ahead, you know what gets to me? All these stories you hear about people being "doored." It happened to a good friend of mine. The driver could have looked before opening his door right into the path of her bike. It was a close call! But often they never do. If drivers are looking at all, it's only for cars. So be careful!
C: That's very true. If you have to stop suddenly, it's important to know how, isn't it?
I: Absolutely. You might want to take some basic precautions even when you're buying a new bike. Make sure your feet can not only touch the ground, but that the ball of your foot can support your weight. The seat may be adjustable, but sometimes the lowest position is actually too high. Try it out at the store.
A: That's good advice. And in my case – I haven't ridden in 20 years – do you have any advice just for getting started? As I said, I'm very nervous!
B: I've heard there are refresher courses …
I: That's right. I taught one recently. Above all, give yourself time. One student had very poor balance. They all should have mastered the basics in a few days, but she took much longer. So don't be too hard on yourself. When you're 100% comfortable, that's when you can plan bike outings!

11.8 page 118 exercise 3C

I = Instructor, E = Eye witness (1–2), R = Reporter

I: Now we're going to watch an eyewitness account from two points of view. We'll then explore what went wrong.
E1: You can't believe how shaken I am right now. I was nearly killed.
R: What happened exactly?
E1: So I was about to cross the street, you know, and this bike, going the wrong way, was speeding toward me. But, of course, I didn't see him because I was looking to the left. I never dreamed in a million years, there would be a bike going against traffic!
R: Very dangerous, I agree.
E1: So I step into the street and see this bike coming right at me! He's turning left. I swear, I screamed at the top of my lungs. I had no idea I could scream that loudly.
R: And then?
E1: He swerved to avoid hitting me. He veered off to the left. And quite fortunately, he screeched to a halt before he knocked someone else over instead. The skid marks were visible on the ground!
I: Now we're going to hear the other side of the story.
R: You were going the wrong way on your bike and nearly caused an accident. Can you tell us –
E2: This city has no respect for bikes. There are no bike lanes. The other side of the street has ongoing construction. I've got to get to work, man!
R: Yes, I sympathize, but what exactly happened?
E2: So this woman, instead of waiting on the sidewalk for the light to change, she was standing in the street. I simply never saw her.
R: That's not good.
E2: And then she started to cross, and … well, she just froze in her tracks, instead of moving out of the way. I mean, I guess she must have gotten frightened because she just stopped dead, I swear. It was awful. I could feel the color draining from my face. I just turned white. You know, one of those heart-stopping moments …
R: I've had them!
E2: A chill went through my body. My hair stood on end. If you could have seen me in the mirror! It was standing straight up. But, I guess I'm lucky to have fast reflexes because somehow I narrowly missed her. I'm still shaking!

11.9 page 118 exercise 3D

1

E1: So I step into the street and see this bike coming right at me! He's turning left. I swear, I (beep) I had no idea I could scream that loudly.
E1: So I step into the street and see this bike coming right at me! He's turning left. I swear, I screamed at the top of my lungs. I had no idea I could scream that loudly.

This is your cyber teacher, Helene. Let's look at the first expression. *To scream at the top of your lungs* means "to scream as loud as you can." And the clue is the next sentence, "I had no idea I could scream that loudly."

2
R: And then?
E1: He (beep). He veered off to the left.
R: And then?
E1: He swerved to avoid hitting me. He veered off to the left.
To swerve means to "veer, or steer suddenly, to one side." The clue is the next sentence, "He veered off to the left."

3
E1: And quite fortunately, he (beep) before he knocked someone else over instead. The skid marks were visible on the ground!
E1: And quite fortunately, he screeched to a halt before he knocked someone else over instead. The skid marks were visible on the ground!
To screech to a halt means "to come to a stop very suddenly." The next sentence gives a clue: "The skid marks were visible on the ground!"

4
E2: And then she started to cross, and … well, she just (beep), instead of moving out of the way. I mean, I guess she must have gotten frightened because she just stopped dead, I swear.
E2: And then she started to cross, and … well, she just froze in her tracks, instead of moving out of the way. I mean, I guess she must have gotten frightened because she just stopped dead, I swear.
To freeze in your tracks means to "be paralyzed with fright." And the next sentence is a clue: "I mean, I guess she must have gotten frightened because she just stopped dead, I swear."

5
E2: It was awful. (beep) I just turned white. You know, one of those heart-stopping moments …
E2: It was awful. I could feel the color draining from my face. I just turned white. You know, one of those heart-stopping moments …
When *the color drains from your face*, your blood flow is protecting your internal organs. This is a response to fright. And the next sentence is, "I just turned white" – another way to express that you are terrified.

6
E2: A chill went through my body. (beep) If you could have seen me in the mirror! It was standing straight up.
E2: A chill went through my body. My hair stood on end. If you could have seen me in the mirror! It was standing straight up.
If *your hair stands on end*, it means "you're so frightened, your hair becomes vertical." And sure enough, he then gives us a clue and says, " If you could have seen me in the mirror! It was standing straight up."
So, as you can see, if you listen carefully, you can often figure out what expressions mean from what comes next. When telling a story, speakers like to repeat themselves for emphasis!

▶ **11.11** *page 121 exercise 6B*

A: Remember that article on online dating I showed you? I want to do some vocabulary with my class, but I've identified 21 possible words and expressions!
B: A great topic, though! *How to stay safe while dating* … Let's take a look.
A: So, first, let me tell you about some of the words I didn't choose.
B: OK. You've given a lot of thought to this.
A: I have. For example, take *to bail*. It's pretty obvious it means "to leave." And students will figure that out when they insert the section titles. Then there's *strike up* a conversation. They can figure out that means "to start" when they see "walking on the beach," "seemed delightful," and "invited her to my house." What else could it possibly mean in this context?
B: You have a point. But on the other hand, *strike up* is a useful phrasal verb. And bail, or even better *bail out* could be a good informal verb to know.
A: So maybe I should let them choose their own words. For example, if they've seen them before, then they may want to look them up so they can use them in their own conversation.
B: Not a bad idea.
A: Then take *utterly*. Even if you have no idea it means "very" or "completely," just try removing it. The sentence still makes perfect sense.
B: True. You could say if you don't need the word to understand the text, keep reading.
A: And then there's stew. I left that out, too. It's obviously something to eat when you see "boiling on the stove." So students will know it's a dish with *rabbit*. And besides, it has nothing to do with dating.
B: You're pretty good at this!
A: It's really just common sense. And *head case*. Forget it. Too informal. They'll figure out it means "crazy."
B: But how will students know when a word is informal?
A: They can only guess. But the key is whether they've seen it before. Reading, of course, includes many examples of the writer's own style. Take, for example, "Does it *jar you*?" Students might not even find the verb *jar* in the dictionary because we generally say "Is it jarring?"
B: Wow, a good reason to cut down on dictionary use, isn't it?
A: Absolutely. I'm going to start by giving them just these five: *to coax, to pop up, to draw on, eligible,* and *to screen*. And I think I'll give the class some helpful hints on whether to look up words. It will be really interesting to see …

▶ **11.12** *page 122 exercise 7B*

B = Bob, A = Andrea
B: The sun is killing me.
A: Well, *someone* didn't put on sunscreen!
B: Let's go for a swim!
A: Do you want to get eaten by a shark?
B: Do I want *what*? Oh, come on, Andrea. There's nothing to worry about.
A: Nothing to worry about? You obviously didn't see the sign over there.
B: I *did* see it, but I'm sure they're just playing it safe. I mean, what are the odds?
A: Pretty high if you ask me! And with your red shorts, they'll spot you from miles away.
B: That doesn't make any sense! Sharks are color blind!
A: Color blind? They *are*? Whatever, I'm not going in the water and neither are you, Bob.
B: No, seriously, the chances are pretty slim – statistically speaking. Let me show you. Give me your phone.
A: Now?
B: Yeah, let me google something. … shark attack odds … Here, listen: "The likelihood of someone getting attacked and killed by a shark …

▶ **11.13** *page 122 exercise 7C*

B: Here, listen: "The likelihood of someone getting attacked and killed by a shark is exceedingly slim – 1 in approximately 11.5 million. There are an estimated 64 attacks each year, but few are fatal.
A: Few. Not none, so the odds might not be in our favor!
B: Look, to put it in perspective, a person is three times more likely to die in a plane crash, 30 times more likely to be killed by a dog and, are you ready for this?
A: Thirty times more likely to be hit by lightening, too. I bet it doesn't say how many sharks die from getting hit by lightening, though.
B: Hah, hah, very funny. And how about this, "The odds of a person being killed by an asteroid are 1 in 200,000, which … "
A: … means you're less likely to be killed by a shark than by an asteroid.
B: Exactly! So, let's jump in.
A: Hey, not so fast!

▶ **11.14** *page 122 exercise 7D*

B: What?
A: You can't take these numbers at face value.
B: It's written right here! The evidence is clear!
A: I think it's anything *but* clear. Look, these statistics are an average of everyone in the world, right? I mean, they divide the number of attacks by the number of people.
B: I suppose.
A: But most people don't live near shark-infested beaches, let alone go swimming where there are sharks.
B: So you're saying the odds would be higher among beach goers?
A: Exactly. Or surfers. These studies assume that any random person might be attacked, which doesn't make any sense! I mean, if you …
B: Andrea, are we really talking about statistics? Right here by the ocean, on our honeymoon?
A: I'm just trying to show you the danger is real!

Audio scripts

B: You worry too much. Come on! Have some fun!
A: I am having fun! But I want to have fun and be safe. And I want you to be safe, too.

11.17 page 124 exercise 10A

P = Professor, L = Linda, B = Brad

P: Today we're going to talk about allergies, a very serious problem. Research shows allergies affect up to 50 million people in the U.S. – that's right, almost 16 percent of the population. As many as 30 percent of adults and 40 percent of children have some kind of allergy. And allergies can be dangerous.
L: Are food allergies more dangerous than say, allergic reactions to medicines?
P: Good question, Linda. Actually, medicines cause the greatest number of fatalities each year, followed by food allergies, and then insect stings. The cause is anaphylactic shock. In fact, almost any substance the body perceives as foreign may cause it.
B: So this is ana-ph... can you spell that for us?
P: Yes, let me write it on the board: A-N-A-P-H-Y-L-A-C-T-I-C. It comes from Ancient Greek.

11.18 page 124 exercise 10B

P: As I was saying, the reaction is called "anaphylactic shock" or more technically "anaphylaxis." It's a severe allergic reaction with rapid onset.
B: Rapid ... excuse me, I didn't catch that.
P: Onset. It starts quickly.
L: That's scary! How can it be prevented?
P: That can be difficult unless you know you have an allergy. If you've had a reaction before, always carry epinephrine so you can give yourself a shot. It's what's called an antidote. It counters the effects of the allergic reaction.
B: A shot! Eww. Forget it!
P: It's better than the alternative, believe me! This is not to be taken lightly.
B: So ... uh ... what kind of symptoms might someone have?
P: Well, anaphylaxis usually attacks several systems at once – the skin, the respiratory system, the gastrointestinal system, and the heart and central nervous system. Symptoms can be varied.
B: In addition to swelling?
P: Yes, you might have hives, itching, a flushed face, swelling ... all at once.
B: Eww!
P: I know. It's not pleasant. And you could have abdominal pain and cramps, wheezing, and other breathing difficulties, headaches, or even anxiety. Some people describe a feeling of impending doom.
B: Umm, Professor Davis. I'm starting to feel nervous. Do you think we could talk about something else?
P: Yes, sure, Brad. But let me just add one more point. If you think you may have allergies, or if you've ever had a suspicious reaction, please see an allergist and get yourself tested. It could be the difference between life and ...
B: Professor Davis! May I be excused? I think I've ...

11.19 page 124 exercise 10C

B: Excuse me ...
P: Welcome back. I hope you're feeling better, Brad.
B: Yes, a little. Thanks. I'm sorry, I just got kind of nervous.
P: That's OK. I can totally understand. So, to continue, the important thing is that the symptoms of anaphylactic shock could have many other causes, an unexpected cramp, for example. That's why it's important to get to the hospital when in doubt.
L: I have cramps when I've eaten too much.
P: Don't we all! Yes, cramps are often pretty harmless, just like fatigue. But if they're severe and are accompanied by other symptoms, they could signal an allergic reaction.
L: And you might get hives from an insect bite. Itching and swelling, too – that is, even when it's not serious.
P: That's absolutely right, Linda. But these aren't normal symptoms when we eat, so if you ever have them, it's best to be on the safe side and seek medical treatment right away.
B: And couldn't a sense of impending doom or confusion be a symptom of something like a heart attack? Or just anxiety, like a panic attack?
P: Yes, it could, Brad. Again, the important thing is to be aware of symptoms in combination. What about wheezing?
L: I'd say it's also a very common symptom of asthma.
P: It is, but here, too, asthma doesn't cause hives or cramps. I can't emphasize it enough: When in doubt, it's essential to seek help, and encourage others to do the same. That's all we have time for today. Next week ...

Unit 12

12.1 page 126 exercise 1A

... which goes to show just how important it is for companies to rethink their existing culture, their way of doing business, and sometimes even their line of products. Success comes from constant innovation, so you could say many bankruptcies **stem from** fear. And innovation **is closely related to** risk and uncertainty, which many companies understandably avoid. It's not always easy for big corporations to move beyond their historical and cultural legacy and leap into the unknown. Old ways of thinking and acting can be incredibly resistant to change. But if you think about the world's most profitable and enduring brands, you know, if you think about the Apples, the Starbucks, the Hondas ... they have one thing in common: They've managed to stay ahead of the curve by constantly reinventing themselves.

12.2 page 126 exercise 1C

P = Presenter, S = Student (1–2)

P: Case in point: Microsoft. Show of hands: Who in this room owns – or has owned – a computer running on Windows? See? Lots of people. In the 80s and 90s, by selling PC software, the company became one of the world's most profitable and successful corporations, but the explosion of mobile computing has given rise to a number of new challenges. Since the mid 2000s, sales of cell phones and tablets have increased worldwide, while PC shipments have plummeted – especially desktops. So, in order to survive in the post-PC era, Microsoft has had to branch out into cloud computing and hardware development, and it seems that the company's efforts are paying off.
S1: Well, I have one of their *Surface* tablets and I think it's great.
P: Funny you should mention that! The *Surface* line had a bumpy start, but its sales eventually skyrocketed – by an impressive 117%!
S2: Erm ... I'm not sure we're living in a post-PC era. I mean, I still have a desktop, and so do some of my friends.
P: That's a good point. Maybe it's too soon to write PCs off. 3D gaming might lead to a renewed interest in high-end computers. If 3D gaming remains popular, the decline in PC sales might level off – and who knows? Sales might even rise – in the near future. It's hard to tell at this point.

12.3 page 126 exercise 1D

P: Here's another fascinating story. You're all familiar with National Geographic magazine, right? What do you associate it with?
S1: The yellow borders!
S2: Lots of beautiful photographs!
P: Exactly! National Geographic was first published in 1888 – yes, 1888 – and with its dazzling photos of wild animals, remote locations, and exotic cultures – just take a look at those pictures! – It soon became an American treasure.
S1: Wow! How can a magazine survive this long?
P: By reinventing itself, just like Microsoft. You see, in the 90s, it seems the magazine had lost of some its edge, and the number of subscribers began to **plunge** – especially young readers, who no longer found it appealing. That was when a man named John Fahey – that's F – A – H – E – Y – came on board and started with a TV channel in 2001.
S2: Oh, I love the National Geographic Channel.
P: So do I! I find it both informative and entertaining. Anyway, as expected, the TV channel **paved the way for** other innovations. For example, to keep up with the digital revolution, the company has built a very robust social media presence.
S1: I follow them on Instagram.

P: And so do dozens of millions of people! Here's something that may surprise you: National Geographic is the top non-celebrity account on Instagram, and the number of followers continues to **soar** month after month! Not only followers, but likes as well.

S2: Interesting! I'm going to check them out. What's the …

▶ **12.6** *page 128 exercises 3A and B*

Right, so in today's episode, I'm going to talk about two songs that have had a sizeable impact on the music industry – and, in some cases, on the world at large. Let me tell you a little bit about each one. The first song was written to raise money for anti-famine efforts in Ethiopia, and it was once the UK's best-selling single. I'm talking about *Do they know it's Christmas*, performed by a charity group called Band Aid, whose lineup included some of the biggest British and Irish musical acts at the time, including Bono, Phil Collins, and Sting, among dozens of other pop stars. The other song I picked for today's episode might come as a bit of surprise, but it was a tremendously influential song – and an irresistibly catchy one at that! I'm talking about Cher's comeback single *Believe*, which topped the charts in dozens of countries when it was released and went on to sell 10 million copies worldwide. *Believe* was a calculated effort. When the producers walked into the studio, their goal was to make a catchy dance tune that would appeal to both Cher's older fan base *and* to club kids, some of whom had never even heard of her! So, they had an idea: Why not take her vocals and tweak them with Auto-Tune, an audio processor that changes people's voices and, in some cases, makes them unrecognizable? To everyone's surprise, Cher didn't refuse to be "auto-tuned," and the song instantly caught on.
Now, why was each song so influential? *Believe* was such a monster hit that the Auto-Tune effect soon spread like wildfire across the music business – especially in R&B and dance music. Today, Auto-Tune – also known as the "Cher effect," has become ubiquitous in the industry, and you'd be hard pressed to find a singer who doesn't use it – at least sparingly – to correct a few imperfections here and there. Which I think is fine, really. It's as if a song were wearing make-up to look prettier. What bothers – and worries – me is that, in my opinion, today most people – regardless of talent – can take a shot at singing if they can fall back on Auto-Tune. It makes you wonder if singers are just one step away from being completely replaced by robots – or soulless zombies that are detached from their art. Now, moving on to the Band Aid song … *Do they know …?* wasn't a tune I instantly warmed up to, and I remember being underwhelmed when I first heard it. But the song eventually grew on me, maybe because of the message it was trying to get across – and the amount of money it went on to raise, of course. What's remarkable about *Do they know …?* is that it showed artists their influence could be used to bring about real change, and this eventually inspired other fundraising anthems such as *We are the world*

and *That's what friends are for*, just to name a few. The song really raised awareness of issues such as famine and hunger. Nevertheless, the biggest charity rock songs ever recorded date back to the 80s and 90s, which makes you wonder if pop and rock artists may have given up trying to make the world a better place, and, if so, why.

▶ **12.10** *page 132 exercise 7C*

Conversation 1
M = Mike, G = Gina

M: Have you ever read the book *Great Expectations*, Gina?
G: By Dickens? Yes, I have, actually – when I was around 12. It made quite an impression on me!
M: So I guess you'd say it's worth the effort? It seems to be about 500 pages.
G: I definitely think it's worth reading, Mike, yes. This book was my first exposure to life in England. A true historical novel.
M: Think I'll get a copy. You know, Jane – my girlfriend – is from London. And I'm looking for something to read on the plane when I go to San Francisco.

Conversation 2
E = Elise, M = Mike, G

E: Excuse me, do you mind if I ask you a question? What's that you're reading?
M: *Great Expectations* by Dickens. Needed something for this long flight!
E: Well, I hope you find it worth your time. Not only is it long, but it's also depressing.
M: Oh, I know, but I'm sure it will be worth it. My girlfriend's from London, and I want to understand her family better.
E: Gee, not sure you'll do that by reading Dickens! Don't you think it might be more worthwhile to take a trip there, instead?
M: Hmm … I guess you have a point. It's a little cheaper this way, though.

▶ **12.11** *page 133 exercise 8C*

Conversation 1
A: Hey, Jim, come here!
B: Why?
A: Big news! I don't want to yell across the room.
B: OK.
A: They promoted me to manager!! (beep) I got promoted to manager!!

Conversation 2
A: What a great hotel! I think I'm going to dive off our balcony into the pool down there.
B: Are you out of your mind? The water is only four feet deep. You could hurt yourself! (beep) You could get hurt!
A: Maybe you're right. It's just that it looks like so much fun, though.

Conversation 3
A: What's wrong? Why are you holding your arm like that?
B: This guy twisted it in the subway! (beep) I got it twisted in the subway!
A: Huh? What do you mean?

B: Well, he was mad at me because he thought I was blocking the door and …
A: That's awful, Luke! Are you sure you're OK?
Conversation 4
A: What are you doing, Marcy?
B: I'm looking to see if we can buy a dog.
A: A dog? Are you nuts? They're not allowed here! You want to cause them to evict us? (beep) You want to get us evicted?
B: They're not? Wow, that's so unreasonable! I had no idea.

▶ **12.12** *page 134 exercise 9A*

P = Professor, M = Michael,

P: Good morning, everyone. You may find my lecture today comical given my name – yes, I know it's Orwell – but rest assured, there's no connection whatsoever to the famous novel, 1984. But the topic is …
M: A utopian society?
P: Yes! You guessed it. We're going to talk about what the elements of an ideal or utopian society might be. That is, the exact opposite of Orwell's totalitarian society. Let's start by brainstorming. What's the very first word that comes to mind when I say "utopia"?

▶ **12.13** *page 134 exercise 9B*

P = Professor, J = Jennifer, M = Michael, O = Oscar

P: What's the very first word that comes to mind when I say "utopia"? Jennifer?
J: I'd say "fun." I know a lot of people think of serious concepts like "democracy" or "justice," but to me, a true utopia makes life just enjoyable and worth living.
M: But wouldn't you say we need a minimum level of serious commitment, too, for a utopia? I mean by government. Access to the basics for a comfortable standard of living – food, education, housing, medical care – don't these need to be universal first?
O: Yeah, and what about "respect" as in "respect for our planet"? We have to conserve resources, reduce pollution … I know it sounds boring to say we need to be "green," but we do.
J: Well, I have no doubt whatsoever that those things will come, too. You see, technological changes will allow us to fix things.
P: Jennifer, could you explain what you mean more specifically?
J: Sure! I read this article the other day and, for one thing, the housing shortage will disappear. You know why? Building will not only go up, but down.
M: Huh? How can we simultaneously be building more and less?
J: No, what I mean is new housing will be built underground. Like 25 storeys under.
P: That's not so far fetched, actually, Jennifer. In Coober Pedy, Australia, for example, residents prefer to live in caves because of the heat. And housing is, in fact, built underground. It gets up to 45 degrees centigrade there.
O: Wow, that's cool. Or maybe I should say, "That's hot"!

Audio scripts

J: That's a good one. Anyway, you know what else? The food shortage will be gone, too. You'll just download your favorite chef's recipe to a 3D printer. Progress will ensure that around the world, everyone is connected.
M: And what about our environment? As Oscar mentioned?
J: No problem ... everyone will have a private drone to get around and they'll be powered with solar energy, so there won't be any emissions whatsoever where we live.
P: Hmm ... What do you think, Michael?

▶ 12.14 *page 134 exercise 9C*

P: These are all very interesting ideas, but this does all sound very futuristic, doesn't it? Is there any evidence whatsoever that any of these changes might actually come about?
J: Well, don't we already see some of them starting? There's been a sharp rise in building up, so why not down, too?
P: Yes, cities have already shown success in building vertically instead of horizontally. So we know it's possible to fit more people. And the thing about hunger, well, hasn't the number of people who are starving been falling steadily? The current statistics show the number of hungry people in the world has dropped to a little under 800 million, which is approximately 200 million fewer than in the early 90s. So, yes, it's a significant drop, but the situation is still pretty catastrophic. The evidence over the last 25 years shows that world hunger cannot be eliminated quickly.
J: But think how easy food production will be once 3D food takes off.
M: But can we ensure that the poor will have access to 3D food? It seems to me that there's more to it than meets the eye.
J: You're such a pessimist!
M: No, I'm not. I'm a realist.
P: For the next class, here's what I'd like you do ... Ask yourself: "Is the world getting better or worse?" Look at the question from different angles, do some research, and write an essay expressing your views.
J: Cool.

Review 6 (Units 11–12)

▶ R6.1 *page 136 exercises 1A and B*

M = Melinda, P = Phil

M: Thief! Thief! Can you believe it? He snatched my purse! I just got my purse stolen! That ...
P: Let's go after him!
M: That's dangerous, Phil. But ... He could have just asked if he needed money.
P: You might say this was easier!
M: Very funny. Looks like I might as well forget about ever seeing my iPhone again!
P: You might want to file a report right away. The sooner, the better.
M: Guess I'll have to. As if I had nothing better to do!
P: Some guy ran off with my wallet once on this very corner. I got it taken right here! That was a couple of years ago, but still ... this might be a bad corner.
M: You did? So where are the police around here? What's the matter? They won't come here because they might have to work too hard?
P: Well, maybe you'll get your bag back if we file a report. It shouldn't be that hard to locate it. Do you have "find my phone" activated?
M: I don't know. I have no idea. All I know is I'm locked out. And now I'm going to miss an important meeting and have to call a locksmith. Not to mention the credit cards, the phone, and ...
P: I know, Melinda. It's a total drag. But really, I think your chances of recovering it might be good.
M: Yeah, right. He could have at least dropped the bag after he took the money! He ...
P: Well, I guess you could say he wasn't exactly thinking about you.

Song lyrics notes and activities

As a general rule, elicit all you can about …
- the artist, their nationality, reasons for being famous, personal life, previous / subsequent hit;
- the song itself: year / video / other uses in soundtracks, TV shows, adverts, etc.;
- the link to the lesson: whether it's lexical, topical or grammatical, and sts' opinion of it / the tune / music / artist;
- the meaning / message behind the lines / song, who the artist(s) might be singing to who, etc.;
- how it sounds: exploit the audio / video whenever you can access it.

Always encourage the class to try to sing the lines and notice elements of pronunciation within them—they're great models for stress, weak forms, unpronounced consonants, elision, links, etc., and can be referred to in order to correct mispronunciation, incorrect use, etc.

Similar to the **Common mistake** exercises, it's often a nice idea to board the song line at the start of class with words missing, an error to correct, extra words to delete, etc. to highlight a potential error they might make with target language from the lesson. Have / Help sts correct it and leave it up throughout the lesson as a reference.

Lastly, if you—or they—don't know the song line we've chosen, or think it dull, get them to suggest a better alternative they do like that links to the lesson topic / language. The aim is always to find links which help sts better remember useful language from the lesson.

1.1

Song line: 'Cause the players gonna play … And the haters gonna hate … Baby I'm just gonna shake … Shake it off. Shake it off

Song: *Shake it off*, released in 2014

Artist: Taylor Swift (American)

Lesson link: phrasal verbs with *off*

Notes: A dance-pop hit, marking Taylor's permanent departure from her earlier country style. It's about how she's learnt to live with and simply shake off all the negative comments about her. The video, shows people expressing their identity through different dance styles, making reference to pop icons like Beyoncé, Lady Gaga and American rappers.

Before 2A, get sts to sing the song line, repeating the words cued by the three dots (play, play, play, etc.) and elicit the song title and artist info from them. Elicit the meaning of 'to shake something / somebody off', mime / elicit a mime of its literal meaning (to shake until something falls off) and provide sts with more examples, e.g. *I need to shake this cold off before work tomorrow* (get rid of), *The thief tried to shake off the police by running into a crowded market* (lose).

1.2

Song line: Some people want diamond rings, Some just want everything, But everything means nothing, If I ain't got you, yeah

Song title: *If I ain't got you*, released in 2011

Artist: Alicia Keys (American)

Lesson link: subject-verb agreement

Notes: In Alicia Keys' words, the song is about "how material things don't feed the soul." It was inspired by the death of American singer Aaliyah in 2001.

After 5A, check if sts recognize the song line, and get them to explain the sentiment and who might be singing to whom. Then, board the line: *But everything means nothing* and ask: *Can you say "Everything mean"? Why not? Is it the same in your language?*

Board a few more blanked lines for sts to complete, e.g.

1. *I need your love. I need your time. When everything ___ (be) wrong, You make it right.* (Calvin Harris & Ellie Goulding)
2. *Nobody ___ (see), nobody ___ (know). We are a secret.* (Zara Larsson)
3. *Every little thing she ___ (do) is magic. Everything she ___ (do) just turns me on.* (Police)
4. *'Cause everybody ___ (cry), And everybody ___ (hurt) sometimes.* (REM)
5. *Dancing in the moonlight. Everybody ___ (feel) warm and bright* (Toploader)

(Answers: 1 's 2 sees, knows 3 does, does 4 cries, hurts 5 's feeling)

1.3

Song line: Take you with me if I can. Been dreaming of this since a child. I'm on top of the world

Song: *On top of the world*, released in 2013

Artist: Imagine Dragons (American)

Lesson link: figurative expressions

Notes: An upbeat song featured on the video game FIFA 13 soundtrack, as well as on its rival game Pro Evolution Soccer 2013. The band's breakthrough single from the album *Night Visions* with a video about conspiracy theories, for example, that that the 1969 moon landing was a hoax, with footage directed by Stanley Kubrick.

While checking answers for 7A, link the expression "to stay on top of things" to the song line, "on top of the world". Explore more expressions with "top", e.g. over the top, to top it all, blow one's top, at the top of one's lungs, top of the line.

Song activities

1.4

Song line: I'm giving you up, I've forgiven it all. You set me free
Song: *Send my love (to your new lover)*, released in 2016
Artist: Adele (British)
Lesson link: using perfect tenses and *set*
Notes: This is Adele's first upbeat, danceable song to top the charts. In the singer's words, it's a "happy you're gone" story about an ex-boyfriend. Adele is well-known for past-relationship reflections in her lyric writing and millions of fans seem to identify with her.

After sts read **Uses of *set*** in 8B, draw their attention to the song line. Elicit the song title, artist, what they know about / think of her, if they can remember the video, and see if they can sing it with the correct links: *you‿up, forgiven‿it‿all*, plus the next line: *we both know we ain't kids no more*. Perhaps you can elicit the chorus too: *Send my love to your new lover. Treat her better. We've gotta let go of all of our ghosts*. Ask: *What's the song about? Is she happy about the end of the relationship? Why / Why not?* Focus on the verb *set* and elicit which verb tense is being used in the song. Remind sts *set* is an irregular verb and, elicit which tense it is here (from the context, it's most likely to refer to the past tense). If appropriate, hold a class vote on their favorite Adele song.

1.5

Song line: When I met you in the summer, To my heartbeat sound, We fell in love, As the leaves turned brown
Song: *Summer*, released in 2014
Artist: Calvin Harris (British)
Lesson link: use of *as*
Notes: A song about the euphoria of a summer romance, its video about a desert drag race followed by a party has over one billion YouTube views.

Before **12A**, board this skeleton and play part of the song for sts to remember the blanked words in pairs. We suggest you include the next two lines as there are further examples of *as*: W___ I m___ y___ in t___ s___, To my h___ s___. We f___ in l___, a___ the l___ t___ b___. And we c___ b___ t___ baby a___ l___ a___ s___ are b___. (And we could be together baby As long as skies are blue)

Focus on the use of *as* in *as long as*. Elicit a meaning / synonym (*while*) and more examples from sts, e.g. *As long as you love me, We could be starving, We could be homeless, We could be broke* (Justin Bieber, 2012).

2.1

Song line: You say you want a leader, But you can't seem to make up your mind, I think you better close it, And let me guide you to the purple rain,'
Song: *Purple Rain*, released in 1984
Artist: Prince (American)
Lesson link: making decisions
Notes: Prince's signature song, it was also soundtrack to the film *Purple Rain*, a rock musical drama in which he starred. Prince once explained in an interview that, being purple the combination of red and blue, 'purple rain' meant blood in the (blue) skies, and that the song was mainly about his personal love and faith in Jesus Christ. Prince was a Jehovah's Witness and gospel themes permeated some of his work.

Before **1D**, ask: *Are you good at making decisions? Do you take long to make up your mind?* In pairs, sts ask and answer *What's the most difficult decision you've ever made? Did you think you made the right choice?* Classcheck a few answers. If possible, play the song line as a dictogloss, as it's very quick and good practice of listening for word segmentation! Then, focus on the song line and check if sts know the song and artist. Ask: *What decision do you think Prince is talking about? Can you sing the chorus? Were you shocked by his death?*

2.2

Song line: Home where my thought's escaping. Home where my music's playing, Home where my love lies waiting, Silently for me Song
Song: *Homeward Bound*, released in 1966
Artist: Simon & Garfunkel (American)
Notes: Written by singer Paul Simon while he toured the UK in 1964, felt homesick and was missing his girlfriend. American duo Simon & Garfunkel split in 1970; henceforth Paul Simon began a successful solo career as guitarist, singer and songwriter

Warm-up. Set the lesson context with the song line. Board a blanked version of the lines, e.g. _____ where my thought's _____ . _____ where my music's _____ , Home where my _____ lies _____ , _____ for me. Tell sts about the song artist and background. Play part of the song only for sts to complete. Paircheck. Re-play, if necessary. Classcheck. Elicit how he feels and why. If time / for homework, ask sts to write their own song line about "home" and / or Google their own song lines.

2.3

Song line: What doesn't kill you makes you stronger. Stand a little taller. Doesn't mean I'm lonely when I'm alone.
Song: *What doesn't kill you*, released in 2011
Artist: Kelly Clarkson (American)
Lesson link: being alone
Notes: Title track from her fifth album, the line "what doesn't kill you makes you stronger" is a common proverb in many languages and cultures. In the 20th Century, it was attributed to German philosopher Frederic Nietzsche.

After 5B, have sts read the song line. Check if they can sing or hum the melody of this dance anthem, and perhaps play the video. Ask: *What's the message of the song?* (empowerment). Focus on the last line, "doesn't mean I'm lonely when I'm alone." Elicit the difference between the two adjectives and ask sts how the meaning would change if you swapped them (i.e. doesn't mean I'm alone when I'm lonely). Ask: *How often do / don't you feel lonely when you're alone? Do you like being completely alone, offline, unreachable?*

2.4

Song line: So many tears I've cried. So much pain inside. But baby it ain't over 'til it's over
Song: *It ain't over 'til it's over*, released in 1991
Artist: Lenny Kravitz (American)
Lesson link: *so many* and *so much*
Notes: The ballad made Lenny Kravitz a mainstream artist, topping charts worldwide. Later, Kravitz won a Grammy award for Best male rock vocal performance every year from 1999 to 2002, and now holds the record for most consecutive Grammy wins in the same category.

Before 8A, get sts to read the song line. Check if they know the melody, if not sing or play part of the song to the class. Highlight the silent *t* in *ain't*, and any other examples they may have seen or heard of this increasingly common slang form of isn't. Focus on and elicit rules for *so many tears* vs *so much pain* in the song. Encourage sts to contrast the target language to their mother tongue equivalents. Ask: *Are "tears" countable in (L1)? How about "pain"? What word(s) do you have for "so many" and "so much"?*

2.5

Song line: There are places I remember all my life, though some have changed
Song: *In my life*, released in 1965
Artist: Beatles (British)
Lesson link: comparing places you have lived
Notes: Lennon first wrote this autobiographical song as a long poem, inspired by a bus route he used to take as a child in Liverpool. The handwritten original is in the British Library in London, and can be seen on the Internet. In 2000, Mojo magazine voted it the best song of all time.

Before 11A, play the song line. See if you can elicit the next line: *Some forever, not for better, some have gone and some remain*. Ask: *What does it make you think of? Do you remember your first home? What was it like? Have you been back there? Has it changed? Or: If you've always lived in the same home, how has it changed through the years?* If time, ask sts to *Think of one place you'll always remember* and describe it to a partner.

3.1

Song line: Jigeumbuteo gal dekkaji gabolkka, Oppa Gangnam Style. Gangnam Style
Song: *Gangnam Style*, released in 2012
Artist: Psy (South Korea singer / rapper, real name Park Jae-sang)
Lesson link: foreign languages
Notes: Gangnam Style was the first video to hit one billion views on YouTube. It went viral in 2012, forced YouTube into an upgrade after it broke the website's hit counter and is nearing three billion views! Gangnam literally means "south of the river" and is a posh district in the Korean capital Seoul, with a heated nightlife. The song mocks "Gangnam lifestyle", that is, the excessive pursuit of image, good looks, success and affluence. The line Jigeumbuteo gal dekkaji gabolkka would literally translate as "Now let's go until the end".

As a warm-up, play part of the music video to sts and check what they know about it. Ask: *Why was this video so successful / popular? Can any of you do the horse riding-esque dance? Do you understand the words in Korean? Does it make any difference if you don't understand them? What other songs have you listened or danced to without understanding what the lyrics were about?*

Song activities

3.2

Song line: I'm gonna raise a fuss, I'm gonna raise a holler. About a workin' all summer just to try to earn a dollar
Song: *Summertime Blues*, released in 1958
Artist: Eddie Cochran (American)
Lesson link: slang expressions that are no longer used
Notes: A rock 'n roll classic, about youngsters being held back by society / their parents. His "summer time blues" are the hardships summer can bring instead of the usual joys. Cochran was 19 when he recorded this but died two years later in a traffic collision.

Use after 5C as another example pre-Make it Personal, or to finish the lesson. Read / Sing the line to see if anybody recognizes it. If not, dictate the following line (the chorus) a word at a time. Enjoy their guesses as to what comes next! *Sometimes – I – wonder –what – I'm – gonna – do – but – there – ain't – no – cure – for – the –summertime – blues*. If possible, have an audio / video version ready so they can see / hear it.

Try to elicit the meaning of "raise a fuss / raise a holler" (to yell, shout, or complain). Cochran uses it to suggest making a noisy commotion about working conditions / salary. Elicit the lesson link (It's an old phrase no longer used) and how it's said now: *to make a fuss, to holler*.

Ask: *Have you ever had the summertime blues? What other great rock n roll songs do you know?*

3.3

Song line: Drench yourself in words unspoken. Live your life with arms wide open. Today is where your book begins. The rest is still unwritten
Song: *Unwritten*, released in 2004
Artist: Natasha Bedingfield (British)
Lesson link: words and self-expression
Notes: A number 1 hit in the UK, the song talks about self-belief and living life to the fullest. It was used as the theme song for MTV show *The Hills* and is often played at graduations.

After 7A, have sts read the song line, interpret what it means, then include it in 7C, as part of the quotes you do / don't agree with activity. Elicit the meaning of drench yourself via a common example, e.g. *I got absolutely drenched in the rain as I had no umbrella*.

Help sts to interpret what she means (Each day is a blank page, it's up to you to fill it.). Ask: *Is she singing to a specific person or is it a more general anthem?* (latter) *Is she optimistic?* (yes) *Do you agree with her?*

The song has a stirring chorus, which a class who are into singing ought to enjoy, as this is becoming a karaoke classic

3.4

Song line: And I promise you kid I'll give so much more than I get. I just haven't met you yet
Song: *Haven't met you yet*, released in 2009
Artist: Michael Bublé (Canadian)
Lesson link: 10C item 2
Notes: Originally a jazz crooner, this very uplifting pop song from his fourth album, *Crazy Love*, took Bublé to mainstream audiences worldwide. He's now sold about 60 million albums. It's about starting again and falling in love again after a bad break up.

Use before or after 10C to help sts associate with and elicit more about Michael Bublé. If possible, bring in a photo and / or show the video. He's a naturalized Italian and has won four Grammys!

Ask sts to read and try to interpret the line. Ask: *Who's he singing to?* (a future partner) *Why is he promising so much?* (He's learnt from past mistakes.) *Why hasn't he met her?* (He's on the rebound and just starting to look for the new love of his life).

3.5

Song line: There's nothing you can do that can't be done … It's easy. All you need is love
Song: *All you need is love*, released in 1967
Artist: The Beatles (British)
Lesson link: accomplishing something if you try
Notes: The song was released on the first live TV broadcast in history, watched by 400 million people in 25 countries, on June 25th 1967.

As a books closed warm-up, board: *You can do anything if you have …*

Elicit and board sts' guesses on how to complete the sentence, e.g. *enthusiasm, determination, energy, enough luck / money, powerful friends*. Then, give them a clue: *The answer I'm after is the chorus of a famous Beatles song* to see if anyone can come up with love.

Books open. Sts read, and hopefully some may be able to sing the line. With a class old enough to know The Beatles, ask: *Which Beatle sang it?* (John Lennon). *Who was your favorite Beatle?* Then ask if they agree with the sentiment in the line, have heard it before, like it, etc.

Elicit / Highlight the weak pronunciation of can (/kən/) compared to the negative (/kænt/). If time, a fun activity to finish the lesson / Unit could be to watch a video of the whole song, and sing it as a class.

Song activities

4.1

Song line: Never forget where you've come here from. Never pretend that it's all real. Someday soon this will all be someone else's dream
Song: *Never forget*, released in 1995
Artist: Take That (British)
Lesson link: dreams
Notes: Singer / writer Gary Barlow's reminder to the band, which included Robbie Williams, when they were about to break up, that they should remember their humble roots and be grateful for their massive success. Their turn "living the dream" was almost over. This chorus is played at Twickenham, London, the world's largest rugby stadium, whenever England's rugby team score.

Use after 1E (or instead of 1E3 if your sts are unable to search online in class). Have sts read and try to remember / sing the line. Elicit all you can about the band, any memories the song brings them and try to elicit why the singer might have written it to the others. The video shows photos of the band as kids and footage of them performing. If you're able to show this, pick up on the theme of childhood dreams, rags to riches, and find out what your sts dreamt about / aspired to as children.

4.2

Song line: Never in my wildest dreams, Did I think someone could care about me
Song: *Wildest dreams*, released in 2012
Artist: Brandy (American)
Lesson link: emphatic inversion
Notes: A beautiful introspective, beat-driven ballad reflecting on falling in love so strongly that it's almost too good to be true. Second single on her sixth album, *Two Eleven*, the video shows her performing it onstage to cheering fans.

Before 4A, focus on the song line, see if anybody knows or can sing it, or the next line *Not just the way you love me*. Elicit guesses as to why it's in the lesson. Sts might come up with the lesson title (not believing what you're told). Focus on the inversion: *Is it a question?* (No) *Why does she use a question form?* (for emphasis), then go into the grammar in 4A. If sts enjoy ballads, you might want to play the chorus to them, to help hook and remember the grammar.

4.3

Song line: But then they sent me away to teach me how to be sensible. Logical, responsible, practical
Song: *Logical song*, released in 1979
Artist: Supertramp (British)
Lesson link: illogical vs. logical thinking
Notes: A song about how the innocence / wonder of childhood quickly gives way to worry / cynicism kids learn to be "responsible adults", i.e. that logic can restrict creativity and passion.

Warm up. Use before asking the lesson question title, as it will help sts think about what is / isn't (il)logical. Focus on the line and see if anyone recognizes / can sing it. Elicit the pronunciation of the four adjectives and pronunciation pattern they illustrate (stress the syllable before the suffixes *-ible* and *-ical*). Elicit as many other examples as they can think of. If teaching Romance language speakers, ask which one is a false friend (they often confuse *sensible* and *sensitive*).

Elicit what they think the song might be about, who *they* are (adults), *me* (*a child*), why this happens and if they think that all the logic imposed on us by adults / general education is a good thing.

4.4

Song line: I don't wanna close my eyes, I don't wanna fall asleep. 'Cause I'd miss you, baby, and I don't want to miss a thing
Song: *Don't wanna miss a thing*, released in 1998
Artist: Aerosmith
Lesson link: our eyes and our emotions
Notes: This rousing ballad was the soundtrack theme to 1998 film *Armageddon*, starring Bruce Willis and Ben Affleck. Singer Steve Tyler's daughter, Liv Tyler, acts in it. Aerosmith's first Billboard number one hit after 28 years on the U.S. rock n' roll scene!

Before 7D, focus on the song line and ask sts to analyze the pronunciation of the letter s in it. Which are /s/ and /z/? Elicit the difference between 'close' verb /kloʊz/ and 'close' adjective /kloʊs/. (Answers I don't wanna close /z/ my eyes /z/, I don't wanna fall asleep /s/. 'Cause /z/ I'd miss /s/ you, baby, and I don't want to miss /s/ a thing)

Ask sts to interpret who's singing to who, where and why. If possible, get them to sing it as dramatically as they can, share any feelings about Aerosmith and / or the song itself, and show the poster for or an extract from the film. If time allows, this is one of the songs we'd recommend you to consider singing right through, as it's easy and dramatic.

Song activities

4.5

Song line: (Freedom!) I won't let you down. (Freedom!) I will not give you up
Song: *Freedom '90*, released in 1990
Artist: George Michael (British-Greek)
Lesson link: the value of freedom
Notes: Real name Georgios Kyriacos Panayiotou, the music video topped the MTV charts, casting the most prominent top models of the time. The song is referring to Michael's past success with Wham!, yet also shows a new side of himself as a new man, who is more cynical about the music business than he had been before. Michael refused to appear in the video and allowed a group of supermodels to appear instead.

As the warm-up, focus on the song line to see if they can sing it / know song title, artist, year. Revise the meaning of *let someone down* (disappoint), and other words they may know ending with the suffix *-dom*, e.g. nouns: *boredom*, *kingdom*, *random*, *stardom*, *wisdom*, and the adverb *seldom*. Elicit interpretation of the line to see if they can find the link to the lesson question title and topic of ex-criminals being given their freedom. Board the questions: *How would you feel on your day of release from prison? What would you do first? Is there anything you would risk going to jail for?* In pairs, take turns asking and answering then move into the lesson title: *Would you hire a former criminal? Would the type of crime make any difference for you? What if the former criminal was family to you?*

5.1

Song line: Yeah, I know, that I let you down. Is it to late to say sorry now?
Song: *Sorry*, released in 2015
Artist: Justin Bieber
Lesson link: failure; letting someone down
Notes: Justin Bieber's first number 1 hit in the year of 2015 – out of 4 from the same album (*Purpose*). He's apologizing to a lost love and asking for a second chance.

After 3E, books closed, wrap up the lesson with the song line. If time, cut up and give the sts in groups a scrambled version of the line, or just scramble it on the board to re-order according to what they know / remember. Open books or play it to check answers. Elicit the lesson link (let sb down), opinions of Justin Bieber and his music, In pairs, sts discuss: *How often do you say sorry to people? When did you last say sorry? Who was it to? What had you done? Did it work?*

5.2

Song line: All is quiet on New Year's Day. A world in white gets underway. I want to be with you, Be with you night and day
Song: *New Year's Day*, released in 1983
Artist: U2
Lesson link: New Year's Day
Notes: U2's first big single, written about the Polish Solidarity Movement, led by activist Lech Walesa, who fought for the end of strict communist rule in Poland in the 1980's. These are the opening lines and talk about a new beginning.

Warm up. Use the song to explore the topic of New Year. Ask: *What do / don't you usually do on New Year's Eve? And on New Year's Day*. Then go into the song line. Interpret / Elicit feelings about the lyric. Ask: *How quiet / lively is New Year's morning in your town? Have you ever seen snow? What does get "underway" mean?* (begin e.g. a meeting / journey / adventure). Encourage sts to find connected speech features and, drill pronunciation: All_is quiet, on_New Year's Day, a world_in_white gets_underway, I want_to be with_you night_and_day. Ask: *Do you know the song chorus?* (I will be with you again). *Which was your best ever New Year's Eve / most successful resolution?*

5.3

Song line: When you try your best, but you don't succeed. When you get what you want, but not what you need
Song: *Fix you*, released in 2002
Artist: Coldplay (British)
Lesson link: effort and not being successful
Notes: Second single from the album *X & Y* about true love, helping in someone's time of need, and learning from your mistakes. Written about Gwyneth Paltrow's father's passing away, when the actress was still married to singer Chris Martin. Used as an anthem by several sports teams, e.g. the LA Kings. The video shows Martin walking around London.

After 6C, get sts to read the song line and elicit feelings about the words, music and the band. Try to elicit the chorus (*Lights will guide you home, And ignite your bones, And I will try to fix you*). Then focus on "succeed". Elicit more words with the same root onto the board: *succeed*, *success*, *(un)successful*, *(un)successfully*, and highlight the stress and consonant doubling. Ask: *When have you tried your best, but not succeeded? Have you ever got what you want, but not what you needed?*

Song activities

5.4

Song line: You and I should ride the coast and wind up in our favorite coats just miles away
Song: *The day we caught the train*, released in 1996
Artist: Ocean Colour Scene (British)
Lesson link: phrasal verb *wind up*
Notes: '90s classic, 'Beatles-esque' indie rock ballad with a catchy "Oh oh la la" chorus from the band's second and post popular album, *Moseley Shoals*. Based on The Who's cult film *Quadraphenia*, it talks about the day the main mod character, Jimmy, caught the train back to the coast (Brighton) to revisit his past glories, only to end up totally deceived and suicidal. The coats referred to are the parkas worn by scooter riding mods in the 60s.

While checking answers for 8B, link the verb *wind up* to the song line. See if anybody knows the line / band and try to elicit the chorus. Explore the uses of "wind" as in *wind* /wɪnd/ (noun), to *wind something up* /waɪnd/ (= to close or end an activity), to *wind somebody up* (= UK: to annoy somebody, US: to make somebody excited), past 'wound' /waʊnd/. Ask sts to write down a few example sentences of their own with the vocabulary from 8B. Paircheck. Classcheck.

5.5

Song line: It's all over the front page. You give me road rage
Song: *Road rage*, released in 1998
Artist: Catatonia (British)
Lesson link: bad drivers
Notes: A rock ballad about the trial of Tracie Andrews who, in 1996, killed her boyfriend Lee Harvey, stabbing him 30 times with a penknife. She told police it was a road rage attack and even appealed on TV to find his killer. But in 1998 she was found guilty of murder.

Do as a warm-up to the lesson topic. Divide the class into small teams and board the words cage and courage as column heads. Elicit the pronunciation of the -age endings /eɪdʒ/ and /ɪdʒ/ then give sts two minutes to brainstorm words for each column. Feedback awarding one point per word each and two points for any original word no other group has, provided they get the pronunciation and spelling right and can explain the meaning.
(Possible answers: **Cage:** age, page, rage, sage, stage, wage, teenage, engage, outrage. **Courage:** manage, (dis)advantage, encourage, shortage, storage, sausage, marriage, carriage, bridge, fridge)

Focus on the song line to see if anyone knows / can sing it. Elicit anything they know or imagine about it. If none know it, get them to guess if the singer is male or female and the context. If possible, play the lines to check, and get them to mimic her rolling "r"s in road rage. Ask: *Do you like the song / Cerys Matthews' voice? Have you ever experienced or heard of cases of road rage?*

6.1

Song line: I got a shelf full of books and most of my teeth. A few pairs of socks and a door with a lock
Song: *Pencil full of lead*, released in 2009
Artist: Paolo Nutini (British)
Lesson link: reading paper books (and not electronic ones)
Notes: A lively song, a great chorus and a distinctive "vintage" trumpet melody all worth playing in class. It's about feeling grateful for and being content with what you do have in life, and not taking things for granted.

After 1F, focus on the song line and check if sts know the song / artist. Share the facts above with the whole class. If appropriate, explore / revise the differences in usage between *have got / got* and get sts to come up with similar lines about simple things they (have) got, e.g. *I got a roof over my head*. If time, explore the full song lyric.

In small groups, sts discuss: *Some people say you can tell a lot about a person by looking at their bookshelf (or lack of one these days). Do you agree? Do you (or your parents) have a bookshelf at home? What are most titles about? Have you bought books and then never read them?* Classcheck.

6.2

Song line: I'm out of touch, I'm out of luck, I'll pick you up when you're getting down
Song: *Lego house*, released in 2011
Artist: Ed Sheeran (British)
Lesson link: using *out of*
Notes: Lego house is a metaphor for a relationship. "I'm gonna pick up the pieces and build a Lego house, if things go wrong, we can knock it down." The video includes Rupert Grint of Harry Potter fame as an obsessive fan.

Focus on the line and elicit all you can about the song / title / artist / melody. Ask: *What's the link to the lesson? (out of) Can anyone sing it? Did you use to / Do your kids play with Lego? What's you favorite Ed Sheeran song?* For fun, and to help consolidate meaning of out of and the phrasal verbs in the line, elicit what the opposite line would be from sts (*I'm in touch, I'm in luck, I'll put / bring you down when you're feeling up!*).

Song activities

6.3

Song line: And baby, you're all that I want, when you're lyin' here in my arms. I'm findin' it hard to believe, We're in heaven.
Song: *Heaven*, released in 1984
Artist: Brian Adams (Canadian)
Lesson link: expression with *heaven*
Notes: A power ballad, in 2002, it was re-recorded by DJ Sammy, whose dance version was very popular in the U.S. and UK. In Adams' video, a guy gets pulled over for drink driving close to a Bryan Adams gig. The girl he was driving ditches him, goes to the show, and meets Adams.

After finishing the "Heaven" short story, focus on the line and obvious link. Elicit all you can about the song / artist / melody, and see if any of them are old enough to have any memories associated with it. Ask: *What's he finding hard to believe?* (the heavenly feeling of being in love) *What's the most romantic song you know? What's your idea of heaven?* Give examples yourself first to get them going, e.g. *Staying at home all day binge watching a great TV series, lying on a deserted beach, hanging out with great friends.*

6.4

Song line: Near, far, wherever you are. I believe that the heart does go on
Song: *My heart will go on*, released in 1997
Artist: Celine Dion (Canadian)
Lesson link: using auxiliaries as rejoinders
Notes: Written for the film *Titanic*, this became Dion's biggest selling song, top selling single of 1998, and won the 1998 Oscar for Best Song From A Film and four Grammys. *The heart going on* refers to the 100-year old survivor, Rose, looking back over her life and shot-lived love affair with the drowned

Before 8A, board the song line with this error: *Near, far, wherever you are. I believe that the hot dogs go on*. See if sts recognize and can correct it. If necessary, give a clue (1998, the film *Titanic*, Celine Dion). Ideally play the video for sts to sing along. Share opinions of the film / song / singer. Highlight the errors and see if they know of any other commonly misheard lyrics. Leave the corrected version on the board for reference for the rest of the class to help sts with emphatic inversion. Point to it as a prompt for self-correction when you hear mistakes either of conjugation or omission of the emphatic form.

6.5

Song line: In my dreams I have a plan. If I got me a wealthy man, I wouldn't have to work at all
Song: *Money*, released in 1976
Artist: Abba (Swedish)
Lesson link: a song from the musical *Mamma Mia*
Note: Follow up single to *Dancing Queen*, the song deals with being poor in a rich man's world, sung by a woman who, despite hard work, can barely make ends meet and so dreams of a well-off man.

After 9D, use / play the song (line) and establish the link (Abba / the musical poster).

From the line, elicit all you can about the melody / chorus (*Money, money, money must be funny, in a rich man's world*). Elicit the following line, which leads into the chorus, via a numbered hangman, a word at a time:

1 ___ 2 ___ 3 ___ 4 ___ 5 ___ 6 ___ 7 ___

In teams, sts have to guess a word at a time (not letters but full words), scoring a point for each correctly guessed word, and two points for the contraction (*I'd*). Give clues to help as necessary, e.g. the last word rhymes with *all*. (Answer: 1 I'd, 2 fool, 3 around, 4 and, 5 have, 6 a, 7 ball).

Elicit what sts know about Abba / their music / history. Ask: *Do you agree with the chorus? Would you ever marry for money? Would you be happy not working, living off someone else?*

7.1

Song line: Isn't it ironic … don't you think? It's like rain on your wedding day. It's a free ride when you've already paid
Song: *Isn't it ironic?*, released in 1995
Artist: Alanis Morrisette (Canadian)
Lesson link: getting married (life stages)
Notes: Third single from third album, *Jagged Little Pill*, ironically, the events she lists (e.g. a traffic jam when you're already late), aren't really 'irony' (use of words to convey the opposite of their literal meaning). In 1996, it won MTV Video Awards for Best Female, Best Editing, and Best New Artist.

Do after 2C. Elicit all you can from the **Song line:** melody, singer, song / album title, etc. Encourage sts to suggest other 'ironical' things, e.g. the next line from the song *It's like good advice that you just didn't take*. Ask: *Have you ever paid for something which you could have got for nothing?* If you choose to play it, highlight the silent *t* in *Isn't it ironic … don't* and elicit other examples from song lines they know (most of them as final *t* are virtually always silent or elided). Then explore the lesson link (weddings): *Have you ever been to wedding / party / event seriously affected by the weather? What's the best / worst wedding you've been to? How do you imagine / remember your own wedding?*

Song activities

7.2

Song line: Wherever you go, whatever you do, I will be right here waiting for you
Song: *Right here waiting*, released in 1998
Artist: Richard Marx (American)
Lesson link: future continuous
Notes: People often associate this classic ballad with Bryan Adams. Marx wrote it as a love letter to his wife, actress Cynthia Rhodes, when she was away shooting a film. In 2013, Spotify UK named it their most popular love song.

Do as lead in to 4A. If possible, cut up / scramble the song line for small groups to order from memory, books closed, then open to check. Elicit the lesson link (the tense), artist and anything they know about him / the song. For fun, they can invent other similar lines, e.g. *However you feel, wherever you kneel, Whoever you meet, I'll wait at your feet.* Ask: *What's the most romantic song / gesture you know?* As an extension, after the grammar, ask sts to search for their own song lines with the future (perfect) continuous.

7.3

Song line: I hear babies crying. I watch them grow. They'll learn much more than I'll ever know. And I think to myself, What a wonderful world
Song: *What a wonderful world*, released in 1967
Artist: Louis Armstrong (American)
Lesson link: babies
Notes: Classic, optimistic ballad about Earth's beauty. Many versions, e.g. by Joey Ramone, which younger classes may enjoy more. Featured in the 1987 film *Good morning Vietnam*. Armstrong's most famous song, but not at all typical of his jazz.

Do after 6B as a break in the reading, to give sts time to forget some of it and so enjoy re-reading it more. Dictate / Board the line with these eight mistakes for sts to correct in pairs, then correct it, ideally by listening if you can play / sing it: *I listen babies cry. I look them grow. They'll learning much more than I'll never know. And I'm thinking myself, What wonderful world*
Ask: *Which of these mistakes have you made? What's the link to the lesson?* (babies) *What does the line / song / singer make you think of? How do you feel when babies cry? Are you optimistic or pessimistic about our babies' futures? How often are you able to pause and reflect on Earth's magical beauty?*

7.4

Song line: If you ever get close to a human, And human behavior. Be ready, be ready to get confused,
Song: *Human behavior*, released in 1993
Artist: Bjork (Icelandic)
Lesson link: human behavior
Notes: Björk's first solo hit is a danceable, animal perspective on humans, with the animals definitely winning. It's about her childhood, feeling more comfortable alone with nature than mixing with chaotic, illogical humans.

Do as lead-in to 9E or to wrap the lesson. Elicit the link (the different ways people behave) and if possible to lesson 7.2 (age-related behavior). Ask: *Who do you think is singing about who?* to elicit the information above and all you can about Bjork, e.g. *How does she dress / behave / sound? What do you think most animals think of humans? Any exceptions? Why might they get confused?* If you can, show part of the official video as it's fun seeing the bear win.

7.5

Song line: Workin' 9 to 5, What a way to make a livin'. Barely gettin' by. It's all takin' and no givin'
Song: *Nine to five*, released in 1980
Artist: Dolly Parton (American)
Lesson link: jobs and making a living
Notes: Lively song Parton wrote for the soundtrack to the eponymous feminist film about life in a US office, starring herself, Jane Fonda and Lily Tomlin. Based on the typewriter sound Parton could make with her long acrylic fingernails, she even recorded her nails as percussion on the track!

Do after 12E to end the lesson / unit and, if time, consider singing the whole song as it's fun and uplifting. Board 9 to 5 and elicit what it makes sts think of (a routine working day), and other famous number combinations / uses they see regularly (24/7, 9/11, 100% sure, etc.). Then focus on the song line and ask: *Is she positive or negative about the working day? What hours would it be in our country?* (e.g. in Spain it might be 9–2 and 5–8).

Song activities

8.1

Song line: No one learned from your mistakes. We let our profits go to waste. All that's left in any case. Is advertising space
Song: *Advertising space*, released in 2005
Artist: Robbie Williams (British)
Lesson link: bad customer service and advertising
Notes: A ballad about a star's tragic fall from grace, making reference to Quentin Tarantino's film *True Romance*, where Christian Slater is able to speak to the spirit of Elvis Presley. In the video, Williams emulates Elvis.

Do after 1E as another angle on "advertising". Books closed, dictate the song line with the last word in each line missing (say "blank" instead) for sts to guess / remember. Get sts to interpret it. Give clues: singer's name, the facts above, and ideally, show him singing it. Ask: *What mistakes did Elvis make?* (overeating, wasting his fortune) *When did he die?* (1977) *What does Robbie Williams mean by "profits going to waste"?* (e.g. his millions could have been much better spent, or that we didn't learn from his errors as other stars have died early in similar ways).

8.2

Song line: Oh cherie amour, pretty little one that I adore. You're the only girl my heart beats for. How I wish that you were mine
Song: *My cherie amour*, released in 1969
Artist: Stevie Wonder (American)
Lesson link: the subjunctive
Notes: French for "my dearest love". Motown soul classic, originally written for Wonder's girlfriend, as "Oh my Marcia". By the time he recorded it, he and Marcia had split up, so it became "My cherie amour."

Do as lead in to 4A then use as another example to match to Grammar rules a–c. Ask their opinion of Stevie Wonder / the song? Ask: *Which of you speaks some French? What other expressions do you know?* Highlight the rhymes at the end of lines 1–3. Ask: *What else rhymes with adore?* (*floor, more, pour, bore, ignore,* etc.).

8.3

Song line: You've got a friend in me. When the road looks rough ahead, And you're miles and miles, From your nice warm bed
Song: *You've got a friend in me*, released in 1995
Artist: Randy Newman (American)
Lesson link: travel and being far away
Notes: Uplifting song originally written as the theme for *Toy Story* and became the theme for *Toy Story 2* and 3 too.

Do after 5D to reflect further on acts of kindness / friendship. Focus on the line and elicit all you can about the artist / song / use in *Toy Story* / melody. Ask: *What's the opposite of rough?* (smooth) *What else can be "rough"?* (the sea) *What does ahead mean?* (further away, in the direction the speaker (or addressee) is travelling. Then explore the line, asking: *What makes a good friend?* Give examples from your own experience.

8.4

Song line: It's a bittersweet symphony, this life. Try to make ends meet. You're a slave to the money, then you die.
Song: *Bittersweet Symphony*, released in 1997
Artist: The Verve (British)
Lesson link: money and making ends meet
Notes: A somber look at routine and everyday life. The video shows singer Richard Ashcroft bumping into people as he walks through a crowded London.

Do after 8B as an additional angle on "money". Books closed, elicit words / phrases they associate first with sugar, then lemons to get sweet and bitter, then elicit the meaning when combined (*bittersweet*). Books open, sts read the line, tell you all they can about artist / melody, perhaps an extract from the well-known video too. Ask: *What does "to make ends meet" mean?* (earn just enough money to live on). Get sts to interpret it, saying if they agree with his negative, matter-of-fact point of view. Ask: *What's the lesson connection? For you, is life a symphony? What other metaphors can you think of for "life"?*

8.5

Song line: I'm in the phone booth, it's the one across the hall. If you don't answer, I'll just ring it off the wall
Song: *Hanging on the telephone*, released in 1978
Artist: Blondie (U.S.)
Lesson link: getting satisfaction by phone
Note: First recorded by The Nerves in 1976, this was Blondie's second single from *Parallel Lines*, later covered by many, e.g. UK girl band Girls Aloud and Def Leppard.

Do either as an alternative warm-up to the lesson. As it's a short, fun song, consider singing it with them. Then board / dictate these questions for sts to answer in groups:
Do you often call but not get an answer? Or refuse to answer when called?
How often are you kept hanging on the telephone?
What's the longest you've ever been kept waiting?
What was the worst thing you've ever had to listen to while waiting?

Song activities

9.1

Song line: I can move to another town, Where nobody'd ask where you are now. L.A. or Mexico, No matter where I go, I can't outrun you
Song: *I can't outrun you*, released in 2008
Artist: Trace Adkins (American)
Lesson link: verbs beginning with out
Notes: Haunting country-soul from Adkins' tenth album *X*, about his devastation after divorce and being unable to outrun a past love. Covered by Thompson Square in 2013.

Do as a lead-in to exercise 2A. Focus on the lesson link (outrun) and it's meaning (run better / faster / further / longer than sb). Highlight the useful expression, *No matter*. Elicit interpretation, asking: *Who's singing to who? Why? Where's he / she living now?* (probably eastern or central USA as he wants to run west or south) *What do you think might happen next?* and feed in the info above.

9.2

Song line: Say something, I'm giving up on you. I'm sorry that I couldn't get to you. Anywhere, I would've followed you
Song: *Say something*, released in 2014
Artist: A Great Big World (American)
Lesson link: three-word phrasal verbs
Notes: Heart-breaking ballad about unrequited love, from the album *Is there anybody out there?* The duo later recorded a version with Christina Aguilera too. It won Grammy for Best Pop Duo / Group Performance in 2015.

Do as a lead-in to exercise 4A. Books closed, board / dictate the song line with the three prepositions missing: *Say something, I'm giving you. I'm sorry that I couldn't get you. Anywhere, I would've followed you*. In pairs, sts work out which ones go where. Elicit guesses, but don't confirm, then books open to check answers. Drill the silent *t* in *couldn't* and *get*.

9.3

Song line: I'm a survivor. I'm not gonna give up. I'm not gonna stop. I'm gonna work harder
Song: *Survivor*, released in 2001
Artist: Destiny's Child (American)
Lesson link: surviving challenging situations
Notes: Contemporary R&B inspired by the reality TV show where contestants vote each other off an island. Beyoncé wrote it after the group lost three members in a year, and a press report compared them to the show, speculating who'd be the last voted off. Resulted in an acrimonious court case between the band members!

Do after 6B to break up the reading. Focus on the line and highlight the very abbreviated form of *going to*. In the lyrics, it sometimes appears as *not gonna* or just *not gon'*. Elicit the lesson link (surviving hardship against the odds), and all you can about the artist / song / info above and get them to interpret the lyric. If time, get sts to brainstorm and share the song lines that most motivate them when things get tough.

9.4

Song line: Something in the way you move, Makes me feel like I can't live without you. It takes me all the way. I want you to stay
Song: *Stay*, released in 2012
Artist: Rihanna (Barbados, guest vocals Mikky Ekko)
Lesson link: overview of verb patterns (pattern a)
Note: Emotive, ballad about uncertainty, vulnerability in a relationship, temptation and the inability to resist true love. Rihanna was only 25 when this became her 27th million-seller!

Do after 8A. Elicit the links to the lesson (pattern a – *Makes me feel*). With an older class, you might ask if they recognize the line *Something in the way you move* (from The Beatles song, *Something*), and see if they can think of other lines / melodies repeated in different songs. A class that enjoy singing might like to try to imitate Rihanna's moving performance.

9.5

Song line: I am beautiful, No matter what they say. Words can't bring me down. I am beautiful in every single way
Song: *Beautiful*, released in 2002
Artist: Christina Aguilera (American)
Lesson link: celebrating beauty regardless of weight, etc.
Notes: Aguilera's signature song, an emotional, uplifting ballad about self-empowerment and inner beauty from her fourth album *Stripped*.

Do as a lead-in to the topic of beauty and dieting. Elicit the lesson link, artist, etc. Ask *Can you remember another song line in this unit with "No matter"* (9.1)? Elicit paraphrases for "bring me down" (upset, depress, get me down, make me unhappy, etc.). Ask: *Who is "they"? How many different ways can you be beautiful?* (physically, through kindness, etc.) Notice the expression *"every single"*. Why *"single"*? (for emphasis). Elicit more examples, e.g. *Every single student in the class likes this song!* Ask: *Which of the ballads in Unit 9 do you prefer?* (9.1, 9.3, 9.4 or this one) and, if time, consider singing their preference to wrap the unit.

Song activities

10.1

Song line: If you wanna be my lover, You gotta get with my friends. Make it last forever, Friendship never ends
Song: *Wannabe*, released in 2000
Artist: The Spice Girls (British)
Lesson link: the nature of friendship
Notes: Their first single and, worldwide, best-seller ever by an all-female group. Carried their "Girl Power" message, a response to all the 90s boy bands. It's about the value of friendship and was named catchiest ever hit single in a 2014 UK scientific study by Manchester's Museum of Science and Industry. Spice Girls manager Simon Fuller created *American Idol*.

Do before, during or after 2. Focus on the song line and elicit the lesson link, other song lines from earlier about friends (8.3), all you can about the band, and more of the song: *I'll tell you what I want, what I really really want*, "Zig A Zig Ahhhh", which is just a nonsense phrase, and title, Wannabe, to see if sts can understand the wordplay: (a 'wannabe' aspires to be like someone else, generally a celebrity).

10.2

Song line: It's my life. It's now or never. I ain't gonna live forever. I just want to live while I'm alive
Song: *Livin' on a prayer*, released in 2000
Artist: Bon Jovi (American)
Lesson link: the life span (living forever)
Notes: Often voted best song of the '80s, about two kids working to make it on their own despite constant hardships. Jon Bon Jovi told The Times in 2010 he never gets tired of singing it.

Do as a lead-in to 3C or to end the lesson, eliciting the links (*want to* + base form, and topic, living longer) Books closed. Board this abbreviated version: ___ ___ life. ___ ___ ___. ___ ___ ___ live ___. ___ ___ ___ ___ live ___ ___ alive.
In pairs, sts try to remember and complete it. With a younger class, perhaps play the hangman word guessing game from 6.5. Open books to check. Elicit the differences between *life*, *live* and *alive*. Elicit all you can about the melody / artist / title / song. Make sure they produce the "*Oh-oh, we're halfway there, oh-oh, livin' on a prayer*" chorus at least. Elicit a definition of "livin' on a prayer" (without concern for your actions, always in trouble and constantly praying God helps you out of it). Ask: *Who would like to live forever? If not forever, how long?*

10.3

Song line: You won't ever find him being unfaithful, you will find him, you'll find him next to me
Song: *Next to me*, released in 2012
Artist: Emeli Sandé (British)
Lesson link: words with both prefixes and suffixes
Notes: Award-winning, R&B, third single from her debut album, *Our Version of Events*. Celebrating having someone stand loyally beside you, come what may.

Do after 6C. Focus on the line, elicit the prefix / suffix lesson link and any other words which sound a bit like *unfaithful*, e.g. *ungrateful*, Elicit all you can about the artist / tune / melody / video. Get sts to analyze the line for features of connected speech (*won't_ever, find_him being_unfaithful*) and elided t in next to. Ask: *What's a synonym for "next to" (beside) and "faithful" (loyal)? Who's singing about who?*

10.4

Song line: I lost a friend, Somewhere along in the bitterness. And I would have stayed up with you all night, Had I known how to save a life
Song: *Save a life*, released in 2010
Artist: The Fray (American)
Lesson link: inverted conditional sentence
Notes: Became a hit after appearing in TV show *Grey's Anatomy*. It's about singer Isaac Slade's experience at a camp for troubled youths, while he was mentoring a teenager who was struggling with addiction.

Do as a lead-in to 8A to show sts they already "know" the grammar! Focus on the inversion (Had I known) and ask: *What's another way to say this? (If I'd known) Why's it inverted?* (for emphasis). For homework, ask sts to search for other songs they like with an inversion.

… Song activities

10.5

Song line: Just say yes, just say there's nothing holding you back. It's not a test, nor a trick of the mind, Only love

Song: *Just say yes*, released in 2009

Artist: Snow Patrol (British)

Lesson link: trying to persuade someone

Notes: Electronic-dance single from collection, *Up to Now*, originally written by front man Gary Lightbody for Gwen Stefani, who declined it. It's about loving someone to the point of exasperation when they show less passion than you.

Do after 11E as a lesson wrap to link to the topic / language of persuasion. For fun, have sts read and mime it to show their comprehension. Can they sing it too as they mime? Elicit anything you can about the artist / song / video / who's singing to who and why and if they're into Snow Patrol. Ask: *What other songs of theirs do you know?* (most are much less dancey). Board questions for sts to discuss in small groups: *What's holding you back from achieving your dream? Have you ever been persuaded to do something you later regretted?*

11.1

Song line: Don't listen to a word I say. Hey! The screams all sound the same. Hey! Though the truth may vary. This ship will carry our bodies safe to shore

Song: *Little talks*, released in 2011

Artist: Of Monsters and Men (Icelandic)

Lesson link:

Notes: Catchy folk song, an imaginary dialogue between a late husband and his wife: maybe she's going crazy or maybe he's actually there? Debut single from this six piece indie band's first album, *My head is an animal*.

Do after 1E. Have sts find the lesson link (*safe*). Ask: *Why isn't it safely?* (talking about the bodies, not the carrying). *Does anybody know the melody / group?* Elicit the song title too, asking: *What might the "little talks" be?* (short husband and wife conversations). In pairs, ask sts to classify the letter *s* in the song line into three groups: /s/, /z/ and /ʃ/:

/s/ listen, say, screams, sound, same, this, safe

/z/ screams, bodies

/ʃ/ ship, shore

Ask: *Do you / Does anyone you know ever talk to people who have died?* giving an example yourself, e.g. *I often say 'Hi' to my grandpa when I walk past his old house. My mum still talks to my dad's photo, even though he died a few years ago.*

11.2

Song line: Oh, I would do anything for love. I would do anything for love, but I won't do that. No, I won't do that

Song: *I'd do anything for love (but I won't do that)*, released in 1993

Artist: Meat Loaf (American)

Lesson link: special uses of modals: won't for refusal

Note: Long, dramatic, global hit, it's a male-female dialog. Each verse mentions two things he'd do for love, then one he won't, back referencing to an ambiguous "that". Video based on *Beauty and the Beast / Phantom of the Opera*.

Do after 4B. Have sts read the song line and find the lesson link. Ask them how many different pronunciations can they find for the letter o:

/oʊ/ Oh, won't, no /ʊ/ would /ʌ/ love /uː/ do /ɔː/ for

Elicit more examples for each sound and highlight spelling patterns. Then get all you can from the **Song line**: melody, singer, song / album title. *Do any of them remember it? Why does he contract will not but not would?* (the rhythm). Ask: *What would / wouldn't you do for love?*

11.3

Song line: Heartbreaks and promises, I've had more than my share. I'm tired of giving my love, And getting nowhere

Song: *Show Me Love*, originally released in 1990

Artist: Robin S (American)

Lesson link: unsuccessful dating

Notes: Remixed as a dance tune in 1992, it became one of the best-known house anthems. Iconic synthesizer bass organ riff.

Do after 5D. See if anybody recognizes the song line, raising a hand (silently) if they do. If you can, play the opening bars to see if more recognize the riff, or remember the chorus *You got to show me love*. All but very young classes should! Elicit what you can about the artist / song / title and what it makes them think of / feel.

Highlight the rhyme, *share* and *nowhere* and elicit others (e.g. *rare, chair, wear, there, they're*).

Ask: *What have you had more of your share of in life? What are you tired of? How often do you feel you're getting nowhere?*

Song activities

11.4

Song line: Baby, this is what you came for. Lightning strikes every time she moves. And everybody's watching her, But she's looking at you
Song: *This is what you came for*, released in 2016
Artist: Calvin Harris (British), featuring Rihanna (Barbadian)
Lesson link: definite and indefinite articles (pattern b, lightning)
Notes: Harris co-wrote this joyful club track with his then girlfriend, Taylor Swift, who used the pseudonym Nils Sjöberg, because they didn't want their relationship to overshadow it. Has a unique 3D-cube video.

Do after 9A. Books closed. Set a task to count how many time they hear the letter s, and dictate it once. Paircheck, dictate again. Then ask: *Which are pronounced /s/ and /z/? Which is different?* (she) Dictate once more. If possible, play an extract to check, or get willing sts to sing it. (Answer: 7 x /s/, 4 x /z/) Focus on the song line and elicit the lesson link. Sts may suggest the picture of lightning in 7C but encourage them to consider lightning in terms of the grammar (pattern b). Ask: *What does lightning make you think of?* Elicit all you can about the Rihanna, the song, the mood it puts them in, etc.

11.5

Song line: I've been through the desert on a horse with no name. It felt good to be out of the rain
Song: *Horse with no name*, released in 1971
Artist: America (American)
Lesson link: safety (horseback riding)
Notes: Based on desert scenery / tranquility singer Dewey Bunnell, encountered. He lived in the UK, so was delighted to avoid the rain! Sts might know it from *Grand Theft Auto* video game.

Use before 11A to cue *horseback riding*, then add *desert survival* as another topic option. Books closed, board **des**ert and des**sert** and elicit the difference. Then board / dictate the line with the prepositions missing for sts to insert them: *I've been the desert a horse no name. It felt good be the rain.*

If possible, play the *la-la-la-la-la-la* section in the background while they do it, then the line itself (or just books open) to check. Elicit what sts know about the band / song / associations with it.

12.1

Song line: The world I love. The trains I hop. To be part of, The wave can't stop. Come and tell me when it's time to
Song: *Can't stop*, released in 2002
Artist: Red Hot Chili Peppers (American)
Lesson link: trends and the word wave
Notes: Energetic, third single from *By the way*, encouraging listeners to live with passion / individuality and cultivate inner, personal energy. The video shows band members doing random, abstract actions.

Do after 2C. Elicit the lesson link (waves) and other types of wave (e.g. *radio, sea, Mexican, trend, series (of attacks), brainwaves*). *What wave is this?* (a movement / uprising of similar-minded people). If possible play / watch the line; it's one of their best-known songs. Ask: *What do you know about the song / band?* See if anybody knows its abrupt final line: *This life is more than just a read-through* (= a rehearsal). Do they agree you only live once / have to make the most of life?

12.2

Song line: I want to thank you for giving me the best day of my life. Oh just to be with you is having the best day of my life
Song: *Thank you*, released in 2000
Artist: Dido (British)
Lesson link: passive forms with gerunds and infinitives
Notes: Touching, soft ballad and biggest hit from Dido's debut album, *No Angel*. The first verse became the chorus in Eminem's *Stan*. In the video, Dido loses her house and possessions for not paying her bills.

Do as a lead in to 4A to exemplify preposition + gerund. If you think sts will know the song, or have seen it enough already during the lesson, books closed, dictate / board with changes for them to spot / correct in pairs: *I so want to say thanks, to you for having given me the best day in my life*. Ask: *Is it correct English?* (all except in which should be *of my life*). *Is it what was written on the page?* (No) If possible, sing / play / watch it to correct (or just books open). Once sts know the melody, get them to sing / fit your version to it for fun. (It fits if you hurry!). Highlight the lesson link and elicit all you can about Dido / the song / Eminem's use of it, etc.

Song activities

12.3

Song line: Good friends we've lost, along the way. In this great future, you can't forget your past, So dry your tears, I say ...
Song: *No Woman no cry*, released in 1975
Artist: Bob Marley and The Wailers (Jamaican)
Lesson link: the future
Notes: First hit single from Marley's album, *Live!* Originally "No, Woman, Nuh cry." *Nuh* is Jamaican for "don't," so it means "Don't cry". Brazilian Gilberto Gil recorded this in 1979.

Do before 6. Elicit the link (future) and get sts to try to remember the previous line (*Good friends we've had*) and the next (*the title itself*). Give a clue if necessary (the world's most famous reggae singer). Elicit all you can about him / his music / legacy / longevity / ever present face on T-shirts, then encourage sts to interpret the song line. (He's leaving his mother / partner / sister / daughter, reassuring her the slum they live in won't get her down, that everything will be alright, so "don't shed no tear." The "Government yard in Trench Town" is the Jamaican public-housing project where Marley lived in the late '50s.)

12.4

Song line: And I'm in so deep. You know I'm such a fool for you. You've got me wrapped around your finger. Do you have to let it linger?
Song: *Linger*, released in 1993
Artist: Cranberries (Irish)
Lesson link: causative with *get*
Notes: Singer Dolores O'Riordan lyrics are about regret, based on a soldier she once fell in love with. The band became one of the mid-'90s biggest. The video is a tribute to Jean-Luc Goddard's film *Alphaville*.

Do as a lead-in to 8. Books closed, board the first letter of each word for pairs to remember and complete: A__ I__ i__ s__ d__, etc.
Play a bit of the song, or give another letter / clues if they get stuck (e.g. the opposite of *shallow*, slightly politer word for *idiot*, mime *wrapping*). Books open or play / listen to check. Ask: *What do you know about the band / song? Who's she singing to, How's she feeling? Why?* Finally, elicit the lesson link (*get* + causative / participle).

12.5

Song line: If you want to make the world a better place, Take a look at yourself, and then make a change
Song: *Man in the mirror*, released in 1998
Artist: Michael Jackson (American)
Note: Fourth of five US number 1 hits from *Bad*, and his best seller since dying in 2009. It's about making a change and realizing it has to start with you. The video compiles raw news footage of everything, from homelessness to racial violence.

Do after 11D as lesson / course wrap. Books closed, board the song with the five articles and two prepositions removed to see if pairs can complete it: *If you want make world better place, Take look yourself and then make change*. As a clue say there are seven missing words. Listen / play / read it to check.

Get sts to interpret the meaning (Always begin with yourself to make this world a stronger, more livable place). Did sts realize it was such a "protest message" song? Do they agree? Elicit the obvious lesson link (improving society).

Phrasal verb list

Phrasal verbs are verbs with two or three words: main verb + particle (either a preposition or an adverb). The definitions given below are those introduced in iDentities.

Transitive phrasal verbs have a direct object; some are separable, others inseparable

Phrasal verb	Meaning
A	
ask someone **over**	invite someone
B	
block something **out**	prevent from passing through (light, noise)
blow something **out**	extinguish (a candle)
blow something **up**	explode; fill with air (a balloon); make larger (a photo)
bring something **about**	cause to happen
bring someone or something **back**	return
bring someone **down**	depress
bring something **out**	introduce a new product
bring someone **up**	raise (a child)
bring something **up**	bring to someone's attention
build something **up**	increase
burn something **down**	burn completely
C	
call someone **back**	return a phone call
call someone **in**	ask for someone's presence
call something **off**	cancel
call someone **up**	contact by phone
carry something **out**	conduct an experiment / plan
cash in on something	profit
catch up on something	get recent information; do something there wasn't time for earlier
charge something **up**	charge with electricity
check someone / something **out**	examine closely
check up on someone	make sure a person is OK
cheer someone **up**	make happier
clean someone / something **up**	clean completely
clear something **up**	clarify
close something **down**	force (a business / store) to close
come away with something	learn something useful
come down to something	be the most important point
come down with something	get an illness
come up against someone / something	be faced with a difficult person / situation
come up with something	invent
count on someone / something	depend on
cover something **up**	cover completely; conceal to avoid responsibility
crack down on something	take severe measures
cross something **out**	draw a line through
cut something **down**	bring down (a tree); reduce
cut someone **off**	interrupt someone
cut something **off**	remove; stop the supply of
cut something **out**	remove; stop doing an action
cut something **up**	cut into small pieces

Phrasal verb	Meaning
D	
do something **over**	do again
do someone / something **up**	make more beautiful
draw something **together**	unite
dream something **up**	invent
drink something **up**	drink completely
drop someone / something **off**	take someplace
drop out of something	quit
dwell on something	linger over, think hard about something
E	
empty something **out**	empty completely
end up with something	have an unexpected result
F	
face up to something	accept something unpleasant
fall back on something	use an old idea
fall for someone	feel romantic love
fall for something	be tricked into believing
figure someone / something **out**	understand with thought
fill someone **in**	explain
fill something **in**	complete with information
fill something **out**	complete (a form)
fill something **up**	fill completely
find something **out**	learn information
fix something **up**	redecorate (a home); solve
follow something **through** / **follow through on** something	complete
G	
get something **across**	help someone understand
get around to something	finally do something
get away with something	avoid the consequences
get back at someone	retaliate, harm someone (for an offense or wrong act)
get off something	leave (a bus, train, plane)
get on something	board (a bus, train, plane)
get out of something	leave (a car); avoid doing something
get something **out of** something	benefit from
get through with something	finish
get to someone	upset someone
get to something	reach
get together with someone	meet
give something **away**	give something no longer needed or wanted
give something **back**	return
give something **out**	distribute
give something **up**	quit
give up on someone / something	stop hoping for change / trying to make something happen

Phrasal verb list

Phrasal verb	Meaning
go after someone / something	try to get / win
go along with something	agree
go over something	review
go through with something	finish / continue something difficult
grow out of something	stop doing (over time, as one becomes an adult)

H

Phrasal verb	Meaning
hand something **in**	submit
hand something **out**	distribute
hang something **up**	put on a hanger or hook
help someone **out**	assist

K

Phrasal verb	Meaning
keep someone or something **away**	cause to stay at a distance
keep something **on**	not remove (clothing / jewelry)
keep someone or something **out**	prevent from entering
keep up with someone	stay in touch
keep up with someone or something	go as fast as

L

Phrasal verb	Meaning
lay someone **off**	fire for economic reasons
lay something **out**	arrange
leave something **on**	not turn off (a light or appliance); not remove (clothing or jewelry)
leave something **out**	not include, omit
let someone **down**	disappoint
let someone / something **in**	allow to enter
let someone **off**	allow to leave (a bus, train); not punish
let someone / something **out**	allow to leave
light something **up**	illuminate
look after someone / something	take care of
look down on someone	think one is better, disparage
look into something	research
look out for someone	watch, protect
look someone / something **over**	examine
look someone / something **up**	try to find
look up to someone	admire, respect

M

Phrasal verb	Meaning
make something **up**	invent
make up for something	do something to apologize
miss out on something	lose the chance
move something **around**	change location

P

Phrasal verb	Meaning
pass something **out**	distribute
pass someone / something **up**	reject, not use
pay someone **back**	repay, return money
pay someone **off**	bribe
pay something **off**	pay a debt
pick someone / something **out**	identify, choose
pick someone **up**	give someone a ride
pick someone / something **up**	lift
pick something **up**	get / buy; learn something; answer the phone; get a disease
point someone / something **out**	indicate, show
pull something **off**	make something happen

Phrasal verb	Meaning
put something **away**	return to its appropriate place
put something **back**	return to its original place
put someone **down**	treat with disrespect
put something **down**	stop holding
put something **off**	delay
put something **on**	get dressed / add jewelry (to the body)
put something **together**	assemble, build
put something **up**	build, erect
put up with someone / something	accept without complaining

R

Phrasal verb	Meaning
run into someone	meet
run out of something	not have enough
run something **by** someone	tell someone something so they can give you their opinion

S

Phrasal verb	Meaning
see something **through**	complete
send something **back**	return
send something **out**	mail
set something **off**	cause to go off, explode
set something **up**	establish; prepare for use
settle on something	choose after consideration
show someone / something **off**	display the best qualities
shut something **off**	stop (a machine, light, supply)
sign someone **up**	register
stand up for someone / something	support
start something **over**	begin again
stick with / to someone / something	not quit, persevere
straighten something **up**	make neat
switch something **on**	start, turn on (a machine, light)

T

Phrasal verb	Meaning
take over from someone	take control from someone else
take something **away**	remove
take something **back**	return; accept an item; retract a statement
take something **down**	remove (a hanging item)
take something **in**	notice, remember; make a clothing item smaller
take something **off**	remove clothing, jewelry
take someone **on**	hire
take something **on**	agree to a task
take someone **out**	invite and pay for someone
take something **out**	borrow from the library
take something **up**	start a new activity (as a habit)
talk someone **into**	persuade
talk something **over**	discuss
team up with someone	start to work with, do a task together
tear something **down**	destroy, demolish
tear something **up**	tear into small pieces
think back on something	remember
think something **over**	consider
think something **up**	invent, think of a new idea

Phrasal verb list

Phrasal verb	Meaning
throw something **away / out**	discard, put in the garbage / trash
tip someone **off**	give someone a hint or warning
touch something **up**	improve with small changes
try something **on**	put on to see if it fits, is desirable (clothing, shoes)
try something **out**	use an item / do an activity to see if it's desirable
turn something **around**	turn so the front faces the back; cause to get better
turn someone / something **down**	reject
turn something **down**	lower the volume / heat
turn someone **in**	identify to the police (after a crime)
turn something **in**	submit
turn someone / something **into**	change from one type or form to another
turn someone **off**	cause to lose interest, feel negatively
turn something **off**	stop (a machine / light)
turn something **on**	start (a machine / light)
turn something **out**	make, manufacture
turn something **over**	turn so the bottom is on the top
turn something **up**	raise (the volume / heat)

Phrasal verb	Meaning
U	
use something **up**	use completely, consume
W	
wake someone **up**	cause to stop sleeping
walk out on someone	leave a spouse / child / romantic relationship
warm (up) to something/ someone	begin to like something or someone
watch out for someone	protect
wear someone/something **out**	damage from too much use
wipe something **out**	remove, destroy
work something **out**	calculate mathematically; solve a problem
write something **down**	create a written record (on paper)
write something **up**	write in a finished form

Phrasal verb list

Intransitive phrasal verbs have no direct object; they are all inseparable

Phrasal verb	Meaning
A	
act up	behave inappropriately
B	
blow over	pass, be forgotten
blow up	explode; suddenly become angry
break down	stop functioning
burn down	burn completely
break out	start suddenly (a war, fire, disease)
break up	end a relationship
C	
call back	return a phone call
carry on	continue doing something; behave in a silly / emotional way
catch on	become popular
check in	report arrival (at a hotel, airport)
check out	pay a bill and leave (a hotel)
cheer up	become happier
clear up	become better (a rash, infection; the weather)
close down	stop operating (a business)
come along	go with, accompany
come back	return
come down	become lower (a price)
come in	enter
come off	become unattached; appear a certain way
come out	appear; be removed (a stain)
come up	arise (an issue)
D	
doze off	fall asleep unintentionally
dress up	wear more formal clothes; a costume
drop in	visit unexpectedly
drop out	quit
E	
eat out	eat in a restaurant
empty out	empty completely
end up	do something unexpected; reach a final location / conclusion
F	
fall off	become unattached
fall through	fail to happen
fill out	become bigger
fill up	become completely full
find out	learn new information
follow through	finish, complete something
fool around	have fun (in a silly way)
G	
get ahead	make progress, succeed
get along	have a good relationship
get back	return
get by	survive
get off	leave (a bus, train)
get on	board (a bus, train)
get through	finish; survive
get together	meet
get up	get out of bed
give up	quit

Phrasal verb	Meaning
go along	accompany; agree
go away	leave a place
go back	return
go down	decrease (a price, number)
go off	explode, detonate
go on	continue
go out	leave (a building / home); socialize
go over	succeed (an idea / speech)
go up	increase (a price, number); be built
grow up	become an adult
H	
hang up	end a phone call
help out	do something helpful, useful
hold on	wait (often during a phone call)
K	
keep away	stay at a distance
keep on	continue
keep out	not enter
keep up	maintain speed / momentum
L	
lie down	recline (on a bed / floor / sofa)
light up	illuminate; look pleased, happy
look out	be careful
M	
make up	end an argument
miss out	lose the chance (for something good)
P	
pass out	become unconscious, faint
pay off	be worthwhile
pick up	improve
play around	have fun, not be serious
pop up	occur unexpectedly
R	
run out	leave suddenly; not have enough (a supply)
rush off	leave in a hurry
S	
show up	appear; arrive at a place
sign up	register
sit down	sit
slip up	make a mistake
stand up	rise (to one's feet)
start over	begin again
stay up	not go to bed
straighten up	make neat
T	
take off	leave, depart (a plane); succeed, achieve success
turn in	go to sleep
turn out	have a certain result
turn up	appear
W	
wake up	stop sleeping
watch out	be careful
wear off	disappear, diminish slowly
wind up	become ultimately
work out	exercise; end successfully

Richmond

58 St Aldates
Oxford
OX1 1ST
United Kingdom

ISBN: 978-84-668-2090-5
DL: M-4709-2016
First Edition: November 2016
© Richmond / Santillana Global S.L.

All rights reserved. No part of this book may be reproduced, stored in a retrieval system or transmitted in any form by any means, electronic, mechanical, photocopying, recording or otherwise, without the prior permission in writing of the Publisher.

Richmond publications may contain links to third party websites. We have no control over the content of these websites, which may change frequently, and we are not responsible for the content or the way it may be used with our materials. Teachers and students are advised to exercise discretion when assessing links.

Publishing Director: Deborah Tricker

Editors: Cathy Heritage, Laura Miranda, Shona Rodger

Proofreader: Shira Evans, Tas Cooper, Fiona Hunt

Project and Cover Design: Lorna Heaslip

Layout: Oliver Hutton (H D Design), Dave Kuzmicki

Picture Researcher: Magdalena Mayo, Arnos Design

Illustrators: Aviel Basil, Ricardo Bessa, John Holcroft, Oivind Hovland, Andres Lozano, lynton@kja-artists, sean@kja-artists

Digital Content: Luke Baxter, Anup Dave

Audio Recording: Motivation Sound Studios

Texts:

p. 32 https://www.mindtools.com/CommSkll/PublicSpeaking.htm
© Mind Tools Ltd, 1996-2016. All rights reserved. "Mind Tools" is a registered trademark of Mind Tools Ltd. Reproduced with permission.

p. 43 http://www.scientificamerican.com/article/why-do-some-people-believe-in-conspiracy-theories/
Reproduced with permission. Copyright © 2016, Scientific American, a division of Nature America, Inc. All rights reserved.

p. 64 *The Way Up to Heaven* extract (first published in *The New Yorker*, 1954). Published in Penguin Books in the collection *Kiss Kiss*, a collection of short stories. Copyright © Roald Dahl Nominee Ltd, 1954. Reproduced with permission.
Illustration for *The Way Up To Heaven* copyright © Eleanor Percival

p. 76 http://listverse.com/2016/01/24/10-things-you-didnt-know-babies-could-do/
Reproduced with permission.

p. 86 http://www.fastcompany.com/3012939/the-true-story-of-amazing-customer-service-from-gasp-an-airline
Used with permission of Fast Company Copyright© 2016. All rights reserved.

p. 98 http://www.huffingtonpost.com/kerri-zane/5-reasons-its-better-to-b_b_2854313.html
Reproduced with permission.

p. 108 https://www.psychologytoday.com/blog/looking-in-the-cultural-mirror/201009/are-american-friendships-superficial
Reproduced with permission of Jefferson M. Fish Copyright© 2016. All rights reserved.

p. 120 http://www.aarp.org/home-family/dating/info-01-2013/online-dating-safety-tips-solin.html
Reprinted from January 9, 2013 AARP.org. Copyright © 2013. All rights reserved.

p. 130 http://www.wired.com/2014/05/victorian-postcards-predict-future/
Reproduced with permission Copyright © 2016 Condé Nast. All rights reserved.

Photos:

500PX MARKETPLACE/Brian Bonham; ALAMY/Kaleidoscope, Steve Stock, BSIP SA, Cultura RM, MBI, Home People, Rob Walls, Alex Segre, Image Source, David Cole, age fotostock, Peter Forsberg, Maurice Savage, RayArt Graphics, CBW, Stock Photo, blickwinkel, Blend Images, AF archive, Richard Levine, Vadym Drobot, Jack Sullivan, SilverScreen, Ian Allenden, Web Pix, Eden Breitz, David Levenson, Ferne Arfin, Ed Rooney, Xinhua, Mike Kiev, Roberto Herrett, Lynne Sutherland, ZUMA Press, Inc., Eric D ricochet69, Nicholas Stratford, Wavebreak Media ltd, World History Archive, Stacy Walsh Rosenstock, epa european pressphoto agency b.v., Clare Gainey; ARNOS DESIGN LTD./David Oakley; CARTOONSTOCK/Eldon Pletcher, Aaron Bacall, Fran; GETTY IMAGES SALES SPAIN/Howard Kingsnorth, HeroImagesCLOSED, Francisco Romero, Eyecandy Images, Hero Images, Thinkstock; GLASBERGEN CARTOON SERVICE/Randy Glasbergen/www.glasbergen.com; ISTOCKPHOTO/Getty Images Sales Spain; OFF THE MARK CARTOONS/Mark Parisi; PBS/PBS Newshour; REX SHUTTERSTOCK/Ricardo Demurez / imageBROKER, Everett Collection, Blend Images, Broadimage, WestEnd61, SNAP; SHUTTERSTOCK NETHERLANDS,B.V.; WATCHMOJO/ www.watchmojo.com; ZUMA PRESS/Bryan Smith; Dr. Cialdini/ www.influenceatwork.com; Eleanor Percival; Chic by CHoice; Alinea Egmont; ARCHIVO SANTILLANA

The Publisher has made every effort to trace the owner of copyright material; however, the Publisher will correct any involuntary omission at the earliest opportunity.

Printed in Brazil by Forma Certa Gráfica Digital
Lote: 792974
Cód: 290520905